THE TRANS GENERATION

The Trans Generation

How Trans Kids (and Their Parents)
Are Creating a Gender Revolution

Ann Travers

 University of Regina Press

Printed and bound in Canada at Marquis. The text of this book is printed on 100% post-consumer recycled paper with earth-friendly vegetable-based inks.

Cover art: Lindsay Morris/INSTITUTE

Library and Archives Canada Cataloguing in Publication

Travers, Ann, author
    The trans generation : how trans kids (and their
parents) are creating a gender revolution / Ann Travers.

Includes bibliographical references and index.
Issued in print and electronic formats.
Co-published by New York University Press.

ISBN 978-0-88977-578-7 (softcover).—ISBN 978-0-88977-579-4 (PDF).—
ISBN 978-0-88977-580-0 (HTML)

1. Transgender children. 2. Parents of transgender children.
3. Transgender people—Identity. 4. Gender identity—Law and legislation.
I. Title.

HQ77.9.T73 2018   306.76'8   C2018-901578-0
C2018-901579-9

10 9 8 7 6 5 4 3 2 1

University of Regina Press, University of Regina
Regina, Saskatchewan, Canada, s4s 0A2
TEL: (306) 585-4758 FAX: (306) 585-4699
WEB: www.uofrpress.ca

U OF R PRESS

We acknowledge the support of the Canada Council for the Arts for our publishing program. We acknowledge the financial support of the Government of Canada. / Nous reconnaissons l'appui financier du gouvernement du Canada. This publication was made possible with support from Creative Saskatchewan's Creative Industries Production Grant Program and with the help of a grant from the Federation for the Humanities and Social Sciences, through the Awards to Scholarly Publications Program, using funds provided by the Social Sciences and Humanities Research Council of Canada.

Canada Council   Conseil des arts
for the Arts   du Canada

Canada

creative
ᴇWAN

To every kid and every parent that I interviewed:
Thank you. You are the beating heart of this book.

CONTENTS

Introduction

People know what they do; frequently they know why they
do what they do; but what they don't know is what what they
do does.
—Michel Foucault

February 17, 1962: Toronto, Ontario. In the hospital, the doctor, in the
usual way, tells my unwed mother, "It's a girl." Fifty-five years later, I
bear both the psychological scars of the effects of the branding of me as
a girl and eventual woman and the wrenching separation from my birth
mother. In the story I tell about myself, I am unable to separate the sex
assignment imposed on me from the sexism and misogyny that were my
due as a girl or from the gender policing and homo-hatred I received for
not being very good at it. Nor, for that matter, can I untangle the privilege of my whiteness and relative wealth from the patriarchal burden of
shame imposed on unwed mothers and their offspring and my own bad
luck in the adoption game. I come from all these things. These social
forces are real; they shape opportunities unequally. I am all these things
and more.

My daughter and I recently discussed the lack of agency that children
typically experience: most kids do not have much say in many things,
and all have absolutely no control over how they come into this world
(out of whose body, in what place and time) or typically who raises them
and how. We are all born into systems of power and privilege, and this
concept of the "sociological imagination," as C. Wright Mills famously
coined it, has a significant impact on our life chances and choices. Our
biographies are shaped by our lived experience in specific geopolitical and historical moments. Context is not everything, but it certainly
counts for a lot.

Being called a "boy" or a "girl" and assigned correspondingly gendered names and pronouns are two of the many dimensions of power

1

that adults exercise over children and that shape how they experience the world. For the most part, this power is taken for granted—so much so that in 2011, a Toronto couple's decision to keep the specifics of their child's genitals private, coupled with a gender-neutral name, Storm, generated heated media and online commentary that signaled a deeply rooted belief in the appropriateness of adults imposing sex categories on children.[1] Parents are expected to do gender work with their children properly. Some, such as Storm's parents, Rogue Witterick and David Stocker, make efforts to resist sex stereotyping by choosing gender-neutral names and resisting the efforts of others to assign gendered clothing, characteristics, and activities to their children on the basis of their assigned birth sex; but the binary sex system is so pervasive that most children succumb, and those who do not typically struggle for support.

I define "transgender" in a broad and historical sense to include people who "defy societal expectations regarding gender." Trans activist Julia Serano notes that "not everyone who falls under this umbrella will self identify as 'transgender,' but all are viewed by society as defying gender norms in some significant way."[2] While Serano and others distinguish between those who are transsexual—individuals who transition from their assigned sex to their affirmed sex—and those who are transgender, the issue of terminology is complicated because individuals understandably have very strong feelings about how they identify. I use the term "transgender" and its shorthand, "trans," interchangeably to speak in very general terms about kids who defy gender norms, but I choose each person's own language to describe them specifically.

I have been traveling in ethnographically rich circles, both socially and as a researcher, offline and online, formal and informal, with transgender kids and their families for over seven years. This book is fairly unique in that I rely on the direct reports of trans kids and their parents to map in time and space the ways in which they are disabled[3] by environments that rely on naturalized binary gender systems. Relying on parents to report the experiences of children and young people is inherently problematic,[4] and I address this limitation by including the voices of a number of trans kids themselves, who describe their experiences in their own words. Doing this is particularly important because, as critical childhood studies scholar James Marten observes, "children may be among the least articulate of all members of society. By the time they are fully literate and aware of the possibilities and challenges posed by their surroundings, they are hardly children at all. And they are, it goes without saying, literally without political power. As a result, it is very difficult to get at their point of view, and most treatments examine institutions, ideas, or policies that shape the lives of children rather than flesh-and-blood youngsters."[5]

Children do have strong feelings about their gender identities, so I draw on the embodied experience—"the suffering"[6]—of my participants in navigating the gendered spaces that disable them as well as the pleasure and empowerment they experience in resisting the dominant narratives that restrict their sex/gender identities and expression. But the perspectives of parents, while not synonymous with those of their children, are very important because they are typically their children's primary adult attachment, and it is parents who most often advocate on their behalf.

For the purposes of this book, "childhood" is defined as an institutionalized stage of life from birth to the "age of majority" (which varies from jurisdiction to jurisdiction across Canada and the United States from 18 to 21 years of age). In discussing the experiences of specific young people, this text uses the term "children" to refer to those 15 years of age and younger, "youth" to refer to those between the ages of 16 and 21, and "kids" to speak more generally about people 18 and under.

My research confirms that trans kids resist the very names and pronouns associated with the sex category that has been assigned to them at birth, which puts them in potential conflict with families, peers, school and sports/recreational institutions and programs, healthcare systems, juvenile justice systems, organizations that provide social support, and work environments. All children do gender work, but the gender work that trans kids do to resist the sex/gender identity assigned to them is particularly powerful in its ability to make the social construction and imposition of binary sex and gender systems more visible. The experiences of trans kids also throw into sharp relief the extensive labor that the people in their environments engage in to impose and naturalize cisgender binary categorization.

Many of the trans kids in my study regularly experience crisis as a result of the restrictive ways in which sex categories regulate their daily lives and put pressure on them to deny their internal sense of who they are in gendered terms. Critical trans activist and legal scholar Dean Spade identifies government identity documents, bathrooms, and sex-segregated facilities as key points of vulnerability and insecurity for trans people,[7] but relationships with sex-defined peers, sex-segregated/sex-differentiated activities and spaces, gender-coded clothing and hairstyles, pronouns and names, access to healthcare, and gender policing by adults and peers also play a significant role. This perspective is reflected in the experiences of many of the kids and parents I spoke with.

In my own life, when I have called sexist assumptions about fundamental male-female difference into question or attempted to interrupt them, as my three children and I navigate the everyday spaces of the daycare, the birthday party, the playground, the classroom, sports and recreation, and so on, I have often been made to feel like a deluded heretic. Parents and caregivers routinely present me with "evidence" that their children's cisgender conformity is fundamental to their nature rather than environmentally mediated. My efforts to provide more, rather than less, gender-neutral space for all kids is intended to redistribute power: to open up options for kids' own gender self-determination, to reverse the privilege that masculinity and male bodies enjoy over femininity and female bodies, and to influence the circulation of cultural and material resources in more equitable ways.

As educational scholar Mark Hellen observes, the majority of transgender children and youth are "non-apparent";[8] the lack of acceptance of gender diversity in their environments leads many to keep themselves hidden. Most trans kids who lack parental acceptance and support and/or appropriate healthcare either adapt to pressure or are driven underground. This is the self-perpetuating logic of "the Thomas Theorem,"[9] whereby "situations that are defined as real become real in their consequences."[10] On the other hand, however, visible trans kids are at higher risk of discrimination and violence. Ultimately, both those who are visible and those who are invisible are vulnerable to high-risk behavior, self-harm, and suicide.

There have always been children who refuse their gender designation—and, truth be told, I was one of them—although most do so in silence. Since the mid-1990s, however, an increasing number of kids are finding it possible to openly resist the sex category assigned to them at birth and to identify themselves in unexpected ways. This agency has become possible as a result of adult transgender activism, the availability of information about LGBT people and identities via the Internet, and emerging social movements on behalf of transgender kids consisting of parents, therapeutic/medical providers, and trans people of all ages.[11] We now see trans kids circulating on TV talk shows, in social media posts, and in mainstream news headlines. This visibility both reflects and contributes to a cultural shift toward advocacy for greater gender openness in Canada and the United States. But cultural spaces of acceptance and support remain few and hard to come by. Trans kids need us to fight for them and along with them, whether they make themselves known to us or not.

In the past five years, some positive changes have come about in law and policy in various jurisdictions in Canada and the United States. In 2014, the province of British Columbia was the first in Canada to allow transgender people, including children, to change the gender marker on their birth certificates without having to undergo sex reassignment surgery. This development was a result of a case brought to the British Columbia Human Rights Tribunal on behalf of Harriette Cunningham, who was 11 years old at the time. "In 2013, with the help of her grandmother and human rights lawyer barbara findlay,[12] Harriette began petitioning local representatives to overturn legislation that required trans people to undergo reassignment surgery before changing the gender on their birth certificates. When Bill 17 passed in 2014, Harriette was the youngest of 30 British Columbians to receive their newly accurate identification."[13] Harriette subsequently appeared before the tribunal to argue for the elimination of gender markers on birth certificates altogether. This goal has yet to be achieved, although as of 2017, BC Care cards for provincial health insurance can now be obtained without a gender marker. In 2014, transgender 11-year-old Tru Wilson's parents launched a human rights complaint on her behalf against the Vancouver Area Catholic Diocese and achieved, via an out-of-court settlement, the desired policy change to recognize transgender girls and boys as their affirmed sex.[14] In March 2016, a human rights complaint between the parents of eight-year-old Bella Burgos and the River East Transcona School Division in Manitoba was resolved in favor of affirming transgender students, including access to washrooms and changing facilities according to their affirmed sex.[15] Similarly, Maine's highest court ruled in 2014 that a transgender student's rights were violated when her school forced her to use a staff bathroom rather than the girl's bathroom.[16] The passage of AB 1266 into law in California, signed by the governor on August 12, 2013, allows children "to participate in sex-segregated programs, activities and facilities," including on the basis of their affirmed gender rather than their birth sex.[17] Since 2004, many school boards on both sides of the border have adopted trans-inclusive policies.[18]

Other potential watershed cases were until recently before the courts, the most high profile being the American Civil Liberties Union's legal challenge on behalf of transgender boy Gavin Grimm's right to use the boys' washroom at his high school. When a lower court upheld Grimm's right to use the boys' washroom, the school district appealed to the U.S. Supreme Court. Many trans people and supporters hoped that this judicial body would establish a federal precedent in support of transgender rights. But a change in the political landscape from an Obama White House that voiced its intention to support transgender students to a Trump administration that included transgender students among its vulnerable targets sent the case back to the lower court, which, in light of the new administration in Washington, subsequently overturned its original decision and ruled against Grimm. A subsequent appeal of that decision appears to have been stalled by Grimm's June 2017 graduation from high school and, hence, his legal standing in the matter before the courts. Trans-oppressive attitudes are persistent in U.S. and Canadian culture and policy, and the increasingly sinister efforts by the Trump administration and many U.S. state governments to resist or roll back legal and policy gains on behalf of trans people indicate the extent to which trans kids remain marginalized and at risk.

As trans kids are a very vulnerable population, I have taken great pains to ensure their anonymity. For this reason, I locate them nationally only and provide very general markers related to their racialization. While this forecloses more nuanced analysis of individual cases with regard to the impact of specific forms of racialization and specific geographical contexts, it is a necessary measure. The threshold of anonymity I provide is such that individual transgender kids and/or their parents are not identifiable. However, communities consisting of transgender children and youth and/or their parents are often closely knit, and some of the stories I report on may be familiar to members of these networks.

Every region of the mainland United States and all regions of Canada with the exception of the Yukon and Nunavut are represented in my research. A greater number of voices participated in this study than are represented here. In two cases, as children aged from the time of the initial interview to a publication date three years later, parents withdrew their participation in order to let their children decide if and when to tell their own stories and out of the increased concern about their children's safety following the election of Donald Trump.

I interviewed 19 transgender kids and 23 parents of transgender kids in Canada and the United States between 2012 and 2017. My overall sample consists of the experiences (some told to me directly and some by their parents) of 36 kids. These kids live in various regions across Canada and the United States and range in age from four to 20. Most of the kids in my study come from middle-class families, but at least five are working class or living in poverty. Of these kids, 15 are Euro-Canadian or Euro-American, meaning they are racialized as white, while the remainder are racialized to some degree as nonwhite, 13 of them visibly so. Of the kids in my study who are racialized as nonwhite, five identify as Asian Canadian or Asian American, six as Black Canadian or Black American, six as Indigenous or Native American[19] to varying degrees, and one as Latinx.[20] I know of four of the kids who are adopted. Three kids live in nonurban areas. The gender identities that these kids affirm put them at odds with traditional notions of binary gender. These identities include gender nonconforming, transgender, trans nonbinary, male, female, boy, girl, trans boy, trans girl, gender neutral, and agender, and several kids require more than a few words to sum up their identities.[21] Wren (11, Black Canadian), for example, described herself this way: "I was born a boy, but I like being a girl."

Most of the trans kids and parents of trans kids whom I interviewed for this book were met through family gender conferences, Facebook networks for parents of transgender kids who are active in supporting their children, and chain referral sampling. Of the parents I interviewed, 19 were mothers (two of whom were partnered with women and five of whom were single parents), and four were fathers (one of whom was partnered with a man). In spite of active support by many of the fathers of trans children, emotional and support work on behalf of trans kids, like other familial emotional and support labor, remains highly feminized. Fathers are often deeply engaged with their kids in general and around their difficulties with trans oppression, but more often mothers negotiate daily challenges and are the spokespeople for the family. In many cases, in two-parent families, queer or straight, both parents attended meetings with school officials to seek accommodation for their kids. Because most of the parents interviewed were located via networks or organizations that support trans kids, the dominant narrative was one of revelation, adjustment, acceptance, and support through advocacy or activism.

I identify my participants by pseudonyms, age, racialization, and nation of residence. After serious deliberation, I decided not to indicate whether a particular participant was "designated male at birth" or "designated female at birth." Identifying my participants by the sex they were assigned at birth is an important way to render visible the power relations at play as sex/gender categories are imposed and the consequences for kids who resist. This analysis does emerge in many of the stories I share, but in describing my participants, I honor their self-definitions. I do so for two reasons: first, because of the way sex markers have been imposed on the kids in my study and how hard they, and often their parents, have had to work to resist this imposed marker; and second, because information about assigned sex satisfies a cis-sexist need to "know" who everyone "really is." In many ways, I think it is valuable to exclude this information entirely. The social disruption I am advocating for in this book can therefore be more fully experienced in the reading.

One of the experiences I have enjoyed the most in the work of this book has been the extent to which I often "forget" the sex category to which my participants were originally assigned: indeed, I rarely think of them in terms of genital variation at all. I find myself unable to remember who anyone "really is," in that trans-oppressive cultural way of needing to know the nature of a person's genitals in order to take them seriously as the gender they affirm. Far from experiencing this "forgetting" as problematic, I find it incredibly freeing, and it actually reflects my vision of a more gender-just future based on the trans-positive perspective that "gender is not genitals."[22] In writing this way, I have endeavored to model a much more open and less biologically determin-istic way of enabling and respecting each person's right to determine their own gender. This is a transformative experience that I would like to see generalized. I acknowledge that the reader may find my failure to identify the assigned sex of my participants frustrating at times, and I hope it comes to be appreciated as a valuable aspect of the experience of reading the book.

An important dimension of gender self-determination involves the creation of new language to allow for a greater range of identities. The English language is less thoroughly gendered than are French and Span-ish, for example, whereby objects and not just people have a gender, but English features explicitly gendered pronouns. In addition to emerg-ing terminology to describe gender identities beyond the binary, new gender-neutral pronouns are being used by trans people of all ages, per-haps the most common being the replacement of "he/him/his" and "she/her/hers" with "they/them/theirs."[23] This is a challenging adjustment for adults, although, as some of my research indicates, young children not only seem to be more adaptable in this regard but often invent new lan-guage for themselves as needed. Stacey, mother of four-year-old Cas-sandra (Euro-Canadian), for example, described how children in one of her older daughter's classes asked after Cassandra by saying, "Where's your brother/sister?" In spite of my own increasing preference to be ad-dressed using "they/them/their" pronouns, I struggle to get this right on behalf of others. Gendered pronouns are such an ingrained habit. To avoid misgendering[24] people as much as possible, I do a lot of back-ground work: there are signs up in my office that say "they/them/theirs," and I have asked my family to refer to me with these pronouns, partly to explore adopting them myself but also to aid me in internalizing them.

I have been deeply affected by my interviews with trans kids and their parents. I intentionally conducted each interview as an act of emotionally invested social action research[25] in support of gender self-determination and reduced vulnerability for trans kids. My heart needed to be open, and I needed to be fully present to do this. As Stef (17, Euro-Asian Canadian) talked about what they had experienced in school (as a transgender girl starting at age five and as a gender-neutral person starting at age 14), for example, I responded by saying, "You have put up with a lot of shit!" To this, I received an emphatic "Yes!" Feeling deeply understood by a compassionate adult is important to children and youth and feeds their resilience. I remain aware of this need in all my interactions with the trans kids with whom I work. Supporting the authority of my participants with regard to their own gender identities is as important to me as it is to learn about who they are and how they are navigating their lives. Unlike traditional, and inaccurate, portrayals of science and academic research as being characterized by so-called objectivity and lack of invested interest, the social action model of research is explicitly designed to develop knowledge that can be used to fight oppression.

There are difficulties involved in writing about vulnerable populations for diverse audiences, and I have encountered these at several stages. There are considerable tensions and debates within trans communities about what is necessary for recognition, equality, and safety. It is a challenge to generate space for this critical analysis while keeping in mind the potential consequences for transgender kids.

The overall purpose of *The Trans Generation* is to make life better for transgender kids in particular and for all kids in general. My general argument in the book is that trans kids are incredibly vulnerable because of the way in which gender identities are imposed on children in general, with particularly negative consequences for trans kids. I document the ways in which unsupportive families, schools, healthcare programs and delivery mechanisms, bathroom facilities, and sports and physical recreation programs harm trans kids and the positive results that come with acceptance and support. A central piece of the book, a chapter titled "Parenting," documents the incredible time, energy, love, intelligence, and courage that supportive parents of trans kids devote to making it possible for their children—and trans kids in general—to show up as who they really are. A key argument of the book relates to how resources for this kind of support are unevenly distributed, particularly with regard to race and class. The theoretical framework I draw on for the book is based on the activism and scholarship of queer and trans scholars of color as it enables a more critical discussion of the lives of transgender kids.

I end the book by applying debates within queer and trans communities about reformist versus more radical social change programs and strategies to the matter of how best to empower transgender kids. I center the most precarious trans kids to argue against an either/or approach to these debates, insisting on the power and value of carefully leveraging rights discourse to achieve measures of immediate harm reduction within the context of a broader anti-oppression framework. The book concludes with the outline of a more comprehensive program for social change. As this book is intended for a mixed audience of academics, students, trans people of all ages, family members and friends of trans kids, and those who care for and work with kids, I provide a brief list of recommendations in Appendix A.

C. Wright Mills once said, "Neither the life of an individual nor the history of society can be understood without understanding both."[26] I hope that this book will contribute to an understanding of how oppressive contexts shape the lives of trans kids and how we can work together both to foster individual resilience and to generate widespread social change.

1

Transgender Kids

Whenever we are crossing the Canadian-U.S. border, my instructions to Wren—and her response—are always the same: "I will be calling you 'he.'" She always asks me why. We have had many discussions about this, and none of them have been satisfactory for either of us. But before we leave home each time, I insist that she refrain from wearing a skirt or a dress until we are across the border. (If we are driving, it's not unusual for us to pull into the nearest shopping-mall parking lot to enable her to "change back" into herself.) Most of the time, she and I are in solidarity in the face of the failure of others to understand who she is or to realize that the categories they impose upon her are contrived and oppressive; but the erasure of her identity is real, and it hurts every time. The last time we flew to the United States, I watched as she came through the security sensor gate behind me. I didn't even notice that one of her fists was clenched until the guard who was waiting to wand her asked her to open her hand. When she did, she revealed a delicate, iridescent pink hair scrunchie. I realized that she was trying to find a way to hang onto herself in the face of this denial of her person. I was stunned by her ingenuity and torn up by the way she was left empty-handed. I don't tell her that security personnel might react intrusively and even aggressively, if they notice she is "really" a boy but presenting as a girl. We might be separated and questioned about the nature of our relationship—I am her adoptive mother—and the standard of care I am providing for her. These things have happened to families that I know. As she grows up, Wren will increasingly engage with gendered and racialized systems that put her at risk. She is only nine years old, and I fear that the truth about the extent of the potential danger lying ahead would harm her development.
—Jordan, parent

On an August afternoon in 2011, I found myself at a AAA baseball game in the U.S. Southwest, standing in a long line at the concession stand because I had promised my daughter a slushy. I was surrounded by kids of all ages. When the one in front of me turned around, she caught the involuntary look of surprise in my eyes and cheerfully called me on it, saying, "You thought I was a boy, didn't you?" "I thought you looked like me," I replied. She looked like I did when I was 11—an unmistakably queer kid. She went on to tell me that people think she is a boy all the time and that she doesn't mind but her mom hates her short haircut. We chatted for a bit, but when we got close to the front of the line, I switched gears and got serious, saying, "I want you to remember me. Remember that I told you that someday, probably when you go to college, you'll meet lots of other people like us, and they will love you. And your life will be great." We stood there for a moment, eyes locked, saying nothing. I felt like I had reached across time to do for her what nobody did for me, and I found doing it empowering and portentous—until later that day, when I realized how elitist it was to assume a college escape plan was in her future.

The light at the end of the tunnel I attempted to provide to the presumably Euro-American kid at the ballgame came from *my* story, which is based on a combination of race and class privilege and good timing; but most transgender kids will never attend postsecondary school, and even most of those who do will be unable to remain in what for me has come to constitute a relatively queer- and trans-positive bubble. The world of the university did and does provide me with a favorable habitat. From what this kid told me about her parents, however, her family may not have the resources to send her to college: her dad ran the concession stand at the ballpark. Her gender nonconformity and her age—just on the cusp of puberty and the greater pressure that "tomboys" experience to conform to feminine norms as they grow into teenagers[1]—triggered my concerns about her vulnerability, and I wanted to throw her a lifeline. In my effort to speak to her, I spoke mostly to myself. She was full of resilience: she was unfazed by the responses of others to her gender nonconformity and really seemed to enjoy engaging with complete strangers about it. This was an important lesson about the tendency to project our own experiences and desires onto the children we feel affinity with. This theme drives the book: how to decenter my own whiteness, class privilege, and professional status to present a more nuanced analysis of transgender kids in North America.

Nine years ago, in 2008, gender educators Stefanie Brill and Rachel Pepper published *The Transgender Child*, a groundbreaking book that provided adult caregivers of and service providers for children who affirm a sex/gender identity other than the one assigned to them practical guidance and a supportive framework for navigating the process of social and/or medical transition. The emergence of affirmative (as opposed to punishing, "corrective," or "reparative") resources such as this one,[2] for networks of parents and professionals focused on supporting transgender children,[3] was in response to critical need. A recent report released by the Williams Institute at the UCLA School of Law concluded that one in every 137 teens between the ages of 13 and 17 identifies as transgender.[4] In *Being Safe, Being Me*, the authors of the Canadian Trans Youth Health Survey noted that nearly two-thirds of the respondents reported self-harm over the previous year, and one in three had attempted suicide.[5] Equally troubling are the figures relating to poverty: one in five younger trans youth (14–18 years) and more than one in three older trans youth (19–25 years) went without food at some point in the previous year because they could not afford it.

In a study investigating school climate, the Egale Canada Human Rights Trust reported that 95% of transgender students felt unsafe in schools, 90% reported being verbally harassed because of their gender variance, and 50% said that their teachers and other adults in positions of authority failed to intervene when anti-queer or trans-oppressive comments were made.[6] Other studies have reported that doctors, teachers, and classmates often misunderstand gender-nonconforming kids,[7] which can result in damaging feelings of social isolation. Many are diagnosed with learning disabilities and/or psychological problems because of stress, depression, and suicidal tendencies.[8] Recent data suggest that a disproportionate number of LGBT youth are homeless. Another study reports, "Most transgender children still live in the shadows, hiding from a world that sees them as freaks of nature. Rejected by their families, many grow up hating their bodies, and fall victim to high rates of depression, drug abuse, violence and suicide."[9] If this is where it can end, where does it begin?

The Two-Sex System

The seemingly "natural" basis of binary sex/gender systems assumes that "sex" is a biological term to describe a binary system of anatomy and that "gender" is a cultural term that describes social expectations of sexed bodies, yet these definitions have been challenged by queer, feminist, trans, and intersex theory. As queer theorist Judith Butler insists, sex "has been gender all along";[10] the very "fact" of the two-sex system is an *ideological* rather than a *naturally occurring* phenomenon.[11] With few exceptions, however, the "realness" of binary sex, and what are assumed to be naturally corresponding gender differences, is received wisdom so absolute that feminist scientific and cross-cultural evidence that establishes sex and gender variation beyond dyadic systems is dismissed.[12] In short, this system continues to operate as a powerful and inflexible social and cultural foundational force. In fact, Canadian and U.S. sex/gender systems appear to be resilient enough to adapt to some transgender disruptions by restabilizing around binary categories, which may lessen the relative precarity of transgender kids who undergo affirmative medical intervention early enough to avoid puberty. In contrast to the view of transgender adults, dominant biomedical models view the prepubescent bodies of children as blank slates that may be subject to the kind of intervention that restabilizes binary gender systems.[13] Transgender scholars Susan Stryker and Paisley Currah pointedly define gender "as a biopolitical apparatus that operates on all bodies to produce unequally distributed life chances; gender privileges not just men over women, but also the legibly or functionally gendered over those who become inhuman waste due to their incoherent, messy, resistant, or ambiguous relationship to biopolitical utility."[14]

Research and anecdotal evidence indicates that children have a strong sense of their own gender identity by the age of three or four and some earlier than that. Indeed, one of the parents I interviewed described how her daughter, Cassandra insisted, "I is a girl," at two and a half years of age. But the circumstances under which children experience gender—both the gender that is imposed on them and the gender they feel themselves to be—are complex and difficult to unpack. Anyone who has spent any time around babies and small children has to have observed how distinct their personalities are and how they bring something uniquely of themselves to every interaction and context. Children are not blank slates, as early approaches to child development and education insisted,[15] but rather are fundamentally social beings who strive for the agency to construct themselves as much as they are constructed by interactions with people and institutions around them. Children engage with their environments in mutual developmental interaction between personal and social systems. Psychoanalyst Adrienne Harris captures this complex relationship in her description of gender as "soft assembly," as "personal and social, personal and political, private and public. Any individual experience of gender is rooted in personal history, collective histories, and the slowly but also rapidly evolving, historically shifting world of bodies, words, and material life."[16] Much as Karl Marx asserted that "men [sic] make their own history, but they do not make it as they please; they do not make it under self-selected circumstances, but under circumstances existing already, given and transmitted from the past,"[17] gender necessarily emerges in context. Children make gender their own, but they are limited by the tools they are given. Transgender kids shine a light on the ways that children do gender and the creativity and determination they bring to this task.

The increasingly visible social movements of trans kids and their parents and caregivers insist that children do know their own gender identities and that they both are and should be the authorities when it comes to any claims about their gender. Yet prevailing attitudes about children and teenagers allow adults to dismiss the statements that young people make about themselves and the world around them. Nonbinary trans kids, or those who do not stick with one transition but retreat, move sideways, or go ahead in a different direction, are cited as examples to reinforce cultural norms and prescriptions that infantilize teenagers and preteens.

While some headway is being made to recognize the capacity of children to determine their own gender, this acknowledgment is extended much less to sexuality. Gender scholar Kathryn Bond Stockton observes that the circulation of transgender children in mainstream media depends on their being constructed as both sexually innocent and fundamentally heterosexual.[18] This is a central contradiction that informs mainstream discourse about children, gender, and sexuality in general. In a groundbreaking study of kindergarten children and gender, critical childhood studies scholar Annika Stafford observes that "discourses of children's innocence and discourses of difference work together to normalize rigidly gendered heterosexuality, compelling children to conform to such norms or face social othering in the form of isolation and persecution for their characteristics that do not fit within the strict boundaries of normalcy."[19] A considerable volume of research tells us that children develop physically and mentally in keeping with access to resources and opportunities.[20] Drawing on new research findings relating to the "plasticity" of the brain, sociologist Raewyn Connell observes that there is strong evidence that social context/interaction drives brain development.[21]

Another factor to consider is what sociologist Barrie Thorne has observed in children and their peer cultures: they are not just passive recipients of society's gender system but rather active interpreters and co-constructors of meaning.[22] Similarly, Connell remarks, "Children deal with the same institutions and with overlapping groups of adults. One of the key competencies children learn is to recognize the prevailing masculinities and femininities in the adult world. Whatever ideology prevails in the gender order, children grow up under its shadow."[23]

Coping Strategies

The kids in this book developed a range of coping strategies to deal with the shadow of the gender order. These include invisibility; trying to make the assigned category work; living a double life; engaging in self-harm; gender and/or sexual nonconformity; socially and/or medically transitioning; branching out beyond the binary; and engaging in education and activism to bring about social change.

Invisibility

All the kids in the book experience dissonance, if not a powerful dis-identification, with and resistance to the binary sex/gender identity imposed on them. The fact that I was able to identify and interview them speaks to the degree of privilege that most of their families (birth, adoptive, or chosen) have been able to rally around their children's gender self-determination. It does not mean that all participants come from relative wealth, however, although many would qualify as middle class. But these trans kids are known to me, and their experiences shed light on the many others who lack the safe environments required to show themselves. Speaking of the relationship between privilege and visibility, Kai, an LGBT youth worker, told me, "Young people are saying directly to me, 'Like I already am so teased and bugged and bullied for these other aspects of my identity that there is no way I'm going to start outing myself on invisible identities.' Like, 'I'll just restrict myself and conform and do whatever I need to do to not have to deal with that aspect of difference because these ones that everyone sees, no matter what I do, are taking up so much of the plate of my energy that I can't even get to that.'"

Sucking It Up

Most trans kids probably try very hard to make a go of being the girl or boy that people around them expect them to be, either because they are not aware of any options or because rejecting one's assigned identity can be overwhelming and difficult to undertake. For some, this process is short-lived, but even those who go on to adopt a more visible strategy often give it a shot. Cameron (18, Euro-Canadian) explained about his experience early on, "I was very passive in some ways, and if my parents told me I was something, then that's what I was. But I never really totally felt like I fit in with girls or like with girls' qualities." Now identifying as a trans guy, Cameron described his experience this way: "I tried really hard to fit in when I was 12 because I still had no idea what was going on; I didn't know that being transgender was even a thing. I never doubted that I was a girl because, you know, I was basically being trained to be a housewife; there were no other options." Michael (17, Asian Canadian) described himself as having tried in his early teens to banish his discomfort about his body and assigned female gender role by putting his heart and soul into an exaggerated performance of femininity. Michael described himself as having been "rather extreme about it," wearing makeup, feminine clothing, high heels, and the like. But, he laughed, "It didn't work." Michael began living as a man at age 16.

Living a Double Life

It is not unusual for trans kids with supportive families to begin the process of transition by presenting and expressing themselves according to their affirmed gender at home before taking on other social spaces. Several kids in the study have safe space for their gender self-determination at home but conform to their assigned category, more or less, everywhere else. Lennox (11, Indigenous/Canada), for example, is currently living a double life that she finds painful. At home, she is a girl, while at school, she is a boy. She explained, "It's difficult because I don't like switching back and forth. It's just hard just because I don't know what to be. I really want to be a girl, but at school, I'm used to being a boy." Lennox feels safe with her family and can absolutely count on their support (her mother is a trans parent activist) but is afraid she would lose her friends and be all alone at school if she showed up as herself. At present, she's not willing to risk doing this, but the stress she experiences around her sex/gender is significant. Like Lennox, Tru Wilson[24] (12, Black/Euro-Canadian/Indigenous) lived a double life for several years, being a girl at home and a boy at school. Tru experienced this situation as torture: "The pain was just too unbearable. People talk about torture and how like in horror movies and how you're hung up by your wrists and like all that stuff, but they don't know torture. They don't know the pain that you go through where it just feels like you're—where it just feels like something's tugging and tugging and tugging at you and pushing down on your body until you feel like you're going to collapse." Other kids who lack safety at home do the opposite: they present as their affirmed gender in social spaces other than their home while conforming at home.

Most of the trans kids in my study have strong parental support, but those with fewer resources (family and financial support for transition or gender self-determination) have still found a way to build community and experience at least some gender authenticity in (often online) peer networks. For this latter population, having to conform to their assigned sex/gender at least some of the time—with regard to clothing, presentation, names, and pronouns—is really painful and consistently results in negative mental health consequences.

Engaging in Self-Harm or Attempting Suicide

Trans kids are disproportionately at risk for self-harm and suicide.[25] Many of the kids I spoke to struggle with depression and self-harm, and their sex/gender identity issues appear to be a factor in these feelings. Trans kids are particularly vulnerable to coercive pressure to conform to societal gender norms, which often results in bullying and gendered harassment by peers and often debilitating social stigmatization.[26]

Many of the kids in the book have struggled, or are struggling, with anxiety and depression related to gender dysphoria (see glossary) or because the gender-restrictive contexts of most of their surroundings contribute to their struggles with mental health. Five kids have attempted suicide, and at least twice that many have engaged in self-harm (primarily cutting). Dylan (15, Euro-American), for example, was living with his working-poor family in a trailer park in a small community in the U.S. when I interviewed him. He reported experiencing extreme "gender dysphoria" and mental anguish at the onset of puberty and continues to be mostly unable to live as the young man he really is. His gender dysphoria is so intense that, he said, "If I don't have a chest binder, I won't leave my house." The compromises that Dylan is regularly forced to make cause him extreme mental anguish: "It's not like I wear dresses and skirts. I thought about it, and it just makes me uncomfortable and really angry, and I'm like 'No.' I usually cry if I have to wear something like that. I hate it so much. But I don't know, like, I usually wear skinny jeans. It's more of a gender-nonconforming thing." Dylan emphasized, "Me coming out as trans was not only self-acceptance, but it was asking others to accept the person that I wanted to be and who I realized that I was." He was looking forward to being able to legally change his name from the feminized one on his birth certificate to "Dylan" when he turns 16, saying, "That will be pretty exciting. Even if they're not using the right pronouns yet, I'll still have my name. My name's important to me."

Dylan reported struggling with depression, self-harm, and multiple suicide attempts, for which he was receiving therapy. The day of the interview, Dylan was off work because he had cut himself badly the night before. Although he knew the wound needed stitches, his terror of hospitals was keeping him away from the emergency room. He assured me that he planned no immediate further self-harm:

I got rid of everything I could have used or would have used, so there's nothing that I'm planning on doing. It's not as bad as it used to be. It is pretty bad still, but I used to cut daily, multiple times a day, two or three times a day. I'd wake up and cut, and before bed I'd cut. And so it got to the point where I didn't see it as such a big deal. They aren't deep or anything—never needed stitches—and then a while ago, I started cutting deeper, where I would need stitches. I actually—when I cut really bad, I have to call my mom, count how many days I can go without.

I found this admission alarming and handled the situation as skillfully as I could—via Skype. I know that all the kids in my study are vulnerable to self-harm and/or suicide, and I try to communicate to them that I believe they are who they tell me they are and that they matter. And I mean it every time. I made several attempts after the interview to reach Dylan to see how he is doing, but I have not been successful. I know there is a good chance that he's busy or he's changed his email address or something like that, but I do worry about him.

Gender and Sexual Nonconformity

Some of the kids in the book are more or less comfortable with the sex identity assigned to them but resist conforming to the sexist gender expectations they encounter. Ray-Ray (16, Euro-Canadian) has always found gender norms confining, both socially and with regard to his self-expression. Ray-Ray identifies as a boy and doesn't think that is going to change, but he has always been gender nonconforming and is often read by others as "different," saying, "I definitely don't fit the stereotype." When he was younger, he wore dresses for special occasions and "would always go to the girl's section with all the colors and sparkles" when shopping for clothes. Ray-Ray's mother, Nadine, herself experienced censure from people in their rural, conservative community for letting her son be "weird." This was why Ray-Ray's family relocated to another part of the country to a "rather hippy," rural environment when he was still quite little. Ray-Ray thinks that because of this relocation, he has "never felt really harshly judged": "which was really good, and I'm glad about that." While Ray-Ray feels fairly sexually fluid, he described the pressure he feels to "identify as something": "because with people partnering up around me, I want to too. And my mom just keeps telling me, 'Well, you've got to try something to see what you like, right?' And I kind of have a really big problem with decisions. I'm kind of scared of making decisions. It takes me a long time. So I think that's part of my problem, like why I haven't been with anybody yet. And also because people really don't know which way I swing probably. So they're not able to approach me." But this makes Ray-Ray uncomfortable too: "If you partner up with somebody who identifies as a woman or a girl for the first time, does that make you straight? I don't feel that way. I feel like I'm still open. That's not a deciding factor." Ray-Ray noted that others assume he is gay because of their investment in gay stereotypes: "People who know me, who have known me since I was little, sometimes mention how it's funny how the first thing I did when I got my dollhouse with all the things for Christmas from my dad was vacuum the whole thing and how I wore dresses and all that. I feel like I *should* be gay, but I don't really know."

All the kids in the book have encountered society's conflation of gender and sexuality, so it was not unusual for some of them to think of themselves as potentially gay, lesbian, or queer before coming to understand that it is their gender identity that is nontraditional. Several of my participants who were designated female at birth began their gender journey by identifying as lesbians or bisexual because they "didn't even know that transgender was a thing," but when their online activity and/ or engagement with the LGBT community exposed them to a range of gender identities, binary and nonbinary, they shifted their attention from their sexuality to their gender and found themselves more "at home." Helen (16, Euro-Canadian), for example, wishes they had known about the existence of nonbinary genders much earlier in their life. They have trouble even naming their gender identity! The first nonnormative identity Helen embraced concerned sexuality: "Yeah, I am a lesbian. . . . But . . . once I found out there were nonbinary genders, I was . . . I think I am one, and I think I like them." Helen described themselves as "one of those people who really needs experience in order to understand things," so it was not until they went to an LGBT camp and met nonbinary people that they understood themselves fully. After all, they observed, "in my town, I am the only nonbinary person I know of." Several of my participants reported having a parent ask them, "Aren't you just gay?" or even "Could you not just live as a gay person?"—imagining that being gay would somehow be easier than being transgender.

Alternative sexual identities are a source of pleasure and self-realization for some and a way station on the way to gender self-determination for others. Quinn (18, Indigenous/Euro-Canadian) said they came out "initially as bisexual": "right before I got into this relationship with a girl, and I started identifying as a lesbian part way through it, and when we broke up about half a year later, I said, 'Well, if I'm attracted to girls, what makes a girl?'" Issues around sexual orientation, at least in conventional terms, stop making sense when people let go of the sex/gender binary. As Quinn explained, "If you're like, 'Oh, I'm attracted to girls,' but a lot of girls don't have vaginas, and when you take into account that there's a huge percentage of the population that's intersex[27] and not as many people are dyadic as most people tend to think, then like what makes a girl or a boy? Nothing really. . . . You're just like, 'Oh no, nothing makes sense anymore.'" Quinn began the process of resisting their assigned gender category by first identifying as "gender queer": "Because it's a term I'd heard used around before and because I was at the time identifying as queer because I wasn't as comfortable with my orientation. Not that I wasn't comfortable, but I didn't really know how to identify: 'Oh no, like I used to think I liked girls, and now I'm having some trouble with this; so I'm queer, and I'm also gender queer, super queer.' I identified myself as 'super queer,' to be honest, a lot of the time."

While sex education in public schools may emphasize consent, safety, consideration, and self-care, at best, as opposed to abstinence and an explicitly anti-LGBT curriculum, at worst, it doesn't always leave open the question about what kinds of sexual/romantic and nonromantic attachments kids ultimately want to establish. This is because the internalization of the model of monogamy forecloses a lot of self-discovery and self-knowledge. Polyamorous and kink communities emphasize consent and communication and model other ways to relate sexually to people that, for some, bring more pleasure and build more community. Some of the kids in this study feel empowered by and are contributing to new language around a range of gender and sexual identities. Quinn said, for example, "If you want to get really, really specific, I am a demi-polyromantic, polysexual, gender-queer individual." Quinn defines themselves as "polyamorous and polysexual and polyromantic": "but I usually just describe myself as queer because that's so much easier, in addition to being a demi-romantic, which is on the aromantic spectrum." Quinn took visible pleasure in providing me with a crash course in newly emerging language around gender and sexual identities:

> This is a fun thing! In addition to having different romantic or sexual orientations like bi, poly, homo, hetero, etcetera, pan, there's also those four romantic orientations, and then you have different degrees sort of. So you have asexual, which I'm sure you know what that is, someone who doesn't experience sexual attraction, and then you have alosexual, which is the opposite. And the same is true for romanticism, and then you have all these different degrees within that. So "demi" is one of those, and "demi" means partial, of course, but specifically in this case, it means after you have a really strong emotional bond with the person. So it takes me like months and months and months of knowing someone in order to develop romantic feelings for them. I don't really get crushes, which is great because none of my friends seem to benefit from them.

Hunter (13, Indigenous/Canada), identifies as a "gay, demi-sexual male who is also polyamorous." He explained, "Demi-sexual means if you start to get to know a person, then you start feeling sexual attraction to them. So the more you know them, the more sexual attraction you feel for them, and like, it's something that you can't actually choose. It basically chooses you, I guess." The way that gender- and sexual-minority people of all ages produce language beyond the limits of binary gender, heterosexuality, and monogamy is an exciting thing to chronicle. This living dictionary of identity and practice is constantly being updated and revised. It reflects grassroots knowledge and community formation/ negotiation rather than top-down diagnosis and categorization by scientific and medical communities (or moral mandates stemming from conservative religious traditions). Trans teens in particular are actively engaging in these processes of knowledge generation and exchange.

In the absence of visible transgender people and people with non-binary identities in the lives of the trans kids in the book, many have developed their own language to explain their dissonance/dysphoria, while others have experienced a "eureka" moment when they learned of the existence of other transgender people. Accessing or developing new language is a key aspect of empowerment for trans kids. For example, Tru described having feelings about not being a boy in first grade that solidified by fourth grade into the knowledge that "I am a girl." With the help of a supportive friendship group, Tru developed her own language to describe a sense of self that was at odds with what was being imposed on her. Tru explained,

> I said that I was "half boy and half girl." And the term "he/she" came to me a little later when I started talking about it with my friends, and they said, "You could—just to like be more simple—you could also call yourself a 'he/she.'" I thought that I was a boy that liked dolls and boys. I didn't know that I could actually change. Then I thought, "What if I could turn into a girl?" And then it started to become a feeling of me being a girl. And then as it grew and got more stronger, it just became a fact, and I knew that I was a girl. I just didn't know how to explain it.

A key facet of Tru's empowerment was finding a way to explain to adults in her family and at her school that they had her gender wrong. As soon as Tru socially transitioned, "everything changed": "It felt so good when we got rid of my boy clothes. It felt so good when I got my very first dolls for Christmas. And it felt so good to hear the first time someone called me Tru and didn't ask if that was right."

Several participants experienced unease with their gender identities and their bodies, an experience that was painfully heightened at puberty, but they lacked the language to make sense of it. Michael started to feel "really different" and depressed around puberty: "Like I didn't feel how I thought a girl should feel like." Michael experienced a sense of dissonance with his assigned sex/gender identity and social standing as a girl, but, he said, "I just thought maybe I'm just a tomboy, right? But that didn't work either [laughs]. Because as a tomboy, guys still treated me as a girl, and you know they're all—they have to be all gentleman-like towards me, and that made me feel kind of like, what's the word? Undignified? I feel like I should be on the same level as them. They shouldn't be treating me differently." It was not a matter of feeling that he was treated unfairly, he said, but rather, "they were just treating me like they would treat any other girl, [softer] like how they were treating other girls." Michael did not have words for his experience until he met a transgender person for the first time, and then everything fell into place for him. He described a chance meeting with a female-to-male (FTM) transgender person through a friend as being "like a spark" (he punctuated this statement by snapping his fingers). Prior to this meeting, Michael had never heard of trans people: "But after I met him, I'm like 'I think this is what all these feelings, all these experiences are.'" He then turned to the Internet for more information.

Transitioning

When a person undergoes *social transition*, the process typically involves announcing a change in gender identity along with new pronouns and often, but not always, adopting a new first name. One begins to "live" as the affirmed gender. Where legally possible, obtaining new government identification featuring the affirmed rather than assigned sex marker is an important part of this process.

Government identification often presents trans people with an insurmountable barrier to social transition. "M" or "F" sex markers on government identification play a fundamental role in imposing a binary-based sex category on kids and in enabling or preventing freedom of movement. Birth certificates include assigned sex markers and are necessary to register for school and many recreational programs and to obtain a healthcare card and passport. Identity documents that contain a sex marker that does not match the way in which one's gender is "read at a glance" or a person's affirmed sex are a source of precarity for transgender people of all ages. Cameron explained why he wanted to legally change his name and sex marker, for example: "I would like to not have the 'F' on the top of my health card and my licenses and my whatever, but I'm not in a position where I can get that changed legally right now." The province he lived in at the time required sex reassignment surgery to change the gender marker on government ID. When I interviewed Levon, parent of Caroline (six, Black American), in 2013, he explained that they would not visit Canada or any other country until their daughter was old enough to have the sex-reassignment surgery that was a requirement for a U.S. passport (the policy was changed in 2014). Levon said it was out of the question for his daughter to have to present as a boy even for a few hours because it would be so damaging to her mental health: "I could never ask her to do that."

Fortunately, some of the restrictive requirements for obtaining government-issued identity documents congruent with affirmed, rather than assigned, sex have been removed. According to the National Center for Transgender Equality, as of 2014, trans people who are U.S. citizens can "obtain a full ten-year passport with an updated gender marker if you have had clinical treatment determined by your doctor to be appropriate in your case to facilitate gender transition. No specific details are required about what type of treatment is appropriate for you."[28] Starting in 2014, trans Canadians became able to obtain passports reflecting affirmed gender without undergoing sex reassignment surgery. As noted earlier, a legal case on behalf of a trans child in British Columbia— Harriette Cunningham—resulted in a change to that province's Vital Statistics Act.[29] Many other provinces have similarly changed requirements.[30] In 2011, Australia introduced a three-gender marker system on its passports, allowing transgender citizens to switch from "M" to "F" or vice versa and intersex citizens to list their gender as "X." As of August 31, 2017, the government of Canada made it possible for citizens to obtain a Canadian passport with "X" as a third option for a gender marker. In March 2017, the province of Ontario introduced the option of "X" "in the sex field of its driver's licence, to ensure the fair, ethical and equitable treatment of people with trans and non-binary gender identity."[31] In the same year, Oregon became the first U.S. state to add the new gender option of "X" to its driver's licenses.[32] While adding "X" as a third option reflects a significant cultural shift toward greater gender inclusion, "X" still marks gender, and it might actually put people traveling with such documents at risk at international borders.

While the ability to obtain government identification congruent with one's gender identity is an extremely significant step with regard to recognition and harm reduction for trans people, many trans people suggest that even *requiring* a gender marker is fundamentally oppressive. Trans activists and allies are fighting for an end to the inclusion of sex markers on government identification entirely.[33] For example, in 2017, a British Columbia parent applied for a judicial review in order to procure a birth certificate for their child without a sex marker.[34] In the same year, three Saskatchewan families of trans kids took their fight for a gender-neutral birth certificate to the province's human rights commission.[35] At the time of this writing, these cases were unresolved.

When a person undergoes *medical transition*, the process includes any or all of the following: puberty-suppression therapy in the case of children to interrupt "natal" puberty; cross-sex hormone therapy; sex reassignment surgery (top and/or bottom); other cosmetic procedures. These medical treatments fall under the wider umbrella of *trans-affirming healthcare*. Puberty-suppression therapy via "hormone blockers" is referred to as the "Dutch protocol" because it originated in Amsterdam. Unlike in Holland, however, many North American clinics support early social transition for children. The term "transition" is most typically understood according to the logics of the sex/gender binary, but it need not be restricted to this. Some people who assert a nonbinary identity, for example, undergo a social and/or medical transition. Some trans people who access affirming healthcare may also socially transition, and some may not; trans people who socially transition may or may not access trans-affirming healthcare. In a number of regions, however, the ability to socially transition or change one's sex marker on government-issued identity documents may hinge on receiving specified medical treatment[36] under the supervision of a licensed professional.

Some of this study's participants volunteered that they were on hormone blockers and/or cross-sex hormones, while others intended or hoped to be. Some volunteered their plans for surgery, while others had no access to appropriate healthcare (because of lack of financial resources or parental support); and still others had no desire to medicalize their gender identities. Many voiced regret about not having been aware of transgender possibilities earlier in their development so that they could have taken hormone blockers to prevent undesired physical changes at puberty. Very few in the study grew up knowing that alternative gender identities were a possibility or that you could "switch."

Branching Out beyond the Binary

One of the accusations leveled at trans people in general and trans kids in particular is that our gender variance is "just a phase," and this attitude can operate by putting pressure on some of us to be more binary conforming, fixed, or fully transitioned than might be optimal. This pressure can have a profound effect on some trans people, making us feel that we must hold fast to a narrative that proclaims the permanence of transition, as if one has finally ended up where one belongs on a linear and binary-based gender-identity highway. Stef, however, has had multiple transitions and is bound to confound some trans people for whom the need to defend the authenticity and permanence of their identity is particularly acute. This feeling is because of the way their story may be taken up by anti-trans activists.

Stef transitioned to Stefanie at age five, legally changed their name and pronouns, and first took hormone blockers and then cross-sex hormones. But when they were 14, Stef said, "I started feeling that I really didn't like gender norms and how, even if I was a female, that I would not fit into certain categories." Stef resists both a binary-based trans narrative of permanence and the kind of criticism of that narrative that legitimates trans-oppressive refusals to acknowledge the "realness" of trans kids' gender identities. Of their time as a girl, Stef refuses to say "it was just a phase" or that it was a mistake: "[being a girl was] just something that I did really want back then, and now I want something different."

Stef learned about and got to know gender-fluid and agender trans people via the Internet, which helped them transition from being a transgender girl to a gender-neutral/agender identity. They decided, "Well, today I'm just going to be Stef." This process of resistance and discovery was aided by an online trans group in which Stef felt safe enough to try out gender-neutral pronouns. This transition was complicated, however, because Stef feared that the trans friends they had made at various camps, conferences, and online spaces—and who had served as a lifeline to keep "Stefanie" going while "she" struggled in trans-oppressive school settings—would turn their back on them if they ceased to be *her*. Much to their relief, Stef has not been abandoned by their friends, but they expressed regret about not being exposed to more options earlier in their life, specifically about gender-fluid and gender-queer identities. While Stef refuses to repudiate their time as a girl or to express regret about the affirming healthcare they received, they believe they may have opted for a less binary-based trans identity at an earlier time if they had known about these possibilities. Stef describes themselves now as "trans identified," saying, "I used to be female, but now I'm androgynous."

The lack of visible nonbinary options limits the embodiments that trans kids are able to explore, which had a significant impact on Kidd (18, Black/Native American). Kidd explained what this lack of information when they were younger denied them: "the chance to express myself and try to figure out who I was in that sense like a lot of other kids did." Although they mostly flew under the radar in high school, only presenting as a girl with close girlfriends, Kidd fully expected to transition to a woman after graduation. They explained, "Throughout my high school career, I actually thought I was completely a transgender girl." But Kidd changed their mind about transitioning when they had the opportunity to explore their gender more after high school.

Kidd moved to another city to live with their older sister, who is a lesbian, after high school. Here, they had the space and support to explore themselves "gender wise, sexuality wise all that good stuff." In this new environment, where Kidd was "more free with being Carmella [the name they give their female persona] all the time," their understanding of their gender identity changed and, so did their plans to transition. Kidd came to an understanding: "I am actually in this middle space that does not exist, and that is when I started doing my research and was like, 'Oh, you know, there is this nonbinary, and I am more like that than anything else.'" Kidd went on to say, "Even though quite a percentage of me was Carmella, there is a percentage of me that is Kidd [the name they give their male persona]. I realized that I am both and neither at the same time. I did not want to completely get rid of Kidd, as he is a part of who I am." As Kidd embraced a nonbinary identity, they abandoned their plans to transition to a woman, explaining, "This kind of rolling who I am feels right." Kidd now identifies as nonbinary, asks to be addressed using "they/them/their" pronouns, and only regrets not being made aware of all the possibilities regarding gender and sexual identity earlier in their life.

Most of the kids in this book view gender as a spectrum. Michael believes that children and young people should be able to "try stuff out, find what fits for you." Some have very politically nuanced understandings of gender-identity issues and resist the sex and gender binary entirely, at least for themselves. Quinn identifies as a "queer, nonbinary, trans person of color" and laments the invisibility of gender-diverse trans people. In their analysis of gender, Quinn emphasized relationships of power and oppression: "The *assigned* female at birth, *assigned* male at birth, it really renders the power dynamic clear, doesn't it?" According to Quinn, "I was sort of thinking maybe I'm bi some time in grade 7, but the gender thing, there wasn't really a lead-in to it; it was just sort of like a giant rock fell from the sky, and suddenly I had to pay attention to it. It was like that, and I started walking around being like, 'Look, there's a rock here,' to all my friends." Some trans kids affirm a binary identity but embrace gender nonconformity, which can be really confusing to people they encounter, adding to the feelings of pressure and stress that these trans kids experience. Cameron, for example, explained why he took some time to feel entitled to define himself as a guy: "every once in a while, I like to throw on a skirt."

Social Change

Many of the trans kids in my study are very open about being trans, partly for their own comfort but also for political reasons: their own difficult experiences lead them to want to create more space for other kids to determine their own genders and find acceptance. Knowing that they have done things that will make things better "for the next trans kid" is a source of great pride to a number of the kids in the book. They have done this in a variety of ways, from engaging in highly visible legal cases and participating in pride parades as openly trans to speaking publicly in support of transgender-inclusive policies (at school boards or in recreation districts, for example). Others are incredibly private and do not wish to be "out there" about anything at all, least of all about their trans status, but they have found quieter ways to make a difference. Some kids feel that participating anonymously in my research is a way for them to contribute to education around trans issues without risking a loss of privacy or putting themselves in harm's way. Not surprisingly, social change approaches among trans kids and their parents mirror tensions within broader queer and trans communities and other social justice struggles.

Significant debates in transgender studies and queer and trans communities include those between queer-identified proponents of transgender identities who model an antiessentialist gender future[37] and transsexual-rights authors and activists[38] who may or may not see themselves under the LGBT umbrella but are concerned about ending the mental distress, discrimination, and violence that transsexuals face.[39] Critics of this latter approach argue that the tendency to limit transgender issues to transsexuality fails to represent the range of visible and invisible individuals and identities and the disproportionate access to appropriate healthcare that is a function of race and class.[40] It is important to see transgender kids against the backdrop of these debates within and between queer and trans communities because these tensions are present in the social movements they and/or their parents interact with. Other tensions within queer and trans communities that are reflected among activist trans kids and their parents relate to a focus on trans identity as a single issue versus an analysis of discrimination against trans people within an overarching system of oppression.

It is true that some transgender kids are "gender conforming"[41] in that they conform to binary identities—though not the category to which they were assigned at birth—and this may be easier for many people to understand and accept and for mainstream institutions to adapt to and integrate; but they are a relatively privileged, albeit extremely vulnerable, minority. This subset often has both the desire for and access to gender-affirming healthcare, and their circumstances may be less insecure than those whose avowed identities are nonbinary or for whom gender-normative clothing, identity documents, hormone therapy, and/or surgery is out of reach or undesirable. But it is also accurate to say that kids who affirm a binary-based trans identity are vulnerable, and those without significant resources and support are even more so. For those who are visible in the face of opposition, the discrimination and bullying they experience from adults and peers is very damaging and greatly increases the risk of mental health struggles, self-harm, and suicide. Those who are invisible often witness trans-negativity and struggle with feelings of isolation and self-hatred.

Trans Kids and Precarity

Given the range of complex experiences trans kids are vulnerable to, it is crucial to situate transgender kids within broader relations of power and oppression, yet existing resources for the public (versus academic critical theory)[42] tend to focus on relatively privileged, rather than socioeconomically marginal, children. A more integrated anti-oppression approach to understanding and supporting transgender kids is required. In the remainder of this chapter, I focus on two trans kids, Wren and Finn (14, Euro-American), to draw together recent theorizing relating to precarity, children and childhood, critical disability, and queer and trans scholarship on the biopolitics of gender and race.

Wren socially transitioned to a female identity when she was seven but, at the age of 11, told me she wishes she had been left alone to be who she was without having to think of or explain herself as *any* gender. I have had the chance to interview her twice, and it is very interesting to track the consistency of her sense of gender identity and how she sees this playing out in the future. When I first interviewed her at age seven, right after she had switched her pronoun, she told me, "I was born a boy, but I like being a girl." At 11, she explained that she felt pressure to transition: "I would not say I wanted to *be* a girl. I just wanted to wear those kinds of clothes, so that people assumed that I'm a boy that likes being a girl. But I didn't. I was actually kind of fine with who I am—just wearing different clothes was what I kind of wanted and having my hair different, longer."

The "effeminaphobia," as gender theorist Eve Sedgwick called it,[43] directed at gender-nonconforming boys is keenly felt by kids such as Wren who are designated male at birth and are gender nonconforming. Wren told me that she thinks she probably would not have felt the need to transition as a girl if people had not made such a big deal about her gender nonconformity. But the microaggressions that Wren endured as a consequence of the gender confusion she provoked in other people—and their insistence on making it *her* problem—translated into too much anxiety for her. I am struck by Wren's tremendous courage to resist what was expected of her rather than conform. Trans activist Julia Serano lauds the courage of all trans kids given the "presence of systemic societal transphobia."[44] But conforming would have come at too great a cost for Wren. Wren told me how she would feel if she had been unable to express her femininity: "I would feel like my true self isn't really my true self, like I'm not in the same body as I used to be, like I'm not in the body I want to be—stuck." But when I asked Wren, at age seven, about her vision of herself in the future, she was very matter of fact in explaining that she did not see transgender womanhood as an option. She told me of her plan to "change back" into a boy when she turned

10. I was a bit surprised to hear this given how stereotypically feminine she is, although I never doubt anyone's assertions about their gender identity. When I interviewed her in 2015, she was 11, and the timeline for changing back had shifted for her; but the vision of her future had not: she was operating in stealth mode at a new school, and she hoped to pass as a girl until she turns 14 or 15, at which point she plans to "change back into a boy." Wren consistently refuses the possibility of trans adulthood for herself, explaining, "I am Black. I don't want to be trans too." Wren's life chances are shaped by the class privilege of her parents, but in seeing no future for herself—literally—she displays a sophisticated and heartbreaking political awareness about the disabling effects of being transgender and subject to anti-Black racism.

Finn[45] is another trans kid who saw no future for himself. In the course of my research, I learned, via his mother's heartbreaking announcement in an online parent group, that Finn had committed suicide at the age of 14. I obtained permission from his mother to share some of what she wrote in a later post to the group.

It's been five weeks since my 14 year old transgender son Finn took his life. We had a discussion that night at dinner about his next Lupron[46] shot, and how we were going to pay for it since we'd just gotten a letter that day of our second denial of state insurance, and had been told by Lupron's owner company, Abbvie, that we were slightly over income and it was unlikely that we'd qualify for their patient assistance program. We couldn't afford the $1400 out of pocket payment. We talked about other options, but he was afraid of the side effect of weight gain. He begged me to do a GoFundMe for him, but I told him we couldn't do it for something ongoing. He left the table upset. Oh, how I wished I would have checked in on him. But he spent most of his time holed up in his room, and I was trying to be respectful of not intruding. Later that night, while I slept in the next room, he quietly left the house and walked to the railroad a few blocks away, and lay his body across the track. It was the 11:00 train.[47]

Finn and many other trans kids find puberty too difficult to bear and, faced with what they see as limited options for the future, choose death. Many of these kids are isolated, but many are also, like Finn, deeply loved and supported by their families and friends. As I picture this beautiful kid lying down on the tracks and remaining there while the train thundered toward him and over him, I am struck by the power of his will. This was no suicide attempt to signal a need for help but rather a grim and determined choice. I see Finn not as a victim of trans oppression but rather as a casualty, because of the obvious agency he displayed in choosing death. That he weighed his options and decided the best decision was to die speaks to the limited agency available to him and the hopelessness about the future he felt. I shared these thoughts with his mother, and she agreed, saying, "I was struck by that mere determination and courage it must've taken to stay on those rails as the train roared down towards him." His mom described Finn as gifted and wise but lacking the maturity to manage his considerable emotional sensitivity. She explained, "He had to lay down that load he was carrying somehow. The hopelessness he felt in the road ahead of him is what broke him that night. But even if he had no problem getting Lupron, he still had his internal demons." But, she said, "if the barriers to taking Lupron were not there, I don't think he would have died that night." For Wren and Finn, like many vulnerable trans kids, being trans is only one dimension of their precarity.

To be alive is to be precarious—it is an inevitable part of the human condition—but we are unequally so. Judith Butler defines precarity as an inevitable social condition in which "one's life is always in some sense in the hands of the other. . . . Survival is dependent on what we might call a social network of hands."[48] In *States of Insecurity*, political theorist Isabell Lorey defines precariousness as "insecurity and vulnerability, destabilization and endangerment," as opposed to "protection, political and social immunization against everything that is recognized as endangerment."[49] Lorey uses the term "precarity" specifically to refer to "naturalized relations of domination, through which belonging to a group is attributed or denied to individuals. Precarity involves social positionings of insecurity."[50] Moreover, Lorey and Butler both contend that modern practices of governing are precisely about this differential distribution of precariousness. The key tension for neoliberal states involves governing via imposing precarity on part of the population but not so much that it results in insurrection. Indeed, Lorey remarks, "Managing this threshold is what makes up the art of governing today."[51]

Lorey draws on the work of Michel Foucault with particular emphasis (for our purposes) on the historical emergence of biopolitical governance. In the West during the 18th and 19th centuries, liberal humanist doctrine combined with population-management strategies offered up by the emerging disciplines of psychology, criminology, and medicine to establish new mechanisms for state governance that marked the modern capitalist nation-state as distinct from former modes of ruling. According to Foucault, the emergence of this modern state necessitated a shift away from power as overt dominance/violence to "biopower."[52] The emergence of biopolitical governance reflected an overall shift from state violence that crudely dictated life or death to state population management that fostered life or disallowed it. In this reading, colonialism, neoliberal capitalism, racialized socioeconomic relations, and heteropatriarchy all can be cited as (closely related) forces that combine to produce a "differential distribution of precarity."[53]

The socioeconomic and cultural legacy of the Enlightenment, capitalist transformation, and colonial appropriation reveals power operating through naturalized categories of sex, gender, sexuality, race, citizenship, ability, and age that are mutually constitutive. White settler nations and neoliberal globalization have their roots in the imperial projects of the emergent modern capitalist nation states of western Europe. The central ideology of these (ongoing) colonial projects is liberal humanism. Liberal humanist philosophy maintains that only humans are capable of reason, and only some humans rise above biological disadvantages related to gender, racialization, social class, sexuality, age, and non-Christian status. Those who are deemed to lack this capacity to be fully human are understood to be "disabled" and are, accordingly, subjugated.[54]

Racialization

Canada and the U.S. occupy huge, varied, and contested geopolitical spaces. Both nations brand themselves as democracies, but each is more accurately understood as a "white settler society,"[55] albeit with different histories of displacing/committing genocide against Indigenous populations and subjugating racialized minorities. White settler societies required land, labor, and capital investment,[56] and these logics explain histories of genocide, slavery, white settlement, and forced migration. These histories provide a crucial genealogy of contemporary socioeconomic inequality wherein gender, race, class, sexuality, and immigration/citizenship status are key axes of inequality and oppression in both countries. Queer and trans scholars of color and antiracist allies, writing in the tradition of critical race and biopolitics, identify hierarchies relating to race, gender, sexuality, class, and disability as an "assemblage" of oppression.[57] Describing sexuality as a heavily racialized "organizing principle of social life" and "a form of power that exists regardless of an individual's sexual identity," for example, sociologist C. J. Pascoe establishes a clear link between children, gender, sexuality, and race in the United States.[58] In *Dude, You're a Fag: Masculinity and Sexuality in High School*, Pascoe speaks of "gender and sexuality regimes" and contends that "gendered power works through racialized selves."[59] In describing the racialized operation of "fag discourse" in a U.S. high school, Pascoe emphasizes that homophobia is not a racially neutral phenomenon: it is mostly white boys who call each other the abject "fag" in order to establish themselves as appropriately masculine. Black American boys in Pascoe's study, however, were less likely than white boys to be on the receiving end of the "fag" epithet, but their less suspect Black masculinity was bifurcated by racist notions of hypersexuality/hypermasculinity on the one hand and their relative impotence in the face of racialized national economic and political systems on the other.

Canadian critical race[60] and Indigenous scholars[61] have written extensively about the white patriarchal construction of citizenship in the national imagination and with regard to the distribution of status and resources. This scholarship emphasizes the role of whiteness and masculinity in colonial/genocidal relationships with respect to Indigenous peoples and racialized and oppressed groups. Black feminist scholars,[62] for their part, have made significant contributions to feminist, queer, and trans analyses of gender and sexuality by demonstrating how these are integrated with race, ethnicity, social class, immigration status, and dis/ability to create privileged and abject categories of people and legitimate, versus deviant, gender and sexual identities and practices. Transgender people of all ages are constituted by, and constitute themselves within, these particular sociohistorical contexts or assemblages.

Queer/trans necropolitics reflects an engagement between critical race and queer and trans scholarship that is uniquely positioned to situate transgender kids in Canada and the U.S. "Necropolitics" emerged as part of a tradition of radical critical race theory that builds on Foucault's analysis of biopower. It is a framework for analysis that identifies "assemblages"[63] of oppression that unevenly distribute resilience versus harm, life versus death, along axes of race, class, sexuality, and gender. Introduced by critical race scholar Achille Mbembe in 2003, necropolitics is consistent with Lorey's vision of the modern state as unevenly distributing precarity in that it defines sovereignty as the power of the state "to dictate who may live and who must die."[64] Some people are awarded life and life-sustaining resources, while others are killed outright, condemned to a "slow death" by virtue of being starved for resources, treated to "social death,"[65] and/or violated on a day-to-day basis. In a similar vein, geographer Ruth Wilson Gilmore defines racism as "the state-sanctioned or extralegal production and exploitation of group-differentiated vulnerability to premature death."[66]

A key feature of the biopolitics of the modern nation-state concerns necropolitics: the rationalization of inhumane treatment, violence, and oppression for the greater good. Subhabrata Bannerjee's introduction of the term "necrocapitalism" emphasizes the mutually constitutive relationships between state and capitalist "necropower" for distributing precarity (for example, in the increasing use of privatized military forces in the so-called war on terror).[67] While Mbembe focuses explicitly on state atrocities on a large scale,[68] queer and trans necropolitical theorizing focuses on systemic racism, classism, and institutionalized state violence (in the form of policing, urban planning, the prison industrial complex, borders, the war on terror, and lack of access to healthcare).[69]

Queer/trans necropolitical theorizing challenges the notion that LGBT organizations and individuals in the West have made gains resulting in changes to law and government policy. Trans and queer scholars of color and antiracist, antipoverty allies[70] have resisted white, middle-class, "homonormative"[71] and "transnormative"[72] milestones because they have failed to attend to issues beyond gender and sexuality. As such, critical queer and trans scholarship resists the assimilation agenda of mainstream LGBT politics.[73] Transgender scholars Riley Snorton and

Jin Haritaworn[74] draw on Mbembe's theory of necropolitics, Duggan's analysis of (white, middle-class) homonormativity, and assemblage theorist Jasbir Puar's concept of homonormative nationalism or "homonationalism,"[75] to formulate an explicitly trans necropolitics that focuses on the day-to-day experiences of racism and poverty for trans people of color.[76] Indeed, trans necropolitical theorizing resonates powerfully with the findings of the 2011 report *Injustice at Every Turn: A Look at Black Respondents in the National [U.S.] Transgender Discrimination Survey*, which concluded that trans people of color in the U.S. experience a relentless barrage of microaggressions. The report revealed that while "discrimination was pervasive" for all respondents who took the national transgender discrimination survey, "the combination of anti-transgender bias and persistent, structural, and individual racism was especially devastating" for black transgender people and other people of color.[77]

Childhood

Scholars in the field of critical childhood studies situate "children" as a socially constructed demographic category—like gender, sexuality, race, class, and disability—that acts as a lens through which we can see more clearly how power operates. These categories can be mobilized to maintain systems of oppression and affect different transgender kids in particular ways. Dean Spade proposes that instead of organizing efforts for change around notions of individual "rights," we identify and critically engage with race, gender, sexuality, class, and immigration status as "vectors of vulnerability and security that intersect to impact life chances," examining how "gender categories are enforced on all people in ways that cause particularly dangerous outcomes for trans people."[78] Critical childhood studies suggests that age is another such vector, with "childhood" generating particular interrelations of precarity that subject "minors" to varying degrees of subordination. Age categories, in concert with other ascribed variables, are used to organize populations with regard to access to care and resources. As critical childhood studies scholar Annette Appell observes, childhood is transitory but foretelling: "Unlike other subordinated groups, children will outgrow their subordination as children, but whether they will be subordinated as adults depends very much on their childhood, that is, their race, class, and gender, or perhaps more accurately the race, class, and gender of their parents."[79] Analyzing children as a socially constructed minority group subject to, and implicated in, relations of oppression is a central piece of the puzzle in order to understand trans kids in all their complexity.

The way we organize children as a disempowered demographic group, and childhood as a cultural system/ideology for imposing and justifying this disempowerment, also returns to the liberal humanist legacy, this time of an age-based binary: innocence/dependence versus rational knowledge/autonomy. The liberal humanist fantasy suggests that the apex of human development is to be antisocial: when you grow up, you rely on no one but yourself. It sees children as innocent and benevolently disempowered by purportedly responsible adults. This view has been sharply criticized by feminists for rendering invisible the extensive care work and interdependence that humans of all ages require to survive. Feminist critiques of liberalism's foundational view of the citizen as autonomous counter it with a fundamental belief in interdependence and group life in which we rely on the care received from others.[80] The ideology of individualism has adapted to neoliberal times and operates powerfully in discourses of governance today that normalize the gutting of social welfare provisions.

The relationship between "transgender" and "childhood" is a troubled one given that children are not typically credited with the ability to authenticate their own gender identities or to know themselves. The experiences of children, who are understood as not yet fully human, are rendered less real, their feelings and desires less important, and their capacity for agency limited at best. The line between childhood and adulthood is further blurred because children's dependence is largely imposed on them and because many of those who are no longer legally minors still lack meaningful autonomy/agency. Given that only adults are recognized as politically capable,[81] a transgender child is by definition disempowered and more precarious.

In contrast to liberal humanist definitions of children and childhood that view children as passive, a more critical definition of children sees them as capable of agency, although to varying degrees, depending on factors such as race, class, gender, and so on. Critical childhood studies scholar Natascha Klocker describes children's agency on a continuum from thinness to thickness, whereby "'thin' agency refers to decisions and everyday actions that are carried out within highly restrictive contexts, characterized by few viable alternatives. 'Thick' agency is having the latitude to act within a broad range of options. It is possible for a person's agency to be 'thickened' or 'thinned' over time and space, and across their various relationships. Structures, contexts, and relationships can act as 'thinners' or 'thickeners' of individual's agency, by constraining or expanding their range of viable choices."[82] Measuring children's agency involves an examination of the nature and frequency of structural barriers or entitlements and "microaggressions."[83] According to sociologist Sonny Nordmarken, "Microaggressions are routine in social interaction; all social actors deliver them. These often unconscious and unintentional messages manifest as brief, unthinking slights, snubs, insults, or other indignities, frequently embedded within a stream of communication. They are verbal, nonverbal, and environmental, and they can appear in facial expressions, body language, terminology, representation, or remarks."[84] Kids are exposed to, and dole out, a range of microaggressions, but the power of adults over children complicates most settings. These microaggressions wash over and through kids and include various forms of racism, state surveillance, criminalization, poverty, sexism/misogyny, coercive sex/gender assignment and policing, queer oppression, trans oppression, and invisibility. Viewing agency as a continuum draws attention to the complexities of inclusion as well as exclusion. I notice that there are often costs to the inclusion and privilege that some of the kids in my study are able to experience, such as the self-hatred and sense of isolation that can come with invisibility or the reluctant binary conformity with which one of my subjects felt he had to comply in order to participate in sport.[85]

Beyond simply limiting the agency, in varying ways, of actual children, however, the social construction of childhood as a disempowered state does much more than control and discipline children; it is mobilized more broadly to justify practices of neoliberal governance that punish other marginal populations. In an examination of sex-offender registries in the United States, for example, educational scholar and prison abolitionist Erica Meiners reported two key findings: first, that the imagined victim in state discourse about sex-offender registries is a (by definition, innocent) white female child; and second, that in practice, sex-offender registries actually disproportionately target and harm those who are some combination of young, LGBT, and visible minority rather than the (exceptional) sexually deviant adult stranger.[86] Meiners noted that a child's minor status, which precludes legal consent, is used to put LGBT and/or visible minority kids and young people engaging in consensual sex on sex-offender registries, with devastating lifelong consequences. Not only do sex-offender registries fail to protect children from far more routine sexual abuse at the hands of adult family members and trusted others, but they inflict harm on children who defy prescribed boundaries.

Western societies lean heavily on constructions of this imaginary innocence and on romanticized discourses of childhood. This "imagined" child, who must be sheltered from unseemly lifestyles and behaviors, lest the child become corrupted or scarred by the experience, turns out to be white, relatively wealthy, a citizen of a wealthy nation of the global north and heterosexual and yet sexually "innocent."[87] There is also a privatization of childhood—as children are defined as dwelling outside the public sphere ("for their own protection")—which masks the power relations at play. These critical perspectives emphasize the ways in which "the child" has generated "languages of contention"[88] with respect to various forms of deviance relating to gender and sexuality as well as class, race, and intelligence.[89] Puar observes, "Historically speaking, settler colonialism has a long history of articulating its violence through the protection of serviceable figures such as women and children, and now the homosexual"[90]—and now, I might add, via the sexually innocent transgender child. The legitimacy of adult authority over children counts on the subliminal link between childhood, innocence, and vulnerability. This innocence, queer scholar Sarah Chinn notes, is an impossible fantasy,[91] yet this imagined child invites normative understandings of sex, gender, race, social class, and citizenship.[92] To adequately empower trans kids, binary sex and gender systems need to be understood as part of a larger assemblage of power relations. I examine how these forces impact the precarity of trans kids via the lens of critical disability scholar Tobin Siebers's theory of complex embodiment: because of its promise in guiding our fight to make the lives of kids such as Wren and Finn literally, more livable.

Disability

Siebers characterizes Western culture as founded on "the ideology of ability,"[93] despite the fact that this flies in the face of the fragility of the human body—our fundamental precariousness. This ideology of ability is fundamental to liberal humanism's hierarchy of humanity and helps to generate an individual's status and qualification for inclusion and access, or exclusion and denial. Colonialism, racialization, patriarchy, class oppression, and "adultism"[94] are all organized around this notion of what it is to be fully human versus not-quite-human, nonhuman,[95] or disabled. Trans kids experience precarity because they are "other" in binary-based schemes of sex/gender differentiation, but the social forces of race, class, age, family, and community support produce variable vulnerability to interpersonal and state violence.

Identity and disability, for Siebers, are socially constructed and complexly embodied; they are "the theories that we use to fit into and travel through the social world."[96] Siebers exhorts scholars to go beyond making general statements about the social construction of identity categories, insisting that we must "map as many details about the construction as possible and . . . track its political, epistemological, and real effects in the world of human beings."[97] In contrast to medical models of disability that define disability "as a property of the individual body that requires medical intervention," the social model of disability defines disability "relative to the social and built environment, arguing that disabling environments produce disability in bodies and require interventions at the level of social justice."[98] Siebers draws our attention to "built environments" that normalize some physical capacities while associating others with disability, which has particular relevance for trans people, as sex-segregated bathrooms and the activities related to urination, defecation, and menstruation that people are unable to opt out of, for example, socially construct visible trans and gender-nonconforming people as deviant, that is, disabled.[99]

The disabling impact of built environments causes suffering for some people, but these shared experiences of suffering—the "dossier"—can be mobilized for resistance.[100] Sharing this dossier of disabling experiences renders power relations that socially construct categories of disability more visible; that is, they enable us to see the blueprint. And if we can see the blueprint, we are better able to modify or dismantle oppressive environments. In seeking resistance strategies to racist and anti-trans systems of oppression, Riley Snorton pointedly asks, "what stories do we need to surround ourselves with for the presents we currently inhabit?"[101]

The kids in the book demonstrated profound determination to realize and disclose their affirmed genders in often forbidding social contexts that disabled them along multiple axes. They engaged in self-directed identity construction despite incredible environmental pressure to go along with the sex/gender assigned to them. Conversations focused on vulnerability and the harms they experienced but also on the pleasure of self-definition and the possibilities inherent in resistance to coercive sex assignment. There is reason to resist the sentimentality of dominant narratives about transgender kids as either helpless victims or heroic resistance fighters, though the stories that follow show that at times these narratives are not misplaced.

Exposing the blueprint of the social construction of binary systems of sex and gender by documenting the experiences of transgender kids is an act of resistance. As Siebers suggests, precarity is embodied, mapped in time and space, in complex ways. Left unchecked, precarity can disable transgender children, but documenting and sharing it can confront, resist, and transform unjust environments. The stories of trans kids and their parents, as related in this book, are important.

In the next four chapters, I pay particular attention to four key questions:

1. Why do some trans kids have more agency and seem to thrive, while others have less resilience and suffer more?
2. How does poverty and gendered and racial violence impact the lives of trans kids?
3. How do we make the lives of trans kids more livable?
4. How might some social change efforts and achievements on behalf of trans kids who are visible and supported by mobilized parents unwittingly marginalize more precarious racialized and/or impoverished cisgender kids?

In chapter 2, I chronicle the many ways that my participants are disabled in school settings and the consequences of this disabling for their current and future precarity.

2

Schools

I think high school is always sort of stressful and big for anyone, but on top of that, I'm coming in as a different person
from other people's perspective. So, in the first few weeks, I
think it was super difficult for me. Lots of people were still
getting my pronouns and name wrong because they were
adjusting, the kids from my old school; I was getting questions. And then at this point, people started to gossip. So the
kids from my elementary school were telling the kids from
other schools that I was trans. And as a result, I started sort
of getting hate from some of them.
—Greg, 13, Euro-Canadian

From 1967 to 1971, I attended an all-white elementary school in Toronto,
Ontario, that served the western-European Canadian middle- and upper-
middle-class families residing on the neighborhood's east side and the
poorer western-European Canadian and southern- and eastern-European
families living on its west side. I do not remember having a classmate who
did not "pass" as white until fourth grade, when I moved out of the neighborhood. Girls and boys had separate entrances to the school building:
we lined up at least 100 yards apart. The playground was sex divided: the
boys had an area that was at least six times bigger than that allocated to the
girls. Girls skipped rope and played jumpsie[1] next to the teachers' parking lot, while boys ran wild, in great swooping arcs on the larger part of
the playground. By third grade, I remember crossing over to the boys'
side on occasion, without censure, as long as I had a legitimate purpose:
running laps because I had joined the cross-country team, for example.
School activities were routinely organized by grouping girls and boys sep-
arately. Although it was a little unusual, I had friends who were boys and
friends who were girls, but rarely did these two groups come together out
of school. For the most part, I moved freely back and forth.

But at school, there was a dress code. Until I was in fourth grade, when the influence of second-wave feminism began to impact Canadian public school culture, girls in Ontario schools were required to wear skirts and dresses—no pants allowed. I hated this dress code, hated the leotards with the crotch that hung down to my knees no matter how often I pulled them up, hated freezing to death before school and at recess when frigid winter winds whipped up from the lake, and hated not being able to wear jeans or pants. Finally, in third grade, I received permission from my teacher to wear pants to school in the winter as long as I wore them under a skirt and took them off as soon as I arrived in the classroom. That this was a huge victory for me indicates how little agency I had around my choice of clothing.

I am a relatively privileged person with regard to key measures of whiteness, class position, and employment in a respected professional field, but as a gender-nonconforming adopted girl who lacked a secure attachment with either parent, one of whom was emotionally abusive, I was dogged by loneliness, depression, and self-hatred throughout my childhood and adolescence. I was occasionally lifted up, just enough, however, by teachers whose regard and warmth carried me along. It happened first in third grade, when my teacher distinguished herself from her predecessors and treated me with warmth and interest. I flourished in her care. Mrs. B. was young—and pretty hip, when I think back—and seemed to like all the things that other adults did not like about me—my smarts, assertiveness, natural confidence, roughness, and athleticism. She must have been a feminist. She liked me, odd girl that I was, and I could feel it; I was starved for it.

Yet not everyone in that classroom flourished—the kids in the bottom-tier reading group, for example, were disabled by a performance-oriented, "skill and drill" delivery model of education and had low status among their peers. There were probably children in that classroom whom I do not remember at all who had a miserable time while I flourished, perhaps had a miserable time, in part, *because* I flourished. There was always a pecking order, whether I had a good teacher who cared about me and the class in general or a teacher whose authoritarianism just reinforced existing hierarchies. In these early school years, I learned how awful it felt to be on the bottom of that pyramid, and I was forever fearful of being consigned there. I wish I could say that I responded less oppressively to this lesson, but I did not. For that to have happened, I would have needed coaching from an adult I trusted. Instead, I learned to hold my own and contributed to the toxic environment brewing around me.

How School Shapes Us

As my own experience indicates and as a number of studies have shown,[2] the 13 years children normally spend in school in Canada and the U.S. shapes personality and worldview and negatively or positively determines future opportunities. School success is a predictor of future economic success, and this outcome corresponds strongly to the socio-economic status of a child's family. For some students, school is a place of learning, opportunity, and social engagement; for others, it is a place where they fail and/or are targeted, defeated, and unsafe. Between these two extremes live a range of others, who do not attract attention, neither thriving nor visibly flailing. Some of these children *appear* to be fine, at least on the outside, but inwardly struggle with depression, anxiety, and shame and/or are living under the shadow of abuse. Some play a waiting game, biding their time until they can get out from under adult thumbs. Yet somehow there always seem to be a few particularly charismatic survivors who bristle with resilience and energy: the flamboyantly queer and incredibly talented; bold and unapologetic girls; racialized kids whose brilliance allows them to, at least partially, transcend the limits of the identities imposed on them. Some burn with a bright inner light and the strength to make the most of the tiniest opportunities. This latter group almost coheres with the promise of liberal individualism and a self-improvement mantra encouraging positive attitudes and hard work. However, relying on these examples is both too easy and naive, for even kids such as these can be crushed by oppressive forces. In C. J. Pascoe's book *Dude, You're a Fag*, for example, one of the kids she focuses on is a 15-year-old racialized, gender-nonconforming boy named Ricky, who is an incredibly talented dancer and choreographer. The failure of the school to protect him from anti-gay and anti-trans violence results in his being pushed out of school.

Schools are a central site where children bump up against an environment built around naturalized but falsely universal abilities: including but not limited to those related to gender and sexual conformity, English-language proficiency, neurotypical learning styles, the "able body," and white, middle-class standards of living and cultural norms. Kids must be enrolled in one form of government-certified school program or another until the age of 16, and so odds are school will be a difficult space for many kids at some point during this exposure, whether as a result of poverty, racialization, neurodiversity, inadequate support, physical confinement, adult authoritarianism, or sheer lack of relevance to the rest of their lives. Additional factors for LGBT kids, in general, and for most of the participants in this study include institutional reliance on binary sex organization, practices of sex segregation and differentiation, and anti-queer and trans-oppressive environments. Sex-segregated and sex-differentiated spaces and activities, both formal and informal, generate profound discomfort for transgender kids who assert their nonnormative gender identities, for those who are invisible, or for those who are just figuring themselves out. Schools are often spaces of psychological difficulty and physical danger for trans kids.

Canadian and U.S. studies clearly indicate that public schools are inhospitable to sexual-minority and transgender students. The 2011 *First National Climate Survey on Homophobia, Biphobia, and Transphobia in Canadian Schools* by the Egale Canada Human Rights Trust produced alarming findings that include the following:

- 79% of transgender students felt unsafe in their schools, particularly with respect to use of washrooms, change rooms, and corridors.
- 63% of transgender students reported having been verbally harassed about their sexual orientation.
- 74% of transgender students reported having been verbally harassed about their gender expression.
- 37% of transgender students reported having been physically harassed.
- 70% of all participating students reported hearing homophobic and transphobic remarks from peers.
- 10% of LGBTQ students and 17% of trans students reported hearing homophobic and transphobic remarks from teachers and school staff.[3]

These findings are echoed in a U.S. study authored by the Gay, Lesbian and Straight Education Network (GLSEN). The *2015 National School*

Climate Survey: The Experiences of Lesbian, Gay, Bisexual, Transgender, and Queer Youth in Our Nation's Schools reports the following:

- 58% of LGBTQ students felt unsafe in their schools because of their sexual orientation, while 43% felt unsafe because of their gender expression.
- 32% of LGBTQ students felt unsafe and/or uncomfortable enough to miss a day of school in the preceding months, while 10% missed four or more days.
- 49% reported experiencing electronic harassment/cyberbullying.
- 60% reported experiencing sexual harassment.
- 98% heard homophobic remarks, with 60% of these hearing this language frequently.
- 96% of LGBTQ students heard negative remarks about atypical gender expression, and of these, 70% heard these remarks frequently.
- 86% heard transphobic remarks, 40% of these frequently.
- 63% of LGBTQ students in this study reported hearing negative remarks about gender expression from teachers and school staff.[4]

The GLSEN report cites policies that specifically targeted transgender students, noting that 51% of trans students were unable to use their preferred name or pronoun, while 60% had been restricted to using a bathroom or change room according to their legal sex.[5] Tellingly, both studies identified sex-segregated spaces in schools, such as bathrooms and locker rooms, as particularly unsafe. Kids' experiences of homo-negativity and trans oppression are heavily influenced by adult authority, a hidden curriculum, and peer culture and tend to crystallize around bathroom and locker-room access and sex-segregated and sex-differentiated sporting practices.

The pressure on kids to act in "gender appropriate" ways, depending on their racial and class location, occurs because of the way that sex/gender is structured into existing institutions such as families and schools.[6] Gendered spaces, sex-segregated spaces, and sex-differentiated activities are often the first place of crisis for trans kids; where they are allowed to go, and who they are allowed to be when in those spaces, is typically restricted by the binary sex marker on their identity documents. Educational institutions use databases that require and perpetuate binary sex markers. Often this crisis can at best be resolved to allow for binary transition, for those who seek it, and tolerance for those who resist its categories altogether. At worst, it provides the basis of, and justification for, the systemic abuse and dehumanization of trans kids.

School-based peer groups—the artificial age-based segregation that characterizes modern schooling—are often challenging for trans kids to navigate. As Edgardo Menvielle observes, "The amount of rejection that children actually experience in the early school years varies significantly from severe to almost none. There is also great variation in children's social competence to secure a social position and to deal with rejection when it happens."[7] Nevertheless, in Menvielle's experience, trans kids "experienced more social difficulties and social anxiety, perhaps related to the enforcement of gender roles in real-time as well as the budding internalization of these rules by the child." Gender-variant kids "may experience significant social isolation" as a result of "a) pervasive girl-boy social segregation that develops in elementary school, b) the preference of many children to associate predominantly if not exclusively with same-sex peers, and c) children's enforcement of gender boundaries, often reinforced by adults."[8] Menvielle goes on to make an observation about the particular vulnerability of feminine boys in the punishing social context of the school, noting that "over time opportunities for friendship across sex groups become fewer. This is particularly marked for feminine boys who tend to receive the brunt of mocking and ridicule for not living up to the normative masculine expectations by other boys, and who also may lose friendships as girls' groups become more closed off."[9] It is important to emphasize that even those who are not personally targeted but who witness the routine homo-negativity and gender bullying that is particularly characteristic of interactions between boys and young men or who witness sexism and misogyny directed at girls and women shape and limit themselves in response.[10]

Hiding, Coping, and Surviving

Ray-Ray is troubled by the homo-negativity he regularly witnesses in high school: he hears other students saying things like "faggot" on a regular basis. Even this is not directed at him for his gender nonconformity, it bothers him because, he said, "my mom is gay" and because his own sexual orientation is up in the air. He finds it particularly disturbing that "people display these behaviors until you mention something, and they're all super apologetic. And it's kind of like, 'Well, you've got to stop doing it to actually mean your apology,' and they don't." From Ray-Ray's perspective, those who tend to make most of the homo-negative remarks are the jocks: "the guys who play basketball, they wear like athletic shorts all the time." Ray-Ray also observes a racial hierarchy at his high school. Although Euro-Canadians—and he is one of them—are a minority in his school, they are disproportionately represented among the "regulars," which is the term he and his friends use to refer to those at the top of the social pyramid. Ray-Ray observes that many of the homophobic jocks he referred to are well represented among the disproportionately white "regulars." Like Ray-Ray, Michael was not targeted himself but found the high school environment fairly anti-queer. According to Michael, the guys who make homo-negative comments are "kind of like not the well-educated group of people." Michael and Ray-Ray's accounts both situate "ignorant" white jocks at the epicenter of gender and sexuality policing.

Much to the dismay of Frank (13, Euro-Canadian), his official documents contain highly feminized first and middle names and the sex designation "F," which has caused serious difficulty, as his high school insists on using his birth name and birth sex on official school documents, including class attendance sheets. Frank explained why it is so important to him to have his gender identity publicly affirmed in school documents: "It's still hard because a lot of those kids are from downtown, not very accepting, so it's hard to have my entire personal information out there just from one little letter; it's my entire personal information in one little letter." While Frank is most afraid of "kids from downtown" who are racialized (Indigenous), impoverished, and really "rough," research suggests that anti-queer and anti-trans peer aggression is just as likely to come from high-status populations, making queer and trans kids a common target of verbal, social, and physical violence. Pascoe makes readers a witness to these events, underscoring the conflation of gender and sexuality: boys who perform masculinity inadequately are branded "fags" or described with female epithets.[11] Gender and sexuality put-downs tend to be used interchangeably.

Trans kids adopt various strategies in response to the sense of crisis they experience around sex-segregated and sex-differentiated spaces and activities in school settings. The freedom to socially transition is one variable key to their agency. There have been legal efforts to bar trans people from using facilities consistent with their affirmed identities in many U.S. states, but a number of schools *are* increasingly adapting to the presence of trans kids, some voluntarily and others because they are legally required to do so. Trans students are typically at the mercy of teachers and are extremely vulnerable; adults have a great deal of power over those who are deemed "minors," and this power is institutionalized in school settings where age-based subordination and binary gender systems combine to lessen the agency of trans kids. That said, there are many people working in school systems who care deeply and work tirelessly to empower trans kids, but commonly received knowledge about gender as a "natural" system can create blind spots and unwitting compliance in trans oppression.

The decisions adults in authority make about whether to respect a trans kid's gender identity have powerful consequences. Greg (13, Euro-Canadian) and Wren have had much better luck than Frank with their schools, where supportive administrators manually changed all their identity markers on class and attendance lists. School principals can override databases to replace assigned gender markers with affirmed ones, but stubborn technocrats and staff who do not understand how to support these students or are deliberately negligent and oppressive can make the situation worse. Hunter describes his experience coming out as trans when attending a special education program for children who are neurodiverse or learning disabled in his school district—he has been diagnosed with fetal alcohol syndrome. Hunter described arriving at school one morning and announcing to his class that he was transgender. His teachers responded by calling his mother to ask "if she was accepting this": "And, of course, she said, 'I wouldn't be sending my kid to the school dressed like this or saying a different name if I wasn't accepting it,' but they called her at least three or four times, like farther apart, and just kept asking the same question. But they would never say anything straight to my face." Hunter was understandably angry that they did not take his word for it. But the multiple calls to his mother speak to another dimension of oppression: Hunter's mother is poor, Indigenous, and a single parent—part of a demographic that is particularly vulnerable to state surveillance, oversight, and child apprehension. These repeated phone calls to her need to be understood within the context of ongoing colonialism.

Since coming out as trans, Hunter acknowledges that his teachers have had some adjusting to do as he has announced "at least three name changes in one class." Hunter has overheard his teachers misgendering him, referring to him by his "dead name" (see glossary) and dismissing the credibility of his transition. The assumption that children's and young people's identities are static and that their exploration of gendered identities, trying on of names, and so on are not to be taken seriously speaks to the disabling effects of binary gender and age subordination as key organizing principles of mainstream schools. That adults at Hunter's school responded to his transition by questioning his authority and that of his mother is consistent with the pervasive ageist assumption that children lack knowledge about, and authority over, themselves and the colonial assumption that Indigenous parents do not know what is best for their children. But socioeconomic privilege is not necessarily a mitigating factor.

Alicia (17, Euro-American) is a member of an upper-middle-class family living in a suburban U.S. community. Alicia experienced bullying and assault while attending a private school for boys. The religious orientation of Alicia's "super Catholic" school seems to have been a contributing factor. Alicia told me she "got bullied a lot": "Most of it was just, you know, people beating you up, throwing your stuff around, breaking your items, just a lot of getting called names and stuff. I got called a lot of [homophobic] names." One of the worst instances happened in a school bathroom when she found herself surrounded by all of the boys in her class: "As soon as I'd finished using the urinal, someone pulled me, threw me down on the ground, and everyone in the class started kicking me, and that was pretty bad. I got a lot of bruises. It happened to a lot of people; it wasn't just me. But it happened often to me." Alicia believes that if her peers had known she was transgender, "it would have been even worse," and this feeling contributed to her decision to remain hidden for years. Complaining to the administration about the assaults and indignities at the hands of peers proved fruitless for Alicia. Her school principal dismissed her complaints, telling her she was bringing it on herself, saying, "You look like a girl. You *should* put up with that stuff." This same message was delivered to Alicia's mother when she complained about the bullying her "son" was experiencing.

The administration's response to these complaints made Alicia feel she was on her own when she later experienced a sexual assault in a school bathroom. She succeeded in fighting off the assault by "stabbing the person a couple of times" with a pencil: "So it never happened again, but seeing as I'd already tried talking to the current principal about that stuff, I didn't really see that there was anybody to really go to about it." Alicia felt that there was no one to turn to, although she said, "Looking back on it, I could even have gone to the police or something, but when you're a kid you just think, 'Oh, no one's going to care and no one's going to listen, so why bother?'" It was only several years later that she shared these experiences with her parents when they were attending family counseling together and her mom and dad were struggling to understand why Alicia experienced so much stress about bathrooms. Left to her own devices, Alicia learned to stand up and fight back: "Before I was out of there, I managed to punch a couple people in the face, and that stopped a lot of the bullying." Leaving the all-boys school for a public high school improved Alicia's situation because she left her antagonists behind and was able to connect with some students who were either LGBT themselves or "less uptight about gender and sexuality."

There were no reliable adult allies that Alicia felt she could turn to as she experienced these harrowing ordeals and no one to whom she could truly show herself. She kept herself hidden until the last year of high school. Her parents became supportive as she transitioned, but she survived on her own for years. Although high school provided a better experience for Alicia, the trans-oppressive actions of the school administration and of one particular teacher created a forbidding environment in which to transition. Two years prior to transitioning, for example, she was pulled out of class and given an in-school suspension for wearing "women's" clothing, something that made no sense to her, as "it wasn't a dress-code violation." She had simply "started trying to expand [her] wardrobe": "You know, just trying to try out new clothing, . . . just a skirt and a top. It was just normal clothes." The gendered nature of the dress code was so taken for granted that no such stipulation was deemed to be necessary.

One of Alicia's high school teachers not only was explicitly anti-trans and racist but required students to perform in trans-oppressive class plays as part of their graded requirements. These plays contained homo-negative and trans-negative jokes. Alicia reported, for example, that her teacher would "have people cross-dressing on the stage, and then he'd make it really disgusting, you know, kiss the person and then have the person not realize it and then have the person get all angry." She described her "entire first two years" as "pretty darn uncomfortable in that class" because her teacher "continually cracked really offensive jokes. Most of his jokes were homophobic." Alicia found that her teacher began targeting transgender people in particular as transgender rights bills gained media attention in her state and around the region. Initially, Alicia stood up to him, telling him that his remarks and jokes were wrong and that he should stop, but the teacher responded by asking her if she was transgender. This question put her on the spot, and she backed down: "After he'd just finished saying all this gross stuff against transgender people, it's just really uncomfortable, especially since I hadn't come out to my teachers and stuff. It was just really stressful." Alicia's teacher was also crudely sexist and racist, making fun of Black students, for example, if "they walked into class wearing new shoes." Even though Alicia liked and excelled in the subject and would have earned a special diploma if she had stayed with it, she quit the class in senior year because she just could not take it anymore.

The majority of transgender kids, as Mark Hellen reminds us, are invisible,[12] and Alicia was one of them. This invisibility masks the harm that a binary and heteronormative social culture causes in school settings. In addition to harming visible queer and trans kids and invisible trans kids such as Alicia, it reinforces sexist and misogynist norms, and the harm that this does, to all of us, should be a call to arms.

A number of the trans kids in this book experienced verbal abuse, threats of violence, and physical violence at school that have made it impossible for them to continue attending, either temporarily or indefinitely. Such interruptions to school attendance have negative mental health consequences and significantly lessen the likelihood of academic success and therefore increase the likelihood of future precarity. Frank's experience is instructive and chilling with regard to the disabling environment of school contexts for (voluntarily or otherwise) visible transgender children.

There are significant differences between Alicia and Frank concerning access to wealth, gender-affirming healthcare, and opportunity.

Alicia was bullied in a wealthy, suburban private school. Frank is a member of a low-income family and lives in a conservative, rural Canadian community that is an eight-hour drive from the big city where his endocrinologist practices and his pro bono lawyer works. His mother, Catherine, is his family's primary breadwinner and has been unable to work for several years. Frank's experience in several schools has been characterized by anti-queer and trans-oppressive abuse by peers as well as teachers. The way the school administration and the school district handled violence furthered Frank's victimization. Frank has spent long stretches of time out of school—the longest period being a year and a half—because it has simply been unsafe for him to attend. He has been fortunate to have a few key allies, including his mother, his younger sister, and a big-city lawyer. They have not been able to keep Frank safe, but they have demonstrated to him that he is worth fighting for and have kept his very bright spark burning.

The disabling impact of coercive gendering began to impact Frank in preschool when, in contrast to the information on his birth certificate, he kept insisting that he was a boy. Preschool staff responded by contacting his mother to express concern and to recommend a behavior-modification program for him. Based on their knowledge of the family's history with domestic violence—Frank's father had assaulted his mother[13]—the preschool staff pathologized Frank's gender expression and assumed a position of authority over Catherine. The smallness of the community meant that this explanation for his gender expression followed Frank to elementary school, where it was adopted by most of the staff. Catherine experienced considerable pressure from both preschool and elementary school staff to put a stop to Frank's determination to live as a boy. Their certainty about the need for Frank to stop was troubling enough that she did try, at times, to get Frank to stop, but she saw the harm this was doing to him and started fighting to have Frank accepted as a boy at school. This battle has been mostly a losing one for both of them.

Frank experienced gender policing and anti-trans bullying from peers, teachers, and school personnel in elementary school. He was systematically misgendered at school and reproached and humiliated for insisting on identifying as a boy. Frank has resisted his assigned sex against fierce opposition for years. The extent of abuse that Frank has experienced in school contexts, without giving in or conforming, is an indication of how strongly he feels himself to be a boy and how incredibly courageous he is. Neither Frank nor his family had any knowledge of transgender people or possibilities until he was 11, when a knowledgeable and compassionate camp counselor he encountered introduced the term "transgender" to him. Catherine has long been lesbian and gay positive, but she had never heard of transgender people either, so they fought this fight on their own, in isolation from trans communities and LGBT resources, for nearly seven years.

Literature on resilience in children demonstrates the value of even a little adult respect and warmth for children who are deeply at risk; somewhere in their social network, someone acknowledges the child or young person and cares about them.[14] This acknowledgment does not remediate their structural oppression, but it does foster resilience in the face of it. Beyond Frank's immediate family, there have been a few adults in positions of authority who went to bat for him. According to Catherine, Frank has had a supportive social worker and a "great kindergarten teacher." As she describes it, the only way Frank would go to school in kindergarten was if his teacher picked him up and walked him to school herself. So she did this, every day, in spite of being a parent herself with children who needed to be dropped off at a different school beforehand. When Frank moved on to first grade, his new teacher was so abusive that he repeatedly ran away from school, frequently showing up at his mother's place of work on the other side of town. It was this pattern of truancy that resulted in Frank being assigned to a social worker, who turned out to be a key support. Frank's former kindergarten teacher noticed what was happening to him in first grade and went so far as to report her colleague to the provincial teachers' association—a huge step for her to take in a small town—and arranged to have Frank transferred back to kindergarten as "her helper" for the remainder of the year.

Sadly, the kindergarten teacher was an exception, as elementary school was an intolerant place filled with misery for Frank. Frank described both the teachers and his peers in elementary school as "brutal," explaining, "When I would tell the teachers that the kids were making fun of me, they didn't get told it's not right to discriminate against other people." In Frank's experience, if he reported it when kids would call him a "fag" or a "girl dyke," it just made the situation worse. Teachers regularly punished and shamed him for insisting he was a boy and would force him to "confess" to "really being a girl" in front of other students. Most of his teachers and the school administrators viewed him as either mentally ill or abhorrently deviant or both and saw it as their legitimate role to correct him and to ignore his mother's instructions to acknowledge him as a boy. The way they went about doing this speaks to the overall harshness of the school environment and the negative impact it would have on all the children in attendance. For example, as Frank's was an inner-city school, local corporations contributed Christmas gifts each year that were sex typed. Although Catherine repeatedly asked that Frank be placed on the "boy list," he would be given a toy stereotypically associated with girls, such as a Barbie, in front of the whole school. In one such instance, when given a doll, Frank ran away sobbing and was then given a detention for refusing to apologize to the corporate donor.

Frank was regularly bullied by a group of boys at school, and the staff condoned this behavior via their inaction. The bullying culminated in a violent sexual assault—off school property—by two of his classmates when Frank was 10 years old. According to Catherine, "Two boys ended up really brutally sexually and physically assaulting Frank. They damaged his septum and some vertebrae and penetrated him with objects. It was really brutal." Frank was hospitalized for five days after the attack. There were two particularly shocking outcomes related to this attack. First, a new social worker assigned to Frank when he was admitted to the hospital failed to make a formal report of the incident. And second, the school failed to implement a viable safety plan to enable Frank to return to school and instead went on to suspend him for refusing to be silent about the assault once he returned.

In the immediate aftermath of the assault, Catherine agreed with the school administration that it was in Frank's best interest to keep him out of school while a safety plan for his return was developed. But when a month went by without a word from the school, Catherine phoned the principal to tell him that Frank would be returning to school and that she expected him to be kept safe. The "safety plan" the school put in place consisted of keeping Frank's assailants in the same class with him and restricting Frank, who loved playing basketball at recess, to the area at the back of the school used by younger children, while the boys who had assaulted him enjoyed their regular access to the larger playground and the basketball hoops. The school seemed to be more concerned about protecting Frank's assailants than it was about protecting him. This attitude was evident when, upon his return to school, Frank was warned not to talk about the assault, or he would be suspended. Frank complied with this order, but when his assailants complained to his teacher that Frank had told friends of his who attended another school about the assault, the principal suspended Frank. Frank attempted suicide the day he was suspended.

Many victims of sexual assault feel their treatment by police and courts constitutes a "second rape."[15] Frank had a similar experience at the hands of school and school district personnel. The harm that authorities at Frank's elementary school have done to him is consistent with the acts of state "abandonment" and "letting die" highlighted by queer/trans necropolitics. That Frank has survived at all speaks to his incredible resilience and the support of his family. Catherine, focused on keeping her son alive, kept Frank at home after his suicide attempt and began a long, difficult, and ultimately unsuccessful fight to get the school to address issues relating to his safety in a meaningful way. Frank was out of school for a year and a half while this fight was going on. Catherine was quick to say that she did not want the kids who assaulted Frank to be criminalized for their actions. She sees their behavior as evidence of their own neglect and mistreatment, as Indigenous children living in poverty and with the damaging effects of ongoing colonialism. As she explains, "I'm not big on punishment; I don't even really support the whole punishment model, but I'm sorry, if it was race, we'd be doing something. But you shouldn't go around making homophobic, transphobic slurs either. When you know damn well that kid knows, and they've been told, and you're still calling my kid a fucking "he/she/it," time to up the discipline maybe." As a self-identified anti-racist ally and a working-class person with a strong labor background, Catherine had no desire to see these children harshly punished or further damaged. She just wanted to see measures taken to protect Frank (and other potential victims) from further harm.

After a year-and-a-half battle that went nowhere, Catherine gave up and enrolled Frank in another school in their district. He attempted to pass as a boy there; but the smallness of the community meant his status of being designated female at birth became widely known, and Frank once again experienced trans-oppressive abuse at the hands of teachers and peers. Fortunately for Frank (and Catherine), a lawyer who specializes in LGBT rights cases learned of Frank's case via word of mouth. This lawyer has worked pro bono on Frank's behalf for several years. This lawyer, Catherine explained, "saved Frank, saved us. She's fought with the school district. They're assholes. They just do what they want. I mean, we're treated better now, because we're lawyered up, right." But even with this legal support, Catherine feels relatively powerless in dealing with the school district: "I don't feel any safer to go up against the district. I know if I went up against the district, they're a little bit nervous about me, because I'm lawyered up, but when push comes to shove, if I had to get into a full-on battle with them, yeah—I wouldn't." The small town that Frank lives in and his family's lack of mobility due to poverty preclude the possibility of Frank reinventing himself in a new environment. But Frank is courageous and determined to stay, as much to fight to make things better for other trans kids as to maintain connections with the people he loves and who love him.

When I interviewed Frank in 2015, he was about to start high school and was excited about it. As stressful as he finds it all, Frank's resilience is evident in that he remains hopeful that each new environment will be better. Sadly, this optimism is often misplaced. I learned in a subsequent conversation with his mother that the principal of the high school was reneging on his earlier promise to remove Frank's dead names and female sex marker from attendance lists (which are posted on the door of each classroom). The principal claimed to be unable to accommodate this request because class lists have to correspond with the provincial database. Catherine responded by telling the principal, "I don't give a shit about any of that. I don't care if you have to manually go around and put 'M' on the class list. That's all I'm asking." This request was not unreasonable—a number of other trans kids I interviewed received this kind of confidentiality about their assigned sex from their schools. Although Frank was unaware of the principal's plans when I spoke with him, he was justifiably afraid that he would be harmed if others at his high school found out that he is trans. Soon after school began that fall, Frank experienced anti-trans bullying that made him afraid for his life, and he was forced to leave school once again.

Under the circumstances, Frank is an astonishingly courageous and resilient kid, but his life chances have been severely compromised by the hostile environments of the various public schools he has endeavored to attend. The assumption that binary sex categories must be determined by professional adults at the time of birth is clearly operating to harm Frank in the school environment and to contribute to his own and his family's precarity.

Tru Wilson's (12, Black/Euro-Canadian/Indigenous) very public story is another compelling example of the way religious schools often provide an added dimension of difficulty for trans kids. Tru's desire to transition in her religiously conservative private school in fifth grade placed her and her family in great conflict with the Roman Catholic Archdiocese of Vancouver, which administered both her school and her family's church. Tru's school provided a particularly difficult context for her transition because of its religious conservatism in general and the requirement to wear gendered uniforms, and, as her mother, Michelle, explained, "there were things where they would separate them by gender too, the girls on this side and boys on that side." Tru had been living as a girl at home and a boy at school for two months at this point, and this double life was causing her severe distress. As she described it, "It was basically torture for me to have to be forced to say that 'I'm Trey.' I wanted so badly to say my name is Tru, but I couldn't. Because at home I'm so used to being Tru, and I love being Tru, and it's just so amazing. But at school, I had to be Trey, and sometimes I couldn't deal with that. When someone called me Trey, I just wanted to shout out and correct them: 'My name is Tru, and you're going to call me that.' I couldn't take it anymore. The pain was just too unbearable." Without clearing it with her parents, Tru took the bold step of informing first her teacher and then the school principal, "I'd really like to wear the girl's uniform. You're infringing on my ability to express myself by making me wear pants." Michelle characterized this action as "incredibly brave," noting that prior to transitioning, Tru was a really shy kid, "not confident in her abilities or her skills. But she had these moments where she would just put herself out there."

The impact on Tru's mental health while she was forced to continue attending school as a boy alarmed her parents: it became clear to them that doing so was no longer viable. On the first day of the new school year, Michelle and Tru's father, Garfield, provided the school with a letter stating that Tru would be attending as a girl from then on, but the school refused to allow her to transition. According to Michelle, "The first time we sat down with the principal, he handed us a letter from their lawyer and said, you know, 'Even though we acknowledge that we need to respect based on the human rights charter [in British Columbia], we need to respect and support, we just want to be sure because this is a big thing to ask of your *son* and shouldn't be anything that's rushed into, and we'd like you to get a second assessment done.' And they gave us a list of doctors, one of which was Dr. Kenneth Zucker[16] in Toronto" (my emphasis). Michelle and Garfield were surprised by the opposition of the school administration and the school board, so, as a family, they weighed their options. Michelle got to work gathering resources by contacting the local LGBT center, where she was given the name of barbara findlay, a lawyer who specializes in advocating for transgender rights. findlay was initially optimistic that the school was open to Tru transitioning, but when the school sent a second letter refusing to allow Tru to transition on the grounds of religious freedom, it was clear they had a fight on their hands. As Tru told it, "I could stay at school and fight for it or go back to my old school, and I wanted to stay at my school so bad, because of all my friends, so I tried to fight. I tried to fight. I tried to stay, but I just couldn't." Tru had a very close group of friends at the school who lovingly supported her transition all the way, and it was extremely hard for her to leave them: "By the time I had almost finished transitioning, it felt like they were a part of me because they were so supportive, and if I left them, then that part of me would have been gone." But after two months of negotiating with the school and the school board, Michelle realized, "They weren't budging. They weren't going to move," and she and Garfield made the difficult decision to remove all three of their kids from the school (and the related religious community) and enroll them at a school where Tru's transition would be supported. As important as it is to focus on the vulnerability of the particular trans kid, this case provides a poignant example of the impact of trans oppression on the child's entire family—especially siblings who are attending the same school.[17]

Michelle and Garfield took time to settle their children into their new school and then had their lawyer file a human rights complaint against the Roman Catholic Arch Diocese of Vancouver.[18] This complaint was settled out of court in Tru's favor to enable future transgender kids to transition.[19] The terms of the settlement included a financial payment, the adoption of a gender inclusive policy in the school district, and a personal apology to Tru from the head of the regional Catholic diocese and its lawyers. Michelle describes taking strength from her Indigenous heritage throughout this process: as a granddaughter of a survivor of Canada's residential school system, she feels strongly that "there's something about people taking ownership for the damage that they've caused. An apology's huge." When Tru learned the terms of the settlement she said, "I felt so good, and for a second, I thought that I'd be able to go back. But then I told myself, 'No.' What they did was almost unforgiveable, and I was trying to be as generous as I could, and I gave them so much time. It was just torture, and I was breaking down, and I was paying less and less attention to my schoolwork, and it felt like my grades were dropping, and I just couldn't do it." Tru and her family have the satisfaction of knowing their efforts have produced social change. The next child who wants to transition at Tru's old school or at any school in the province will have to be formally accommodated.

A number of the kids in this book encountered considerably less difficulty in transitioning at their schools, which had a positive impact on their overall well-being. Socially transitioning at school typically, but not necessarily, depending on the school, requires a formal diagnosis of gender dysphoria and/or a letter from a doctor or clinician stipulating the necessity, from a health standpoint, of allowing the child to live in their affirmed gender. Wren's transition from gender-nonconforming boy to gender-conforming girl may have been the most seamless—it required no documentation or formal process, which was largely a result of the background work her parents had done to ensure that their (at the time) gender-nonconforming "son" started school in a welcoming environment. When Wren was four and approaching school age, her parents were worried that "he" would be targeted for gender policing if they enrolled "him" in public school, so they looked around for a more gender-inclusive alternative. Jordan, one of Wren's parents, explained, "At the time, we understood Wren as a gender-nonconforming boy. We didn't want 'him' to stop wearing dresses and skirts unless 'he' wanted to stop wearing dresses and skirts, not because 'he' was being teased or pressured."

There was no perfect school for Wren, but a "good enough," not very expensive private school in a completely inconvenient location vis-à-vis Wren's parents' places of employment ("but we did it anyway") was chosen because of the openness and willingness of the staff to work to create a safe space for Wren's gender nonconformity. In spite of the staff's lack of experience with transgender students or kids who were as gender nonconforming as Wren, they recognized that antibinary/antisexist work would benefit not only Wren but everyone in the school. Wren attended this "kind of hippy," as Jordan described it, Canadian private school from kindergarten through fourth grade, and it was during this time that she transitioned. The summer before she was to start second grade, Wren let her parents know that she wanted to be referred to with female pronouns. Her social transition at school, such as it was, was accomplished when Jordan sent an email to all the parents seeking carpool participants, referring to Wren as "my daughter" rather than "my son"—with no explanation. Jordan described this moment as "a beautiful nonevent."

While gender categories still played a role in the school, there was a lot of mixed, as opposed to divided, gender play through all grade levels, and Wren's teachers—and sometimes her classmates—often interrupted general incidents of sexism and specific queries about Wren's gender. As luck would have it, when Wren was in third grade, her new-to-the-school teacher was gender-nonconforming themselves with a gender-nonconforming child of their own. This teacher worked consciously to break down gender divisions in the social dynamics of the class. Wren told me that she felt that every teacher at her school "has done something about the boy/girl thing." The school proved to be a "good enough" environment for Wren to transition from boy to girl.

While Wren's transition was a "nonevent," Esme's was a carefully planned and scripted one. Esme (10, Euro-Canadian) transitioned as a six-year-old in first grade in the middle of the school term. In a process carefully managed by her parents—primarily her mother—and the school administration, an information session was held for parents of children in Esme's grade, and a local trans-positive expert delivered an in-class workshop to Esme's class to prepare them to welcome her as a girl. Esme hung out in another part of the school while this workshop happened. She revealed that she had a hard time reentering the classroom because though she very much wanted this transition, it came with a lot of anxiety for her: "The first day that they talked to the kids I got really kind of freaked out. I was in first grade, right? So I started crying. No one was teasing me or anything; it was just—if you tell someone something, it just feels a bit new to you." Esme went on to say, however, that although she was "crying in the morning, the rest of the day passed like normal; no one said anything about it." Things have gone relatively smoothly since. Occasionally Esme will be asked *the* question: "Are you a boy or a girl?" And although this microaggression makes her feel "kind of weird," she just says "girl" and gets on with it.

Switching Schools to Transition

Some trans kids move from school to school to escape trans oppression or to facilitate transition: some kids leave one school as their designated gender and arrive at another in their affirmed gender. When Canaan (18, Euro-Canadian) was 14, he switched high schools in order to transition to male at the beginning of ninth grade, but his desire for anonymity was completely negated by the actions of an ignorant but well-meaning teacher. His mother, Shari, reported learning that on the first day of classes, Canaan's teacher—who had just recently received LGBT sensitivity training—announced to the entire class that Canaan was transgender, thinking that publicly identifying and welcoming him constituted sensitivity and support. Canaan was devastated by this announcement. It defeated the entire purpose of changing schools and exposed him to gossip and harassment for the next four years of high school. It also misrepresented his identity. According to Shari, Canaan does not identify as transgender. He identifies as male. This difference is very important to him. What is so troubling about this incident is that the teacher thought he was being supportive: it reveals how much care needs to go into teacher training about trans issues and the importance of allowing kids to control the sharing of information about their gender identities.

Prior to Nina's understanding her child, Martine (12, Euro-Asian Canadian) as a transgender girl, she worked to get the school to be more gender and sexuality inclusive and to intervene in the gender bullying that Martin, whom she understood to be her "son" at the time, was experiencing. She recalled asking the principal if the school "could talk about things like homosexuality, like years back, and the school wasn't comfortable with that": "Then I asked one of the teachers, 'Can you read maybe one book on diverse families?' She said, 'No.' That was it. So I was alone dealing with that. I'd say, 'Well, we had a situation of bullying on the bus: they called Martin a girl, and she downplayed it. She said, 'Well, that's not really bullying.' I said, 'Well, if it makes "him" cry, and they're doing it again.'" Nina was similarly unsuccessful later when she asked the school to allow her daughter to transition. "I had meetings. I had the hospital come to the school. I met with the principal a lot, and basically she had almost never heard of this. I would come in and say, 'I need to talk about this issue.' 'Oh, okay. Well, all right,' and downplay my observation. And they'll say, 'But Martin looks so much like a boy here.'" Nina felt strongly that the school was pathologizing her as a parent rather than taking her concerns seriously, especially when a school board psychologist attended one of the meetings Nina had with the principal. During this meeting, the psychologist "did not say a word": "I was there for an hour and a half, and he just listened to me. Again, I felt like a hysterical mother." What really upsets Nina is that "while this is happening, the principal won 'Principal of the Year.'"

Martine transitioned as soon as she finished elementary school, and her mother reported, "We were able to breathe." Nina was relieved no longer to have to keep the secret. She explained, "We were hiding it. She was a girl at home, a boy at school, a boy outside. We were mixed up with the pronouns. It was a gray zone. I couldn't stand it. You know, 'Hide the dress! Don't be yourself, hide it,' just ugh. So now we are all breathing easier." As one of the benefits of living in a major urban center, Martine was able to enroll in a high school in another zone of the city where she could begin as a girl. Her mother explained that there, "Nobody knows her. She just started off as a girl, and that's it." This is an example of how complex the tension between secrecy and privacy can be. As this story illustrates, for transgender students such as Martine, gender policing and harassment affect mental health, school attendance, and achievement.

Stef transitioned from designated male at birth to a transgender girl at age five and then to a gender-neutral identity at age 14. When I interviewed them at age 17, Stef described experiencing a frequent lack of safety while attending various schools as a transgender girl and having to switch schools a lot. Stef explained, "Some schools were too hard for me [because of peers] bullying me a lot," and school personnel failed to protect them or were part of the problem. Stef ended up attending four high schools before ultimately switching to an adult education program in their school district. Stef's mother, Kazuko, explained that in one case, "Stef went to a new school, everything was cool. They were like, 'Just tell us which washrooms you want to use, and everything's fine.' They were very, very open. And then they lost the director that was the contact person for us, and he moved to another school. Then it started getting complicated. And then Stef decided, you know what, . . . so we just switched to adult ed." That Stef found it difficult, but not impossible, to attend school as a transgender girl but not as a nonbinary person speaks to the overwhelming binary organization of school institutions and settings. This is one of the ways in which there are limits to the transitions that are possible in school settings.

Greg planned his transition to coincide with the beginning of high school and started taking hormone blockers the year before. He walked out of his elementary school on the last day of the school year and immediately got his hair cut, came out to his friends via Facebook, and became a boy named Greg from then on. Prior to this carefully managed transition, he got himself organized emotionally and psychologically to deal with negative responses: "I set this rule for myself, which I still go by today, is if anyone was not accepting or not nice about it, I would simply cut them out of my life." Most of his friends have stuck by him.

Greg and his parents worked with his high school over the summer to make sure he could enroll as a boy. In this regard, he feels lucky to have been the second rather than the first openly transgender student to attend his high school. Greg described the school as "incredible" because the administration alerted all of his teachers in advance to ensure that they were prepared to act supportively if Greg encountered difficulties with his peers. Some trans students feel safer when their teachers are aware of their status because they can be on top of any class dynamics that emerge, while others—Canaan, for example—consider their status to be confidential medical information.[20] Even though Greg's legal documents had yet to be changed, the school worked around this by manually putting an "M" beside Greg's name on the attendance sheet. At first, the school wanted him to use a staff bathroom, but Greg refused and went on to use the boys' bathroom without incident. However, because some of the kids at his high school knew Greg from before his transition, word got out that he was transgender. Reactions ranged from confusion to "hate," but Greg had enough resilience and support to cope with the negative reactions.

Similarly, Michael purposefully transitioned between high school and university: "I had already planned it out, right, once I leave and I go to university, and I'm just going to change my name. And I was just like, 'I'm not going to interact with you guys' [*laughs*]." While still in high school, Michael kept a low profile, making sure to fly under the radar by keeping his head down and dressing in unisex style, but he "didn't bind back then": "So you could tell I was a girl." As he described it, he was "kind of a lonerish." Being disconnected from his surroundings in high school seems to have been what Michael needed at the time.

After graduating, Michael learned that another trans guy had attended his high school at the same time. Michael said that probably, like everyone else, he "thought she was a tomboy . . . or he [Michael corrected himself]." It speaks to the extent of their efforts to blend in that they were unable to see each other. They have since been in touch, and though it might have been helpful to know each other while in high school, not every trans person experiences the value of trans solidarity. There are trans people of all ages who avoid other trans and gender-nonconforming people, particularly visible ones, at least in certain spaces, because they are not ready for, or are uninterested in, being visible themselves.

As these stories indicate, the ability to change schools is an option for some trans kids but is impossible for many others. Moving kids out of hostile school environments is obviously not an option for everyone, especially in rural areas where either there are no alternatives or the community is too small to allow for anonymity. Changing schools requires parental consent and access to other resources, such as transportation, money for school fees, parental advocacy and know-how, and is further mediated by variables including racialization, class position, and language spoken in the home. For kids with multiple "special needs," a safe place to transition may come into conflict with other aspects of their precarity.

Homeschooling is an option for some trans kids who either do not want to attend or lack the safety they would need to participate in formal school settings, but it too involves interaction with administrative bodies committed to the binary model and extensive parental resources. One of the mothers in the study, Luna, homeschools her four children, and therefore she has to work with a homeschooling "base school" in her region. Of Luna's four children (Euro-Canadian), one is comfortable enough with their assigned sex, one is a 16-year-old trans girl, another is a seven-year-old nonbinary trans person, and the youngest "has yet to declare." Luna described how their family "put the school really on the spot around how they were going to manage having an out trans student": "And the interesting part of this is that actually, in the end, the most difficult facilitation was around my kid Otter, who is seven, because Otter is a borderlands person, a both/neither person around gender, and this is proving to be radically more challenging." Registering Otter for school turned out to be "massively difficult" because in the province the family lives in, "they have this computer system where there is this one box, and in that box there has to be an 'M' or an 'F.' And the eldest child was like, 'As long as I can control what goes in the box, I can make a choice, and I'm going to be happy with it.' Otter is like, 'You may not put an 'M' or an 'F' in that box because I am a both/neither person, and I refuse to have that letter associated with me.'" This experience speaks to the challenges that trans kids who defy binary intelligibility face in navigating school systems and school environments. Only Luna's tenacity and experience dealing with administrative systems enabled her to contest this limitation.

Many of the book's participants deeply resent the power and authority that adults in school have over them. Quinn identifies as nonbinary and was waiting until the end of the year—when they graduated from high school—to report two teachers for anti-trans behavior. Some of Quinn's teachers use correct pronouns and insist that their classmates do so as well, but, Quinn said, others "would sooner laugh at me than use my pronouns and frequently do." Quinn has two teachers, in particular, who refuse to use correct pronouns, even though they have asked them to do so repeatedly. One of these teachers accuses Quinn of changing their pronouns just to seek attention. According to Quinn, this teacher "throws her hands up in the air and says, 'Quinn, you don't have to make it so hard for me all the time. I'm an old woman. I can't just conform just to make one person happy. You're just going to have to deal with it,'" on occasion leaving the room in a huff in the middle of class. Sometimes when this happens, Quinn hears it from frustrated classmates, who say things like, "Why don't you just get over it? It's not that bad." These microaggressions hurt and disempower Quinn, and they have responded with the overlapping strategies of doing what they had to do to survive/resist and engaging in activism to achieve change (as part of their school's gay-straight alliance).

On occasion, Quinn's classmates are supportive. For example, in their last two years of high school, Quinn frequently wore a T-shirt with their pronouns on it—"they them their." One day when they were wearing it, one of their teachers "just kept on misgendering" Quinn: "He was using me as an example, and he kept on going, 'she, she, she.' So I actually turned my shirt around, and I was like, 'Here, you obviously can't get it, so here are my pronouns. They're on my shirt. If you forget, look at me while you are talking about me and read my shirt.' And he just started laughing and used 'she.'" But this time, first one then more of their classmates backed them up: "This one kid in my class slammed his hands down on the desk and started screaming at my teacher: 'Mr. X, you're being such a jerk. Can't you see that you're hurting Quinn. You don't have to be so mean to them. Why are you doing this?' And then he got up and left, and my entire class was like, 'Yeah, Mr. X, you don't have to be such a rude jerk. We know you're old and angry.'" Quinn felt both empowered by this support and fearful that it might lead to retaliation from the teacher. Peer support has the potential, in such a context, both to empower and to disempower, both to decrease and to increase the precarity of trans kids by upsetting the adults who have power over them. As far as Quinn knows, they are the only person at the school who uses "they/them/their" pronouns and are therefore readily identifiable. Quinn is understandably concerned that reporting these teachers before the end of the year could affect their grades: "It's sort of a horrible thing that I have to think about. How can I make sure that these adults, who have a lot of power over me— especially because they control my marks in a grade 12 year, and they're already really into weird power-trippy dynamics—how can I make sure that they don't hurt me?"

Trans kids adopt various strategies to survive or even thrive within the disabling environments and systems of formal schooling, including remaining invisible, avoidance via absenteeism or dropping out, transitioning—often switching schools to do so—and surviving, resisting, and fighting back. Their experiences bring the blueprint of the binary gender system into sharp relief and have the ability to suggest appropriate ways for transforming schools away from the ideology of heteronormativity and cisgender ability that is so damaging for trans kids.

Transitioning *in* School versus Transitioning *the* School

When schools have "allowed" the trans students in this study to transition, they have not transitioned the school *away* from binary sex differentiation. But to lessen the precarity of all kids, and trans kids in particular, we should be working toward a gender-inclusive school that forgoes—and explicitly counters—the disabling force of binary gender systems. The students whose stories are told here use qualifying language to describe even "successful" transitions in school settings.

For example, in spite of describing a supportive high school administration as "incredible," Greg had some misgivings. Although he acknowledged the administration did take some action whenever he reported experiences of trans oppression, "it never feels like they are taking enough action. It sort of feels like they are not taking it as seriously as they should be." While Greg felt fairly comfortable at his high school, he was still dealing with frequent microaggressions, which took a toll. His remarks speak to the limited extent to which this binary-based climate was targeted for change. Greg's school was still organized, formally and informally, by the binary sex/gender system of heteropatriarchy; he was supported in switching his identity from one to the other, but the fraught *system itself* was not examined as a subject for transition. Instead, how he was treated as an individual by other individuals—while a crucial dimension—became the principal focus and obscured the larger picture. Enabling and supporting transitions for binary-conforming trans kids *is* a crucial dimension of harm reduction, as Greg's, Esme's, and Tru's cases highlight in a positive sense and Frank's and Stef's underscore so negatively. Yet this focus fails to address the impact of binary gender systems on invisible trans kids, such as Alicia and Lennox, and on all those whose identities and behaviors are marginalized in other ways.

To illustrate this issue, Wren's transition is illuminating. When she was known as a gender-nonconforming boy, Wren's first school was one of her safer places, yet while Wren's transition at school was fully supported and relatively seamless, it raises questions about the role the school could have played in *transitioning the environment* around her. Jin (13, Euro-Canadian) is a gender-nonconforming kid who enrolled at Wren's school after leaving an unsafe public elementary school environment. One of Wren's parents, Jordan, and Jin's mother, Mickey, articulated a common assessment of the private school their children attended together as a "kind of hippy" place. More meaningful work to destabilize gender systems, however, had yet to be undertaken. For example, although pleased that all the kindergarten children used the girls' washroom, they noted there were still sex-segregated bathrooms for everybody else, although these were not, to their knowledge, policed. Wren and Jin used the girls' bathroom without incident. Both Jordan and Mickey, however, felt that the elimination of sex-segregated bathrooms, with regard to signage if not more extensive structural change, *could* have happened but that they would have had to initiate it and lead the social justice and educational work to motivate and execute it.

Like many of the parents of trans kids who become advocates and activists, both Jordan and Mickey are academic researchers whose work includes a focus on gender. As a result, they were able to share resources and expertise with school staff. For example, during the years that Jin attended the school, Mickey and her partner, Ry, shared resources, donated gender-inclusive and trans-inclusive children's books, initiated numerous meetings with the teachers about gender-inclusive education across the ages (including about the school's physical-education program, change rooms for swimming classes, and the older grade's year-end sleepover camp). Jordan provided the school principal with a copy of Gender Spectrum's "Gender Inclusive Schools" and, along with Mickey, met with the principal and another teacher to talk about undertaking some related projects for change.

While there was enthusiasm from all involved about undertaking the work of fully transitioning the school, after the first meeting with Jordan, Mickey, and school personnel, the difficulties in scheduling a second meeting, given the external obligations of everyone involved, stalled the conversation. This result speaks to the extraordinary demands already placed on the time and energy of people who *are* invested in the well-being of children—parents and teachers alike. Without budgetary resources to implement school district policies that target school systems and culture for change, action is dependent on donated labor. Under these circumstances, often the best outcome one can hope for, it seems, is that individual trans kids will be accommodated.

Transitioning School Board Policy

As an example of structural change at the school board level, in 2014, the Vancouver School Board (VSB), which is also my home district, updated its (2004) A: Foundations and Basic Commitments (ACB) "Lesbian, Gay, Bisexual, Transgender, Transsexual, Two-Spirit, Questioning Policy" to more effectively address inclusion issues relating to lesbian, gay, bisexual, trans, two-spirit,[21] and questioning (LGBT2Q) youth, a policy later referred to as the "sexual orientation and gender identities" policy (ACB-R-1). The role of a staff person, the part-time "Anti-homophobia and Diversity Teacher Mentor," was central in this process, as she provided support to staff and LGBT2Q kids and their parents in the district and worked with the Pride Advisory Committee, consisting of LGBT2Q community members, to draw the school board's attention to aspects of the policy that needed improvement. The VSB committed the district and all its schools to addressing anti-harassment in particular: "The board will strive to prevent, and to provide effective procedures to respond to any language or behaviour that degrades, denigrates, labels, or stereotypes students on the basis of their real or perceived sexual and/or gender identities and/or gender expression, or that incites hatred, prejudice, discrimination, or harassment on such bases." The new policy stipulates that the VSB will

- provide bathroom access according to affirmed gender category;
- use affirmed names and pronouns as requested;
- use affirmed names in all school correspondence when requested by the student and/or the student's parents (with the exception that information relating to a child's gender transition would not be shared with parents or guardians without the child's permission);

- invite participation by trans students in physical education and sex-segregated recreational and competitive athletic activities in accordance with their gender identity;
- resist directing students to reparative therapy programs or services;
- use professional development funds to deliver workshops for teachers and administrators on LGBT2Q+ inclusive curricula;
- provide learning resources in languages and formats easily accessible to ESL students and their families, where possible.

The policy update addressed bathroom and change-room access specifically with requirements about access to these spaces:

- "[They will be] assessed on a case-by-case basis with the goals of maximizing the student's social integration, ensuring the student's safety and comfort, minimizing stigmatization, and providing equal opportunity to participate in physical education classes and sports." This assessment prioritizes the comfort and safety of transgender students.
- "Trans students shall have access to the washroom and change room that corresponds to their gender identity. Students who desire increased privacy will be provided with a reasonable alternative washroom and/or changing area."
- "The decision with regard to washroom and change room use shall be made in consultation with the trans student."

Finally, the policy addressed the institutional framework of sex-segregated activities with the directive that "schools will reduce or eliminate the practice of segregating students by sex. In situations where students are segregated by sex, trans students will have the option to be included in the group that best corresponds to their gender identity."[22]

While this policy was a significant step forward to support transgender students, I know that anecdotally little has changed on the ground in schools and classrooms, and the policy is often only accidentally or voluntarily applied in the classroom. Sasha (six, Euro-Canadian) regularly bumps up against the binary organization of her VSB classroom, for example. According to her mom, Sonja, Sasha's classroom teacher regularly organizes the children as "boys" and "girls," which means that Sasha has to choose which gender to be when neither of the categories speaks to her. She experiences this situation as incredibly stressful and difficult. The overarching culture of binary normativity remains substantially unchallenged, and yet getting an update passed by the VSB was an important achievement. Gestures of acceptance and tolerance and public statements of support for queer and trans kids do make a difference; otherwise the Christian Right would not mount such fierce opposition to them.[23] But while measures such as these are meaningful—and difficult to achieve—they do not go nearly far enough. And policies without sufficient budgetary resources for staff training do little to change school cultures.

Furthermore, schools typically do not adopt measures for trans inclusion until a visible transgender kid shows up. This reluctance reflects a superficial rather than a substantive approach and means that issues relating to binary gender culture and gender policing typically receive little attention otherwise. This attitude is inadequate for the well-being of all of the kids at the school and is limiting for the trans kids who feel safe enough to become visible and in the identities they feel comfortable exploring and asserting. In Pascoe's recommendations for change as a result of her research at "River High," she identifies the need for legal protections for girls from sexual harassment and queer and gender-nonconforming youth from homophobia and transphobia.[24] But without teachers and administrators who are specifically trained and required to enforce policies, legal and policy change alone are insufficient. There is a dire need for proactive change to create more inclusive learning environments for all students. These include supporting gay-straight alliances, altering gendered school practices, and providing pro-LGBT2Q resources and education for all students.

* * *

Any analysis of the experiences of trans kids in schools needs to start from the premise that many school environments are unsafe for many kids and that issues of trans inclusion, or lack thereof, take place within a context of neoliberal restructuring.[25] Thus, teachers and school administrators are constantly being asked to do more with less, which relegates much of what they accomplish in their non-face-to-face teaching time to volunteer effort. Without a key person willing and able to drive the work of change, "good enough" environments for trans kids seem like a lottery win. This situation will not change until substantially increasing school budgets becomes a societal priority.

How many of the kids in our school systems are at risk of losing that inner spark not only because of trans oppression and homo-negativity but also because of the overlapping violence of misogyny and sexism, racism, poverty, ableism, authoritarianism, intolerance for neurodiversity, or ignorance and neglect? How many come to school hungry for food, safety, affection, or regard and yet fail to receive these and struggle accordingly? It is challenging to provide kids with safe and affirming environments and connections with others, but it is crucial to their development and the resilience and vitality of our communities. A key aspect of this safety is enabling their agency to name and claim preferred gender identities that they negotiate for themselves.

Efforts to specifically reduce the precarity of transgender students in school settings cannot be isolated from general measures for promoting child welfare (such as universal school breakfast and lunch programs, incidental fee-free learning, and adequate resources to support varied learning styles). Support for trans kids, therefore, needs to be grounded in a broader anti-oppression perspective.[26]

Changing school contexts to decrease the precarity of transgender kids requires a systemic approach to eliminating formally sex-segregated and sex-differentiated spaces and activities. This approach can combine with school-community-based initiatives to transform school culture within a broad-based movement to oppose neoliberal restructuring of social welfare, public school, and municipal systems. Schools that do allow kids to transition often fail to confront head-on the problems of sexism and misogyny associated with the binary gender system of heteropatriarchy but, rather, allow it to remain largely undisturbed. The appropriate focus for schools should be on *transitioning the school community away from the binary system of gender* and finding ways to interrupt and change other oppressive dynamics.

3

Spaces

When [Wren] was five, still so small really, she told me that
the bathrooms at the church we attend made her sad. She
stood before me as she said this, a small and anguished
child, frozen between two doors. She literally did not know
where to go—but she knew that loss would be the result of
either choice she made.

—Jordan, parent

As evidence of the change in the air today, the church that Wren and
her family attend recently designated all the bathrooms in the building
as "welcoming bathrooms," meaning that they are for everyone to use
regardless of gender identity.[1] It is too late to spare Wren the traumatic
experience referred to in the epigraph, but it will make a difference
for all the trans kids—whether visible or invisible—who follow in her
footsteps.

Issues relating to transgender inclusion in schools, as well as in public
spaces more broadly, tend to crystallize around bathroom and locker
room access because these spaces are central to the maintenance of the
binary gender order. Canadian and U.S. institutional and public culture
relies on binary sex difference as foundational. But extensive scholarship
has revealed the two-sex system to be a social construct rather than a
natural system.[2]

A socially constructed binary system is perhaps most obviously built
into the lived environment via sex-segregated facilities (bathrooms and
locker rooms) and sex-differentiated activities. Sex-segregated and sex-
differentiated environments are, unsurprisingly, sites of crisis for most
trans kids. In this chapter, the disabling impact of the institutionalization
of the binary sex system is made manifest in spatial terms, particularly
in the public/private spaces of bathrooms and locker rooms that certify
and regulate membership in gendered social groups and participation

in public life. As a requirement of public spaces, bathrooms are central to citizenship, and to use them, one must be readable at a glance or be, to use Judith Butler's term, "intelligible."[3] It is in the regulation of such spaces that binary gender is produced and becomes embodied. It is no surprise, therefore, that the "bathroom problem" is a pervasive theme in much queer and trans literature and scholarship. As queer scholar Jack Halberstam[4] emphasizes, "the bathroom problem . . . severely limits [the ability of gender-nonconforming people] to circulate in public spaces and actually brings them into contact with physical violence as a result of having violated a cardinal rule of gender: one must be readable at a glance."[5] The difficulties that trans and gender-nonconforming people of all ages confront in public spaces when needing to urinate, defecate, empty a colostomy bag, deal with menstruation, or other immediate and urgent acts of bodily maintenance that require privacy reveal a "blueprint" for the social construction of sex difference.

In a study of the disempowering experiences that gender-nonconforming women have with sex-segregated bathroom facilities in the United Kingdom, geographer Kath Browne introduces the term "genderism" to articulate the process whereby "those who transgress the accepted dichotomy of sex are policed." The bathroom is where "sites and bodies are mutually constituted within sexed power regimes." Browne emphasizes that "gendered spaces are *disabling* environments; it is the normative constructions of sex that are both built into, and interact in, everyday spaces that (re)produce the 'abnormal.'"[6]

The bathroom problem is not solely about gender nonconformity, however. As basic requirements of public spaces, bathrooms are central to access and therefore citizenship,[7] but this access is unevenly embodied. One need only think of the ways in which homeless, impoverished, racialized, and disabled people and survival sex workers are dehumanized and at times criminalized for performing urgent bodily functions in the street, denied privacy due to lack of sufficient public facilities and the prerogative of private enterprises to restrict access to their bathrooms. When out in public and badly needing a bathroom, the privileged among us are able to purchase something in order to gain access to the bathroom in a store or coffee shop. Indeed, white, middle-class privilege often enables people to access bathrooms without having to buy anything at all: our humanity is intelligible, and we are correspondingly treated with respect and/or kindness. In contrast, lack of bathroom access produces disabling consequences that further acts to exclude the marginalized from public space and civic participation.

Sex-segregated bathrooms reinforce sex difference and are a crucial part of the pervasively gendered environments in which children circulate. One of the ways kids know that they are not performing their assigned gender adequately is by how people react to them when they enter sex-segregated spaces or participate in sex-differentiated activities. The bathroom is one of the most urgent of these spaces. As Browne observes, the "moments where boundaries of gender difference are overtly (en)forced can illustrate how sites and bodies are mutually constituted within sexed power regimes."[8] Sociologist Judith Lorber views sex-segregated bathrooms as an intrinsic part of "the bureaucratic structure and the process of control of public space" that "replicates the supposed biological base of the gendered social order and the symbolic separation of men's and women's social worlds."[9] If privilege is defined as freedom from injustice, then bathroom privilege goes unnoticed by the majority of people who conform to gender norms and/or other aspects of socioeconomic privilege, yet it is a site of injustice for many, including the majority of trans people of all ages.

Gender Policing in Bathrooms

The experiences of the trans kids in this study underscore the damaging consequences of sex-segregated bathroom facilities in general and the denial of access on the basis of gender self-determination in particular. The trans kids in this study had troubling stories related to bathroom access, from gender policing to feeling trapped in or forced to use the wrong bathroom. Trans kids do experience acts of extreme violence (as happened to Alicia and Frank), but more often they are the victims of microaggressions from peers and adult authority figures who say, "You don't belong here," which minimizes their authority over themselves, negatively impacts their physical, social, and emotional well-being, and highlights the ways in which barriers to bathroom access produce social and/or physical disability. Peers typically play a central role in gender policing in school contexts. Often in school bathrooms, kids are unsupervised, and safety is lacking. Alicia's experience with violence in the bathroom at her private boys' school is telling in this regard. Many kids in the book avoided going to the bathroom, at school and in public, by purposely dehydrating themselves or by holding it, to the point that they risked permanent health consequences.

Several kids had to change schools because the administration in the former school refused to support an acceptable bathroom solution. For example, Sean (9, Euro-Canadian) is a gender-nonconforming girl. Starting in kindergarten and continuing throughout the time she attended that particular public school, a group of boys terrorized her and other gender-nonconforming girls by preventing them from using the girls' bathroom. According to her father, Hal,

> When she would try and go down to the washroom, there would be a group of boys—sometimes from her class sometimes from another class—who would see her in the hall, and she would try to go into the girls' room, and they would block her and say, "No, you are a boy. You can't go in the girls' room." I think one time she even went down towards the boys' room, and then the boys said, "No, you can't come in here," and these boys just gathered around her. They were bigger than her, and they would do this.

Sean's parents took this issue up with the school administration, expecting them to be equally concerned and to take effective action on Sean's behalf, but that is not what happened. Instead, the situation was dismissed, and they were given vague promises about an anti-bullying program being introduced in the future. While the administration failed to act, Hal reported

> Sean ended up doing this over and over again and holding it and being so scared to go that by the next year, she developed a whole series of bladder problems, and it was incredibly painful for her to pee. She often couldn't pee. She would be crying and screaming sometimes for an hour, and it would be like this every day. We finally took her to the hospital. . . . We went to a urologist, and they took a scan of her, and they basically said that she had so embodied that fear and through her actions of holding it in, it had actually changed the shape inside, like with her organs and her ability to control her bladder.

Sean's parents eventually learned that the same thing was happening to four or five other girls who had short hair whom these boys judged to be inadequately feminine. Powerless to protect her in this context, Sean's parents moved her to a different public school. For her part, Sean vowed she would never cut her hair short or wear pants again. This gender policing is a chilling example of the misogyny and gender terrorism many girls experience that more broadly includes slut shaming, sexual harassment, sexual violence, and rape culture and how early on in life some boys begin to participate in these oppressive dynamics.

Silver's mother, Sherene, had a similar story to tell, but Silver (six, Indigenous/Euro-Canadian) ultimately faced the harshest treatment from *adults* at her school. According to Sherene, Silver is consistently read by people who do not know her as a boy; Silver is okay with this in general, but it presents problems with regard to bathroom access. For example, when Silver was in first grade, she was "mistaken" for a boy by another girl in the bathroom and, in spite of her insistence that she was a girl, was told to leave. Unlike Sean, who experienced gender policing as an expression of dominance, the gender policing that Silver experienced in this instance seems to have reflected fear more than malice; girls are taught to fear boys and often have reason to. "Silver left the bathroom, and she went to the boys' bathroom. And then a teacher found her, so she still hasn't gone pee by this time, and she's probably six years old in grade 1. So the teacher sent her to the principal's office because she was in the boys' bathroom, which isn't allowed. And so she peed her pants." What Silver learned from these encounters was that she had nowhere to go to pee. For two weeks after this incident, "she peed her pants every day. She started bringing an extra shirt so she could tie it around her waist to cover up the pee." Sherene was deeply concerned for her daughter's well-being: "I started leaving work, taking my lunch. I'm driving across town at lunch time and taking her to pee and then leaving work so I could be there at the end of the day. Obviously it wasn't sustainable, but she was scared to go into the bathroom even with me."

Sherene's familiarity with the public school system in the district, and with educational systems more generally, made her a strong advocate for her daughter. She started by calling in the school district's part-time anti-homophobia staff person to address issues of school culture. When this failed to resolve the bathroom crisis for Silver, Sherene asked the principal to let Silver use the staff bathroom. According to Sherene, the principal responded by saying, "No. If we do that for her, we have to do it for everyone": "And I said, 'Look, they're doing it at universities all over the place. I've looked around a bit, and this isn't a big request, this isn't a strange request, and you actually have a kid in your school who requires some safety.' And she said, 'No. If we do it for her, we have to do it for everyone else.' I said, 'Well, do it for everyone then.' And she said, 'We can't do it,' and I said, 'Fine,' and I moved her." Moving to a different school in the district that immediately accommodated Silver's need for a gender-neutral bathroom without question solved the problem at school. But bathrooms in public spaces continue to be unsafe for Silver, and she needs an adult to accompany her. Sometimes this is a problem, particularly when Silver is with her dad (Silver's parents are separated). Once when Silver was with her dad at a park near his house, for example, she had to go to the bathroom. She asked her dad to take her back to his house a block away, but he refused, telling her to use the bathroom at the park. Feeling unsafe to do so, Silver wet her pants and ended up calling her mother to come and get her.

This fear of sex-segregated public bathrooms is widespread among trans kids. Dara, the mother of Davis (11, Asian American), described "a whole world of anxiety and managing" that Davis explained to her that "'she' had to do, with people perceiving 'her' as a boy in the wrong bathroom if 'she's' in the girls' bathroom." Although Davis was pretransition, Dara suspected her child would actually feel more comfortable in the boys' bathroom but was not willing to endure the process of coming out to peers and teachers that that would entail. Dara went on to tell me that Davis's class "had to make hopes, wishes, and dreams for fourth grade, and 'her' hope for fourth grade is that 'her' school would create a bathroom for both boys and girls, but then 'she' decided not to reveal that." Davis's teacher found a way to be on Davis's side by introducing a support structure and coaching Davis's peers to be bathroom buddies to mitigate their classmate's disabling experience of the bathroom. This gave Davis a feeling of safety while at school, but public bathrooms in other places continued to be terrifying. In a subsequent interview, Dara said that her son had transitioned, in part by switching schools, and was a much happier, less anxious child as a result.

Quinn told me, "I never really let on how much shit I have to deal with in bathrooms. I've been attacked in bathrooms in a way that I got out unscathed, but because I'm agile and a fast runner." They think this happens because "someone thinks that you don't fit in in a bathroom well enough": "Like, I guess I send out super trans vibes, because I can be wearing a dress in a women's washroom and be wearing a ton of makeup and people will walk in, give me double looks, look at the sign on the bathroom door, and then keep staring at me the whole time, which is super uncomfortable. And this happens whichever washroom I use, and bathrooms are essentially—like the signs on them as long as they're gendered, it might as well say, 'Get yelled at and get beat up.'" Quinn reports being spat at and shoved in public washrooms but "not so much in school bathrooms." They say that most of the difficulty they experience in using public bathrooms comes from adults. On occasions when they are challenged about being in the "wrong" bathroom, Quinn explained, "Sometimes I have to claim to be a gender I'm not in order to stay safe, mostly in bathrooms in public, not so much at school." They have had the most frightening experiences in public men's bathrooms when "wearing something that wasn't like 'super masculine'": "You can get some very negative feedback because people either think you're a 'tranny,' as they would put it and as I've been called multiple times, or that you're a boy in a dress, which is always confusing to them. It's mostly been when people walk in, see you washing your hands at a sink, and no matter how much you hunch over and try to hide yourself, they can see you in the mirrors, and they see your face, and they decide that you're not acceptable to be in this washroom, and then they might corner you." Quinn finds that women can be unpleasant but not as threatening as some of the men they have encountered: "Women just usually whis-per about you and like give you very passive-aggressive looks because I guess that's how society trains us to be, which is horrible in its own right, but I've been screamed at by women in women's bathrooms before."

Quinn takes deliberate measures to minimize risks to their safety when using public bathrooms, including sizing up public washrooms for ease of exit should the need arise and appearing confident. Quinn noted, "The biggest safeguard, honestly, for washrooms is to just ooze confidence and swagger, but that's so hard because if you're attacked in some situations, then, like, you're going to be terrified going to washrooms in a similar location or if it looks similar or if you see someone who looks like the person who tried to hurt you." In contrast, at school, Quinn feels empowered to resist gender policing in the bathroom. When kids at school look at them weirdly in the bathroom, Quinn takes some pleasure in educating them: "It's mostly the new kids every year who look really, really concerned and confused, and then we have a conversation—I'm not using 'conversation' as a euphemism; we literally have a conversation. It's usually pretty one-sided, but they either are totally okay with it afterwards or they avoid me like the plague, which is fun." Being a member of their school's gay-straight alliance means that Quinn feels more empowered in school environments because they know they are not alone and have the advantage of being able to call on a collective voice.

Frank's devastating experiences in elementary school at the hands of teachers included experiencing psychological torture around bathroom access. Frank described feeling consistently humiliated by teachers around issues of bathroom use: it was one of the principal ways they imposed a female identity on him. One of the ways teachers repudiated his male identity on a daily basis was by forcing him to use the girls' bathroom and punishing and humiliating him when he used the boys'. They instilled in Frank such a sense of shame and self-surveillance that he reported to his teachers when he did use the boys' bathroom. On these occasions, he was given detentions. Frank is deeply offended by every aspect of this experience when he thinks about it now. He explained why being forced to use the wrong bathroom is so traumatic for him: "It is really simple things like using the bathroom that you don't want to use that can really hurt people: it embarrassed me so much. I cried, and I hid in the bathroom every single time. Every time I had to use the bathroom, I would hide in there until I made sure no one was in the hallway and nobody was in the bathroom, which was hard because it was in the main hallway. I hid in there for over half an hour sometimes."

Some kids experience gender dysphoria and *feel* like they are in the wrong bathroom, even though no one is physically preventing them from using the one they would prefer. Tru Wilson, for example, grew up feeling out of place in the boys' bathroom and longed to use the girls'. Lennox initially vocalized a desire for "bathrooms to be bathrooms" rather than sex-segregated spaces, saying that she wished for "a bathroom for everyone to use, like it's a boy-and-girls' bathroom; that's what I wish they had at school." But it soon became clear in our conversation that Lennox was most drawn to the girls' bathroom. When asked what she would do if she was able to choose between a gender-neutral bathroom and the girls' bathroom, her eyes lit up, and she said unequivocally, "The girls." As a trans child who is invisible outside her home, Lennox keeps her desire to use the girls' bathroom secret and finds having to use the boys' bathroom painful. For her, being able to use the girls' bathroom is crucial to living fully as a girl but is not something she is prepared to do at the moment.

Gender-Neutral or No-Gender Bathrooms

For some kids, neither sex-segregated bathroom is the right one. Stef, for example, identifies as gender neutral and describes using washrooms this way: "horrible for me because a lot of people kind of look at me, and they're kind of like, what the f——? What's going on here?" Stef regularly experiences a dilemma around which bathroom to use. They experience greater safety in girls' washrooms, find girls' washrooms to be cleaner, more likely to have mirrors and to be stocked with toilet paper, and because privacy is really important to them, more likely to have stalls with doors that close and lock. But when they use them, they said, "then everyone thinks I'm a girl, so then, well, shit, but I'd rather be safe and not get asked too many questions like, 'You're in the wrong washroom. Please get out of here.'" One of the worst experiences Stef has had to deal with around bathroom access occurred on a school trip to another country: "[Local men] wouldn't allow me to go into the washrooms, so I had to be escorted into the washroom by my teacher, which really sucks, and then escorted out of the washroom." For the sake of independence and comfort, Stef started using the girls' washroom on this trip but then encountered resistance from their teacher, who stopped them from going into the girls' washroom, saying, "I understand why you're going into the girls' washroom, but didn't you say that you were a boy?" Stef responded, "No, I'm not a boy. I already told you what my situation was, and I told you that if anyone is offended or anything, please talk to me. But expect that I will be doing what I need to do to *survive*" (my emphasis). The relationship between bathroom access and empowerment is clear: bathroom access is a survival issue. Like other kids I talked to, Stef found so-called gender-neutral public washrooms often to be inadequate:

> What schools and a lot of public places try to pass off as a gender-neutral washroom are often, like, one-stall rooms, which also don't make me feel terribly safe because when someone tries like knocking on the door 20 times or something like that, and where they have a child and they want to pee or something, and then they're really angry that someone is inside the washroom that they think is for like moms and stuff like that or dads who have babies and stuff like that or teenagers. And I don't really like the little, small, shitty little washrooms that they try to pass off as gender-neutral washrooms, which is really just like a family washroom that you just put "gender neutral" on.

Quinn experiences a similar dilemma: they use the girls' washroom most of the time because "the boys' washrooms are disgusting": "Like the boys pee everywhere, and there's toilet paper everywhere, and there's usually not toilet paper or soap. So I use the girls' just for cleanliness, generally speaking. However, being in the girls' washroom, generally speaking, I'm perceived as a girl being in the girls' washroom, and that makes me very uncomfortable. So I use the boys' whenever it's hygienic." The stall doors in either bathroom have no locks (which Quinn attributes to budget shortfalls), so they have to be held closed. And menstrual pad and tampon disposal bins are not provided in the stalls, which poses a particular risk for trans boys. When I asked Quinn if they are able to find gender-neutral washrooms when out in public, they spat back, "There's never a gender-neutral washroom." Where they do exist, the vast majority of bathrooms that are not gender designated are marked for the physically disabled or adult-led family groupings.

Stacey, Cassandra's mother, reported that, upon seeing a washroom with a sign indicating that it is a washroom for the "handicapped/men/women," her daughter said, "I wish all bathrooms were like that. Then you could just go to the bathroom." Frank is in full agreement, saying, "I don't think anyone should be assigned to a strict gendered bathroom. I think bathrooms should be gender neutral." Frank cited the example of the open, gender-neutral washroom facilities provided at an annual conference for transgender adults and children and their families: "They even put signs over top of the little 'guy' and 'girl' signs, and it says, 'gender-neutral bathroom.' I think that's the best situation—the best thing to do." Political scientist Heath Fogg Davis suggests that the most meaningful challenge to sex-segregated bathrooms is to convert all bathrooms into "unisex or no-gender bathrooms" by "removing urinals and building additional private stalls in their place."[10] Bathroom access is foundational for well-being, and the trauma trans kids experience when denied it has serious social and mental and physical health consequences.

The trans kids in the book applied various, often situational, strategies to navigate bathroom access: remaining invisible, avoidance, making situational choices to survive, pursuing medical transition, and resisting/fighting back. Trans kids weigh the often-conflicting needs of gender self-determination, physical urgency, and self-protection in employing these strategies. The need for safety, by means of invisibility, for example, often comes with negative mental health consequences of its own. Social acceptance for gender-affirming, or nonbinary, bathroom access empowers trans kids.

Political Conflict around Transgender Bathroom Access

The space available for girls with penises, boys with vulvas, and children who identify outside the gender binary entirely is fearfully contracted in North American culture, as evinced by the recent rise of "bathroom bills" in the U.S. that stipulate that trans people must use public bathrooms in accordance with the sex they were assigned at birth. Recent legislation and policy debates regulating the access that transgender people have to these spaces in the United States and Canada expose trans oppression at its vilest and most disabling.

United States

HB2. In the United States, many states have considered trans-oppressive state "bathroom bills," driven by moral panics about men masquerading as women in order to sexually attack women and girls, with special hyperbole devoted to the specter of an innocent (white) female child being victimized in the bathroom by a man masquerading as a woman.[11] These bills are designed to prevent trans people from using bathrooms and locker rooms and other sex-segregated facilities according to their affirmed gender identities.[12] Anti-trans bathroom bills reinforce a cisgender binary sex system by restricting people to using bathrooms congruent with their "sex at birth." Only one state, North Carolina, however, has been successful in passing such a bill—House Bill 2 (HB2)—although a number are still pending.[13] The state legislature of North Carolina passed HB2 in March 2016 to negate a Charlotte city ordinance prohibiting discrimination against LGBTQ people. According to journalist Mark Stern, "HB2 nullified this ordinance, and any other municipal law that provided greater protections than state law. Since state law doesn't protect LGBTQ people, HB2 nullified all local LGBTQ nondiscrimination ordinances. More controversially, it also regulated the use of government bathrooms, including those in public schools and universities. Under HB2, individuals had to use the bathroom that corresponded to their 'biological sex,' as listed on their birth certificate. In many states, it is difficult or impossible for trans people to alter their birth certificate. So this provision effectively bars countless trans people from using government bathrooms."[14]

The immediate fallout from the passage of HB2 led to its partial repeal. After HB2 was passed, the state lost millions of dollars in business as the National Basketball Association (NBA), the National Collegiate Athletic Association (NCAA), and many headline performers, including Bruce Springsteen, canceled their events in the state. The subsequent electoral defeat of Pat McCrory, the North Carolina governor who championed HB2, was just the beginning of his employment woes. McCrory recently complained about his inability to find work, claiming, "Even after I left office people are reluctant to hire me, because, 'Oh my gosh, he's a bigot,' which is the last thing I am."[15] This pressure forced the partial repeal of HB2 by the state legislature on March 30, 2017. Its replacement, House Bill 142 (HB142), appears to be an equally damaging piece of legislation for LGBT rights in North Carolina, but it seems to have mollified the state legislature's more mainstream critics.[16] According to Stern, HB142 is "just as odious." The bill forbids "state agencies, boards, offices, departments, institutions," and "branches of government," including public universities, from regulating "access to multiple occupancy restrooms, showers, or changing facilities." It applies this same rule to "local boards of education," meaning these boards cannot pass trans-inclusive policies. Instead, local governments, public universities, and school boards would have to wait for permission from the General Assembly to protect trans people. . . . That's not the end of it. HB 142 would also impose a years-long moratorium on local LGBTQ nondiscrimination ordinances. The bill would bar any city from "regulating private employment practices or regulating public accommodations" until December 1, 2020. Stern goes on to note that "there is nothing to stop the General Assembly from extending this moratorium as its expiration date draws closer."[17]

GAVIN GRIMM: G.G. V. GLOUCESTER COUNTY SCHOOL BOARD. Other potential watershed cases have stalled before the courts, the most high profile being the legal challenge of the American Civil Liberties Union (ACLU) on behalf of transgender boy Gavin Grimm's right to use the boys' washroom at his high school. The ACLU and its Virginia affiliate took Grimm's school board to court in 2015 to fight the policy that restricted transgender students to gender-neutral washrooms. The policy in question was adopted in 2014, two months after Grimm had begun using the boys' washroom. According to the ACLU, the policy contravenes the provisions of Title IX of the U.S. Education Amendments of 1972, a federal law prohibiting sex discrimination by schools and that requires all institutions receiving federal government funding to implement gender equity. Grimm's case was dismissed by a U.S. district court, but he successfully appealed it to the U.S. Court of Appeals for the Fourth Circuit, which overturned the ruling. When a subsequent lower court upheld Grimm's right to use the boys' washroom, the school district appealed to the U.S. Supreme Court, which, in August 2016, temporarily stayed the Fourth Circuit ruling while it considered the case. This occurred within a changing political context, however: In 2016, the Obama White House voiced its intention to support transgender students. Many trans people and supporters hoped that the Supreme Court would therefore establish a federal precedent in support of transgender rights.[18] According to *Advocate* reporter Trudy Ring, a ruling by the Supreme Court in favor of Grimm would have set a precedent likely to produce rulings against North Carolina's HB2 and other state anti-trans bathroom bills.[19]

But the 2016 presidential election produced a change in the political landscape to a Trump administration that included transgender students among its vulnerable targets by officially withdrawing the Obama directive about supporting trans students. The new attorney general, Jeff Sessions, insists that federal protections under Title IX do not include gender identity.[20] The Supreme Court responded to this change by refusing to hear Grimm's case and returning it to the lower court, which, in light of the new administration in Washington, subsequently overturned its original decision and ruled against Grimm. Grimm graduated from high school in June 2017, and this change in his status was employed by the U.S. Court of Appeals for the Fourth Circuit to insist that a "lower court must sort out whether Grimm still has enough of an affiliation to his alma mater to pursue the case."[21]

Canada

BILL C-279 AND BILL C-16. At the federal level in Canada, Bill C-279, commonly referred to as "the bathroom bill," to "amend the Canadian Human Rights Act to include gender identity as a prohibited ground of discrimination" and to amend the Criminal Code to include "gender identity as a distinguishing characteristic," was introduced into the Canadian federal legislature in 2013.[22] The bill failed to pass through necessary levels of government at this time, however, but Bill C-16 was introduced and passed after the Trudeau government took power in 2016. Bill C-16 explicitly adds transgender rights to the *Canadian Charter of Rights and Freedoms*. As of June 2017, all provinces and territories in Canada include gender-identity protections in their human rights codes. These provisions can be leveraged by trans students and their parents to ensure access to bathrooms and change rooms in accordance with their affirmed gender. The case advanced by the mother of Bella Burgos provides a powerful example.

ELIZABETH BURGOS V. RIVER EAST TRANSCONA SCHOOL DIVISION. In the summer of 2014, Isabella (Bella) Burgos announced to her family that she was transgender—that she had "felt like a girl in a boy's body for four years."[23] With the full support of her parents, Bella returned to school that fall as a girl. In spite of the initial welcome from students and staff, Bella's safety and well-being were compromised when the parent of another child at the school complained about Bella using the girls' bathroom. This parent not only complained to the school principal but "yelled at the child and her older brother and lobbied other parents outside the school."[24] The school responded to this complaint by insisting that Bella use a gender-neutral bathroom rather than the girls' bathroom. Bella's parents were concerned about the negative impact this "segregation" would have on Bella's transition. According to Bella's father, Dale, "You want to make sure they feel welcome and happy at the decision they made. . . . Because this is probably the biggest decision she'll ever have in her whole life."[25]

Dale Burgos reported that Bella was harassed at the school by staff as well as by the aforementioned parent. "Our daughter was followed by staff to see which bathroom she used. She was approached by a janitor at one point. There were many instances like this in the school."[26] Insisting that access to the bathroom consistent with Bella's affirmed gender identity is a human right, Bella's mother, Elizabeth, filed a complaint with the Manitoba Human Rights Commission in October 2014, alleging that the school's insistence that Bella stay out of the girls' bathroom amounted to discrimination on the basis of gender identity. In this complaint, Bella's parents insisted that the school district needed to support transgender students with explicit and supportive policy provisions and provide students and school personnel with appropriate education and training.[27] They also contended that the school had failed to protect Bella from trans-oppressive bullying by the parent who yelled at her. In March 2016, the human rights complaint between Elizabeth Burgos and River East Transcona School Division was resolved in favor of Bella and her family. This constituted a significant win for transgender students in general. According to Kelly Barkman, superintendent and CEO of River East Transcona School Division, the agreement allows "for transgender students to have the right to use the washroom they identify with and the guidelines, if you look at it, do get into things such as resources, professional development, not only for the staff, but for the students."[28]

Successful human rights complaints such as this one and the out-of-court settlement guaranteeing transgender inclusion achieved by Tru Wilson and her family are clear indicators that transgender kids in Canada have legal rights to access bathrooms and change rooms according to their affirmed gender. But assumptions about fundamental differences between only two sexes and male athletic superiority create particular obstacles for trans kids who wish to participate in sport and physical recreation.

Challenges Associated with Sport and Physical Recreation

I turn here to the ways in which the regulation of gendered bodies accomplished by sex-segregated bathrooms is duplicated and amplified in the spaces of the change room and the sex divided and differentiated worlds of sport participation. Like bathrooms, sex-segregated and sex-differentiated sport and physical recreation spaces, facilities, and programs—including day and sleepaway camps, activities, and uniforms—place transgender kids in harm's way. These facilities and spaces are predicated on the taken-for-granted assumption that there are only two, fundamentally different sexes[29] and that boys and men have an across-the-board unfair athletic advantage over girls and women.[30]

For trans kids who transition to a binary identity, sport participation typically requires a switch from one gendered space to another, often but not always requiring medicalization for eligibility. I begin this discussion with the well-publicized case of Texas high school trans wrestler Mack Beggs. In 2017, Mack, then 17, was forced to wrestle in the girls' competition rather than the boys' in the Texas state championship—he went on to win. Beggs began undergoing testosterone therapy in October 2015, but his request to wrestle as a boy was turned down by the state's officiating body for school sports. The state requirement that student athletes participate in accordance with the assigned sex on their birth certificate (altering requires a court order) meant that Beggs had to decide whether to wrestle against girls or not at all. He chose to wrestle against girls rather than quit, in spite of feeling strongly that he should be competing against boys because, as he said, "I'm a guy." Reporter Christina Cauterucci described the "spectacle of an undefeated teenage boy demolishing his female opponents—or advancing after they forfeited—because officials won't validate his trans identity" as having "caused a confused uproar in the Texas high-school wrestling community. And, in the process, it has exposed the farcical conundrums that arise from trying to impose hard, abstract boundaries on the messy reality of gender."[31] Cauterucci noted that parents of female competitors, as well as the audience, booed Beggs as he participated and that parents and coaches claimed that he was cheating: "arguing that testosterone, often used as a steroid performance enhancer, gives Beggs an unfair advantage."[32] What is particularly interesting is that the assumptions that there are only two sexes and that testosterone provides an "unfair" athletic advantage are untroubled not only by anti-trans complaints about Beggs's participation while taking the hormone but by some trans-positive arguments in favor of allowing trans boys and trans men to participate in their affirmed sex category.

For example, when Dale Hansen, a Texas sportscaster, spoke out on behalf of Beggs's right to wrestle against boys, he argued that Beggs should not be penalized for a "genetic mix-up at birth."[33] This particular defense of Beggs's right to wrestle against boys takes both an ableist and a biological determinist approach grounded in a medical model of disability by making being transgender tantamount to having a "birth defect." Hansen also takes for granted the faulty logic of fundamental male athletic superiority. This is a clear indication that issues relating to transgender participation in sport cannot be understood independently from the historical role of sport in normalizing and reinforcing the ideology of the two-sex system and the widespread gender inequality (male superiority) that accompanies it.

Modern Sports' Role in Normalizing the Two-Sex System

Modern sport emerged in Europe and its colonies in the late 19th and early 20th centuries. From the outset, sport was a male-supremacist "civilizing"[34] and capitalist project[35] that represented, among other things, a backlash against the increasing power of middle- and upper-class white women[36] and the burgeoning working class. Sport was explicitly designed to emphasize sex difference, socialize boys and men into orthodox masculinity, enforce heterosexuality,[37] further the goal of white middle- and upper-class morality and leadership within Western imperialist projects,[38] and importantly, at least at the professional level, provide a return for capital investment. Any analysis of sport needs to have an intersectional footprint,[39] as race, class, sexuality, gender, and nation constitute relations of power and privilege[40] working in and through sport that are far from simplistic.

While sport at the international level (and much of the world) is organized around binary notions of biological difference between males and females,[41] queer feminist science[42] reveals the extent to which the taken-for-granted two-sex system is constituted by ideological assumptions about its existence.[43] It is no accident, for example, that queer feminist science scholar Anne Fausto-Sterling's *Sexing the Body* begins with a devastating critique of sex-verification testing at the highest levels of sport to establish the failure of science to demarcate boundaries between male and female bodies.[44] The measuring of bodily capacity that national and international sport is purportedly organized around underscores its significant cultural role in the hierarchical demarcation of sex boundaries. By virtue of sex-segregated sporting spaces and grossly unequal cultural and economic spaces, sport in Canada and the U.S. and much of the world is organized through taken-for-granted Eurocentric patriarchal models of binary sex difference. That these socially generated boundaries are culturally understood as natural and unmediated by social forces makes them all the more difficult to challenge.

The revelation that this two-sex system is ideological rather than natural underscores the role of sport in showcasing a vision of a stark biological divide between male and female bodies that is intricately bound up with gender injustice for women and gender transgressors throughout society. As sport sociologist Mary Jo Kane notes, the establishment of gender difference is a "product of patriarchal social construction."[45] "Male" and "female" bodies are produced, in corporeal terms, in social contexts that assume and privilege male athletic competence at the expense of female physical development.[46] Kane demonstrates that the gender binary paradigm in sport is grounded in biologically deterministic notions of gender polarity and features an emphasis on difference and the dismissal and deliberate invisibility of similarities between male and female athletes. This invisibility is essential for upholding male dominance and is achieved through the symbiotic relationship between mainstream sport and mainstream sport media.[47] Kane insists that a more accurate model for sport reporting would portray a gender continuum. Critical feminist sport scholars focus on the role of sport in contributing to gender inequality by reinforcing orthodox masculinity and perpetuating sexism.[48] As it stands, the institutionalization of the two-sex system *as natural* contributes to the cultural and economic marginalization of women, gays and lesbians, and transgender people in the world of sport and beyond.

For trans people of all ages, the sex segregation of sport is a key obstacle to participation. Within this field is an emergent subset of research that views the sex segregation of amateur and professional sport as deeply problematic.[49] In *Playing with the Boys: Why Separate Is Not Equal*, political scientist Eileen McDonagh and journalist Laura Pappano identify "coercive" as opposed to "voluntary" sex segregation for girls and women as the cornerstone of sports' contribution to gender inequality.[50] The predominant sex segregation of many sports and sex differentiation of activities within some less segregated sports (for example, gymnastics and figure skating) or different rules (for example, in basketball, golf, tennis, and volleyball) play an important role in normalizing gender inequality by packaging, showcasing, and emphasizing differences between male and female bodies to celebrate masculine superiority and justify extensive opportunity structures and disproportionate patterns of remuneration for male athletes.[51] The fact that the names of professional women's sport associations need to be specifically gendered while men's remain unmarked (for example, Ladies Professional Golf Association versus Professional Golf Association; Women's National Basketball Association versus National Basketball Association) is a powerful indicator of the cultural assumption that sport is a male realm. Sport is simply assumed to be a male prerogative unless an exception is marked. Understood in this light, privileged networks for resource distribution associated with and enabled by mainstream sport depend on fierce patrol of its borders. The regulation of the bodies of women and transgender people reflects the extent to which we, as interlopers, must be carefully policed.

Transgender athletes present a challenge to sex-segregated sporting institutions and programs whether they, as individuals, are interested in doing so or not. Concerns about transgender participation in sport tend to center on assumptions that a transgender woman has presumably been exposed to higher levels of testosterone prior to transitioning, and therefore this testosterone should be considered a "performance-enhancing drug." According to critical sport scholar Sarah Teetzel, however, comparisons between transgender women athletes and steroid use for the purpose of doping are misguided; past exposure to higher levels of testosterone produces no evidence-based comparative advantage.[52] Despite this fact, David McArdle notes that the United Kingdom's Gender Recognition Act of 2004 granted sport an exception to the requirements for legal recognition of transgender persons, fearing that transgender women, by virtue of their past lives as (presumably testosterone-saturated) "men," would dominate women in sport.[53] The underlying assumption of sex-segregated sporting spaces is that someone who is born male naturally has an "unfair advantage" when competing against women in sport.[54] In spite of documented overlaps between male and female athletic performance, these ideas continue to characterize and structure mainstream sporting policies and lean heavily on a Western trope of white, female frailty.[55]

The role of sport in normalizing and reinforcing binary sex ideologies and gender inequality is evident in the gender policing that occurs in change rooms and when people are participating in sport and physical recreation. As educational scholar Elizabeth Meyer observes, "Most traditional extracurricular activities have subtexts that subtly and overtly teach that certain forms of masculinity and femininity are valued over others. The clearest example of such an activity is that of elite amateur and professional athletic teams and the cheerleaders and dance squads that accompany them."[56] Sociologist of sport Michael Messner characterizes youth sports in the United States as reproducing "soft essentialist narratives that appropriate the liberal feminist language of choice for girls, but not for boys, thus serving to re-create and naturalize class-based gender asymmetries and inequalities."[57]

Barriers for Trans Kids

Sex-segregated sport and leisure facilities create a crisis for trans kids as a result of three different types of barriers: issues of access resulting from the sex-segregated structure of many sports, programs, and facilities; problems relating to participation in sex-differentiated activities within gender-integrated sports/activities; and difficulties relating to the climate of these environments. Because of these factors, many trans kids drop out or avoid physical activity altogether. Those for whom sport participation is a priority struggle to find ways to do so.

The assumption that male athletic superiority is a biological certainty is pervasive in Canadian and U.S. culture, and many of this study's participants and their parents echoed these sentiments. Dave (17, Euro-Canadian), for example, described himself as having participated in many sports when he was still presenting as a girl, but he stopped upon transition. As a man, Dave considers himself to be newly uncompetitive in the sports he previously played successfully as a girl. He feels he is too small to play hockey and overmatched in table tennis. Jenny, the mother of Nick (11, Asian Canadian), took for granted the athletic superiority of boys her son's age, attributing their superior skill level to male puberty. She observed that "their strength level [is much greater]" and therefore presents an obstacle to her son's participation.

Although many sport and physical recreation activities are formally sex segregated, some parents choose to enroll their gender-nonconforming and trans children in sex-*integrated* activities. Formal sex segregation in sport has received critical attention, but sex-integrated activities remain problematic. Gender-integrated environments provide a lower barrier in general because they do not force the issue in the same way, but they remain problematic and not just because of the extent to which sex-segregated changing/locker-room facilities are the norm. Within integrated sports and physical recreation programs, formal and informal rules often require different activities and uniforms for boys and girls. In gymnastics and dance, for example, boys and girls wear different uniforms and are required to train their bodies to perform in different ways that reflect, and reassert, widespread cultural beliefs in binary sex and male superiority. Given that 99% of the kids who participate in gymnastics will not reach the elite heights of the sport, non-gendered uniforms and instruction on all the equipment would benefit the majority, and transgender and gender-nonconforming kids could be spared sex segregation and differentiation in this arena. In Canada and the U.S., however, this is not the norm. As such, children's bodies are subjected to the gendered muscle development and physical differentiation that renders the resulting differences to appear as "natural."

Seeing the so-called sex differences in gymnastics produced through social practice and repetition gave Sean's father, Hal, a more critical perspective. Hal observed how sex-differentiated activities in gymnastics actually created gendered bodies. When Sean first enrolled in gymnastics, she was deeply disappointed to learn that she would not be able to work on the rings because they are designated as an apparatus for men and boys. According to Hal, "Sean had her heart set on doing the rings, but the rings are not allowed to her. But she started gymnastics with a Brazilian coach, who came and asked the girls, 'Can anybody do a chin-up?' But nobody could. And then Sean came and just ripped off nine chin-ups, and he was so excited he took her to all the other coaches. But she came back to me and said, 'I dunno what to do because I can't do the rings.'" Hal observed how this rule reinforced assumptions about sex differences: "The thing, too, that strikes me is that the boys that are struggling. They're not as strong as her, but they're doing it every day. And in a few years hence, they will become proficient, strong at this. And if Sean does not end up doing those exact muscle-building things, she will not. So then it will become this self-perpetuating dynamic that's going on." This is an example of the way that the "gender continuum" of overlapping sport performance is rendered invisible via social practices, with the result that the natural basis of sex segregation, sex differentiation, and male "unfair advantage" goes unquestioned.

Even in integrated community-center dance classes, it is often impossible to register kids without sharing information about their sex. Such information is assumed to be essential and is used to organize children's participation in gender-appropriate ways. Many feminist parents who actively resist sex stereotyping are deeply troubled by the way sex markers are deployed to socialize children in distinctly gendered ways. Like many gender-nonconforming boys, Cody (five, Euro-American) routinely gets "mistaken" for a girl. According to Cody's mother, Zimm, Cody has long hair and a "mixed" wardrobe, likes superheroes, rough-and-tumble play, pretty things, and ballet. In his current ballet class, they "dress the boys and girls in different clothes." Zimm described the challenges that this differentiation poses for Cody and subsequently for her:

> He is supposed to wear a uniform. He's supposed to wear black leggings and a white shirt. And the girls are supposed to wear a black leotard, and they can wear pink tights, and they have pink ballet shoes. And he has black ballet shoes, and I was so worried that he was going to flip his shit because he did not get to wear the pink ones [*laughs*] and the pink tights. It turned out not to be a problem, and he's willing to go along with it. I

mean, it does visually distinguish him, as like clearly he is one of the boys in the dance class, with his really long, blond hair that several weeks ago he wanted me to put up in a bun.

Jordan described the difficulties they and their partner encountered in attempting to find a dance class for their (at the time) gender-nonconforming son:

> When Wren was four and still identifying as a boy, "he" took a ballet course through the community center, and because "he" wanted the leotard and the tutu that the girls had—there were no other boys in the class—I got them for "him." And "he" basically blended in until my use of the male pronoun in a conversation with "his" teacher outed "him" as a "boy." I asked the teacher to keep letting "him" dance as a girl, and it seemed to be going fine until the little performance at the end of the class. Wren was dancing in "his" pink leotard and tutu in the special performance, in front of all the parents and friends of the dancers. When it ended, the teacher called out to "him" in front of everyone and instructed "him" to bow, not curtsy, saying that "boys should bow, not curtsy." Everyone there looked very puzzled, and Wren was mortified.

Like many parents when they encounter overt discrimination against their children, Jordan marshaled their resources:

> I was angry about it and didn't sign Wren up there again. Instead, I went through a long and arduous process to find a dance class where my "son" could dance like the girls without censure. I was surprised at how difficult it was. I did find one of the really serious programs that allowed it. But when I chatted with other parents before, during, and after the dance class, I found myself avoiding using any pronouns to refer to Wren because I felt I had ruined things for "him" in the community-center class by outing him as a boy. But this avoidance felt really, really weird.

Gender essentialism is clearly "harder"[58] in some sports than others, as a result of the way certain sports are organized. Tight and revealing uniforms—such as swimsuits—present more of a challenge to transgender kids than do the bulkier uniforms that athletes wear in other sports.

Feminist sport scholars are increasingly challenging the appropriateness of sex-segregated teams and sex-differentiated activities.[59] My own research on gender and sport[60] is part of this tradition in part because the sex-segregated structure of many sport and physical recreation spaces make participation complicated for trans kids. The difficulties faced by kids who want to identify outside the binary are often extraordinary. Neither side of the binary is right for some, and this produces a sense of crisis because fully mixed spaces (gender integrated with unisex rules and uniforms) for sport and physical recreation are rare.

Jordan's account of finding a dance class where Wren, pretransition, could wear a pink outfit and dance "as a girl" exemplifies how parents must draw on socioeconomic privilege when negotiating so-called sex-integrated physical recreation spaces. Less privileged families would not have had the funds or access or time to travel to the "appropriate" dance class for Wren. Others may have had to settle for a local community-center class if they could afford one at all. If Jordan had not been able to devote the time, energy, and know-how to navigating these spaces, Wren would have had to either quit dancing, dance as a boy and wear the boys' outfit, or put up with the occasional misgendering, shaming, and censure from the teacher. The ability to support and advocate for trans kids is not evenly distributed. What about those whose parents are not able to leave work to attend their kids' sports events in order to run interference for them? What about families whose lack of economic resources leaves them with few or no options for sport participation?

Climate: Issues of Informal Inequality

Adding women as participants, tolerating gay teammates, and enabling trans participants who undergo medicalized binary transition do not, on their own, change the overall cultural role of an enterprise that normalizes binary sex systems via gender inequality, homophobia, and trans oppression. According to a University of British Columbia study, "Are We Leveling the Playing Field? Trends and Disparities in Sports Participation among Sexual Minority Youth in Canada," lesbian, gay, and bisexual teens are 50% less likely than their heterosexual counterparts to participate in sports.[61] While the study does not address transgender participation specifically, it is logical to assume that the binary

normative nature of most sport programs combines with heteronormativity to discourage participation by queer and trans kids. This is borne
out in the research shared here and corroborated by data in the 2013
GLSEN report indicating that "11% were prevented or discouraged from
participating in school sports because they were LGBTQ."[62]

Locker Rooms

Very much like bathrooms, locker rooms are spaces that impose binary
gender structures and regulate access on the basis of intelligibility. Being
included with same-gender peers is an important aspect of transition for
many kids. But in group discussions at conferences or news interviews, I
have witnessed a few parents of trans kids talking about the importance
of their children being able to bond with their same-gender peers in the
locker room without any acknowledgment of the extent to which male
locker rooms in particular can be toxic environments with regard to
misogyny and for gender and sexual minorities.[63] One of my participants, Cory Oskam[64] (16, Euro-Canadian), emphasized how necessary
it was to use the same locker room as everyone else in order to participate in team bonding, but he also did his part to change the climate of
the locker room. When Cory first transitioned, his school suggested he
use a gender-neutral space, but he purposefully positioned himself as
fundamentally male (rather than the trans, nonbinary identity he feels
greater affinity for) to enable himself to dress with the team. At times,
however, he found the locker room to be an uncomfortable space. Once
while in a boys' hockey dressing room, Cory experienced discomfort as
one of his teammates made homo-negative remarks to the group. Corey
handled this incident by waiting until he was alone with the guy to ask
him, "Dude, why do you say those things?" It takes courage to stand up
to boys and men who are performing orthodox masculinity. On a number of occasions since then, Cory has heard "faggot" and "pussy" used
as pejoratives in the locker room, bringing to mind Pascoe's observation
that "fag" is used as an abject category in the construction of adolescent
masculinity.[65] Cory explained why hearing the guys in his locker room
use these terms to "really put down women" was something he experienced as "really offensive": "I do identify as someone who was female at
one point. And I do identify, like, as female once in a while. So it was

not pleasant to hear." When this occurred on his hockey team, Cory complained to his coach: "'They're saying these words that make me feel uncomfortable,' and he's like, 'Yeah, those are words that shouldn't be said in the dressing room.' And then they were addressed in just a very anonymous fashion, by the coach saying like, 'I've heard that there's bad language in the dressing rooms, and that needs to go away.' And it really did stop." Dave, however, drew on the homophobic climate of the locker room to deflect attention away from his post-top surgery chest and to keep himself safe. When a boy asked him, "Why do your nipples look so weird?" Dave responded, "Dude, why are you looking at my nipples?"

Coping Strategies

Trans kids and their parents in my study applied four strategies to negotiate barriers to participation in sport and physical recreation: continuing to play as their assigned sex; avoiding or quitting sport; participating in recreational activities that are less sex divided/differentiated; and transitioning—with or without undergoing medical treatment.

Some trans kids remain invisible to enable them to fit in and so participate in sport on the same principle. For others who are visibly gender nonconforming, sport participation can be very challenging. Ray-Ray's mother, Nadine, shared an example of the ongoing labor she has had to engage in to enable her son to continue to participate in the sport of running:

> Ray-Ray took off one time in a race—this was probably about grade 5 or 6—and there was a guy standing on the edge of the field to tell the kids when they can cut in. He's one of the officials. He takes off running across the field yelling at the top of his lungs with the megaphone, "There's a girl on the track." And I was out there, and I jogged beside him, and I said, "That's a boy. He's my son. His name is Ray-Ray, and he'll probably win." And I walked away. That's how bad it was, and Ray-Ray just went—he just persisted, but other kids I know who are gender nonconforming would be horrified.

Ray-Ray has been competing in track since he was in third grade, and he is regularly marshaled away from the boys' competition and toward the girls. "His name is Ray-Ray Marvolo," Nadine explained, but "they would move his name to the girls' marshaling list when they saw his long hair, and then the guy marshaling the girls would stand there yelling his name until one of the other kids who knew who he was would say, 'He's not a girl; he's a boy.' And the guy still wouldn't get it. And I would often have to go to the marshaling tent. In fact, I almost always went to the marshaling tent to get him sorted and racing as a boy." Nadine shared this and other examples to emphasize how crucial it has been for her to run interference at every track-and-field event Ray-Ray attends. She regularly has to say, "This is my son; he is a boy." Without Nadine's advocacy at track meets, things would have been much harder for Ray-Ray.

In contrast to Ray-Ray's negative experience playing on a boys' soccer team, where his teammates treated him as an outsider because of his gender nonconformity, his experience with his high school's mixed-sex Ultimate Frisbee team has been positive. Some sex differentiation is built into the game—a certain number of girls or women are required to be on the field at all times—but the sport provides a more welcoming place for Ray-Ray. Even though he now stands six foot two, Ray-Ray is often read by opponents as a girl. This is actually an advantage for his team because they are often short of girl players. Ray-Ray told me that his coach asked him if he would be okay to continue "playing as a girl," and he happily agreed. He remarked that he finds this "kind of funny and fun!"

Several kids in this book stopped participating in particular sports or stopped playing sports altogether when they transitioned. While this represents a loss for some, such as Dave and Nick, others were happy to quit. According to Ingrid, the mother of Ziggy (15, Euro-American), when he was given the option of dropping out of physical education, he jumped at it. He experienced his school's reluctance to allow him to participate in physical education as a boy as a blessing. Ingrid explained, "Ziggy hated PE, and when the principal gave him the option of quitting [a course that was normally compulsory], he was thrilled." At the time of the interview, Ziggy was happily participating in his school's marching band, where gender has not been an issue for him.

Kids who defy cisgender binary categorization tend to experience frequent gender policing from children and adults alike. This comes in the form of the most common question: "Are you a boy or girl?" As a result, some trans kids who want to play sport present themselves as their affirmed rather than their birth sex. Going "stealth" works better for trans kids who embrace a binary identity and who are able to pass, either because they are younger or because they undergo medical treatment (as Dave and Cory did).

Jordan wonders how much Wren's decision to transition to female pronouns two years ago had to do with wanting to dance and dress the way she likes without having to constantly explain herself to children and adults. Jordan reported that Wren's participation in a day-camp program two years ago was the impetus for her transition from gender-nonconforming boy to a girl in every facet of her life: "During the sign-up process, Samantha [Jordan's partner] asked her, 'Do you want to go to camp as a boy or a girl?' Which I thought was really, like, neat. I was so focused on trying to make the overall environments more gender flexible that I never thought about asking Wren that. But Wren said, 'a girl,' without any hesitation, so that's how Samantha signed her up. She showed her how to change privately with her bathing suit in the change room. And Wren was totally successful, and I think it gave her a lot of confidence."

When Wren encounters bodily changes at puberty, her parents are prepared to provide their daughter with access to hormone blockers, but they will follow Wren's lead, even though sometimes "it's a tricky balancing act" to figure out what kind of support to provide. As a 10- and 11-year-old, Wren has participated as a girl on several sex-segregated teams without incident. This has not been complicated because the rules for transgender participation in her district do not require medical treatment until the age of 13. But Wren has just been selected for a competitive girls' hockey team outside of school, and policies in her region require transgender kids to provide documentation proving that they are under the treatment of a medical professional. Wren has been going back and forth about whether to take hormone blockers. She told me that she really does not want to, but she does not want to get outed or kicked off the team either. She is in a tough spot and does not know what to do about it.

Indeed, the sex-segregated structure of sport may be a deciding factor in driving some trans kids to undergo medical treatment or to transition along binary lines. According to Diane Ehrensaft, author of *Gender Born, Gender Made: Raising Healthy Gender-Nonconforming Children* and a psychologist with a clinical practice in the San Francisco Bay Area specializing in trans and gender-nonconforming children, the desire to participate in sport is a major factor driving gender-liminal youth to undergo binary transition.[66]

This dynamic was true for Cory, who is more comfortable with a non-binary identity and wanted to undergo testosterone therapy *and* continue to play on a girls' hockey team. In girls' hockey, he was an elite goalie with good prospects for college scholarships; but on the boys' team, there is a deeper pool of goalies and he felt he would be unexceptional. Taking testosterone was important for Cory because he did not want to develop breasts or have a period. He thus had to balance his desire to participate in girls' hockey with his need to shape his body in a manner consistent with his gender identity. Cory's former name was Anneke—and this is something he is very open about. Indeed, he had a very public gender-nonconforming identity of "just Anneke" from age eight to 13, but he found it necessary to affirm a male gender identity in order to access testosterone. Cory explained that his desire to take testosterone ultimately took precedence over his desire to continue to play girls' hockey. "Just Anneke" was just not working anymore.

Most, but not all, of the stories relating to bathroom access and sport participation come from, or concern, kids who have parental support for expressing their gender in whatever way they feel most comfortable. Most, but not all, of these parents are professionally educated and relatively economically privileged. Trans kids should not have to depend on luck or their family's cultural and economic capital to navigate public institutions or secure legal representation, nor should they have to depend on their parents' ability to move them to a different school or team—or, in some cases, another community—to experience safety and inclusion in the bathroom, in the change room, and on the playing field. More precarious transgender kids face extreme hardship in these environments.

Sport Policy Changes

The International Olympic Committee (IOC) arrived at a policy for the participation of transgender athletes in 2004. Colloquially known as the "Stockholm Consensus,"[67] it allowed fully (hormonally and surgically) transitioned athletes, with legally affirmed gender identities, to compete in their reassigned sex category.[68] This policy required transsexual athletes to undergo complete hormonal transition at least two years prior to competing in an Olympic event, to undergo genital-reassignment surgery, and to have documents proving legal recognition of their new sex by their home governments. In testament to the preeminence of the IOC in making sport policy, many international and national sporting bodies followed the IOC's lead in developing identical policies.

The Stockholm Consensus was widely criticized by sport scholars on the grounds that genitals are irrelevant to athletic performance, that the expense and/or invasiveness of surgery is a barrier for many athletes, and that many governments refuse to supply legal documents designating the appropriate legal sex identity.[69] In an influential 2010 report, *On the Team: Equal Opportunity for Transgender Student Athletes*, LGBT educator and sport scholar Pat Griffin and National Center for Lesbian Rights (NCLR) Sports Project director Helen Carroll deemed the Stockholm Consensus's requirement for hormonal and surgical treatment inappropriate for high school athletes aged 13–17. In this report, they refute the discourse of unfair male advantage by placing a higher priority on the benefits of participation over competition, arguing, "A transgender student athlete at the high school level shall be allowed to participate in a sports activity in accordance with his or her gender identity irrespective of the gender listed on the student's birth certificate or other student records, and regardless of whether the student has undergone any medical treatment."[70] Finding male and female adolescent athletic performance to be comparable, the report recommends that transgender high school students should be eligible to compete on whatever team they choose without undergoing a medicalized "sex change." At the college level, however, the report recommends that participation by transgender athletes require a formal diagnosis of "gender identity disorder" (now "gender dysphoria") by a licensed professional. Nevertheless, provisions are less invasive than in the Stockholm Consensus. The report urges that early-transitioning trans female athletes who used hormone blockers during adolescence and who currently take cross-sex hormones should be immediately eligible to participate in college sports, while those who transition after puberty should be required to undergo only one year of cross-hormone therapy prior to participation. Trans male athletes do not require any hormone therapy to be eligible to compete on men's teams but, once they have begun testosterone therapy, may no longer compete on women's teams. This protocol for participation in college-level athletics was adopted by the National Collegiate Athletics Association (NCAA) in 2011 and the Canadian University Athletics Association (CUAA) in 2012.

The 2011 IOC Regulations on Hyperandrogenism, known as the "Consensus Statement"[71] on sex reassignment and hyperandrogenism, responds to critics of the Stockholm Consensus by mirroring NCAA and CUAA policies. The Consensus Statement must be understood, however, within the context of controversy around sex testing for women athletes in elite amateur sport.

The IOC and its affiliates finally discontinued the long-reviled, scientifically unfounded practice of sex-verification testing for *all* women competitors prior to the 2000 Olympic Games,[72] but the IOC's hegemonic role in normalizing the two-sex system and male superiority continued via the provisions of the new Consensus Statement and ongoing but selective sex testing of women athletes. This was most dramatically evident in the recent case of the gender-troubling figure of South African runner Caster Semenya, whose "masculine" appearance became a subject of concern among competitors and sporting officials when she won the 800-meter World Championship in Berlin in 2009.[73] Semenya was forced to undergo invasive sex testing in order to continue competing. While the results of the tests have never been officially confirmed, the new Consensus Statement on hyperandrogenism and women athletes was a response to the controversy surrounding Castor Semenya as well as Indian runner Santhi Soundarajan.[74] The policy allows for women whose testosterone levels are deemed higher than "normal" to undergo treatment to normalize their levels and continue to compete.[75]

The circumstances under which Semenya was permitted to compete in the 2012 Olympics in London, where she won a silver medal, are unknown. But what we do know is that four other female athletes were identified as having hyperandrogenism and barred from competing. As sport scholar Lindsay Pieper chronicles, these athletes were taken to "Nice and Montpellier, France, for treatment. . . . The doctors recommended that the athletes undergo a corrective measure to ensure their future participation in sport. . . . The specialist also performed 'feminizing vaginoplasty,' and aesthetic (re)construction of the vagina. Put simply, the doctors completed an unnecessary operation that did not alleviate a health issue and then executed plastic surgery to ensure that the women's genitals aligned with accepted anatomical compositions."[76] This incident produced protest that came to a head in 2014 when Indian sprinter Dutee Chand was targeted for testing by the Sports Authority of India (SAI). When her testosterone levels were deemed to be "too high" to be naturally occurring in a "woman," Chand was given the option of undergoing surgery and hormonal treatment or no longer being eligible to compete. The SAI's policies in this matter lined up with those of the International Association of Athletics Federation (IAAF), which had in turn followed the lead of the IOC in setting such policy. Chand took her case to the Court of Arbitration for Sport (CAS) which, in 2015, "suspended the International Association of Athletics Federations' hyperandrogenism rules for two years."[77] The ruling stipulated that new evidence had to be provided by the IAAF within that time frame if Chand and other women like her are to be barred from competing. That new evidence is still pending. This ruling by the CAS did something unprecedented in international and national sporting policy: it questioned the long-held conviction, in the sport world and beyond, that testosterone levels are a clear indicator of sex identity and that the relative lack of this hormone among women explains across-the-board so-called female athletic inferiority. While this ruling pleased feminist scientists and social justice scholars and activists, the prejudice and hostility from other competitors and sport media continued to surround Semenya and other female athletes deemed too muscular to be "normal" women.

Although the IOC disagrees with the CAS ruling in the Chand case, there were no regulations in place for the 2016 Olympic Games in Rio, and none are expected for the PyeongChang 2018 games either. According to the IOC, "we are still awaiting the resolution of the Dutee Chand case."[78] When Semenya won a gold medal in the 800-meter race at the Rio Olympics in 2016, one of her competitors, Lynsey Sharp from Great Britain, who came in sixth, gave a tearful interview on the track in which she complained about the suspension of the hyperandrogenism rule: "I have tried to avoid the issue all year. You can see how emotional it all was. We know how each other feels [*seemingly referring to her white competitors*]. It is out of our control and how much we rely on people at the top sorting it out. The public can see how difficult it is with the change of rule but all we can do is give it our best."[79] *Guardian* reporter Andy Bull put it this way: "The unpalatable but unavoidable fact is that while neither of the other two medalists, Burundi's Francine Niyonsaba and Kenya's Margaret Wambui, have identified as hyperandrogenic, both have been subjected to the kinds of innuendo that Semenya herself experienced in 2009."[80] As political scientist Heath Fogg Davis observes, allegations that athletes such as Semenya are "actually men" are "often intertwined with racism and homophobia. Black female athletes who are muscular, dark-skinned, and competitively dominant such as Semenya have historically been and continue to be stereotyped as masculine and ugly, and thus failing to measure up to hegemonic feminine standards of being the kind of woman that straight men sexually desire."[81]

The IOC has obviously been scrambling to produce research to prove that testosterone levels impact performance outcomes. On July 3, 2017, *Guardian* reporter Joanna Harper announced that a study, published by Stephane Bermon and Pierre-Yves Garnier in 2017, purports to link testosterone levels to performance outcomes in male and female elite athletes. In referencing this study, Harper speculates that we may see the "reinstatement of rules imposing a maximum level of *male* sex hormones in athletes competing as female" and that "Caster Semenya could be forced to undertake hormone therapy for future Olympics" (my emphasis).[82]

In 2016, the IOC announced a new policy specific to transgender athletes: transgender athletes are now eligible to compete in the Olympics without having undergone sex reassignment surgery. The IOC's new transgender policy mirrors the NCAA and CUAA policy on transgender sport participation. While it is an improvement over the prohibitive requirements of the Stockholm Consensus, it continues to reflect an ideological commitment to a two-sex system (albeit a more complicated one) and an unquestioning belief in male athletic superiority. Transgender women are required to follow a hormone regime that negates the "performance-enhancing" effects of testosterone, while transgender men are not required to submit to any hormonal regime in order to participate as men in men's sports. Speaking about the NCAA policy on which the new Consensus Statement is modeled, sociologist Adam Love observed that while such policies on transgender participation are less restrictive than the Stockholm Consensus, "they embrace, perhaps even more explicitly, . . . the language of female physical inferiority," as they allow "male-to-female transsexuals to continue their participation on men's teams" but do not "grant similar rights to female-to-male transsexuals to continue participating on women's teams."[83]

The new policy on transgender participation is based on the norms of the Consensus Statement and took effect at the 2016 Summer Games, but, to my knowledge, no transgender athletes competed. The limited nature of inclusion permitted by the IOC continues to reinforce binary-based understandings of sex difference and is consistent with *gender-conforming*, as opposed to *gender-transforming*, transgender inclusion.[84] Gender-conforming policies of inclusion tend to be conservative in that they reify, rather than challenge, the sex binary that is instrumental in gender inequality, homo-negative trans oppression. Transgender people of all ages who do not conform to binary understandings of sex difference and resist identities grounded in male or female categories, who do not successfully "pass" as boys or girls or men or women, or who are unable to access trans-affirming healthcare are typically left out when it comes to participation in amateur or elite sport.

Although *On the Team* has been the most influential report to inform intercollegiate policies in the U.S. and Canada, other reports have also developed measures for transgender inclusion. The U.S. Transgender Law and Policy Institute's *Guidelines for Creating Policies for Transgender Children in Recreational Sports* emphasizes the importance of students' ability to participate in sport on the basis of their affirmed gender. This report disputes assumptions of male athletic advantage among preadolescent children, stating that no "hormonally-based advantage or disadvantage between girls and boys exists" prior to adolescence, that "gender segregation in children's sports is purely social," and that "individual variation with respect to athletic ability *within* each gender is much more significant than any group differences between boys and girls."[85]

The U.S. LGBT Sports Foundation has developed a "model policy" for sport participation. The "All 50"[86] policy is "based on a single principle: transgender high school student-athletes will compete in the gender in which they identify and have a positive sport experience."[87] While stipulating that all students have the right to participate in a sex category other than that which they were assigned at birth, the policy recommends the formation of a Gender Identity Eligibility Committee, one member of which must be either a physician or a mental health professional. The single criterion for this committee's determination is listed as "sincerity." There is no mention of required medical treatment in the document. This model policy represents a step forward for binary-based transgender student athletes, but it falls short by lacking provisions for nonbinary trans kids and recommendations for overhauling the sex-segregated and sex-differentiated structure of much high school sport. In *Sport in Transition: Making Sport in Canada More Responsible for Gender Inclusivity*, the Canadian Centre for Ethics in Sport speaks out against sex-verification testing, acknowledging that the science of sex difference is flawed science and therefore not a basis for organizing sport. With regard to transinclusion, it states, "Where feasible, transitioning sport will aim for the widest and easiest possible inclusion by supporting integrated sport activities."[88]

In a report published by the Canadian Teachers Federation, *Supporting Transgender and Transsexual Students in K-12 schools: A Guide for Educators*, teachers and administrators are instructed to enable transgender and/or gender-nonconforming kids to participate fully in all activities, including physical education and sport, in a manner consistent with their affirmed and consistent gender identity, with no requirement for medical treatment. The report *is* explicit that this includes locker-room, change-room, and bathroom access for transgender students but, importantly, prescribes making private facilities available to *any* student who requires them for any reason.

In *Questions and Answers: Gender Identity in Schools*, the Public Health Agency of Canada states that "school policies that segregate students by gender ignore and stigmatize individuals who challenge the typical 'male' or 'female' notions and can cause emotional and psychological distress for students" and that "gender-variant youth should be allowed to join sports teams according to their self-identified gender as opposed to requiring them to join based on their biological sex."[89] Obstacles to implementing such policies and their impact require further research.

High school policies for transgender participation in sport are uneven in the United States. The site where the "model policy for transgender students on high school teams" document can be found—TransAthlete.

com—provides a color-coded map of the U.S., according to the nature of the high school policy for transgender student athletes in each
state.[90] Green represents "inclusive—no medical hormones or surgery
required" (California, Colorado, Connecticut, Florida, Maryland, Mas-
sachusetts, Minnesota, Nevada, New Hampshire, Rhode Island, South
Dakota, Utah, Vermont, Virginia, Washington, Wyoming). Yellow is defined as "needs modification, case-by-case or individual review" (Alaska,
Arizona, Delaware, Georgia, Illinois, Iowa, Kansas, Kentucky, Maine,
Michigan, Missouri, New Jersey, New Mexico, New York, North Dakota,
Ohio, Oklahoma, Oregon, Pennsylvania, Wisconsin). Red is defined as
"discriminatory—requires birth certificate or surgery and hormone wait
period" (Alabama, Idaho, Indiana, Louisiana, Nebraska, North Carolina, Texas). Blue represents states with no policy (Arkansas, Hawaii,
Mississippi, Montana, South Carolina, Tennessee, and West Virginia). It
speaks to the traction that transgender rights has generated in the past
decade that 16 of the 50 U.S. states have such low-barrier policies for
trans participation at the high school level. However, recommendations
for transgender inclusion in high school sport at the national level, in
either the United States or Canada, have yet to be adopted, and it is too
soon to tell how recently introduced policies will work in practice. The
decision by the Trump administration to retract the federal government
support of transgender students promised by the Obama administration is an obvious source of concern. Many trans activists are optimistic
about the role of the courts in using Title IX to defend the rights of trans
students, but we have yet to see how this will play out.

In Canada, to date, there are four provinces that have adopted transgender policies for athletic participation at the high school level. These
include the Manitoba High Schools Athletic Association, BC School
Sports, the Alberta Schools' Athletic Association, and the Ontario Federation of School Athletic Associations.[91] If I apply the color-coded
model from TransAthlete.com, Alberta, British Columbia, and Manitoba are green, while Ontario is yellow (for transgender females only).
Various school boards, including Toronto, Edmonton, and Vancouver,
include provisions for the participation of trans kids in physical education and sport. The language of the "gender and sexual diversity" policy
of the Vancouver School Board includes the recommendation that sex-
segregated activities be eliminated wherever possible, but, to my knowl-

edge, there are no Canadian public school policies that focus on sex integration in athletics. The extent to which provincial and territorial human rights codes in the *Canadian Charter of Rights and Freedoms* may be invoked to enable the participation of trans kids in sport is something to keep an eye on. To date, however, there appear to be no public school policy provisions in either Canada or the U.S. for nonbinary trans athletes who resist participation in either of the traditional sex categories.

The implications of this policy evolution for trans kids are uncertain, but it is reasonable to predict that kids such as Mack Beggs who undergo medicalized binary-based transitions will be the easiest to accommodate. Trans kids and their parents/guardians navigate these social environments and barriers to participation, often placing them in a crisis that can only be resolved by deciding not to transition or by choosing medicalized binary transition. Most trans kids in Canada and the U.S. are still running into significant barriers to participation.

* * *

Targeting gender systems, and their intersections with other systems of oppression, is the most effective way to improve the quality of life and opportunities for transgender and gender-nonconforming adults, youth, and children, while granting everyone gender self-determination. But this action needs to take place within an appreciation of the wider socioeconomic context. In keeping with neoliberal restructuring, Canadian and U.S. sports at the local and participatory (versus competitive) level have lost government funding, while professional and elite amateur sport franchises and programs receive the bulk of government funding.[92] Reinvesting in more accessible community-based, gender-integrated physical recreation programs would extend greater access to trans kids and reverse trends toward profit-driven investment in elite amateur athletics in the service of nationalism.

Sport and physical recreation programs and spaces that normalize the gender binary and female inferiority in conjunction with systems of privilege based on race and class need to be targeted. Love urges us to shift "away from the sex segregated two-sex system as much as possible . . . not only for the inclusion of transgender athletes but also as a means of promoting gender equity more broadly."[93] Yet how do we increase transgender inclusion without eliminating spaces for girls and young women to develop skills and confidence? To avoid undoing much of the progress that has been made in increasing the participation of girls and women in sport, McDonagh and Pappano suggest we target "coercive" as opposed to "voluntary" sex segregation for girls and women, given that the former is largely responsible for gender inequality.[94] Gender integration of all sporting spaces may simply have the negative impact of exposing girls and women to more sexism and misogyny so must be accompanied by significant anti-sexist and pro-LGBT initiatives. Advocacy and activism should target the binary gender system and its intersection with other systems of oppression (sexism, racism, classism) within sport and extend gender self-determination to all.

The "green" standard, to borrow the color scheme provided by TransAthlete.com, for bathroom and change-room access and sport participation, whereby affirmed gender is respected no questions asked, is ideal for kids who are comfortable with binary categorization but fails to address the role of sex-segregated spaces and sex-segregated and sex-differentiated activities in general in normalizing the ideology of the two-sex system and disciplining most of us to comply with it. Trans kids signal the need to reconfigure space and social practice away from these gender-oppressive dynamics.

4

Parents

We left everything. Everyone was like, "Well, are your other
kids going to stay here?" I'm like, "No. We're leaving as family. We came in as a family. We're leaving as a family because
we support every member of our family. How could we let
our other kids be part of a community that rejects their sibling? Are you fucking kidding me? Like what are you thinking? No."
—Michelle, parent

There are some kids and parents of kids for whom there was no
"coming-out" moment, because they either very obviously failed to conform to traditional gender norms or were "persistently and consistently
insistent"[1] about being a boy or a girl in spite of their assignment to
the so-called opposite category. Some kids, such as Cory, never needed
to come out because they were never "in," meaning they were always
read as gender nonconforming or, as in Ray-Ray's case, always took full
advantage of the freedom they had to express themselves by wearing
dresses and sparkly things and playing with "cross-gender" toys.

It might seem strange that I am positioning a chapter on parenting
and families after ones that focus on schooling and then bathrooms and
sport/physical education: the "family" is listed in every sociology textbook I have ever seen as the primary or first agent of socialization that
a child encounters. And families are typically, after all, profoundly gendered spaces. Indeed, in spite of being far from the norm, the socially
constructed heterosexual, cisgender nuclear family is a key ideological
building block of white-supremacist and colonial-capitalist heteropatriarchal societies such as Canada and the United States. But one of the
things I focus on in this chapter is the extensive (mostly) maternal labor
that is required to reduce the precarity of transgender kids both within
family and friendship networks and in gendered environments outside

the home. I discuss the significance of parent-led activist networks in promoting the well-being of trans kids and the way in which unevenly distributed cultural capital and material resources tend to drive activism on behalf of more privileged rather than more precarious transgender kids.

This chapter tells the stories of the work that my parent participants engage in, with heart and soul, on behalf of their kids and that has often come at considerable cost to their own mental and physical health. I also explore the costs and benefits of transition and trans oppression to the family as a whole and the role siblings play in supporting trans kids.

Family Acceptance and Support

Family acceptance is known to be the most significant variable with regard to mental health outcomes for trans kids.[2] According to Edgardo Menvielle, "Resiliency in the child is best achieved through a supportive family environment that fosters the development of self-esteem and social competences. . . . Our assumption is that GID [gender identity disorder][3] in children represents normal developmental variation. Consistent with an affirmative goal, parents are encouraged to unconditionally value their child, acknowledge his or her difference, assist their child in navigating schools and society, and advocate for changes in the family and community to minimize social hazards."[4] Psychologists Augustus Klein and Sarit Golub report "family rejection as a predictor of suicide attempts and substance misuse among transgender and gender-nonconforming adults,"[5] and we can extrapolate from this data to confirm the importance of family support for trans kids. In general terms, parents have a great deal of power over their children, and their support or lack thereof plays a central determining role in the degree of agency trans kids have. One study shows high rates of violence by parents against gender-nonconforming children and youth.[6] Much of the resilience that transgender kids are able to marshal depends, to begin with, on the extent of their parents' or caregivers' resources—cultural and material—and then the degree to which these resources are available to them. Both significant degrees of social inequality and the collective power of adults over children create variations in precarity among trans kids.

All the parents who directly participated in my research approached their children's gender identities with openness and encouraged the kids themselves to explore what felt right for them in the context of at least a somewhat-open, versus a binary-restrictive, vision of the gender landscape. The kids in the book who affirm binary or nonbinary identities took the lead in claiming these identities themselves. My observations in forums for parents of trans kids, online and offline, reveal some significant differences in how supportive parents approach their kids' assertion of a nontraditional sex/gender identity, with a minority viewing being trans in a manner consistent with a medical model of disability and belief in a two-sex system. The most consistent principle that parents articulated about their children's gender, however, was that their kids should be the ones to determine it. Parents collectively presented me with a dossier of evidence about the damage we do when we fail to listen to kids' voices and the benefits that result, not just for the kid but for the people around them—in the family and beyond—from recognizing kids' authority to self-define their own gender identities.

Child-Centered Parenting

Starting in early childhood, some of the kids in my study insisted on being seen as a gender other than the one they had been assigned at birth, and their families took them seriously, providing acceptance, support, and advocacy on their behalf and often on behalf of trans kids more generally. Many of these families are led by parents who intentionally worked to establish their family as a space free of sexism and gender stereotypes. Cassandra's parents, for example, had determinedly established a gender-neutral tone to their household. As Cassandra's mother, Stacey, describes it, "in our house, toys are toys, hair is hair, clothes are clothes. We actually had only gender-neutral toys in our house for a very long time." Cassandra was asserting "'I is a girl' at two and a half." Her mom responded, "Well, boys have a penis, girls have a vulva," thinking that perhaps her child did not understand anatomy and that it was time to explain. After that, Cassandra settled on being "both" for a while. But Cassandra's distress and behavior around her assigned gender identity prompted Stacey to educate herself, going "on the hunt for research" and buying "every resource possible" about transgender people and issues.

When Cassandra was around four, Stacey introduced the possibility of transgender identity to her: "I kind of described transgender to her in terms of 'most girls have a vulva, some girls are born with a penis—not many, some—but just different, and that's okay, and vice versa.'" And since then, Cassandra has "identified mostly as a girl."

The wisdom of supporting Cassandra as a girl was reinforced for Stacey and her husband by the changes in Cassandra's personality once her self-identification as a girl was honored. Stacey reports that prior to Cassandra's transition, she had wondered if her daughter was "on the autism spectrum because she wasn't making eye contact with people." But the new level of confidence Cassandra displayed posttransition indicated to Stacey how much Cassandra's being unable to assert a gender identity that she felt authentic about was compromising her ability to socially interact and be at ease. Stacey noted that this drastic change in Cassandra's behavior is what helped her husband: "because he was still struggling a little bit, but I think that's what helped him start doing some of the reading, seeing that the change in her behavior was so drastic." Increased social confidence is one of the benefits that a number of parents of trans kids have identified as resulting from affirming their children's gender identity.[7]

Cassandra's particularly strong gender conformity as a girl has occasionally puzzled Stacey and her husband because of their determination to help their children go beyond stereotypical gender identities and behavior. Stacey said, "I've got four girls, and she is the most feminine of all of them." I wonder if some trans kids who affirm a binary identity, however well supported they are at home, feel pressure to do more gender work in the world than they otherwise might if they had never had to resist the imposition of an identity that felt so fundamentally wrong to them in the first place. But then again, some folks, whether cisgender or trans, experience a powerful affinity with binary-based femme identities or masculine identities. We have seen the damage that radical feminist denunciation and gender policing of butch-femme relationships among lesbians has done, for example, and I, like Stacey, firmly believe that questioning the authenticity of anyone's gender self-determination is oppressive.[8]

The parents of Simon (seven, Euro-Canadian), Hilary and Andrew, also built feminist resistance to gender stereotypes into their family culture and rather successfully at that, because Simon was not their first child to express a nonnormative gender identity. Hilary's oldest son was designated male at birth and often talked about wishing he was a girl when he was six or seven. But Hilary reported that he went on to settle into being a cisgender male and expressing comfort about having done so. Hilary described him as having "fallen into the script of manhood as most men do," explaining, "I do think he probably has an inherent wider range, but I think, like most men, he has given up quite a bit of it." But this experience with her older son "primed [her] to be open to that," with the assumption that "you grow out of it." But that is not what happened with Simon.

Simon began insisting that he was a boy from the time he was two and a half. Unlike his brother, Simon demonstrated no gender fluidity at all. He was "consistently expressive about being male, and he didn't want to be a girl, didn't want to have long hair, didn't want to wear girls' clothes." When he was young, Simon became obsessed with lions, wanting in particular "to be a boy lion." Hilary and Andrew, as "good feminists," kept telling Simon that "girls are cool, girls can have adventures, girls can do all these things and be as tough as you want to be, and a girl lioness is so fierce and does all the hunting," and his response was, "I don't care. I need a mane, and I need to be a boy lion." Hilary explained how she feels when she looks back: "That was one of his ways of telling us who he was, by looking outside the species." She sees Simon as trying to express that he was really a boy in a variety of ways before she and her husband were ready to hear it.

Hilary and Andrew initially viewed Simon as a tomboy, but, Hilary said, "it just progressed to this point where whenever I saw something about transgender kids in the news, I would just automatically send it to my husband, Andrew, 'just for your information, just because it seems like we might be headed towards needing to deal with this.'" Hilary undertook the labor of educating both herself and Andrew about transgender issues so that they could respond appropriately to Simon. Although they began to think of Simon as transgender, Hilary and Andrew tried to put it off by saying "things like, 'well, there's things you can do when you're an adult to deal with this, but kids don't get to make that decision.'" They did this because they wanted to wait, to be sure, in case Simon, like his older brother, changed his mind. But Simon never wavered. Instead, he kept coming to his mother and asking what he needed to do to make sure he did not become a girl: "Just a little tap, tap, tap, 'tell me what to do to make sure this doesn't happen.' It was that that made me see how much that meant to him."

While Simon accepted Hilary's explanation that only grown-ups get to transition, she knew she "was lying by saying that it wasn't available to him": "By that point, I knew about hormone blockers, and so I didn't understand why I was trying to put them off. I mean, obviously I was probably trying to put them off for my own comfort." When Hilary realized that it was she and not Simon who was not ready for his transition, she got out of the way. After all, she explained, "the amount of trust he was placing in me made it more heartbreaking to realize that I might be leading him astray." Hilary quickly became convinced that it was time for Simon to transition. She explained to her husband, "He has all these friends to whom he is just a boy even if they're using female pronouns. So why are we not jumping on this? Like, quick, while they're six years old, and if we say now, 'He's a boy,' they will be like, 'Okay.' Let's do it now before it turns *political*" (my emphasis). She reflected on the moment she asked Simon if he would like to live as a boy: "I knew that as soon as I said it, I would never be able to take it back. I knew that as soon as I opened that gate, he would be so far through it and gone that there would be no reboxing him up. So, I mean, instinctually I knew that we were keeping him in a box."

Hilary expressed a bit of uneasiness about the role she played in enabling Simon's transition, however, because he did not appear to be in "sufficient distress" to qualify for the more typical narrative of imminent self-harm and/or suicide that is often used to justify social transition for children. It seems clear to me, however, that Simon was, in Ehrensaft's words, "insistent, persistent and consistent"[9] about his gender identity and that his parents took him seriously. When not extreme, distress can be difficult to measure, but more to the point, we need to create environments for kids to determine their own gender identities without trauma being associated with it. Early acceptance without the necessity of severe distress has obvious and positive implications for trans kids' mental health. Such a path may occur more readily in some anti-sexist and queer-positive households,[10] but other parents who have never given much thought to gender have responded very supportively to their children simply because they are deeply oriented to respecting children's voices or because the child's distress is so worrying.

Quinn's family responded to Quinn's news about their nonbinary gender identity with acceptance and support. When I interviewed Quinn, their family was still going through some adjustments, particularly with regard to their dad remembering to use the right pronouns. But Quinn's family has been creative about this issue, with their mom coming up with the idea of a pronoun jar. Quinn explained that "it costs 50 cents for every wrong pronoun." Quinn's mom demonstrated real sensitivity to them by doing this. Quinn appreciates the pronoun jar, particularly because, they explained, "my mom suggested it too because I would be way too scared to suggest this on my own just because of—not because I'm scared of my parents or how they'd react but because so many people have taught me that my gender identity isn't important enough."

Hunter described himself as "the third generation of queer" in his family and found his mother immediately in support of his newly disclosed identity. Hunter felt particularly happy about his family's response "after hearing about so many other people not being accepted and thrown out of their houses." Although his mom has been really supportive of his transition, the family is struggling hard to make ends meet. Hunter's mom is the sole breadwinner, supporting Hunter and his grandparents. Hunter reported, "There is not much food in my house, so I basically eat maybe once a day." That his mother found $110 to pay for his first prescription of testosterone and assorted supplies because the paperwork for provincial support had yet to go through speaks to the commitment this family has to supporting Hunter.

Some families can point to a specific moment when their children let them or somebody else know about the dissonance they experienced about their assigned sex/gender. In some cases, this occurs within the context of a warm and secure relationship between parent and child that is undisturbed by the revelation. The first person whom Helen told about their nonbinary identity, for example, was their mom, and both Helen's expectations and their mother's response were positive. "I was just like, 'I think I am gender queer, and I want to change my name.' I think I was more scared about the name part than the gender part because my mom is pretty progressive." It took Helen's mom a little while to get used to their new name and pronouns, but "she was cool with it."

Nina described herself as having "noticed something early." As early as age two, Martine consistently played only with stereotypical "girl" toys (dolls, not trucks) and went on to fixate on princesses. "We'd all laugh and say, 'Oh, "he's" in touch with "his" feminine side, and ha ha ha, no wonder, "he" has three sisters, no wonder, no wonder.'" By the time Martine started kindergarten, however, Nina began to worry about how fixated she was on stereotypically feminine toys, interests, and clothing. Nina was puzzled by this but mostly just figured her "son" was gay, which did not particularly trouble her. But starting at age six, Martine started to assert that she was a girl. Nina was concerned enough to talk with her pediatrician about this issue several times, and this doctor ended up referring Martine to a gender clinic.

Since transitioning, Martine is happier and enjoying more success at school, but Nina is careful not to overplay the role of transition as addressing every difficult aspect of her daughter's life—unlike, as she has observed, some of the kids in their local support group for whom transition appears to be a "magic bullet." But everyone in their family is doing better since Martine's transition; they are relieved that the time for keeping secrets about her gender identity is over, now that she is living as a girl and attending a high school in a district outside their neighborhood. Nina reports that Martine has gone from being an unhappy, lonely kid with few interests to someone who has friends. But they've gone from keeping Martine's identity as a girl secret to keeping her identity as a trans girl secret. I am not sure how this will play out.

Some children watch and wait to see how their parents respond to other LGBT people and issues relating to transgender people in the news. Some of these children stay invisible to protect themselves when they observe family hostility to queer and trans people, while others see evidence of queer and trans-positive attitudes as a sign that they are safe to show themselves. The kids I interviewed engaged in a range of activities (including persistent, consistent insistence,[11] coming out, strategic action, self-harm, suicide attempts, and mental health struggles) and experienced a range of feelings (fear, appreciation, openness, forgiveness, consideration, self-hatred, resilience, desolation, and loss) with regard to or as a consequence of relaying their nontraditional gender identities to their families.

Managing Family Reactions

The outcome for Michael and his family has been quite positive, but Michael carefully planned for the immediate negative reaction he expected his mom to have. Michael anticipated some difficulty telling his mother and father, explaining that, although divorced themselves, they are very "traditional." Michael lives with his mother and stepfather and managed his coming-out moment very carefully by writing his mom a letter and going to stay at a friend's house for a few days to avoid dealing with her initial reaction. As expected, "she was quite shocked, and she just kind of freaked out." Her response was more confusion than judgment, however: "She just kind of like, 'Oh my God, what's going on?' It was scary for her." His mother went from shock to denial, even calling on a gay male friend to talk some sense into Michael by warning him that he might not have children or a family or that he could get hurt. According to Michael, "Those things that he said did kind of sadden me a little bit, you know, because those might happen." But Michael was not deterred. "I stood my ground. No matter what she said, I'm like, 'No, this is—I'm serious about this.'"

Things were difficult between Michael and his mom for a month or so until his mom sought out a psychologist to help them work through things together. She specifically looked for and found a Chinese Canadian psychologist who spoke her native language and who specialized in child and youth gender issues. Michael and I laughed when he told me the psychologist's name because he is well known in the Canadian trans community as a warm and caring gender-affirming mental health provider. Michael and his mom and then his dad, who was less unsettled by Michael's announcement, worked with the psychologist to assist everyone in adjusting and supporting Michael. Michael told me that his dad initially asked him, "Are you sure you are not just a lesbian?" Asking if a child or youth might not "just be gay" is not an uncharacteristic response for parents of a kid who comes out as trans. But Michael's family put in the effort to give him the support he needed and he described himself as having a "good" relationship with both his parents as well as his stepfather. As Michael's case exemplifies, a lot of emotional labor on the part of trans kids themselves is required, even in the best case scenarios, to manage their gender identities within family contexts.

Cameron's experience with his family is at the other end of the spectrum. He comes from a fundamentalist Christian family in which he was homeschooled and completely isolated—except for the Internet—until he left home at 17. In preparation for coming out to his family, Cameron found another place to live and carefully packed up his things the night before his high school graduation. His father responded to Cameron's announcement by calling him "an abomination." During our (Skype) interview when Cameron told me what his dad had said, I leaned in toward the computer monitor and said, "You are not an abomination." I could see so much pain on his face as he softly whispered, "Yeah, I figured that out. But yeah, that's probably one of the things that stuck with me the most." The experience of Enrique (17, Latinx) with his father was not quite as horrible, but his dad's resistance to his gender identity made it clear to Enrique that he needed to move out and cut financial ties. Fortunately for Enrique, he found a home with his boyfriend's more accepting family and was doing well at the time of the interview.

Coming Out via Self-Harm and/or Suicide

Unfortunately, it is not unusual for parents to learn about their kids' nonnormative gender identities via their self-destructive actions. Some kids struggling with their assigned sex/gender category express their gender dysphoria through mental health struggles, self-harm, and even suicide attempts. Young people in general have higher suicide rates than adults do, but those who are LGBT and/or racialized are particularly vulnerable.[12] Whether trans kids are visibly gender nonconforming or not, the anxiety and distress many feel is harmful to their mental and physical health. It is actually not unusual for family members to become aware that their child does not feel "like a girl" or "like a boy" because the kid manifests anxiety or depression, engages in self-harm, or attempts suicide. I have spoken with only one parent—Finn's mom—whose child succeeded in killing himself, but I have interviewed kids who have attempted suicide and/or their parents. Whether successful or not, suicide attempts by kids are sometimes evidence of extreme gender distress, in probably far more cases than we are aware of.

Nathan (17, Euro-Canadian/Indigenous) was 15 when he tried to kill himself. The aftermath of his suicide attempt created the necessary opening for him to tell his family that he is male and about the agony he experiences about being forced to live as a girl and in a female body. I first interviewed his mother, Nora, when Nathan was 16. Nathan had been pushed out of school by anti-trans bullying and death threats the previous year. At the time, Nora described her son as being in a deep depression and cutting himself on a regular basis. Nathan's desire to obtain male government identification and enroll in a different school as a boy was thwarted because, at the time, the province he lived in required top surgery to change the sex marker on his identity documents. Nathan had the love and acceptance of his family, but the cost of surgery was completely beyond their resources. Nora described herself as being very frightened that Nathan would kill himself: "I'm to the point now where when I go to bed every night, I knock on his door, I tell him, 'I'm going to bed,' and I say, 'I love you.' If Nathan falls asleep before I go to bed, and he doesn't answer me when I knock on that door, I fly into a panic, because he didn't answer. That's the point that my life has gotten to."

Dylan attempted suicide when he was 13. He was living with his (very religious) grandmother at the time, and she, along with an aunt and an uncle, responded to his announcement that he is trans by verbally disowning him. Dylan's family struggles with poverty. His father is dead, and he currently lives with his mom and her boyfriend in a trailer park. From his comments, it seems clear that Dylan's mother cares about him but lacks the emotional and financial resources to give him the support that he really needs. This scenario played out when he came out to her as trans after his suicide attempt:

> We were just standing in my bedroom, watching TV. I'm just folding the laundry, super casual. I said, "Mom, I think I'm trans." And she's like, "Why do you think that?" "Because I'm trans." That was pretty much as far as that went. There really wasn't a reaction. I had been in therapy, and my mom didn't react because my therapist was talking at that point in time about how I don't respond well to reaction—like instant reactions when they're negative. So I think that she just was trying to be what was going to upset me the least.

Dylan's mom struggles with his gender identity, however, and this comes out in her continual use of female pronouns and his dead name. This situation is painful for him, and he fears that she may not give permission for him to take testosterone; she has been very clear that he is going to have to find a way to pay for it himself.[13]

Dylan has had a really tough time with some members of his family around his gender transition, but there have been small but significant moments of acceptance and support. His stepfather, for example, has found a way to be on Dylan's side. Recently, when ordering fast food, Dylan's stepfather used male pronouns to refer to him for the first time: "I wasn't wearing my chest binder, I wasn't trying to pass, and the guy at the counter said, 'Can I take your order, gentlemen?' I was like, 'French fries.' He was like, 'I want a number six, and he wants a large fries.' '*He*.' That was huge. I cried. And then he started apologizing for not using my pronouns and name, and I'm like, 'No, this is perfect.'" And Dylan's grandmother has recently started talking with him again.

Hilary and Andrew, in contrast, view unconditional acceptance as a core responsibility of parenting and are uncomfortable when people treat them as if they are being heroic. Simon's parents are Euro-Canadian and middle class and, judging from my conversation with Hilary, highly intelligent, thoughtful, and well-informed people. Hilary describes the neighborhood where her family lives as "really, really liberal": "Like all the professors and doctors all live in the neighborhood, and they're all very educated and liberal. So publicly, nobody is going to say anything negative about us." But the way her neighbors tend to praise Hilary and Andrew for supporting Simon makes her feel uncomfortable at times: "I do get the feeling, sometimes, that when people are saying positive things about our parenting, that what they're thinking is, 'Thank God it's you and not me,' like when they're too effusive: 'Oh, you're such good parents.' 'No, we're actually letting our kid be themselves.' I don't actually feel like this is a superhuman thing, but sometimes when they go on about it a little too much, it feels like only a superhuman parent could deal with it."

While I agree very much with Hilary that parenting to enable gender self-determination should be a given, it certainly is not. The ways in which binary gender organizes people, relationships, and spaces requires an incredible amount of labor to resist. This chapter brings to light the phenomenal amount of care, advocacy, and activism required by parents to push back against cisgendered environments that harm their children. The resources—time, energy, money, connections, and know-how—required to resist social forces that render one's children precarious is not unique to parents of trans kids but is characteristic of families of more precarious children in general. For many of the kids in my study, after a brief period of adjustment, their parents responded to their gender declaration by consciously creating more space for them to determine their own gender identities and working hard to marshal resources on their behalf.

Emotional Labor and Care Work

Most of the parent advocacy on behalf of transgender kids in North America is engaged in by white, middle-class, and well-educated mothers, many of whom appear to be heterosexual.[14] Political scientist Kimberley Manning explains this demographic limitation as occurring within a neoliberal context where "health, education, and social care are relegated to the private sphere" such that "publicly tackling transphobia is only possible for those who can afford the costs of time, labor, finances, and risk." Parents "relying on reduced incomes, new immigrants, and others living on the margins of a reduced state, may have little capacity to engage in visible advocacy work."[15] For more marginalized families, "the emotional labor necessary to protect one's family from the mutually constitutive violence of transphobia, racism, and/or poverty as it is enacted by society and the state" is ongoing: the oppression of their kids is not the exception that it often is for more privileged parents.[16]

White, middle-class parents of trans kids are disproportionately able to mobilize in defense of their vulnerable trans kids, whether the kids themselves are racialized as white or not. Kai, a parent and an LGBT2Q youth worker, addressed this demographic reality by asking, "How do we protect young people who don't have privileged activists as parents? What empowerment strategies do we offer?" Hilary, too, reflected on the politics of race and class privilege in movements involving parents of trans kids: "I sometimes look at the families that look like mine (Euro, middle class, with a young, passing trans child), and I think there is a trend towards using our entitlement and privilege as our primary weapon in our child's defense—and then in our own defense when we feel uncomfortable. Our society prioritizes the righteousness of white mothers defending their children in a way that we don't for Black mothers and Indigenous mothers." Indeed, Manning points out that "it can become easy to lose sight of the struggles of parents who may not teach at a university, for example, and of the racialized transgender kids who are at far greater risk of violence than are our own white children."[17]

Some parents *are* simply more equipped to engage in trans-affirming care work than others are, and socioeconomic privilege is a significant dimension of this differential ability. Race and class inequality does disproportionately enable relatively wealthy and/or white trans kids to circulate in mainstream and social media because the resources parents are able to leverage (time, know-how, money, contacts, training, "respectability," etc.) are racialized and classed. The capacity to engage in voluntary labor—in practical terms—is unevenly distributed along racial, class, and ethnic lines, but another dimension concerns the extent to which parents themselves endure oppression that impacts their overall well-being.

Like care work in general, the parenting of trans kids is gendered as women's work, and it is primarily, although by no means exclusively, mothers who provide the support and advocacy to enable their children to transition.[18] Sociologist Arlie Hochschild introduced the gendered nature of care work in 1983, and since that time, numerous scholars have attempted to document "the less easily measurable emotional and management practices associated with meeting others' needs, and in some ways, meeting one's own needs."[19] Sociologist Amanda Watson observes that women are disproportionately charged with ameliorating "the emotional burdens of neoliberal capitalism," and this "cultural expectation on women to juggle or balance—by becoming agile or flexible—is a form of affective labor that is disciplinary, and divides women into 'deserving' or 'undeserving' mothers based on this ability."[20]

Forms of Care Work

Affirming parents of trans kids work really hard to create safety in the social environments and spaces that their children circulate in. Although not exclusively and often with the support of the children's fathers, heterosexual mothers of trans kids dominate parent networks and social movements. Given the gendered nature of emotional and affective labor in general in Western societies, it is not surprising that the frontline fight has been led by women, most of whom, but not all, are able to call on a degree of race and class privilege and/or the cultural capital that comes from experience engaging in other social justice struggles. The kinds of care work mostly mothers perform decrease the precarity of trans kids and include the following: educating themselves and other family members and friends; affirming and emotionally supporting trans kids and supporting the family as a whole in the face of trans oppression/blowback; running interference and protecting kids from anti-trans aggressions large and small; educating people in positions of authority; fighting to create safety in the spaces and institutions kids have to navigate; locating and accessing appropriate resources; helping their kids recover from trauma; coaching kids to enable them to handle the situations they encounter and to build resilience in the face of oppression; and working for social change on behalf of trans kids in general. Family support is a crucial factor for decreasing precarity, but it cannot substantially mitigate poverty, racism, and trans-oppressive violence. Although parental activism and advocacy on behalf of trans kids is not limited by race and class privilege, the cultural capital and the resources necessary to advocate effectively are available only to a minority of the families that are committed to supporting their trans kids.[21]

An often-significant dimension of emotional labor engaged in by parents of trans kids concerns educating themselves about what is going on with their children and managing their own process of adjustment, which require accessing resources and critically engaging with their own reactivity. Doing so is necessary either to respond constructively to their children's expression of a nontraditional gender identity or to create the space, and sometimes even the language, for kids to affirm such an identity—as some trans kids need their parents to figure out what is happening for them before they can know themselves. This is what Dara had to do to enable Davis, for example, to express who he is.

I first met Dara about six years ago, when we both attended a conference for transgender children and their families. Neither of us, as it happened, had children with us: I was attending as a researcher, and Dara came alone because her child was far too anxious in general to manage such an experience. Dara told me that she came to the conference because she sensed that there was a gender dimension to her child's discomfort in the social world. Dara is highly attentive to her child, which gave her the insight to know that she would need to learn more about children who experience dissonance with their assigned sex in order to support him. Her instincts were correct. Dara described the process of needing to get "informed enough to start talking with 'her' [at the time]." Once they started to talk and Dara introduced language about various gender options, Davis gained clarity about his identity and desire to live as a boy and became able to express this to her.

Victor, Greg's father, is one of several dads I interviewed who took the lead in undertaking the affective labor that made it possible for his son to open up about being a boy. It was Victor who created the safety that Greg needed and who helped support Greg's mom in her own process of adjustment. Greg had been really struggling with his mental health prior to his transition, and one particularly bad night led to a breakthrough. Greg was in such distress that Victor took him to the emergency room, but once there, they waited for five hours without seeing a psychiatrist and ended up deciding to head home. A conversation that Victor initiated in the car on the way home gave Greg the freedom he needed to speak his mind. Victor had begun to suspect that Greg might be trans and had done some online research to learn more about it. Greg told me that his father asked him, "Have you ever felt like you're someone else?": "And I said, 'Yes.' And he asked me if I felt like I was a boy. And I said, 'Yes.'" Greg remembers his dad telling him that "no matter what," Greg was "still his child." Greg found this "really, really good to hear." The process of self-education that Victor undertook gave Greg the affirmation and support he needed to then come out to his mother, who had a little more trouble accepting the news at first. Victor then went on to help convince Greg's mom that allowing their son to transition was the healthiest option.

In contrast to parents who had to help their children express their gender dissonance, Kazuko, Stef's mother, found herself confronted with a child who "just screamed out" at her, "in a very affirmative tone, saying that, 'No, I'm not a boy. I'm a girl.'" In response, Kazuko "started to research and check things out and started to realize that, yes, [her] child had more of a female identity than male." As a result of her research, Kazuko came to believe that accepting a child's affirmed gender identity was much more beneficial than trying to change it. This resonated with Kazuko's child-centered approach to parenting in general, so with great courage, she registered Stef in school as a girl and went about achieving a legal name change.

A key aspect of caring labor by parents involves providing their kids with the gender recognition they so badly need. Sociologist Jane Ward introduced the concept of "gender labor" to describe the dimension of care work enacted by queer femmes within intimate relationships with trans men.[22] Being seen/recognized and valued for who you are is a key dimension of mental health and social stability. Mothers of trans kids are typically, although not exclusively, the people in kids' lives who provide them with this affirmation and reassurance.

It is not hard for Hilary to imagine what would have happened to Simon if he had been born to a family that would not accept him: "I see him as so sensitive that I'm too scared to ponder how much he could've been broken." She remarked that when she meets adult transgender people, she has trouble understanding how they made it through their childhood "without anyone seeing that [they] are in distress." Hilary told me, "I think it's much more crushing to endure a hardship when you are also enduring putting your identity aside. Like, when you have a solid foundation of who you are and knowing that the people around you believe in who you actually are, it's a lot easier to take that adversity."

For some parents, the process of accepting and supporting their trans child is very fraught. It takes some time, as Manning observes, for some parents to shift out of shame and disbelief and into activism on behalf of trans kids, especially if exposed to adult "experts" who pathologize their children's gender nonconformity.[23] Some parents feel shame or regret about taking a bit of time to work through this process rather than immediately accepting their children's assertion of their gender identity. In Frank's case, for example, Catherine experienced intense pressure— first from preschool and then from elementary staff—to refuse to accept Frank as a boy. Because of this resistance, Catherine acknowledged that there were times when she forced Frank to wear girls' clothes: "I just feel sick about that now. I wish I would have known the word 'trans' and what that meant. I'm a really strong person, and had I had some literature, had I known, I could have not fucked up, right? Because those experiences—I mean, Frank was being bombarded outside the home and from extended family, and it makes me sick that I contributed to that. And I mean, I did the best I could with the information I had, but it's shitty to look back and know that that's damaging to that little person." But Catherine soon recognized the harm that misgendering Frank was doing to him and went on to resist the efforts of others to gender police him. She has been his strongest supporter ever since. And Frank speaks only positively about his mom, describing her as "very experienced and open-minded and accepting." He remembers telling her that he was a boy, and his mom "just kind of went along with it": "She thought that I would grow up to be a tomboy and a lesbian. Obviously that's not the case, but I think my mom would be the first person who actually listened to me from day one."

Nina feels considerable shame about the time it took for her to come around to be the supporter and advocate that Martine needed: "My biggest shame is that I said, 'No, you're not. Stop it. Stop it.' I'm ashamed of that, but I know it's a normal reaction. I wasn't like, evil, but I still feel that that was wrong. But I just didn't know. I would say, 'Stop giving me a headache.'" Nina was under extreme duress at the time as a result of an overwhelming burden of family responsibilities, which, along with the lack of information about transgender identities in her social context, played a significant role in her initial refusal to listen to Martine's assertions about being a girl. Nina knows she did the best she could with the information and resources she had at the time, but she wishes it had been different and that she could have acknowledged Martine as a girl much earlier. But Nina is a dedicated parent who has worked very hard to create safety for Martine.

One of the main reasons otherwise-LGBT-positive parents sometimes resist their children's trans identities is because they are afraid of what lies in store for them. Trans and gender-nonconforming people in North America, at least in dominant Eurocentric cultural spheres, have been an extremely marginalized and often criminalized population. In spite of shifting social contexts that provide some measure of recognition and tolerance, parents fear that their children will be subject to discrimination, hatred, and violence—in short, that their life chances will be profoundly compromised. It is not unusual for parents to hope that their children can find a balance between authenticity and conformity that will enable them to put together a livable life. But parents' coming face to face with the negative consequences of denial and the positive impact of affirming their kids' gender self-determination often shifts many into the role of advocacy and activism. In this role, they wrestle with various strategies for providing their kids with the best life chances. As Luna described it, however, the fear for the safety of her trans daughter, Taya (16, Euro-Canadian), never entirely goes away:

> My most raw fear is for her safety and well-being. I fear the intolerance that I am seeing in the world and I guess, even though I strongly believe— and all the research is coming out now to say affirmation is the best parenting path—there are always the people who call me late at night or drop emails in my box or hand-delivered letters in my mailbox that say, "You will be responsible if there is a terrible outcome," like "if somebody harms your kid or if your kid harms herself, it will be on your head because you didn't discourage them from this path." And I guess there's just always that little nagging feeling of, you know, is there a better way of supporting, am I missing anything, is this the best that I can do in terms of assuring her confidence, all my kids' confidence, that they absolutely have the right to be whatever they are and absolutely have the right to engage with the world in a fair or more equitable way? Sometimes there are days when the outside world feels like it has so much more power than I do.

This undercurrent of fear is one thing that all parents of vulnerable children have in common, however differently situated they are in being able to ameliorate it.

All of the parents I spoke with, often unprompted, remarked on the very obvious positive outcomes that acceptance, their own and others', had for their kid. Dara is a professor who has used all her resources to gather information and to develop supports for her highly precarious son. Davis experiences multiple dimensions of precarity that negatively impact his agency, and Dara has worked tirelessly both to change the environments that negatively impact him and to foster the resilience that he will require to navigate the world. Although not without friends, Davis experienced the social dynamics of school as an outsider. Dara explained that since he started elementary school, he experienced such high anxiety on the playground that he was unable to play at recess. That changed posttransition: "For the first time since he was in first grade, he is now playing at recess. He is either playing basketball, playing four squares, playing capture the flag. He was a wallflower for years. For years, I've been talking to them [the school]: 'How do we help him do recess?' 'How do we help him just be with somebody? Just to get on the playground.'" Davis's transition has not been a miracle cure, but it has helped. Dara sees it in this way: "The gender transition has really made it possible for—it's like he has more of himself to bring to situations that are going to be difficult anyway because he finds social situations difficult." Once he began to feel comfortable being a boy around his parents (trying out his new name and pronouns), Davis relied on Dara to communicate for him or to act as his representative in every social sphere he transitioned in, including facilitating a change in schools and running workshops for staff—free of charge—on gender-inclusive practices. Gender transition and the social acceptance Davis has experienced have empowered him to deal with his general social anxiety more effectively.

Andrew gives Hilary a lot of credit for leading Simon and their family through transition in the timely way that she did. She said, "He's so cute. He just wants to give me all these accolades for the transition because he says that he wouldn't have realized that we needed to do it." Andrew tells Hilary that she has "saved Simon a surgery, and he won't have to get top surgery, and thank God for that. Getting on top of it way before puberty was really helpful." In a follow-up interview two years later, when Simon was nine, Hilary noted how Simon's plans for his future embodiment have shifted, and he is considering going through puberty rather than taking blockers. She attributes this to her son's "broad community of vibrant nonpassing trans mentors [who have] removed his fear of 'being trans wrong' because he sees these real, lovable people with awkward, interesting, livable lives, and he knows that he can fall anywhere on the spectrum and still just resemble these wonderful people that he already knows." Hilary worked hard to build this trans-diverse community for Simon and observed that it has paid off in terms of his resilience: "[It has] removed my fear of his suicide risk, because I know that it will be much harder for him to feel isolated when he's seen so many people who are just like him. It's harder for him to feel helpless when he sees people just like him who are changing the world."

Some families take longer to accept and adjust to their children's gender revelation. As mentioned earlier, Greg's mother took a little longer than his dad to accept him as a boy. According to Greg, "She was asking me, you know, 'Maybe it's a phase. Maybe, you know, how could you know for sure, you're only 13?' And she was asking, 'Why can't you just live as a gay girl?'" Greg understands that his mother's questions and concerns stemmed from fear for what a trans identity meant for his future quality of life and concerns about the health impacts of potential medical procedures. It helped when the doctor told Greg's mother, "Yes, your child is indeed transgender; no, this is not a phase." The doctor reassured Greg's mother, although, Greg said, "Personally I don't think it should require his validation."

In Tru's case, her mom, Michelle, was initially much more accepting than was her dad, Garfield. I interviewed Tru and Michelle together in 2015, and at one point in the interview, Michelle directed her remarks to Tru: "We were unsure how to deal with it because it was making Daddy uncomfortable, and people were concerned about your safety and your well-being and whether or not you were going to be bullied and what was appropriate behavior." Garfield brought his experience of being subjected to racist bullying when he was a child to the matter of his "son's" gender presentation. Michelle explained, telling Tru, "He didn't want you to go through that too." And Tru added, "And Dad wasn't really used to coming home from work and seeing his little boy running toward him in a princess dress." Tru said that her dad's discomfort made her nervous about telling her parents what was really happening for her. Instead, she chose to be strategic. She said she was "worried that they would react badly, that [she] would get in trouble for thinking it," and she decided to just say she "was a boy and a girl." Michelle and Garfield both responded with acceptance and support to this announcement, taking Tru out to the store and buying her clothes from "across the aisle" for the first time. Tru's parents took efforts to educate themselves, at her mother's prompting, and have become not only accepting and supportive of her but very public activists on behalf of trans people of all ages.

Like many parents, Tru's parents took some time to become the advocates she needed. "She was waiting for us to catch up," Michelle explained. Michelle was initially uncertain about what they should be doing about Tru's gender nonconformity. She started doing a lot of research about it and came to an understanding: "For boys to persist past those gender norms, it says the more it continues, there's a higher chance of your child being gay. And that was one thing I latched onto and just thought, 'Oh well, "Trey's" probably gay,' like 'big whoop'—you know, good to know now. But there was a really small percentage of that who identified as trans." Michelle sought out support, seeing first a psychiatrist and then a psychologist specializing in gender issues in children because, she said, "I wanted Garfield to be able to hear that us supporting our child is not detrimental to our child's development. I needed us to be on the same page, and I needed reassurance for me too." As Michelle described it, "As a parent, you are wanting that validation that what you're doing is the best thing for your child, because it's scary. As parents, we don't necessarily know what we're doing. Like, every day you don't know what you're doing. No matter how many other kids you have, it's always different, right?" Michelle and Garfield came to understand that Tru's well-being was at stake and that they needed to support her and her desire to live as a girl, so they told her, "We're going to fight for you to be Tru full-time, like all the time. And from here on in, we want you to be Tru."

Educating the other parent can be much more difficult than it was for Michelle, however. One of the challenging things that Nina has had to do was educate her ex-husband about transgender issues so that he, too, can support Martine as a girl. This was difficult because part of the problem was that Martine did not feel safe presenting as a girl around her dad and his wife. Because Martine's dad was not seeing it, he took that as evidence that Martine was not really a girl. It took multiple conversations for Nina to make him understand that he and his wife needed to provide Martine with the safety she needed to show up as herself.

For some parents of trans kids, they are unable to get the other parent on board, which has terrible consequences both for the kid and for the affirming parent. It is very difficult for a trans kid to have even one parent who does not support them, and it also places immense stress on the affirming parent. In some cases, this leads to divorce. Indeed, the nonaffirming parent may object so much to their child's transition that they take legal action to try to block it. This happened in the province of British Columbia in April 2016 when a father pursued legal action to stop the hormone-blocker therapy his trans son was undergoing with the consent of his mother, who was the custodial parent.[24] Lou, Stef's "bio dad," as Kazuko refers to him, took Kazuko to court. Lou had been supportive of "Stephen's" first transition to "Stefanie" but "started to freak out" when he learned that "Stefanie" was not wanting to have sex reassignment in the future. When Stef transitioned to an androgynous identity, Lou's opposition became extreme. Kazuko described this as devastating: "He wouldn't even respect the name change. He wouldn't respect calling Stef 'Stef.' It was, you know, 'Your name is Stefanie unless you change it legally,' 'You're a girl.' So it became very disastrous for the relationship. And to the bio-dad, it was more of, 'if you are going to identify as a female, there's only one way, and you have to have the surgery.'" Kazuko described Lou as being very homophobic but able to understand transsexuality as long as it was binary conforming in every way. Lou took Kazuko to court to try to stop Stef from transitioning away from Stefanie, claiming "parental alienation as well as trying to get shared custody." It took two years in court, and the judge ruled in Kazuko's favor. But Kazuko described the difficulties of going through this ordeal without support: "I was kind of alone. I had message boards, but that doesn't help when you need someone to talk to." It was up to Kazuko to provide the love and support to keep first Stefanie and then Stef resilient and alive in body and soul through ongoing socially traumatic experiences, and Lou's opposition to Stef's gender-neutral transition was a major source of trauma in itself.

Many parents have more than one child, so they need to take into account the needs of their other kids and the impact of having a transgender sibling. As psychologists Laura Edwards-Leeper and Norman Spack observe, "The child's wishes are not the only factor: the impact of the social transition on the child's siblings should be taken into consideration. Often, we find that siblings are the most supportive members of the family of the gender dysphoric child, often coming to accept the social transition quickly and becoming a primary ally when their gender dysphoric sibling is teased by peers. However, in other cases, the social implications of having a severely gender dysphoric brother or sister can be devastating."[25] Michelle, Garfield, and Tru and her two siblings had to make difficult decisions about how to proceed around Tru's transition because it affected everybody in the family. As Michelle explained,

> It was so scary because we went through the whole discussion as a family.
> Like are we going to have to leave town? Are we going to be able to talk to

our family anymore? Are we going to have support? Are we going to have to have really shitty conversations where we have to kick people out of our lives because they're assholes and can't deal with this? What's the best thing? Do we go stealth for her? Do we live open? Do we completely start our lives over just for her, you know, and how fair is that to the other kids?

Many of the siblings of the trans kids in my study have easily adjusted to their sibling's gender transition, often becoming their earliest and greatest defenders. Frank's younger sister, Marina, for example, regularly gets right in there to protect him from bullies. And Stacey described Cassandra's older sister, Brenda, as having only a little difficulty with Cassandra's transition initially because "she was concerned for her dad because he'd be the only boy in the family. So she was worried about daddy. Once Dan reassured her that he was okay, Brenda has been very accepting and easy going." Stacey recalled picking Brenda up from school one day: "I had all the kids with me, and a little boy in her class was like, 'Brenda, which one's your brother-sister? Which one's your brother-sister?' Right? And Brenda says, 'I just—I have a sister.'" Stacey supported Brenda around Cassandra's transition with great care and intention to ensure that "she had the tools and the language to deal with the kids at school." This support included doing role-play with Brenda to help her answer the kinds of questions other kids might ask her and asking the school counselor to check in on Brenda at recess to make sure she was doing okay.

Patrick, Wren's brother, was more resistant, however, to her transition, expressing sadness and frustration around feelings that he was losing his "brother." Patrick was almost four when Wren transitioned, and his initial response was sadness and resistance. Jordan, one of Wren's parents, recalled him saying, "I don't want Wren to be my sister. I want *him* to be my brother." Patrick needed a lot of coaching about respecting Wren's decisions about her gender identity, including the importance of not disclosing that she was designated male at birth. Patrick has outed his sister as "having a penis" several times, as recently as when he was six and she was nine. Wren understandably refuses to be enrolled in the same summer camp as her brother for this reason. Jordan had to explain to Patrick, on multiple occasions, that he was making his sister unsafe and that she needs to be the one to decide if and when to disclose. As

Patrick's parent too, Jordan wrestled with this issue, saying that "he's just talking about his reality, his life," understanding how hard it is for Patrick to keep any of his thoughts to himself in general. Patrick understands the situation now, but that required both coaching and maturity. Jordan acknowledged that Wren has yet to entirely forgive Patrick for his previous behavior.

Managing and educating extended family and friends requires a great deal of time and energy as well as a lot of insight and patience. On Simon's behalf, for example, Hilary sent out an email to her and Andrew's extended families announcing Simon's transition. This email resulted in both support and some resistance. One very valuable source of support has been an older gay relative, adored by everyone in the family, who has spoken out in support of Simon. He performed a crucial role in encouraging the rest of his family to accept and support Simon. Nina described the support she received from her parents as pivotal in helping her be there for her daughter. She described the "great blessing" of support for Martine that she received from her father as he lay dying. "On his deathbed, he said, 'Just let it be,' and that was great for me."

Jordan, a trans nonbinary person themselves, found themselves blamed by members of their partner's extended family for Wren's gender nonconformity. According to Jordan, "Members of my extended family said something along the lines of, 'It figures Jordan would have a transgender child.'" Jordan explained what is ironic about this attitude, however: "Following Wren's lead has brought about my own more explicit trans emergence, not the other way round." But Jordan reported having worked hard, "on principle, from the outset to create space" for all their children "to experience and represent themselves away from the constraints of the gender binary": "It kills me how little space I have been able to create for them in spite of all my efforts."

Luna has been surprised by interactions with members of her extended family because they have had years to get on board about her children's affirmed gender identities and seemed to get it but then behave in really hurtful ways. Luna explained, "The latest really challenging dynamic is that on Stanley's side of the family, there are very few girls born in the last several generations. And right now Stanley's brother's partner is pregnant, and there's all this family flapping about 'it's the first girl,' like 'it's the only girl,' like 'oh, in this sea of boys, this is the first and only daughter,' right? And it's so painful, like for Taya to stand there." Luna described how she interrupts conversations such as these that render her daughter invisible. In this case, she intervened by saying, "'I have a daughter, you know.' And you should have seen the expressions on people's faces, like they were nonplussed and confused—and this is nine years into the journey. You would think nine years into the journey people would have sort of taken some responsibility to figure it out a little better than that. So how do we engage with that part of the family?" Luna finds this situation very challenging because she values extended family and building relationships with people who have diverse opinions but, she said, "I just don't want to expose Taya to that idea, which is actually quite prevalent, that somehow there is a hierarchy of women and where exactly she falls and it's not at the top anyway."

For many of the families I have come to know, accepting and supporting their child's affirmed gender identity has not been without its costs. I've heard reports about grandparents, best friends, aunts, uncles, and cousins who have been barred from the house for their refusal to use correct pronouns and names, for their refusal to stop asking "why?" or because of anti-trans ranting. Parents have struggled so hard to create more safety for their children at school, on the playground, and at the rec center and have often met with great resistance. But the one place most of them are able to exert control over is the threshold of the family home. Granted, doing so requires economic independence from family members, which is (obviously) not always the case. But many of the parents have drawn the line at the door. Catherine explained, "I'm at a place now where I'll have the conversation, I'll be supportive, and I'll be kind, and I'll remind you, but there comes a point where, 'get on board or get out of the house,' because I'm sick of this." She has had to tell her parents and her sister that "they can't come over anymore, because they kept saying 'she.'" Catherine has drawn this line because she recognizes how harmful it is to Frank. Nathan's mom, Nora, echoes the sentiment, describing how she kicked a friend out of her house for refusing to call Nathan by his name: "'Jane,' I said, 'if you don't get the fuck out of my house now,' I said, 'I will be arrested here tonight.'" Nora's brother-in-law is not allowed in the house either for the same reason.

Shielding Transgender Kids from Harm

Jordan has run interference for Wren with other children as well as adults and consciously tries to open up space around gender in children's worlds: "Some kids would say to me, 'Is she a boy or a girl?' And I would just say, 'That's a really interesting question, isn't it? How come it's so important for us to figure that out?' And then they would respond, 'Well is she?' And I would say, 'It's like there it is, isn't it? Like what does it feel like to not know?' And then they would not answer but look at me like I'm just out of my fucking tree."

Engaging in care work to shield a trans kid from harm requires a lot of time, knowledge, social skills, and foresight. Parent advocates have to anticipate problems before they happen if they are to spare their children even some of the damaging consequences of oppression. Doing this can mean speaking with adults in a variety of contexts (the eye doctor, day camps, the school, recreation activities) that your child will interact with—in advance. It involves a lot of educational and affective labor, which adds to parental overload and calls on a great deal of cultural capital.

Part of the typical work of supporting trans kids involves absorbing as many microaggressions on the kids' behalf as you can—to spare them the negative mental health consequences of ignorance and oppression. A number of parents reported doing behind-the-scenes work to prepare people and environments to be less damaging to their kids. Cory's mom, Nicole, for example, shielded him from all kinds of adult resistance to his playing hockey, first as a gender-nonconforming girl and then as a trans boy. It was only years later that Cory found out about the extent of work his mom had engaged in on his behalf because keeping it hidden was one of the ways she shielded him from anxiety. For the same reason, Catherine worked hard behind the scenes to try to get Frank's new high school to ensure that his correct gender marker and name were on all official school documents. She wanted Frank to be able to experience inclusion as a matter of course; her inability to accomplish this was traumatic for both of them.

Parents often do a lot of the work involved in explaining their trans children to others. Kazuko described the effort involved in "trying to explain to people": "People think that Stef has reverted 'back' to the male identity. And I keep saying that Stef is on a different level now. They are embracing the masculine and feminine sides of themselves, being an androgynous identity, or gender queer or gender fluid. I think it's just going beyond what the binary is." But ultimately, parents have to help their children develop the resilience and skills to handle things on their own. The necessity for doing this is something that parents of more precarious children often feel acutely.

Building Resilience

While some parents fear that their child's transgender identity may be exposed and result in negative repercussions, Hilary, instead, fears secrecy. She feels strongly that too much privacy "feels really dangerous," that if Simon "has to keep it a secret, then it could be used against him." Hilary has communicated to Simon that being trans does not have to be a secret because she "wanted him to grow up embracing that": "I didn't want to step on any of that. I want him to grow up with activism tools so that he never feels hopeless. I want him to grow up able to answer any questions without shame so that he never associates any of this with feelings of shame." Trans kids and their parents obviously make decisions about visibility and disclosure in vastly varying social contexts with access to considerably different information and resources.

Eva is both proud of her gender-nonconforming son, Peter (six, Euro-Canadian), and worried about the difficulties he may face in his future: "I'm very proud of him for having the self-confidence to wear what he wants to wear to school and to continue wearing it, regardless of what people are saying. I think that's pretty amazing. I guess I'm worried that that's going to change one day." Eva defines Peter's gender identity as "very much a boy," reporting that he "has no difficulties with calling himself a boy, with going to the boys' washroom; he's very centered on being a boy. He very rarely has said he wished he was a girl, and he hasn't said that in quite a long time. So he's a very confident child. He seems quite happy to be who he is." At times, however, Eva worries that supporting Peter and his gender nonconformity may actually be increasing his precarity, explaining, "As a parent, you wonder, am I putting him in a situation where he's going to come home crying because somebody teased him?" As many parents of trans and gender-nonconforming kids do, Eva wonders where her son's gender nonconformity comes from, saying, "I think it would be pretty interesting just to know if he would be interested in wearing dresses if most of his friends at school were boys and how much of this has to do with his interests, because a lot of the girls are wearing dresses, or how much of it has to do with how much he loves *Frozen* and identifies with Elsa?" Concerns such as these relate to ongoing debates about nature versus nurture with regard to sex/gender, and I cannot help but wonder what it would look like if we puzzled as much about the source of gender conformity in cisgender girls and boys rather than naturalizing their gendered presentation and behavior to the extent that we do as a culture. Feminists do this work, but it often seems we have lost the battle for the mainstream since the 1970s, if we ever really had it: the critique of sex typing kids seems to have become more and more esoteric as the social worlds in which children circulate become bluer and pinker all the time.[26]

One of the things that many parents of trans kids do is coach their kids to stand up for themselves. Eva admires Peter's confidence in general and his resistance to sexist gender norms in particular. Because she observes how frustrating it is for Peter when other adults restrict his gender options, Eva invests time and energy in helping him learn to stand up for himself and coaching him about how to respond to various scenarios. She shared a particularly frustrating example: "We went to a shop with sun hats, because we needed to buy him a sun hat. And he picked out a pink one, and I was going to buy it for him. I was actually at the register, and the woman at the counter said to me, 'We have another store just across the street, and we have some hats in blue.' And he left the store—just walked out of the store." Eva felt it was important to her son's resilience to restore his confidence in his original choice:

> I went out after him and said, "Oh, it's fine. Why don't you get this hat?" And he said, "No, I don't want it," and I said, "Because of what she said?" And he said, "Yes," and I said, "You know what she is?" I think I might've said, "She's stupid," or something like that, you know, and I said, "If you want to wear this hat, you should wear this hat, and you shouldn't let this get in the way. If you really like the hat, let's go get it." And I went back and said, "Did you know he was perfectly happy about getting the hat before you said that?" She said, "Oh, well, I didn't mean anything by it." I

said, "Well, we were perfectly happy with the hat." So anyway, I managed
to persuade him to come back to the store and buy the hat, and he did.
And he wore it quite happily for the rest of the summer.

This kind of intervention is labor-intensive for Eva, but she undertakes it
to build Peter's resilience, to push back against people and environments
that constrain him and to enable him to develop the ability to do this for
himself. But this is demanding work, and Eva herself finds "educating
people all the time" tiring.

Hilary, too, sees fostering resilience in her children as a central part
of her role as a parent. Speaking of Simon, she said, "I have to remember
that it's on him to develop the skills to deal with this, that I cannot fix
it so it will be smooth forever. All I can do is raise a resilient kid." Kazuko's educational and employment background helped her figure out
how to build Stef's resiliency in the face of trans oppression. "[After]
reading everything that I read, one of the most important conclusions
that I came out with was that Stef has to see other people like them and
be part of something bigger." Kazuko's own gender and sexual nonconformity had taught her "the importance of building community, to not
feel alone." She shared this sense of purpose on her child's behalf: "I
wanted my child to build resiliency. I didn't want the thought of suicide,
the violence. . . . I wanted just to build the kid's self-confidence and do
everything to create a child whose adaptation techniques are ready for
whatever's out there and then just try and protect them as best as I can
while they were younger, hoping for the best."

Kazuko worked hard to connect her then-trans daughter with
LGBTQ and trans communities and resources from the get-go. "We
went to the United States when Stef was six to make sure that they met
other kids like them. We went everywhere." She regularly traveled with
Stef to camps and conferences in the U.S. and Canada and drove into the
nearest major city to provide Stef with a trans-affirming peer and adult
environment several times a month. When Stef was old enough to go to
LGBTQ youth camps, Kazuko sent them. Kazuko explained, "That was
one of my goals, that it would be beneficial for Stef to be around like-
minded and similar-living kind of people in their community so that
they know they're not alone, that they know that there's an openness out
there that exists, because the school year can be really tough because

of the ignorance and whatnot of people—so to build that strength and the bonds that friendship can have." Kazuko also facilitated Stef's use of Skype to connect with trans kids all over North America. The importance of the Internet and social media for enabling access to information and community was a recurrent theme in my interviews with trans kids and their parents.[27]

Sometimes cultivating resilience meets resistance from the kid, however. Jordan, for example, described a sticky situation: Wren holds what Jordan considers to be a fairly unrealistic belief that nobody remembers that she "used to be a boy." Believing it necessary to foster resilience in Wren, Jordan has spoken rather matter-of-factly to her about the likelihood that she will encounter someone who knows her from before, that she will be outed, and that her transgender identity is nothing to be ashamed of. Jordan is very careful to frame this very real possibility as an accidental rather than an aggressive act. Like other parents of trans kids, Jordan employs role-play to help Wren prepare for a scenario in which her trans identity is revealed by a kid or adult who means her no harm or by someone who asks her if she is a boy or girl. Jordan reported that Wren "hates this": "But I feel that leaving her unprepared for the likelihood of such an occurrence would be a failure on my part." Jordan told me, though, that there are damaging things that happen that they or Samantha never share with Wren. A friend of Jordan's got in touch on one occasion to say that they had happened to cross paths—in a bar—with a parent of a child from Wren's former school. Upon discovering that Jordan was a mutual acquaintance, the parent exclaimed—with great excitement—"Jordan's daughter has a penis!" Jordan was furious and "phoned this guy up and read him the riot act. He apologized and sounded really sincere, but Goddamn!" Jordan is convinced that telling Wren about incidents such as this would negatively impact her mental health.

Many of the parents of trans kids in this book devoted significant time and energy to trying to make their children's schools safe and welcoming places for trans kids to navigate: by laying the groundwork, educating staff, other parents, and children; facilitating transition; and advocating for their child. Several mothers went so far as to deliver gender-inclusive training workshops for teachers and other school personnel—free of charge—while many others did this work less formally via countless meetings with teachers and school staff. Still others provided schools with trans-inclusive resources and made connections with appropriate organizations on the school's behalf. It is not unusual at all for parents of trans kids to do this work gladly: they do it free of charge because they are just so happy to be able to do it, given how damaging things are to their children if business as usual continues. Some of these parents started out having expertise around gender issues, while others became experts through their efforts to educate themselves and others in support of their children.

Dara, for example, has engaged in serious gender work with all the schools Davis has attended. Davis has multiple bases of precarity that are not mitigated by the relative wealth of his family alone. The amount of labor that Dara engages in to empower her son is staggering—she has the cultural capital and financial resources to do this, and it is still so intensive. In addition to the time she has spent supporting her highly anxious son, coaching him to become more resilient, obtaining professional support, and driving to a city three hours away once a month to see his endocrinologist, Dara regularly spends huge amounts of time and energy working with school staff—voluntarily providing numerous workshops about creating gender-inclusive practices.

Stacey too has been hard at work educating herself, her children, her husband, her extended family, her school community, and the school staff. In her first discussion with the principal about Cassandra being a girl in spite of the male gender marker on her birth certificate, Stacey reported, "The principal kind of looked at me like I had my head on backwards." But as a result of Stacey's efforts, the principal ultimately agreed to accept Cassandra as a girl at the school. But Stacey considers this to be just the starting point for trans inclusion: she wants to ensure that Cassandra has the space and support to continue to explore her gender as she is going through school. With that goal in mind, Stacey took care to be proactive in instructing school staff about appropriate responses. In order to do so, she had to be able to anticipate situations that would come up. Stacey gave an example: "[I] asked that they don't correct, if they say things like—I would prefer that they don't even say, 'Boys line up here, girls line up there'—but if they do that and she picks the girls' lineup, I ask them not to correct her. Or if she picks the boys' lineup, I ask them not to correct—like shove her over to the other line."

It would clearly be beneficial to all children if gender were not used to organize kids at school.

When Hilary came to terms with the fact that Simon was a boy, she started organizing herself to work with the school to enable him to transition. That involved locating LGBT resources in her local community that helped her work with the school. She described the process of finding appropriate support as challenging: "Now that I think about it, I went through so many phone calls figuring out how to approach it." She finally found the right person to talk to when she made contact with a woman who ran a safe-schools program for her local school board. The LGBT resource person she found via the school district was a huge help, but Hilary had to be prepared for legal action, particularly around bathroom access. The school initially responded to news of Simon's impending transition by designating a gender-neutral bathroom and, "fairly predictably," wanting Simon to use it. But because of her research, Hilary said she "knew where this was going" and came prepared. "I went in prepared to do battle. I went in with lists, prepared to be like, 'If you take this position that he has to use the gender-neutral bathroom, you're going to lose and you're going to be on the wrong side of history.' I don't know if I would've had what it takes to go to the media and start a lawsuit over it, but I was prepared to threaten it for sure. I knew that in terms of a human rights challenge, it wouldn't stand to isolate a child like that." I am convinced that the gender work that these parents do benefits all of the children—cis and trans—with whom the adults they train come in contact.

Sometimes creating safer space for one's trans child necessitates a move from one school to another or even one part of the country to another. One of the reasons Ray-Ray's family moved across the country, for example, was to provide him with a more conducive environment for his gender nonconformity. The ability to move schools or locations to decrease the precarity of a trans kid requires a constellation of material and social resources that are very unevenly distributed.

The support of family cannot mitigate poverty, but it does contribute to resilience. I checked in with Nora a year after my initial interview and learned with great relief that Nathan was doing much better. A few months after our first conversation, Nora reported that Nathan somehow found a sense of resolve and decided to get a job to pay for his top

surgery. His family helped him find employment in the fast-food industry and supported him in saving up enough money. He had the surgery
in June 2016, and I saw a subsequent picture of him, standing proud, in
a family photo. Nathan still struggles with depression but is doing much
better. While his is a story of individual and family resilience, his financial inability to obtain the bottom surgery that he needs to feel whole is
a significant factor that continues to compromise his well-being.

Parents of trans kids often become accidental activists, becoming
radicalized around trans issues only because of the difficulties their kids
experience. But as a result of advocating for their own children, many
parents become well educated and serve as valuable no-cost resource
providers for other parents of trans kids and older trans kids themselves.
Kazuko, who had been damaged by her own experience of isolation in
advocating for Stef, for example, took it upon herself to create more
resources for parents of trans kids, believing that connecting parents
with each other is really important. As an activist, she is involved in
an organization that does training in the schools relating to supporting
transitioning kids. Kazuko takes great pride in her ability to help parents
of other trans kids: "I brag about that I can find anything, anywhere,
any time, you know. Like, just tell me what you need, and I'll get it." The
enjoyment of at least some dimension of privilege (wealth, education,
experience as an activist) is typically necessary to enable parents to play
these kinds of leadership roles. But this voluntary labor contributes to
reducing the precarity of transgender kids more generally. Many parents
of trans kids apply their volunteer labor to fill the gap in available services and care for trans kids and their families.

As I documented earlier in the book, some families have been able
to access the legal support necessary to make human rights complaints
on behalf of their children. This was the case for Tru Wilson and Bella
Burgos, whose cases achieved real change that will benefit trans kids in
each of their provinces. The option for families to pursue legal action
in an effort to prevent their children from experiencing discrimination
and trans oppression is disproportionately available to relatively privileged families. However, Frank and Catherine have been fortunate to receive extensive pro bono support from a lawyer who specializes in trans
rights, while in the U.S., organizations such as the National Center for
Lesbian Rights (NCLR) and the American Civil Liberties Union (ACLU)

have taken a leading role in advocating for trans kids and footing the bill for many legal challenges.

Parents of Trans Kids as a Social Movement

A social movement of parents of transgender kids has been one of the driving forces behind the emergence of visible trans kids, support networks for families, legal and policy changes, and the burgeoning sector of affirming professional healthcare targeted to children. A minority of these parents are trans themselves and/or visibly racialized and/or male identifying, but much of the cultural power of movements of parents of trans kids lies in female cisgender conformity, presumed or actual heterosexuality, dominant narratives of motherhood, and middle-class whiteness.

However radical the more mainstream-appearing mothers of trans kids among this movement may actually be, their ability to project as nonthreatening and motherly enables them to intervene on behalf of queer and trans kids in ways that are less available to those of us who are some combination of queer, trans, racialized, or male presenting. These moms are particularly effective at engaging in social change efforts in kids' spaces, addressing issues of children, gender, and sexuality that have previously been mostly forbidden or are more risky when queer, and/or trans adults or men undertake this labor. Queer and trans adults have played a role in addressing queer and trans oppression in educational content and contexts, but the power of mostly white, middle-class, heterosexual cisgender moms to challenge schools and other institutions to change the way they do gender cannot be overstated.

Collateral Precarity

Trans oppression not only harms the trans kids themselves but has a ripple effect on all who love and care for them. In this sense, having a trans kid can result in a family experiencing what I refer to as *collateral precarity*. All of the parents I interviewed deeply regret the difficulty that their children experience and the trauma to the whole family that often accompanies this difficulty, but none of them regret their children's nontraditional gender identities.

Negative mental and physical health consequences often accrue to parents as they try to protect their kids from microaggressions, partly because of the effort involved but also because being unable to keep our children safe is a devastating experience for most parents. Seeing Stef mistreated and struggling to protect them, for example, has taken a toll on Kazuko. Stef explained the single most important reason that they did not commit suicide: "the reaction my mom would have. That terrified me, and I didn't want my mom to go through anything else, because she already had two big depressions. So that's pretty much the reason why I didn't kill myself." Supporting Stef has also cost Kazuko professionally. She described her current white-collar employment this way: "a really nice cushy, quiet job which is way below my intelligence and way below my qualifications, but it's quiet/nonstressful." Kazuko has prioritized the taxing work of supporting Stef and other parents of trans kids over career advancement and recognition.

In Frank's case, the violence and trans oppression he experienced sent shockwaves through his entire family. The stress resulting from the sexual assault on Frank and its aftermath required Catherine to go on long-term disability; as her family's sole breadwinner, this put them in poverty: "We lost our car, and we had to move to a cheaper place in a worse neighborhood." Catherine described the severity of the poverty they endured in the aftermath of the assault, saying, "We were chopping up furniture!" When I first interviewed her, Catherine had been off work for two and a half years. As she explained, "Since this has happened to Frank and since some of the community's response, I couldn't hold my shit together." Catherine dreams of moving to a big city and leaving their small town behind, but the monumental tasks of finding a new job and securing housing are more than she can handle at the moment. She explained, "When you've been kicked down, it's hard to—I don't believe in myself anymore. Like, I always felt pretty strong and pretty confident, and that's gone right now. I don't feel like, 'Fuck this, we can move and I'll find work, and we'll be good.' I don't feel that way anymore." Catherine described herself as having been fundamentally changed by the traumatic ordeal of trying to get the school to take appropriate action to protect Frank: "It killed me, it killed me. I will never be the same person. I've been in therapy for—well, since it happened, it's been two and a half years." There are significant costs to parents and families, costs that include negative consequences for economic security, professional advancement, loss of family and friends, parental overload and (mostly maternal) mental and physical health, and loss of activities, spaces, community, feelings of safety, and privacy.

For trans kids who do not have family support, the risk of self-harm and suicide, as well as poverty and criminalization, are disproportionately high. But often families' own precarity is so extreme that their efforts to support their child fall far short of what they need. Hunter is marginalized in multiple ways: neurodiversity, indigeneity, poverty, and gender. He has been attending what appear to be a series of "special education"—although we no longer call them that—programs and receiving services from his province's child welfare department for a number of years. Fortunately, this contact with the government has not resulted in his removal into care, as is so common for Indigenous children in Canada, but rather has put him in touch with crucial resources, including his participation in a group for transgender children and teens facilitated by a psychologist who is well respected by the local trans community for his affirmative-care ethos and advocacy work. Since I interviewed Hunter, however, he and his family were driven by severe poverty to move across the country to be closer to family support. This had the result of isolating Hunter completely from any kind of LGBT support not available within his immediate family or via the Internet and cutting off his access to affirming healthcare.

Collateral Benefit

Without prompting, a number of the parents I interviewed talked about the benefits they and their families have gained as a result of having a transgender family member. These include a really meaningful sense of accomplishment about their abilities to advocate and engage in social change, opportunities for intellectual and social development relating to greater understanding of structures of oppression, more space for everyone in the family to explore their own gender identities, a newfound sense of community with LGBT people and other parents of trans kids and meaningful new connections to LGBT and other social justice movements, and more authentic relationships with family and friends. During my second interview with Dara, when I asked her if she had ever imagined that parenting was going to be this hard, she burst out laughing and said, "No, not in a million years. This is taking me on a journey that I never imagined. I wouldn't change it for anything. It's, like, not even just about gender, the whole gender and race and developmental issues and where he's about to be tested for learning disabilities and just the whole early trauma and then, later, the rest of his life are just—it's incredible."

Limits to Radical Social Change

There are gender-essentialist and binary-normative narratives at play within some transgender networks and communities, and parent networks are no exception. For some, being transgender *is* "being trapped in the wrong body," which is equated with a medicalized disorder. Some transgender people and supporters look to the scientifically discredited "science of sex difference"[28] to ground the certainty they feel that transgender men are born with male brains and female bodies while transgender women are born with female brains and male bodies.

None of the parents of transgender kids whom I interviewed expressed their understanding of their children's gender nonnormativity in this way. Most of the parents in the book have a relatively nuanced understanding of diverse gender-identity possibilities. A few parents hung on to fairly stereotypical understandings of gender difference (referencing their children as having always preferred to play with trucks versus dolls, for example, as evidence of gender nonnormativity), but all followed their children's lead with an attitude of general openness about gender as a spectrum. While none of the parents I interviewed narrowly understood being transgender as a necessarily medicalized identity, in my travels to various conferences and in online spaces, I have encountered parents of trans kids who play a part in reconstituting transgender children within a stabilized gender binary: by taking for granted the inevitability and universal appropriateness of hormone therapy and surgical treatment options and/or by leaving homophobia, patriarchy, and misogyny unacknowledged. I heard one parent at a family conference, for example, say that he sees his transgender child as having a "birth defect" that needs to be medically repaired. Kazuko has come across this attitude as well. Not only did Stef's biological father, Lou, feel this way, but, Kazuko recalled, "There was a parent on one of the parent sites that we navigate. She was like, 'Oh, my God, my kid wants to stop the blockers. It's the end of the world.' I'm like, 'Whoa, wait a second. [*Laughs*] You know, this is still the child's body, and maybe the child wants to have the fertility to be able to save the eggs or save the sperm or whatnot. And maybe the body changes. They don't want to have that blocking anything. They want to go with the natural process and let whatever is be.'" Indeed, the radicalization that some parents of trans kids experience as a result of their children's resistance to traditional gender expectations is limited to gender and, even then, often fails to be critical of heteropatriarchy as an oppressive system. Troublingly, at least before the election of Donald Trump and the increased visibility of anti-LGBTQ white supremacists, not an insignificant number of white parents take it for granted that the main threat to the safety of trans kids comes from nonwhite (ignorant/conservative) communities. This assumption defies reality and plays into racist and xenophobic social practices and trans-/ homonationalist agendas. As Manning points out, "The relatively few numbers of parents of color publicly advocating for their transgender children is . . . not due to cultural mores more conservative than those found in religiously conservative white families and communities, as is sometimes suggested, but rather a direct outcome of racist structures that exhaust and exclude."[29]

But the employment of gender-essentialist explanations for affirmed male and female identities among trans kids should not seem surprising at all given that pervasive gender essentialism is so culturally dominant, especially in the spaces where children circulate.[30] I suspect that some parents of trans kids adopt this perspective early on in the process as they struggle to make sense of the way their children's gender identity is turning their world upside down but that this perspective shifts over time as they engage in community building and activism with trans and queer adults.

Radical Potential

There are possibilities for greater radicalization of the mostly relatively privileged parent activists who make up these social movements, as a result of their engagement with diverse trans communities. I attended the "Gender Odyssey" adult and family conference in Seattle several years ago, for example, and found myself listening to a powerful keynote by an Asian American transgender woman, a former president of San Francisco Pride, who talked openly about her experiences of family rejection, discrimination, racism, and survival sex work. As I listened to this powerful speaker, I found myself looking around at the 200 or so people who filled the room. The audience was equal parts white, middle-class, heterosexual couples and a somewhat racially diverse group of (presumably) trans and queer adults. I watched the mostly straight, mostly white parents earnestly nodding with recognition and seeming personal connection to the activist moments in LGBT history that the speaker referenced, such as the Stonewall riot and the central role that trans women played in leading that fight against police violence. This really got me thinking about the extent to which some previously "unwoke" parents of trans kids are being radicalized. I know that many parents of trans kids made space for their transgender kids because they already had queer or feminist sensibilities and attachments to social justice issues more broadly. But I am certain that some came late to the party, which fills me with hope: that knowledge of the ways environments and institutions harm their otherwise privileged children will translate to engagement with anti-oppression social change movements more broadly.

Hilary came to parenting with a strong social justice orientation to begin with, but she described how having a transgender child opened her eyes to the struggles that more precarious families face in raising their children: "It was the first time I really had to confront that idea. I got it that other people had to raise their children in these much more visceral, under threat kind of ways. I got it and I mourned for it, but I get it at a different level now." Hilary also described how a friend helped her understand that the kind of social change work necessary to resist the precarity imposed on disenfranchised children is at odds with white, middle-class notions of appropriate behavior. Hilary referred to the "number-one criticism people have about parents who have transgender children" as "being the way of putting their children out there; politically as an activist, as a parent, you're using your children for activist purposes, and people find this quite unforgivable." Hilary described how her friend identified the privilege underneath this judgment: "She said, 'As white, middle-class parents, we have this expectation that we would never, ever use our children politically, but nobody ever raises those same questions about a Black family that might choose to send their child to the first nonsegregated school. . . . When your child is marginalized, sometimes you have to put your child in the line of fire to ensure a better future for them.'" This statement resonated powerfully for Hilary, but she acknowledged, "It's just really hard for us to have that conversation when it's privileged parents and marginalized children because we don't have a script. I mean, parents expect to be able to pass their privilege on to their children. That is something I've really struggled with: having to make peace with the fact that my son will never get to be as safe as I get to be."

* * *

The extent to which the social movement of parents of trans kids is able to harness its power to really make a difference in reducing the precarity of trans kids will depend, in large part, I am convinced, on the extent to which trans oppression is understood to be part of larger systems of inequality and oppression and resisted accordingly. The most precarious trans kids are caught up in the necropolitics of racism, colonialism, enforced poverty, sexism, misogyny, and so on that shape their lives as or more profoundly than—but always in combination with—the imposition of a cisgender identity on them.

In the awful year that followed Trump's election and inauguration, with disturbing attacks on the gender self-determination of transgender kids and adults and on racialized, undocumented, and religious minorities, I have wondered about the extent to which social movements made up of parents of trans kids will be willing and able to form coalitions with other vulnerable groups. One of my purposes in writing this book is to encourage relatively privileged parent activists to think of transgender kids in all their diversity and to work in coalition with other marginalized communities to generate safety for kids who are even more unsafe than their own, to use their relative privilege to create more space at the table for everyone.

I view the care work of mothering as mitigating precariousness by definition, but for whom? To use a metaphor I loathe for a moment, that of the lifeboat, I ask, how do we get all the children in the boat—and, by necessity, in order to accomplish that, all their families in the boat? I have never felt a greater sense of purpose than I do as a parent, and I honestly fear how I might respond to a situation in which only a few children could be saved. It is highly likely that I would do anything to make sure that my children get in the boat, that I would do whatever I could to divert scarce resources to my own kids, not because they are of my blood (they are not) but because they are of my heart. But this metaphor of too few boats for too many people is what neoliberalism is all about: an illusion of a zero-sum game in which losers must exist in order for winners to be crowned.

5

Supportive Healthcare

As a nonbinary trans person specifically who is not interested in surgeries or any type of medical procedures, I don't
feel like I'm trapped in the wrong body. It's more that I'm
trapped in other people's perceptions of my body.
—Quinn, 18, Indigenous/Euro-Canadian

In December 2015, the Centre for Addictions and Mental Health
(CAMH) in Toronto, Ontario, closed its Child, Youth and Family Gender Identity Clinic and terminated the employment of its director, Dr.
Kenneth Zucker. This was a move that many critics feel was long over-
due, both reflecting and signaling a sea change in the clinical landscape
vis-à-vis the treatment of transgender and gender-nonconforming children in North America. Zucker is a prominent psychiatrist specializing
in the treatment of gender-nonconforming and transgender children
who has become a person of controversy over the years because of his
profoundly influential advocacy of a harmful "reparative" or "corrective"
model of treatment. Zucker's influence on the medicalization and psychiatric management of gender nonconformity in children in Canada
and the U.S. has been profound: he recently chaired the Working Group
for the Sexual and Gender Identity Disorder Section for the 2013 fifth
edition of the *Diagnostic and Statistical Manual* (*DSM*) that replaced the
diagnosis of gender identity disorder in children (GIDC) with gender
dysphoria (GD).

As an indication that debates about appropriate healthcare for transgender kids are far from over, however, a January 11, 2016, petition was
circulated in opposition to Zucker's firing and the closing of CAMH. It
was signed by some 508 "professional clinicians and academics" who
expressed concern about the impact of trans activism on academic freedom. Along with several other scholars and activists, I responded by
developing and circulating a counterpetition in support of the closing of

CAMH and emphasizing the need for accessible affirmative healthcare for trans people of all ages. This petition had more than 1,500 signatures when we submitted it.

In spite of this petition battle, the issues involved are multiple and very complex. I was surprised and deeply troubled, for example, to find queer feminist science scholar Anne Fausto-Sterling's signature on the original petition in support of Zucker, as her work has been a frequent touchstone in my own scholarship. I begin this chapter with a brief overview of the medicalization of gender nonconformity in children in North America. Bringing the hybrid assemblage–critical disability theoretical lens I introduced in chapter 1 into engagement with my interview data allows me to consider the transgender child in potentially new ways: as a particular expression of the multiple ways in which gender is experienced and assembled in North American contexts.

In keeping with critical disability scholar Tobin Siebers's instructions to go beyond merely identifying disability as a social construction to "look for the blueprint," to identify aspects of the built environment that produce disabled bodies/persons, I trace the recent history of the corrective medicalization of childhood gender nonconformity as one facet of the blueprint of the social construction of binary gender. A second facet I examine is the application of puberty-suppression therapy with the institutional—if not necessarily the recipients'—goal of enabling binary gender conformity and assimilation. I conclude that access to affirming medicalized transgender identities is limited by other dimensions of precarity, notably race, class, and binary gender conformity, such that much affirming medicalization inevitably tends to operate in a transnormative way. I draw on the work of trans scholar Julian Gill-Peterson to observe how this context and these processes operate to position less precarious transgender children as (proto-)citizen-consumers and more precarious transgender children as have-nots in a racialized neoliberal biomedical market.[1]

Gender-nonconforming children have been identified as a clinical population and subject to increasing medicalization in North America since the 1960s, a process that added a clinical dimension to the gender policing that children experience in daily life.[2] Pioneers in this field capitalized on moral panics around homosexuality and transsexuality to develop diagnostic and treatment regimens that targeted mostly gender-nonconforming boys for gender-reparative therapy.[3] Like lesbian and gay "conversion therapy,"[4] these ongoing but increasingly illegitimate treatment programs use varying techniques aimed at "repairing" children's gender nonconformity, typically blaming parents in general and mothers in particular for having done a poor job of gender socialization in the first place. The work undertaken to formally pathologize gender nonconformity in children and establish a legitimate subfield of research in North America culminated in the inclusion of the gender identity diagnosis in children (GIDC) in the third edition of the *Diagnostic and Statistical Manual* in 1980.[5] GIDC persisted until 2013, when, under the leadership of the aforementioned Dr. Zucker, it was revised to the less pathological but still binary-gender-normative gender dysphoria (GD).

The achievement of a formal diagnosis in 1980 provided the researcher clinicians who were studying and treating gender-nonconforming children with legitimacy and contributed to the process of normalization regarding binary sex and gender logic in the United States and Canada. This subfield took as its foundation binary sex categories as naturally cohering with normalized gender identities and gendered behaviors. According to this logic, gender nonconformity was seen as pathological and in need of correction. Researcher and trans advocate Jake Pyne describes the medicalization of childhood gender nonconformity as a form of governance that enclosed gender-nonconforming children and their families in a web of surveillance and gender policing.[6] One of the most well-known programs that operated in the 1970s—the UCLA "feminine boy project"—made headlines in 2011 when a former patient committed suicide at the age of 38. The family of the boy, known as Kraig in the scientific literature, described him as having been totally broken by treatment to curb his gender nonconformity, including severe beatings that his father was instructed to administer.

There is considerable debate within trans and queer communities about the role that the GIDC diagnosis has played and that the revised diagnosis of gender dysphoria continues to play in regulating gender identities. Queer gender and sexuality scholars Eve Sedgwick and Phyllis Burke were among those who sharply criticized the initial GIDC diagnosis, seeing it as a replacement for the diagnosis of homosexuality as a mental illness that was jettisoned by the American Psychiatric Association in 1973 as a result of successful pressure from gay and lesbian clinicians and activists.[7] While treatment regimens targeting child-hood gender nonconformity were initially oriented to preventing both adult homosexuality and transsexuality, the removal of homosexual-ity from the *DSM* in 1980 produced a shift away from concerns about sexual identity and toward preventing gender nonconformity. In this way, gender-reparative therapy nimbly adapted to the success of gay and lesbian activism against the pathologization of same-sex sexuality by focusing on eliminating gender-nonconforming behaviors in children, to the extent that, queer sociologist Karl Bryant argues, it *produced* ho-monormative (gender-conforming) homosexuals. Bryant observes that the "homophobia critique" of GIDC left transsexuality as well as other nonnormative expressions of neurodivergence as legitimate targets for prevention.[8] Trans and "mad pride"[9] activists have criticized lesbian and gay social movements for legitimating relations of power that operate via the construction of normal versus deviant subjectivities.

Many feminist, queer, and trans critics challenge the foundational as-sumption of binary gender norms that informs both the original and subsequent diagnosis. In 2004, queer feminist scholar Judith Butler characterized the GIDC diagnosis as contributing to the gender dis-tress of gender-nonconforming children that its advocates purported to correct. She brought the concept of "intelligibility" to bear on GIDC, observing that power generates the range of possibilities for legible iden-tities and expression. To be outside these parameters is to experience precarity: to risk abandonment, even death.[10] One study disputes the binary relationship between gender normality and gender deviance en-coded in the *DSM*, claiming instead, "Our results clearly show that a non-unitary sense of gender identity, a wish to be the other gender and dissatisfaction with one's sexed body are not unique to trans people, but are also common, albeit to a lesser degree, in the 'normal' population."[11]

Bryant provides keen insight into these debates by observing that a formal diagnosis is far from being the first step in medicalization and may even produce opportunities to restrict medicalization. He points out that the significant research and treatment activity that began in the early 1960s was simply formalized with the publication of the third edition of the *DSM* in 1980; prior activity was already constitutive of medicalization in its own right but flew under the radar. The formal diagnosis of GIDC became a lightning rod for criticism and a mechanism for limiting the medicalization of gender-nonconforming children; it shone a spotlight on harmful reparative therapy practices that yielded criticism and activism. Feminist and lesbian and gay activists and critics played a significant role in making the all-encompassing corrective regimes (of psychiatry, social services, family, and school) visible in their employment of shame, manipulation, and brutality in the name of child welfare.[12]

Trans people and our allies face significant dilemmas around the diagnosis, relating to the role it plays in enabling access to healthcare, social transition, and legal rights on the one hand versus the oppressive role it plays in naturalizing cisgender binary normativity on the other. In spite of concurrence with the substance of critiques, many trans activists, scholars, and allies insist that eliminating the diagnosis will do more harm than good, arguing instead for harm reduction as the appropriate political strategy.[13] Psychologist Jemma Tosh, for example, insists that the elimination of the diagnosis would have terrible consequences for many trans people, including greater risk of mental distress, vulnerability to violence and discrimination, self-mutilation, and suicide.[14] She urges scholars and professionals to foresee the potential harm of our debates and recommendations for actual trans people.

Affirmative Transgender Healthcare

In recent years, there has been what Pyne refers to as "a paradigm shift" in the treatment of gender-nonconforming and transgender children toward affirmation and harm reduction.[15] An ever-expanding body of research shows that an affirmative approach and family support produce the best outcomes for transgender kids and young people. In 2011, the World Professional Association for Transgender Health (WPATH)[16] took a position against gender-reparative therapy, stating that any therapy that seeks to change the gender identity of a patient is unethical. This position has been reflected in legal change in certain jurisdictions as well. For example, in 2014, California passed the Student Success and Opportunity Act to ban reparative therapy and require schools to permit transgender children to participate in activities and to access spaces and facilities according to their affirmed gender categories; in 2015, the province of Ontario (home to CAMH) passed a law prohibiting gender-reparative therapy.

Trans activist Julia Serano notes the role of activism in bringing about a shift in the clinical treatment of transgender people of all ages toward an affirming approach. An affirming approach has been established as the best practice for increasing the life chances of transgender kids. This approach "challenges societal transphobia (rather than reinforcing it, as the gender-reparative therapy approach does)" and "favors an individual approach for each child, rather than pushing all children toward the same end goal (e.g., gender conformity)."[17]

As high-profile, government-funded gender-identity treatment programs that target gender nonconformity for correction lose legitimacy, publicly and privately funded gender clinics featuring affirming models of treatment for trans kids are springing up in many North American centers. Via these clinics, kids who affirm the "opposite" gender identity to the one they were assigned or who question their gender identities may be eligible for puberty-suppression therapy. Unlike in Holland, where the model of puberty-suppression therapy for trans kids originated, however, many North American clinics support early social transition for children. Social transition is a key way for transgender children to explore the extent to which a change in gender will bring about a lessening of the anxiety and distress they experience. Puberty suppression extends this period of exploration by delaying the development of secondary sex characteristics.

Affirming treatment focuses on enabling kids' families to accept and affirm their children's gender identity, supporting them in dealing with the mental health consequences of trans oppression and providing assistance and advocacy as the kids and their families navigate gendered environments. While the affirming treatment model does not steer patients toward any particular gender identity, when desired, hormone blockers and cross-sex hormones can be used to manipulate the body's growth patterns to correspond with prevailing Eurocentric binary sex norms.

Puberty-suppression therapy for transgender kids is designed to enable them to postpone puberty while they consider their options and to enable kids who choose to medically transition to visibly conform to binary sex norms, an ability that is associated with reduced precarity. In the clinical literature surrounding gender-affirming practice, the first goal of puberty-suppression therapy is to "buy time" for the child or young person before committing to irreversible development of secondary sex characteristics. The second goal is a "more 'normal' and satisfactory appearance" after transition—a far more gender-normative capacity for passing and "realness" than has been available for adult transition.[18] In most cases, children who have been designated female at birth and who undergo puberty-suppression therapy will not need top surgery as part of gender confirmation surgery, and children who have been designated male at birth will not need to manage the residues of voice change, facial hair, skeletal development, and a visible Adam's apple, for example.

Trans kids remain a highly contested population, however, as anti-trans critics are generating a moral panic around the access of some trans kids to affirming healthcare, with the accusation that "doctors and parents [are] turning children transgender." This panic, Serano notes, relates to the cis-sexist claim that trans people "have taken their precious and perfect cisgender bodies, and transformed them into defective transsexual ones" while attempting to use constructions of childhood innocence to gain political traction.[19] Anti-trans authors of newspaper articles and opinion pieces express fear that some cisgender children are being pushed into the "wrong" puberty that will ultimately require expensive medical procedures to reverse.[20] The irony is that early transition for trans kids who need it provides them with the opportunity to avoid future and expensive medical procedures to reverse the development of unwanted secondary sex characteristics.

Flawed as anti-trans arguments are, however, even trans and trans-positive scholars and activists who strongly support access to an affirming model of trans healthcare for all who need it have concerns about how it operates within systems of power more broadly. The emergence of affirmative (as opposed to punishing and reparative) care resources and networks of parents and professionals focused on supporting trans kids *is* a response to a critical need, but I and others have observed that these resources are disproportionately available to relatively privileged (albeit vulnerable) rather than socioeconomically precarious trans kids.[21] I am also concerned about the way in which the deployment of these resources within social contexts that remain binary normative may impose limited transgender possibilities on children and young people and leave sexist and misogynist underpinnings of social, economic, and political life more generally untouched.

In the remainder of this chapter, I engage with a central dilemma: how can we protect and greatly expand existing access to affirming healthcare for all who need it while at the same time troubling the consequences of the privileging of an often-binary-conforming and inaccessible model of transgender embodiment/inclusion in society more broadly? I frame the topic of medicalization in this way because the varied experiences of trans kids in Canada and the United States are necessarily shaped by ongoing colonialism, neoliberal capitalism, racialized socioeconomic relations, and heteropatriarchy, conditions that produce a "differential distribution of precarity" that make some lives and not others *livable*.[22]

A key aspect of this dilemma relates to the risk involved in criticizing the way trans-affirming medical resources are being shaped and delivered when

1. these resources are literally life altering and life saving for many trans people;
2. many trans people of all ages lack these resources; and
3. transgender people in general are so vulnerable.

I fear that any criticism of affirming healthcare will have the unintended consequence of limiting access to it by feeding anti-trans agendas. But my knowledge of the history of social justice struggles in the West tells me one thing: when social justice movements construct themselves as "single issue" and foreclose critical discussion about the ways in which privilege operates within them, internal hierarchies such as those relating to race, class, gender, sexuality, (dis)ability, citizenship, and so on are reinforced.

What the Kids Want

The kids in my study have various plans for "transition." Some are already on hormone blockers or cross-sex hormones, while others intend to access this therapy in the near future. My participants experience varying degrees of dissonance between their assigned sex and how they define/name themselves and, for many but not all, gender dysphoria about their physical embodiment. Some kids take blockers because of gender dysphoria—to enable them to feel at home in their bodies—and are not trying to pass; some have various plans regarding surgery, while others reported having no access to affirmative health-care because they lack parental support and/or financial resources. And some have no desire to medicalize their gender identities. Several of my participants, in fact, voiced regret about not having been aware of non-binary transgender possibilities earlier in their own development. Three interrelated themes relating to medicalization and precarity emerged from my interviews with the kids and their parents: the trauma of the "wrong" puberty and the need for intervention, barriers to accessing affirmative care, and nonbinary troubles.

The Trauma of the "Wrong" Puberty and the Need for Intervention

Puberty is a pivotal time both for kids who have identified as transgen-der or resisted their assigned sex/gender for years and for kids whose transgender identities coalesce via a sense of crisis as secondary sex characteristics emerge. The trauma of the wrong puberty is a central theme that runs through my interview data. While hormone blockers can be understood to be an aspect of the blueprint of the social con-struction of binary gender, it would be a mistake for us to reduce them to this: many of the trans kids in my study experience puberty suppres-sion not as a reconsolidation of binary gender but rather as a desperately needed source of liberation and relief from gender dysphoria and/or nonintelligibility. Gender dysphoria and trans oppression have a sig-nificant impact on trans kids' mental health and relationships to their bodies. According to Dara, Davis "started his period on his 11th birth-day": "The place he was in the first 48 hours, I thought I was going to lose my kid. He was so, like—he just sunk so low. He could hardly talk. He just shut down, and it was awful. So it's good actually to live through that. Because I think certainly for me but for him too, it really clarified that this was not okay, that this was not how he wanted his life to be." Many of the trans kids in my study either do engage or have engaged in self-harm (primarily cutting and suicide attempts) that they explic-itly relate to the gender dysphoria they experienced with the onset of puberty. Kazuko firmly believes that hormone blockers saved Stef's life, explaining, "It was something that was necessary at that point. There was already so much anxiety around everything else that the blockers, at the moment of time when they took it, freed them from a lot of the anxiety." Greg also experienced mental distress around puberty and started to cut himself. But he was able to disclose his self-harm to a caring and supportive school counselor who, as required by law, alerted Greg's parents. Greg's parents were deeply concerned for his well-being and used their resources to enable him to access appropriate mental health support and, subsequently, trans-affirming healthcare. Greg described going on blockers as "a huge relief." Fortunately for Greg, his parents came on board fast. In some such instances, however, parents respond with emotional abuse and/or physical violence or by forcing their children to undergo reparative therapy. The fact that trans kids are minors is a significant dimension of precarity, as parents or legal guardians play a central role in their ability to fashion for themselves a livable life, via acceptance, financial and practical resources that enable therapy and medical treatment, and, crucially, permission/consent.

Greg reported that his parents gave their consent for puberty suppression because they understood blockers to be fully reversible, in contrast to the cross-sex hormones or surgery that they found more worrisome. As Greg explained, "They liked the idea that blockers would give me another year or two to really sort of see if this is really what I want. So I think that it was just a win-win situation: for me, because I knew my parents were okay with it, and they would probably feel more at ease. And I was also more at ease knowing that I wouldn't have to continue through puberty." This intervention was crucial for Greg's well-being.

Some of my participants experienced painful unease with their bodies at puberty but did not have language to make sense of it, and this was a factor in their inability to access appropriate and timely affirming healthcare. Michael, for example, described himself as starting to feel "really different" and depressed around puberty but unaware that being trans was even an option until he met a transgender person. He is now on testosterone (T) and on the waiting list for top surgery in his province.

Like so many trans kids, the Internet was the starting point for Cameron in making sense of difficult feelings about his body. Cameron grew up homeschooled and isolated in a rural, fundamentalist Christian family. He "tried really hard to fit in" as a girl because he "didn't know that being transgender was even a thing." But, he said, "puberty freaked me out so much. I would scream and cry if my mom mentioned bra shopping or buying pads, and I just never knew why." Cameron was not exposed to LGBTQ people until he was 14 and got to meet some through an online writing site. They provided him with the space and the language to begin to make sense of his own experience of trauma around puberty.

I first interviewed Nathan's mother, Nora, when top surgery seemed completely out of reach. At the time, she told me that her son hated his postpubertal body so much that he engaged in more or less constant self-harm: "I think it was 10 when he started his period. When all that stuff started, that's when all the sports stopped. That's when anything to do with being outside and being seen stopped." Nathan hates his body, he "can't stand it," and because of this, Nora told me, "he continues to cut himself." Nathan has cut himself so much that "the tops of his legs and the tops of his arms are scarred up for life." Nora has "tried so many things to stop it": "It's actually gotten to the point where, like, me and my husband said, 'Well, if he's cutting himself, he's not trying to kill himself.' That's how bad it is. And I never thought I'd ever say that about one of my youngsters." Nora is not overstating the fear that many parents of trans kids have with regard to the possibility of their child committing suicide.

When Martine was seven, Nina made an appointment for her at a gender clinic. When Martine heard about it, she asked, "Does the doctor have the machine?" "What machine?" Nina responded. "The machine where you walk in as a boy and walk out as a girl." Parents and kids are vulnerable to doctors and psychologists who are culturally positioned as experts. Trans-oppressive professionals can do a lot of damage, and trans-positive professionals can be life saving. As Kazuko observed, "I think wherever you are, if you've got that one good doctor, because there's always that questionable one that can end up ruining your entire perception of stuff and make it hard on you. Because we've had doctors and psychologists that have told parents, like, the worst things ever, and the parent believes them because that's the doctor, right?" Esme's family was fortunate to find that "one good doctor" early on in the process. Esme has insisted that she is a girl since preschool and has been under the care of a trans-affirmative doctor since she was six. She told me, "I know I'm going to get the hormone blockers and the estrogen," explaining how she would feel if she were to grow a beard and have her voice get very deep: "I wouldn't feel like I was—that I was in the right body." Esme is really clear that growing up to be a man—"with a beard and everything"—is not what she wants. With the support of her parents, she will forgo "male" puberty and be one of the new generation of trans people who will be able to assimilate more effectively than were previous generations who were unable to prevent their bodies from developing in undesirable ways.[23] Esme may or may not wish to find a way to be visible as a transgender person, but it will likely be up to her. At present, she eagerly participates in pride celebrations and enjoys being visibly transgender. And unlike some trans girls, Esme does not regard her penis as a problem. Esme displays flexibility around her physical embodiment, explaining, "It doesn't really depend on what middle parts you have, you know? It doesn't really matter which one you have. It's just who you decide to be. Like, just say you have the same middle part as someone else: it doesn't mean you're the same as them, right? You can choose who you want to be." Because of her parental support and access to trans healthcare (family economic security and provincial and private health insurance), Esme *can* choose. The flexibility that some transgender kids experience around their bodies, however, is constrained by social contexts. Decisions to transition are also influenced, to varying degrees, by binary-normative contexts.

Children in general are socialized to internalize the sex/gender binary, and trans kids are no more or less than cisgender ones. Binary-conforming trans kids themselves are not reinscribing or reinforcing the gender binary; this is being done by environments that restrict legitimate gender identities, trans and cis, to binary-normative ones. But the solution is not to question the gender self-determination of or to deny affirming healthcare to binary-identifying trans kids any more than it is to prevent cisgender kids from identifying as girls or boys.

While I focus on trans kids, it would be interesting to learn how many cisgender girls become uncomfortable with their female identity once they hit adolescence. The state of grace for tomboys often runs out in this period.[24] Some of my female-to-male trans participants told me that when they hit adolescence and experienced this increased pressure to conform to feminine norms, they actually really tried to "go for it," meaning they went all out to conform to gender expectations for girls—

makeup, dresses and skirts, and high heels—but could not find the right fit. I wonder how many cisgender girls feel this way when they experience the weight of new expectations for appearance and behavior and are exposed to greater sexism and misogyny but, unlike trans boys, do not see transitioning away from a female identity to be desirable.

Most of the parents of trans kids I interviewed resisted binary-restrictive views of gender and sought to create as much space for their child to explore their gender identity as possible. Parents followed their children's lead and did not seek to impose any identity on them. But as feminist and masculinity scholars have demonstrated for decades, overarching binary-normative social contexts leave their mark on all children, even as some find ways to resist. This is as true for transgender as it is for cisgender children. Affirming trans health resources are deployed within social contexts that are organized on the basis of the sex/gender binary. As such, these contexts operate to limit transgender possibilities and reinforce the essentialist foundations of patriarchy and misogyny.

Several of the parents I interviewed talked about having mixed feelings about their children accessing affirming healthcare, but not because they resisted their kids' nonnormative gender identities but because medicalization poses a dilemma for some feminist parents. For parents who hold a critical perspective on the two-sex system and attendant gender binary, medicalization poses a dilemma. On the one hand, they resist both the naturalness and oppressive nature of the binary gender order and want their children to express themselves without these limits. On the other hand, their kids may clearly identify as a boy or girl and need to be recognized as such for the sake of their mental health and agency as a person. Dara, for example, initially struggled to reconcile her critical feminist perspective on the socially constructed nature of binary gender systems with Davis's severe crisis at the onset of puberty. But she could see that puberty was "profoundly traumatic to him" and "wasn't going to work," that medical intervention was necessary if he was to survive. In the end, this understanding made the decision to grant her consent an easy one.

Eva, parent of Peter, contextualized her concerns about the medicalization of transgender children within the increasing medicalization of children in general. Saying, "I think a lot of things are being medicalized," Eva articulated a critique of the for-profit pharmaceutical industry and the employment of medicalization as a tool of social control, citing the example of the diagnosis of attention-deficit/hyperactivity disorder (ADHD) and attendant pharmaceutical intervention that is being increasingly applied to children who struggle to adapt to relatively sedentary days in school classrooms.

Barriers to Accessing Affirming Healthcare

The politics of trans visibility versus the ability to assimilate or "pass" are complex. Trans scholar Tey Meadow observes that "the smallest gender outlaws" have "deeply different trajectories and life chances"[25] than did the adult trans people who have gone before them, owing to the ability of these youngsters to take hormone blockers. Forgoing natal puberty enables a subsequently less complicated medical transition and greater ability to pass as their affirmed sex in the future should they choose to do so. Different trajectories for trans kids, therefore, are considerably shaped by binary conformity and socioeconomic privilege. According to Siebers's logic, if we identify being transgender as a disability, one of the blueprints of the social construction of binary gender is puberty-suppression therapy. Critical perspectives on biomedicine as implicated in relations of oppression come into play.

It is not being transgender, per se, that increases the likelihood of self-harm and suicide among trans kids but rather cultural and social prejudice that does the damage. This is true whether one is visible or not, but visibility does correlate to a higher level of suicide risk and lower quality of life. According to Brynn Tannehill, board member of the Trans United Fund, "Being *seen* as transgender or gender non-conforming increases suicide risk."[26] This higher risk is mitigated by trans-affirmative healthcare that enables transgender people to pass. In a study comparing quality-of-life outcomes for trans women with and without access to facial feminization surgery, for example, surgeons Tiffany Ainsworth and Jeffrey Spiegel stated the following conclusion: "Transwomen have diminished mental health-related quality of life compared with the general female population. However, surgical treatments . . . are associated with improved mental health-related quality of life."[27] According to the U.S. Surgeon General and the National Action Alliance for Suicide Prevention,

Suicidal behaviors in LGBT populations appear to be related to "minority stress," which stems from the cultural and social prejudice attached to minority sexual orientation and gender identity. This stress includes individual experiences of prejudice or discrimination, such as family rejection, harassment, bullying, violence, and victimization. Increasingly recognized as an aspect of minority stress is "institutional discrimination" resulting from laws and public policies that create inequities or omit LGBT people from benefits and protections afforded others.

Individual and institutional discrimination have been found to be associated with social isolation, low self-esteem, negative sexual/gender identity, and depression, anxiety, and other mental disorders. These negative outcomes, rather than minority sexual orientation or gender identity per se, appear to be the key risk factors for LGBT suicidal ideation and behavior.[28]

While the decision by trans kids and their families to opt for hormone blockers may or may not be undertaken with the goal of passing in mind, it does play a role in enabling trans kids to assimilate as adults if they wish to, an ability strongly linked to reduced future precarity.

The framework of queer/trans necropolitics is a powerful lens for situating queer and trans lives within systems of oppression, focusing as it does on systemic racism, classism, and institutionalized state violence as axes of precarity that shape which categories of queer and transgender members of the social body live and which either die or are politically, socially, culturally, and economically abandoned. As this lens draws attention to "contemporary carceral and medical industries as key growth sectors in the Neoliberal era,"[29] it supports an exploration of the ways in which the life-affirming resources that enable transition for the trans kids who are able to access them have a necropolitical footprint for others without such access.

Socioeconomic dimensions of precarity are racialized in Canada and the United States and generate vulnerability to interpersonal and state violence. While I welcome (and celebrate) the harm reduction flowing from the "paradigm shift" from corrective to affirming medicalization of transgender kids in Canada and the U.S., I am concerned that the current neoliberal context means that access to this kind of healthcare is restricted to relatively resource-rich trans children. Julian Gill-Peterson emphasizes "the enforced precarity of the lives of many transgender children, particularly of color."[30] Indeed, aspects of precarity related to racialization and poverty receive little to no attention in scholarly literature, in resources for transgender kids and their families, or in mainstream or (trans-/homonormative) LGBT media.

In both Canada and the United States, there is a socioeconomic divide with regard to access to treatment. Dara reports, for example, that the annual cost of a hormone-blocking implant for Davis is US$25,000. His family has good health insurance, and Dara expected it to be covered; but she and Davis's dad are able to pay for it themselves if they have to. While doing so would place a strain on their finances, Dara acknowledged her family's relative privilege, knowing that for so many other families, this is completely out of reach. From being so in touch with her own child's precarity, Dara expressed a sense of desperation that other trans kids are unable to access such necessary resources and support.

In the United States, some private insurers cover hormone therapy and/or gender confirmation surgery, but many do not. In the U.S. gender-affirming clinical practice of Edwards-Leeper and Spack, the psychologists unsurprisingly observe, "We have witnessed a socioeconomic divide in regard to who is able to obtain treatment in our clinic."[31] While under the (now-jeopardized) provisions of the Affordable Care Act (ACA), discrimination against transgender people by insurance providers is prohibited, the remedy requires a legal challenge with attendant financial and/or cultural capital. It is too soon to tell what the implications of potential reform of the ACA may be for this issue, but there are obvious reasons to be fearful.

In contrast to the U.S., access to trans healthcare is partially mediated by the availability of public insurance in Canada, but race- and class-based and geographic factors that enable and obstruct access cut across national borders. Canadian provincial healthcare policies regarding treatment for transgender people vary from province to province, and there are always at least some upfront costs (such as paying a licensed professional for a diagnosis of gender dysphoria) and incidental costs such as travel, accommodation, and time off work for parents of kids in rural settings or provinces without transgender healthcare resources. Some provinces cover surgery only for adults, and in any case, wait times for publicly funded surgeries are long. Only some provinces cover the cost of blockers and hormones, while the costs of related medications, for depression and anxiety, for example, are unevenly funded. The quality of medical care in remote communities in general is poor, while Indigenous reservations in Canada and the U.S. are severely and systematically underresourced. This situation is complicated by the fact that the violent imposition of binary gender systems on Indigenous peoples has been part of the (ongoing) process of colonization.[32]

Some of my participants have supportive parents whose insurance policies and personal wealth have enabled access to affirming healthcare. There are some for whom cost is an occasional barrier and some for whom it is an insurmountable one. Many of my participants expressed significant frustration and anguish about lack of access to affirming treatment—whether because they could not afford it or because they were not old enough to access treatment without parental permission or both. For several trans kids in my study, lack of access to affirmative healthcare has had devastating consequences. Prior to Nathan's success in finding a job and raising enough money to pay for his top surgery, Nora reported being "terrified, constantly": "And it's all because of this damn top surgery. And I am literally terrified, because I know for a fact that once he gets this done, he's gonna be a completely different child. And it kills me that I can't do anything. I told him—I was like, 'Honey, if I owned my home, I would sell the fucking thing. I would do whatever it takes.'" The two years that Nathan spent out of high school because he could not get new government ID without top surgery cost him the opportunity to graduate with his peers. When last I spoke with his mother, he was still working on his high school diploma via adult education.

Enrique, for example, left home because of his father's unwillingness to accept his transition, and this interrupted his education. He moved in with his boyfriend's family and in this context is receiving emotional and financial support (his boyfriend's mother has been paying for his testosterone). But we know from numerous reports from social service organizations and research studies that many kids in Enrique's situation find themselves on the street. When I interviewed Dylan in 2015, he was living with his working-poor family in a trailer park in the U.S. He reported experiencing extreme gender dysphoria and mental anguish but was not at a place in his life where it was possible to live as a boy/man.

Dylan's economic and social vulnerability raises alarm as it affects his ability to obtain hormones and to live fully as a man, both things that seem profoundly necessary for his well-being. He reported struggling with depression, self-harm (cutting), and multiple suicide attempts, for which he was receiving therapy. According to Dylan, the catalyst for his first suicide attempt was a combination of "a pretty violent relationship" and "really bad gender dysphoria" at the onset of puberty.

Dylan has been told by his doctor that he has to wait until he is 16 to start testosterone, and even then his mother's consent will be required. He thinks she will give it, but he said, "She told me that she would not be paying for it." Dylan has started working at a minimum-wage service job and is hopeful that Medicaid will cover the necessary doctor appointments. But he knows that "all of the testosterone will be completely out of pocket because it's not covered." Dylan lives in a small community without any trans healthcare and will depend on someone else to take him into the city to see the transgender specialist he has been referred to. Like most young trans people, Dylan depends on the adults in his life for access to healthcare.

Economic security does not necessarily translate to access to affirming healthcare, however. As emphasized earlier, kids are limited by their social subordination to the adults who have immediate power over them. Alicia, for example, hails from an economically secure family but did not initially feel she could count on her parents for support. So at 16, she took matters into her own hands by making her own hormones in a high school science lab. Unbeknownst to her teacher or her parents, Alicia provided herself with hormone therapy for several months: "I'd taken a couple of chemistry classes, a genetics class, and some biology classes. And I had a bit of an ulterior motive. I think I did a pretty good job with that," Alicia said with pride. Once she told her parents and gained their support, their insurance and personal wealth ensured that she began to receive medically supervised cross-sex hormone therapy. But I have to hand it to her for her creativity and ingenuity in providing herself with affirming healthcare.

Speaking of two "classes" of transgender people emerging in Canada and the United States on the basis of access to and consumption of affirming healthcare is both instructive and simplistic. Barriers to accessing the affirming healthcare that aids the ability to pass include poverty, lack of health insurance, lack of family support, geographic inaccessibility, binary nonconformity, mental health issues/trauma, and coming to understand or being enabled to understand oneself as trans too late to redirect puberty. While transgender resilience is heavily influenced by multiple dimensions of privilege, other factors such as body type (the mutability of more androgynous versus stereotypically sex-typed physical features) and individual hardiness and resourcefulness also come into play. But for trans kids, their position as minors in the care of parents or state agencies and variations in their socioeconomic status are key elements of precarity.

Issues relating to racialization go beyond access, however. Gill-Peterson positions the medicalization of transgender children as always already steeped in sexism, racism, and ableism by exposing the field of endocrinology as a racialized project from the get-go, whereby the "discovery" of the body's hormone systems took place within a white, colonial, and heteropatriarchal context: "Biomedicine is at the forefront of the contemporary politics of sex, gender, sexuality, and race . . . , and the transgender child is emerging as one of its newest anchors."[33] Gill-Peterson describes the Tanner scale, the "five-point diagram of 'normal' puberty progression," as a eugenic device in that it is deployed racially to prescribe puberty-suppression therapy for Black and Latina girls, whose purported earlier puberty reflects "the much older colonial hypersexualization of and medical interest in the genitals of the black and brown female body."[34] The Tanner scale universalizes Eurocentric binary sex norms.

Nonbinary Troubles

In my interviews with Cameron, Helen, Quinn, Stef, and Kidd, they lamented the lack of childhood exposure to nonbinary people/identities, while Wren wishes that she had been left alone to be who she was without having to think of herself or explain herself in terms of any gender. Some of the kids and young people in my study have very nuanced understandings of gender-identity issues and see themselves as at odds with the gender binary. Quinn, for example, identifies as a "neurodivergent queer, nonbinary, trans person of color" and resists the imposition of power that allows anyone to assign gender to anyone else.

Many kids who identify as nonbinary, however, need trans-affirming healthcare. But in most contexts, the current process for accessing affirming healthcare depends on being diagnosed with gender dysphoria, and this frame sets limits on the embodiments available to transgender kids, at least officially: one is required to convince a licensed clinician that one *has* gender dysphoria in order to transition socially and/or medically. The script for such an encounter is readily learned via trans sites on the Internet, but not all nonbinary kids are sophisticated enough to adapt their story to fit with the binary narrative or comfortable with misrepresenting their gender identity. Their desperation for treatment or accommodation usually wins out, and there is considerable anecdotal evidence that some therapists collude in constructing a false binary narrative out of respect for their clients' right to gender self-determination and/or as a harm-reduction measure.

Cory Oskam, for example, took hormone blockers for four years to stop his body from undergoing "female" puberty. Cory wanted very much to take testosterone but was stalled because he was uncomfortable defining himself as male. The requirement that he claim a male identity as a condition for gaining access to testosterone was imposed on Cory, and he refused this condition for some time. The first time Cory met with a therapist for the necessary psychological assessment in the hope that he would be approved for testosterone met with failure. He was open about his nonbinary gender identity, and the therapist determined that he was not "trans" enough" and denied him the necessary paperwork. Cory was devastated by this determination and put things on hold for a few years. But his desire to go on T persisted, and he adopted a more sophisticated strategy with the next therapist he saw: "I answered the questions 'correctly' I guess. I was saying that, 'Yeah, I was born in the wrong body,' you know. 'I want testosterone.' . . . They asked me, 'Do you want breasts?' And I was like, 'No.' And 'Do you want to go through puberty now?' 'Male puberty? Yes. Not female puberty.' So I guess I just answered the questions correctly and got T." Now that he is on testosterone, Cory is assumed to be male, observing, "Testosterone does do its own thing, and I do look more male. And I am perceived as like a cis now in the world even though I don't identify as one."

While nonbinary trans people of all ages are becoming more culturally visible, most of the representation relating to trans kids continues to be binary conforming in nature and, as such, poses limited challenges to oppressive binary-normative cisgender environments. I am certainly not arguing that trans kids are pressured to take blockers and/or hormones against their will—I do not believe this to be the case. Rather, I am concerned that the social context of binary gender conformity that trans kids find themselves in is often so oppressive that hormone blockers and eventual cross-sex hormones may be essential for their very survival. My concern is that by altering their embodiment to conform to binary gender systems—in order to survive, thrive, and construct a livable life—some trans kids become the site of another individualized medical solution to a social problem that leaves structures of oppression untouched, including those of racialization and poverty that shape which kids are able to thrive in this way. As gender scholars Elizabeth Bucar and Finn Enke observe, "The vast majority of transsexual-identified individuals in the United States will not have a single surgery related to sex change, due to lack of access and/or lack of desire. Thus, any media coverage that focuses primarily on SRS [sex reassignment surgery; see "gender confirmation surgery" in the glossary] disproportionately excludes from its purview poor people, people of color, all gender variance that is not medically mediated, and the countless ways in which trans masculine and trans feminine people negotiate the sex/gender expectations of the culture around them."[35] At the same time, I need to emphasize that it is deeply problematic to be critical in *any* way of trans kids who conform to binary norms either because they self-define as boys or girls or as a means of reducing their precarity. After all, gender-conforming cisgender kids are rarely censored for doing just this. When trans-affirming children's physician Johanna Olson-Kennedy[36] gave a keynote address at "Gender Odyssey" a number of years ago, I asked her a question about the unintended potential of affirming healthcare for reinforcing the binary gender order. Her response was sharp and instructive, and I have never forgotten it: "Don't put the onus for the gender revolution on the shoulders of transgender children—they are just trying to survive." Singling out trans kids as a point of intervention against binary normativity would be especially cruel given their particular vulnerability; it would amount to another form of gender policing and run counter to the principle of gender self-determination for all, wherever one locates oneself on the gender spectrum, that I advocate in this book.

An Emergent Gender-Affirmative Industry

If someone had told me when I was 10 years old that I could take hormone blockers to avoid getting my period and growing breasts and be accepted as a "borderlands person," as one of my seven-year-old participants described themselves, I would have done it in a heartbeat. But the emergence of a "gender-affirmative industry" in which a great many people become invested for their livelihood and the entrenchment of a pharmaceutical industrial complex that sells chemical solutions to social problems to individual consumers and for-profit medicalization bears critical scrutiny. As Hilary remarked, there is tremendous potential in new technologies: "I feel like what's going to happen in the next 10 years, we could be 3-D printing stem cells into penises." But the interests of for-profit medical and pharmaceutical industries, as opposed to a more socially just public healthcare model, are a dynamic that trans scholars of color point to with concern.[37]

In the current neoliberal context, gender identity becomes something that is, to a degree, bought and sold. But instead of justifying opposition to trans-affirming healthcare that places the burden for resisting oppressive binary systems on the shoulders of transgender people, this critical scrutiny should encompass the multiple ways in which products and services aimed at binary gender conformity are marketed to and consumed by cisgender people as well.[38] Critical trans scholars and activists draw our attention to the ways in which the technologies of trans-affirming medicalization are unfairly singled out for critical scrutiny. In viewing the body as "an open technical system," Gill-Peterson resists a good/bad view of the medicalization of trans embodiment by demonstrating that such "technicity"—meaning the ability to use technology to modify the body, a capacity that is reflected in both taken-for-granted and novel practices, from clipping one's toenails to organ transplants—is widespread.[39] This perspective reveals the transphobia behind a singular focus on the body-modifying practices of hormone therapy and/or gender confirmation surgery "as a betrayal of the human's integrity."[40]

* * *

Binary gender systems provide an overarching framework of meaning that shapes and somewhat contains resistance as much as conformity.

As long as binary gender systems are in place, there are limits set on the scope of gender self-determination available to kids. Targeting binary gender systems for transition, rather than binary-conforming trans kids, is the appropriate strategy to widen the scope of gender self-determination available to all. This project is entirely compatible with the fight to expand access to trans-affirming healthcare.

Trans advocacy and activism by transgender people and our allies achieved at least a partial (and still highly contested) paradigm shift from gender-reparative to gender-affirming medicalization. I do not intend to minimize this accomplishment, but I do wish to subject this paradigm shift to critical scrutiny with regard to its unintended consequences. As a basis for my conclusion to this chapter, I return to the directive by Michel Foucault that I used to open the book: "People know what they do; frequently they know why they do what they do; but what they don't know is what what they do does."[41] Given the extent to which racialized, impoverished, and non-binary-conforming trans kids are denied recognition and care, transgender have-nots will continue to experience a heightened layer of precarity around gender nonconformity that complicates "the state-sanctioned or extralegal production and exploitation of group-differentiated vulnerability to premature death," to return to Ruth Gilmore's definition of racism.[42] By enabling some trans kids to reduce their precarity by accessing trans-affirming healthcare, disparities among transgender people are emerging in new and troubling ways. In spite of the increasing visibility of transgender people, we see binary gender normativity restabilizing itself as a basis for transgender inclusion. But access to such care is unevenly distributed to the extent that less precarious trans kids are being positioned as (proto-) citizen consumers in a racialized biomedical market that reflects and exacerbates existing socioeconomic divides. This is what what we have done is doing: we are enabling the survival of some trans kids and not others. Unless we engage meaningfully to challenge white supremacy, colonialism, and capitalist exploitation, it is what we will continue to do.

Conclusion

Beyond Hope

If I'm not vocally outraged at every injustice against trans people, I'm teaching Simon that some trans people are beyond hope and I'm leaving room for him to be beyond hope one day. I try to make the case that the vibrancy and health and inherent value of the entire trans spectrum is vital to our kids, no matter how much privilege they have, because it teaches them to value their transness, rather than only feeling valuable if they are overcoming transness. We can't free them from the box of their assigned gender just to put them in another box of "the right way to transition" or "the right way to be trans." And the truest way to build their self-esteem so that they can stand against bigotry and violence is to build pride that is without limits or qualifications.
—Hilary, parent

LGBT activism in Canada and the U.S. over the past decade in particular has been successful in achieving significant changes in legal and policy landscapes for LGBT people of all ages, although more uniformly in Canada than in the United States. LGBT social movements have used human rights or anti-discrimination legislation to resist discrimination on the basis of sexual and/or gender identity. There are now consequences for discriminating against lesbian, gay, bisexual, and transgender people in many jurisdictions and institutions.

Canada legalized same-sex marriage in 2005. In November 2015, newly elected Canadian prime minister Justin Trudeau announced that his government would "introduce legislation that will make gender identity a 'prohibited ground for discrimination under the Canadian Human Rights Act' and make the transgender community an 'identifiable group protected by the hate speech provisions of the *Criminal Code*.'"[1] Bill C-16, an act to amend the Canadian Human Rights Act and the Criminal Code, was introduced by member of Parliament and justice minister Jody Wilson-Raybould, passed in the House of Commons on October 18, 2016, and by the Senate to become law on February 14, 2017.

The Trudeau government engaged in unprecedented symbolic support of LGBT communities when, on June 1, 2016, the rainbow/pride flag was raised on Parliament Hill for the first time, and later that month Trudeau became the first prime minister to participate in a pride parade when he marched in Toronto. He was also front and center at the Vancouver pride parade later that summer. Many provincial governments and the government of the territory of Nunavut have protections for gender identity enshrined in their Human Rights Code. In July 2016, the British Columbia government explicitly added "gender identity and expression" to its Human Rights Code.

In 2011, Hillary Clinton, in her capacity as U.S. secretary of state, declared that "gay rights are human rights."[2] State bans on same-sex marriage were ruled unconstitutional by the U.S. Supreme Court in 2013. More recently, on May 9, 2016, U.S. attorney general Loretta Lynch announced that the federal government was taking the North Carolina state legislature to court over HB2—its controversial law requiring transgender people to use the bathroom corresponding to their birth sex. The Obama administration followed this statement on May 13, 2016, by sending a letter to every school district in the U.S. directing them to allow transgender students to use the bathroom appropriate to their *affirmed* gender identity. According to *New York Times* journalists Julie Davis and Matt Apuzzo, the letter lacked the force of law but contained "an implicit threat: schools that do not abide by the Obama administration's interpretation of the law could face lawsuits or a loss of federal aid."[3] The letter from the Obama administration clearly communicated the federal government's intention to include gender identity as a protected category under the gender-equity provisions of Title IX.

Too many LGBT people in Canada and the U.S. have been harmed by laws and social policies that are no longer on the books to dismiss the value of this pro-LGBT social and political change. Educational scholars Therese Quinn and Erica Meiners, for example, make a strong point when they state that "the gains of the LGBT movements in education—

including visibility, policy, curriculum, and climate—were almost unimaginable a decade ago."[4] The successful employment of human rights discourse has effectively changed policies in a number of Canadian and U.S. school districts to stipulate that trans kids be treated according to their affirmed gender. Crucial institutional changes relating to access to new identity documents and sex-segregated spaces on the basis of affirmed rather than assigned sex and access to trans-affirming healthcare are producing better outcomes for some trans kids. As a result of a series of legal challenges in many provinces and their spillover effects, people of all ages are now able to obtain new government identification with an affirmed gender marker without the requirement of surgery. Reparative therapy to correct sexual and/or gender "deviance" has been banned by law in the states of California (2012) and New Jersey (2013), the District of Columbia (2014), and the province of Ontario (2015).

I began writing this book in 2015, amid unprecedented, yet far from mainstream, support for lesbian, gay, and transgender rights in Canada and the United States. In addition to the statements of support from the high-level politicians in Canada and the United States just noted, in some cases, there have been financial consequences for governments that advocate blatant homo-negativity and trans-negativity.[5]

While LGBT rights have been enshrined at the federal level in Canada and at the provincial level in all but two provinces, the current conservative shift in the political landscape of the United States and its chilling effect north of the 49th parallel have increased the precarity of vulnerable trans children. The 2016 U.S. presidential election resulted in a dramatically different social and political landscape for vulnerable groups across the nation, LGBT people and trans kids among them. Though many Canadians appear to feel smugly superior about Canadian inclusiveness, viewing racism and intolerance as a U.S. rather than a Canadian problem, ongoing patterns of oppression (colonial, racist, misogynist, and heteronormative) persist as foundational components of Canadian institutions and culture.[6]

In the first 100 days of the Trump presidency, executive orders radically deepened forces of precarity for Muslim people, racialized immigrants and undocumented people, people of color in general, Jews, refugees, the poor, Indigenous people, people with disabilities, women, and gay, lesbian, and trans people. Trump specifically targeted trans kids for persecution on February 22, 2017, when he announced that he was revoking the directive by the Obama administration to interpret gender-equity provisions in Title IX to allow trans students to use bathrooms and locker rooms consistent with their affirmed gender identities. Any hope that the Supreme Court would step in and issue a landmark ruling in support of transgender rights was dashed on March 6, 2017, when the court specifically referenced Trump's revocation of the Obama directive to refer the Gavin Grimm case back to the lower courts. The result there was no less discouraging.[7] The Trump administration reversed or attempted to reverse, as in the case of the right of transgender persons to serve openly in the military,[8] a number of pro-LGBT decisions of the Obama administration.

This climate has the potential to silence disagreement among various groups of LGBT people—about what strategies are appropriate and who benefits from so-called wins—with calls for unity. But calls for unity along any demographic line reflect the limitations associated with single-issue social movements in general: they center on the interests of the relatively privileged, so racialization, sexism, misogyny, and economic deprivation are either overlooked or tokenized. The experiences of working-class women and women of color, for example, have been overshadowed in the white, middle- and upper-class agendas of mainstream feminism, while wealthy, white, gay men have driven the agendas of LGBT organizations and social movements. Indeed, Dan Savage's "It Gets Better" campaign, initiated in response to the suicides of gay teens, has been criticized by anti-racist activists and scholars for speaking only to those lesbian and gay people who are not otherwise oppressed. It therefore fails to acknowledge that for many racialized and impoverished LGBT teens, it *does not get better*.[9] These teens do not leave oppression and tyranny behind as they grow to adulthood and move out into a more welcoming world; they remain dogged by discrimination and poverty, continue to be vulnerable to self-harm and suicide, and are disproportionately at risk for spending time in prison. The queer or the trans aspect of their oppression cannot be abstracted from the trauma of racialization and poverty that makes them disproportionately precarious. Many of the legal and policy gains for trans kids noted earlier are life enhancing at minimum and life saving in many cases, but they disproportionately benefit less precarious trans kids. As Catherine, Frank's mother, sees it,

There is this kind of little movement I've seen where people want to put this positive spin on life for trans folks. And I can't speak for trans adults, and I can't speak for trans kids, but as a parent of a trans kid, I can certainly tell you nothing has changed. What's changed is that we have some really amazing supports in our lives. In our community, the school district hasn't changed the way they do daily business. I get frustrated when it's, like, Caitlyn Jenner—good on her, that's awesome, but that is not the reality. They only focus all of the attention on all of the celebrities and everybody who's famous just to distract people from the real problems that are going on. They need to focus more attention on people who don't have money to get proper reassignment surgeries, who aren't able to be who they want to be because they're poor or they don't live in places that are accepting.

Advances in LGBT rights have taken place at the same time that we have seen widening social inequality, the expansion of a racialized prison industrial complex, ongoing colonial relationships with Indigenous peoples, and severe cutbacks to public education and social services. These contexts continue to disproportionately increase the precarity of LGBT people, including trans kids, who are impoverished, racialized, and undocumented residents of Canada and the United States.

LGBT scholars and activists of color and their allies draw attention to the ongoing violence of settler colonialism, the prison industrial complex, and neoliberal restructuring and trouble historically inaccurate narratives of Western progress and national myths of foundational social justice propagated by Canadian and U.S. (under Obama) political leaders when making pro-LGBT statements.[10] For example, when announcing that the federal government was filing a civil rights lawsuit against the state of North Carolina to declare its bathroom bill discriminatory, Loretta Lynch, the U.S. attorney general at the time, invoked the mythical narrative of the U.S. as a justice-seeking country, making reference to "the founding ideals that have led this country—haltingly but inexorably—in the direction of fairness, inclusion and equality for all Americans." Lynch identified similarities between North Carolina's bathroom bill and Jim Crow laws and opposition to same-sex marriage rights, acknowledging "a recognizably human fear of the unknown, and a discomfort with the uncertainty of change," while insisting that "this is not a time to act out of fear. This is a time to summon our national virtues of inclusivity, diversity, compassion and open-mindedness." Lynch stated that North Carolina's anti-trans bathroom legislation provides no benefit to society—and rather harms "innocent Americans." The implication is that harm remains the just deserts of the "noninnocent": racialized, impoverished, incarcerated, disabled, undocumented, street-drug-addicted, and suspected (brown) terrorists. In an unprecedented statement, toward the end of her announcement, Lynch spoke directly and movingly to the transgender community on behalf of the Obama administration: "No matter how isolated or scared you may feel today, the Department of Justice and the entire Obama Administration wants you to know that we see you; we stand with you; and we will do everything we can to protect you going forward. Please know that history is on your side. This country was founded on a promise of equal rights for all, and we have always managed to move closer to that promise, little by little, one day at a time. It may not be easy—but we'll get there together."[11] Although such homonationalist statements obscure structures of oppression, they have cultural power that lessens some of the precarity experienced by the trans kids in this book. Two things are true here: it was definitely better for some trans kids under Obama, but that administration was far from heroic. And things are definitely better for some trans kids under the Trudeau government in Canada than they were under Stephen Harper, but Trudeau's loyalty to big business and resource extraction and his government's refusal to equitably fund Indigenous children in Canada indicates little to no meaningful redistribution of wealth and power. This is because legal and policy reform often leaves structures of oppression untouched.

What's Wrong with Rights?

Movements that focus on achieving transgender rights and changing government policies rely on legal discourse as a strategic frame and view these initiatives as key mechanisms for improving the life chances of transgender people of all ages. These are part of broader LGBT campaigns and typically focus on achieving two key measures:

- The inclusion of gender identity and expression as protected categories in human rights statutes and public policies that recognize these rights by enabling transgender people to access sex-segregated facilities and sex-differentiated activities according to their affirmed gender

- The enactment of hate crime legislation as protection from anti-queer and anti-trans violence

The basic rights that LGBT movements have achieved and that I benefit from include freedom from discrimination and police persecution, marriage rights/benefits for same-sex couples, and the right to adopt and retain custody of children. On a visceral level, when I stand in the dugout as a coach at a Little League game, although I experience feelings of otherness at times, I am still able to do so as an openly queer and gender-nonconforming person. That this was not possible in the past but is now is not a small thing, and frankly, it is not something I imagined possible when I was 16. Nevertheless, there is considerable debate among scholars and activists within trans communities about the appropriateness of prioritizing legal rights over working collectively to oppose state and corporate power. Much of this debate mirrors that within lesbian, gay, and queer communities and scholarship about the appropriateness of "marriage equality" as a primary goal of LGBT movements. According to this logic, gays and lesbians push for recognition as fully human, that is, respectable people, thereby qualifying them for the rights and responsibilities that go along with full citizenship. Critics argue, however, that this perspective only rehabilitates and reinforces oppressive liberal humanist hierarchies and systems of governance and expands the power of the state (especially through punitive measures) while normalizing private (familial) responsibility for social security.[12] In this sense, previously abject but comparatively privileged (white, middle- and upper-class, avowedly monogamous) lesbian and gay people are "folded into life" or welcomed into the nation and accorded citizenship.[13] Trans scholar Eric Stanley applies this analysis to trans movements, lamenting the "normalizing force of mainstream trans politics in the U.S."[14]

These debates necessarily relate to political strategy as well as endgame: are rights provisions, hate crime laws, and pro-LGBT statements by politicians the goals our social movements should pursue? What tactics are appropriate: legal challenges, political lobbying, or direct action? Radical critiques emphasize the failure of rights-oriented campaigns and measures to redistribute wealth and resources even as they expand legal and cultural recognition. These debates are paralleled within other social justice movements relating to women, racialized minorities, and children, among others.

Radical democratic theorist Nancy Fraser defines gender justice, and by extension democracy, in terms of "participatory parity," that is, economic and cultural equality for women.[15] For Fraser, gender justice is a foundational requirement of democracy and involves both recognition (legal and cultural inclusion) and the redistribution of material resources. While women, alongside other overlapping groups marked by mutually constitutive relations of sexism, colonialism, racialization, and class formation, were initially excluded from formal citizenship in self-proclaimed Western "democracies," this is no longer the case,[16] although this process of enfranchisement was geographically and racially staggered.[17] Yet in spite of the achievement of formal citizenship (for those who have documents), a great deal of evidence reveals that there are significant gaps between the legal status of women in these nations and full gender equality and that inclusion has particularly benefited women who are white, relatively well-off, and able to mobilize.[18]

In Canada, critical race scholar Sherene Razack observes that a gendered and racialized two-tier structure of citizenship was established through conquest and the Indian Act and subsequently by Canada's 2001 Anti-Terrorism Act.[19] Stephen Harper's Conservative government expanded the state's powers in Canada in 2015 when Bill C-51 allowed citizenship to be stripped from Canadian-born persons of foreign-born parents convicted of certain crimes. Feminist sociologist Sunera Thobani similarly positions citizenship in the Canadian context as a prize, as a tool for the domination and exclusion of others, rather than as a fundamentally emancipatory category.[20] Citizenship in Canada, from this perspective, is symbolically associated with whiteness, and whiteness acts as the unspoken norm against which racial difference is measured.[21] Furthermore, in jockeying for citizenship, white outsiders—women, workers, LGBT people—often trade on their race privilege at the expense of solidarity with other excluded groups. In this way, Thobani observes, "citizenship serves as a status that mobilizes national subjects, classed and gendered as they may be themselves, in defense of the institution against the claims of those designated as undeserving outsiders."[22] Various categories of exclusion, such as race, class, disability, and sexuality, intersect powerfully with the lack of legal and political recognition accorded children, who qualify as temporary *noncitizens*.

There are insider and outsider divisions within queer and trans communities. Mainstream LGBT movements narrowly focus on sexual and gender identity in pursuit of legal rights and recognition without complicating other subtexts of citizenship or seeking to redistribute wealth accordingly. Jasbir Puar observes that "any single-axis identity politics is invariably going to coagulate around the most conservative normative construction of that identity, foreclosing the complexities of class, citizenship status, gender, nation, and perhaps most importantly in the context of very recent events, religion."[23] In writing about queer movements, educational scholar Kevin Kumashiro observes that a single-issue focus on sexuality risks "complying with other oppressions and excluding their own margins," to the extent that "such movements become just like the mainstream except with different identities taking center stage."[24] This has the inevitable result of privileging queer and trans people who are disproportionately white, documented, middle and upper class, and gender conforming. If recognition can be measured in terms of rights and the formal privileges and responsibilities of citizenship, then what is necessary for redistribution? And to what extent do some relatively privileged trans-rights activists ignore or neglect these issues?

What Is Wrong with Punishment?

Over the past 30 years, a phenomenal expansion of the U.S. prison industrial complex has dovetailed with massive cuts to public institutions and programs of support for the most economically vulnerable. Understanding hate crimes legislation in this context links it to the ever-expanding punishment apparatus of the state, a state with a demonstrated record of disproportionately incarcerating people of color and poor people, in which groups the most vulnerable LGBT people are to be found. According to a 2017 report by the Williams Institute at the UCLA School of Law, incarceration of lesbian, gay, and bisexual people is three times that for the general population.[25] While not rivaling the United States and Russia, the two nations with the highest percentages of their populations in prison, Canada's prison population is expanding fast and is equally racialized: Indigenous and Black Canadian people are disproportionately subject to incarceration.[26] Hate crime legislation in Canada emerged in response to racism and religious persecution and is defined as "any criminal offense against a person, group or property that is motivated by hatred or prejudice towards an identifiable group." In addition to race and religion, sex or sexual orientation is included as an identifiable group.[27] A queer/trans necropolitics framework draws our attention to the fact that the employment of state repression against offenders as a measure for improving the lives of transgender people fails to provide justice, given the disproportionate policing and security measures that target and incarcerate people who are racialized, Indigenous, poor, migrants, LGBT, youth, and disabled. From this perspective, many trans people have more to fear from the state than they have to look forward to with regard to protection.

Queer/trans necropolitical scholars argue that LGBT support for hate crime legislation actually calls on the power of the state and state violence to protect LGBT people from violent "others." They note that this same state violence was only too recently used *against* LGBT people and continues to be used against Indigenous, racialized, impoverished, and undocumented people. By securing "human status" without questioning its foundation in liberal humanist ideas that are ultimately oppressive, privileged queer and trans people become complicit in that oppression. While many mainstream LGBT organizations celebrate the classification of anti-LGBT violence as a hate crime, a more critical analysis draws our attention to the disproportionate criminalization of racialized and impoverished persons for hate crimes against LGBT persons, thus perpetuating structural racism and classism and reinforcing state violence. Furthermore, punishment of this nature fails to protect *all* LGBT people from harm by instead *individualizing* anti-gay and anti-trans violence. The structural violence of heteronormativity and patriarchal sex/gender systems thus go unaddressed.[28] From this perspective, hate crime provisions represent elite LGBT interests and reinforce the security apparatuses of the carceral state, that is, the prison industrial complex. A carceral state inflicts great harm on vulnerable populations, queer and trans kids among them.

Privileged LGBT subjects often cite hate crimes against transgender women of color as justification for hate crime legislation and state recognition of transgender rights, but they do not adequately take up the central role of racialization and enforced poverty that generates this violence. Trans scholars of color Riley Snorton and Jin Haritaworn introduce the "traumatized citizenship model" to describe the way in which more privileged transgender subjects are able to leverage the violence waged against trans women of color to increase their legal standing.[29] From this perspective, the recognition of equal rights of citizenship (protection from discrimination) and access to state protection that the privileged "we" gain as a result of these strategies constitute collusion and perpetuate harms equally heinous.

In the U.S., President Obama signed the Matthew Shepard and James Byrd Junior Hate Crimes Prevention Act in 2009. On the surface, this recognition and repudiation of interpersonal violence against LGBT people and people of color was a watershed moment. After all, 40–50 years earlier, police were raiding gay and lesbian bars in the U.S. and Canada and beating and imprisoning patrons with impunity.[30] In a discussion of "queer investments in punishment," trans scholar Sarah Lamble notes that race- and class-privileged LGBT people's support for hate crimes legislation and harsh punishment for offenders means "many LGBT communities now partly measure their citizenship status on whether the state is willing to imprison other people on their behalf."[31] This issue is complicated by the lack of evidence that hate crime laws deter people from acts of violence.

Consider this case in point. A compelling example of the harm that hate crime legislation can deliver to already-marginalized people is the prosecution *as an adult* of Richard Thomas, a 16-year-old Black American boy, for his assault on a gender-nonconforming teen in the state of California. In "The Fire on the 57 Bus in Oakland," *New York Times Magazine* author Dashka Slater reports that, on November 4, 2013, an 18-year-old agender teenager named Sasha Fleischman was seriously injured when another teenager on the bus set their skirt on fire. At the time of the assault, Sasha, who is Euro-American and middle class, was attending an alternative private school in Berkeley. Richard, her assailant, was a resident of one of the city's poorer neighborhoods. He had experienced significant trauma-related losses over the course of his life. Richard was attending a high school with a graduation rate below 50% and was academically struggling. At the time of the assault, Slater states that Richard "was having trouble understanding his schoolwork and wanted to be tested for learning disabilities. He was worried about graduating. And the violence around him was pressing in. That fall, another friend, this one from Oakland High, was shot. At the end of October, while walking to the store in an unfamiliar neighborhood with his cousin Gerald, Richard was robbed at gunpoint by two teenage boys who took his money, his phone, his coat and his shoes."[32] Sasha was asleep on the bus when Richard and two of his friends began to ridicule them for their gender nonconformity. Richard and his friends decided to set Sasha's skirt on fire, expecting that the fabric would merely smolder and wake up its wearer and that this would somehow be "funny." Richard applied the lighter to Sasha's skirt, but the skirt went up in flames and seriously burned Sasha's legs. Surveillance footage from the bus was used to identify Richard, and he was arrested the next day. The county district attorney used her discretion to charge him with a hate crime and as an adult. Slater notes that hate crime legislation was introduced in the 1980s as a result of moral panics around skinhead attacks; offenders accused of a hate crime were subject to tougher sentences than if they had committed the same crime against a person who was not a member of a persecuted minority. Charging Richard as an adult denied him the anonymity legally provided to juveniles and increased the probability that he would do time in an adult facility.

When Richard was questioned by police about his motives for the attack, he stated, "I'm homophobic. I don't like gay people." His lawyer argued, however, that it made no sense to describe a child's nascent opinions as "hate." Even Sasha's parents objected to Richard being tried as an adult, while Sasha was uncertain about what kind of penalty was appropriate. "I know he hurt me," Sasha said. "He did something that's really dangerous and stupid. But then again, he's a 16-year-old kid, and 16-year-old kids are kind of dumb. It's really hard to know what I want for him." In a letter of apology to Sasha, Richard wrote, "I am not a thug, gangster, hoodlum, nor monster. I'm a young Black-American male who's made a terrible mistake. . . . I've also been hurt a lot for no reason, not like I hurt you, but I've been hurt physically and mentally so I know how it feels, the pain and confusion . . . of why me; I've felt it before plenty of times." Slater goes on to note that the National Center for Lesbian Rights, the Transgender Law Center, and the American Civil Liberties Union of Northern California wrote letters to District Attorney

O'Malley asking her to reconsider the charges, challenging the appropriateness of trying juvenile offenders as adults. The district attorney held fast, however, and Richard agreed to a plea bargain of seven years, the bulk of which would be served at an adult facility.[33]

Without dismissing for a moment the harm done to Sasha and the serious nature of the assault, is this what should have happened? Will this make LGBT kids safer? Is the criminalization of youth aggression a solution? The issues raised by critics of hate crime measures are also at play, albeit on a smaller scale, with regard to the adoption of punitive anti-bullying policies in many school districts.

The School-to-Prison Pipeline

Many school boards have passed anti-bullying and/or anti-homophobia policies that contest what has long been a normalized practice of targeting queer and gender-nonconforming children (as well as those who are racialized, visibly impoverished, physically and/or neurologically disabled, in care, fat,[34] or marginalized according to other markers of difference) for harassment and abuse. There is no question that official statements that this kind of behavior is inappropriate are an improvement over the long-standing normalization of such violence. In a 2012 report, titled *The Health of Canada's Young People: A Mental Health Focus*, the Public Health Agency of Canada defined bullying as "a form of repeated aggression where there is an imbalance of power between the young person who is bullying and the young person who is victimized. Power can be achieved through physical, psychological, social, or systemic advantage, or by knowing another's vulnerability (e.g., obesity, learning problem, sexual orientation, family background) and using that knowledge to cause distress." The report goes on to note that victims "tend to have high levels of emotional problems, while young people who bully tend to have the highest levels of behavioural problems. Young people who are involved in both bullying others and being victimized tend to have elevated levels of both emotional and behavioural problems, with this group of young people having the highest level of emotional problems and the second highest level of behavioural problems."[35]

As of July 2013, anti-bullying laws have been passed in all 50 U.S. states, and some Canadian provinces have anti-bullying legislation. Considerable research has demonstrated that punitive anti-bullying policies, rather than representing progress with regard to social justice, fail to protect vulnerable LGBT kids and instead contribute to a "school-to-prison pipeline" for racialized and disabled children and youth. This is true in both Canada and the United States. Educational researchers Therese Quinn and Erica Meiners echo social justice lawyer Andrea Ritchie's characterization of antibullying laws as "mini hate crime laws" in the way that they are "likely to both reflect and reinforce dominant sets of power arrangements."[36] In the past two decades, many public school districts in North America have passed "zero-tolerance" anti-bullying policies, often in an effort to protect themselves from legal action.[37] Child and youth studies scholars Monique Lacharite and Zopito Marini cite the 2005 case of *Jubran vs. North Vancouver School District #44* in Canada, in which a student took his school district to court because he was subjected to extreme bullying for years. The ruling assigned legal responsibility to the school district for failing to uphold its student code of conduct. While the case was a victory in the sense that it placed the responsibility for keeping students safe squarely on the school's shoulders, increasing the punishing capacity of schools has had very negative consequences for vulnerable students. Lacharite and Marini observe that Canadian courts and schools are "showing a new intolerance for bullying and establishing the need to classify bullying as a crime."[38]

Evidence suggests that anti-bullying school policies do not make LGBT kids safer because they individualize anti-gay and anti-trans aggression rather than attending to heteronormative structural factors and because they punish troubled kids rather than marshaling appropriate resources on their behalf.[39] In Lacharite and Marini's analysis of the zero-tolerance policy outlined as part of Ontario's Safe Schools Act, they observe that the policy "outlines specific punishments for inappropriate behaviors by using suspension and expulsion more often as well as police involvement and disciplinary measures." They go on to note, however, that the policy did not "include room for exception or unusual circumstance, and as it was employed more and more, expulsion and suspension rates rapidly increased, leading to another problem altogether, . . . an increase in dropout rates."[40]

Numerous scholars employ the metaphor of a racialized "school-to-prison pipeline" to describe the trajectory for kids rendered precarious by racialization and/or poverty or other dimensions of socially constructed marginality, noting that strong-armed anti-bullying policies actually reinforce institutional racism by exposing more kids to criminalization, family intervention, and systems of law enforcement. Research indicates that Indigenous, Black American and Black Canadian, immigrant youth of color, and disabled and LGBT kids are disproportionately targeted for discipline practices that push them out of school.[41] Such exclusion is a strong predictor of precarity, as many of these children in fact drop out, become poverty stricken, and are later incarcerated. A 2013 ACLU report titled "What Is the School to Prison Pipeline?" "concluded that students of color and disabled students are disproportionately suspended, expelled, and sent into the justice system, in comparison to white and nondisabled students."[42] Quinn and Meiners observe, "These gendered and racialized practices of removing students from their educational settings—the most dramatic educational sanction available—start in preschools, as indicated in a 2005 survey of 40 states' prekindergarten programs."[43] Yet this is business as usual. As critical childhood studies scholar Lucia Hodgson observes, "The criminalization of black children is a major component of their social oppression."[44] The school-to-prison pipeline contributes to precarity in that it is "a complex network of relations that naturalizes the movement of youth of color from schools and communities into under- or unemployment and permanent detention. . . . Because schools are sites of surveillance that are neither race nor gender-neutral, these laws entrench extant relationships to law enforcement. Criminalization in and outside of schools is a process of racialization, through which youth of color are normalized as those who are 'bad' and 'in trouble.'"[45] As desperate as Catherine was to protect Frank, she was cognizant of the need to avoid criminalizing the two Indigenous boys who sexually assaulted him, knowing that their behavior reflected their own trauma and marginalization. Her knowledge is consistent with research that indicates that bullying and interpersonal violence are often multidirectional. According to a recent study, "33% of the students who reported high involvement in bullying or victimization did so as dual participants, that is, they were involved in both."[46] Another study notes that students are often bullied because they are visibly impoverished and often resort to violence as a mechanism of defense.[47]

In the context of ongoing cuts to school budgets, policies that respond to student behavioral problems by allowing expulsion are attractive. Quinn and Meiners observe that if teaching staff are cut and those remaining are pressured to meet the needs of the same number of students, there is a greater likelihood that authoritarian systems of discipline and oppressive relationships will exist.[48] While queer critics of the school-to-prison pipeline emphasize that gender- and sexual-minority kids experience substantial and long-lasting harm in communities and schools, anti-bullying policies exemplify "how a carceral state can take up the harm and violence experienced, as well as the desires of communities for systemic change, to advance agendas that do little to make communities safer for those who are non-heterosexual and/or non-gender-conforming."[49] Quinn and Meiners observe that restorative or transformative justice practices are emerging in schools and communities in the United States in opposition to tactics of punishment and isolation.[50] These alternatives are severely underfunded, while more and more resources are being pumped into carceral facilities. Programs that address oppressive structures and cultures in schools that cause harm to students and teachers in a variety of ways are badly needed.

Reform versus Radical Change

If the rights framework has such clear limitations, to what extent, then, does it make sense to pursue "rights" for transgender kids? Does it inevitably serve only the interests of less precarious trans kids? After all, trans kids are striated by privilege with regard to their ability to exercise these rights. But while rights initiatives are limited, I am convinced that abandoning them would be a mistake. Rights *do* deliver important measures of harm reduction and can be strategically important in challenging oppressive cultures. Anti-homophobia and trans-inclusive policies that recognize and value gender and sexual diversity by focusing on changing school culture to be more inclusive do challenge oppressive aspects of heteropatriarchy and are not irrelevant, or the Christian Right would not mobilize so forcefully against them.

The discourse of rights can be a powerful tool for undermining oppressive constructions of human/not quite human/subhuman subjects. In Judith Butler's articulation of her "new gender politics," she argues that rights are foundational to social justice struggles and insists, "When we struggle for rights, we are not simply struggling for rights that attach to my person. . . . We are struggling to be conceived as persons. . . . If we are struggling not only to be conceived as persons, but to create a social transformation of the very meaning of personhood, then the assertion of rights becomes a way of intervening into the social and political process by which the human is articulated."[51] Siebers, too, links rights to the acknowledgment of human status and insists on the value of a social, rather than a medical, model of disability to challenge barriers to citizenship. Claiming citizenship via seeking rights, according to Siebers, has the potential to reveal the blueprint of social oppression, to show that disability is constructed rather than naturally occurring: "Disability seen from this point of view requires not individual medical treatment but changes in society. Social constructionism has changed the landscape of thinking about disability because it refuses to represent people with disabilities as defective citizens and because its focus on the built environment represents a common cause around which they may organize politically."[52]

Critical citizenship scholar Naila Kabeer articulates an "inclusive" or "horizontal" conceptualization of citizenship based on collective, as opposed to individualistic, criteria. This definition of citizenship focuses on relationships *between* citizens as much as it does on "the more traditional 'vertical' view of citizenship as the relationship between the state and the individual." Kabeer notes that "it is the collective struggles of excluded groups which have historically driven processes of social transformation."[53] This definition of citizenship echoes Fraser's concept of participatory parity as a measure of social justice. Indeed, critical citizenship scholar Ruth Lister makes this connection explicitly by invoking it to bestow "cultural citizenship."[54] Kabeer's definition of inclusive citizenship, like Siebers's vision of rights as a tool for social change, draws inspiration from political philosopher Hannah Arendt's definition of citizenship as "the right to have rights," that is, the right to be regarded as fully human.[55] An inclusive definition of citizenship focuses attention on the structural issues relating to resources for claiming and contesting citizenship and exclusion. Citizenship is as much a resource in itself as are the means (material and cultural) for embodying it and enacting social change. This link between rights and citizenship targets social structures, including state power, that privilege heteronormativity and cisgender binary normativity in concert with poverty and racism. Rights are an important tool for reducing the precarity of trans kids, but rights must be pursued within a broader anti-oppression strategy.

The value of obtaining trans rights in shaping cultural climate has been driven home very sharply by the damaging change in tone that emerged in the early days of the Trump administration. Rights do matter, as they shape cultural climates and legitimate student experiences of discrimination and provide avenues for recourse. According to the Canadian Civil Liberties Association, "Studies have shown that LGBTQ students feel safer and more accepted when they know their schools have policies and procedures that explicitly address homophobia." School board policies that entitle students to form gay-straight alliances are also crucial, as they "contribute to making school safer for LGBTQ students."[56] And a recent article in the *Guardian*, by Nicola Davis, announced a "drop in teenage suicide attempts linked to legalization of same-sex marriage." In this article, Davis reports that lesbian, gay, and bisexual students feel safer and report better mental health indicators in states where marriage equality has been achieved, as evidenced by a 14% drop in suicide attempts among lesbian, gay, and bisexual teenagers that is linked to states that have legalized same-sex marriage.[57] Rights- and policy-oriented changes do make improvements in aspects of the lives of some queer and trans students.

The federal enforcement of Title IX gender equity provisions in the U.S. to enable transgender students to use bathroom and change-room facilities consistent with their affirmed gender identities, promised by the Obama White House, signaled to trans people of all ages that we matter and that hatred and fearmongering should not guide policies that concern us. The subsequent change in tone from the White House emboldened anti-trans and anti-LGBT rhetoric and policy making. This shift speaks to the value of mobilizing rights as part of a broad-based anti-oppression strategy to empower transgender kids. In the final section of this chapter, I outline the general principles of a strategy that leverages rights within an anti-oppression model of transformational social change to reduce the precarity of *all* transgender kids.

Transforming Disabling/Oppressive Environments and Building Agency

The stories about the suffering and pleasure of trans kids that I have documented in this book reveal the importance of gender self-determination for all kids, the specific harms experienced by trans kids as a result of exposure to cisgender-normative environments and trans-oppressive policies and practices, and the ways in which multiple bases of oppression combine to render some trans kids more precarious.

Neither Wren, who is alive, nor Finn, who is no longer alive, could see a future for themselves as trans people. Their assessment of reality is chilling but instructive and guides me in making recommendations for empowering particularly precarious trans kids. Social movements dedicated to supporting trans kids need to focus on the needs of the most precarious by combining work to achieve specific measures to enable gender self-determination with a focus on transforming environments to meaningfully support all kids. In contrast to the more typical subtext of trans kids as relatively privileged, we need to keep the most precarious trans kids in mind in our social change efforts. What are the forces and structures that are currently disempowering *these* kids? How do forces of oppression relating to racism, poverty, colonialism, and sexism, for example, combine with imposed gender systems to place some transgender kids in particular at terrible risk. This work occurs within a context where even relatively privileged trans kids are incredibly vulnerable. But radical change will require social movements on behalf of trans kids to build powerful coalitions with other marginalized communities to protect the many vulnerable kids in our midst and the vulnerable adults they will grow up to be. As Kimberley Manning observes, "Under the glare of the media spotlight personal testimonials can contribute to the erasure of some trans* lives: it can become easy to lose sight of the struggles of parents who may not teach at a university, for example, and of the racialized transgender kids who are at far greater risk of violence than are our own white children."[58]

For the 1995 co-authored book *In School: Our Kids, Our Teachers, Our Classrooms*, former Canadian National Hockey League star Ken Dryden spent a year observing in a Canadian high school. Through this process, he determined that education was being delivered to those he called "the front-row kids" by teachers who, for the most part, had been front row kids themselves. Dryden saw "back-row kids" engaging via resistance and so worried the most about the "middle-row kids," whose educational needs were being neglected. He advocated restructuring public education to specifically target middle-row kids.[59] I see an important parallel for movements in support of trans kids. The visible kids are the ones with the most support, yet even with this support, they are very vulnerable. But centering social change efforts around these kids will not produce a sufficient increase in life chances for the most precarious trans kids. If instead we direct our social change efforts to increasing the agency of the most precarious trans kids, this will incorporate the gender self-determination needs of more privileged trans kids.

We must invest culturally and materially in the most vulnerable kids and their families, by establishing a baseline of security for all not only by reversing cuts to social services, school budgets, community centers, and healthcare services but by recommitting to and radically expanding a welfare state model. Components of this model include guaranteed housing and basic income for all, a public not-for-profit model of healthcare, and equitable nation-to-nation relationships with Indigenous peoples that include reparations for land theft.

Key points of contact between trans kids—apparent or nonapparent—and the public sector include education, the healthcare system, social services for children and families, the criminal justice system, and community centers. In general, we should advocate for the training of public-sector service providers to adopt gender- and sexual-diversity inclusion and affirming approaches and to be able to identify and intervene on behalf of kids who are experiencing gender coercion or anti-gay or anti-trans peer or adult aggression. Identifying basic needs and ensuring that they are available to all is a core component of a broad-based anti-oppression agenda.

As I see it, we have four key tasks. First, we must find ways to put pressure on social institutions and spaces to generate room for all kids to determine their own gender identities within a wider range of possibilities. Second, we must strive to ensure that gender-affirming healthcare becomes available to everyone. Third, we need to target gender systems for dismantlement while respecting and supporting people for whom binary gender identity has resonance. Finally, and most importantly, the most precarious trans kids need to be at the center of all our social change efforts: this can be accomplished only through a redistribution of cultural and material resources and the abolition of incarceration as a system of social control. It is beyond the scope of this book to engage in a discussion of how to radically reform criminal justice and prison systems, but I and other prison abolitionists emphasize that punishment regimes are the wrong end of the social stick to invest in: incarcerating nonviolent members of vulnerable communities reinforces the vulnerability of those communities and hence the precarity of trans kids. But the institutional and cultural shift necessary to decrease the precarity of trans kids directly addresses many of the primary factors that determine the likelihood that one will spend time in prison. Anti-racist and anti-poverty activists have long documented the role of oppression, poverty, and trauma in leading to the criminalization of already vulnerable people and the use of state violence and imprisonment as tools of containment and social control. A radical shift away from punishment and toward intense social and material investment in children to protect them from abuse, coercion, and violence is the most effective way to empower transgender kids.

Long-term goals for transforming harmful environments include removing gender as a mandatory identity category for government documentation, investing cultural and material resources heavily in the most vulnerable children, providing safety nets for all community members to ensure a baseline standard of living above the poverty level, transforming inequitable and colonial relationships with Indigenous peoples, ensuring access to gender-affirming healthcare within the context of a no-barrier public healthcare model more generally, abolishing prisons, and engineering a cultural shift away from practices that naturalize and reinscribe human hierarchies toward egalitarian patterns of interaction and decision making that by necessity include an open-ended gender spectrum. Thinking in terms of the most precarious transgender kids is a powerful orientation for a vision of a more just and equitable future for all of us.

* * *

When I traveled by car from Canada to the U.S. in 2016, a Euro-Canadian, visibly gender-nonconforming, middle-class, designated female at birth, nonbinary, trans masculine person, with my Black Canadian daughter in the car, I felt confident in my own power in the world—so confident that when I realized I had forgotten my passport, I didn't panic. I explained to my daughter that I was optimistic we would be let through, but I was careful to point out that this would be because of my whiteness and visible class privilege and that—unjust as it is—it would be unsafe for her to approach the border with the same sense of entitlement when she is old enough to travel on her own. As I expected, the border agent allowed me to enter the U.S. on the basis of my British Columbia driver's license alone. This is what entitlement *feels* like: confidence, positive expectation, legitimacy. I want this for all of us.

As I prepared to undertake a subsequent cross-border trip with my daughter in 2017, just after the election of Trump, I worried about my phone being searched, about my relationship with my daughter being questioned by border guards, about my "gender issues." I was anxious about the trip and anxious about the future. Nothing untoward happened that day, but the experience of anxiety was significant in itself. I realized I had gotten used to being seen as respectable.

The first Sunday after the election, the Black American preacher at Mount Zion Baptist Church in Seattle, Washington, delivered a powerful sermon about the necessity of principled action for social justice. Speaking to a primarily Black congregation that had experienced so much oppression, he acknowledged the temptation to give in to cynicism and hopelessness. Instead of giving up, however, he urged the congregation to go beyond hope to engage in the "politics of the broken-hearted: to stand in the tragic gap between cynicism and idealism." I believe that gap is where most parents of particularly precarious kids live.

I came to parenting with a keen commitment to make space for my children to resist the constraints of gender and racism and to let their hearts grow big with self-regard and kindness for others. The research and advocacy I do on behalf of trans kids comes from places of hurt, regret, and desire for redemption in my own history, and in this sense, it is extraordinarily selfish. I wish I had been allowed to be, and had the courage and support to be, a happier and kinder child and young person, but in parenting and interacting with kids to enable them to be authentic, happier, and kinder than I was, I find my own tragic gap and the core political and intellectual purpose of my mature years as a scholar.

I find it heartbreaking that Wren sees no future for herself as a black trans woman. But I see flashes of possibility and resilience in her. When we were talking about the difficulties involved in being different, Wren observed that these same difficulties can be gifts. So I asked her if she thinks being trans is a gift. This is what she said: "I've heard of gifted as in magical—like mutant. If you're transgender, you are basically kind of like a mutant. There are things that are harder for you, but there are things that you can really do and are really amazing. Like you're special in your own special way. Like you're an X-Man." I hope that Wren will someday find a way to claim all of herself. For all I know, she will do this by coming to see herself, literally, as some kind of an *ex-man*. But it is not enough for us to hope that she and other trans kids are able to find this space: we have to go beyond hope and build a big enough lifeboat for all of them—and, by extension, all of us.

ACKNOWLEDGMENTS

Over the past few years, I have noticed a change in my reading habits: I now begin each book or article with the acknowledgments. This is because they allow me to see the author both in context and as a person. Similarly, I wrote this book as a member of a number of overlapping kinship networks and communities, and I wish here to honor the people who hold me up, keep me grounded, educate and challenge me, and make space for my work.

My editor, Ilene Kalish, believed in this project from the outset and helped me in all phases of the work. She set high standards and was invested in my success. I am incredibly lucky to have had her stewardship and encouragement. Shari Dworkin and Jodi O'Brien offered early encouragement and ongoing support and directed me to Ilene Kalish and NYU Press. What a gift! I owe a huge debt of gratitude to Jane Ward and Georgiann Davis, who, as reviewers, were the absolute model of outstanding academic peer review: deeply engaged with the work and generous with constructive feedback that pushed me in all the right ways.

Delia Douglas, Michael Hathaway, Jenny Shaw, Wendy Chan, Gwen Bird, and Nadine Boulay read earlier versions of the work and gave me encouragement and valuable feedback. I am specifically grateful to Delia Douglas for generously pushing me to address racism and colonialism in more meaningful ways. This has profoundly shaped my scholarship. Kathleen Millar and Jenny Shaw were particularly helpful as I worked to theorize precarity. Amanda Watson helped me integrate theorizing relating to affective labor to describe the gendered nature of reproductive care work. Ken Clement and Jack Saddleback were generous with their time in sharing their insights about the particular challenges experienced by two-spirit and gender-nonconforming Indigenous kids. Wallace Wong shared important insights from his clinical practice with trans kids and encouraged me to write this book. Patti Bacchus helped me understand school board policies relating to LGBT kids. Andrea Fatona assisted me with appropriate terminology and provided a valuable sounding board for making sense of the complex relationships relating to racialization and transness. barbara findlay filled in gaps in my understanding of legal matters relating to trans issues in Canada, while Asaf Orr and Helen Carroll did so for the USA. Jennifer Marchbank, Lindsey Freeman, Jessi Jackson, Kari Lerum, Dara Culhane, Amie McLean, and Kathleen Millar assured me that my work was important and bolstered my resilience when challenges emerged. Marina Morrow, Brian Burtch, Sharalyn Jordan, Jennifer Marchbank, Rodney Hunt, Elizabeth Saewyc, Mary Ann Saunders, Brenda Jamer, Jennifer Thomas, and Megan Simon helped me get a research program on trans kids under way. Jennifer Marchbank, Sharalyn Jordan, and Nadine Boulay have been generous and inspiring colleagues in our shared project relating to supports for trans kids in the Greater Vancouver area. Bev Neufeld provided encouragement and expertise around grant writing, while Megan Simon was totally indispensable in our eventual success in securing a major grant. Suzanne Norman has been my go-to person for questions around publishing. Jennifer Breakspear, while executive director of Qmunity, worked with me to get a community-based research project under way that paved the way for this book. Tiffany Muller-Myrdahl provided peer support around developing a writing timeline. Nadine Boulay and Alex Werier assisted with the nuts and bolts of preparing the manuscript.

A number of scholars with particular expertise relating to transgender kids influenced my work and were valuable and generous sounding boards. They include Cindy Holmes, Kimberley Manning, Jake Pyne, Elizabeth Meyer, Annie Pullen Sansfacon, Jennifer Marchbank, Karl Bryant, Julie Temple Newhook, and Julian Gill-Peterson. In addition, four parents of trans kids thoughtfully shared feedback with me about some of the conclusions I came to in a talk I gave relating to the book.

The CRIRAFETS (Critical Race and Feminist Technoscience Reading Group), consisting of Kathleen Millar, Michael Hathaway, Stacy Pigg, Coleman Nye, Jessi Jackson, Lindsey Freeman, Amanda Watson, and Nick Scott, provided intellectual companionship during a pivotal year of writing.

The Canadian Institute for Health Research, the Social Sciences and Humanities Research Council of Canada, and Simon Fraser University's Faculty of Arts and Social Sciences provided funds in support of my research. SFU's Office of the Vice-President, Research provided funds to assist with preparing the manuscript for publication. The Department of Sociology & Anthropology at Simon Fraser University continues to provide an encouraging environment for critical teaching and scholarship. My own office perches on the end of the hallway of the Department of Gender, Sexuality and Women's Studies. In addition to providing my research project on trans kids with office space, they have welcomed me as their own for years now. I have benefited immeasurably from their warmth and goodwill.

Marilyn Gates, you fed my resilience first when supreme good fortune landed me in your undergraduate class in 1986 and then as a colleague, when you told me to write from the gut. Your fingerprints are all over this manuscript.

Kendry, you made me a mom. Your arrival was the beginning of the best part of my life, and your companionship at close to 20 academic conferences has been such a joy. You inspire me with your courage. Langston, I love how hard we can laugh at the same thing without ever having to say anything. Thank you for all the elephants, all the hugs, and all the baseball games. Hanna, you gave me enough time to get it right. Thank you so much for that. I love to love the dog with you. Charlie, Jack, and Thunder, you have made my office furry enough to feel like home over the years. And dog kisses are magic.

Gwen, my biggest thanks and appreciation are reserved for you: first, for all the practical labor you dedicated to enabling me, otherwise known as "the grumpy and demanding houseguest" that you put up with off and on for three years, to write this book; second, and most importantly, for the emotional labor you dedicate to me and to our children—to this quirky little family we built and hold together. This has been the real difference maker. Your steadfast love and belief in me allowed me to open a vein and let this book pour out. I can never thank you enough—but I will try. One vacation at a time . . . one retirement plan at a time . . .

APPENDIX A

Recommendations

Immediate and significant harm reduction for trans kids can be achieved via short-term goals/interventions with regard to key points of contact between kids, their parents, and the public sector. Many of them target kids as a whole for benefit; this is necessary given what we know about the invisibility of many transgender kids, race- and class-based differences among trans kids, and the harm that restrictive and sexist gender categories inflict on the many kids who would not categorize themselves as trans or gender nonconforming.

SCHOOLS
- Transition school spaces and practices away from sex/gender categories
- Integrate gender- and sexuality-inclusive sex and gender education curricula into the mainstream to support gender self-determination for all
- Address sexism, racism, and other bases of oppression by integrating an anti-oppression approach into the school curriculum
- Invest more resources into schools to enable them to be sites of individual and community empowerment

BATHROOMS, LOCKER ROOMS, AND SPORTS
- Provide low-barrier public bathroom access for everyone—all gender, all age, all color, all ability, all neighborhood, all income
- Provide all-gender multiuser and single-user bathroom and change-room facilities and educate people of all ages about bathroom and change-room etiquette
- Prioritize no-user-fee, sex-integrated sport and recreational opportunities for people of all ages and incorporate egalitarian values in the organization and culture of these activities

- Eliminate male-only sex-segregated sport at all levels of play while maintaining girl- and women-only sporting spaces with no-questions-asked trans-inclusive boundaries as an interim measure
- Invest public funds in community-based sport and recreation programs rather than elite athletics

PARENT ACTIVISM

In outlining recommendations for parent activism, I wish to acknowledge that much of this work is already being undertaken and that I am highlighting the importance of certain kinds of action rather than pretending to offer instructions.

- Embrace open-ended gender self-determination for everyone
- Engage in parent-to-parent peer support
- Have as a central goal the transitioning of environments away from binary gender systems and attendant systems and cultures of patriarchy and misogyny
- Form coalitions with other marginalized groups to decrease the precarity of all kids
- Fight for the expansion of public resources accessible to all kids and their families: shelter, food, education, recreation, child care, social welfare, citizenship
- Pool resources (cultural and material) and work very consciously to address socioeconomic barriers to parent participation

AFFIRMING HEALTHCARE

- Develop a public-health model of all-gender trans-affirming medicalization (low-barrier access) in the context of a public-health delivery model in general (one tier for everyone)
- Lower the age of consent to lessen the social subordination of children and young people
- Transition social spaces and institutions away from sex/gender categories

APPENDIX B

Resources

TEXTS

Young-Adult Fiction / Personal Memoir

Coyote, Ivan E. *One in Every Crowd*. Vancouver, BC: Arsenal Pulp, 2012.

Gino, Alex. *George*. New York: Scholastic, 2015.

Gold, Rachel. *Being Emily*. Vancouver, BC: Arsenal Pulp, 2012.

Kulkin, Susan. *Beyond Magenta: Transgender Teens Speak Out*. Somerville, MA: Candlewick, 2014.

Lowrey, Sassafras. *Lost Boi*. Vancouver, BC: Arsenal Pulp, 2015.

———. *Roving Pack*. Vancouver, BC: Arsenal Pulp, 2012.

Peters, Julie Anne. *Luna*. Vancouver, BC: Arsenal Pulp, 2006.

Spoon, Rae. *First Spring Grass Fire*. Vancouver, BC: Arsenal Pulp, 2012.

Wood, Jennie. *A Boy like Me*. United States: 215 Ink, 2014.

Children's Books

Beam, Cris. *I Am J*. Boston: Little, Brown, Books for Young Readers, 2011.

Bladacchino, Christine. *Morris Micklewhite and the Tangerine Dress*. Toronto: Groundwood Books, 2014.

Coyle, Carmela LaVigna, and Mike Gordon. *Do Princesses Wear Hiking Boots?* New York: Cooper Square, 2003.

Coyote, Ivan E. *Tomboy Survival Guide*. Vancouver, BC: Arsenal Pulp, 2016.

Garvin, Jeff. *Symptoms of Being Human*. New York: Balzer + Bray, 2016.

Girard, M.-E. *Girl Mans Up*. New York: HarperCollins, 2016.

Goto, Hiromi. *Half World*. Toronto: Razorbill Canada, 2009.

———. *The Water of Possibility*. Regina, SK: Coteau Books, 2001.

Hall, Michael. *Red: A Crayon's Story*. New York: Greenwillow Books, 2015.

Herthel, Jessica, and Jazz Jennings. *I Am Jazz*. New York: Dial Books, 2014.

Hoffman, Sarah, and Ian Hoffman. *Jacob's New Dress*. Park Ridge, IL: Albert Whitman, 2014.

Kilodavis, Cheryl, and Suzanne DeSimone. *My Princess Boy*. New York: Aladdin, 2010.

Thom, Kai Cheng. *A Place Called No Homeland*. Vancouver, BC: Arsenal Pulp, 2017.

Wittlinger, Ellen. *Parrotfish*. New York: Simon and Schuster Books for Young Readers, 2007.

Yolen, Jae, and Heidi E. Y. Stemple. *Not All Princesses Dress in Pink*. New York: Simon and Schuster Books for Young Readers, 2010.

Resources for Trans Kids

Andrews, Arin. *Some Assembly Required: The Not-So-Secret Life of a Transgender Teen*. New York: Simon and Schuster Books for Young Readers, 2014.

Bornstein, Kate. *My Gender Workbook: How to Become a Real Man, a Real Woman, the Real You, or Something Else Entirely*. New York: Routledge, 2013.

Bornstein, Kate, and Sara Quin. *Hello Cruel World: 101 Alternatives to Suicide for Teens, Freaks, and Other Outlaws*. New York: Seven Stories, 2006.

Egale Canada Human Rights Trust. "Two Spirits, One Voice." ("A community based initiative that seeks to bolster supports for persons that identify both as LGBTQ and Indigenous—Two Spirit people. Funded through the Ministry of Community Safety and Correctional Services, this program works with educators, healthcare workers, law enforcement and other community service providers.")

Jennings, Jazz. *Being Jazz: My Life as a (Transgender) Teen*. New York: Crown Books for Young Readers, 2016.

Pessin-Whedbee, Brook, and Naomi Bardoff. *Who Are You? The Kid's Guide to Gender Identity*. London: Jessica Kingsley, 2016.

Sharman, Zena, ed. *The Remedy: Queer and Trans Voices on Health and Health Care*. Vancouver, BC: Arsenal Pulp, 2016.

Stigma and Resilience among Vulnerable Youth Centre. *Canadian Transgender Youth Health Survey*. Vancouver, BC: Stigma and Resilience among Vulnerable Youth Centre, 2013. (National survey with Canadian youth who identify as transgender or gender-queer and are between the ages of 14 and 25, based on 900 responses from transgender youth from all provinces and territories except Nunavut and the Yukon.)

Taylor, Catherine G., and Tracey Peter. *Every Class in Every School: Final Report on the First National Climate Survey on Homophobia, Biphobia, and Transphobia in Canadian Schools*. Toronto: Egale Canada Human Rights Trust, 2012.

Testa, Rylan Jay, and Deborah Coolhart. *The Gender Quest Workbook: A Guide for Teens and Young Adults Exploring Gender Identity*. Oakland, CA: Instant Help, 2015.

For Parents/Family

Angello, Michele, and Ali Bowman. *Raising the Transgender Child: A Complete Guide for Parents, Families, and Caregivers*. Berkeley, CA: Seal, 2016.

Brill, Stephanie A., and Lisa Kenney. *The Transgender Teen: A Handbook for Parents and Professionals Supporting Transgender and Non-Binary Teens*. Jersey City, NJ: Cleis, 2016.

Brill, Stephanie A., and Rachel Pepper. *The Transgender Child*. San Francisco: Cleis, 2008.

Duron, Lori. *Raising My Rainbow: Adventures in Raising a Fabulous, Gender Creative Son*. New York: Broadway Books, 2013.

Ehrensaft, Diane, and Edgardo Menvielle. *Gender Born, Gender Made: Raising Health Gender-Nonconforming Children*. 3rd rev. ed. New York: The Experiment, 2011.

Ehrensaft, Diane, and Norman Spack. *The Gender Creative Child*. New York: The Experiment, 2016.

Erikson-Schroth, Laura, and Jennifer Finney Boylan, eds. *Trans Bodies, Trans Selves: A Resource for the Transgender Community*. New York: Oxford University Press, 2014.

Evans, Cheryl B. *I Promised Not to Tell: Raising a Transgender Child*. Self-published, available on Amazon, 2016.

Hubbard, Eleanor A., and Cameron T. Whitley. *Trans-Kin: A Guide for Family and Friends of Transgender People*. Boulder, CO: Bolder, 2012.

Kane, Emily W. *The Gender Trap: Parents and the Pitfalls of Raising Boys and Girls*. New York: NYU Press, 2012.

Kreiger, Irwin. *Helping Your Transgender Teen: A Guide for Parents*. Ashford, CT: Genderwise, 2011.

Nealy, Elijah C. *Transgender Children and Youth: Cultivating Pride and Joy with Families in Transition*. New York: Norton, 2017.

Pepper, Rachel. *Transitions of the Heart: Stories of Love, Struggle, and Acceptance by Mothers of Transgender and Gender Variant Children*. Berkeley, CA: Cleis, 2012.

Travers, Robb, Trans PULSE Project, and Canadian Electronic Library. *Impacts of Strong Parental Support for Trans Youth*. Toronto: Trans PULSE Project, 2012.

For Policy Makers/Educators

Balsam, Kimberly F., Yamile Molina, and Keren Lehavot. "Alcohol and Drug Use in Lesbian, Gay, Bisexual, and Transgender Youth and Youth Adults." In *Principles of Addiction: Comprehensive Addictive Behaviors and Disorders*, edited by Peter M. Miller et al., vol. 1, 563–574. San Diego, CA: Elsevier, 2013.

Bloomfield, Veronica E., and Marni E. Fisher, eds. *LGBTQ Voices in Education: Changing the Culture of Schooling*. New York: Routledge, 2016.

Cahill, Sean. "Black Sexual Citizenship: Understanding the Impact of Political Issues on Those at the Margins of Race, Sexuality, Gender, and Class." In *Black Sexualities: Probing Powers, Passions, Practices, and Policies*, edited by Juan Battle and Sandra L. Barnes, 190–212. New Brunswick, NJ: Rutgers University Press, 2010.

Canadian Rainbow Health Coalition, Transcend Transgender Support & Education Society, and Vancouver Coastal Health Authority. *Caring for Transgender Adolescents in B.C.: Suggested Guidelines*. Canadian Electronic Library. Saskatoon, SK: Transcent; Vancouver, BC: Vancouver Coastal Health, 2006.

Cianciotto, Jason, and Sean Cahill. "Lesbian, Gay, Bisexual, and Transgender Youth: A Critical Population." In *LGBT Youth in America's Schools*, edited by Jason Cianciotto and Sean Cahill, 9–35. Ann Arbor: University of Michigan Press, 2002.

Coupet, Sacha M. "Policing Gender on the Playground: Interests, Needs, and the Rights of Transgender and Gender Non-conforming Youth." In *Children, Sexuality, and the Law*, edited by Sacha M. Coupet and Ellen Marrus, 186–223. New York: NYU Press, 2015.

Fedders, Barbara. "Gender at the Crossroads: LGBT Youth in the Child Welfare and Juvenile Justice Systems." In *Children, Sexuality, and the Law,* edited by Sacha M. Coupet and Ellen Marrus, 224–254. New York: NYU Press, 2015.

Fisher, Emily S., and Karen Komosa-Hawkins, eds. *Creating Safe and Supportive Learning Environments: A Guide for Working with Lesbian, Gay, Bisexual, Transgender, and Questioning Youth and Families.* New York: Routledge, 2013.

Fisher, Sylvia K., Jeffery M. Poirier, and Gary M. Blau, eds. *Improving Emotional and Behavioral Outcomes for LGBT Youth: A Guide for Professionals.* Baltimore: Paul H. Brookes, 2012.

Mallon, Gerald P. *LGBTQ Youth Issues: A Practical Guide for Youth Workers Serving Lesbian, Gay, Bisexual, Transgender, and Questioning Youth.* Rev. ed. Arlington, VA: CWLA, 2010.

———, ed. *Social Work Practice with Transgender and Gender Variant Youth.* London: Routledge, 2009.

McDermott, Elizabeth, and Katrina Roen. "Troubling Gender Norms: Gender Non-Conforming Youth" and "Trans and Genderqueer Youth Online." Chapters 4 and 5 in *Queer Youth, Suicide, and Self-Harm: Troubled Subjects, Troubling Norms,* 62–102. London: Palgrave Macmillan, 2016.

Meyer, Elizabeth, and Annie Pullen Sansfaçon, eds. *Supporting Transgender and Gender Creative Youth: Schools, Families, and Communities in Action.* New York: Peter Lang, 2013.

Miller, S. J. *Teaching, Affirming, and Recognizing Trans and Gender Creative Youth: A Queer Literacy Framework.* Queer Studies and Education. London: Palgrave Macmillan, 2016.

Nova Scotia Department of Education and Early Childhood Development. *Guidelines for Supporting Transgender and Gender-Nonconforming Students / Student Services.* Halifax: Nova Scotia Department of Education and Early Childhood Development, 2014.

Orr, Asaf, and Joel Baum. *Schools in Transition: A Guide for Supporting Transgender Students in K–12 Schools.* American Civil Liberties Union, Gender Spectrum, Human Rights Campaign, National Center for Lesbian Rights, and National Educational Association, 2016.

Pullen, Christopher. *Queer Youth and Media Culture.* Basingstoke, UK: Palgrave Macmillan, 2014.

Russell, Stephen T., and Jennifer K. McGuire. "The School Climate for Lesbian, Gay, Bisexual, and Transgender (LGBT) Students." In *Toward Positive Youth Development: Transforming Schools and Community Programs,* edited by Marybeth Shinn and Hiorkazu Yoshikawa, 133–149. New York: Oxford University Press, 2008.

Russell, Stephen T., Amanda M. Pollitt, and Jennifer M. Elsevier. "School Environment for LGBTQ/Sexual Minority Youth." In *International Encyclopedia of the Social and Behavioral Sciences,* edited by James D. Wright, 86–90. London: Elsevier, 2015.

Sadowski, Michael. "Respecting the 'T' in LGBTQ." In *Safe Is Not Enough: Better Schools for LGBTQ Students.* Cambridge, MA: Harvard Education Press, 2013.

Simkins, Sandra. "The Special Needs of Lesbian, Gay, Bisexual, and Transgender Youth." In *When Kids Get Arrested: What Every Adult Should Know*, 175–178. New Brunswick, NJ: Rutgers University Press, 2009.

Taylor, Catherine G., and Tracey Peter. *Every Class in Every School: Final Report on the First National Climate Survey on Homophobia, Biphobia, and Transphobia in Canadian Schools*. Toronto: Egale Canada Human Rights Trust, 2012.

Vaccaro, Annemarie, Gerri August, and Megan S. Kennedy. *Safe Spaces: Making Schools and Communities Welcoming to LGBT Youth*. Santa Barbara, CA: Praeger, 2012.

WEBSITES

Egale Canada Human Rights Trust: http://egale.ca
Addresses LGBTQI2S human rights

Families in TRANSition: A Resource Guide for Parents of Trans Youth:
www.rainbowhealthontario.ca/resources/families-in-transition-
a-resource-guide-for-parents-of-trans-youth/

The first comprehensive Canadian publication to address the needs of parents and families supporting their trans children; summarizes the experiences, strategies, and successes of a working group of community consultants—researchers, counselors, parents, and advocates, as well as trans youth themselves; provides the stories of parents and youth along with practical and sensitive parent-to-parent and professional therapeutic advice; written and published by CTYS (Central Toronto Youth Services) with the support and collaboration of many community members and organizations, especially P-FLAG Toronto (Parents Family and Friends of Lesbians and Gays) and Transceptance (a Toronto support group for parents of trans youth)

Gender Creative Kids: http://gendercreativekids.ca
Provides resources for supporting and affirming gender-creative kids within their families, schools, and communities, based in Canada

Gender Fork: http://genderfork.com
"A supportive community for the expression of identities across the gender spectrum"

Gender Odyssey: www.genderodyssey.org
Provides education and support of families raising gender-variant, gender-nonconforming, gender-fluid, cross-gender, and transgender children and adolescents; holds annual conferences

Gender Spectrum: www.genderspectrum.org
Provides education, training, and support to help create a gender sensitive and inclusive environment for all children and teens

LGBTQ Resources and College Affordability: www.affordablecolleges.com/resources/
lgbtq-college-resources/
A guide to LGBTQ colleges that breaks down the individual components that make a campus LGBTQ friendly and is intended to help you navigate potential schools

NCLR: National Center for Lesbian Rights: www.nclrights.org/our-work/transgender-law/transgender-youth/
Provides resources for transgender youth
PFLAG Transgender Network: www.pflag.org/transgender
Trans Active: www.transactiveonline.org
An internationally recognized nonprofit focused on serving the diverse needs of transgender and gender-nonconforming youth, their families, and allies
TransAthlete.com
Transgender Equality: www.transequality.org
Trans Kids Purple Rainbow Foundation: www.transkidspurplerainbow.org
An organization supporting trans youth—in schools, in the media, and against homelessness
Trans Parenting: www.transparenting.com
Provides support and educational resources to parents and their advocates raising a gender-independent child
TransParents: http://transparentusa.org
"Provides support, information and resources to help parents confidently navigate their gender independent child's personal journey of self-discovery to authentic living"
Trans Student Educational Resources: www.transstudent.org
Trans Youth Equality Foundation: www.transyouthequality.org
Provides education, advocacy, and support for transgender and gender-nonconforming children and youth and their families; based in Portland, Maine; includes a podcast, TransWaves
TransYouth Family Allies (TYFA): www.imatyfa.org
"Empowers children and families by partnering with educators, service providers, and communities, to develop supportive environments where gender may be expressed and respected with a vision towards a society free of suicide and violence in which all children are respected and celebrated"

FILMS

Growing Up Trans. The Passionate Eye. Canadian Broadcasting Corporation, 2016.
Pink Boy. Documentary by Eric Rockey. 2016. http://pinkboyfilm.com
Transforming Gender. Doc Zone. Canadian Broadcasting Corporation, 2015. www.cbc.ca/doczone/episodes/transforming-gender
The Youth and Gender Media Project. New Day Films, 2011.
Four short films "that capture the diversity and complexity of gender nonconforming youth. These award-winning films provide students and educators with unique tools to explore critical questions about gender identity and family acceptance, and are ideal for discussions about bullying and inclusiveness."
- *Creating Gender Inclusive Schools*
- *I'm Just Anneke*
- *The Family Journey: Raising Gender Nonconforming Children*
- *Becoming Johanna*

APPENDIX C

The Kids

Name	Age	Ethnicity/racialization	Country
Alicia	17	Euro-Canadian	U.S.
Cameron	18	Euro-Canadian	Canada
Canaan	18	Euro-Canadian	Canada
Caroline	6	Black American	U.S.
Cassandra	4	Euro-Canadian	Canada
Cody	5	Euro-American	U.S.
Cory Oskam	16	Euro-Canadian	Canada
Dave	17	Euro-Canadian	Canada
Davis	8; 11	Asian American	U.S.
Dylan	15	Euro-American	U.S.
Enrique	17	Latinx	U.S.
Esme	10	Euro-Canadian	Canada
Finn	14	Euro-American	U.S.
Frank	13	Euro-Canadian	Canada
Greg	13	Euro-Canadian	Canada
Helen	16	Euro-Canadian	Canada
Hunter	13	Indigenous	Canada
Jin	13	Euro-Canadian	Canada
Kidd	18	Black/Native American	U.S.
Lennox	11	Indigenous	Canada
Martine	12	Euro-Asian Canadian	Canada
Michael	17	Asian Canadian	Canada
Nathan	15; 17	Euro-Canadian/Indigenous	Canada
Nick	11	Asian Canadian	Canada
Peter	6	Euro-Canadian	Canada
Quinn	18	Indigenous/Euro-Canadian	Canada
Ray-Ray	16	Euro-Canadian	Canada

Name	Age	Ethnicity/racialization	Country
Sasha	6	Euro-Canadian	Canada
Sean	9	Euro-American/Canadian	Canada
Silver	6; 8	Indigenous/Euro-Canadian	Canada
Simon	7; 9	Euro-Canadian	Canada
Stef	17	Euro-Asian Canadian	Canada
Taya	16	Euro-Canadian	Canada
Tru Wilson		Black Canadian/ Euro-Canadian/Indigenous	Canada
Wren	9; 11	Black Canadian	Canada
Ziggy	15	Euro-American	U.S.

GLOSSARY

AFFIRMED SEX/GENDER; SELF-AFFIRMED SEX/GENDER: the sex/
gender one self-defines as

AFFIRMING HEALTHCARE; GENDER-AFFIRMING HEALTHCARE;
TRANS-AFFIRMING HEALTHCARE: any combination of hormone blockers, cross-sex hormones, and surgery to achieve physical
consistency with one's self-defined sex/gender, and/or mental health
support to address the negative consequences of trans oppression

AGENDER: a descriptor for a person who does not identify according
to sex/gender systems; includes nonbinary gender identities and not
identifying with the gender system at all

ALOSEXUAL: people for whom sexual pleasure is a solitary pursuit, if
indeed it is pursued at all

ASEXUAL: someone who does not experience sexual arousal/
attraction

ASSEMBLAGE: a sociohistorical convergence of hierarchy and
oppression

ASSIGNED SEX/GENDER AT BIRTH: a doctor's medical pronounce-
ment that "it's a girl" or "it's a boy," which is the basis of legal sex
identity, the binary-normative sex/gender category imposed on
infants

ASSIMILATION: the ability of a trans person to be read in social situations as cisgender (also see STEALTH)

BINARY NORMATIVITY: the assumption that there are only two sexes
and that these two sexes are markedly different

BINARY SEX/GENDER SYSTEMS: sociopolitical and economic systems based on a binary view of sex

BINDER/BINDING: the practice of using tensor bandages or custom-
ized compression garments to flatten breasts to create the impression of a more typically masculine chest structure

BIOPOLITICS: the integration of biology with political power

BIOPOWER: the employment of population management for political ends; the political control of bodies

BLACK: racialized members of the African diaspora

BOTTOM SURGERY: removal of uterus (hysterectomy) and ovaries (ovariectomy) and surgical construction of a penis (phalloplasty) to create more typically male genitals; surgical removal of the penis and construction of the vagina (vaginoplasty) to create more typically female genitals

CHILDHOOD: a socially constructed stage of life from birth to young adulthood

CHILDREN: the demographic group from birth to age 15

CISGENDER: the state of correspondence between assigned sex/gender at birth and self-identity; a normative category

CIS-SEXISM: the assumption that congruence between assigned sex/gender at birth and self-identity is the norm

CONVERSION THERAPY; CORRECTIVE/REPARATIVE THERAPY: psychological/psychiatric treatment designed to "cure" gay, lesbian, and trans and gender-nonconforming people

CROSS-SEX HORMONES: hormones associated with the "opposite" sex/gender category that are sometimes employed by trans people to achieve greater physical consistency with their self-defined sex/gender or to reduce vulnerability to discrimination and violence

DEAD NAME: the inappropriately gendered name imposed on and subsequently repudiated by a trans person

DEMI-ROMANTIC: romantic attachment based on the prior establishment of emotional intimacy

DEMI-SEXUAL: sexual attraction based on the prior establishment of emotional intimacy

DIAGNOSTIC AND STATISTICAL MANUAL (*DSM*): the "bible" of the American Psychiatric Association; the central diagnostic and treatment resource for the psychiatric and psychological professions

EURO-AMERICAN: a person living in the United States who is racialized as white/has European ancestors

EURO-CANADIAN: a person living in Canada who is racialized as white/has European ancestors

EUROCENTRIC: institutions and/or belief systems that place people of European heritage who are racialized as white at the center of leadership, knowledge production, and importance; typically associated with a view of whiteness as consistent with civilization and dominant notions of rational progress

FEMALE TO MALE (FTM): a trans person assigned female at birth who has medically and/or socially transitioned to a male identity

GAY-STRAIGHT ALLIANCE (GSA): clubs or student groups designed to reduce homo-negativity and support LGBT students, most typically at the high school level

GENDER CONFIRMATION SURGERY: surgical procedures that enable the body to conform to gender identity, including but not limited to chest reconstruction, genital reconstruction, and facial reconstruction; also referred to by the less preferred terminology of "sex reassignment surgery"

GENDER CONFORMING: consistent with normative binary sex/gender stereotypes or characteristics

GENDER DYSPHORIA (GD): the distress or dissonance that people of all ages may experience when their sex/gender identity is in conflict with the sex/gender identity they were assigned at birth or that their physical characteristics signal to others; a somewhat less pathologizing but still binary-oriented diagnosis that replaced GIDC (see below) in the fifth edition of the *DSM* in 2013

GENDER ESSENTIALISM: the assumption that biology plays a significant determining role in gender identity, which does not vary from one sociohistorical context to another

GENDER FLUID: a descriptor for someone for whom gender varies over time or an identity that resists binary categorization

GENDER IDENTITY DISORDER IN CHILDREN (GIDC): a diagnosis whose inclusion in the third edition of the *Diagnostic and Statistical Manual* in 1980 reflected the formal medicalization of gender nonconformity in children; a diagnosis whose focus is children who fail to conform to the sex/gender assigned to them at birth

GENDER LIMINAL: a descriptor for someone whose sex/gender identity is ambiguous (in the context of a sex/gender binary)

GENDER NEUTRAL: a descriptor for a person or place not organized according to sex/gender systems

GENDER NONCONFORMING: unwilling or unable to conform to binary sex/gender norms

GENDER QUEER; NONBINARY: someone who does not conform to binary sex/gender norms

GENDER SELF-DETERMINATION: the right of every person to know and be known according to an internal sense of gender identity

HETERONORMATIVE: people, spaces, and social practices organized on the basis of the centrality of the heterosexual couple

HOMONATIONALISM: homonormative nationalism; when privileged LGBT people express loyalty to the nation-state and/or when states position themselves as progressive on the basis of their inclusion of relatively privileged LGBT people

HOMONORMATIVITY: when more conservative/privileged LGBT people (white, wealthy, binary-gender conforming) experience social inclusion without troubling broader patterns of hierarchy and oppression

HOMOPHOBIA: fear and hatred of lesbian gay bisexual and queer people on the basis of an assumed norm of heterosexuality

HORMONE BLOCKERS: puberty-suppression therapy via medical intervention

HYPERANDROGENISM: a condition of women who are considered to have natural testosterone levels above the so-called normal female range

INDIGENOUS: the original inhabitants of a geographic territory; the preferred term for first peoples in general residing within the borders of the Canadian nation-state

INTERSEX: people whose genetic/reproductive traits defy simple binary sex categorization

LATINX: a gender-neutral ethnic descriptor for people of Latin heritage in the U.S. and Canada

MALE TO FEMALE (MTF): a trans person assigned male at birth who has medically and/or socially transitioned to a female identity

MICROAGGRESSIONS: "the death of 1,000 cuts"; daily and seemingly benign forms of oppression that, experienced collectively, produce trauma

MINORITY STRESS: the mental health consequences of oppression

MISGENDER: to apply a sex/gender descriptor or pronoun that is inconsistent with a person's self-defined sex/gender identity

NATIVE AMERICAN: the preferred term for Indigenous/first peoples in general residing within the borders of the U.S. nation-state

NECROCAPITALISM: the relationship between death and capitalist relations of production

NECROPOLITICS: the relationship between death and political power

NECROPOWER: the relationship between death and power

NEURODIVERSITY: the recognition that neurological variation among humans is normal, in opposition to a socially constructed mental state as the norm according to which variation is measured and pathologized

NONBINARY; TRANS NONBINARY: a descriptor for someone who identifies outside binary gender systems

PANSEXUAL: a descriptor for someone who is attracted to people regardless of sex/gender identity

PASSING: the ability to be intelligible to others in terms of one's self-defined gender identity

PHALLOPLASTY: surgical construction of a penis from the patient's own living tissue

POLYAMOROUS: being capable of or desiring intimate sexual relationships with more than one partner

POLYSEXUAL: typically refers to those who are attracted to trans, nonbinary, or genderqueer people but can also refer to people who are attracted to multiple genders

PRECARIOUSNESS; PRECARITY: the fundamental vulnerability that is characteristic of human life and the ways in which this fundamental vulnerability is striated

PRONOUNS: the gendered nouns used to refer to specific persons

RACIALIZATION: the social and historical process whereby a more powerful group imposes a framework of biological inferiority onto another

SEX REASSIGNMENT SURGERY: see GENITAL CONFIRMATION SURGERY

SOCIAL TRANSITION: the process of beginning to live as the sex/gender that one self-defines as

STEALTH: descriptor for a transgender person who passes or for whom information about their transgender status is kept private

TANNER SCALE: a normative scale for measuring physiological development according to a Eurocentric binary sex model

TITLE IX: the 1972 U.S. legislation that requires all institutions receiving federal funds to maintain gender equity

TOMBOY: a masculine, gender-nonconforming, or inadequately feminine girl

TOP SURGERY: a double mastectomy and nipple grafts for a male-contoured chest; breast implants and chest reconstruction for a female-contoured chest

TRANS: short form for "transgender"

TRANS BOY: a child or young person assigned female at birth who self-defines as a boy

TRANS-EXCLUSIVE RADICAL FEMINISTS (TERFS): a conservative/trans-oppressive strain of radical feminism that views gender in essentialist terms, or as inevitably linked to the genitals one is born with, and that sees transgender women as men masquerading as women

TRANSGENDER: an umbrella term for people who defy simplistic adherence to binary sex/gender categories

TRANS GIRL: a child or young person assigned male at birth who self-defines as a girl

TRANSINCLUSION: policies and practices related to transforming trans-oppressive/binary-normative environments to include people of all genders

TRANSNORMATIVE: a descriptor for relatively privileged transgender people who are willing and able to assimilate to binary gender systems and norms without calling into question broader relations of oppression

TRANS OPPRESSION: the discrimination and harm experienced by trans and gender-nonconforming people

TRANSPHOBIA: fear and hatred directed at those who do not conform to binary sex/gender systems and a mechanism for maintaining these systems

TRANSSEXUAL: a person who medically and socially transitions from their assigned sex at birth to their self-defined sex/gender

TWO-SPIRIT: A First Nations / Indigenous / Native American term to describe a person who has both a masculine and a feminine spirit; can relate to gender nonconformity or same-sex sexuality or both

VAGINOPLASTY: surgical construction of a vagina

NOTES

INTRODUCTION

1. Witterick, "Dancing in the Eye of the Storm," 21.
2. Serano, "Detransition, Desistance, and Disinformation."
3. I rely on the theorizing of critical disability scholar Tobin Siebers, in *Disability Theory*, to use the term "disabled" to refer to the way in which built environments confer privilege on some people and act to disable others. I elaborate on this topic at greater length in chapter 1.
4. Blum-Ross, "What Does It Mean for Children to Have a 'Voice' in Research?"
5. Marten, "Childhood Studies and History," 52–53.
6. Siebers, *Disability Theory*, 28.
7. Spade, *Normal Life*, 32.
8. Hellen, "Transgender Children in Schools," 92.
9. Thomas and Thomas, *Child in America*, 301.
10. Macionis and Gerber, *Sociology*, 132.
11. Meadow, "Child," 57–59.
12. barbara findlay deliberately spells her name without capitalization.
13. Underwood, "Ms. Chatelaine."
14. Canadian Press, "Human Rights Complaint."
15. Cloutier, "Transgender Girl's Human Rights Complaint."
16. Stout, "Transgender Teen Awarded $75,000 in School Restroom Lawsuit."
17. Queer Voices, "California's Assembly Bill 1266 for Transgender Student Rights Signed."
18. For example, the San Francisco Unified School District in 2004, the Toronto School Board in 2012, the Edmonton School Board in 2011, and the Vancouver School Board in 2014.
19. The preferred identity term for the peoples who, for over 10,000 years, have occupied the continent they refer to as "Turtle Island," on which the Canadian and U.S. white settler states were established, on the Canadian side of the border is "Indigenous," while south of the border, Indigenous peoples tend to self-identify as "Native American."
20. "Latinx" is a recently introduced gender-neutral term to describe persons of Latin American descent.
21. Most kids and parents use sex and gender terminology interchangeably; for example, it is not unusual for someone to define themselves as "male" in one

moment and a "boy" in another without implying different meanings. This is not something I feel it is necessary to investigate or trouble; rather, it reflects nonacademic common language.

22. Not to mention intersex individuals, whose genitals are ambiguous as far as binary categorization goes.

23. There is a literary and popular-culture history to troubling gendered pronouns, often in feminist science fiction. Think of the opening to science fiction writer Ursula K. Le Guin's 1969 book *The Left Hand of Darkness*, "The king was pregnant" (7) and the use of "Sir" to refer to Captain Janeway on *Star Trek* and Marge Piercy's use of "per" as a replacement for "him/her" in her 1976 novel *Woman on the Edge of Time*.

24. To misgender someone is to refer to them with gendered terms or pronouns that do not correspond to their affirmed identity.

25. Kapoor and Jordan, "Introduction," 4.

26. Mills, *Sociological Imagination*, 3.

CHAPTER 1. TRANSGENDER KIDS

1. Halberstam, *Female Masculinity*; Chinn, "I Was a Lesbian Child."

2. Pyne, "Gender Independent Kids."

3. Meadow, "Child."

4. Herman et al., "Age of Individuals Who Identify as Transgender."

5. Veale et al., *Being Safe, Being Me*.

6. Taylor and Peter, *Every Class in Every School*, 23.

7. See, for example, Hellen, "Transgender Children in Schools."

8. See, for example, Grossman and D'Augelli, "Transgender Youth and Life-Threatening Behaviors."

9. Goldberg and Adriano, "I'm a Girl"

10. Butler, *Gender Trouble*, 14.

11. Fausto-Sterling, *Sexing the Body*.

12. See, for example, Connell, *Gender*; Jordan-Young, *Brain Storm*; Karkazis et al., "Out of Bounds?"

13. Castañeda, "Childhood."

14. Stryker and Currah, "General Editors' Introduction," 303.

15. Matthews, "Window on the 'New' Sociology of Childhood."

16. Harris, *Gender as Soft Assembly*, 175.

17. Marx, "Eighteenth Brumaire of Louis Bonaparte," 595.

18. Stockton, *Queer Child*, 8.

19. Stafford, *Is It Still a Boy?*, 3–4.

20. See, for example, Dowling, *Frailty Myth*; Jordan-Young, *Brain Storm*.

21. Connell, *Gender*.

22. Thorne, *Gender Play*.

23. Connell, *Gender*, 103–104.

24. Her real name, as requested.

25. Crissman et al., "Transgender Demographics."

26. See, for example, Brill and Pepper, *Transgender Child*; Brill and Kenney, *Transgender Teen*; Ehrensaft, *Gender Born, Gender Made*.

27. There is considerable debate within scientific communities about the percentage of intersex people in the overall population. Feminist science scholar Anne Fausto-Sterling, in *Sexing the Body*, estimates that 1.7% of the population is intersex, while one critique of her research, by Leonard Sax ("How Common Is Intersex?") claims that the percentage is 100 times lower than that. The United States Affiliate of the Organization of Intersex International webpage claimed the 1.7% figure in 2015.

28. National Center for Transgender Equality, "Understanding the Passport Gender Change Policy."

29. Government of British Columbia, "Change of Gender Designation."

30. An intersex birth certificate was issued recently; see Levin, "First US Person to Have 'Intersex' on Birth Certificate."

31. Government of Ontario, Ministry of Transportation, "New 'X' Gender Option Now Available."

32. Wamsley, "Oregon Adds a New Gender Option."

33. See, for example, the Gender-Free I.D. Coalition: http://gender-freeidcoalition.ca.

34. Zeidler, "Parent Fights to Omit Gender."

35. S. Mills, "Gender-Neutral Birth Certificate Fight."

36. Ranging from hormone therapy to surgery depending on jurisdiction.

37. See, for example, Burke, *Gender Shock*; Butler, *Gender Trouble*; Halberstam, *Female Masculinity*; Halberstam, *In a Queer Time and Place*; Noble, *Sons of the Movement*; Travers, "Queering Sport"; Travers and Deri, "Transgender Inclusion."

38. For example, Namaste, *Invisible Lives*; Namaste, *Sex Change, Social Change*.

39. Elliot, *Debates in Transgender, Queer, and Feminist Theory*.

40. Holman and Goldberg, "Ethical, Legal, and Psychosocial Issues."

41. Travers, "Queering Sport."

42. See, for example, Gill-Peterson, "Technical Capacities of the Body"; and Saketopoulou, "Minding the Gap."

43. Hatred of the female and the feminine; Sedgwick, *Epistemology of the Closet*.

44. Serano, "Detransition, Desistance, and Disinformation."

45. His real name, as per his mother's wishes.

46. Hormone blockers.

47. Finn died in June 2017.

48. Butler, *Frames of War*, 14.

49. Lorey, *State of Insecurity*, 10.

50. Ibid., 12.

51. Ibid., 2.

52. Foucault, *Birth of Biopolitics*.

53. Butler, *Frames of War*, 25.

54. Siebers, *Disability Theory*, 12.

55. Thobani, *Exalted Subjects*.

56. Glenn, "Settler Colonialism as Structure," 57.

57. See, for example, Gill-Peterson, "Technical Capacities of the Body"; Gosset, "Silhouettes of Defiance"; Haritaworn, "Loyal Repetitions of the Nation"; Haritaworn, Kuntsman, and Posocco, *Queer Necropolitics*; Kumashiro, *Troubling Intersections of Race and Sexuality*; Kumashiro, *Troubling Education*; Puar, *Terrorist Assemblages*; Puar, "Homonationalism as Assemblage"; Puar, "Q&A with Jasbir Puar"; Snorton and Haritaworn, "Trans Necropolitics"; Weheliye, *Habeas Viscus*.

58. Pascoe, *Dude, You're a Fag*, 10.

59. Ibid., 55.

60. See, for example, the works of Sherene Razack, Sunera Thobani, Eva Mackey, and Delia Douglas.

61. See, for example, Coulthard, *Red Skin, White Masks*; and Simpson, *Dancing on Our Turtle's Back*.

62. Crenshaw, *Fighting the Post–Affirmative Action War*; Higgenbotham, "African American Women's History"; P. Collins, *Black Feminist Thought*; P. Collins, *Black Sexual Politics*; hooks, *Feminist Theory from Margin to Center*; hooks, *Yearning*; hooks, *All about Love*; Lorde, *Sister Outsider*; McKittrick, *Sylvia Wynter*; and Williams, *Alchemy of Race and Rights*.

63. Assemblage refers to integrated systems of oppression: an intricate web of social history / social forces that surround us and impact experience in embodied ways. See, for example, Puar, *Terrorist Assemblages*.

64. Mbembe, "Necropolitics," 11.

65. Berlant, "Slow Death."

66. Gilmore, *Golden Gulag*, 28.

67. Bannerjee, "Necrocapitalism."

68. Such as colonialism, the Nazi concentration camps, apartheid, and the Israeli occupation of Gaza.

69. See, for example, Snorton and Haritaworn, "Trans Necropolitics"; Haritaworn, Kuntsman, and Posocco, *Queer Necropolitics*; Puar, *Terrorist Assemblages*.

70. Noble, *Sons of the Movement*; Noble, "My Own Set of Keys"; Noble, "Our Bodies Are Not Ourselves"; Spade, *Normal Life*; Stanley, "Gender Self-Determination"; Stanley and Smith, *Captive Genders*; Stryker, "Transgender History, Homonormativity, and Disciplinarity."

71. In *The Twilight of Equality: Neoliberalism, Cultural Politics, and the Attack on Democracy*, Lisa Duggan coined the term "homonormativity" to describe "a politics that does not contest dominant heteronormative assumptions and institutions, but upholds and sustains them, while promising the possibility of a demobilized gay constituency, and a gay culture anchored in domesticity and consumption" (50). Duggan purports that visible white and/or "respectable" (middle-class consumers) LGBT individuals who conform to binary sex and gender norms have achieved rights and experience a measure of inclusion, without having unsettled the foundations of oppression.

72. Susan Stryker proposed this terminology in correspondence with Jasbir Puar; Stryker, personal communication, 2016.

73. Jasbir Puar, for example, builds on Duggan's concept of homonormativity in *Terrorist Assemblages* to describe assimilationist, rights-oriented LGBT campaigns, coining the terms "homonationalism" (homonormative nationalism) and "queer necropolitics." In this sense, previously abject but comparatively privileged (white, middle- and upper-class) queer and trans people are being "folded into life," welcomed into the nation, accorded with citizenship. From this perspective, the newly welcomed among the transgender community are more likely to be transnormative at least to some extent (binary conforming, middle class, white). Similarly, in "Settler Homonationalism: Theorizing Settler Colonialism within Queer Modernities," Scott Morgensen describes the way in which privileged LGBT subjects buy into the community as "naturalizing settler colonialism" (121).

74. Snorton and Haritaworn, "Trans Necropolitics."

75. Homonormative nationalism: Puar, *Terrorist Assemblages*.

76. In the introduction to *Queer Necropolitics*, Jin Haritaworn, Adi Kuntsman, and Silvia Posocco emphasize that "social inclusion is realized through practices of 'letting die,' that is, through dying in abandonment. Letting die, abandonment, and differential belonging are directly connected to the operations of forms of governance in late liberalism that determine some subjects as morally deserving, while simultaneously justifying punitive measures for those deemed undeserving as necessary, just, and rational" (7–8).

77. Grant et al., *Injustice at Every Turn*, 2.

78. Ibid., 29.

79. Appell, "Pre-political Child of Child-Centred Jurisprudence," 20.

80. Butler, *Frames of War*.

81. The boundary between childhood and adulthood is linked to the "age of majority," which varies from 18 to 21 depending on jurisdiction in Canada and the U.S.

82. Klocker, "Example of 'Thin' Agency," 85.

83. Pierce, "Psychiatric Problems of the Black Minority."

84. Nordmarken, "Microaggressions," 130.

85. I return to this topic in more detail in chapter 3.

86. Meiners, "Offending Children, Registering Sex."

87. Stockton, *Queer Child*, 5.

88. Carter, *Quality of Home Runs*, 23.

89. Stockton, *Queer Child*.

90. Puar, "Rethinking Homonationalism," 338.

91. Chinn, "I Was a Lesbian Child," 158.

92. See, for example, Hodgson, "Childhood of the Race"; Meiners, "Trouble with the *Child* in the Carceral State."

93. Siebers, *Disability Theory*, 288.

94. Flasher, "Adultism," 521.

95. Weheliye, *Habeas Viscus*, 4.
96. Siebers, *Disability Theory*, 281.
97. Ibid., 289.
98. Ibid., 284.
99. I address the disabling role of bathrooms and other facets of sex segregation specifically in chapter 3.
100. Siebers, *Disability Theory*, 28.
101. Snorton, comments at "Trans-of-Color Roundtable Discussion," Trans* Studies Conference, Tucson, AZ, 2016.

CHAPTER 2. SCHOOLS

1. Rubber bands were linked together and held by one girl at each end to form a modified sort of high jump. The goal was to jump over the rope of rubber bands, and you were allowed to use a foot to pull it down to jump over. It was incredibly acrobatic, and the girls who were good at it were astonishing in their athleticism. I was pretty good at it, and I missed it when I moved on to middle school, where we are all too cool to play like that anymore.
2. For example, OECD, *Equity and Quality in Education*.
3. Taylor and Peter, *Every Class in Every School*, 15–18.
4. GLSEN, *2015 National School Climate Survey*, 4–6.
5. Ibid., 5.
6. Berkowitz and Ryan, "Bathrooms, Baseball, and Bra Shopping."
7. Menvielle, "Comprehensive Program," 359.
8. Ibid., 359–360.
9. Ibid., 360.
10. Pascoe, *Dude, You're a Fag*.
11. Ibid.
12. Hellen, "Transgender Children in Schools."
13. Frank's father is no longer on the scene, and a court order prohibits him from contact.
14. See, for example, Hoffman, "Risky Investments."
15. Madigan and Gamble, *The Second Rape*.
16. Dr. Kenneth Zucker is a prominent psychiatrist specializing in the corrective treatment of trans and gender-nonconforming children. I situate Dr. Zucker in the treatment field more thoroughly in chapter 5.
17. Menvielle, "Comprehensive Program."
18. Private schools in British Columbia receive government funding and are subject to the British Columbia Human Rights Code.
19. The family decided to settle out of court rather than spend years fighting the case. They did not want to put Tru through that.
20. Asaf Orr, attorney for the National Center for Lesbian Rights, insists that transgender status is confidential medical information and should be treated by all school personnel accordingly; person communication, 2015.

21. "Two spirit" is a term embraced by a number of Indigenous communities in Canada and the United States to refer to community members who are neither male nor female or whose sexuality cannot be described as heterosexual.

22. Vancouver School Board, "ACB-R-1."

23. As it did in Vancouver and typically throughout Canada and the U.S. for LGBT-positive measures in schools.

24. Pascoe, *Dude, You're a Fag*, 166–167.

25. Meiners, "Trouble with the *Child* in the Carceral State"; Quinn and Meiners, "From Anti-Bullying Laws and Gay Marriages."

26. Meyer, *Gender and Sexual Diversity in Schools*.

CHAPTER 3. SPACES

1. This chapter is partly based on a previous chapter published in *Child's Play*, edited by Michael Messner and Michela Musto: Ann Travers, "Transgender and Gender Nonconforming Kids and the Binary Requirements of Sport Participation in North America." Since that publication, policy analysis has been updated, and additional interviews have been conducted.

2. See, for example, Fausto-Sterling, *Sexing the Body*; Karkazis et al., "Out of Bounds?"

3. Butler, *Undoing Gender*, 34.

4. Some of the authors I cite in this manuscript published their work under first names they no longer attach to themselves, and I follow their current lead in identifying them. While this frustrates bibliographic systems and sometimes makes locating a source a little less straightforward, affirming their gender self-determination and self-naming is a crucial aspect of a trans-positive politics.

5. Halberstam, *Female Masculinity*, 23.

6. Browne, "Genderism and the Bathroom Problem," 335, 336, 339 (my emphasis).

7. Ibid.; Molotch and Nolen, *Toilet*.

8. Browne, "Genderism and the Bathroom Problem," 336.

9. Lorber, *Breaking the Bowls*, 35–36.

10. H. Davis, *Beyond Trans*, 80.

11. Cavanagh, *Queering Bathrooms*; Meiners, "Offending Children, Registering Sex."

12. T. Ring, "Supreme Court to Hear Gavin Graham Case."

13. For a comprehensive overview of state attempts to pass anti-trans bathroom legislation, see Kralik, "'Bathroom Bill' Legislative Tracking."

14. Stern, "HB2 'Repeal' Bill."

15. Abramson, "North Carolina Governor."

16. The NBA announced after the partial repeal that it will hold its 2019 All-Star Game in North Carolina.

17. Stern, "HB2 'Repeal' Bill."

18. Davis and Apuzzo, "US Directs Public Schools."

19. T. Ring, "Supreme Court to Hear Gavin Graham Case."

20. Lopez, "Trump's Justice Department Just Rescinded a Memo."

21. Marimow, "Case of Virginia Transgender Teen."
22. Open Parliament, Bill C-16.
23. Ricci, "Transgender Child Told You Can't Use Girls' Bathroom."
24. "Family of Bella Burgos."
25. Quoted in Ricci, "Transgender Child Told You Can't Use Girls' Bathroom."
26. "Family of Bella Burgos."
27. Cloutier, "Transgender Girl's Human Rights Complaint."
28. Ibid.
29. Karkazis et al., "Out of Bounds?"
30. The underlying assumption of sex-segregated sporting spaces is that someone who is born male naturally has an "unfair advantage" when competing against women in sport. Assumptions of unfair advantage lean heavily on a Western trope of white, female frailty (to justify a long-reviled and scientifically unfounded practice of sex-verification testing). Assumptions of female inferiority rest on the ideology of the two-sex system, and this ideology plays a significant cultural and economic role in the devaluation of women, gays and lesbians, and transgender people. See, for example, Cavanagh and Sykes, "Transsexual Bodies at the Olympics"; Dowling, *Frailty Myth*; Love, "Transgender Exclusion and Inclusion in Sport"; Sullivan, "Gender Verification and Gender Policies"; Sykes, "Transsexual and Transgender Policies in Sport."
31. Cauterucci, "Trans Boy Who Won the Texas Girls' Wrestling Title."
32. Ibid.
33. Wong, "Texas Sportscaster Shreds Trans Phobes."
34. Carter, *Quality of Home Runs*, 13.
35. T. Collins, *Sport in Capitalist Society*.
36. Bullough and Bullough, *Cross Dressing*.
37. Pronger, *Arena of Masculinity*.
38. Carrington and McDonald, "Marxism, Cultural Studies and Sport."
39. Ibid.; Banet-Weiser, *Most Beautiful Girl in the World*; Crenshaw, *Fighting the Post–Affirmative Action War*; Douglas and Jamieson, "Farewell to Remember"; Douglas, "Wages of Whiteness"; Dworkin and Wachs, *Body Panic*; Collins, *Black Sexual Politics*; Travers, "Thinking the Unthinkable"; Travers and Deri "Transgender Inclusion and the Changing Face."
40. Puar, *Terrorist Assemblages*.
41. Kirby and Huebner, "Talking about Sex"; Davis, *Beyond Trans*; Pieper, *Sex Testing*.
42. Butler, *Undoing Gender*; Butler, *Gender Trouble*; Fausto-Sterling, *Sexing the Body*; Halberstam, *Female Masculinity*; Haraway, *Modest_Witness*; Haraway, *Simians, Cyborgs and Women*; Jordan-Young, *Brain Storm*; Pieper, *Sex Testing*.
43. Jordan-Young, *Brain Storm*; Karkazis et al., "Out of Bounds?"
44. To justify a long-reviled and scientifically unfounded practice of sex-verification testing for women athletes only, the International Olympic Committee (IOC) and its affiliates finally discontinued the practice of sex-verification testing for all women competitors prior to the 2000 Olympic Games.

45. M. Kane, "Resistance/Transformation," 191.
46. See, for example, Dowling, *Frailty Myth*; Pronger, *Arena of Masculinity*; J. Ring, *Stolen Bases*.
47. See, for example, Birrell and McDonald, *Reading Sport*; Messner, *Power at Play*; Messner, Dunbar, and Hunt, "Televised Sports Manhood Formula"; van Sterkenburg and Knoppers, "Dominant Discourses about Race/Ethnicity."
48. See, for example, Broad, "Gendered Unapologetic"; Cahn, *Coming on Strong*; M. Hall, *Girl and the Game*; Heywood and Dworkin, *Built to Win*.
49. See, for example, Cohen, *No Girls in the Clubhouse*; Dowling, *Frailty Myth*.
50. McDonagh and Pappano, *Playing with the Boys*, 6.
51. Burstyn, *Rites of Men*.
52. Teetzel, "On Transgendered Athletes, Fairness and Doping."
53. McArdle, "Swallows and Amazons."
54. Sykes, "Transsexual and Transgender Policies in Sport."
55. Travers, "Thinking the Unthinkable."
56. Meyer, *Gender and Sexual Diversity in Schools*, 9.
57. Messner, "Gender Ideologies, Youth Sports," 151.
58. Ibid.
59. Travers, "Sport Nexus and Gender Injustice"; McDonagh and Pappano, *Playing with the Boys*; J. Ring, *Stolen Bases*; Cohen, *No Girls in the Clubhouse*.
60. Travers, "Sport Nexus and Gender Injustice"; Travers "Queering Sport"; Travers, "Women's Ski Jumping"; Travers, "Thinking the Unthinkable," Travers and Deri, "Transgender Inclusion."
61. Doull et al., "Are We Leveling the Playing Field?"
62. GLSEN, *2015 National School Climate Survey*, 5.
63. Sabo, "Myth of the Sexual Athlete."
64. His real name, by request: Cory is a very public trans activist, and being visible as a trans person is very important to him.
65. Pascoe, *Dude, You're a Fag*, 51.
66. Ehrensaft, personal communication, 2012.
67. IOC Medical Commission, "Statement of the Stockholm Consensus on Sex Reassignment in Sports."
68. Sykes, "Transsexual and Transgender Policies in Sport."
69. Cavanagh and Sykes, "Transsexual Bodies at the Olympics"; Love, "Transgender Exclusion and Inclusion in Sport."
70. Griffin and Carroll, *On the Team*, 25.
71. Pieper, *Sex Testing*, 182.
72. Cavanagh and Sykes, "Transsexual Bodies at the Olympics"; Pieper, *Sex Testing*.
73. Nyong'o, "Unforgiveable Transgression of Being Caster Semenya."
74. Pieper, *Sex Testing*.
75. In "On Transgendered Athletes, Fairness and Doping: An International Challenge," Sarah Teetzel successfully uncouples concerns about testosterone as a performance-enhancing substance from concerns about steroid use in sport by

establishing that the performance-enhancement effect resulting from doping is far greater than any advantage, if such advantage exists at all, from past or present levels of testosterone predating or resulting from gender transition. Indeed, Teetzel regards the latter as negligible.

76. Pieper, *Sex Testing*, 183.
77. BBC Sport, "Dutee Chand Cleared to Race."
78. Carr, "Here's What the 2018 Olympic Gender Regulations Look Like."
79. "Tearful Lynsey Sharp."
80. Bull, "Caster Semenya wins Olympic gold but faces more scrutiny."
81. H. Davis, *Beyond Trans*, 112.
82. Harper, "Using Testosterone to Categorise."
83. Love, "Transgender Exclusion and Inclusion in Sport," 380.
84. Travers, "Queering Sport."
85. U.S. Transgender Law and Policy Institute, *Guidelines for Creating Policies*, 2–3.
86. Referring to all 50 U.S. states.
87. LGBT Sports Foundation, "All 50."
88. Canadian Centre for Ethics in Sport, *Sport in Transition*, 29.
89. Public Health Agency of Canada, *Questions and Answers*, 9.
90. TransAthlete.com, "K–12 Policies."
91. The Alberta organization is a voluntary organization, while the other three have set policies that must be complied with.
92. Gruneau, "There Will Never Be Another Gordie Howe."
93. Love, "Transgender Exclusion and Inclusion in Sport," 382.
94. McDonagh and Pappano, *Playing with the Boys*, 6.

CHAPTER 4. PARENTS

1. Ehrensaft, *Gender Born, Gender Made*.
2. Pyne, "Gender Independent Kids."
3. GIDC was the diagnosis listed in the *Diagnostic and Statistical Manual* from 1980 to 2012.
4. Menvielle, "Comprehensive Program," 363.
5. Klein and Golub, "Family Rejection as a Predictor," 193.
6. Roberts et al., "Childhood Gender Nonconformity."
7. Meadow, "Child."
8. Nestle, *Persistent Desire*.
9. Ehrensaft, personal communication, 2012.
10. Certainly not those headed by trans-exclusive radical feminists!
11. Ehrensaft, personal communication, 2012.
12. Grossman and D'Augelli, "Transgender Youth and Life-Threatening Behaviors."
13. Dylan is not the first transgender person in his family. His older sister is a transgender woman whose own struggles with poverty (Dylan reported that she was homeless for some time) have been a barrier to her obtaining trans-affirming healthcare.

14. Manning, "Attached Advocacy and the Rights of the Trans Child."
15. Ibid., 584.
16. Ibid., 585.
17. Ibid., 590.
18. Ibid.
19. Watson, "Accumulating Cares," 27.
20. Ibid., 262–263.
21. Manning et al., "Fighting for Trans* Kids."
22. Ward, "Gender Labor."
23. Manning, "Attached Advocacy and the Rights of the Trans Child," 583–584.
24. Allen, "Court Ruling a Victory for Transgender Boy."
25. Edwards-Leeper and Spack, "Psychological Evaluation and Medical Treatment," 331.
26. E. Kane, *Gender Trap*.
27. Nora, however, worries about trans kids using the Internet to learn about themselves because "often the first thing you find when you Google something is the suicide stats."
28. Connell, *Gender*; Jordan-Young, *Brain Storm*; H. Davis, *Beyond Trans*.
29. Manning, "Attached Advocacy and the Rights of the Trans Child," 585.
30. E. Kane, *Gender Trap*.

CHAPTER 5. SUPPORTIVE HEALTHCARE

1. Gill-Peterson, "Technical Capacities of the Body."
2. E. Kane, *Gender Trap*; Serano, "Detransition, Desistance, and Disinformation."
3. Bryant, "Making Gender Identity Disorder of Childhood."
4. Psychological/psychiatric treatment designed to "cure" gay, lesbian, and trans and gender-nonconforming people.
5. American Psychiatric Association, *Diagnostic and Statistical Manual*, 3rd ed.
6. Pyne, "Governance of Gender Non-conforming Children," 79.
7. Sedgwick, "How to Bring Your Kids Up Gay"; Burke, *Gender Shock*.
8. Bryant, "In Defense of Gay Children?"
9. "Mad pride" activists resist the stigma associated with mental illness and challenge neuronormativity, insisting that neurodiversity is a feature of humanity; Fitzpatrick, "Trans Activists, Don't Throw Mad People under the Bus!"
10. Butler, *Undoing Gender*, 8.
11. Joel et al., "Queering Gender," 314.
12. Bryant, "Diagnosis and Medicalization."
13. Winters, "Proposed Gender Dysphoria Diagnosis in the DSM-5."
14. Tosh, *Perverse Psychology*, 14.
15. Pyne, "Gender Independent Kids," 3.
16. Formerly the Harry Benjamin International Gender Dysphoria Association.
17. Serano, "Detransition, Desistance, and Disinformation."
18. Giordano, "Lives in a Chiaroscuro," 580.

19. Serano, "Detransition, Desistance, and Disinformation."

20. Such as Wente, "Transgender Kids"; Singal, "How the Fight over Transgender Kids."

21. Gill-Peterson, "Technical Capacities of the Body"; Meadow, "Child."

22. Butler, *Frames of War*, 25.

23. Meadow, "Child."

24. Chinn, "I Was a Lesbian Child"; Halberstam, *Female Masculinity*.

25. Meadow, "Child," 58.

26. Tannehill, "Truth about Transgender Suicide" (my emphasis).

27. Ainsworth and Spiegel, "Quality of Life of Individuals," 1019.

28. U.S. Department of Health and Human Services, Office of the Surgeon General and National Action Alliance for Suicide Prevention, *2012 National Strategy for Suicide Prevention*, 122.

29. Haritaworn, Kuntsman, and Posocco, introduction to *Queer Necropolitics*, 16.

30. Gill-Peterson, "Technical Capacities of the Body," 414.

31. Edwards-Leeper and Spack, "Psychological Evaluation and Medical Treatment," 323.

32. Morgensen, "Settler Homonationalism."

33. Gill-Peterson, "Technical Capacities of the Body," 412.

34. Ibid., 413.

35. Bucar and Enke, "Unlikely Sex Change Capitals of the World," 323.

36. Johanna Olson-Kennedy is an adolescent-medicine physician specializing in the care of trans and gender-nonconforming children and youth. She is an assistant professor at the Children's Hospital of Los Angeles.

37. Haritaworn, Kuntsman, and Posocco, introduction to *Queer Necropolitics*, 16.

38. For example, plastic surgery, razors, and cosmetics.

39. Gill-Peterson, "Technical Capacities of the Body," 408.

40. Ibid., 407.

41. Quoted in Dreyfus and Rabinow, *Michel Foucault*, 187.

42. Gilmore, *Golden Gulag*, 28.

CONCLUSION

1. Government of Canada, "Bill C-16."

2. Capehart, "Clinton's Geneva Accord."

3. Davis and Apuzzo, "US Directs Public Schools."

4. Quinn and Meiners, "From Anti-Bullying Laws and Gay Marriages."

5. As noted in chapter 3, for example, the passage of HB2 had significant financial consequences for the state of North Carolina.

6. See, for example, Razack, "Gendered Racial Violence"; Mackey, *House of Difference*.

7. I have summarized this case in the introduction.

8. There is critical debate within queer and trans communities about the value of being able to serve openly in the military, given its role in spreading violence across

the globe; however, it is important to note that for many low-income Canadians and Americans, many of whom are members of visible minorities, the military is a much-needed source of employment and is often the only route available for postsecondary education.

9. Grzanka and Mann, "Queer Youth Suicide."
10. Puar, *Terrorist Assemblages*; Snorton and Haritaworn, "Trans Necropolitics"; Haritaworn, Kuntsman, and Posocco, *Queer Necropolitics*; Morgensen, "Settler Homonationalism"; Meiners, "Trouble with the *Child* in the Carceral State."
11. Lynch, "Attorney General Loretta E. Lynch."
12. For example, Duggan, *Twilight of Equality*; Puar, *Terrorist Assemblages*; White-head, *Nuptial Deal*.
13. Puar, *Terrorist Assemblages*, 10, xii.
14. Stanley, "Gender Self-Determination," 90.
15. Fraser, "Feminist Politics in the Age of Recognition," 27.
16. Lister, "Inclusive Citizenship."
17. Indigenous women were enfranchised in 1950 in Canada, although the lack of ballot boxes until 1962 made this legal capacity meaningless. In the United States, Native American women received the right to vote in 1924, and Black women received the right to vote along with white women in 1920; but until the 1965 Voting Rights Act, minority voting rights were largely symbolic.
18. Regarding the University of British Columbia's pursuit of diversity via the hiring of white women, see Thobani, "After UBC Ousted Arvind Gupta as President."
19. Razack, *Casting Out*, 4.
20. Thobani, *Exalted Subjects*.
21. See, for example, Krebs, "Hockey and the Reproduction of Colonialism in Canada"; and Denis, *We Are Not You*.
22. Thobani, *Exalted Subjects*, 76.
23. Puar, "Q&A with Jasbir Puar."
24. Kumashiro, *Troubling Intersections of Race and Sexuality*, 5.
25. Williams Institute, "Incarceration Rate of LGB People."
26. Correctional Investigator, *Annual Report*; Brosnahan, "Canada's Prison Popula-tion."
27. Government of Canada and the Province of British Columbia, "What Is a Hate Crime?"
28. Meiners, "Trouble with the *Child* in the Carceral State."
29. Snorton and Haritaworn, "Trans Necropolitics," 73.
30. In contrast, there has been no interruption of police violence against people of color, as evinced by the attention the Black Lives Matter movement has brought to the many Black people who have been murdered by police and security forces. See www.blacklivesmatter.com.
31. Lamble, "Queer Investments in Punitiveness," 151.
32. Slater, "Fire on the 57 Bus in Oakland."
33. Ibid.

34. I use "fat" not in a pejorative sense but in keeping with the way fat activists have reclaimed the term.
35. Freeman et al., *Health of Canada's Young People*, 167.
36. Quinn and Meiners, "From Anti-Bullying Laws," 157.
37. Berlowitz, Frye, and Jette, "Bullying and Zero-Tolerance Policies."
38. Lacharite and Marini, "Bullying Prevention and the Rights of Children," 313–314.
39. Fields et al., "Beyond Bullying."
40. Lacharite and Marini, "Bullying Prevention and the Rights of Children," 306–307.
41. See, for example, Berlowitz, Frye, and Jette, "Bullying and Zero-Tolerance Policies"; Gebhard, "Pipeline to Prison"; Hodgson, "Childhood of the Race."
42. Berlowitz, Frye, and Jette, "Bullying and Zero-Tolerance Policies," 3.
43. Quinn and Meiners, "From Anti-Bullying Laws and Gay Marriages," 158–159.
44. Hodgson, "Childhood of the Race," 41.
45. Meiners, "Ending the School-to-Prison Pipeline," 553.
46. Lacharite and Marini, "Bullying Prevention and the Rights of Children," 299.
47. Berlowitz, Frye, and Jette, "Bullying and Zero-Tolerance Policies," 13–14.
48. Quinn and Meiners, "From Anti-Bullying Laws," 161–163.
49. Meiners, "Trouble with the *Child* in the Carceral State," 132.
50. Quinn and Meiners, "From Anti-Bullying Laws," 168.
51. Butler, *Undoing Gender*, 32–33.
52. Siebers, *Disability Theory*, 73.
53. Kabeer, *Inclusive Citizenship*, 23, 21–22.
54. Lister et al., *Gendering Citizenship in Western Europe*, 9–10.
55. Arendt, *Origins of Totalitarianism*.
56. Canadian Civil Liberties Association, *Information Guide: LGBTQ Rights*.
57. N. Davis, "Drop in Teenage Suicide Attempts."
58. Manning, "Attached Advocacy and the Rights of the Trans Child," 590.
59. Dryden and McGregor, *In School*.

BIBLIOGRAPHY

Abramson, Alana. "North Carolina Governor Who Signed Bathroom Bill Says People Are 'Reluctant' to Hire Him." *Time*, March 15, 2017. www.time.com.

Ainsworth, Tiffany, and Jeffrey Spiegel. "Quality of Life of Individuals with and without Facial Feminization Surgery or Gender Reassignment Surgery." *Quality of Life Research* 19 (2010): 1019–1024.

Allen, Samantha Wright. "Court Ruling a Victory for Transgender Boy." *Prince George Citizen*, April 28, 2016. www.princegeorgecitizen.com.

American Civil Liberties Union. "This Court Decision in the Gavin Grimm Case Will Bring Tears to Your Eyes." April 10, 2017. www.aclu.org.

———. "What Is the School-to-Prison Pipeline?" 2013. www.aclu.org.

American Psychiatric Association. *Diagnostic and Statistical Manual*. 3rd ed. Washington, DC: American Psychiatric Association, 1980.

———*Diagnostic and Statistical Manual*. 5th ed. Washington, DC: American Psychiatric Association, 2013.

Appell, Annette. "The Pre-Political Child of Child-Centred Jurisprudence." In *The Children's Table: Childhood Studies and the Humanities*, edited by Anna Mae Duane, 19–37. Athens: University of Georgia Press, 2013.

Arendt, Hannah. *The Origins of Totalitarianism*. Orlando, FL: Harvest Books, 1973.

Banet-Weiser, Sarah. *The Most Beautiful Girl in the World: Beauty Pageants and National Identity*. Berkeley: University of California Press, 1999.

Bannerjee, Subhabrata. "Necrocapitalism." *Organization Studies* 29 (2008): 1541–1563.

BBC Sport. "Dutee Chand Cleared to Race as IAAF Suspends 'Gender Test' Rules." July 27, 2015. www.bbc.com.

———. "Dutee Chand: I Lost All My Honour in Landmark Gender Case." July 28, 2017. www.bbc.com.

Berkowitz, Dana, and Maura Ryan. "Bathrooms, Baseball, and Bra Shopping: Lesbian and Gay Parents Talk about Engendering Their Children." *Sociological Perspectives* 54, no. 3 (2011): 329–350.

Berlant, Lauren. "Slow Death (Sovereignty, Obesity, Lateral Agency)." *Critical Inquiry* 33, no. 4 (2007): 754–780.

Berlowitz, Marvin J., Rinda Frye, and Kelli M. Jette. "Bullying and Zero-Tolerance Policies: The School to Prison Pipeline." *Multicultural Learning and Teaching*, 2015, 1–19.

Birrell Susan, and Mary G. McDonald, eds. *Reading Sport: Critical Essays on Power and Representation*. Boston: Northeastern University Press, 2000.

Blum-Ross, Alicia. "What Does It Mean for Children to Have a 'Voice' in Research?" Connected Learning Research Network, August 18, 2016. http://clrn.dmlhub.net.

Brill, Stephanie, and Lisa Kenney. *The Transgender Teen: A Handbook for Families and Professionals Supporting Transgender and Non-binary Teens*. Jersey City, NJ: Cleis, 2016.

Brill, Stephanie, and Rachel Pepper. *The Transgender Child: A Handbook for Families and Professionals*. San Francisco: Cleis, 2008.

Broad, Kendal L. "The Gendered Unapologetic: Queer Resistance in Women's Sport." *Sociology of Sport Journal* 18 (2001): 181–203.

Brosnahan, Maureen. "Canada's Prison Population at All-Time High." CBC News, November 25 2013. www.cbc.ca.

Browne, Kath. "Genderism and the Bathroom Problem: (re)Materialising Sexed Sites, (re)Creating Sexed Bodies." *Gender, Place & Culture* 11, no. 3 (2004): 331–346.

Bryant, Karl. "Diagnosis and Medicalization." In *Sociology of Diagnosis*, edited by P. J. McCann and David J. Hutson, 33–57. Bingley, UK: Emerald, 2011.

———. "In Defense of Gay Children? 'Progay' Homophobia and the Production of Homonormativity." *Sexualities* 11, no. 4 (2008): 455–475.

———. "Making Gender Identity Disorder of Childhood: Historical Lessons for Contemporary Debates." *Sexuality Research and Social Policy* 3, no. 3 (2006): 23–29.

Bucar, Elizabeth, and Finn Enke. "Unlikely Sex Change Capitals of the World: Trinidad, United States, and Tehran, Iran, as Twin Yardsticks of Homonormative Liberalism." *Feminist Studies* 37, no. 2 (2011): 301–328.

Bull, Andy. "Caster Semenya Wins Olympic Gold but Faces More Scrutiny as IAAF Presses Case." *Guardian*, August 21, 2016. www.theguardian.com.

Bullough Vern L., and Bonnie Bullough. *Cross Dressing, Sex, and Gender*. Philadelphia: University of Pennsylvania Press, 1993.

Burke, Phyllis. *Gender Shock*. New York: Doubleday, 1990.

Burstyn, Varda. *The Rites of Men: Manhood, Politics and the Culture of Sport*. Toronto: University of Toronto Press, 1999.

Butler, Judith. *Frames of War: When Is Life Grievable?* London: Verso, 2009.

———. *Gender Trouble: Feminism and the Subversion of Identity*. New York: Routledge, 1990.

———. *Undoing Gender*. New York: Routledge, 2004.

Cahn, Susan K. *Coming on Strong: Gender and Sexuality in Twentieth-Century Women's Sport*. Cambridge, MA: Harvard University Press, 1995.

Canadian Centre for Ethics in Sport. *Sport in Transition: Making Sport in Canada More Responsible for Gender Inclusivity*. Ottawa: Canadian Centre for Ethics in Sport, 2012.

Canadian Civil Liberties Association. *Information Guide: LGBTQ Rights in Schools*. July 2014. http://ccla.org.

Canadian Press. "Human Rights Complaint Prompts New Gender Policy in Vancouver Catholic Schools." Canadian Broadcasting Corporation, July 16, 2014.

Canadian Teachers Federation. *Supporting Transgender and Transsexual Students in K–12 Schools: A Guide for Educators*. Ottawa: Canadian Teachers Federation, 2012.

Capehart, Jonathan. "Clinton's Geneva Accord: 'Gay Rights Are Human Rights.'" *Washington Post*, December 7, 2011. www.washingtonpost.com.

Carr, Grace. "Here's What the 2018 Olympic Gender Regulations Look Like." Daily Caller, July 3, 2017. http://dailycaller.com.

Carrington, Ben, and Ian McDonald. "Marxism, Cultural Studies and Sport: Mapping the Field." In *Marxism, Cultural Studies and Sport*, edited by Ben Carrington and Ian McDonald, 1–12. New York: Routledge, 2009.

Carter, Thomas. *The Quality of Home Runs: The Passion, Politics, and Language of Cuban Baseball*. Durham, NC: Duke University Press, 2008.

Castañeda, Claudia. "Childhood." *Transgender Studies Quarterly* 1, nos. 1–2 (2014): 59–61.

Cauterucci, Christina. "The Trans Boy Who Won the Texas Girls' Wrestling Title Exposes the Illogic of Anti-Trans Policy." *Slate*, February 27, 2017. www.slate.com.

Cavanagh, Sheila. *Queering Bathrooms: Gender, Sexuality, and a Hygienic Imagination*. Toronto: University of Toronto Press, 2010.

Cavanagh, Sheila, and Heather Sykes. "Transsexual Bodies at the Olympics: The International Olympic Committee's Policy on Transsexual Athletes at the 2004 Athens Summer Games." *Body and Society* 12 (2006): 75–102.

Chinn, Sarah E. "'I Was a Lesbian Child': Queer Thoughts about Childhood Studies." In *The Children's Table: Childhood Studies and the Humanities*, edited by Anna Mae Duane, 149–166. Athens: University of Georgia Press, 2013.

Cloutier, Danelle. "Transgender Girl's Human Rights Complaint against School Division in Winnipeg Resolved." CBC News, March 11, 2016. www.cbc.ca.

Cohen, Marilyn. *No Girls in the Clubhouse: The Exclusion of Women from Baseball*. Jefferson, NC: McFarland, 2009.

Collins, Patricia Hill. *Black Feminist Thought: Knowledge, Consciousness and Empowerment*. New York: Routledge. 1990.

———. *Black Sexual Politics: African Americans, Gender, and the New Racism*. New York: Routledge, 2005.

Collins, Tony. *Sport in Capitalist Society: A Short History*. New York: Routledge, 2013.

Connell, Raewyn W. *Gender: In World Perspective*. 2nd ed. Cambridge, UK: Polity, 2009.

Correctional Investigator. *Annual Report of the Office of the Correctional Investigator: 2014–2015*. Cat. No. PS100E-PDF. Ottawa: Government of Canada, 2015.

Coulthard, Glen Sean. *Red Skin, White Masks: Rejecting the Colonial Politics of Recognition*. Minneapolis: University of Minnesota Press, 2014.

Crenshaw, Kimberlé. *Fighting the Post–Affirmative Action War*. New York: Essence Communications, 1998.

Crissman, Halley P., Mitchell B. Berger, Louis F. Graham, and Vanessa K. Dalton. "Transgender Demographics: A Household Probability Sample of US Adults, 2014." *American Journal of Public Health* 107, no. 2 (2017): 213–215.

Davis, Heath Fogg. *Beyond Trans: Does Gender Matter?* New York: NYU Press, 2017.

Davis, Julie Hirschfield, and Matt Apuzzo. "US Directs Public Schools to Allow Transgender Access to Restrooms." *New York Times*, May 12, 2016. www.nytimes.com.

Davis, Nicola. "Drop in Teenage Suicide Attempts Linked to Legislation of Same-Sex Marriage." *Guardian*, February 20, 2017.

Denis, Claude. *We Are Not You: First Nations and Canadian Modernity*. Peterborough, ON: Broadview, 1997.

Douglas, Delia D. "Forget Me . . . Not: Marion Jones and the Politics of Punishment." *Journal of Sport and Social Issues* 32, no. 10 (2014): 3–22.

———. "Private Mark Graham, an Un/Known Soldier: Not Just Any Body Can Be a Citizen." *Gender, Place and Culture: A Journal of Feminist Geography* 22, no. 7 (2014): 1007–1022.

———. "The Wages of Whiteness: Confronting the Nature of Ivory Tower Racism and the Implications for Physical Education." *Sport, Education and Society* 18, no. 4 (2013): 453–474.

Douglas, Delia D., and Katherine M. Jamieson. "A Farewell to Remember: Interrogating the Nancy Lopez Farewell Tour." *Sociology of Sport Journal* 23, no. 2 (2006): 117–141.

Doull, Marion, Ryan J. Watson, Annie Smith, Yuko Homma, and Elizabeth Saewyc. "Are We Leveling the Playing Field? Trends and Disparities in Sports Participation among Sexual Minority Youth in Canada." *Journal of Sport and Health Science*, October 24, 2016. doi:10.1016/j.jshs.2016.10.006.

Dowling, Colette. *The Frailty Myth: Women Approaching Physical Equality*. New York: Random House, 2000.

Dreyfus, Hubert L., and Paul Rabinow. *Michel Foucault: Beyond Structuralism and Hermeneutics*. Brighton, UK: Harvester, 1982.

Dryden, Ken, and Roy McGregor. *In School: Our Kids, Our Teachers, Our Classrooms*. Toronto: McClelland and Stewart, 1995.

Duane, Anna Mae, ed. *The Children's Table: Childhood Studies and the Humanities*. Athens: University of Georgia Press, 2013.

Duggan, Lisa. *The Twilight of Equality: Neoliberalism, Cultural Politics, and the Attack on Democracy*. Boston: Beacon, 2004.

Dworkin, Shari L., and Faye Linda Wachs. *Body Panic: Gender, Health, and the Selling of Fitness*. New York: NYU Press, 2009.

Edwards-Leeper, Laura, and Norman P. Spack. "Psychological Evaluation and Medical Treatment of Transgender Youth in an Interdisciplinary 'Gender Management Service' (GEMS) in a Major Pediatric Center." *Journal of Homosexuality* 59, no. 3 (2012): 321–336.

Ehrensaft, Diane. *Gender Born, Gender Made: Raising Healthy Gender-Nonconforming Children*. New York: The Experiment, 2011.

Elliot, Patricia. *Debates in Transgender, Queer, and Feminist Theory: Contested Sites*. Farnham, UK: Ashgate, 2010.

"Family of Bella Burgos Ready to Go though Mediation over Human Rights Complaint." *Winnipeg Free Press*, April 15, 2014. www.winnipegfreepress.com.

Fausto-Sterling, Anne. *Sexing the Body: Gender Politics and the Construction of Sexuality*. New York: Basic Books, 2000.

Fields, Jessica, Laura Mamo, Jen Gilbert, and Nancy Lesko. "Beyond Bullying." *Contexts*, November 20, 2014.

Fitzpatrick, Cat. "Trans Activists, Don't Throw Mad People under the Bus!" *Feministing*, February 11, 2016. http://feministing.com.

Flasher, Jack. "Adultism." *Adolescence* 13, no. 51 (1978): 517–523.

Foucault, Michel. *The Birth of Biopolitics: Lectures at the Collège de France, 1978–79*. Basingstoke, UK: Palgrave Macmillan, 2008.

Fraser, Nancy. "Feminist Politics in the Age of Recognition: A Two-Dimensional Approach to Gender Justice." *Studies in Social Justice* 1, no. 1 (2007): 23–35.

Freeman, John G., Matthew King, and William Pickett, with Wendy Craig, Frank Elgar, Ian Jannsen, and Don Klinger. *The Health of Canada's Young People: A Mental Health Focus*. Ottawa: Public Health Agency of Canada, 2011.

Gebhard, Amanda. "Pipeline to Prison: How Schools Shape a Future of Incarceration for Indigenous Youth." *Briarpatch*, September 1, 2012. http://briarpatchmagazine.com.

Gender Spectrum. "Gender Inclusive Schools." Accessed August 23, 2015, www.genderspectrum.org.

Gill-Peterson, Julian. "The Technical Capacities of the Body: Assembling Race, Technology, and Transgender." *Transgender Studies Quarterly* 1, no. 3 (2014): 402–418.

Gilmore, Ruth Wilson. *Golden Gulag: Prisons, Surplus, Crisis and Opposition in Globalizing California*. Berkeley: University of California Press, 2007.

Giordano, Simona. "Lives in Chiaroscuro: Should We Suspend the Puberty of Children with Gender Identity Disorder?" *Journal of Medical Ethics* 34 (2008): 580–584.

Glenn, Evelyn Nakano. "Settler Colonialism as Structure: A Framework for Comparative Studies of U.S. Race and Gender Formation." *Sociology of Race and Ethnicity* 1, no. 1 (2015): 52–72.

GLSEN. *The 2015 National School Climate Survey: The Experiences of Lesbian, Gay, Bisexual, Transgender, and Queer Youth in Our Nation's Schools*. New York: GLSEN, 2015. www.glsen.org.

Goldberg, Alan B., and Joneil Adriano. "I'm a Girl: Understanding Transgender Children." ABC News, June 27, 2008. http://abcnews.go.ca.

Gosset, Che. "Silhouettes of Defiance: Memorializing Historical Sites of Queer and Transgender Resistance in an Age of Neoliberal Inclusivity." In *The Transgender Studies Reader 2*, edited by Susan Stryker and Aren Aizura, 580–590. New York: Routledge, 2013.

Government of British Columbia. "Change of Gender Designation on Birth Certificates." Accessed May 3, 2017, www2.gov.bc.ca.

Government of Canada. "Bill C-16: An Act to Amend the Canadian Human Rights Act and the Criminal Code." http://openparliament.ca.

Government of Canada, and the Province of British Columbia. "What Is a Hate Crime?" KnowHate. Accessed May 3, 2017, http://hatecrimebc.ca.

Government of Ontario, Ministry of Transportation. "New 'X' Gender Option Now Available on Ontario Driver's Licences." Ontario Newsroom, March 20, 2017. http://news.ontario.ca.

Grant, Jaime M., Lisa A. Mottet, Justin Tanis, with Jack Harrison, Jody L. Herman, and Mara Keisling. *Injustice at Every Turn: A Report of the National Transgender Discrimination Survey*. National Centre for Transgender Equality, 2011. www.thetaskforce.org.

Griffin, Pat, and Helen Carroll. *On the Team: Equal Opportunity for Transgender Student Athletes*. NCLR, Women's Sports Foundation, and It Takes a Team. 2010.

Grossman, Arnold H., and Anthony R. D'Augelli. "Transgender Youth and Life-Threatening Behaviors." *Suicide and Life-Threatening Behaviors* 37, no. 5 (2007): 527–537.

Gruneau, Richard. "There Will Never Be Another Gordie Howe." Unpublished discussion paper, 2014.

Grzanka, Patrick, and Emily Mann. "Queer Youth Suicide and the Psychopolitics of 'It Gets Better.'" *Sexualities* 17, no. 4 (2014): 369–393.

Halberstam, Jack. *Female Masculinity*. Durham, NC: Duke University Press, 1998.

———. *In a Queer Time and Place: Transgender Bodies, Subcultural Lives*. New York: NYU Press, 2005.

Hall, M. Anne. *The Girl and the Game*. Toronto: Broadview, 2002.

Haraway, Donna. *Modest_Witness@Second_Millenium.FemaleMan©Meets_Onco-Mouse™*, New York: Routledge, 1997.

———. *Simians, Cyborgs, and Women: The Reinvention of Nature*. New York: Routledge, 1991.

Haritaworn, Jin. "Loyal Repetitions of the Nation: Gay Assimilation and the 'War on Terror.'" *DarkMatter* 3 (2008). www.darkmatter101.org.

Haritaworn, Jin, Adi Kuntsman, and Silvia Posocco. Introduction to *Queer Necropolitics*, edited by Hin Haritaworn, Adi Kuntsman, and Silvia Posocco, 1–28. Abingdon, UK: Social Justice, 2014.

———, eds. *Queer Necropolitics*. Abingdon, UK: Social Justice, 2014.

Harper, Joanna. "Using Testosterone to Categorise Male and Female Athletes Isn't Perfect, but It's the Best Solution We Have." *Guardian*, July 3, 2017. www.theguardian.com.

Harris, Adrienne. *Gender as Soft Assembly*. Hillsdale, NJ: Analytic, 2005.

Hellen, Mark. "Transgender Children in Schools." *Liminalis*, 2009, 81–99.

Herman, Jody, Andrew R. Flores, Taylor N. T. Brown, Bianca D. M. Wilson, and Kerith J. Conron. "Age of Individuals Who Identify as Transgender in the United States." Williams Institute, University of California Los Angeles School of Law, 2017. http://williamsinstitute.law.ucla.edu.

Heywood, Leslie, and Shari L. Dworkin. *Built to Win: The Female Athlete as Cultural Icon*. Minneapolis: University of Minnesota Press, 2003.

Higgenbotham, Evelyn Brooks. "African American Women's History and the Metalanguage of Race." *Signs* 17, no. 2 (1992): 251–274.

Hochschild, Arlie. *The Managed Heart: Commercialization of Human Feeling*. Berkeley: University of California Press, 1983.

Hodgson, Lucia. "Childhood of the Race: A Critical Race Theory Intervention into Childhood Studies." In *The Children's Table: Childhood Studies and the Humanities*, edited by Anna Mae Duane, 38–51. Athens: University of Georgia Press, 2013.

Hoffman, Diane M. "Risky Investments: Parenting and the Production of the 'Resilient Child.'" *Health, Risk, and Society* 12, no. 4 (2010): 385–394.

Holman, Catherine White, and Joshua M. Goldberg. "Ethical, Legal, and Psychosocial Issues in Care of Transgender Adolescents." *International Journal of Transgenderism* 9, nos. 3–4 (2006): 95–110.

hooks, bell. *All about Love: New Visions*. New York: HarperCollins, 2000.

———. *Feminist Theory from Margin to Center*. Cambridge, MA: South End, 1984.

———. *Yearning: Race, Gender, and Cultural Politics*. New York: Routledge, 1990.

IOC Medical Commission. "Statement of the Stockholm Consensus on Sex Reassignment in Sports." October 28, 2003. www.olympic.org.

Joel, Daphna, Ricardo Tarrasch, Zohar Berman, Maya Mukamal, and Effi Ziv. "Queering Gender: Studying Gender Identity in 'Normative' Individuals." *Psychology & Sexuality* 5, no. 4 (2014): 291–321.

Jordan-Young, Rebecca. *Brain Storm: The Flaws in the Science of Sex Differences*. Cambridge, MA: Harvard University Press, 2010.

Kabeer, Naila. *Inclusive Citizenship: Meanings and Expressions*. London: Zed Books, 2005.

Kane, Emily W. *The Gender Trap: Parents and the Pitfalls of Raising Boys and Girls*. New York: NYU Press, 2012.

Kane, Mary Jo. "Resistance/Transformation of the Oppositional Binary: Exposing Sport as a Continuum." *Journal of Sport and Social Issues* 19 (1995): 191–218.

Kapoor, Dip, and Steven Jordan. "Introduction: International Perspectives on Education, PAR and Social Change." In *Education, Participatory Action Research, and Social Change*, edited by Dip Kapoor and Steven Jordan, 1–14. New York: Palgrave Macmillan, 2009.

Karkazis, Katrina, Rebecca Jordan-Young, Georgiann Davis, and Silvia Camporesi. "Out of Bounds? A Critique of the New Policies on Hyperandrogenism in Elite Female Athletes." *American Journal of Bioethics* 12, no. 7 (2012): 3–16.

Kirby, Sandra, and Judith Huebner. "Talking about Sex: Biology and the Social Interpretations of Sex in Sport." *Canadian Woman Studies* 21, no. 3 (2002): 36–43.

Klein, Augustus, and Sarit Golub. "Family Rejection as a Predictor of Suicide Attempts and Substance Misuse among Transgender and Gender-Nonconforming Adults." *LGBT Health* 3, no. 3 (2016): 193–199.

Klocker, Natascha. "An Example of 'Thin' Agency: Child Domestic Workers in Tanzania." In *Global Perspectives on Rural Childhood and Youth: Young Rural Lives*, edited by Ruth Panelli, Samantha Punch, and Elsbeth Robson, 83–94. New York: Routledge, 2007.

Kralik, Joellen. "'Bathroom Bill' Legislative Tracking." National Conference of State Legislatures, July 28, 2017. www.ncsl.org.

Krebs, Andreas. "Hockey and the Reproduction of Colonialism in Canada." In *Race and Sport in Canada: Intersecting Inequalities*, edited by Janelle Joseph, Simon Darnell, and Yuka Nakamura, 81–105. Toronto: Canadian Scholars Press, 2012.

Kumashiro, Kevin K. *Troubling Education: Queer Activism and Anti-Oppressive Pedagogy*. New York: Routledge, 2002.

———. *Troubling Intersections of Race and Sexuality: Queer Students of Color and Anti-Oppressive Education*. New York: Rowman and Littlefield, 2001.

Lacharite, Monique, and Zopito A. Marini. "Bullying Prevention and the Rights of Children: Psychological and Democratic Aspects." In *Children's Rights: Multidisciplinary Approaches to Participation and Protection*, edited by Tom O'Neill and Dawn Zinga, 297–324. Toronto: University of Toronto Press, 2008.

Lamble, Sarah. "Queer Investments in Punitiveness: Sexual Citizenship, Social Movements and the Expanding Carceral State." In *Queer Necropolitics*, edited by Jin Haritaworn, Adi Kuntsman, and Silvia Posocco, 151–171. Abingdon, UK: Social Justice, 2014.

LeGuin, Ursula K. *The Left Hand of Darkness*. New York: Ace Books, 1969.

Lemert, Charles. *Dark Thoughts: Race and the Eclipse of Society*. New York: Routledge, 2002.

Levin, Sam. "First US Person to Have 'Intersex' on Birth Certificate: 'There's Power in Knowing Who You Are.'" *Guardian*, January 11, 2017. www.theguardian.com.

LGBT Sports Foundation. "'All 50': The Transgender-Inclusive High School Sports and Activities Policy and Education Project." Accessed May 2016, www.transathlete. com.

Lister, Ruth. "Inclusive Citizenship: Realizing the Potential." *Citizenship Studies* 11, no. 1 (2007): 49–61.

Lister, Ruth, Fiona Williams, Anneli Anttonen, Jet Bussemaker, Ute Gerhard, Jacqueline Heinen, Stina Johansson, and Arnlaug Leira. *Gendering Citizenship in Western Europe: New Challenges for Citizenship Research in a Cross-National Context*. Bristol, UK: Policy, 2007.

Lopez, German. "Trump's Justice Department Just Rescinded a Memo Protecting Transgender Workers." *Vox*, October 5, 2017. www.vox.com.

Lorber, Judith. *Breaking the Bowls: Degendering and Feminist Change*. New York: Norton, 2005.

Lorde, Audre. *Sister Outsider: Essays and Speeches*. New York: Crossing, 1984.

Lorey, Isabell. *State of Insecurity: Government of the Precarious*. London: Verso, 2015.

Love, Adam. "Transgender Exclusion and Inclusion in Sport." In *Routledge Handbook of Sport, Gender and Sexuality*, edited by Jennifer Hargreaves and Eric Anderson, 376–383. New York: Routledge, 2014.

Lynch, Loretta E. "Attorney General Loretta E. Lynch Delivers Remarks at Press Conference Announcing Complaint against the State of North Carolina to Stop

Discrimination Against Transgender Individuals." Justice News, U.S. Department of Justice, May 9, 2016. www.justice.gov.

Macionis, John J., and Linda M. Gerber. *Sociology*. Toronto: Pearson, 2011.

Mackey, Eva. *The House of Difference: Cultural Politics and National Identity in Canada*. New York: Routledge, 1999.

Madigan, Lee, and Nancy C. Gamble. *The Second Rape: Society's Continual Betrayal of the Victim*. New York: Macmillan, 1991.

Manning, Kimberley Ens. "Attached Advocacy and the Rights of the Trans Child." *Canadian Journal of Political Science / Revue Canadienne de Science Politique* 50, no. 2 (2017): 579–595.

Manning, Kimberley, Cindy Holmes, Annie Pullen Sansfacon, Julia Temple Newhook, and Ann Travers. "Fighting for Trans* Kids: Academic Parent Activism in the 21st Century." *Studies in Social Justice* 9, no. 1 (2015): 118–135.

Marimow, Ann E. "Case of Virginia Transgender Teen Gavin Grimm Put Off by Appeals Court." *Washington Post*, August 2, 2017. www.washingtonpost.com.

Marten, James. "Childhood Studies and History: Catching a Culture in High Relief." In *The Children's Table: Childhood Studies and the Humanities*, edited by Anna Mae Duane, 52–53. Athens: University of Georgia Press, 2013.

Marx, Karl. "The Eighteenth Brumaire of Louis Bonaparte." In *The Marx-Engels Reader*, 2nd ed., edited by Robert C. Tucker, 594–617. New York: Norton, 1978.

Matthews, Sarah. "A Window on the 'New' Sociology of Childhood." *Sociology Compass* 1, no. 1 (2007): 322–334.

Mbembe, Achille. "Necropolitics." *Public Culture* 15, no. 1 (2003): 11–40.

McArdle, David. "Swallows and Amazons, or the Sporting Exception to the Gender Recognition Act." *Social and Legal Studies* 17, no. 1 (2008): 39–57.

McDonagh, Eileen, and Laura Pappano. *Playing with the Boys: Why Separate Is Not Equal in Sports*. New York: Oxford University Press, 2007.

McKittrick, Katherine, ed. *Sylvia Wynter: On Being Human as Praxis*. Durham, NC: Duke University Press, 2014.

Meadow, Tey. "Child." *Transgender Studies Quarterly* 1, nos. 1–2 (2014): 57–58.

Meiners, Erica. "Ending the School-to-Prison Pipeline / Building Abolition Futures." *Urban Review* 43 (September 2011): 547–565.

——. "Offending Children, Registering Sex." *Women's Studies Quarterly* 43, nos. 1–2 (2015): 246–263.

——. "Trouble with the *Child* in the Carceral State." *Social Justice* 41, no. 3 (2011): 120–144.

Menvielle, Edgardo. "A Comprehensive Program for Children with Gender Variant Behaviors and Gender Identity Disorders." *Journal of Homosexuality* 59, no. 3 (2012): 357–368.

Messner, Michael A. "Gender Ideologies, Youth Sports, and the Production of Soft Essentialism." *Sociology of Sport Journal* 28 (2011): 151–170.

——. *Power at Play: Sports and the Problem of Masculinity*. Boston: Beacon, 1995.

Messner, Michael A., Michele Dunbar, and Darnell Hunt. "The Televised Sports Man-hood Formula." *Journal of Sport and Social Issues* 24, no. 4 (2000): 380–394.

Meyer, Elizabeth J. *Gender and Sexual Diversity in Schools*. New York: Springer, 2010.

Mills, C. Wright. *The Sociological Imagination*. New York: Oxford University Press, 1959.

Mills, Sarah. "Gender-Neutral Birth Certificate Fight Reaches Sask. Courts." 980AM CJME, July 10, 2017. www.cjme.com.

Molotch, Harvey, and Laura Nolen. *Toilet: Public Restrooms and the Politics of Sharing*. New York: NYU Press. 2010.

Morgensen, Scott. "Settler Homonationalism: Theorizing Settler Colonialism within Queer Modernities." *GLQ: A Journal of Lesbian and Gay Studies* 16, nos. 1–2 (2010): 105–131.

Namaste, Viviane. *Invisible Lives: The Erasure of Transsexual and Transgendered People*. Chicago: University of Chicago Press. 2000.

———. *Sex Change, Social Change: Reflections on Identity, Institutions and Imperial-ism*. Toronto: Women's Press, 2005.

Nestle, Joan. *Persistent Desire: A Femme-Butch Reader*. Boston: Alyson, 1992.

Noble, Bobby Jean. "'My Own Set of Keys': Meditations on Transgender, Scholarship, Belonging." *Feminist Studies* 37, no. 2 (2011): 254–268.

———. "Our Bodies Are Not Ourselves: Tranny Guys and the Racialized Class Politics of Incoherence." In *Transgender Studies Reader 2*, edited by Susan Stryker and Aren Aizura, 248–258. New York: Routledge, 2014.

———. *Sons of the Movement: FtMs Risking Incoherence on a Post-Queer Cultural Land-scape*. Toronto: Women's Press. 2006.

Nordmarken, Sonny. "Microaggressions." *Transgender Studies Quarterly* 1, nos. 1–2 (2014): 129–134.

Nyong'o, Tavia. "The Unforgiveable Transgression of Being Caster Semenya." *Women and Performance: A Journal of Feminist Theory* 20, no. 1 (2010): 95–100.

OECD. *Equity and Quality in Education: Supporting Disadvantaged Students and Schools*. Paris: OECD, 2012. www.oecd-ilibrary.org.

Open Parliament. "Bill C-16." Accessed August 25, 2017, OpenParliament.ca.

Pascoe, C. J. *Dude, You're a Fag*. Berkeley: University of California Press, 2007.

Pieper, Lindsey P. *Sex Testing: Gender Policing in Women's Sports*. Urbana: University of Illinois Press, 2016.

Pierce, Chester M. "Psychiatric Problems of the Black Minority." In *American Hand-book of Psychiatry*, 2nd ed., edited by Silvano Arieti, vol. 2, 512–523. New York: Basic Books, 1974.

Pronger, Brian. *The Arena of Masculinity: Sports, Homosexuality and the Meaning of Sex*. New York: St. Martin's, 1990.

Puar, Jasbir. "Homonationalism as Assemblage: Viral Travels, Affective Sexualities." *Jindal Global Law Review* 4, no. 2 (2013): 23–43.

———. "Q&A with Jasbir Puar." *DarkMatter*, May 2, 2008. www.darkmatter101.org.

———. "Rethinking Homonationalism." *Journal of Middle East Studies* 45 (2013): 336–339.

———. *Terrorist Assemblages: Homonationalism in Queer Times*. Durham, NC: Duke University Press. 2007.

Public Health Agency of Canada. *Questions and Answers: Gender Identity in Schools*. Ottawa: Public Health Agency of Canada, 2010.

Pyne, Jake. "Gender Independent Kids: A Paradigm Shift in Approaches to Gender Non-conforming Children." *Canadian Journal of Human Sexuality* 23, no. 1 (2014): 1–8.

———. "The Governance of Gender Non-conforming Children: A Dangerous Enclosure." *Annual Review of Critical Psychology* 11 (2014): 79–96.

Queer Voices. "California's Assembly Bill 1266 for Transgender Student Rights Signed by Governor Jerry Brown." *Huffington Post*, February 2, 2016. www.huffingtonpost.com.

Quinn, Therese, and Erica R. Meiners. "From Anti-Bullying Laws and Gay Marriages to Queer Worlds and Just Futures." *QED: A Journal in GLBTQ Worldmaking* 1 (2013): 149–175.

Razack, Sherene. *Casting Out: The Eviction of Muslims from Western Law and Politics*. Toronto: University of Toronto Press, 2008.

———. "Gendered Racial Violence and Spatialized Justice: The Murder of Pamela George." *Canadian Journal of Law and Society* 15, no. 2 (2000): 91–130.

Ricci, Talia. "Transgender Child Told You Can't Use Girls' Bathroom." *Global News*, October 3, 2014. http://globalnews.ca.

Ring, Jennifer. *Stolen Bases: Why American Girls Don't Play Baseball*. Urbana: University of Illinois Press, 2009.

Ring, Trudy. "Supreme Court to Hear Gavin Grimm Case: Huge Implications for Trans Students." *Advocate*, February 4, 2016. www.theadvocate.com.

Roberts, Andrea, Margaret Rosario, Heather Corliss, Karestan Koenen, and S. Bryn Austin. "Childhood Gender Nonconformity: A Risk Indicator for Childhood Abuse and Posttraumatic Stress in Youth." *Pediatrics* 129, no. 3 (2012): 410–417.

Sabo, Don. "The Myth of the Sexual Athlete." In *Reconstructing Gender: A Multicultural Anthology*, edited by Estelle Disch, 263–267. Boston: McGraw-Hill, 2003. Originally published 1994.

Saketopoulou, Avgi. "Minding the Gap: Intersections between Gender, Race, and Class in Work with Gender Variant Children." *International Journal of Relational Perspectives* 21, no. 2 (2011): 192–209.

Sax, Leonard. "How Common Is Intersex? A Response to Anne Fausto-Sterling." *Journal of Sex Research* 39, no. 3 (2002): 174–178.

Sedgwick, Eve. *Epistemology of the Closet*. Berkeley: University of California Press, 1990.

———. "How to Bring Your Kids Up Gay." *Social Text* 29 (1991): 18–27.

Serano, Julia. "Detransition, Desistance, and Disinformation: A Guide for Understanding Transgender Children Debates." *Medium*, August 2, 2016. www.medium.com.

Siebers, Tobin. *Disability Theory*. Ann Arbor: University of Michigan Press, 2008.

Simpson, Leanne. *Dancing on Our Turtle's Back: Stories of Nishnaabeg Re-creation, Resurgence and a New Emergence*. Winnipeg, MB: ARP Books.

Singal, Jesse. "How the Fight over Transgender Kids Got a Leading Sex Researcher Fired." *New York*, February 7, 2016. http://nymag.com.

Slater, Dashka. "The Fire on the 57 Bus in Oakland." *New York Times Magazine*, January 29, 2015. www.nytimes.com.

Snorton, Riley. "Trans-of-Color Roundtable Discussion." Trans* Studies Conference, Tucson, AZ, 2016.

Snorton, Riley, and Jin Haritaworn. "Trans Necropolitics: A Transnational Reflection on Violence, Death, and the Trans of Color Afterlife." In *The Transgender Studies Reader 2*, edited by Susan Stryker and A. Aizura, 66–76. New York: Routledge, 2013.

Spade, Dean. *Normal Life: Administrative Violence, Critical Trans Politics, and the Limits of Law*. Cambridge, MA: South End, 2011.

Stafford, Annika. "Is It Still a Boy? Hetero/Gender Normativity in Kindergarten." Ph.D. diss., University of British Columbia, Vancouver, 2013.

Stanley, Eric. "Gender Self-Determination." *Transgender Studies Quarterly* 1, nos. 1–2 (2014): 89–91.

Stanley, Eric, and Nat Smith, eds. *Captive Genders: Trans Embodiment and the Prison Industrial Complex*. Oakland, CA: AK, 2011.

Stern, Mark Joseph. "The HB2 'Repeal' Bill Is an Unmitigated Disaster for LGBTQ Rights and North Carolina." *Slate*, March 30, 2017. www.slate.com.

Stockton, Kathryn Bond. *The Queer Child: Or Growing Sideways in the 20th Century*. Durham, NC: Duke University Press, 2009.

Stout, David. "Transgender Teen Awarded $75,000 in School Restroom Lawsuit." *Time*, December 2, 2014. www.time.com.

Stryker, Susan. "Transgender History, Homonormativity, and Disciplinarity." *Radical History Review*, no. 100 (2008): 145–157.

Stryker, Susan, and Paisley Currah. "General Editors' Introduction: Decolonizing the Transgender Imaginary." *Transgender Studies Quarterly* 1, no. 1 (2014): 303–307.

Sullivan, Claire F. "Gender Verification and Gender Policies in Elite Sport: Eligibility and 'Fair Play.'" *Journal of Sport and Social Issues* 3, no. 5 (2011): 400–419.

Sykes, Heather. "Transsexual and Transgender Policies in Sport." *Women in Sport and Physical Activity Journal* 15, no. 1 (2006): 3–13.

Tannehill, Brynn. "The Truth about Transgender Suicide." *Huffington Post*, November 14, 2015. www.huffingtonpost.com.

Taylor, Catherine, and Tracey Peter. *Every Class in Every School: Final Report on the First National Climate Survey on Homophobia, Biphobia, and Transphobia in Canadian Schools*. Toronto: Egale Canada Human Rights Trust, 2011.

"Tearful Lynsey Sharp Says Rule Change Makes Racing Caster Semenya Difficult." *Guardian*, August 21, 2016. www.theguardian.com.

Teetzel, Sarah. "On Transgendered Athletes, Fairness and Doping: An International Challenge." *Sport in Society* 9, no. 2 (2006): 227–251.

Thobani, Sunera. "After UBC Ousted Arvind Gupta as President, It Made the University Whiter." Rabble.ca, March 4, 2016.

———. *Exalted Subjects: Studies in the Making of Race and Nation in Canada.* Toronto: University of Toronto Press, 2007.

Thomas, William I., and Dorothy Swaine Thomas. *The Child in America: Behavior Problems and Programs.* New York: Knopf, 1928.

Thorne, Barrie. *Gender Play: Girls and Boys in School.* New Brunswick, NJ: Rutgers University Press, 1993.

Tosh, Jemma. *Perverse Psychology: The Pathologization of Sexual Violence and Transgenderism.* London: Routledge, 2014.

TransAthlete.com. "High School Policies for Transgender Student Athletes." Accessed August 2017. www.transathlete.com.

———. "K–12 Policies." Accessed August 2017, www.transathlete.com.

Travers, Ann. "Queering Sport: Lesbian Softball Leagues and the Transgender Challenge." *International Review for the Sociology of Sport* 41, nos. 3–4 (2006): 431–446.

———. "The Sport Nexus and Gender Injustice." *Studies in Social Justice* 2, no. 1 (2008): 79–101.

———. "Thinking the Unthinkable: Imagining an 'Un-American,' Girl-Friendly, Women- and Trans-Inclusive Alternative for Baseball." *Journal of Sport and Social Issues* 37, no. 1 (2013): 78–96.

———. "Transgender and Gender-Nonconforming Kids and the Binary Requirements of Sport Participation in North America." In *Child's Play: Sport in Kids' Worlds,* edited by Michael A. Messner and Michela Musto, 179–201. New Brunswick, NJ: Rutgers University Press, 2016.

———. "Women's Ski Jumping, the 2010 Olympic Games, and the Deafening Silence of Sex Segregation, Whiteness, and Wealth." *Journal of Sport and Social Issues* 35, no. 2 (2011): 126–145.

Travers, Ann, and Jillian Deri. "Transgender Inclusion and the Changing Face of Lesbian Softball Leagues." *International Review for the Sociology of Sport* 46, no. 4 (2011): 488–507.

Underwood, Katie. "Ms. Chatelaine: Harriette Cunningham, Trans Rights Trailblazer." *Chatelaine,* December 23, 2015. www.chatelaine.com.

U.S. Department of Health and Human Services (HHS), Office of the Surgeon General and National Action Alliance for Suicide Prevention. *2012 National Strategy for Suicide Prevention: Goals and Objectives for Action.* Washington, DC: HHS, September 2012.

U.S. Transgender Law and Policy Institute. *Guidelines for Creating Policies for Transgender Children in Recreational Sports.* 2009.

Vancouver School Board. "ACB-R-1: Sexual Orientation and Gender Identities Policy." June 2014. www.vsb.bc.ca.

van Sterkenburg, Jacco, and Annelies Knoppers. "Dominant Discourses about Race/Ethnicity and Gender in Sport Practice and Performance." *International Review for the Sociology of Sport* 39, no. 3 (2004): 301–321.

Veale, Jamie, Elizabeth Saewyc, Helene Frohard-Dourlent, Sarah Dobson, Beth Clark, and the Canadian Trans Youth Health Survey Research Group. *Being Safe, Being Me: Results of the Canadian Trans Youth Health Survey*. Vancouver, BC: Stigma and Resilience among Vulnerable Youth Centre, School of Nursing, University of British Columbia, 2015.

Wall, John. "Childism: The Challenge of Childhood to Ethics and the Humanities." In *The Children's Table: Childhood Studies and the Humanities*, edited by Anna Mae Duane, 68–84. Athens: University of Georgia Press, 2013.

Wamsley, Laurel. "Oregon Adds a New Gender Option to Its Driver's Licenses: X." Oregon Public Broadcasting, June 16, 2017. www.opb.org.

Ward, Jane. "Gender Labor: Transmen, Femmes, and Collective Work of Transgression." *Sexualities* 13, no. 2 (2010): 236–254.

Watson, Amanda. "Accumulating Cares: Women, Whiteness, and the Affective Labor of Responsible Reproduction in Neoliberal Times." Ph.D. diss., Institute of Feminist and Gender Studies, Faculty of Social Sciences, University of Ottawa, 2016.

Weheliye, Alexander. *Habeas Viscus*. Durham, NC: Duke University Press, 2014.

Wente, Margaret. "Transgender Kids: Who Decides?" *Toronto Globe and Mail*, January 17, 2017. www.theglobeandmail.com.

Whitehead, Jaye Cee. *The Nuptial Deal: Same-Sex Marriage and Neo-Liberal Governance*. Chicago: University of Chicago Press, 2011.

Williams, Patricia J. *The Alchemy of Race and Rights*. Cambridge, MA: Harvard University Press, 1991.

Williams Institute, UCLA School of Law. "Incarceration Rate of LGB People Three Times the General Population." Accessed August 2017, http://williamsinstitute.law.ucla.edu.

Winters, Kelley. "The Proposed Gender Dysphoria Diagnosis in the DSM-5." *GID Reform Weblog*, June 7, 2011. http://gidreform.wordpress.com.

Witterick, Rogue. "Dancing in the Eye of the Storm: The Gift of Gender Diversity to Our Family." In *Chasing Rainbows: Exploring Gender Fluid Parenting Practices*, edited by Fiona J. Green and May Friedman, 21–42. Bradford, ON: Demeter, 2013.

Wong, Curtis M. "Texas Sportscaster Shreds Trans Phobes in Must-See Broadcast." *Huffington Post*, March 3, 2017. www.huffingtonpost.com.

Zeidler, Maryse, "Parent Fights to Omit Gender on B.C. Child's Birth Certificate." CBC News, June 30, 2017. www.cbc.ca.

INDEX

Note: participants are indexed under their pseudonyms

International Praise for *The Wrong Mother*

'Sophie Hannah just gets better and better. Her plots are brilliantly cunning and entirely unpredictable. The writing is brilliant and brings us uncomfortably close to the dark, ambivalent impulses experienced by the parents of difficult, demanding children.'   —*The Guardian*

'Sophie Hannah's ingenious, almost surreal mysteries are so intricately constructed that it's impossible to guess how they will end.'   —*Daily Telegraph*

'The fresh and the original have been Hannah's hallmark since her debut, *Little Face*. *The Wrong Mother* is her most accomplished novel yet. As the revelations tumble forth, the tension is screwed ever tighter until the final shocking outcome. Exemplary.'   —*Daily Express*

'Hannah is fast developing a reputation as one of the best new thriller writers around. This (*The Wrong Mother*) leaves you wrong-footed throughout, with a corker of a twist.'   —*The London Paper*

'*The Wrong Mother* is a pacy page-turner and a searing account of the challenges of motherhood.'
  —*The Scotsman*

'This is a superior exercise in storytelling that takes time away from the killer-on-the-loose cop chase to reflect on the chillingly plausible thin line between parenting and psychosis.'   —*Financial Times*

'It's the psychological depth that ensures Sophie Hannah's novels stand out in a crowded market.'   —*Bookseller*

PENGUIN BOOKS

THE WRONG MOTHER

SOPHIE HANNAH is an award-winning poet who won first prize in the Daphne du Maurier Festival Short Story Competition. She is the author of *Little Face*, an international bestseller. Sophie lives in Yorkshire, England, with her husband and two children.

SOPHIE
HANNAH

the
wrong
mother

PENGUIN BOOKS

PENGUIN BOOKS

Published by the Penguin Group
Penguin Group (USA) Inc., 375 Hudson Street, New York, New York 10014, U.S.A.
Penguin Group (Canada), 90 Eglinton Avenue East, Suite 700, Toronto,
Ontario, Canada M4P 2Y3 (a division of Pearson Penguin Canada Inc.)
Penguin Books Ltd, 80 Strand, London WC2R 0RL, England
Penguin Ireland, 25 St Stephen's Green, Dublin 2, Ireland (a division of Penguin Books Ltd)
Penguin Group (Australia), 250 Camberwell Road, Camberwell,
Victoria 3124, Australia (a division of Pearson Australia Group Pty Ltd)
Penguin Books India Pvt Ltd, 11 Community Centre,
Panchsheel Park, New Delhi – 110 017, India
Penguin Group (NZ), 67 Apollo Drive, Rosedale, North Shore 0632,
New Zealand (a division of Pearson New Zealand Ltd)
Penguin Books (South Africa) (Pty) Ltd, 24 Sturdee Avenue,
Rosebank, Johannesburg 2196, South Africa

Penguin Books Ltd, Registered Offices: 80 Strand, London WC2R 0RL, England

First published in Great Britain under the title *The Point of Rescue* by Hodder & Stoughton 2008
Published in Penguin Books 2009

5 7 9 10 8 6

PUBLISHER'S NOTE
This is a work of fiction. Names, characters, places, and incidents are either the product of the
author's imagination or are used fictitiously, and any resemblance to actual persons, living or
dead, business establishments, events, or locales is entirely coincidental.

LIBRARY OF CONGRESS CATALOGING-IN-PUBLICATION DATA
Hannah, Sophie, 1971–
The wrong mother / Sophie Hannah.
p. cm.
ISBN 978-0-14-311630-1
1. Married women—Fiction. 2. Psychological fiction. I. Title.
PR6058.A5928W76 2009
823'.914--dc22 2009027521

Printed in the United States of America

For Susan and Suzie

the wrong mother

1

Monday, 6 August 2007

Or your family.

The last three words are yelled, not spoken. As Pam elbows her way through the crowd in front of me, I hear nothing apart from that last spurt of viciousness, her afterthought. She made it four syllables instead of five: 'Or your fam-ly'; four blows that thump in my mind like a boxer's jabbing fist.

Why bring my family into it? What have they ever done to Pam?

Beside me, several people have stopped to stare, waiting to see how I will react to Pam's outburst. I could shout something after her but she wouldn't hear me. There is too much noise coming from all directions: buses screeching around corners, music thumping out of shop doorways, buskers beating unsubtle notes out of their guitar strings, the low metallic rumble of trains into and out of Rawndesley station.

Pam is moving away from me fast, but I can still see her white trainers with luminous patches on the heels, her solid, square body and short, aubergine-coloured spiky hair. Her livid departure has cut a long, straight furrow out of the moving carpet of people. I have no intention of following her, or looking as if I am. A middle-aged woman whose shopping bags have carved deep pink grooves into the skin on her arms repeats, in what she probably imagines is a loud whisper, what Pam said to me, for the benefit of a teenage girl in shorts and a halter-necked top, a newcomer to the scene.

I shouldn't care that so many people heard, but I do. There is nothing wrong with my family, yet thanks to a purple-haired midget I am surrounded by strangers who must be convinced that there is. I wish I'd called Pam that to her face instead of letting her have the last word. The last three words.

I take a deep breath, inhaling traffic fumes and dust. Sweat trickles down both sides of my face. The heat is thick; invisible glue. I've never been able to handle hot weather. I feel as if someone is blowing up a concrete balloon inside my chest; this is what anger does to me. I turn to my audience and take a small bow. 'Hope you enjoyed the show,' I say. The girl in the halter-necked top smiles at me conspiratorially and takes a sip from the ridged plastic cup she's holding. I want to punch her.

Once I've out-stared the last of the gawpers, I start to march in the direction of Farrow and Ball, trying to burn off some of my indignant energy. That's where I was going, to pick up paint samples, and I'm damned if I'll let Pam's tantrum change my plans. I push through the mobile crush of bodies on Cadogan Street, elbowing people out of my way and enjoying it a bit too much. It's myself I'm furious with. Why didn't I reach out and grab Pam by her ridiculous hair, denounce her as she had denounced me? Even an uninspired 'Fuck off' would have been better than nothing.

Inside Farrow and Ball someone has turned the air-conditioning up too high; it whirs like the inside of a fridge. The place is empty of customers apart from me and a mother and daughter. The girl has bulky metal braces on her top and bottom teeth. She wants to paint her bedroom bright pink, but her mother thinks white or something close to white would be better. They squabble in whispers in the far corner of the shop. This is the way people ought to argue in public: quietly, making sure that as few words as possible are overheard.

I tell the sales assistant who approaches me that I am just browsing, and turn to face a wall of colour charts: Tallow, String, Cord, Savage Ground. I'm supposed to be thinking about paint for Nick's and my bedroom. *Tallow, String, Cord* ... I stand still, too full of rage to move. The sweat on my face dries in sticky streaks.

If I see Pam again when I leave here, I'll knock her to the ground and stamp on her head. She's not the only one who can take things up a notch. I can overreact with the best of them.

I can't shop if I'm not in the mood, and I'm definitely not in the mood now. I leave the chilled air of Farrow and Ball behind me and head back out into the heat, embarrassed by how shaken I feel. I scan Cadogan Street in both directions but there is no sign of Pam. I probably wouldn't knock her to the ground—in fact, I definitely wouldn't—but it makes me feel better to imagine for a few seconds that I am the sort of person who strikes quickly and ruthlessly.

The multi-storey car park is on the other side of town, on Jimmison Street. I sigh, knowing I'll be dripping with sweat by the time I get there. As I walk, I rummage in my handbag for the ticket I'll need to feed into the pay-station slot. I can't find it. I try the zipped side pocket but it's not there either. And I've forgotten, yet again, to make a note of where I left my car, on what level and in which colour zone. I am always in too much of a hurry, trying to squeeze in a shopping trip that has been endlessly postponed and has finally become an emergency between work and collecting the children. Is there something about work I need to remember? Or arrange? My mind rushes ahead of itself, panicking before any cause for panic has been established. Do I remember where I put the scoping study I did for Gilsenen? Did I fax my sediment erosion diagrams to Ana-Paola? I think I did both.

There's probably nothing important that I've forgotten, but it would be nice to be certain, as I always used to be. Now that I have two small children, my work has an added personal resonance: every time I talk or write about Venice's lagoon losing dangerous amounts of the sediment it needs to keep it healthy, I find myself identifying with the damn thing. Two strong currents called Zoe and Jake, aged four and two, are sluicing important things from my brain that I will never be able to retrieve, and replacing them with thoughts about Barbie and Calpol. Perhaps I should write a paper, complete with scientific diagrams, arguing that my mind has silted up and needs dredging, and send it to Nick, who has a talent for forgetting he has a home life while he is at work. He is always advising me to follow his example.

Only forty minutes to get to nursery before it closes. And I'm going to waste fifteen of those running up and down concrete ramps, panting, growling through gritted teeth at the rows of cars that stubbornly refuse to be my black Ford Galaxy; and then because I've lost my ticket I'll have to find an official and bribe him to raise the barrier to let me out, and I'll arrive late at nursery again, and they'll moan at me *again*, and I haven't got my paint samples, or the toddler reins I was supposed to buy from Mothercare, to stop Jake wriggling free from my grasp and launching himself into the middle of busy roads. And I can't come into Rawndesley again for at least a week, because the Consorzio people are arriving tomorrow and I'll be too busy at work . . .

Something hits me hard under my right arm, whacking into my ribs, propelling me sharply to the left. I reel on the kerb, trying to stay upright, but I lose my balance. The tarmac of the road is on a slant, tilting, rising up to meet me. Behind me, a voice yells, 'Watch out, love—watch . . .' My mind, which was hurtling in the direction of anticipated future catastrophes, screeches to a halt as my body falls. I see the bus coming— almost on top of me already—but I can't move out of its path. As if it is happening somewhere far away, I watch a man lean forward and bang his fist on the side of the bus, shouting, 'Stop!'

There's no time. The bus is too close, and it isn't slowing down. I flinch, turning away from the huge wheels and using all the power in my body to roll away. I throw my handbag and it lands a few feet in front of me. I am lying in between it and the bus, and it occurs to me that this is good, that I am a barrier—my phone and diary won't get crushed. My Vivienne Westwood mirror in its pink pouch will be undamaged. But I can't be lying still. I must be moving; the tarmac is scraping my face. Something shunts me forward. The wheels, pressing on my legs.

And then it stops. I try to move, and am surprised to discover that I can. I crawl free and sit up, preparing myself for blood, bones poking through torn flesh. I feel all right, but I don't trust the information my brain is receiving from my body. People often feel fine and then drop dead soon afterwards; Nick is for ever accosting me with gloomy anecdotes from the hospital to that effect.

My dress is shredded, covered in dust and dirt. My knees and arms are grazed, bleeding. All over me, patches of skin have started to sting. A man is swearing at me. At first it appears that he is wearing beige pyjamas with a funny badge on them; it is a few seconds before I realise he's the bus driver, my almost killer. People are shouting at him, telling him to lay off me. I watch and listen, hardly feeling involved. There has already been shouting in the street today. This afternoon, screaming in public is normal. I try to smile at the two women who have nominated themselves as my main helpers. They want me to stand up, and have taken hold of my arms.

'I'm all right, really,' I say. 'I think I'm fine.'

'You can't sit in the road, love,' one of them says.

I'm not ready to move. I know I can't sit in the road for ever—the team from the Consorzio are coming, and I have to cook supper for Nick and the kids—but my limbs feel as if they've been welded to the tarmac.

I start to giggle. I could so easily be dead now, and I'm not. 'I've just been run over,' I say. 'I can sit still for a few seconds, surely.'

'Someone should take her to a hospital,' says the man who hit the side of the bus.

In the background, a voice I sort of recognise says, 'Her husband works at Culver Valley General.'

I laugh again. These people think I have time to go to hospital. 'I'm fine,' I tell the concerned man.

'What's your name, love?' asks the woman who is holding my right arm.

I don't want to tell them, but it would sound churlish to say so. I could give a false name, I suppose. I know which name I would give: Geraldine Bretherick. I used it recently, when a taxi driver was showing too much interest in me, and enjoyed the feeling that I was taking a risk, tempting fate a little bit.

I am about to speak when I hear that familiar voice again. It says, 'Sally. Her name's Sally Thorning.'

It's odd, but it's only when I see Pam's face that I remember the firm, flat object that rammed into my ribs. That's why I fell into the road. Pam has a face like a bulldog: all the features squashed in the middle. Could the hard flat thing have been a hand?

'Sally, I can't believe it.' Pam crouches down beside me. The skin around her cleavage wrinkles. It is dark and leathery, like a much older woman's; Pam isn't even forty. 'Thank God you're all right. You could have died!' She turns away from me. 'I'll take her to hospital,' she tells the people who are bending over me, their faces full of concern. 'I know her.'

In the distance, I hear someone say, 'That's her friend,' and something in my brain explodes. I stand up and stagger backwards, away from Pam. 'You hypocrite! You're not my friend. You're an ugly, evil gremlin. Did you push me into the road deliberately?' Today it is normal to slander people in the street. But the onlookers who until now have been keen to help me don't appear to know this. Their expressions change as it dawns on them that I must be mixed up in something bad. Innocent people do not fall in front of buses for no reason.

I pick up my handbag and limp towards the car park, leaving Pam's astonished face behind me.

*

When I pull into Monk Barn Avenue with my cargo of children, an hour later than usual, I still have that lucky-to-be-alive feeling, an unreal glow that coats my skin, even the patches that are throbbing, where the blood is congealing into scabs. It's similar to how I felt after I had Zoe, with diamorphine coursing through my veins: unable to believe what has just happened.

I am pleased to see my house for the first time since we bought it. Relieved. Given a choice between being dead and living here, I would choose the latter. I must remember to say this to Nick next time he accuses me of being too negative. I still think of it as our new house, although we've lived here for six months and it's only a flat, part of what must once have been a spacious, elegant house that had some integrity. More recently, a team of architectural philistine vandals has divided it into three, badly. Nick and I bought a third. Before we moved here we lived in a three-hundred-year-old three-bedroom cottage in Silsford with a beautiful enclosed garden at the back that Zoe and Jake loved. That Nick and I loved.

I pull up beside the kerb, as close to our house—flat—as I can get, which today is reasonably close; it won't be too much of a slog getting the children and their bags and toys and comfort blankets and empty bottles to the front door. Monk Barn Avenue is two neat rows of four-storey Victorian terraces with a narrow strip of road in the middle. It wouldn't be so narrow if there were not cars parked bonnet to bumper along both sides, but there are no garages, so everybody parks on the street. This is one of my many gripes about the place. In Silsford we had a double garage with lovely blue doors . . .

I tell myself not to be absurdly sentimental—garage doors, for Christ's sake—and turn off the ignition. The engine and radio fall silent and in the silence the thought rushes back: Pam Senior tried to kill me today. *No. She can't have.* It makes no sense. It makes as little sense as her screaming at me in the street.

Zoe and Jake are both asleep. Jake's mouth is open as he snores and grunts softly, his plump cheeks pink, sweaty brown curls stuck to his forehead. His orange T-shirt is covered in stain islands, remnants of the day's meals. Zoe, as always, looks neater, with her head tilted and her hands clasped in her lap. Her curly blonde hair has expanded in the heat. I send her to nursery every day with a neat ponytail, but by the time I arrive to pick her up the bobble has vanished and her hair is a fluffy gold cloud around her face.

My children are breathtakingly beautiful, which is odd because Nick and I are not. I used to worry about their obvious perfection, in case it meant they were likely to be snatched by a ruthlessly competitive parent (of which there are many in Spilling), but Nick assured me that the blotchy-faced, snot-encrusted little characters at Kiddiwinks nursery look every bit as irresistible to their parents as Zoe and Jake do to us. I find this hard to believe.

I check my watch: seven fifteen. My brain is blank and I can't decide what to do. If I wake the children, either they will be manic after their early evening recharge and up causing chaos until ten o'clock, or they'll be groggy and whiny and have to be rushed straight to cot and bed, which will mean they will miss their supper. Which will mean they will wake up at five thirty and shout 'Egg-IES!'—their pet name for scrambled eggs—over and over again until I haul my exhausted body out of bed and feed them.

I pull my mobile phone out of my handbag and dial our home number. Nick answers, but takes a while to say, 'Yeah?' His mind is on something else.

'What's up?' I ask. 'You sound distracted.'

'I was just . . .' Full marks to me. Nick is too distracted, apparently, even to finish his sentence. I hear the television in the background. I wait for him to ask me why I'm late, where I am, where the children are, but he does none of these things. Instead, he startles me by chuckling and saying, 'That is *such* bollocks! As if anyone's going to fall for that!' I know from long years of experience that he is talking to the *Channel 4 News*, not to me. I wonder if Jon Snow finds him as irritating as I sometimes do.

'I'm outside, in the car,' I tell him. 'The kids are both asleep. Turn the news off and come and help.'

If I were Nick, I would be outraged to find myself on the receiving end of a command like this, but he is too good-humoured to take offence. When he appears at the front door, his dark curly hair is flat on one side, which I know means he has been lying on the couch since he got in from work. On my phone I can still hear Jon Snow.

I lower my window and say, 'You forgot to put the phone down.'

'Jesus, what happened to your face? And your dress? Sally, you're covered in blood!'

That's when I know I'm going to lie. If I tell the truth, Nick will know I'm worried. He'll be worried too. There will be no chance of pretending it never happened.

'Relax, I'm fine. I fell over in town and got a bit trampled, but it's nothing serious. A few scrapes and bruises.'

'A *bit* trampled? What, you mean people actually walked over you? You look a state. Are you sure you're okay?'

I nod, grateful that it never occurs to Nick not to believe me.

'Shit.' He sounds even more concerned as his eyes move to the back seat of the car. 'The kids. What shall we do?'

'If we let them sleep, we could be sitting in the car till nine o'clock and then they'll be up bouncing on the sofa cushions until midnight.'

'If we wake them, they'll be a nightmare,' Nick points out.

I say nothing. I would rather have the nightmare now than at nine o'clock, but for once I don't want to be the one to decide. One of the main differences between me and Nick is that he goes out of his way to put off anything unpleasant, whereas I would always prefer to get it over with. As he regularly points

out, this means that I actively seek out the problems he sometimes gets to avoid altogether.

'We could order a takeaway, bring a bottle of wine outside
and eat in the car,' Nick pleads. 'It's a warm night.'

'*You* could,' I correct him. 'I'm sorry, but you're married to
someone who's too old and knackered and grumpy to eat pizza
in her car when there's a perfectly good kitchen table within
reach. And why only one bottle of wine?'

Nick grins. 'I could bring two if that'd swing it.'

I shake my head: the party-pooper, the boring grown-up
whose job description is to spoil everyone's fun.

'You want me to wake them up.' Nick sighs. I open the car
door and ease my wounded body out. 'Jesus! Look at you!' he
shouts when he sees my knees.

I giggle. Somehow, his overreaction makes me feel better.
'How did an alarmist like you ever get a job working in a hospital?' Nick is a radiographer. Presumably he would have been
sacked by now if he made a habit of startling prone patients by
shouting, 'Jesus! I've never seen a tumour that size before.'

I open the boot and start to gather together the children's
many accessories while Nick makes his first tentative advance
towards Zoe, gently urging her to wake up. I am a pessimist by
nature, and guess that I have about twenty seconds to get
through the front door and well away from the danger zone before the children detonate. I grab all the luggage and my house
key (Nick has, of course, forgotten to put the door on the latch
and it has swung closed), and head for shelter. I sprint up the
path with nursery bags and blankets trailing in my wake, let
myself in, and, gritting my teeth against the pain that I know
will come when I try to bend and unbend my stinging knees,
begin my ascent.

Number 12A Monk Barn Avenue has one extraordinary feature: it consists almost entirely of stairs. Oh, there's a strip of
hall, and a narrow stretch of landing, and if you're really lucky
you might stumble across the odd room, but basically what we

bought was stairs in a good location. A location, crucially, that we knew would guarantee places at Monk Barn Primary School for Zoe and Jake.

Perversely, I already resent the school for making me move house, so it had better be good. Last year it was featured in a television documentary, the verdict of which was that there were three state primaries—Monk Barn, one in Guildford and one in Exeter—that were as good as any fee-paying prep school in the country. I'd have opted to pay, and stay in our old house, but Nick had a miserable time as a teenager at a very expensive public school, and refuses even to consider that sort of education for our children.

From our bathroom window there's a good view of Monk Barn Primary's playground. I was disappointed when I first saw it because it looked ordinary; I'd uprooted my family to be near this place—the least they could have done was carve some scholarly Latin texts into the concrete.

I wince as I drag my battered, stiffening body up the first stretch of stairs, past the downstairs loo, the bedroom that Zoe and Jake share, and the bathroom. The centrepiece of our flat is a large rectangular obstruction that looks as if it might have been sculpted by Rachel Whiteread. Inside this white-walled blockage is the house's original staircase that now leads to flats 12B and 12C. It annoys me that there is a big box containing someone else's stairs inside my home, one that eats up half the space and means I keep having to turn corners. When we first moved here, I kept leaping to my feet as I heard what sounded like a stampede of buffaloes on the landing. I soon realised it was the sound of our neighbours' footsteps as they went in and out, that the thudding wasn't coming from inside my new home—it only sounded as if it was.

As I limp past the kitchen, I hear screams from the road. The children are awake. Poor Nick; he would never suspect that I rushed inside to avoid having to deal with the mayhem I knew was coming. I turn another corner. Nick's and my bedroom is a few steps up on the left. It is so small that, if I stood in the doorway and allowed myself to fall forward, I would land on the bed. The idea appeals to me, but I keep going until I get to the lounge, because that's the only room that has a view of the street, and I want to check that Nick is holding his own against the combined forces of Zoe and Jake.

Tutting at the browning banana skin that perches like an octopus on the arm of the sofa, I walk over to the lounge window. Nick is on his knees on the pavement with a wailing Zoe tucked under one arm. Jake is lying in the road—in the gutter, to be precise—red in the face, screaming. Nick tries to scoop him up, fails, and nearly drops Zoe, who screams, 'Dadd-ee! You nearly dropped m-ee!' She has recently learned how to state the obvious and likes to get plenty of practice.

Our neighbours Fergus and Nancy choose this moment to pull up in their shiny red two-seater Mercedes. Roof down, of course. Fergus and Nancy own the whole of number 10 Monk Barn Avenue in its original form. When they pull up in their sports car after a hard day's work, they can go straight inside, pour themselves a glass of wine and relax. Nick and I find this incredible.

I open the lounge window to let some air in, put the phone back in its holder, and turn off the TV. The best way to stop my wounded skin from stiffening is to keep moving—this is what I tell myself as I quickly repair the lounge: cushions back on the sofa, TV guide back on the coffee table, Nick's jacket to the wardrobe, race down to the kitchen with the banana skin. If I ever leave Nick for another man, I'm going to make sure it's someone tidy.

Back in the lounge—our only large room—I unpack the nursery bags, sorting things into the usual five piles: empty milk bottles and juice cups, dirty clothes, correspondence that needs attention, junk that can be binned, and artwork that must be admired. The children are still howling. I hear Nick trying, as tactfully as possible, to fend off Fergus and Nancy, who always want to stop for a chat. He says, 'Sorry, I'd better . . .' Jake's yelping drowns out the rest of his words.

Nancy says, 'Oh dear. Poor you.' She might be addressing Nick or either of the children. She and Fergus often look anxious when they see us struggling with Zoe and Jake. Now they probably think something terrible has happened at nursery—a rabid dog on the loose, perhaps. They'd be horrified if I told them this was normal, that tantrums on this scale are a twice-daily occurrence.

By the time Nick manages to lug the kids up to the kitchen, I have put on a load of washing, wiped all the surfaces, spooned some defrosted shepherd's pie into two bowls and put it in the microwave. My children spill into the kitchen like survivors from the wreck of the *Titanic*: damp, unkempt and full of complaints. I tell them in a bright voice that it's shepherd's pie for tea, their favourite, but they appear not to hear me. Jake lies face down on the floor and sticks his bottom in the air. 'Bottle! Cot!' he wails. I ignore him, and continue to talk brightly about shepherd's pie.

Zoe sobs, 'Mummy, I don't *want* shepherd's pie for supper. I want shepherd's *pie*!'

Nick zigzags around her to get to the fridge. 'Wine,' he growls.

'You're *having* shepherd's pie, darling,' I tell her. 'And you, Jakie. Now, come on—everyone sit down at the table!'

'Nooo!' Zoe screams. 'I don't want that!'

Jake, seeing Nick pouring wine into two glasses, sits up and points. 'Me!' he says. 'Me turn.'

'Jake, you can't have wine,' I tell him. 'Ribena? Orange squash? Zoe, you don't want shepherd's pie? What do you want, then? Sausages and baked beans?'

'Noooo! I said—Mummy, listen. I said, I don't want shepherd's pie, I want shepherd's *pie*.'

My daughter is very advanced for a four-year-old. I'm sure none of her contemporaries would think of such a simple yet brilliant way to infuriate a parent.

'Want dat!' Jake points again at Nick's wine. 'Want Daddy drink! Srittle!'

Nick and I exchange a look. We are the only people in the world who understand every word Jake says. Translation: he wants to sit on the sofa with a glass of wine and watch *Stuart Little*. I can relate to this. It's almost exactly what I want to do, give or take the odd detail. 'After supper, you can watch *Stuart Little*,' I tell him firmly. 'Now, Zoe, Jake, let's all sit down at the table and you can have some nice shepherd's pie, and you can tell me and Daddy all about your day. We can have a nice family chat.' I sound like a naïve idiot even to myself. Still, you have to try.

Nick picks Jake up off the floor and puts him in a chair. He wriggles off and wipes snot all over Nick's trousers. Zoe clings to my leg, still insisting that she both does and doesn't want shepherd's pie. 'Okay,' I concede, moving mentally to Plan B. 'Who wants to watch *Stuart Little*?' This suggestion attracts an enthusiastic response from the junior members of the household. 'Fine. Go and sit on the sofa, and I'll bring your supper in there. But you have to eat it all up, okay? Otherwise I'll turn the TV off.' Zoe and Jake run out of the room, and begin to clamber up to the lounge, giggling.

'They won't eat it,' Nick tells me. 'Zoe'll sit with hers on her lap, mashing it around with her fork, and Jake'll throw his on the floor.'

'Worth a try,' I call over my shoulder as I race upstairs with a bowl of shepherd's pie in each hand.

Jake reaches the top of the stairs first. When Zoe's head appears a second or two later, he smacks her lightly on the nose. She hits him back and he falls into me. I fall too, and spill both bowls of food. When Nick arrives to see what's happened, he finds Zoe bawling on the stairs, Jake bawling in the lounge doorway, and me on my hands and knees on the carpet, collecting fluffy mincemeat, carrots, mushrooms and lumps of potato to put back into the bowls.

'Right,' says Nick. 'If everybody stops crying *right now* ... you can have some chocolate!' He's got a half-unwrapped Crunchie bar in his hand and is holding it as a highwayman might hold his gun, pointing it at the children. I see undiluted desperation in his eyes.

Zoe and Jake are writhing on the floor, demanding both chocolate and *Stuart Little*. 'No chocolate,' I say. 'Bed! Right now!' I abandon the shepherd's pie clear-up operation, pick them up and carry them downstairs to their room.

Utterly determined to complete the task I have set myself no matter what obstacles I encounter, I finally manage to get Zoe into her nightie and Jake into his pyjamas and sleeping bag. I tell them to wait while I get their bedtime milk, and when I come back to their room, they are sitting side by side on Zoe's bed. Zoe has her arm round Jake. They both smile up at me. 'I brushed my teeth, and Jake's, Mummy,' says Zoe proudly. I notice a pink and a blue toothbrush protruding from under Jake's cot, and large white smears on the carpet and on Jake's left cheek.

'Well done, darling.'

'Tory?' says Jake hopefully.

'Which story do you want?'

'Uttyumbers,' he says.

'Okay.'

I take Dr Seuss's *Nutty Numbers* off the shelf and sit down on the bed. I read it without interruption, and Zoe and Jake take turns to lift the flaps and find the hidden pictures. When I've finished, Jake says, 'Gain,' so I read it again. Then I put Zoe in her bed and Jake in his cot and sing them their goodnight song. I made it up when Zoe was a baby, and now Nick and I have to sing it every night while the children laugh at us as if we're eccentric old fools, singing a song that contains their names and lots of words that don't exist.

I kiss them goodnight and close their door. I don't understand children. If they're shattered and want to go to bed, why don't they just say so?

I find Nick sitting cross-legged on the floor, a dustpan and brush idle in his lap. He is watching the news again and drinking his wine, surrounded by small piles of cold shepherd's pie. Nick loves every sort of news: 24, Channel 4, CNN. He's hooked. Even when nothing of any interest is happening, he likes to hear all about it. 'How were they?' he asks.

'Fine,' I tell him. 'Sweet. Aren't you going to . . . ?' I point at the mess.

'In a sec,' he says. 'I'm just watching this.'

It's not good enough. Not now, not on the day that somebody tried to kill me. Is it possible to push a person under a bus and not be trying to kill them?

'You could do both at the same time,' I say. 'Watch the news and clear up the mess.' Pointless; it's the sort of comment someone like Nick doesn't understand.

He looks at me as if I'm crazy.

'I'm just saying, it'd be more efficient.'

When he sees I'm serious, he laughs. 'Why don't I just go straight to the last day of my life?' he says. 'That'd be really efficient.'

'I'm going to ring Esther,' I say through gritted teeth, picking up the phone to take into the bathroom. A warm bath with lots of lavender-scented bubbles in it will make everything all right.

'Remember to make dinner and sleep and have tomorrow's breakfast at the same time,' Nick calls after me. 'It's more efficient.'

He is joking, and has no idea that I often do cook and make phone calls simultaneously. I've made entire meals one-handed, or with the phone tucked under my chin.

I turn on the hot tap and dial Esther's number. Hearing my voice, she says what she always says. 'Have you saved Venice yet?'

'Not yet,' I tell her.

'Damn, you're slow. Pull your finger out. Decontaminate those salt-marshes.'

I work three days a week for the Save Venice Foundation, which Esther thinks is a hilarious and sensationalist name for an organisation. We have been best friends since school. 'Talking of slow . . .' She groans. 'The Imbecile is *such* an imbecile. You know what he did today?' Esther works at the University of Rawndesley. She's secretary to the head of the history department. 'A load of e-mails came through to me that he needed to look at and respond to, right? Six, to be exact. So I forwarded them to him, and—because I know what an imbecile he is—I gave him two options: either he could reply directly, himself, or he could tell me what he wanted me to say and I'd reply for him. Two clear options, right? You understand the choice on offer?'

I say I do, and hope her story won't go on too long. I want her to listen, not talk. Does that mean I've decided to tell her?

'Three hours later, I get seven e-mails in my inbox, from the Imbecile. One tells me that he has replied to all the messages himself. Great, I think. The other six are the replies, to all sorts of important bods in the world of history academia—yawn!— that he thinks he's sent to the bods, but that in fact he's sent to me. He just clicked on reply! He doesn't know that if someone forwards you an e-mail and you click on reply, you're replying to the forwarder, not the sender of the original message! And this guy's the head of a university department!'

Her irate tone makes me weary. I ought to be angry, but instead I am numb.

'Sal? You there?'

'Yeah.'

'What's wrong?'

I take a deep breath. 'I think a childminder called Pam Senior might have tried to kill me this afternoon.'

❋

Pam has never been Zoe and Jake's childminder but she's one of our regular babysitters and she helped Nick when I was away for a week last year. She is usually cheerful and chatty, if a little opinionated about things like dummies and the MMR vaccine. When I saw her in Rawndesley I was pleased; I thought it would save me a phone call. On weekday evenings I'm often so tired by the time I've made and eaten supper that I find it hard to produce full, cogent sentences.

I called out to Pam and she stopped, apparently pleased to see me. She asked after Zoe and Jake, whom she calls 'the bairns', and I told her they were fine. Then I said, 'Are you still okay to have Zoe for the autumn half-term week?' I had my mum or Nick's mum lined up for most of the school holidays, but both were busy that week in October.

Pam looked shifty, as if there was something she wasn't telling me. The expression on my face must have been tragically-let-down-needy-working-mother to the power of a hundred as I anticipated being hit by a sudden childcare catastrophe. As indeed I was.

Monk Barn Primary's autumn half-term coincides with a conference I have to attend. Most of the Venetian environmental scientists as well as experts from all over the world who are working on how to preserve Venice's lagoon are convening for five days in Cambridge. As one of the organisers, I have to be there, which means I have to find someone to look after Zoe. I tried nursery first, hoping they'd have her back just for the week, but they're full. Once Zoe leaves at the beginning of September, another child will take her place. So I thought of Pam, who had helped me before.

'No probs,' she said when I asked her three months ago. 'I've stuck it in the diary.' There was no element of uncertainty, nothing about pencilling it in and confirming later. Reliability, I would have said before today, is Pam's main characteristic. Her navy blue NatWest Advantage Gold diary is never out of her hands for long.

Pam appears to have no interests. She is single, and her social life, from what I can tell, revolves entirely around her parents, with whom she still goes on holiday every year. They stay in hotels that belong to the same chain, all over the world, and clock up reward points that Pam is very proud of. Whenever I speak to her she gives me her latest score, and I try to look impressed. She has also told me defiantly that she and her mum always make sure to leave hotel rooms spotless: 'There'd have been nothing for the maid to do after we left—nothing!'

She doesn't read books or go to the cinema or theatre, or watch television. She isn't keen on exercise of any sort, though she always wears lilac and pale pink sportswear: jogging bottoms or cycling shorts, and skimpy Lycra vests under zip-up tracksuit tops. Art doesn't interest her: she once asked me why I have 'all those blobby pictures' on my walls. She isn't a fan of cooking or eating out, DIY or gardening. Last year she told me she was giving up babysitting at weekends because she needed more time for herself. I have no idea what she might do with that time. She once said that she and her parents were going on a course to learn how to make stained-glass windows but she never mentioned it again and nothing ever seemed to come of it.

Today, in answer to my question about the autumn half-term, she said, 'I've been meaning to ring you, but I've not had a minute.' She was trying to sound casual, but her squirming gave the game away.

'There isn't a problem, is there?' I asked.

'Well . . . there's a bit of a snag, yeah. The thing is, a neighbour of mine's having to go into hospital that week, and . . . well, I feel awful about cancelling on you, but I've kind of said I'll have her twins for the week.'

Twins. Whose mother would be paying Pam double what I'd be paying for Zoe. Was she seriously ill? I wanted to ask. A single parent? I needed to know that Pam was letting me down for a good reason.

'I thought we had a firm arrangement,' I said. 'You told me you'd put it in the diary.'

'I know. I'm really sorry, but, like I say, this lady's going into hospital. I can try and find you someone else, perhaps. Tell you what, why don't I ask my mum? I bet she'd do it.'

I um-ed and ah-ed. A large part of me was tempted to say, 'Yes, please!', the part that yearned to overlook all inconvenient details for the sake of being able to think of the matter as resolved. Sometimes—no, often—I feel as if my brain and life will shatter into tiny pieces if I am given one more thing to sort out. As it is, I start each day with a list of between thirty and forty things I need to do. As I blast my way through the hours between six in the morning and ten at night, the list goes round and round in my head, each item beginning with a verb that exhausts me: ring, invoice, fax, order, book, arrange, buy, make, prepare, send . . .

It would have been a great relief to be able to say, 'Thanks, Pam, your mum'll do nicely.' But I've met Pam's mother. She's short and very fat and a smoker, and moves slowly and with difficulty. In the end I said no thanks, I'd find someone else myself. I couldn't resist adding, nosily, that I hoped Pam's neighbour would make a speedy recovery.

'Oh, she's not ill,' said Pam, as if I ought to have known. 'She's going in for a boob job. She'll be in and out in a couple of days, but the thing is, her husband's away that week and so's her sister, so she's got no help, and you can't lift anything heavy after a boob job, so she won't be able to lift the twins. They're only six months old.'

'A boob job? Are you serious?'

Pam nodded.

'When did she ask you?' I must be missing something, I thought.

'A couple of weeks ago. I'd say I'd have Zoe as well, only I'm not allowed more than three at a time, and I've already got another child booked in for that week.'

'I don't understand,' I said, keeping my voice level. 'I rang you to organise this months ago. You said you'd put it in the diary. When your neighbour asked you, why didn't you just say no, that you're already booked up?'

Pam's mouth twitched. She doesn't like to be challenged. 'Look, I thought I'd be okay with four, just for the week, but my mum said—and she's right—that it's not worth breaking the rules. Childminders aren't allowed more than three at a time. I don't want to get into any trouble.'

'I know, but . . . sorry if this sounds petty, but why are you apologising to me instead of to your neighbour, or the parent of this other child?'

'I thought you'd take it better than either of the other mums. You're more approachable.'

Great, I thought: punished for good behaviour. 'Would it make any difference if I said I'd pay double? If I paid whatever the twins' mum was going to pay you, just to look after Zoe? I will, if that'll make a difference.' I shouldn't bloody well have to, this is outrageous, a voice in my head was shouting. I smiled my most encouraging smile. 'Pam, I'm desperate. I need someone to look after Zoe that week, and she knows you and really likes you. I don't think she'd be happy going to someone she doesn't know so well . . .'

All the warmth was draining from Pam's face as I spoke. Watching her eyes, I felt as if I was transforming into something disgusting in front of her, as if my skin was turning to green slime. 'I'm not trying to rip you off,' she said. 'I don't want more money out of you. What do you think this is, some kind of scam?'

'No, of course not. I just . . . look, I'm sorry, Pam, I don't want to whinge, but I'm a bit upset about this. I can't believe you can't see it from my point of view. I've got a really important conference that I *have* to go to. I've spent months setting it up. I can't not go, and Nick needs to work too—he's used up all his holiday this year. And you're letting me down for the sake of some woman who wants bigger boobs? Can't she get her silicon implants another time?' At no point did I raise my voice.

'She doesn't want bigger boobs! She's having a breast *reduction*, actually, not that you'd care! Because she's got chronic backache and it's ruining her life and her children's lives, because she can't get out of her bed some days, she's in that much agony!'

I started to backtrack and make apologetic noises—of course, if I'd misunderstood, if it was a genuine medical problem—but Pam wasn't listening. She called me a snobby bitch and said she'd always known I was trouble. And then she started screaming at me to get the fuck out of her face, to leave her alone, that she had never liked me, that she wanted nothing to do with me, never wanted to see me again as long as she lived. Or my family.

I cannot imagine ever yelling at anyone the way Pam yelled at me, not unless they'd harmed my children or set fire to my house. I say this to Esther and she says, 'Or pushed you under a bus.' She giggles.

'She didn't push me.' I sigh, pulling my hair away from my neck so that my skin is touching the cool rim of the bath. The water isn't as warm as I normally have it because it's so humid tonight and even the idea of hot water on my wounds is painful. 'If she'd pushed me, she wouldn't have come over and tried to help, would she?'

'Why not?' says Esther. 'People often do things like that.'

'Like what? Which people?' I stir the cloudy water with my toes, annoyed that there isn't more foam; I should have emptied the bottle. The bathroom is another thing that irritates me about our flat. It's too narrow. If you sit on the loo and lean forward, you can touch the cupboard door with the tip of your nose.

'I don't know which people,' Esther says impatiently. 'I just know I've heard of that kind of thing before: the guilty party helps his victim in order to look innocent.' In the background, I hear her microwave beeping. I wonder what she's heating up tonight—a ready meal or leftover takeaway. A fleeting pang of envy for Esther's single, hassle-free life makes me close my eyes. She lives alone in a spacious purpose-built flat at the top of a curvaceous, design-award-winning tower block in Rawndesley, with a large balcony that overlooks both the river and the city. Two whole walls of her lounge are made of glass, and—the thing I find hardest to bear—she has no stairs.

'Anyway, I doubt she was trying to kill you. She probably saw you walking ahead of her, saw a bus coming along, and was so angry that she couldn't resist. That'd explain why she was all smiles once you'd been hurt—she realised she'd turned her revenge fantasy into reality and regretted it.'

Esther is an enthusiastic imaginer of scenarios. She is wasted at Rawndesley University; she ought to be a film director. Over the years she has been certain that her boss the Imbecile is: gay, a Jehovah's Witness, in love with her, a Scientologist, a Freemason, bulimic and a member of the BNP. Usually I find her flights of fancy entertaining, but tonight I want seriousness and sense. I'm exhausted. I'm worried about summoning the energy to climb out of this bath.

'Rawndesley was heaving today,' I say. 'Someone could easily have knocked into me by mistake.'

'I suppose so,' Esther grudgingly admits.

'Oh, God. I can't believe I called Pam an ugly gremlin. I might even have called her evil. I think I did. I'll have to ring her and apologise.'

'Don't bother. She'll never forgive you, not in a million years.' Esther chuckles. 'Did you really call her that? I'm having trouble imagining it. You're so prim and proper.'

'Am I?' I say wearily. There are things about me that Esther doesn't know. Well, one thing. She once warned me not to tell her anything that really needs to stay secret: 'If it's a good story, I won't be able to resist telling everyone.' I had the impression she was using the word 'everyone' in its fullest sense.

'So you don't think I need to . . . tell the police or anything?'

Esther squawks with laughter. 'Yeah, right. What are they going to do, appeal for witnesses? I can see the headline now: "The Notorious Bus-pushing Incident of 2007".'

'I haven't even told Nick.'

'God, don't tell him!' Esther snorts, as if I've suggested telling my window cleaner: someone entirely irrelevant. 'By the way, that story about the neighbour and the agonizing back-ache? Complete crap. The woman's got six-month-old twins, right?'

'Yeah.'

'So, she's been breast-feeding like the clappers and her tits have gone all droopy. She wants to swap them for new, perky ones. The medical gubbins is strictly for emotional blackmail purposes, a way of forcing her husband to part with the cash.'

I hear Nick yelling my name. I ignore him, but he keeps calling me. Normally he gives up almost immediately. 'I'd better go,' I tell Esther. 'Nick wants me. It sounds urgent.'

'Nick? Urgent?'

'Unlikely but true. Look, I'll ring you back.'

'No, take me with you,' Esther orders. 'You know how nosey I am. I want to hear what's going on in real time.'

I make a rude face at the phone, then balance it on the side of the bath as I wrap a towel round myself. Too late, I realise it's white and might end up with smears of red on it. I know we're out of Vanish, so that's two new items for my list: buy more stain-remover, wash blood out of towel.

I take the phone up to the lounge. Nick is still sitting beside the mounds of shepherd's pie on the carpet, still watching BBC News 24. 'Have you seen this?' he says, pointing at a photograph of a woman and a young girl on the screen. A mother and daughter. Across the bottom of the picture there's a caption that tells me their names. They are dead; the caption says that too. I try to take it in: the words and the photograph together. The meaning. 'It's been all over the news for days,' said Nick. 'I keep forgetting to tell you. Not often Spilling makes the national headlines.'

Through a fuzzy layer of shock, I become aware of several things. The woman looks like me. It's frightening how similar we look. She has the same thick, long, wavy dark brown hair, so brown it's almost black. Mine feels like wire-wool when it gets too dry, and I bet hers does too. Did. Her face is long and oval-shaped like mine, her eyes big and brown with dark lashes. Her nose is smaller than mine and her mouth slightly wider, and she's prettier than I am, but still, the overall effect . . .

Nick doesn't need to explain why he wanted me to see her. He says, 'They lived about ten minutes from here—I even know the house.'

'What's going on?' Esther's voice startles me. I wasn't aware I had the phone pressed to my ear. I can't answer her. I am too busy staring at the words on the screen: 'Geraldine and Lucy Bretherick deaths: police suspect mother killed herself after killing her daughter.'

Geraldine Bretherick. No, it can't be her. And yet I know it must be. A daughter called Lucy. Also dead. *Oh, God, oh, God.* How many Geraldine Brethericks can there be who live in Spilling and have daughters called Lucy? *Geraldine Bretherick.* I nearly pretended it was my name today after my accident, when I didn't have the guts to tell the women helping me that I'd rather be left alone.

'Are you okay?' Nick asks. 'You look a bit odd.'

'Sally, what's going on?' demands the voice at my ear. 'Did Nick just say you look odd? Why, what do you look like?'

I force myself to speak, to tell Esther that everything is fine but I have to go—the kids need attention. People who don't have children never challenge that excuse; they shut up quicker than a squeamish chauvinist at the mention of 'women's troubles'. Unless they're Esther. I cut her off mid-protest and take the battery out of the phone so that she can't ring back.

'Sally, don't . . . Why did you do that? I'm waiting for a call about cycling on Saturday.'

'Ssh!' I hiss, staring at the television, trying to focus on the voiceover, what it's saying: that Mark Bretherick, Geraldine's husband and Lucy's father, found the bodies on his return from a business trip. That he is not a suspect.

Nick turns back to the screen. He thinks I'm eager to watch this because it's the sort of news I 'like', because it's domestic and not political, because the dead woman is a mother who looks as if she might be my twin, and lives near us. And the dead girl . . . I check the caption again, trying to use as many facts as I can get my hands on to beat down the horrible haze that's fogging up my brain. Maybe I got it wrong, maybe the shock . . . but no, it definitely says 'deaths'. Lucy Bretherick is dead too.

The girl in the photograph looks nothing like Zoe, and I can't explain the relief I feel. Lucy has long dark hair like her mother's, and she's wearing it in two fat plaits, one with a kink in it, so that it turns halfway down and points back towards her neck. Her two hair bobbles have white discs with smiling faces on them. Her grin reveals a row of straight, white, slightly prominent teeth. Geraldine is also smiling in the photograph, and has her arm draped over Lucy's shoulder. One, two, three, four smiles—two on the faces and two on the bobbles. I feel sick.

Geraldine. Lucy. In my head, I've been on first-name terms with these people for a little over a year, even though they have never heard of me. Even though we've never met.

The voiceover is talking about other murder-suicide cases. About parents who take their children's lives and their own. 'Little girl was only six,' says Nick. 'Doesn't bear thinking about, does it? Mother must have been fucked in the head. Sal, put the battery back in the phone, will you? Can you imagine how that child's dad must feel?'

I blink and look away. If I'm not careful, I will start to cry. I can feel the pressure at the back of my eyes, in my nose. If I do, it won't occur to Nick that I have never before been reduced to tears by a news report. Usually if children are involved I shudder and order him to change channels. It's easy to put horror to one side if one isn't personally involved.

At last the picture disappears. I couldn't take my eyes off it and I'm pleased it's gone. I don't want to see those faces again, knowing what happened. I nearly ask Nick if any of the news reports he's seen have explained why—why did Geraldine Bretherick do this? Do the police know? But I don't ask; I can't cope with any more information at the moment. I'm still reeling, trying to make it part of what I know about the world that Mark Bretherick's wife and daughter are dead.

Oh, Mark, I'm so sorry. I want to say these words aloud but of course I can't.

When I next focus my attention on the screen, three men and a woman are talking in a studio. One man keeps using the phrase 'family annihilation'. 'Who are these people?' I ask Nick. Their faces are solemn, but I can tell they're enjoying the discussion.

'The woman's our MP. The bald guy's some pompous wanker sociologist who's helping the police. He's written a book about people who kill their families—he's been on telly every night since it happened. The guy with glasses is a shrink.'

'Are . . . are the police sure? The mother did it?'

'It said before they're still investigating, but they reckon it's a murder by the mother followed by suicide.'

I watch the bald sociologist's pale lips as he speaks. He is saying that female 'family annihilators'—he makes quote marks in the air—have been much less common than male ones until now, but that he is certain there will be more in due course, more women who kill their children and themselves. Across his chest, a caption appears: 'Professor Keith Harbard, University College London, Author of *Homewreckers: Extreme Killing Within the Family*'. He is talking more than anyone else; the other speakers try and fail to interrupt his flow. I wonder what he would classify as a moderate killing.

The woman sitting beside him, my MP, accuses him of scare-mongering, says he has no business making such grim predictions on the basis of no evidence. Does he know how counter-intuitive it is for a mother to kill her own offspring? This case, she says, if indeed it does turn out to be murder-suicide, is a freak occurrence, will always be a freak occurrence.

'Mothers do kill their own kids, though.' Nick joins in the debate. 'What about that baby that was thrown off a ninth-floor balcony?'

It's all I can do to stop myself from screaming at him to shut up. At all of them. None of them knows anything about this. *I* don't know anything about it. Except . . .

I say nothing. Nick has never been suspicious of me and he must never be. I shiver as I imagine something terrible happening to my own family. Not as terrible as this, what's on the news, but bad enough: Nick leaving me, taking the kids every other weekend, introducing them to his new wife. *No.* That can't happen. I must behave as if my connection with this story is the same as Nick's: we are both concerned strangers with no personal knowledge of the Brethericks.

Suddenly the discussion is over, and there is a man on the screen, with an older man and woman on either side of him. All three of them are crying. The man in the middle is speaking into a microphone at a press conference. 'Are they relatives?' I ask Nick. Mark would be too upset to talk about the deaths of his wife and daughter. These people must be close friends, perhaps his parents and brother. I know he has a brother. There's no family resemblance, though. This man has dark brown hair with streaks of grey in it, sallow skin. His eyes are blue, with heavy lids, and his nose is large and long, his lips thin. He is unusual-looking but not unattractive. Perhaps these are Geraldine's relatives.

'I loved Geraldine and Lucy with all my heart,' says the younger of the two men, 'and I will always love them, even now they're gone.'

Why didn't Mark tell me his wife was the image of me? Did he think it would make me angry? Make me feel used?

'Poor sod,' says Nick.

The man at the microphone is sobbing now. The older man and woman are holding him up. 'Who is he?' I ask. 'What's his name?'

Nick looks at me strangely. 'That's the madwoman's husband,' he says.

I am about to tell him he's wrong—this man is not Mark Bretherick, looks nothing like him—when I remember that I am not supposed to know this. The official story, the one Mark and I drafted together, is that we never met. I remember us laughing about this, Mark saying, 'Although obviously I won't go round *saying* I've never met or heard of a woman called Sally Thorning, because that'd be a bit of a giveaway!'

The madwoman's husband. Nick is laid-back about day-to-day life, but I've never met anyone more black and white about anything that qualifies as an important issue. He wouldn't understand at all if I told him, and who could blame him?

I say quietly, 'I don't think that's the husband, is it?' Impartial, uninvolved.

'Of course it's the husband. Who do you think he is, the milkman?'

As Nick speaks, another caption appears, black letters on a strip of blue that cuts the weeping man with the long nose and heavy-lidded eyes in half. My mouth opens as I read the words: 'Mark Bretherick, husband of Geraldine and father of Lucy'.

Except that he isn't. He can't be. I know, because I spent a week with Mark Bretherick last year. How many can there be in Spilling, with wives called Geraldine and daughters called Lucy?

'Where do they live?' I ask Nick in a stretched voice. 'You said you knew the house.'

'Corn Mill House—you know, that massive dobber mansion near Spilling Velvets. I cycle past it all the time.'

I feel faint, as if every drop of blood in my body has rushed to my head and filled it, pushed out all the air.

I remember the story, almost word for word. I have a good memory for words, and names. *It didn't even used to be a corn mill. There was a corn mill nearby, and the people who owned it before us were pretentious gits, basically. And Geraldine loves the name. She won't let me get rid of it, and believe me, I've tried.*

Who said that to me?

I spent a week with Mark Bretherick last year, and the man I'm looking at is not him.

Police Exhibit Ref: VN8723
Case Ref: VN87
OIC: Sergeant Samuel Kombothekra

GERALDINE BRETHERICK'S DIARY, EXTRACT 1 OF 9 (taken from hard disk of Toshiba laptop computer at Corn Mill House, Castle Park, Spilling, RY29 0LE)

18 April 2006, 10.45 p.m.

I don't know whose fault it is, but my daughter now believes in monsters. They are never mentioned in our house, so she must have picked it up at school, like God (about whom she'd heard so little at home that for the first few months she called him Gart—Mark found this hilarious) and her obsession with the colour pink. Education, even the fraudulent (sorry, creative) Montessori variety that we pay through the nose for, is no more than a process of brainwashing—it does the opposite of train children to think for themselves. Anyway, Lucy's terrified of monsters now, and insists on sleeping with a night light on and her bedroom door open.

The first I knew of it was when I put her to bed yesterday at eight thirty, turned the light out as I always do and closed the door. I felt the usual sweeping relief all through my body (I don't think I could explain to anyone how important it is to me to be able to close that door) and I punched the air in triumph as I often do, though never if Mark is watching. I don't mean to do it, but my arm moves before my brain has time to stop it. I feel as if I've escaped from prison—all my dread disappears; even the certainty that it will return tomorrow can't stifle my joy. When Lucy goes to bed, my life and home are my own again and I can be myself, free, doing whatever I want to do without fear, thinking about whatever I want to think about for a few precious hours.

Until yesterday, that is. I closed the door, punched the air, but before I was able to take more than a couple of steps towards freedom, I heard a loud wailing noise. Her. I froze, trying to close my ears from the inside. But I wasn't mistaken, it wasn't a cat outside or a car coming up the lane, or bell-ringers at the church across the fields (though it's bliss when this happens the other way round: you hear a faint whine or some other high-pitched noise that you're certain is your child wanting attention, *more* attention, and then—oh, thank you, Gart!—it turns out to be only a car alarm, and you're saved). But I wasn't, because the source of the awful whining noises was my daughter.

I have a rule that I've made for myself, and that I stick to *come what may*: whatever I feel inside, however I feel like behaving towards Lucy, I do the opposite. So when she cried after I'd closed her door, I went back into her room, stroked her hair and said, 'What's the matter, love?' because what I really wanted to do was drag her out of her bed and shake her until her teeth fell out.

There must be parents who are so strict and terrifying that their children make sure never to annoy or incon-venience them. Those are the people I both envy and loathe. They must be cruel, vicious, intimidating ogres, and yet—lucky them—their children tiptoe round them trying not to be noticed. Whereas my daughter's not at all frightened of me, which is why she screamed after I closed her door, even though she was absolutely fine: bathed, fed, kissed, hugged, the blessed recipient of at least three bedtime stories.

I need her not to be around in the evenings. Evenings! Anyone would think I meant from six until midnight or something extravagant like that. But no, I settle for a mere two and a half hours between eight thirty and eleven. I am physically unable to stay up any later than that, because every minute of my day is so exhausting. I run around like a slave on speed, a fake smile plastered to my face, saying things I don't mean, never getting to eat, enthusing wildly over works of art that deserve to be chopped up and chucked in the bin. That's my typical day—lucky me. That's why the hours between half past eight and eleven must be inviolable, otherwise I will lose my sanity.

When Lucy told me she was scared of monsters getting her in the dark, I explained as reasonably and kindly as I could that there was no such thing as a monster. I kissed her again, closed the door again, and waited on the landing. The screams got louder. I did nothing, just listened for ten minutes or so. I did this partly for Lucy's sake—I knew there was a danger (*never* underestimate the danger or something awful might happen) of my smashing her head against the wall because I was so furious with her for taking up ten extra minutes, minutes that were mine, not hers. I cannot spare her any time apart from what I already give her, not even a second. I don't care if that sounds bad—it's the truth. It's important to tell the truth, isn't it, if only to yourself?

When I was certain I had my rage under control, I went back into her room and reassured her, again, that monsters weren't real. But, I said—ever the understanding, reasonable mummy—I would leave the landing light on. I closed the door, and this time I got halfway downstairs before she started screaming again. I went back up and asked her what was wrong. The room was still too dark, she said. She insisted that I leave the landing light on and her door open.

'Lucy,' I said in my best authoritative-but-kind voice, 'you sleep with your door closed. Okay, love? You always have. If you want, I'll open the curtains a bit so that some light comes in from outside.'

'But it'll get dark outside soon!' she screamed. By this point she had worked herself up into hysterics. Her face was snot-streaked and red. My palms and the skin between my fingers started to itch, and I had to press my hands together to stop myself from punching her.

'Even when it's dark, some light will come in, I promise. Your eyes'll adjust, and then the sky won't look quite so black.' How do you explain to a child the grey illumination of the night sky? Mark's the intellectual in our family, the one worth listening to. (What does Mummy know about anything of any importance? Mummy has sold her soul. She contributes nothing worthwhile to society. That's what Daddy thinks.)

'I want my door open!' Lucy howled. 'Open! Open!'

'Sorry, darling,' I said. 'I know you're scared, but there's really no need to be. Goodnight. See you in the morning.' I walked over, pulled her curtains half open, left the room and closed the door.

Her screams intensified. Screams for which there was no cause; her room was no longer dark in any way. I sat cross-legged on the landing, fury ripping through my body. I couldn't comfort Lucy any more because I couldn't think of her as a scared child—the screams were too much like a weapon. I was her victim now and she was my torturer. She could ruin my evening, and she knew it. She can ruin my whole life if she wants to, whereas I can't ruin hers because a) Mark would stop me, and b) I love her. I don't want her to be unhappy. I don't want her to have a horrible mother, or to be abandoned, or to be beaten, so I'm trapped: she can make me suffer as much as she wants and I can't retaliate in kind. I have no control—that's what I hate more than anything.

The shrieks showed no sign of stopping. If I hadn't known better, I'd have thought Lucy was being burned alive in her bedroom, from the noise she was making. After a while she got out of bed and tried to open the door herself. I held on to the handle from the outside to keep it shut. Then she really started to panic. She isn't used to doors that won't open. I still couldn't feel anything but rage, though, and I knew I had to wait, so I sat there until Lucy's voice grew hoarse, until she was begging me to come back in, not to leave her alone. I don't know how long it was—maybe half an hour—before I started to feel sorrier for her than I felt for myself. I stood up, opened her door and went back into the room. She was in a heap on the floor and when she saw me she grabbed my ankles and started babbling, 'Thank you, Mummy, thank you, oh, thank you!'

I picked her up and sat her on my lap in the chair by her window. Sweat dripped from her forehead. I calmed her down and cuddled her, stroking her hair. Once she has made me angry, I can only be kind like this when she's reached the point of total despair and all the fight has gone out of her. Anything less and it's hard for me to see her as deserving of sympathy, this well-fed, beloved child who has everything a girl of her age could want—a secure home, an expensive education, nice clothes, every sort of toy, book and DVD, friends, foreign holidays—and who is *still*, in spite of it all, complaining and crying.

When Lucy is desperate, grateful and limp with the relief of having been forgiven, I find it easy to feel the way a mother should. I wish I could awaken this protective feeling in myself more easily. Once she was sick before I could bring myself to comfort her, and I vowed I'd never let it go that far again.

I patted her back and she soon fell asleep on my knee. I carried her over to her bed, laid her down and covered her with her quilt. Then I left the room and closed the door. I had won, though it had taken a while.

I didn't say anything to Mark about what had happened, and I was sure Lucy wouldn't either, but she did.

'Daddy,' she said at breakfast this morning, 'I'm scared of monsters, but Mummy wouldn't let me have the door open last night and I was frightened.' Her lip trembled. She stared at me, wide-eyed with resentment, and I realised that my tormentor, my torturer, is only a child, a naïve little girl. She is not as scared of me as I often fear she is, or as I am of myself, or as she should be. It's not her fault—she's only five.

Daddy sided with his precious daughter, of course, and now there is a new system: door open, suitable night light in place (not too bright but bright enough). I can't object without revealing my own irrationality. 'It makes no difference to us whether her door's open or closed,' Mark said when I tried to persuade him to change his mind. 'What does it matter?'

I said nothing. It matters because I need to close that door. This evening, instead of feeling that I had successfully shut Lucy away at half past eight, I tiptoed round the house imagining I could hear her breathing and snoring and turning over, rustling her covers. I felt her presence with every molecule of my body, invading territory that was rightfully mine.

Still, it's not that bad. As my terminally cheerful mother insists on telling me whenever I dare to complain, I'm luckier than most women: Lucy is a good girl most of the time, I have Michelle to help me, I don't know how lucky I am, it's hard work but it's all worth it, and everything is basically 'hunky-dory'. So why do I wake up every Saturday morning feeling as if I'm about to be suffocated for forty-eight hours, wondering if I'll survive until Monday?

Spoke to Cordy on the phone today and she told me Oonagh is also preoccupied with monsters. Cordy blames the children in Lucy and Oonagh's class who are from 'the other side of the tracks' (her expression, not mine). She said, 'I bet their thick parents have been stuffing their heads full of nonsense about fairies and devils, and they've passed it on to our kids.' She sounded quite cross about it. She says you pay through the nose to send your daughter to a private school where you trust she won't encounter any 'white trash', but then she does because some white trash types have lots of money. 'From setting up chains of tanning studios and pube-waxing emporia,' she said bitterly. I didn't ask what 'emporia' were.

What else? Oh, yes, a man called William Markes is very probably going to ruin my life. But he hasn't yet, and I admit I'm not in the most positive state of mind at the moment. Let's wait and see.

2

8/7/07

It struck DC Simon Waterhouse that, as usual, everything was wrong. He was feeling this more and more lately. The lane was wrong, and the house was wrong—even its name was wrong—and the garden, and what Mark Bretherick did for a living, and the fact that Simon was here with Sam Kombothekra in Kombothekra's silent, fragrant car.

Simon had always objected to more things than would offend most people, but recently he had noticed he'd started to baulk at almost everything he came into contact with—his physical surroundings, friends, colleagues, family. These days what he felt most often was disgust; he was full of it. When he had first seen Geraldine and Lucy Bretherick's dead bodies, his mouth had filled with the undigested remnants of his last meal, but even so, their deaths didn't stand out in his mind in the way he knew they ought to. Each day he worked on this case he felt sickened by his own numbness in the face of such horror.

'Simon? You okay?' Kombothekra asked him as the car lurched over the deep potholes in the lane that led to Corn Mill House. Kombothekra was Simon's new skipper, so ignoring him wasn't an option and neither was telling him to fuck off. Wanting to tell him to fuck off was wrong, too, because Kombothekra was a fair and decent bloke.

He had transferred from West Yorkshire CID a year ago, when Charlie had deserted. Selfishly, she didn't leave altogether—she still worked in the same nick, so Simon had to see her around the building and suffer her stilted, polite greetings and enquiries about his well-being. He'd rather never see her again, if things couldn't be how they were.

Charlie's new job was a travesty. She must know that as well as I do, thought Simon. She was head of a team of police officers who worked with social services to provide an encouraging and positive environment for the local scum, to discourage them from re-offending. Simon read about her activities in the nick's newsletter: she and her underlings bought kettles and micro-waves for skag-heads, found mind-expanding employment for coke-dealers. Superintendent Barrow was quoted in the local press talking about caring policing, and Charlie—with her new, fake, photo-opportunity smile—was head of the care assistants, arranging for all the scrotes to have their arses wiped with extra-soft toilet tissue in the hope that it'd turn them into better peo-ple. It was bullshit. She ought to have been working with Simon. That was the way things were meant to be: the way they used to be. Not the way they were now.

Simon hated Kombothekra calling him by his Christian name. Everyone else called him Waterhouse: Sellers, Gibbs, In-spector Proust. Only Charlie called him Simon. And he didn't want to call Kombothekra 'Sam' either. Or even 'Sarge'.

'If you're unhappy about something, I'd rather you told me,' Kombothekra tried again. They were coming to the point where the pitted lane divided in two. The right-hand branch led to the cluster of squat, grey industrial buildings that was Spilling Vel-vets, and was smooth, concreted over. The track on the left was too narrow and contained even more craters than the wider lane. Twice before on his way to Corn Mill House, Simon had met a car coming in the opposite direction and had to reverse all the way back to the Rawndesley road; it had felt like driving backwards over a rough stone roller-coaster.

Mainly, Simon was unhappy about Charlie. Without her he felt increasingly cut off, unreachable by other human beings. She was the only person he'd ever been close to, and, worst of all, he didn't understand why he'd lost her. She'd left CID because of him—of that Simon was certain—and he had no idea what he'd done wrong. He'd risked his job to protect her, for fuck's sake, so what was her problem?

None of this was Kombothekra's business or what he'd meant. Simon forced his mind back to work. Plenty of negative feeling there too. He didn't think Geraldine Bretherick had killed her daughter or herself; he was staggered that most of the team seemed to favour this hypothesis. But he'd been wrong in the past—spectacularly so—and the Brethericks' minds and lives felt utterly foreign to him.

Mark Bretherick—and Geraldine, Simon assumed—had chosen to live in a house at the bottom of a long lane that was almost impossible to drive down. Simon would never buy a house with such an approach. And he'd be embarrassed to live in one that was known by a name instead of a number; he would feel as if he was pretending to be an aristocrat, inviting trouble. His own home was a neat rectangular two-up two-down cottage in a row of similar neat rectangles, opposite an identical row across the street. His garden was a small square of lawn bordered by thin strips of earth and a tiny paved patio area, also square.

A garden like the Brethericks' would have terrified him. It had too many components; you couldn't look out of one window and see all of it. Steep terraces crammed full of trees, bushes and plants surrounded the house on all sides. Many were in flower, but the colours, instead of looking vibrant, appeared sad and reckless, swamped by too much straggly green. A blanket of something dark and clingy climbed up the walls, blocking some of the windows on the ground floor and blurring the boundary between garden and house.

The terraces led down to a large rectangular lawn at the back, which was the only tidy part of the garden. Below the lawn was a ramshackle orchard that looked as if no one had set foot in it for years, and beyond that a stream and an overgrown paddock. At the side of the house stood a double greenhouse that was full of what looked to Simon like tangled, hairy green limbs and troughs full of murky water. Ropes of foliage pressed against the glass like snakes pushing to escape. In the wide driveway at the side of the house were two free-standing stone buildings that appeared to have no use. Each was probably big enough to house a family of three. One had a dusty, long-since-defunct toilet with a cracked black seat in one corner. The other, a young bobby at the scene had told Simon, used to be a coal store. Simon didn't know how anyone could bear to have two buildings on their land that did nothing, were nothing. Waste, excess, neglect: all these things disgusted him.

Between the two outbuildings, a flight of stone steps led up to a garage, the access to which was from Castle Park Lane. If you climbed to the top of the steps and looked down, you might think Corn Mill House had fallen off the road and landed upright in a hammock of untamed greenery. The house itself had a black-tiled hipped roof but the rest of it was grey. Not solid grey, like the filing cabinets in the CID room, but a washed-out ethereal grey like a damp, misty sky. In certain lights it was more of a sickly beige. It gave the house a spectral look. No two windows were in alignment; all were odd shapes and rattled in the wind. Each one was divided into smaller panes by strips of black lead. The enormous living room and the not-much-smaller entrance hall were wood-panelled on all sides, which made for a dark and sombre look.

There were no window sills, which was disconcerting: the glass was set into the stone of the walls. Simon thought it made the place feel like a dungeon. Still, he had to admit that he hadn't come here in the best of circumstances; he'd been called in after the balloon had gone up at the nick, had arrived knowing he'd find a dead mother and daughter. He supposed it wasn't the house's fault.

Mark Bretherick was the director of a company called Spilling Magnetic Refrigeration that made cooling units for low-temperature physicists. Not that Simon had a clue what that entailed. When Sam had explained it to the team at the first briefing, Simon had pictured a huddle of shivering scientists in thin white coats, their teeth chattering. Mark had conceived and built up the company himself and now had a staff of seven working for him. Very different, Simon imagined, from being given your purpose and instructions by someone who was paid more than you. *Am I jealous of Bretherick?* he wondered. *If I am, I'm sicker in the head than I've ever been.*

'You think he did it, don't you?' said Sam Kombothekra, parking on the concrete courtyard in front of Corn Mill House. Twenty cars could have parked there. Simon hated men who cared about impressing people. Was Mark Bretherick in that category or did he need parking for that number of cars? Did he feel he deserved more than the average man? Than, say, Simon?

'No,' he told Kombothekra. *Don't invent stupid opinions and ascribe them to me.* 'We know he didn't do it.'

'Exactly.' Kombothekra sounded relieved. 'We've been over him with a microscope: his movements, his finances—he didn't get a professional in to do the job. Or if he did, he didn't pay them. He's in the clear, unless something new turns up.'

'Which it won't.'

A man called William Markes is very probably going to ruin my life. That's what Geraldine Bretherick had written in her diary. Typed, rather. The diary had been found on the laptop computer that lived on an antique table in a corner of the lounge— Geraldine's computer. Mark had his own, in his home office upstairs. Before she had given up her job to look after Lucy, Geraldine had worked in IT, so clearly computers were her thing, but even so . . . what sort of woman types her personal diary on to a laptop?

Kombothekra was watching him keenly, waiting for more, so Simon added, 'William Markes did it. He murdered them. Whoever he is.'

Kombothekra sighed. 'Colin and Chris looked into that and got nowhere.' Simon turned away to hide his distaste. The first time Kombothekra had referred to Sellers and Gibbs as 'Colin and Chris', Simon hadn't known who he was talking about. 'Unless and until we find a William Markes who knew Geraldine Bretherick—'

'He didn't know her,' said Simon impatiently. 'She didn't know him. Otherwise she wouldn't have said "a man called William Markes". She'd just have said "William Markes", or "William".'

'You don't know that.'

'Think of all the other names she mentioned, people she knew well: Lucy, Mark, Michelle. Cordy. Not "a woman called Cordelia O'Hara".' Simon had spent two hours yesterday talking to Mrs O'Hara, who had insisted he too call her Cordy. She'd been adamant that Geraldine Bretherick had killed nobody. Simon had told her she needed to speak in person to Kombothekra. He'd doubted his own ability to convey to his sergeant, in Cordy O'Hara's absence, how persuasive her account of Geraldine Bretherick as someone who would commit neither murder nor suicide had been. It was far more perceptive and detailed than the usual 'I can't believe it—she seemed so normal' that all detectives were familiar with.

But either Mrs O'Hara hadn't bothered to seek out Kombothekra and repeat her insights to him, or else she had failed to make any impact on his certainty that Geraldine was responsible for both deaths. Simon had noticed that Kombothekra's softly spoken politeness cloaked a stubborn streak that would not have achieved its goals nearly so often were it more overt.

'Michelle Greenwood wasn't someone Geraldine Bretherick knew well.' Kombothekra sounded apologetic about contradicting Simon. 'She babysat for Lucy from time to time, that was all. And, yes, she referred to her husband and daughter in the diary as "Lucy" and "Mark", but what about "my terminally cheerful mother"?'

'There's a clear difference between inventing your own private, comic labels for friends and family and saying "a man called William Markes". Don't tell me you can't see it. Would you ever describe the Snowman as "a man called Giles Proust"? In a diary that no one else was meant to read?' Come to think of it, Simon had never heard Kombothekra refer to Inspector Proust as 'the Snowman'. Whereas Simon, Sellers and Gibbs often forgot that it wasn't his real and only name.

'Okay, good point.' Kombothekra nodded encouragingly. 'So, where does that take us? Let's say William Markes was someone Geraldine didn't know. But she knew *of* him . . .'

'Obviously.'

'. . . so how could someone she doesn't know and has never met be in a position to ruin her life?'

Simon resented having to answer. 'I'm a disabled, gay, Jewish communist living in Germany in the late 1930s,' he said wearily. 'I've never met Adolf Hitler, and I don't know him personally . . .'

'Okay,' Kombothekra conceded. 'So something she'd heard about this William Markes person made her think he might ruin her life. But we can't find him. We can't find a William Markes—even with the surname spelled in all its possible variations—who had any connection with Geraldine Bretherick whatsoever.'

'Doesn't mean he doesn't exist,' said Simon as they got out of the car. Mark Bretherick stood in the porch, watching them with wide, stunned eyes. He had flung open the front door while they were still undoing their seat belts. The same had happened yesterday. Had he been waiting in the hall, peering through the leaded stained glass? Simon wondered. Walking round his enormous house, searching every room for his missing wife and daughter, who were as alive in his mind as they'd ever been? He was wearing the same pale blue shirt and black corduroy trousers he had worn since he'd found Geraldine and Lucy's bodies. The shirt had tide-marks under the arms, dried sweat.

Bretherick stepped outside, on to the drive, then immediately reversed the action, retreating back into his porch as if he'd suddenly noticed the distance between his visitors and himself and didn't have the energy.

'She wrote a suicide note.' Kombothekra's quiet voice followed Simon towards the house. 'Her husband and her mother said there was no doubt the handwriting was hers, and our subsequent checks proved them right.' Another thing Kombothekra did all the time: hit you with his best point, the one he'd been saving up, at a moment when he knew you wouldn't be able to reply.

Simon was already extending a hand to Mark Bretherick, who seemed thinner even than yesterday. His bony hand closed around Simon's and held it in a rigid grip, as if he wanted to test the bones inside.

'DC Waterhouse. Sergeant. Thank you for coming.'

'It's no problem,' said Simon. 'How are you bearing up?'

'I don't think I am.' Bretherick stood aside to let them in. 'I'm not sure what I'm doing, if anything.' He sounded angry; it wasn't the bewildered voice Simon had grown used to. Bretherick had found a fluency; each word was no longer a struggle.

'Are you sure this is the best place for you to be? Alone?' asked Kombothekra. He never gave up. Bretherick didn't answer. He'd been adamant that he wanted to return home as soon as the forensic team had finished at Corn Mill House, and he'd refused the police's repeated attempts to assign him a family liaison officer.

'My parents will be here later, and Geraldine's mum,' said Bretherick. 'Go through to the lounge. Can I get you a drink? I've managed to work out where the kitchen is. That's what happens when you spend more time in your own home than half an hour at the beginning of the day and an hour at the end of it. Pity I was never here while my wife and daughter were still alive.'

Simon decided he'd leave that one for Kombothekra to respond to, and the sergeant was already saying all the right
things: 'What happened wasn't your fault, Mark. Nobody is responsible for another person's suicide.'

'I'm responsible for believing your stories instead of thinking
for myself.' Mark Bretherick laughed bitterly. He remained
standing as Simon and Kombothekra sat down at either end of a
long sofa that wouldn't have looked out of place in a French
palace. 'Suicide. That's it then, is it? You've decided.'

'The inquest won't be heard until all the relevant evidence
has been collated,' said Kombothekra, 'but, yes, at the moment
we're treating your wife's death as suicide.'

On one wall of the lounge, twenty-odd framed drawings and
paintings hung from the wood panelling. Lucy Bretherick's art-
works. Simon looked again at the smiling faces, the suns, the
houses. Often the figures were holding hands, sometimes in rows
of three. In some the words 'mummy', 'daddy' and 'me' were
floating nearby, in mid-air. If these pictures were anything to go
by, Lucy had been a normal, happy child from a normal, happy
family. How had Cordy O'Hara put it? *Geraldine wasn't just
content, she was radiantly happy. And I don't mean in a stupid,
naïve way. She was realistic and down-to-earth about her life—
she took the piss out of herself all the time. And Mark—God, she
could be hilarious about him! But she loved her life—even silly
little everyday things made her excited: new shoes, new bubble
bath, anything. She was like a kid in that respect. She was one of
those rare people who enjoyed every minute of every day.*

Witnesses, especially ones close to the victim, could be unre-
liable, but still . . . Kombothekra needed to hear what Simon
had heard. Cordy O'Hara's words felt more real to him than the
words in Geraldine Bretherick's suicide note.

The Brethericks had celebrated their ten-year wedding anniversary three weeks before Geraldine and Lucy had died. Simon
noticed that the anniversary cards were still on the mantelpiece.
Or back on the mantelpiece, rather, since the scene-of-crime and

forensic teams had presumably moved them at some stage. If Simon had still been working with Charlie, he'd have talked to her about the anniversary cards, about what was written in them. Pointless to talk to Kombothekra about it.

'One of my suits is missing,' Bretherick said, folding his arms, waiting for a response. He sounded defiant, as if he expected to be contradicted. 'It's an Ozwald Boateng one, brown, double-breasted. It's disappeared.'

'When did you last see it? When did you notice it was gone?' Simon asked.

'This morning. I don't know what made me look, but . . . I don't wear it very often. Hardly ever. So I don't know how long it's not been there.'

'Mark, I don't understand,' said Kombothekra. 'Are you implying that this missing suit has some bearing on what happened to Geraldine and Lucy?'

'I'm more than implying it. What if someone killed them, got blood on his clothes and needed something to wear to leave the house?'

Simon had been thinking the same thing. Kombothekra disagreed; his oh-so-sensitive tone made that apparent, to Simon at least. 'Mark, I understand that the idea of Geraldine committing suicide is extremely distressing for you—'

'Not just suicide—murder. The murder of our daughter. Don't bother trying to be tactful, Sergeant. It's not as if I'm going to forget that Lucy's dead if you don't say it out loud.' Bretherick's body sagged. He put his arms around his head, as if to protect it from blows, and began to cry silently, rocking back and forth. 'Lucy . . .' he said.

Kombothekra walked over to him and patted him on the back. 'Mark, why don't you sit down?'

'No! How do you explain it, Sergeant? Why would my suit have disappeared, apart from the reason I've given you? It's gone. I've searched the whole house.' Bretherick swivelled round to face Simon. 'What do you think?'

'Where did the suit normally live? In the wardrobe in your bedroom?'

Bretherick nodded.

'And you definitely haven't removed it? Left it in a hotel or at a friend's house?' Simon suggested.

'It was in my wardrobe,' Bretherick insisted angrily. 'I didn't lose it, imagine it or donate it to charity.' He wiped his wet face with his shirt sleeve.

'Might Geraldine have taken it to the dry-cleaner's before . . . say, last week?' Kombothekra asked.

'No. She only took clothes to the cleaner's when I asked her to. When I ordered her to, because I'm too busy and important to make sure my own clothes are clean. Sad, isn't it? Well, they're not clean any more.' Bretherick raised his arms to reveal new damp patches on his shirt, superimposed over the dry sweat stains. 'You might well wonder why I'm so upset.' He addressed the coving on the ceiling. 'I hardly ever saw my wife and daughter. Often they were there but I didn't look at them—I looked at the newspaper or the television, or my BlackBerry. If they hadn't died, would I ever have spent time with them, enough time? Probably not. So, if I look at it that way, I'm not really going to be missing much, am I? Now that they're dead.'

'You spent every Saturday and Sunday with them,' said Kombothekra patiently.

'When I wasn't at a conference. I never dressed Lucy, you know. Not once, in the whole six years of her life. I never bought her a single item of clothing—not one pair of shoes, not one coat. Geraldine did all that . . .'

'You bought her clothes, Mark,' said Kombothekra. 'You worked hard to support your family. Geraldine was able to give up work thanks to you.'

'I thought she wanted to! She said she did, and I thought she was happy. Staying at home, looking after Lucy and the house, having lunch with the other mums from school . . . Not that I knew any of their names. Cordy O'Hara: I know that name *now*, I know a lot about my wife now that I've read that diary.'

'Which dry-cleaner's did Geraldine use?' Simon asked.

A hard, flat laugh from Bretherick. 'How should I know? Was I ever with her during the day?'

'Did she tend to shop in Spilling or in Rawndesley?'

'I don't know.' His expression was despondent. He kept failing new tests, ones he hadn't anticipated. 'Both, I think.' He sank into a chair, began to mutter to himself, barely audible. 'Monsters. Lucy was scared of monsters. I remember Geraldine wittering on about night lights, vaguely—I could hardly be bothered to listen. I thought, You sort it out, don't bother me with it, I'm too busy thinking about work and making money. You sort it out—that was my answer to everything.'

'That's not what the diary says,' Simon pointed out. 'According to what Geraldine wrote, you were concerned enough to persuade her to let Lucy sleep with her door open.'

Bretherick sneered. 'Believe me, I didn't give my daughter's fear of monsters a second thought—I thought it was a phase.'

'Children go through so many, it's natural to forget about them once they've passed.' Kombothekra had a seven-year-old and a four-year-old, both boys. He carried photos of them in his wallet, in the same compartment as his money. The pictures fell out whenever he pulled out a note; Simon often found himself having to scoop them up off the floor.

'Geraldine didn't write that diary, Sergeant. I know that now.'

'Pardon?'

Simon watched Kombothekra's eyes widen: a satisfying sight.

'The man who wrote it knew enough about her life to make it convincing. I've got to hand it to him—he knew more about Geraldine and Lucy's lives than I did.'

'Mark, you're letting your—'

'I let my family down in many ways, Sergeant. Too many to count, too many to bear. There's not a lot I can do for them now, but I'll do the one thing that's within my power. I'll refuse to accept

your feeble theory. There's a murderer out there. If you don't think
you can find him, tell me and I'll pay someone else to do it.'

Kombothekra was starting to look uncomfortable. He never
issued direct challenges and hated even more to receive them.
'Mark, I understand how you feel, but it's a big leap from a suit
going missing to opening a full-scale murder enquiry when there
are no obvious leads or suspects, and when a suicide note was
found at the scene. I'm sorry.'

'Have you found William Markes yet?'

Simon tensed. That would have been his next question too.
He didn't like the idea of himself and Bretherick as allies and
Kombothekra the outsider, didn't want to identify too closely
with this stranger's thought processes in case they took him
closer to his pain. Bretherick, he knew, was picturing William
Markes—insofar as one could picture a stranger—leaving Corn
Mill House carrying a bundle of bloodstained clothes and wearing a brown Ozwald Boateng suit. As was Simon. Well, a brown
suit, anyway. The fancy name meant nothing to Simon, apart
from 'bound to be ludicrously expensive'.

'I want to know who he is,' said Bretherick. 'If Geraldine
was . . . seeing him . . .'

'We've found nothing to suggest Geraldine was involved with
another man.' Kombothekra smiled, making the most of this
opportunity to say something that was both true and encouraging. 'So far the name William Markes has drawn a blank but . . .
we're doing our best, Mark.'

Doing, or have done? Simon wondered. Originally there
were three teams working on the case. Now, with Mark Bretherick ruled out as a suspect, nothing to indicate Geraldine
wasn't responsible for both deaths and a suicide note to suggest
that she was, the investigation had been scaled down to Simon,
Sellers, Gibbs and Kombothekra. With Proust waiting in the
wings to shower them with his icy disapproval when they least
deserved it—his idea of team leadership. Simon doubted any

further attempts would be made to track down the William Markes mentioned in the diary.

He needed a piss, and was about to excuse himself when he remembered: there was no toilet in Corn Mill House apart from those that were in the two bathrooms upstairs. Simon had asked Bretherick during an earlier visit and been told that converting the large pantry beside the utility room into a downstairs shower room had been next on the list of home improvements. 'Won't happen now,' Bretherick had said.

Geraldine's body had been found in the large, sunken en-suite bathroom, a small flight of steps down from the master bedroom, and Lucy's in the second, smaller—though still large—bathroom on the landing next to her bedroom. Simon thought about the contrast: the bathtub full of bloodstained water in the en-suite, so red it might have been pure, undiluted blood, and the pristine white marble of the house bathroom, the clear water, Lucy's unmarked body, her submerged face. The floating strands of hair, like black seaweed in the water. *Polished limestone steps leading down to one bath, the other in the middle of the floor* ... Both focal points. Almost as if the rooms were stage sets, had been designed to present these two monstrous deaths as dramatically as possible.

Simon decided to wait. He wouldn't go into either of those rooms again unless he was compelled to.

'My mother-in-law, Geraldine's mum ... she's asking to read the diary,' said Bretherick. 'I don't want her to. I haven't told her how bad it is. It'll destroy her. Unlike me, she'd believe Geraldine wrote those things because the police believe it.' His voice was full of scorn. 'What should I say? What normally happens in cases like this?'

There are no other cases like this, thought Simon. He hadn't seen any, at any rate. He'd seen a lot of stabbings outside nightclubs, but not mothers and daughters dead in matching white bathtubs with funny curled-over tops and gold claw feet ... *as if the bath might suddenly run towards him, disgorge its contents over him . . .*

'That's a tough decision to make.' Kombothekra was patting Bretherick again. 'There's no right answer. You have to do whatever you think is best for you, and for Geraldine's mother.'

'In that case I won't show it to her,' said Bretherick. 'I won't upset her unnecessarily because I know Geraldine didn't write it. William Markes wrote it. Whoever he is.'

'I knew it was trouble,' said Phyllis Kent. 'At that first meeting, I told the superintendent. I turned round and said to him, "This'll be nothing but trouble." Not for him, not for you lot, so you won't care. Trouble for me. And I was right, wasn't I?'

Charlie Zailer allowed the manager of Spilling Post Office to finish her tirade. They stood side by side looking at a photograph of a grinning PC Robbie Meakin. The picture was attached to a small red postbox on the wall, to the right of the post office counter area, and advertised Meakin as one of Spilling's community policing team. 'Culver Valley Police—working to build safer communities.' The slogan, in large bold capitals, looked slightly threatening, Charlie thought. There was a phone number for Meakin beneath the photograph, and an appeal for members of the public to contact him about any topic that might concern them.

'I turned round and said to the superintendent, "Why does it have to be red? Our postbox outside is red, for proper letters. People'll confuse it." And they have. They turn round and say to me all the time, "I think I posted my letter in the wrong box." Course, it's too late by then. Your lot have been in and taken everything, and their correspondence has gone missing.'

'If anything comes to us by mistake, I'm sure we do our best to send it on,' said Charlie. What sort of idiot would fail to notice the large police logo on the box, the obvious differences between this and a normal postbox? 'I'll speak to PC Meakin and the rest of the team and check that—'

'There was a lady came in this morning,' Phyllis went on. 'She was in a right state. She'd posted a letter in there to her boyfriend and it never got to him. I turned round and said to her, "It's not my fault, love. Ask the police about it." But I'm the one who gets the aggro. And why won't the superintendent come in here and talk to me about it? Why's he sent you instead? Is he too embarrassed? Realised what a bad idea it was? It's all very well you turning round and saying to me . . .'

On and on it went. Charlie yawned without opening her mouth, wondering how Phyllis Kent managed to be both in front of and behind everyone she spoke to: 'I turned round and said, he turned round and said, you turned round and said . . .' There was an identical police postbox in the post office at Silsford, and, as far as Charlie knew, there had been no complaints about that one. The market research she'd commissioned last year had proved unequivocally that people wanted as much community policing as possible, as visible and accessible as possible.

Charlie suspected Phyllis Kent savoured grievances. She would have to start going to the supermarket if she wanted to avoid being buttonholed by the woman. It was a shame; Spilling Post Office was also a shop—a rather efficient one, Charlie thought. It was small, L-shaped and sold one variety of everything she needed, so she didn't have to waste time choosing between rows of the same thing. Sliced white bread and mild cheddar could be found alongside more unexpected items: tinned pickled octopus, pheasant pâté. And it was on Charlie's route home from work. All she had to do was pull in by the side of the road, get out of her car, and the door of the post office was right in front of her. It couldn't have been more convenient. Charlie had started to base her day-to-day planning around what she knew Phyllis stocked: Cheerios for breakfast, a bottle of Gordon's gin and a box of Guylian chocolates as birthday presents for her sister Olivia. For a bath, Radox Milk and Honey—the only bath oil Phyllis sold. It lived beside the freezer cabinet, on the third shelf down, between Colgate Total tooth-paste and Always extra-long sanitary towels with wings.

'I'll make sure PC Meakin returns any post that comes to us by mistake,' Charlie promised, once Phyllis's rant had ground to a halt.

'Well, it's no good returning it to me, is it? It wants posting in a proper box, like the one outside.'

'Anything with a stamp and an address on it that's clearly not for us, we'll undertake to send on to its rightful owner.' Charlie didn't know how to sound more reassuring. She had no grander, more impressive promises up her sleeve, so she hoped Phyllis would be content with this one.

But the post office manager was not a woman to whom contentment came easily. 'You're not going, are you?' she said, as Charlie started to inch towards the door. 'What about the lady?'

'Lady?'

'The one who came in this morning. She reckons there's a letter to her boyfriend in there, in your box. No one's been to empty it for days, and she wants her letter. I turned round and said to her, "Leave it to me, love. I'll make sure that superintendent comes and gets your letter out for you. This mess is all his fault in the first place!"'

Charlie swallowed a sigh. Why didn't Phyllis's lady phone her boyfriend? Or e-mail him? Or put a brick through his window, depending on the nature of the message she wanted to convey. 'I'll make sure PC Meakin comes as soon as he can.'

'Why can't you open the box?' said Phyllis. 'I thought you said you were a sergeant.'

'I don't have the key.' Charlie decided to risk being honest. 'Look, this postbox isn't really my responsibility. I only offered to come because Robbie Meakin's off on a week's paternity leave and . . . well, I needed to do my shopping.'

'I've got the key,' said Phyllis, a triumphant gleam in her eye. 'I keep it here behind the counter. But I'm not allowed to open the box. A police officer has to open it.'

Charlie could no longer hold her two bulging carrier bags. She lowered them to the floor gently to avoid breaking the eggs and lightbulbs. So Phyllis had the key. Why did she have to be so irritatingly law-abiding? She could easily have opened the box, fished out the letter to the boyfriend and left the rest of the contents untouched. Why was she bothering Charlie when she could have dealt with it herself?

And if Phyllis hadn't been such a stickler for the rules ... There would be nothing to stop a less scrupulous person having a nosey in the box whenever they fancied, perhaps even stealing letters when the police weren't around—which, let's face it, was most of the time. Whose ludicrous idea was it to leave the key at the post office? Charlie would have liked to turn round and say a few things to that person.

She rubbed her sore hands while Phyllis went to fetch the key. Her fingers were numb; the handles of the carrier bags had cut off her circulation. While she waited, she pulled her phone out of her handbag and deleted a dozen saved text messages which, in an ideal world, she would have liked to keep. But it was something to do. She was terrified of being unoccupied. There was no danger of that at work, or at home, where there was more than enough DIY to keep her busy. Charlie had stripped the walls and floors of her house just over a year ago and was rebuilding the rooms one by one, starting from scratch. It was a long, slow process. So far she'd done the kitchen and made a start on her bedroom. The rest of the house was plaster and floorboards. It looked abandoned, as if it was waiting for vagrants and rats to move in.

'Couldn't you have kept the old furniture until you bought new?' her sister regularly grumbled, wriggling on a wooden kitchen chair that was understudying indefinitely for the comfortable armchair Charlie would one day buy for the lounge. Olivia was ideologically opposed to slumming it. The round contours of her figure were not suited to right angles and hard seats.

'I wouldn't have kept myself if there'd been any choice,' Charlie had told her. 'I'd have replaced me with someone better.'

'No shortage of candidates there,' Olivia had shot back merrily, trying to goad Charlie into sticking up for herself.

The truth was, Charlie didn't want to get the house finished; what would happen after that? What would be her project? Could she find anything big enough to leave no room for thinking or feeling? Old wallpaper was easy to strip down and replace with something more cheerful; despair wasn't.

Phyllis Kent emerged from the back office with the key in her hand. She passed it to Charlie and stood back, ready to make an infuriating comment as soon as one occurred to her. Charlie wondered if Phyllis had read about her in the papers last year. Some people had, some hadn't. Some knew, some didn't. Phyllis seemed the sort who might make an ill-judged remark if she did know, and she'd said nothing so far, but Charlie wasn't going to allow herself to imagine she was in the clear. She'd done that too many times before and been floored when, almost as an afterthought, whoever she was talking to had suddenly mentioned it. It felt a bit like being shot in the back—the emotional equivalent.

Most people Charlie knew well were understanding, non-judgemental. Every time she was told it wasn't her fault, something inside her faded. They didn't even think enough of her to be honest and say, 'How the hell could you have been so stupid?' Charlie knew what they were all thinking: *It's too late, so we might as well be nice.*

She unlocked the box and took out the four envelopes and one loose scrap of lined paper that were inside. Two of the envelopes were addressed to Robbie Meakin, one had no name or address written on it, and a bulging one that looked as if it might burst at the seams was addressed to a Timothy Lush and had a first-class stamp on it. 'Here's your lady's letter,' said Charlie, pitying poor Mr Lush. He'd have to wade through at least seven pages of—*don't leap to premature conclusions,*

Charlie—aimless emotional snivelling, and try to work out what to do next. Charlie had been tempted, many times since last spring, to write a letter of exactly that sort to Simon. Thank God she'd restrained herself. Telling people how you felt was never a good idea. It was bad enough feeling it—why would you want to let it loose in the world?

Phyllis whipped the envelope out of Charlie's hand and dropped it in the metal tray under the counter's glass window, as if prolonged contact with human skin might cause it to burst into flames. Charlie threw the two Meakin envelopes back into the box and unfolded the lined sheet of paper. This was also a letter to Meakin, from Dr Maurice Gidley FRS OBE, who had been out for a meal at the Bay Tree in Spilling last week and been pestered by teenagers on his way back to his car. The youths hadn't attacked him but they had taunted him in a manner that he described as 'unacceptable and intimidating'. He wanted to know if anything could be done to prevent 'ne'er-do-wells' loitering outside his favourite restaurants, which, he informed Meakin, were the Bay Tree, Shillings Brasserie and Head 13.

Ah, yes, Doctor, of course. The 2006 Ne'er-do-wells Act . . . Charlie smiled. She'd have liked to tell Simon about Dr Gidley's absurd note, but she didn't have that sort of conversation with him any more. And now she didn't even have his text messages. She regretted deleting them already, even though she could remember many of them word for word: 'It's a serious one. Time to sober up and face the music.' This had been Simon's reply to an enquiry from Charlie about his hangover after a particularly boozy work night out. 'Walking, floating, air, sky, moonlight, etc': that had been her favourite of Simon's texts. She'd been mystified when she'd got it, hadn't understood it at all. Later, she'd asked him what it meant.

'The Snowman was looking for you. Those are the lyrics from *The Snowman*. You know, Aled Jones. I mixed the words up to make it cryptic, in case your phone fell into the wrong hands.'

Charlie had deleted it. *Stupid idiot.* Stupid for pressing a button that would destroy something she knew she wanted to keep, stupid for wanting to keep it in the first place. Simon's unspectacular, no longer relevant words from over a year ago. *God, I'm a pathetic cow.*

She put Dr Gidley's letter back in the box and used her thumbnail to open the fourth envelope, the one that wasn't addressed to anybody. It was probably hate mail or porn, Charlie guessed. Blank, sealed envelopes were usually bad news.

'Are you allowed to open that?' Phyllis's voice floated over her shoulder.

Charlie didn't answer. She was staring at the short, typed letter, at first aware of nothing except that it was a chance. To reestablish contact. Too good to miss. Charlie blinked and looked again to check that the words 'Geraldine and Lucy Bretherick' were still there. They were. This was current, the case Simon was working on at the moment. Him and the rest of the team.

Charlie missed them all. Even Proust. Standing in his office, being patronised and hectored by him . . . Sometimes when she walked past the CID room she could feel her heart leaning towards it, straining to go in, to go back.

'Please forward this to whoever is investigating the deaths of Geraldine and Lucy Bretherick,' the letter said. It was only one paragraph long, printed in a regular but small sans-serif typeface. 'It's possible that the man shown on the news last night who is meant to be Mark Bretherick is not Mark Bretherick. You need to look into it and make sure he's who he says he is. Sorry I can't say more.'

That was it. No explanation, no name or signature, no contact details.

Charlie pulled her phone out of her bag. She highlighted Simon's number on the screen, her finger hovering over the 'call' button. *All you need to do is press it. What's the worst that can happen?*

Charlie knew the answer to that one from past experience: *worse than you can possibly imagine, so there's no point trying.* She sighed, scrolled up, and rang Proust instead.

3

Tuesday, 7 August 2007

Someone followed me this morning. Or else I'm going insane.

I head for my desk, keeping my eyes down and reminding myself to take deep breaths as I cross the large, open-plan office. The advantage of everybody being so visible is that we tend to go out of our way not to notice one another, to pretend we work in closed, private rooms.

I turn on my computer, open a file so that it looks as if I'm working. It's an old draft of a paper I'm presenting in Lisbon next month: 'Creating Salt-marsh Habitats Using Muddy Dredged Materials'. That'll do.

Is there any evidence that taking deep breaths ever made anyone feel better?

Someone followed me in a red Alfa Romeo. I memorised the registration: YF52 DNB. Esther would tell me to ring the DVLA and sweet-talk them into giving me the name of the car's owner, but I'm not good at sweet-talking, and although every Hollywood film contains at least one maverick office-worker eager to break company rules and give confidential information to strangers, in the real world—in my experience, at any rate—most employees are champing at the bit to tell you how little they can do for you, how absolutely forbidden they are to make your life one iota easier.

I've got a better idea. I pick up the phone, ignore the broken dialling tone that tells me I have messages, dial 118118 and ask to be put through to Seddon Hall Hotel and Spa. A man with a Northern Irish accent asks me which town. 'York,' I tell him.

'Oh, right, got it.' I hold my breath, silently urging him not to ask me the question that always makes me want to bash my head against something hard. He does. 'Would you like to be put through?'

'Yes. That's why I said, "Can you put me through?"' I can't resist adding. *Think for yourself, dork. Don't just stick to the script, because every time you do that, every time one of your colleagues does it, it's five seconds of my life wasted.*

Even if someone isn't trying to kill me, I still haven't got any life to spare. I try to find this funny and fail.

The next voice I hear is a woman's. She gives me the good-morning-Seddon-Hall spiel that I've heard several times before. I ask her to check if a man called Mark Bretherick stayed at Seddon Hall between Friday, 2 June and Friday, 9 June 2006. 'He was in suite number eleven for the first two nights, then in suite fifteen.' I can picture both rooms clearly, on the top floor of the courtyard bit, on the galleried landing.

The pause before she speaks suggests she might have watched the news lately. 'Could I ask your name, please?'

'Sally Thorning. I was a guest at the hotel at the same time.'

'Do you mind me asking why you need this information?'

'I just need to check something,' I tell her.

'I'm afraid we don't normally—'

'Look, forget Mark Bretherick,' I cut her off. 'That probably wasn't his name. There was a man who stayed at Seddon Hall from the second to the ninth of June last year and I need to know who he was. He booked suite eleven for the whole week, but then there was a problem with the hot—'

'I'm sorry, madam,' the soft-voiced receptionist interrupts me. I can hear her computer whirring; she's probably looking at his name on her screen right now. 'I don't mean to be unhelpful, but we can't give out guests' names without a good reason.'

'I've got a good reason,' I tell her. 'Whoever that man was, I spent the week with him. He told me he was Mark Bretherick, but I don't think he was. And, for reasons that I can't go into because of my own confidentiality policy, I really need to know his name. Urgently. So, if you could check your records . . .'

'Madam, I'm really sorry—I'm afraid it's unlikely that we've kept records from that far back.'

'Yeah, right. Course it is.'

I slam down the phone. So much for sweet-talking. Was I too honest, or not honest enough? Or did I sound like a bossy cow? Nick says I sometimes ask questions in a way that makes people pray they won't know the answer.

Last night—because I had to do something—I waited until Nick went to bed and wrote a letter to the police about the Brethericks. It contained almost no information, only that the man identified as Mark Bretherick on the news might be someone else. On my way into work this morning I stopped at Spilling Post Office and put it in the police postbox. By now someone might have read it.

They'll think I'm a crank. I told them the bare minimum. Anybody could have written what I wrote, to get attention or cause trouble—a drunk teenager, a bored pensioner, anyone. They'll put me straight in the Wearside Jack category.

I think about what I told the Seddon Hall receptionist: whoever that man was, I spent a week with him. I could have written that in my letter to the police without giving away my identity. Why the hell didn't I? The more detailed my account, the more likely they would have been to believe me. If I explained everything, how and why it happened . . . Suddenly I feel a burning need to share the full truth with somebody. Even if it's only the police, even anonymously. For over a year I've kept it completely secret, telling the story to myself but no one else.

I highlight the draft of my salt-marsh habitats article and delete it, leaving only the heading in case someone looks over my shoulder. Then I start to type.

7 August 2007

To whom it may concern

I have already written to you once about the Brethericks. I posted my first letter this morning at about eight thirty, on my way to work. Like this one, it was anonymous. I am writing again because, after posting my last attempt, I realised that it would be easy for you to dismiss me as a time-waster.

I can't tell you my name for reasons that will become clear. I am female, thirty-eight, married and a mother. I work full-time, and the work I do is professional. I am university educated and have a PhD. (I'm saying this because I can't help thinking it will make you take me more seriously, so I suppose that makes me a snob too.)

As I said in my last letter, I have reason to believe that the Mark Bretherick I saw on the news last night might not be the real Mark Bretherick. This story may seem irrelevant at first but it isn't so please bear with me.

In December 2005, my boss asked me if I could go on a work trip abroad, for the week of Friday, 2 June to Friday, 9 June 2006. At that time my children were very young and I was working full-time, juggling several different projects and not getting much sleep. Every day felt like a struggle. I told my boss I didn't think I'd be able to do it. Since having my second child, I hadn't been away from home for more than one night at a time. To go away for a whole week didn't seem fair on my husband and the children, and I felt utterly drained when I imagined getting home afterwards and having to clear up the mess that would have accumulated in my absence. It simply didn't seem worth it. I felt slightly disappointed at having to turn down the work because it sounded like an interesting project, but I barely gave it a thought because I was so sure it was out of the question.

I told my husband later, expecting him to say, 'Yeah, there's no way you could have gone,' but he didn't. He looked at me as if I was mad and asked why I'd said no. 'It sounds like the opportunity of a lifetime. If anyone asked me, I'd go like a shot,' he said.

'I can't. It's impossible,' I told him, thinking he must have forgotten we had very young children.

'Why not? I'll be here. We'll manage fine. I might not stay up till midnight every night ironing socks and hankies like you do, but who cares?'

'I can't,' I said. 'If I go away for a week, it'll take me two weeks to get on top of everything once I get back.'

'You mean at work?' he said.

'And at home,' I said. 'And the kids'll really miss me.'

'They'll be absolutely fine. We'll have fun. I'll let them eat chocolate and go to bed late. Look, I can't look after the kids *and* keep the house tidy,' he said, (he could, of course, but he genuinely believes that he can't) 'but we can hire some help.' He mentioned the name of a woman who babysat for us regularly.

As he outlined a possible plan—and I can remember this as vividly as if it happened yesterday—a weird feeling started to grow inside me. At the risk of sounding melodramatic, it felt like some kind of explosion or revelation: I could go. It was possible. My husband was right, the children would be absolutely fine. And I could ring them every morning and every evening, so that they could hear my voice and I could reassure them that I was coming back soon.

Whoever you are that's reading this: I'm sorry to make it so personal. But if I don't tell you all this, the rest won't make sense. It's not a justification, just an explanation.

A week away, I thought. A whole week. Seven unbroken nights. I could catch up on my sleep. At that point my husband and I were getting up three or four times a night, and each time we might be up for an hour or more, trying to settle a wakeful child. And we were both working full-time as well. It didn't seem to bother my husband. 'What's the worst that can happen?' he used to say. 'We'll be tired, that's all. It's not the end of the world.' (My husband is the sort of person who would say that even if he bumped into someone who was holding a large nuclear bomb and wearing a name-badge that said 'Nostradamus'.)

I rang my boss and told him I could go after all. I hired the babysitter that my husband had mentioned, and within a couple of days my trip was arranged. I would be staying in a five-star hotel in a country I'd never been to before. I started to fantasise about the trip. All the work stuff would happen during the day, leaving my evenings free. I could have long, hot baths and lovely room service dinners that I wouldn't have to cook myself. I could go to bed at nine thirty and sleep until seven the next morning—that was the most alluring prospect of all. I'd assumed, without even re-alising it, that my relationship with proper sleep was over for good.

What had so recently seemed impossible quickly be-came a necessity. Every time I had a stressful day at work or a bad night with the kids, I recited the name of the place I was going to in my head—the hotel and the city. If I could manage until then, I told myself, I'd be fine. I'd spend that week refreshing my mind and body, repairing all the damage that had been done by years of overwork and refusing to rest. (I am a workaholic, by the way. I didn't even take any real time off when my children were born—I just worked from home as much as I could for the first six months, sitting at my computer while they slept in their baby-bouncers next to my desk.)

The trip was scheduled for June last year. In March, my boss told me the project had been cancelled. My trip was off, just like that. It's the closest I've ever come to crying in a professional situation. I think my boss could see how disappointed I was because he kept asking me if I was okay, if everything was all right at home.

I wanted to scream at him, 'Everything is absolutely f***ing great at home, as long as I can get away from it for just one week!' I honestly couldn't imagine how I would manage without the break I'd been banking on. Reconciling myself to going without wasn't an option. I needed something, a substitute. I asked my boss if he could send me somewhere else. The company I work for does similar sorts of work for many different organisations, so it didn't seem too unrealistic a request. Unfortunately my boss had no equivalent trip to offer me.

Feeling absolutely wretched, I turned to leave his office, but he called me back. He gave me a stern look and said, 'If you need to get away, go. Take a week off, go on holiday.' I blinked at him, wondering why I hadn't thought of it myself. He then ruined it by adding, 'Take the kids to the seaside,' but I could feel the smile forming on my face. He'd planted a seed in my mind.

I decided I would go away, on my own, without telling anyone. I pretended that the trip had not been cancelled, and booked myself into a spa hotel, safely far away from where I live. I would relax, recuperate, and come back a different person. I didn't feel guilty for lying to my husband, not at that point. I convinced myself that if he knew he would approve. Once or twice I considered telling him. 'Oh, by the way, my work trip was cancelled, but I thought that instead I'd go and spend a week lying beside a swimming pool in a white towelling bathrobe. Oh, and it's going to cost us about two and a half thousand quid—is that okay?'

He might not have minded, but I wasn't prepared to risk it. And, actually, even if he'd said, 'Fine, go ahead,' I couldn't have done it. I couldn't have done it openly—left my kids for a week and swanned off to have orange-blossom oil rubbed into my back. I had to lie about it because it seemed so frivolous, so entirely unnecessary. And yet—and I don't know how to convey to you how much—it was absolutely, desperately necessary for me at that point in my life. I felt as if I might die if it didn't happen.

I set off on the morning of Friday, 2 June, not even bothering to pack the things I'd have needed if I'd been going on the work trip. My husband would never in a million years notice something I'd left at home and think, Hang on, why hasn't she taken that? He doesn't notice anything, which I suppose makes him easy to lie to.

The hotel was unbelievably beautiful. On my first afternoon there, I had a full-body massage (I'd never had one before) and it was like nothing I'd ever experienced. I fell asleep on the table. I woke up six hours later. The therapist explained to me that she'd tried to wake me by shaking a set of bells in front of my face and saying my name, but I was sound asleep. Then she'd read the form I'd filled in at the spa's reception and seen that I'd rated my stress level, on a scale of one to ten, as twenty, so she decided to let me sleep.

When I woke up, I felt unbelievably different. I wasn't at all tired. I couldn't remember the last time I'd felt like that—not since I was at university. All the different parts of my brain felt clean, efficient and ready to go. That night, from the hotel's plush bar, I phoned my husband. I told him I'd arrived at my hotel. He'd forgotten its name. I told him I would be out and about most of the time and that if he needed to contact me my mobile was the easiest way. But I couldn't avoid saying the name of the hotel I was supposed to be staying in, a hotel on the other side of the world. And a man heard me.

As I was putting my phone back in my bag, I looked up and saw him watching me. He had dark auburn hair,

green eyes, pale skin and freckles. His face was boyish, the
sort that will never look old. His drink was in front of
him—something short and colourless. I noticed the blond
hairs on his forearms. I remember he was wearing a blue
and lilac striped shirt with the cuffs rolled up, and black
trousers that were moleskin, I think. He grinned. 'Sorry,'
he said. 'I shouldn't have been eavesdropping.'

'No, you shouldn't,' I agreed.

'I wasn't,' he quickly explained, looking a bit flustered.
'I mean, not deliberately.'

'But you heard, and now you're wondering why I lied
about where I am.' I don't know why, but I told him—
about the cancelled work trip, my massage, my six-hour
sleep. He kept saying that I didn't need to explain myself
to him, but I wanted to, because my reason for lying, I
thought, was about as benign as they come. It was self-
defence, basically. I really believed that and still believe it.
He laughed and said he knew how hard it could be. He
had a daughter too: Lucy.

We started talking properly. He introduced himself to
me as Mark Bretherick. He was married to Geraldine, had
been for nearly nine years. He told me he was the director
of a magnetic refrigeration company, that he made fridges
for scientists to use that were much colder than normal
fridges—nought degrees Kelvin, which is the coldest possible temperature. I asked him if they were white and square,
with egg compartments in their doors. He laughed and said
no. I can't remember exactly what he said next but it was
something to do with liquid nitrogen. He said that if I saw
one of his fridges, I wouldn't recognise it as a fridge. 'It
hasn't got Smeg or Electrolux written on it. You couldn't
put your stuffed olives or your Brie in there,' he said.

After we'd been talking for a while, it emerged that
he lived in Spilling. At the time I lived in Silsford—a
short drive from Spilling—and we couldn't get over the

coincidence. I told him about my work, which he seemed to find interesting—he asked me lots of questions about it. He mentioned his wife Geraldine all the time and seemed to be very much in love with her. He didn't say this, but it was clear she was very important to him. In fact, I smiled to myself because, although he was obviously highly intelligent, he was also one of those men who cannot utter a sentence without it containing his wife's name. If I asked him what he thought about something (as I did many times, not that evening but later, during the course of our week together), he would tell me, and then immediately afterwards he would tell me what Geraldine thought.

I asked if she worked. He told me that for years she ran the IT helpdesk at the Garcia Lorca Institute in Rawndesley, but that she'd always wanted to stop working when she had a child, and so when Lucy was born she did. 'Lucky her,' I said. Although I would hate not to work, I felt a pang of envy when it occurred to me how easy and calm Geraldine's life must be.

On that first night at the bar, Mark Bretherick said one odd thing that stuck in my mind. When I asked him if he thought I was immoral for lying to my husband about where I was, he said, 'From where I'm sitting, you seem pretty close to perfect.'

I laughed in his face.

'I'm serious,' he said. 'You're *im*perfect, and that's what's perfect about you. Geraldine's a perfect wife and mother in the traditional sense, and it sometimes makes me . . .' He stopped then and turned the conversation back to me. 'You're selfish.' He said this as if he found it admirable. 'Practically all you've told me tonight is what you need, what you want, how you feel.'

I told him to sod off.

Far from being put off, he said, 'Listen. Spend the week with me.' I stared at him, speechless. The week? I'd been wondering whether I even wanted to spend the next ten minutes with him. Plus, I wasn't sure what exactly he meant. Until he added, 'I mean, properly. With me, in my room.'

I told him he had a phenomenal cheek. I was quite rude to him. 'You want a week of sex with someone you regard as worthless before returning to your perfect life with the perfect Geraldine. Bugger off.' That was what I said to him, pretty much word for word.

'No!' he said, grabbing my arm. 'It's not like that. Listen, I've probably said it all wrong, but . . . what you said before, about needing to come away this week and sleep and rest because you'd never had the chance before and you wouldn't again, well . . .' He looked as if he was struggling for the right words. He didn't find them. Eventually his face sort of crumpled and he turned away from me. 'Forget it,' he said. 'You're probably right. I'll bugger off, as instructed.'

His vehemence had shocked me, and his sudden dejection was as much of a surprise. He looked as if he might cry, and I felt guilty. Maybe I'd misjudged him.

'What?' I asked.

He sighed, leaning over his drink. 'I was going to say that sleep and rest aren't the only things you don't get enough of once you've had a child.'

'You mean sex?'

'No.' He almost smiled. 'I meant adventure. Fun. Not knowing exactly what's going to happen.'

I couldn't speak. If only he hadn't said that, if only he'd said something else, I'd have been fine. I'd have been able to stand my ground.

'You know, I'm away a lot for work,' he said. 'Overnight. Often. One or two nights at a time, once or twice a month. This time it's a week. And whenever I check into another hotel on my own and throw my overnight bag down on the bed, I think to myself, I don't know what I want more—sleep or adventure. Should I order dinner in my room, watch telly in bed, get my head down early and wake up late, or should I go down to the hotel bar and try to pick up an exotic woman?'

I laughed. 'So tonight you opted for the latter.' Though for him I could hardly have been exotic. I lived less than half an hour's drive from his house. 'Didn't you say Lucy was five?' I said. 'She must be sleeping by now.'

He looked miserable, as if he wished I hadn't said that. 'I can't remember the last good night I had,' he said. He seemed needy, yet at the same time strong and determined. Almost angry. I suppose I found him intriguing.

'Shit,' I said. 'No one warned me it might get worse.'

'It might.' Unexpectedly, he grinned. 'But it could also get better. For a bit. Say, this week. Couldn't it?'

I had never been unfaithful to my husband before. I never will again. I am not the unfaithful type. I hate the whole idea of infidelity. 'You're wasting your time,' I told him.

'You can't, in all conscience, say no,' he said. 'I'd be too embarrassed. The only way you can save me from the fate of massive humiliation is by saying yes.'

I knew I ought to be finding him more annoying by the second, but I was starting to like him. 'Sorry,' I said. 'I can't. I told you, I need to rest. Spending a week with another man—that'd be a big deal for me. It'd send me into panic mode, and I'd go home in a worse state than I was in when I left.' Part of me couldn't believe I was taking this seriously enough to give him such a considered response.

'It could be this week only,' he said. 'We wouldn't have to keep in touch. We're both happily married, neither of us wants to break up our family. We've both got a lot to lose. We're parents—in other words, nobody expects us to do anything secret or exciting ever again.'

He was right. My best friend, who was and still is single, was always telling me I was prim and proper, just because she occasionally saw me trying to persuade my children to eat broccoli, or changing the TV channel if someone was being hacked to pieces on the screen. She thought I'd become a boring mumsy type, and this idea enraged me. And I found this man—Mark Bretherick—physically attractive, especially when he promised that we could confine our adventurous activities, as he called them, to the daytime and early evening, so that I could still have my seven nights of unbroken sleep.

We didn't share a room. We never spent a night in the same bed. By ten thirty each evening, we were back in our separate suites. But we ate together, had massages together, sat in the outdoor hot tub and the hammam together—and obviously we did the obvious.

One evening, in the restaurant, he started to cry. For no reason, it seemed. He burst out of there, embarrassed, and when he came back he asked me to forget it had happened. I worried he was starting to fall for me, having second thoughts about not keeping in touch once our week together was over, but he seemed all right again after that, so I stopped worrying.

However terrible it sounds, I didn't feel guilty. I thought about a book I'd read as a teenager, *Flowers for Algernon*. I don't remember who wrote it, but it's about a retarded man who (I can't remember how) suddenly becomes clever and fully aware. Perhaps he takes a drug of some kind, or someone experiments on him. Anyway, for a while he is bright enough to realise he was retarded and isn't any longer. He feels as if a miracle has happened. He falls in love and starts to live a full, happy life. And then the effect of the drug or experiment starts to wear off, and he realises he will soon be retarded again, unable to think clearly—he will lose this brilliant new life that is so precious to him.

That's how I felt, like that man, whatever his name was. I knew I only had a week, and I had to cram everything into it, all the things my life lacked—rest, adventure, being able to concentrate on myself, my own needs. More importantly, I felt I would be able to do everything I had to do more happily and more efficiently when I got home. I was certain my husband would never find out, and he hasn't.

And then last night I saw the news. I saw a man who was supposed to be Mark Bretherick, and he wasn't the same person. Maybe the man I met could only do the things he did—the things we both did—as somebody else, which would be understandable. But, whoever he was, he must have known the Bretherick family well because he knew so much about them—enough to convince me that he was one of them.

The story I've just told you might have nothing to do with the deaths of Geraldine and Lucy Bretherick. If it doesn't, I apologise for wasting your time. But I can't get it out of my head that the two things might be connected. Geraldine and Lucy Bretherick died several days ago, and my husband tells me it's been on the news and in the papers every day. I didn't know this—I don't think I've sat down with a newspaper since my first child was born—but if it's true then the man I met in the hotel last year is bound to have seen the reports. He will have guessed that by now I know he isn't who he told me he was. I know this sounds totally crazy, but yesterday somebody pushed me into the road and I was very nearly run over by a bus. Today I was followed by a red Alfa Romeo, registration YF52 DNB.

I'm sorry I can't tell you the name of the hotel, or my name or any more than I've told you. If by any chance

you find out who I am during the course of your investigation, please, please contact me at work and do not let
my husband find out about any of this. My marriage
would be over if he did.

A low, rasping voice from behind me jolts me out of my seat. 'I
see dead people,' it says. I make an undignified whimpering
noise as I whirl round to see who is behind me.

It's Owen Mellish, my least favourite colleague. My body sags
as if it's been punctured. I turn back to my screen and quickly
click on 'close file', feeling my face heat up. Owen is laughing
loudly and slapping his knee, pleased to have given me a fright.
His short, paunchy body, squeezed into a tight green T-shirt and
ripped denim shorts, is sprawled in a swivel chair which he rocks
back and forth with one of his trunk-like hairy legs.

'I see dead people,' he says again, louder, hoping to attract
laughter from nearby colleagues. I want to rip out his stupid
goatee beard hair by hair.

No one responds.

Owen gets impatient. 'Haven't you all seen *The Sixth Sense?*'
We tell him that we have.

'That woman that's been on the news—Bretherick. The one
who killed her sprog and herself—she's a dead ringer for Sal,
isn't she? Spooky!'

I've never met anybody with a more irritating voice. Owen
sounds, all the time, as if he badly needs to clear his throat.
Every time he speaks you can hear the phlegm rattling inside
him; it's disgusting.

'You will be dead soon if you don't learn how to drive.' He
laughs. 'Before, on the road. What was that all about?' He is
looking at his audience, not at me. He wants to belittle me in
front of everybody. *Like Pam Senior yesterday, yelling at me in
the street.* It must have been Owen who beeped his horn at me
when I came to a standstill outside our building earlier.

'Sorry,' I mumble. 'I'm tired, that's all.'

'It's all right.' Owen pats me on the back. 'I'd be in a state too if I were you. You know, legend has it that if your doppelgänger dies, you die too.'

'Is that a fact?' I grin at him to show that his words have had no effect. Actually, that's not true. They've made me feel more robust. Owen could never be anything other than utterly prosaic. Hearing him drone on about doppelgängers inspires me to pull myself together. So what if Geraldine Bretherick looked like me? Plenty of people look like plenty of other people and there's nothing sinister about it.

I don't dislike many people, but I do dislike Owen Mellish. He thinks he's witty, but all his jokes are against other people. They're jibes concealed behind a thin veil of humour. Once when I rang the office to say I was stuck in traffic and had been for nearly an hour, he laughed at me and said triumphantly, 'I came in at sparrow's fart and there was barely a car on the road.'

Owen is a sediment modeller, and unfortunately I have to work with him on almost every project I undertake. He creates computerised hydrodynamic models of sediment structures, and I can't work without them. The programs he writes can apply any conceivable tidal or water change, natural or man-made, to sediment with any ratio of silt to sand to cohesive mud, any flock-size. It constantly annoys me to think that, without Owen and his computer, my work would be far less accurate.

At the moment he and I are working together on a feasibility study for Gilsenen Ltd, a large multinational that wants to build a cooling plant on the Culver Estuary. Our job is to predict future levels of contaminant concentrations and industrial enrichment, in the event of the plant being built. We have to deliver our final report in two weeks' time, and Gilsenen has to pretend to care; it's crucial to its image that it appears ecologically responsible. So I have to speak to Owen often, and hear his rattling voice, and I can't get it out of my head that his wife had their first child only four months ago and two months later

Owen left her for another woman. Now he takes his new girl-friend's daughters to the park every weekend, and even has a photo of them on his desk at work, but he never mentions his own son, who was born with a serious heart defect. It's a pity his computing expertise doesn't extend to making a mathematical model that can assess the effect on a baby of being abandoned by his father.

'"To whom it may concern".' Owen's looking at my screen, reading my words aloud. 'What's that? Making a will, are you? Very sensible. What happened to your face, anyway? Hubby been beating you again?'

I grab my mouse and try as quickly as I can to close the file I thought I'd already closed. Do I want to save the changes? In my flustered state, with Owen looking over my shoulder, I click on 'no' by mistake. 'Shit!' I open the file again, praying. *Please, please . . .*

There is no God. It's gone. The draft of my salt-marsh article has been resurrected.

I push past Owen, out of the office and into the corridor. All that effort—gone in the time it took to press a button. *Shit.* Would I have sent it? I doubt any police force anywhere in the world has ever received a letter like it, but I don't care—every word of it was true, and writing it made me feel better for as long as it lasted. I ought to go back to my computer and start from scratch but that's a prospect I can't face at the moment.

I try to focus on despising Owen but all I can think about, suddenly, is the red Alfa Romeo. Writing to the police was a way of pushing it aside. Now that my letter's disappeared, I can't avoid it any more.

I first noticed it on the way to nursery. It was behind me almost constantly, and all I could do was stare at it helplessly, worrying. Normally, car time is grooming and breakfast time for me, the only chance I get to brush my hair, put on my perfume, eat a banana. Today, I felt watched, and couldn't bring myself to do any of those things.

I couldn't see the driver of the Alfa Romeo because of the sun reflecting off his windscreen. *Or hers.* I thought of Pam but I knew this wasn't her car. She drives a black Renault Clio. When I turned left into Bloxham Road, where the children's nursery is, the Alfa Romeo went straight on. I was relieved, and even laughed at myself as I lifted Jake out of his car seat, while Zoe waited patiently on the pavement beside me holding her shiny pink handbag with pink and blue butterflies on it. My daughter is obsessed with handbags; she won't leave the house without one. Inside today's choice she's got fifty-pence in ten- and twenty-pence pieces, a pink plastic car key and fob and a multi-coloured plastic bead bracelet.

'Nobody's following us. Silly Mummy,' I said.

'Why, who did you think it was?' Zoe asked, surveying the empty road, then scrunching up her face to examine me more closely.

'No one,' I said firmly. 'There's no one following us.'

'But you thought there was, so who did you think it might have been?' she persisted. I smiled at her, proud of her advanced reasoning skills, but said nothing.

I dropped the children off and, on my way out of the building, bumped into Anthea, the manager, who is in her mid-fifties but dresses like a teenager, in crop-tops and visible thongs. She gave me another dressing-down, twirling her long streaked hair round her index finger as she spoke. I'd been late to collect Zoe and Jake four days in the past fortnight, and I'd forgotten to bring in a new packet of nappies for Jake so the girls had had to use nursery spares when they changed him. Heinous crimes, both. I apologised, mentally added 'Buy new nappies, try harder not to be late' to my list, and ran back to the car, swearing under my breath. I had a lot to do at work today and didn't have time for Anthea's lectures. Why didn't she just charge me for any spare nappies Jake used? Why didn't she charge me extra if the staff had to stay longer on the days when I was late? I would happily have paid them double, or even quadruple, for that extra hour. I'd still only have had to write one cheque at the end of the month. I don't care about spending money, but I get twitchy at the thought of losing even a second of valuable time.

On the way to the post office to post my anonymous letter to the police, I kept checking my rear-view mirror. Nothing. I'd got halfway to Silsford before I saw the red Alfa Romeo again. Same number plate. Sunlight bounced off the windscreen and I still couldn't see the driver; a dark shape was all I could make out. I tasted bitter coffee in the back of my throat, mixed with bile.

I pulled over by the side of the road and watched the Alfa Romeo speed ahead of me and out of sight. It could be a coincidence, I told myself: I'm not the only person who lives in Spilling and works in Silsford.

I forced myself to calm down and started my car again. All the way to work I checked my mirrors every few seconds like a learner driver under the beady eye of her instructor. There was no sign of the Alfa Romeo, and by the time I got to Silsford I'd decided it was gone for good. Then, as I turned the corner to get to HS Silsford's car park, I saw a red Alfa Romeo parked at the far end of the road, on the right. I gasped, my heartbeat racing to keep up with my brain. This could not be happening. I accelerated, but the Alfa started to move as I approached and was round the corner and away before I could catch a glimpse of the driver.

I braked hard, slamming my fist down on the steering wheel. The registration. I'd been so shaken up by the sight of the red car that I hadn't checked the number plate. I sat perfectly still in the driver's seat, unable to believe my own stupidity. *It has to be the same one*, I thought. *How many people drive Alfas?* A horn beeped loudly behind me. I realised I was in the middle of the road, blocking the traffic in both directions. I waved an apology to whoever was behind me—sodding Owen Mellish, as it turns out—and swerved left into HS Silsford's underground car park.

The 'HS' in the company's name stands for hydraulics solutions. We're spread over the top five floors of a rectangular tower block that nevertheless manages to look short and fat. It's all dark metal and mirrors on the outside, and beige and white on the inside, with square brown suede sofas, potted plants and little water sculptures in the plush reception area.

I work here two days a week, and for the Save Venice Foundation three days a week. Save Venice wanted someone from HS Silsford on secondment part-time for three years. Almost everybody in the office applied, tempted by the prospect of the all-expenses-paid trips to Venice. I can't prove it but I'm sure Owen went for it and has never forgiven me for being chosen over him. Every day, I vow not to allow him to wind me up.

Not bothering with the deep breaths this time, I steel myself and march back to my desk. 'Madam Snoot just phoned for you,' Owen calls out when he sees me. 'She wasn't very happy when I told her you were off skiving somewhere, not at your desk.'

'On Tuesdays and Wednesdays I don't work for her,' I snap.

'Ooh, touchy.' He grins. 'I'd listen to your voicemail if I were you. I know you're scared of her really.'

There are two messages from Natasha Prentice-Nash, or Madam Snoot as Owen calls her. She's the chairman of the Save Venice Foundation and insists on that title rather than 'chairperson' because she claims that isn't a word. Esther has also left two messages for me—at 7.40 and 7.55 this morning—which I delete and resolve to ignore. I listen to the rest: one from nursery, left at 8.10, one from Monk Barn Primary School at 8.15, one from Nick at 8.30, who says, 'Oh, hi, it's me. Nick. Um . . . Bye.' He doesn't tell me what he wants, or say that he will phone back. He doesn't ask me to phone him.

After Nick's comes a man's deep, plummy voice that I don't recognise. I picture plump cheeks, white teeth and a thick pink tongue above some sort of cravat. Not that I even know what a cravat is. 'Hello, this is a message for, um, Sally. Sally Thorning.'

Whoever this man is, he doesn't know me well enough to ring me at 8.35 on a Tuesday morning. 'Hello, Sally, it's, um, it's Fergus here. Fergus Land.' I frown, puzzled. Fergus Land? Who's he? Then I remember: my next-door neighbour, the male half of open-topped-sports-car Fergus and Nancy. I smile to myself. His cheeks *are* plump. Good guess.

'This is a bit odd,' says Fergus's recorded voice. 'You may well have difficulty believing it, but I assure you it's true.'

My mind freezes. I can't cope with another odd thing, not today.

'I've just this minute sat down with a library book, one I took out of Spilling Library last week. About the Tour de France. I've just bought a new mountain bike, you see.'

What does it have to do with me? I wonder.

'Anyway, far-fetched as it sounds, I found Nick's driver's licence inside the book. You know, the little pink photocard one. He obviously borrowed it too, at some point—I know he's a cycling aficionado—and perhaps he used the licence as a bookmark or something, but anyway . . . I've got it. I don't want to drop it through your letterbox, since I know other people live in your building, but if you want to pop round later to collect it . . .'

I feel weak with relief, and decide to overlook Fergus's dig about the inadequate size and situation of my home in comparison with his. Nick left his driver's licence in a library book. It's typical, but not sinister. I try not to be irritated by the image of Fergus at home with his feet up, reading.

I haven't got the energy to speak to Natasha Prentice-Nash, so I phone Nick's mobile. 'Fergus next door has found your driving licence,' I tell him.

'Have I lost it?'

'Yes. It was in a library book about the Tour de France.'

'Oh, yeah.' He sounds pleased. 'I was using it as a bookmark.'

'You left a message,' I say. 'What did you want?'

'Did I?'

'Yes.'

'Oh, right, yeah. Nursery rang. They said you weren't answering your phone.'

'I might have missed one or two calls,' I say vaguely. 'Things have been a bit hectic today.' I stopped answering my mobile after Esther's four attempts to ring me on it between six and half past seven this morning. She knows something is up and is determined to find out what it is. 'What did nursery want?'

'Jake's hurt his ear.'

'What? I've only just dropped him off. Is it serious?'

My husband ponders this. 'They didn't say it was.'

'Did they say it wasn't?'

'Well . . . no, but . . .'

'What exactly happened?'

'I don't know.'

'They must have said something!'

'Nothing apart from what I've told you,' says Nick. 'They just said Jake hurt his ear, but he's fine now.'

'Well, if he's fine, why did they bother ringing? He can't be fine. I'd better call them.'

I cut Nick off and ring Anthea, who tells me that Jake is as jolly as ever. He scratched his ear, that's all, cried a bit and cheered up soon afterwards.

'We did notice that his fingernails need cutting,' Anthea says in an apologetic tone, as if reluctant to interfere.

'Whenever we cut them, he shrieks as if we're putting his neck on the block for the guillotine,' I tell her, knowing I sound defensive. 'I hate doing that to him.' *Neck on the block for the guillotine?* Did I really say that? Has Anthea even heard of a guillotine? Her idea of history is probably last year's *Big Brother*.

'Poor little thing,' she says, and I feel guilty for being such a snob. When I was a teenager, any form of snobbery elicited from me a torrent of fierce indignation. When my mother dared to suggest that I ought not to go out with Wayne Moscrop, whose father was in prison, I followed her round the house for weeks, shouting, 'Oh, right! So I suppose I can only date people whose dads aren't in prison, is that it? Is that what you're saying? So obviously if Nelson Mandela had a son, even if he was helping to lead the struggle against apartheid, you wouldn't want me to go out with him either!'

If Zoe ever acquires a boyfriend who has any connection with a correctional facility, I will have to pay him to forget all about her and tactfully disappear. I wonder how much that might cost. If he's noble and principled, like Nelson Mandela's imaginary son, he might stand his ground however much money I offer him.

'So . . . I don't get it,' I say to Anthea. 'If Jake's okay, why did you ring Nick? And leave a message for me?'

'We have to notify parents of any physical injury, however small. That's the policy.'

'So you don't need me to come and get Jake?'

'No, no, he's absolutely fine.'

'Good.' I tell Anthea about my October half-term dilemma and hint that I would be willing to buy her any number of diamond-studded thongs if she could possibly bend the rules and create a place for Zoe just for that week. She says she'll see what she can do. 'Thank you,' I gush. 'And . . . you're really sure Jake's okay?'

'Honestly, it was just a small scratch. He hardly even cried. There's a tiny pink mark on his ear, but you probably wouldn't even notice it.'

Wearily, I thank her, end the call and ring Pam Senior. She's not in, so I leave a message—a grovelling apology. I ask her to ring me back, hoping that as soon as I hear her voice I will know instantly that she didn't try to kill me yesterday. Muttering, 'She ought to be the one apologising to me,' under my breath, I ring Monk Barn Primary. The secretary wants to know why I haven't filled in a new pupil registration form and an emergency contact form for Zoe. I tell her I haven't received any forms.

'I gave them to your husband,' she says. 'When he brought Zoe in for the open evening.'

In June. Two months ago. I tell her to put new ones in the post and make sure the envelope is addressed to me. 'I'll get them back to you by the end of the week.'

Spend the week with me. That's what he said, Mark Bretherick or whoever he was, after I told him how long I was staying, that first night in the bar. He was also staying for a week. *This time it's a week*, he said. Business. But I didn't hear him cancelling any meetings, and he certainly didn't go to any. I assumed he'd decided to abandon work in favour of me, but surely there would have been the odd phone call . . . I saw his mobile phone in his room, but I didn't see him use it, not once.

Oh, my God. I grip the edge of my desk with both hands. He changed rooms. From eleven to fifteen. He told me there was no hot water in his bathroom, but how likely is that in a three-hundred-pound-a-night hotel? I didn't hear him talking to any of the hotel staff about it. One morning he just told me he'd changed. Upgraded. 'I was in a "Classic" suite before,' he said. 'Now I'm in a "Romantic" one.'

What if he had only ended up at Seddon Hall because he'd followed me? Because I looked so much like Geraldine. And then, because it was short notice, he couldn't get the same room for a whole week . . .

I can't stand this any longer: not knowing anything, not doing anything. I turn off my computer, grab my bag and run out of the office.

As soon as I'm in my car with the doors locked, I ring Esther. 'About time,' she says. 'I was just deciding not to be your friend any more. The only thing that might change my mind is if you tell me what's going on. You know how nosey I am—'

'Esther, shut up.'

'What?'

'Listen, this is important, okay? I will tell you, but not now. I'm about to go to a place called Corn Mill House, to speak to somebody called Mark Bretherick.'

'The one on the news, whose wife and daughter died?'

'Yes. I'm sure I'll be fine, but if by any chance I don't phone you within two hours to say I'm out of there and safe, phone the police, okay?'

'Not okay. Sal, what the *fucking hell* is going on? If you think you can fob me off with—'

'I promise I'll explain everything later. Just, please, please, do this one thing for me.'

'Has this got anything to do with Pam Senior?'

'No. Maybe. I don't know.'

'You don't *know*?'

'Esther, you mustn't say anything about this to Nick. Swear you won't.'

'Ring me in two hours or I'm calling the police,' she says as if it was her idea. 'And if you can't explain or go into detail then, *I'll* push you under a bus. All right?'

'You're a star.'

I drop my phone on the passenger seat and head for Corn Mill House.

Police Exhibit Ref: VN8723
Case Ref: VN87
OIC: Sergeant Samuel Kombothekra

GERALDINE BRETHERICK'S DIARY, EXTRACT 2 OF 9
(taken from hard disk of Toshiba laptop computer at Corn
Mill House, Castle Park, Spilling, RY29 0LE)

20 April 2006, 10 p.m.

I don't think I'm going to be able to be friends with Cordy
for much longer. Which is a shame, as she is one of the
few people I like. She phoned me a couple of hours ago
and told me she's fallen in love with another man, someone with whom she has spent a total of two weekends.
She says she knows it's crazy but she's only got one life
and she wants to be with him. Dermot knows about it,
apparently, and is devastated. I don't blame him, I told
her. Last year she insisted he have a vasectomy. He wasn't
keen but he did it for Cordy's sake, so that she wouldn't
have to keep taking the pill.

She said she couldn't stay with Dermot just because
he'd had 'the snip'. 'I'm not that self-sacrificing,' she said.
'Would you be?'

I didn't know what to say. I was thinking, Yes, I must
be. For the past five years I have felt as if I'm trapped in a
small chamber inside a submarine that's lost its oxygen
supply, and I've done nothing about it. I continue to do
nothing about it. This evening I was in the kitchen chopping chorizo for supper, and Lucy came up behind me,
wrapped her arms round my legs and started to sing a
song she'd learned at school. Loudly. I felt that fluttery
panic in my chest again, as if I'm a butterfly struggling to
escape from a thick, closed fist. That's how I always feel
when Lucy throws her arms round me unexpectedly. I said,

'Hello, darling, that's a nice cuddle,' as the old familiar scream started up in my head: no space, no calm, no choices, and this is going to last for ever . . .

Eventually I told Cordy that, yes, in her position I would be self-sacrificing and stay. Her response was an anguished groan. I felt sorry for her, and was about to take back my words—how did I know what I would do?—when she said, 'I don't think I can stay. But . . . only seeing Oonagh at weekends, it's going to break my heart.'

Mine iced over as soon as I heard these words. 'You mean . . . if you left you wouldn't take Oonagh with you?' I asked, trying to sound casual. And then it all came out: the 'masterplan'. Cordy said that if she leaves Dermot she will let him keep Oonagh. 'I couldn't live with myself if I took her away from him,' she said. 'I mean, it's not as if he can have more kids, is it? And it's my fault. I'm the one who's wrecking the marriage.' She started crying then.

Cordy is not stupid. I'm sure she will succeed in fooling everybody apart from me. Her leaving—when it happens, as it undoubtedly will—will have nothing to do with this new man and everything to do with her being desperate to shake off her child, to be free again. People talk about being 'tied down' in the context of marriage, or living with somebody, but that's rubbish. Before we had Lucy, Mark and I were entirely free.

The ingenious part is that no one will condemn Cordy for abandoning Oonagh. She will pretend she's being self-sacrificing, putting Dermot's needs before her own, heart-broken to be separated from her precious daughter.

'I'm sure Dermot would still let me see Oonagh a lot,' she sobbed. 'She can stay with me every weekend, and in the holidays. Maybe we could even do fifty-fifty, and Oonagh could have two homes.'

'A lot of men wouldn't want to be the main one to look after a child,' I told her, thinking of Mark, who would be hopeless. I don't think he's ever prepared a meal for Lucy. Or for anyone, come to think of it. 'Are you sure Dermot does? Maybe he'd prefer Oonagh to live with you as long as he could have access whenever he wanted.'

Cordy said, 'No, Dermot's not like that. He's a brilliant father. He's done everything, right from the start. We've shared all the childcare, everything. I know he'd want Oonagh to stay with him.'

'Right,' I said, feeling my chest fill with white-hot envy. That was when I knew I wouldn't be able to stand it. If Cordy escapes and starts a whole new life, if she manages to discard Oonagh and look like a saintly martyr in the process, I won't ever be able to speak to her again.

4

8/7/07

'There's been a development.' Sam Kombothekra addressed the whole team but his eyes kept swerving back to Simon. 'I've just taken a call from a Sue Slater, a legal secretary for a firm of solicitors in Rawndesley that specialises in family law. Two weeks before Geraldine and Lucy Bretherick's bodies were found, Mrs Slater took a call from a Geraldine Bretherick, who gave her name and asked to be put through to a lawyer. Mrs Slater didn't think anything of it until she heard the name on the news. It was an unusual name so it stuck in her mind.'

'Kombothekra's an unusual name,' said Inspector Giles Proust. 'There must be thousands of Brethericks.' The sergeant laughed nervously and Proust looked gratified.

'Apparently Mrs Bretherick asked to speak to "somebody who deals with divorces, custody cases, that sort of thing"— that's a word-for-word quote. When Mrs Slater asked her if she needed to engage a lawyer's services herself, she seemed to lose her nerve. She said it didn't matter and put the phone down. Mrs Slater said she nearly didn't ring in, but in the end she thought she ought to, just in case it turned out to be important.'

'Very public-spirited of her.' The Snowman leaned against the wall of the CID room, passing his mobile phone from one hand to the other. Every few seconds he glanced at its screen. His wife Lizzie was away all week on a cookery course. Proust had allowed her to go—it was the first time in thirty years that she'd left the marital home for more than one night, he'd told Simon—on the condition that she 'kept in touch'. 'I'm sure she will, sir,' Simon had said, resisting the urge to add, 'I believe they have telephones in Harrogate.' Lizzie had left yesterday morning, since when the Snowman had been keeping in touch with a frequency that amounted to surveillance. He'd phoned Lizzie five times yesterday and three times today. And those were only the calls Simon had witnessed, calls with no purpose other than to track Lizzie's movements, as far as Simon could make out. 'She's in her hotel room,' Proust would mutter darkly every so often, or, 'She's in a shop buying a sweatshirt. Apparently it's chilly there.' Because Proust was Proust, the responding words 'We don't give a shit' went unspoken.

To the left of the inspector's bald head was a large rectangular whiteboard on to which Geraldine Bretherick's suicide note had been transcribed. Below it, also in black marker pen, someone had copied out the letter that had been posted in PC Robbie Meakin's box at Spilling Post Office: 'Please forward this to whoever is investigating the deaths of Geraldine and Lucy Bretherick. It's possible that the man shown on the news last night who is meant to be Mark Bretherick is not Mark Bretherick. You need to look into it and make sure he's who he says he is. Sorry I can't say more.'

Proust had been cagey about how this note had made its way to his desk from Spilling Post Office. Simon didn't doubt for a second that Charlie had passed it on. Which meant she'd chosen to go to Proust instead of him. So how come Simon hated the whole world at the moment apart from her?

'Well, Sergeant?' Proust asked Kombothekra. 'Is Mrs Slater's contribution important?'

'It is, sir. At least, I believe it is. It's possible Geraldine Bretherick wanted to leave Mark Bretherick and phoned this law firm—Ellingham Sandler—for that reason. Because she wanted to find out, before she initiated anything, what her chances were of getting custody of Lucy.'

'Would she have wanted custody?' asked Proust. 'On the basis of the laptop diary, I'd say not.'

'She talks about her friend Cordy leaving her husband and letting him keep their daughter,' said Chris Gibbs, rubbing his thick gold wedding ring with the fingers of his right hand. 'Might there be a connection there?' Gibbs had got married a little over a year ago. Ever since, he had turned up at work each day with a strange gloss on his thick dark hair, and wearing clothes that smelled, in Simon's opinion, like those colourful plastic devices you sometimes saw in toilet bowls, designed to replace foul smells with aggressive floral ones that were even more offensive.

'You mean Geraldine might have been phoning on Cordy's behalf?' said Colin Sellers, scratching one of his bushy sideburns. If he didn't watch out, they'd take over his entire face. Simon thought of the dark green plant that clung to the walls of Corn Mill House.

'Was it you who spoke to Mrs O'Hara, Waterhouse?'

Simon inclined his head in Proust's direction. Since Kombothekra had taken over from Charlie, Simon had made a point of saying as little as possible in team meetings. No one had noticed; it was a protest with no audience, specially designed for minimum effect.

'Speak to her, again. Find out if she changed her mind about letting her husband keep the daughter to appease her guilt and asked Geraldine Bretherick to phone a lawyer for her.'

Simon allowed his scorn to show on his face. Cordy O'Hara wasn't timid or inert. She'd have phoned a lawyer herself.

'I didn't mean that, sir,' said Gibbs. 'Geraldine was envious of Mrs O'Hara being able to get shot of her daughter—she said so in the diary, explicitly. Maybe it inspired her to try the same thing.'

'That'd be a bit extreme, wouldn't it?' said Sellers. Seeing the rest of the team's expressions, he held up his hands. 'I know, I know.'

All eyes fixed on the enlarged photographs of the crime scenes that took up a quarter of a wall: the matching high-sided white bathtubs with gold claw feet, the clear water in one bath and the livid red water of the other, the curled tendrils of wet hair that formed a corona around each face like the black rays of a dead sun. Simon couldn't bring himself to look at the two faces. Especially the eyes.

'I should probably say . . .' Kombothekra glanced down at his notes. 'Custody—it's not called that any more. Mrs Slater told me lawyers talk about residency these days, and primary carers. The family courts look at everything from the child's point of view.'

'That would seem to be a foolish way to proceed,' said Proust.

'It's not about one of the parents winning and one losing. It's about what's in the child's best interests. Whenever possible they try to come up with some sort of joint residency arrangement.'

'Sergeant, fascinating as this insight into our nation's social and legal history may be—'

'I'll get to the point, sir,' said Kombothekra, his Adam's apple working frantically as it always did when he was the focus of negative attention. 'It's just a hypothesis, but . . . Geraldine Bretherick hadn't worked since her daughter was born. She didn't have any savings; her husband brought in all the money. Money equals power, and women who stay at home with young children day in day out often lose confidence.'

'That's true, sir,' Sellers chipped in. 'Stacey's always banging on about it. Now she's persuaded me she needs to learn French, and I'm forking out for a two-hour lesson every week. She's talking about signing up at the sixth form college to do an AS level. I can't see how it'll make her more confident, unless she's planning to move to France, but . . .' He shrugged.

'Mid-life crisis,' Gibbs diagnosed.

Simon dug his nails into his palm, sickened by the deliberate stupidity. If Stacey Sellers was lacking in confidence, chances were it had nothing to do with not speaking another language and everything to do with Sellers' years-long affair with Suki Kitson, a much younger woman who made her living singing in restaurants, hotel bars and, occasionally, on cruise ships. If Sellers wanted to save money, he should trying packing Suki in and seeing what happened. Maybe Stacey would decide she could live without learning French after all.

'A lot of stay-at-home mums start to feel that the outside world is no longer their domain, if you like—' Kombothekra went on.

'I don't like.' Proust lurched forward, shaking out his arms, as if suddenly aware that he'd been still for too long. He aimed his mobile phone at Kombothekra. 'If I'd wanted a commentary on societal norms I'd have phoned Émile Durkheim. A Frenchman, Sellers, so no doubt your wife knows all about him. It's bad enough that we've had that self-promoting idiot Harbard foisted on us without you turning into a sociologist as well, Sergeant. Stick to the facts and get to the point.'

None of the team had enjoyed working with Professor Keith Harbard, but Superintendent Barrow had insisted; CID needed to be seen to be bringing in outside expertise. Familicide, as some newspapers and television commentators had called it, was too sensitive and newsworthy a crime to be dealt with in the usual way. Particularly when the killer was a woman, a mother. 'We need all the whistles and bells on this one,' the superintendent had said. What they'd got was a fat, balding academic who bandied about the phrase 'family annihilation', especially when there were cameras pointed at him, and mentioned the titles of books and articles he'd written to anyone who would listen; who blatantly thought he was the mutt's nuts, as Sellers had so aptly put it.

'Despite what the computer diary says, most mothers aren't willing to give up their children when it comes down to it,' said Kombothekra. 'And if Geraldine killed Lucy and herself—which we believe she did—that suggests she needed her daughter with her even in death. Yes, she might fleetingly have envied Cordy O'Hara, but that doesn't mean she'd honestly have wanted to abandon Lucy. If she had, she could have done it at any time. What was stopping her?'

Leaving no pause for anyone to answer, he went on, 'Mark Bretherick is a rich, successful man. Wealth and success equals power. It's possible Geraldine feared she wouldn't stand a chance of winning a court case against him.' Kombothekra smiled anxiously at Simon, who looked away quickly. He didn't want to be mistaken for an ally. He wished Sellers and Gibbs would invite Kombothekra to the pub now and again. That'd take the pressure off Simon, take away the feeling that he ought to be doing something he wasn't. Sellers and Gibbs had no excuse; their unwelcoming attitude had nothing to do with Charlie. They disliked Kombothekra's politeness. Behind his back Simon had heard them refer to him as 'Stepford'. Sellers and Gibbs were only capable of civilised behaviour on occasions such as today's briefing, when they feared being impaled on the Snowman's icicle-sharp sarcasm.

'Remember the story of King Solomon, Sergeant?' said Proust. 'The real mother chose to let the other woman keep the child rather than chop it in half.' When the inspector realised that three-quarters of the team was staring at him, mystified, he changed the subject. 'This business about women and their depleted confidence is nonsense! My wife didn't work for years when our children were small, and I've never known a more confident woman. I was the breadwinner, yes, but Lizzie behaved as if every penny of it had arrived as a result of her hard work, not mine. I regularly came home at dawn after a series of scuffles with the most unprepossessing specimens our community had to offer, only to be told that my shift couldn't possibly have been as gruelling as hers. As for the power she wields in our family, it's frightening.' The inspector glanced at his phone. 'All this twaddle about women losing confidence. Would that it were true.' His eyes met Simon's. Simon knew they were thinking the same thing: would Proust have said what he'd just said quite so explicitly if Charlie had still been the skipper?

Simon couldn't stand much more of this. '"You", not "we",' he said to Kombothekra. '*You* believe Geraldine Bretherick killed Lucy and then herself. I don't.'

'It was only a matter of time . . .' Proust muttered.

'Come on,' said Sellers. 'Who else could have done it? There was no break-in.'

'Someone Geraldine let in, obviously. Several sets of fingerprints were found in the house that we haven't identified.'

'That's standard. You know it is. They could be anyone's—someone who came to measure for new curtains, anyone.'

'Who else would have a motive to kill both of them, mother and daughter, apart from Mark Bretherick?' asked Gibbs. 'And he's in the clear.'

Kombothekra nodded. 'We know Geraldine and Lucy Bretherick died on either the first or second of August, probably the first, and we've got fifteen scientists at the Los Alamos National Laboratory in New Mexico who've told us Mark Bretherick was there from July the twenty-eighth until August the third. He's alibi-d up to the hilt, Simon, and there are no other suspects.' Kombothekra smiled, sorry to be the bearer of bad news.

'There's one,' said Simon. 'One we haven't managed to find yet. William Markes.'

'Not that again, Waterhouse.' Proust slapped the wall. 'And don't think you can sneak that "yet" past me. "Yet"—as if you might still find him. Every conceivable corner of Geraldine Bretherick's life has been turned inside out, and there's no William Markes.'

'I don't think we should give up looking for him.'

'It's not a question of giving up, Simon. We've run out of places to look. None of Geraldine's friends or family have heard of him. We've tried the Garcia Lorca Institute where she used to work . . .'

'Maybe there's a Williamo Marco on the books.' Gibbs chuckled.

'... and they couldn't help us either,' Kombothekra told Simon. 'We've eliminated every William Markes on the electoral register—'

'Maybe one of them was lying,' said Simon. 'It'd be easy, if no one knew he had any connection with Geraldine except the two of them.'

'Waterhouse, what are you suggesting we do?' Proust's voice was slow and clear.

'Go back over all the William Markeses. Investigate them as thoroughly as we've investigated Mark Bretherick. And I'd extend that to anyone called William Marx spelled M-a-r-x as well. And M-a-r-k-s, without the e.'

'Excellent idea,' said the Snowman, frost coating his every word. 'Let's not leave out Gibbs' Williamo Marco—though it would be Guillermo, surely. And what about men called William Markham or Markey, just to be on the safe side?'

'We can't do it, Simon,' Kombothekra blurted out; Proust's verbal torture methods made the sergeant jumpy, Simon noticed. 'We haven't got the time or resources.'

'Money has a way of turning up when the people who matter think something's important,' said Simon, trying to beat down the anger that was stewing inside him. 'Markham, Markey—yes. Mark-my-fucking-words, Marks & Spencer, whatever his fucking name is, the man who was probably going to ruin Geraldine Bretherick's life.' Simon took a deep breath through clenched teeth. 'We keep going until we find him.'

Proust's advance was a perfect straight line. He got as close as he could, then stared up at the underside of Simon's chin. Simon kept his eyes fixed on the board opposite him. The Snowman's bald head was a shiny pink blur on the edge of his vision. 'So you're allowing the possibility that Mrs Bretherick got the name wrong,' the inspector said in a voice that was almost a whisper.

'She described him as "a man called William Markes",' said Simon. 'As I've said repeatedly, I take that to mean she didn't know him very well, if at all. She might have got his name wrong.'

'I agree,' said Proust, swinging round to inspect Simon's stubble from the other side. 'So where shall we start? Shall we first eliminate the Peter Parkers, or should we start with all the Cyril Billingtons we can get our hands on?'

'Those names aren't even vaguely similar—' Simon began.

'So a woman can be wrong about a name, and it's up to Detective Constable Waterhouse—the all-seeing, all-knowing—to decide exactly how wrong she can be!' Proust bellowed. Gobbets of his saliva struck Simon's cheek. Kombothekra, Sellers and Gibbs froze in awkward postures. Sellers' hand, which had been on its way down now that he'd finished fiddling with his sideburn for the time being, stuck out in mid-air. The three detectives looked as if they needed to be sprayed with antifreeze. Once again, the Snowman had justified his nickname.

'Listen to me and listen carefully, Detective Constable.' Proust jabbed Simon's neck with his index finger. That was a first. Verbal abuse Simon was used to; the prodding was new. 'Peter Parker is my mechanic and Billington's my uncle. Decent law-abiding citizens both. I'm sure you don't need me to tell you why we're not going to start snouting around in their private affairs on the off-chance that Mrs Bretherick might have been mistaken when she typed the name William Markes. Do I make myself clear?'

'Sir.'

'Splendid.'

'What about the note from Spilling Post Office?' Simon challenged the inspector's retreating back. 'The note that *someone* passed on to you. Mark Bretherick might not be Mark Bretherick. Are we going to investigate that?'

'Gone are the days, Waterhouse, when the police were able to dismiss attention-starved cranks as the fruit-bats that they inevitably turn out to be. Your sergeant will be giving this *new information* his full attention, won't you, Sergeant?'

A few seconds before Kombothekra found his voice. 'I've already made a start. So far it looks as if Bretherick's who he says he is.'

'Waterhouse probably believes his real name is William Markes.' Proust snarled. 'Eh, Waterhouse?'

'No, sir.' Simon was thinking about the cards, the two ten-year-wedding-anniversary cards on the mantelpiece at Corn Mill House. He could picture them clearly. Both were large, A3 size. One had curved edges, swirly silver writing—'For my darling husband, on our anniversary'—above a picture of a yellow flower. The other was pink and padded, with the number 10 and a bouquet of roses on the front. The roses were tied with a pink bow. Simon had memorised what was written inside the cards. Why? So that he could discuss it with Sellers and Gibbs, see what they thought? Proust? They'd laugh him all the way out of the building, any of them would. Even well-meaning Sam Kombothekra.

No, he didn't think Mark Bretherick was William Markes, not necessarily. But those cards . . .

'If it were up to me, we'd have someone watching Spilling Post Office,' he said. 'Whoever wrote that note's got more to say. He or she might write another longer letter in the next few days. If we can get hold of that person, we'll have a lead and possibly a suspect.'

'I'd like to put *you* on a lead, Waterhouse,' was Proust's response.

'Simon, we've got a suicide note'—Kombothekra pointed to the whiteboard—'and a diary that makes it clear Geraldine Bretherick was depressed.'

'A diary that was found on a computer.' Simon sounded like a truculent child even to himself. 'No hard copy, no notebook version. Who types their diary straight on to a computer? And why are there only nine entries, all from last year? Not even nine recent, consecutive days—nine random days from April and May 2006. Why? Can anyone tell me?'

'Waterhouse, you're embarrassing yourself.' Proust belched, then looked at Sam Kombothekra as if he expected to be chastised for his lack of etiquette.

'I've got a copy of this article for each of you.' Kombothekra picked up the bundle of paper that had been on the table next to him since the beginning of the briefing. It was as if Simon wasn't there, had never spoken. Why had he bothered? 'It's Professor Harbard's latest publication,' said Kombothekra.

'We already know what that ego-maniac thinks,' Proust snapped. 'That Geraldine Bretherick was responsible for both deaths. I stand by what I said at the time: he knows no more than we do. He knows *less* than we do. He wants this death to be a family annihilation—a thoroughly repugnant phrase which *he* probably invented—because then he gets to air his nonsense predictions on national television: within five years every mother in the country will be driving herself and her offspring off the nearest cliff or some such guff!'

'He's studied many murder-suicide cases similar to this one, sir,' said Kombothekra, his tone as benign as if the Snowman had just offered him a toasted teacake. Kombothekra felt sorry for Professor Harbard; he'd as good as admitted it to Simon during one of their awkward, mainly silent drives to Corn Mill House. 'It can't be easy for the man, can it?' he'd said. 'He's called in by the super, as an expert, then finds himself in the middle of us lot, being treated like an intruder and a cretin.' Simon had wondered if Kombothekra was talking about himself, his own experience.

To Simon, Harbard had seemed as thick-skinned as a cactus. He was a bad listener. When other people spoke, he nodded impatiently, licking his lips every few seconds and murmuring, 'Yes, yes, okay, yes,' revving up for his next turn under the spotlight. The only time he'd listened attentively was when Superintendent Barrow had popped in to give the team a pep-talk, reminding them of Professor Harbard's eminence in his field, how lucky they were that he'd offered his services.

'I've underlined the paragraph that I think constitutes new information,' said Kombothekra, putting a copy of the stapled article into Simon's hands and taking the opportunity to bestow another smile upon him. 'At any rate, I can't remember Professor Harbard telling us this in person. In paragraph six he says that family annihilation is not a crime that can be attributed to social exclusion or poverty. Most commonly it occurs among the affluent upper-middle classes. Harbard argues that this is because of the need to keep up appearances, to present an image of perfect family life, happiness, success. In the higher socio-economic echelons, image matters more . . .'

'Please don't talk to me about echelons, Sergeant,' said Proust.

'. . . people want to be the envy of their friends, so they put on a front. And sometimes, when the more complicated and painful reality of life intrudes—'

'That's crap,' Simon interrupted him. 'So because the Brethericks were upper-middle class and had money, that means Geraldine's a murderer and a suicide?'

Proust glared at Kombothekra, rolled up his copy of Professor Harbard's article and launched it at the bin in the corner of the room. It missed.

'What about the GHB?' Simon wondered if he could make some headway as the lesser of two evils now that the Snowman was angry with Kombothekra. 'Why did Geraldine Bretherick take it herself? Where did she get it?'

'Internet,' Gibbs suggested. 'It's not hard to get hold of. As for why, GHB's fast replacing Rohypnol as the most popular date-rape drug in the country.'

'Would a woman like Geraldine Bretherick, given everything we know about her, buy illegal drugs on the Internet?' said Simon. 'This is a woman who runs the Parents and Friends Committee at her daughter's school, whose kitchen bookcase is full of books called *Fish Dishes to Make Your Child's Brain Grow* and shit like that.' Unwillingly, he looked at Kombothekra. 'Have we heard back from HTCU yet about the computer?' The high-tech crime unit was referred to as 'Hitcoo' by everyone in CID apart from Proust.

The sergeant shook his head. 'I've been chasing and chasing. No one can tell me why it's taking so long.'

'I bet they'll find no GHB was ordered from Geraldine Bretherick's laptop. And I didn't mean why GHB instead of Rohypnol, I meant why any drug? Okay, in Lucy's case I can understand it—she wanted Lucy to pass out so that all she'd have to do was push her under the water. So that Lucy wouldn't feel any pain. But why take it herself? Think of how much she had to do and do efficiently: kill her daughter, write a suicide note, turn on her computer and open that diary file, leave it on the screen so that we'd find it when we arrived, kill herself—wouldn't she want a clear head?'

'Slashing your wrists hurts,' said Sellers. 'Maybe she wanted to dull her own pain. There was more GHB in Lucy's urine than in her mother's, a lot more. It looks as if Geraldine only took a bit, to take the edge off her fear, probably—make everything a bit hazy around the edges. And that's exactly what happens, that's what a small dose of GHB does.'

'We know that but how did she?' Simon fired back at him. 'What, did she type "date-rape drugs" into Google and take it from there? I can't see it. How would she know how much to take?'

'There's no point speculating,' said Proust briskly. 'The computer chaps will tell us what Geraldine Bretherick did and didn't do with her laptop.'

'We also need them to tell us when that diary file was first opened,' said Simon. 'If it was created on the day she died, for example. In which case the dates at the top of the entries are fake.'

'All this we shall find out in due course.' Proust picked up his empty 'World's Greatest Grandad' mug, dropped his mobile phone into it and glanced towards his office. He'd had enough. 'What about Mr Bretherick's missing suit, Sergeant?'

' 'That's my action,' Sellers told him. 'Lucky me—all the dry-cleaners within a thirty-mile radius of Corn Mill House.'

'Charity shops as well,' Kombothekra reminded him. 'My wife sometimes takes my clothes and gives them to charity without telling me.'

'Mine used to, until I made my displeasure known,' said Proust. 'Perfectly good jumpers she used to give away.'

'And if we find out the suit wasn't given to any dry-cleaner or charity shop? What then?' asked Simon.

Proust sighed. 'Then we'll have an unsolved mystery of a missing suit. I hope you can hear how *Secret Seven* that sounds. The evidence will still point to Geraldine Bretherick being responsible for her own death and her daughter's. I don't like it any more than you do, but there's not a lot I can do. We're only following up the Oswald Mosley suit angle because it's important to Mr Bretherick. Sorry if that leaves you feeling let down, Waterhouse.' Proust took his empty mug and phone and headed for the small cubicle in the corner of the room, three sides of which were glass from waist height upwards. It looked like the lifts you sometimes saw on the outsides of buildings. The inspector went in, slamming the door behind him.

To avoid the sympathy in Kombothekra's eyes, Simon turned to the whiteboard. He knew the wording of the Brethericks' ten-year-anniversary cards by heart, but not Geraldine's suicide note. There was something insubstantial about it, too slippery for his mind to latch on to. He read it again:

I'm so sorry. The last thing I want to do is cause any hurt or upset to anyone. I think it's better if I don't go into a long, detailed explanation—I don't want to lie, and I don't want to make things any worse. Please forgive me. I know it must seem as if I'm being dreadfully selfish, but I have to think about what's best for Lucy. I'm really, truly sorry. Geraldine.

Superimposed over Geraldine's words in Simon's mind were the words of her friend, Cordy O'Hara: *Geraldine was always planning, arranging, whipping out her diary. I saw her less than a week before she died and she was trying to persuade me and Oonagh to go to EuroDisney with her and Lucy next half-term.*

Simon turned his back on Kombothekra, Sellers and Gibbs and headed for the Snowman's cubicle. He hadn't finished with him yet.

Proust looked up and smiled when Simon appeared in his office, as if he'd invited him. 'Tell me something, Waterhouse,' he said. 'What do you make of DS Kombothekra? How are you finding working with him?'

'He's a good colleague. Fine.'

'He's replaced Sergeant Zailer and you can hardly bring yourself to look at him.' Proust trumped Simon's lie with the truth. 'Kombothekra's a good skipper.'

'I know.'

'Things change. You have to adjust.'

'Yes, sir.'

'You have to adjust,' Proust repeated solemnly, examining his fingernails.

'Have you ever heard of anyone writing their diary straight on to a computer? The file wasn't even password-protected.'

'Have you ever heard of anyone putting Tabasco sauce on spaghetti bolognese?' Proust countered amicably.

'No.'

'My son-in-law does it.'

What could Simon say to that? 'Really?'

'I'm not trying to encourage you to take an interest in my son-in-law's eating habits, Waterhouse. I'm making the point that whether you've heard of something or not heard of it is irrelevant.'

'I know, sir, but—'

'We're living in the technological age. People do all sorts of things on their computers.'

Simon lowered himself into the only free chair. 'People who kill themselves leave suicide notes. Or sometimes they don't,' he said. 'They don't leave suicide notes *and* diary entries to ram the point home. It's overkill.'

'I think you've hit upon the perfect word there, Waterhouse, to describe Geraldine Bretherick's actions: overkill.'

'The note and the diary are . . . they're different voices,' said Simon, frustrated. 'The person who wrote the note doesn't want to hurt anyone, wants to be forgiven. The diary-writer doesn't care who gets hurt. We know the note's Geraldine's handwriting. I say that means she definitely didn't write the nine diary entries.'

'If you mention William Markes, Waterhouse . . .'

'The voice in the diary is analytical, trying to understand and describe the experience of day-to-day misery as accurately as possible. Whereas the note—it's just one platitude after another, the feeble voice of a feeble mind.'

Proust stroked his chin for a while. 'So why didn't that occur to your man William Markes?' he asked eventually. 'He's faking Geraldine Bretherick's diary—why didn't he take the trouble to get the tone right? Is he also feeble-minded?'

'Tone of voice is a subtle thing,' said Simon. 'Some people wouldn't notice.' *Like Kombothekra. And Sellers and Gibbs.* 'There's no mention of suicide in the suicide note, sir. Or of killing Lucy. And it's not addressed to anyone. Wouldn't she have written, "Dear Mark"?'

'Don't be dense, Waterhouse. How many times have you been called out to a body swinging from a beam? When I was a PC it used to happen every now and then. Some poor blighter who couldn't take it any more. I've read my fair share of suicide notes and I've yet to read one that says, "I'm sorry I'm about to slit my wrists, please forgive me for committing suicide." People tend to skirt round the gruesome details. They talk metaphorically about what they're doing. As for "Dear Mark"—come on!'

'What?'

'She wrote the note to the world she was leaving behind, not only her husband. Her mother, her friends ... Writing "Dear Mark" would have made it too hard, too specific—she'd have had to picture him alone, bereft ...' Proust frowned, waiting for Simon's response. 'Besides, there's something you haven't thought of: if William Markes was the killer, why would he allow us to find his name on the computer, plain as day? He wouldn't.'

He's trying to convince me.

'I don't understand you, Waterhouse. Why did you change your mind?'

'Sir, I've never believed that Geraldine Bretherick—'

'One minute Charlie Zailer's the last person you're interested in, the next you're staring after her with your tongue hanging out every time she passes you in the corridor. What changed?'

Simon stared at the grey ribbed carpet, resenting the ambush. 'Why did Geraldine Bretherick slit her wrists?' he said stubbornly. 'She had the GHB she'd bought. On the Internet. She'd given Lucy enough to make her pass out, so that she could drown her in a bath full of water without any fuss. Why not do the same when it came to killing herself?'

'What if she botched it?' said the Snowman. 'Miscalculated, and woke up a few hours later—wet, naked and groggy—to a distraught husband and a dead daughter? I think you'd agree that Geraldine Bretherick's wrists were slashed by someone whose intention was unambiguous. They cut downwards, not across. What do we say?'

'But—'

'No, Waterhouse. What do we *say*? Alliterate for me.'

'Across for attention, down for death,' Simon recited, feeling like the biggest idiot in the world. As he spoke, Proust pretended to be a conductor, waving an imaginary stick with one hand. *Twat.*

Simon was about to leave when he realised what the Snowman had said: 'they', not 'she'. 'You agree with me,' he said, feeling light-headed. 'You also don't think she did it, but you don't want to say so in case you turn out to be wrong. You don't want things to get sticky between you and your shiny new sergeant. And you don't need to take that risk'—he leaned on the desk—'because you've got me. I'm a convenient mouthpiece.'

'Convenient? You?' Proust laughed, flicking through the papers on his desk. 'I think you've got the wrong man, Waterhouse.'

Simon thought back over the previous hour: his own sullenness. His swearing, which had gone unremarked upon. He thought about the amount of time he'd been allowed in which to air his allegedly foolish theories, and about Colin Sellers traipsing round every dry-cleaner's within a thirty-mile radius of Corn Mill House . . .

'You agree with me,' he said again with more certainty. 'And you know me: the more you heap on the mockery, the more you let them all talk shit out there, the harder I'll try to prove you all wrong. Or rather, to prove *you* right. How've I been doing so far?'

'Waterhouse, you know I never swear, don't you?'

Simon nodded.

'Waterhouse, get the fuck out of my office.'

5

Tuesday, 7 August 2007

Corn Mill House has all the grandeur, character and atmosphere that my flat lacks. I can't decide if it's beautiful or forbidding. It looks a little like the home of a witch, made of pale grey gingerbread, the kind one might stumble across in a forest clearing in the early morning mist or evening twilight.

Some of the small panes of glass in the leaded windows have cracks in them. The building is large, arts and crafts style, and looks from the outside as if it hasn't been touched since the early 1900s. It makes me think of an old jewel that needs dusting. Whoever built it cared enough to position it perfectly, at the top of one steep side of Blantyre Moor. From where I'm standing I can see right across the Culver Valley. The house must once have been opulent. Now it looks as if it's hiding its face in the greenery that grows all around it and up its walls, remembering better days.

My mind fills with images of winding staircases, secret passages that lead to hidden rooms. What a perfect house for a child to grow up in . . . The thought twists to a halt in my head as I remember that Lucy Bretherick won't grow up. I can't think about Lucy being dead without shivering with dread at the thought of something terrible happening to Zoe or Jake, so I push my thoughts back to Geraldine. Did she love this house or hate it?

Just walk up the drive and ring the bell.

It sounds like a bad idea. I went over and over it in my mind as I drove here, and I couldn't think of one reason why it was the right thing to do, but that made no difference. I knew I had to do it. That's still the way I feel, standing here at the bottom of the uneven lane, staring at Corn Mill House. I have to speak to Mark Bretherick, or the man I saw on the news. I have to do it because it's the next thing; I don't care that it isn't sensible. Esther's always accusing me of being prim, but I think deep down I'm more of a risk-taker than she is. Sensible is just a costume I wear most of the time because it suits the life I've ended up with.

I walk towards the house, crunching pebbles beneath my feet. It rained last night, and there are snail-shells all over the pink and white stones. I keep telling myself that after I've done this, after I've followed my mad impulse and come out on the other side of whatever's about to happen to me, things will be clearer—I'll have less to fear.

I left my car on the top road, safely far away and out of sight. I can lie about my name, but not my number plate. As I press the doorbell, I try to think about what I'm going to say, but my mind keeps switching off. Part of me doesn't believe this is real. The grimy tiles of Corn Mill House's porch floor swim in front of my eyes like the bottom of a kaleidoscope, a shifting mosaic of blue, maroon, mustard, black and white.

He might not be in. He might be at work. No, not so soon afterwards.

But he isn't at home. I press the bell again, harder. If nobody opens the door, I have no idea what I'll do. Wait for him to come back? He's bound to be staying with relatives . . .

No. He will be in. He's there. He's coming to the door now. Maybe the man I met at Seddon Hall was right: maybe I am selfish, because at this moment I firmly believe Mark Bretherick is about to open the door purely because I want and need him to.

Nothing happens. I take a few steps back, away from the porch, and look around me at the garden that slopes down and out of sight on all three sides of the house apart from the one that has the road above it. The word 'garden' is inadequate as a description; these are grounds.

He's not here because he isn't Mark Bretherick, he's lying, and this is not his home.

Something touches my shoulder. I lose my footing as I turn, see a blurred face, hear a horrible crunch beneath my feet. It's him, the man I saw on television last night. And I've trodden on a snail, cracked its shell.

'Sorry, I've . . . I've crushed one of your snails,' I say. 'Well, not *yours*, but you know what I mean.' I assumed the right words would come to me when I needed them; more fool me.

I look up at him. He's wearing gardening gloves that are covered in mud and holding a red-handled trowel in one hand. It looks odd with his blue shirt, which is the stiff-collared sort most men would save for work. There are sweat stains under the arms, and his jeans are brown at the knees, probably from kneeling in earth. He is standing close to me and it's an effort not to wrinkle my nose; he smells stale, as if he hasn't washed for days. His hair looks almost wet with grease.

I am about to start to explain why I'm here when I notice the way he's staring at me. As if there's no way he's going to take his eyes off me in case I disappear. He can't believe I'm standing in front of him . . . A dizzy, nauseous feeling spreads through me as I realise the harm I might be doing to this man. How could I not have anticipated his reaction? I didn't even think about it. What's wrong with my brain?

'I'm sorry,' I say. 'This must be a shock for you. I know I look a lot like your wife. I was shocked too, when I saw on the news . . . when I heard what had happened. That's why I'm here, kind of. I hope . . . oh, God, I feel awful now.'

'Did you know Geraldine?' His voice shakes. He moves closer, his eyes taking me apart. I know one thing straight away: I am not at all afraid of him. If anyone's frightened, it's him. 'Why . . . why do you look so much like her? Are you . . . ?'

'I'm nothing to do with her. I didn't know her at all. I happen to look like her, that's all. And actually, that's *not* why I'm here. I don't know why I said that.'

'You look so like her. So like her.'

I am certain that this man is looking at my face for the first time. He hasn't a clue who I am. Which means he hasn't been following me in a red Alfa Romeo; he didn't push me in front of a bus yesterday.

'Are you okay?' he asks eventually. He has dropped the trowel on the drive and taken off his gloves. I didn't even notice.

I realise I've been standing like a statue, saying nothing. 'What's your name?' I ask him. 'It said on the news your name was Mark Bretherick.'

'What do you mean, "it said on the news"?'

'So you are Mark Bretherick?'

'Yes.' His eyes are glued to me. This is what a person in a trance would look like.

What am I supposed to say next? That I don't believe him? I want him to prove it? 'Can I come in? I need to talk to you about something and it's complicated.'

'You look so like Geraldine,' he says again. 'It's unbelievable.' He makes no move towards the house.

Five seconds pass. Six, seven, eight. If I don't take the initiative, he might stand here studying my face until day turns to night.

'What happened to you?' He points at the cuts on my cheek.

'We need to go inside,' I say. 'Come on. Give me your key.' It's odd, but I don't feel presumptuous, or even awkward any more. For now, he is aware of nothing but my face.

He searches his pockets, still staring at me. It's a relief when finally he hands me the key and I can turn away from him.

I unlock the front door and walk into a large, dark room, nearly as tall as it is wide, with polished wooden floorboards and wood-panelled walls. An elaborate design of blue stucco covers the ceiling, makes me think of a stately home. There are two big windows, both largely uncovered by whatever plant is growing up the walls outside, and the front door is wide open, yet the room seems as dark as if it were underground. The low-hanging chandelier light is on but seems to make no difference. It's as if the dark walls and floor are sucking up the light.

In front of me is a log-burning stove that's been lit and is blazing, even though it's August. Still, the hall is cool. Side by side in the middle of the room, directly in front of the stove, are two matching chairs that look like antiques: slim, armless, S-shaped to follow the curve of a person's back, upholstered in a cream, silky fabric. To my right, a staircase protrudes into the hall, with solid wooden banisters on both sides. Eight steep steps lead to a small square landing, after which further steps lead off to the left and to the right. One of the windows is a bay with a window-seat, a half-hexagon that has a faded burgundy velvet cushion going all the way round it. Against the wall behind me there is a large fish-tank and a chaise-longue.

Mark Bretherick—how else can I think of him?—walks past me and sits in one of the two chairs in front of the fire. 'The lounge is full of bin-bags,' he says.

I lower myself into the chair next to his. He's not looking at me any more. He's staring at the glowing coals and logs through the stove door. I'm still chilly, even now that I can feel the warmth on my face. I look at the window nearest to me and see a drop of water on the stone beneath the glass, like a single tear trickling into the room.

'Cold,' he says. 'The old ruin. This room's always freezing.'

'It's cooler today than it was yesterday,' I say. 'Yesterday it was sweltering.' I fill the air between us with pointless words to make the occasion of our meeting appear less bizarre.

'That was Geraldine's nickname for it—the old ruin. We did our bedroom and the bathrooms when we first bought it, but nothing else. Everything else could wait, Geraldine said.'

'It's a beautiful house.'

'Plenty of time, she said. Thirty thousand pounds each bath-room cost me. Geraldine thought they were the most important rooms in the house. I had to take her word for it. I was never in the house.'

'What do you mean?'

He turns to face me. 'I almost can't stand the sight of you,' he says.

'I'm sorry.'

He shakes his head. Every time he moves, the hard, sharp smell of dirt wafts towards me. 'That's where I found their bod-ies. Did you know that?'

'Where?'

'In the baths upstairs. Geraldine was in one and Lucy was in the other. You didn't know that?'

'No. All I know is what I saw on the news last night.'

'Do you know what GHB is?'

'You mean GBH? Grievous bodily harm?'

His mouth laughs, though his eyes are remote, empty. 'You hear about things like this, things that are so far . . . beyond . . . and you wonder how people can carry on living after they hap-pen. How can they be hungry or thirsty? How can they tie their shoe-laces or comb their hair?'

'I know. I've thought that.'

'When you rang the bell I was sorting out the flowerbeds.'

I am sitting beside him, but I am light years away from his grief. I can feel it like an iron barrier between us.

He looks at me again. 'Wait here. I want to show you some-thing.' He springs out of his chair. It's enough to make me leap up too. Unpredictable; I don't like unpredictable. I know I wouldn't be able to stand it if he showed me anything to do with Geraldine or Lucy's deaths. What if he's gone up to one of the bathrooms? What's he going to have in his hands when he returns? I picture a knife, a gun, an empty pill bottle.

I don't know how Geraldine killed her daughter or herself. It's a question I don't think I can bring myself to ask.

I run my hands through my hair. What the hell am I doing here? What am I hoping to achieve? It can't be helping him to have me here. I should open the door and run.

My phone rings and I jump. I answer it quickly, to stop its mundane trill from polluting the mournful silence. Too late, I realise I could have switched it off; that would have had the same effect. It's Owen Mellish from work. 'Naughty girl,' he says. 'Where've you disappeared to?'

'I can't talk now,' I tell him. 'Is there a problem?'

'Not for me. But I thought I should let you know that Madam Snoot's phoned twice since you left the office. She wasn't pleased to hear you'd decided to take the day off. I told her you'd probably gone shopping.'

'I'll ring her. Thanks for letting me know.' I cut him off before he has a chance to enrage me further. I can hear ominous creaks above my head. I don't know if I've got time to phone Natasha Prentice-Nash before Mark Bretherick reappears, or whether I can do it without him hearing me, but I'm not sure I can stay here unless I do something ordinary. I need to take my mind off the man upstairs and his dead family, the souvenirs he might be about to show me.

I stand as far away from the stairs as I can, highlight Natasha's name on my phone's screen and press the call button. She answers after two rings and says her name, putting her heart and soul into the vowel sounds as she always does. 'It's Sally,' I whisper.

'Sally! At last. We've got a bit of a problem, I'm afraid. The Consorzio gang have arrived.'

'Oh. Okay.'

'Well, it isn't okay, really. There's been some kind of misunderstanding at their end about the documentary.'

'Don't tell me it's off.' I close my eyes, wishing I could say, 'Actually, I'm not Sally Thorning. I'm someone who's standing in for her, but I've only taken over the easy parts of her life.'

'I spoke to the producer today,' says Natasha. 'She's still keen.'

'Great. So . . .' I feel painfully self-conscious. There's a door to my left. As quietly as possible I open it and slip through to an even larger room. It's a lounge, though nothing like the one in my flat. 'Lounge' is too casual a word to describe it—drawing room would suit it better. Like the hall, it's dark and wood-panelled and could almost be an elegantly proportioned cave that has been refurbished for the gentry, the temporary bolt-hole of a king in hiding. I don't have time to notice much else about the room before my eyes are drawn to the black bin-bags. There must be at least a dozen, in a heap on the Persian carpet in front of the fireplace.

'Vittorio seems to think he and Salvo are both being inter-viewed, but Salvo says you and he agreed he'd be interviewed alone,' Natasha is saying. 'He's accusing us of messing him around.'

I sigh. 'Him and Vittorio together—that's always been the plan. Salvo doesn't like it, but he's known about it for ages.'

'Could you ring and butter him up, then? Tell him how im-portant he is? You know the sort of thing he wants to hear.'

I'd rather tell him how intensely irritating he is. I tell Natasha I'll do my best to pacify him and she dismisses me with a curt 'Ciao.' I switch off my phone and put it in my bag, then open the door and lean out into the hall. There is no sign of Mark, no sound coming from upstairs. What will I do if he doesn't come back soon? How long will I wait before going to check that he's all right? Or leaving? It seems unlikely that I will do either.

I walk towards the pile of bin-bags that look so out of place on the elaborately patterned rug. I pull open the one nearest to me, taking care not to rustle the plastic any more than I have to. Apart from a pair of small pink Wellington boots on top, it's full of women's clothes. Geraldine's: lots of black trousers—velvet, suede, corduroy, no jeans—and cashmere jumpers in all colours. Did she collect cashmere? I look in another bag and find dozens of bottles, tubes and sprays, and about twenty paperback books, mostly with pastel-coloured covers—peach, lemon yellow, mint green. Beneath these there is something with a hard edge, something that swings into my ankle as I move the plastic sack, making me grunt through clenched teeth.

I look over my shoulder to check I'm safe, then reach to the bottom of the bag and pull out two chunky wooden frames. Photographs of Geraldine and Lucy. Quickly, I hold them at a distance, not ready for the shock of seeing them so close to me. Geraldine is smiling, standing with her head tilted to one side. She's wearing a white scoop-neck T-shirt, a black gypsy skirt, silver sandals with straps round the ankles and black sunglasses on her head like a head-band. She's got the arms of a silver-grey sweater tied round her waist. There's a cherry blossom tree behind her and a squat, flat-topped building, painted blue, with white blinds at the windows. She's leaning against a red brick wall.

I bring the picture closer, staring, feeling my heartbeat in my ears. My arms are shaking. I know that place, that stubby blue building. I've seen it. I'm pretty sure I've stood where Geraldine is standing in this photograph, but I can't remember when. The last thing I wanted to discover was another connection between Geraldine and me. But what is it? Where is it? My mind races round in circles, but gets nowhere.

The picture of Lucy, which I can look at only briefly, has the same background. Lucy is sitting on the brick wall, wearing a dark green pinafore dress and a green and white striped shirt, white ankle socks and black shoes, her two thick plaits sticking out on either side of her head. She's waving at the camera. At whoever was holding the camera . . .

Her father. The words pierce me like a cold needle. The man upstairs, whoever he is, is throwing away photographs of his wife and daughter. Of Mark Bretherick's wife and daughter. Jesus Christ. And I allowed myself to feel safe around him, in his house.

I don't stop to think. I yank the bag's yellow drawstring and close it, without replacing the photographs. I'm taking them with me. I run to the door, out into the hall, and freeze, nearly dropping the pictures. He's there, back in his chair in front of the stove. His head bent, gazing down at his lap. Has he forgotten I'm here? I stare in horror at the photographs in my hand, hanging in the air between us. If he turned now, he'd see them. *Please don't turn.*

I unzip my handbag and stuff them in, pulling out my phone. 'Sorry,' I say, waving it in the air, a cartoon gesture. 'My mobile rang and . . . I thought I'd take it in there. I didn't want to . . . you know.' *I can't do this. I can't stand here with photographs of Geraldine and Lucy in my handbag and talk to him as if nothing's changed.*

My fingers tug at the zip but my bag won't close. I hold it so that it hangs behind my body. If he looked closely he would see the edges of the frames poking out, but he hasn't even glanced in my direction. There's a pile of A4 paper on his lap. White, with print on it. That's what he's looking at. 'I want you to read something,' he says.

'I have to go.'

'Geraldine kept a diary. I knew nothing about it until after she was dead. I need you to read it.'

I baulk at the word 'need'. In his chair, with his long legs crossed at the ankles and those pages on his knee, he looks harmless once again. Frail. Like a daddy-long-legs that you could brush with your hand and it would fall to the ground.

'You haven't asked me what I want.' I inject what I hope is a reasonable amount of suspicion into my voice. 'Why I'm here.'

His eyes slide to the floor. 'Sorry,' he says. 'Bad manners. Bad host.'

'Last year, I met a man who told me his name was Mark Bretherick. He claimed to live here, in Corn Mill House, and to have a wife called Geraldine and a daughter called Lucy. He told me he had his own company, Spilling Magnetic Refrigeration . . .'

'That's my company.' A whisper. His eyes are sharper and brighter suddenly as he turns to face me. 'Who . . . who was he?

What do you mean, he told you? He pretended to be me? Where did you meet him? When?'

I take a deep breath and tell him an edited version of the story, describing the man I met at Seddon Hall in as much detail as I can. I leave out the sex because it's not relevant. *Just something bad and wrong I needed to do so that I could come home and be good again.*

Mark Bretherick listens carefully as I speak, shaking his head every so often. Not in mystification; almost as though I'm confirming something, something he's suspected for a while. *He has someone in mind. A name.* Hope mixed with fear starts to stir inside me. There's no getting away from it now; he's going to tell me something I'll wish I didn't know. Something that led to a woman and a little girl being killed.

I finish my story. He turns quickly away from me, rubbing his chin with his thumb. Nothing. Silence. I can't stand this. 'You know who he is, don't you? You know him.'

He shakes his head.

'But you've thought of something. What is it?'

'Do the police know?'

'No. Who is he? I know you know.'

'I don't.'

He's lying. He looks like Nick does when he's bought a new bike that costs a thousand pounds and he's pretending it only cost five hundred. I want to scream at him to tell me the truth but I know that would only make him even more unwilling to talk. 'Is there anyone you can think of who envies you, who might have had a thing about Geraldine? Someone who might have wanted to pretend to be you?'

He passes the bundle of paper across to me. 'Read this,' he says. 'Then you'll know as much as I do.'

When I look up eventually, once I've read each of the nine diary entries twice and taken in as much as I can, there is a mug of black tea on a slatted wooden table by the side of my chair. I didn't notice him bringing either. He paces in front of me, up and down, up and down. I struggle not to let my revulsion show; this woman was his wife.

'What do you think?' he says. 'Is that the diary of someone who would kill her daughter and herself?'

I reach for my drink, nearly ask for milk but decide not to. I take a gulp that scalds my mouth and throat. The mug is covered in writing: 'SCES '04, The International Conference on Strongly Correlated Electron Systems, July 26–30 2004, Universität Karlsruhe (TH) Germany'.

'It's not the Geraldine I knew, the person who wrote all that. But then she says, doesn't she? She's got that part covered. "Whatever I feel inside, I do the opposite." '

'She didn't write it every day,' I say. 'From the dates, I mean. It's only nine days in total. Maybe she only wrote it when she felt really down, and on other days she didn't feel like that at all. She might have been happy most of the time.'

His anger surprises me. He knocks the drink from my hand, sending it flying across the hall, spraying tea everywhere. I watch the mug's arc through the air, watch it fall on to the window seat as he yells, 'Stop treating me like I'm mentally impaired!' I duck, making a hard shell of my body to fend off an attack, but he is already kneeling beside me, apologising. 'Oh, my God, I'm sorry, I'm so sorry, are you okay? Christ, you could have got third-degree burns!'

'I'm all right. Honestly. Fine.' I hear the tremor in my voice and wonder why I'm rushing to reassure him. 'It went on the floor, not on me.'

'I'm so sorry. I don't know what to say. God knows what you must think of me now.'

I feel dizzy, trapped. 'I didn't mean to make you angry,' I tell him. 'I was trying to find something positive to say. The diary's horrible. You obviously know it is, and I didn't want to make you feel worse.'

'You couldn't.' His eyes seem to issue a challenge.

'Okay, then.' I hope I'm not about to break my own personal stupidity record. 'Yes, I think this is the diary of someone who might kill her daughter. No, I don't think it's the diary of someone who would kill herself.'

He watches me closely. 'Go on.'

'The writer . . . the voice throughout seems to be screaming self-preservation at all costs. If I had to guess what sort of woman wrote it, I'd say—look, this is going to sound awful.'

'Say it.'

'Narcissistic, spoilt, superior—her way of doing things is better than everyone else's . . .' I bite my lip. 'Sorry. I'm not very tactful.' A ruthless ego, I add silently. Someone who starts to see other people as worthless and expendable as soon as they become obstacles to her getting her way.

'It's all right,' says Mark Bretherick. 'You're telling me the truth. As you see it.' For the first time, I hear a trace of anger in his voice.

'Some of what she's written is exactly what I'd expect,' I say. 'Being a parent can be massively frustrating.'

'Geraldine never had a break from it. She was a full-time mum. She never said she wanted a break.'

'Everybody wants a break. Look, if I had to look after my kids full-time, I'd need strong tranquillisers to get me through every day. I can understand her exhaustion and her need to have some time and space for herself, but . . . locking a child in a dark room and letting her scream for hours, pulling the door shut so she can't get out, and that stuff about having to make her suffer in order to feel protective and loving towards her; it's sick.'

'Why didn't she ask me to hire help? We could have afforded a nanny—we could have afforded two nannies! Geraldine didn't have to do any of it if she didn't want to. She told me she wanted to. I thought she was enjoying it.'

I look away from the anger and pain in his eyes. I can't give him an answer. If I'd been Geraldine, married to a rich company director and living in a mansion, I'd have ordered my husband to stock up on a full team of servants the instant I emerged from the maternity ward. 'Some people are better than others at asking for what they need,' I tell him. 'Women are often very bad at it.'

He turns away from me as if he's lost interest. 'If he can pretend to be me, he can pretend to be her,' he says, blowing on his cupped hands. 'Geraldine wasn't narcissistic—the very opposite.'

'You think someone else wrote the diary? But . . . you'd have known if it wasn't Geraldine's handwriting, wouldn't you?'

'Does that black print look like handwriting to you?' he snaps.

'No. But I assumed—'

'Sorry.' He looks disgusted, mortified to find himself having to apologise again so soon after the last time. 'The diary was found on Geraldine's computer. No handwritten version.'

There's a sour taste in my mouth. 'Who is William Markes?' I ask. 'The man she said might ruin her life?'

'Good question.'

'What? You don't know?'

He barks out a laugh without smiling. 'As things stand, you know more about him than I do.'

My breath catches in my throat. 'You mean . . . ?'

'Ever since I first read that diary, I've had a name in my head with no one to attach it to: William Markes. Then out of the blue you turn up. You're Geraldine's double, physically, and you tell me you met a man who pretended to be me. But we know he wasn't. So at the moment we've got no name to attach to the man you met in the hotel.' He shrugs. 'I'm a scientist. If I put those two facts together . . .'

'You come to the conclusion that the man I met last year was William Markes.'

Sometimes, convenience has the appearance of logic: you link two things because you can, not because you must. *I'm also a scientist.* What if the two unknowns are unrelated? What if the man at Seddon Hall lied because he was breaking the rules for a week and wanted to cover himself, not because he's a psychopath capable of murder?

If William Markes, whoever he is, faked Geraldine's diary after killing her, why did he include his own name? Some kind of complicated urge to confess? Being a scientist and not a psychologist, I have no idea if that's plausible.

'You need to tell the police. They've given up looking for William Markes. If they hear what you've just told me . . .'

I am on my feet. 'I've got to go,' I say, pulling my bag out from where I left it behind the chair. I wrap my arms around it so that he doesn't see the frame edges. 'Sorry, I . . . I've got to pick up my kids from nursery at lunchtime today, and I've got some shopping to do first.' A lie. Tuesday and Thursday are Nick's days, the days when bags go astray and bills and party invitations vanish into thin air.

I have never, not once, collected Zoe and Jake at lunchtime. Their gruelling nursery regime is one of the many things I feel guilty about.

'Wait.' Mark follows me across the hall. 'What hotel was it? Where?'

I pull open the front door, feel more real as the fresh air hits my face. It's sunny outside, only a few feet from where I am now, but still the light looks far away. 'I don't remember the name of the hotel.'

'Yes, you do.' He looks sad. 'You will tell the police, won't you?'

'Yes.'

'Everything? The name of the hotel?'

I nod, my heart tightening with the deception. *I can't.*

'Will you come back?' he asks. 'Please?'

'Why?'

'I want to talk to you again. You're the only person who's read the diary apart from me and the police.'

'All right.' At this point I will say anything I have to if it means I can leave. He smiles. There is a hardness in his eyes: not pleasure but determination.

I have no intention of ever returning to Corn Mill House.

*

I drive to Rawndesley, feeling shell-shocked from my encounter with Mark, needing to forget everything to do with him, with what's happened. In the Save Venice Foundation's office, I spend several hours trying and failing to sort out the mess that Salvo, Vittorio and the TV producer have, between them, created. Natasha Prentice-Nash doesn't comment on my bruised face, nor does she thank me for coming in on a Tuesday or apologise for landing something on me that shouldn't be part of my job purely because I'm the only person in the office with basic social skills. By five o'clock I can't stand it any more, so I head for home.

There's no one there when I get back. Looking up through the car window, I see that our lounge curtains are open. Normally at this time they're closed, with the warm glow of the lamp behind them so that Zoe and Jake can watch whatever CBeebies has to offer without sunlight interfering with the picture.

I climb out of the car, dragging my handbag after me, and look up and down the street for Nick's car. It's not there. Even so, I shout out my family's names as I let myself into the flat. I look at my watch: quarter to six. Maybe the children are still at nursery. Nick might have left work late. Not that he's ever done that in all the years I've known him. It must be nice, I've often thought, to have a job like that.

A horrible possibility occurs to me. What if Nick's forgotten he's supposed to be picking up Zoe and Jake? No, he'd still be back by now. He's never later than five thirty. All I want is to come home to my normal messy, noisy house, two boisterous children and a husband holding out a glass of wine. So where are they?

I run upstairs to the kitchen. My stomach twists with worry when I see there's no note on the table. Nick always leaves a note; I've finally managed to drum it into him that I worry if I don't know where he is. At first he said things like, 'What's there to worry about? I mean, I'm obviously somewhere, aren't I?' Zoe and Jake are obviously somewhere too; the problem is that it's not at all obvious to me where that somewhere is, and that's not good enough.

Where could they be?

As I turn to leave the room, to search all our other rooms and each of our many carpeted steps for the note Nick had bloody well better have left, I see a flash of colour at the edge of my vision. The work-surface on both sides of the sink is covered in pools of bright red, some small, some bigger. There are red smears all over the kitchen wall. Blood. *Oh, no. No, please . . .*

On the floor, light reflects off small pieces of something on the lino. Broken glass.

I leap up the stairs three at a time to get to the lounge. I grab the phone and am about to ring the police when I notice a scrap of paper on top of the television: 'Gone to Mum and Dad's for tea,' Nick has written on it. 'Back eight-ish. Was going to make spag puttanesca for kids' tea, but smashed passata jar—will clear up later!' I've pressed the nine button twice before the significance of Nick's words reaches my brain. I throw the phone on to the sofa and run back to the kitchen, where I start to laugh like a maniac. Passata. Of course. All over the room. The police had a lucky escape; I would have been their most hysterical caller of the day.

I sit down at the table and cry for what seems like a long time, but I don't care. I'll cry for as long as I damn well want. In between sobs, I shout at myself for being a self-indulgent fool.

After a while I calm down and pour myself a glass of wine. I haven't got the energy to clear up the mess. The soul-shaking terror has gone, but I can still feel the hole it blasted through me. Mark Bretherick must have felt the same, except for him the nightmare didn't end. Instead, it became his life. Panic can't last indefinitely. It must eventually have stopped, leaving only the horror—cold, without the distraction of frenzy, stretching on and on.

I shudder. The idea is unbearable. *Thank God I don't know what it feels like. Thank God nothing worse has happened to Zoe and Jake than Nick's mum's atrocious cooking.*

I retrieve my handbag from the hall, pull out the two framed photographs and take them up to the lounge, stopping off at the kitchen to collect my wine on the way. Now that I know Nick and the children are safe, I'm relieved to be alone. I sit on the sofa and lay the photos out beside me. That low red brick wall, the cherry blossom tree, the stunted blue building with the white blinds . . . I know I've seen these things before, but where? A spark flares in my memory: I hear myself saying, 'It's a bit odd that they've painted the outside blue, isn't it? It's not exactly in keeping with the surroundings.' Who was I speaking to? My mind cranks slowly into action, blunt and fuzzy after two days with no respite and almost no food, two days of fielding one shock after another.

'*It's owned by BT. I think it's a telephone exchange. I don't mind the blue. At least it's not grey.*' Nick. Nick said that. Suddenly, full knowledge floods in: it's the owl sanctuary at Silsford Castle. The blue BT building is behind it, across a small field. We've been to the sanctuary twice with the children, once when Jake was a tiny baby and then again about three months ago. Our second visit was more controversial. Zoe wanted to adopt an owl and so did Jake, and they both cried for ten minutes when I said they would have to share. They demanded one each. Eventually Nick had a brainwave and explained solemnly that owls, like children, were better off with two parents. Zoe and Jake saw the logic of this: they had a mum and a dad, so it was only proper that Oscar the Tawny should too.

I pick up the photograph of Lucy Bretherick. The wall she's sitting on is about twenty metres from Oscar's cage. If that. I wrap my arms tightly round my body, trying to squeeze out the fear that's starting to gnaw at me. I don't know what any of this means. All I know is that the Brethericks seem to be coming closer all the time.

I run down the six steps to Nick's and my bedroom, throw open the doors of my wardrobe and pull things off the top shelf until I see the black, unironed lump I'm looking for—a T-shirt with a doodle of an owl printed on it, in white. And underneath, in white cursive-style letters, 'The Owl Sanctuary at Silsford Castle'. Nothing ambiguous about that. Anyone who saw me wearing this T-shirt would know I'd been there.

This is what I was wearing when I caught the train to York on my way to Seddon Hall. It's what I always wear if it's summer and I'm travelling; it's the only T-shirt I've got that's not too smart to waste on a journey or too scruffy to leave the house.

I need to find out if the photographs of Geraldine and Lucy were taken before I went to Seddon Hall or after.

Brilliant, Sally. How are you going to do that, exactly? Ring Mark Bretherick and ask for more details about the pictures you stole from his house?

I run back to the lounge, pick up one of the wooden frames and start to dismantle it. Some people write dates on the back of their photos—that's my only hope. Even as I'm prising open the little metal clasps, injuring my fingertips, I'm wondering why it matters. So what if these pictures were taken before the second of June last year? My brain is jammed; I can't explain to myself why it's important.

Finally, the back of the frame comes loose. I throw it on the floor, and find myself looking at a blank white rectangle. There's no date on the back of the picture. Of course there isn't. Geraldine Bretherick was a mother. I don't have time to put my photographs in frames or albums any more, let alone label them with dates for posterity—they live in a box in my wardrobe. Sorting out that box has been one of my New Year's resolutions two years running. Maybe it'll be a case of third time lucky.

I'm about to reassemble the frame when I notice something at the bottom of the picture's white flip-side: a very faint line going all the way across. I work the long nail of my middle finger—the only nail I haven't yet lost on the household-chore battlefield—into the corner of the frame to dislodge the photograph.

Two pictures fall out on to the carpet. My muscles tense when I see the second one. It was tucked behind the photograph of Geraldine and is almost an exact replica. A woman is standing by the red brick wall, in front of the cherry tree and the telephone exchange. She's dressed in faded blue jeans and a cream shirt. Unlike Geraldine, she isn't smiling. There's a lot that's different. This woman has a square face with small, blunt features that make me think of twists in flesh-coloured Plasticine. She's less attractive than Geraldine. Her hair is dark but short, unevenly cut in a deliberate way, longer on one side than the other—a fashion statement. She's wearing high-heeled leather boots, a brown leather jacket and deep red lipstick. Her arms hang at her sides; she looks as if she's been posed.

I stare and stare. Then I pick up the framed picture of Lucy and very slowly start to undo the clasps on the back. *Crazy. Of course there won't be.*

There is.

Another replica: a young girl, about Lucy's age, also sitting on the wall. Like Lucy, she's waving. A girl with thin, mousy brown hair, the sort of brown that is indistinguishable from a dull grey. She's so skinny that her knee joints look like painful swellings in her stick-like legs. And her clothes . . . no, they can't be . . .

I gasp when I hear someone in the flat, feet running up stairs, a stampede. More than one person, definitely. I'm panicking, wondering where I'm going to hide the pictures, the open frames, and how I'm going to explain myself, when I realise it can't be Nick and the children; I didn't hear the front door and there are no eager voices. I rub the back of my neck, trying to smooth out the knots of tense muscle that feel like ganglia at the top of my spine. *Get a grip, Sally.* This happens at least twice a day, and I should know better than to let it freak me out. The sound is coming from our unique feature, our blockage. It must be somebody who lives above us going up the main stairs, the ones that both are and aren't in the middle of our flat.

The skinny girl in the photograph is wearing Lucy Bretherick's clothes. Same shirt, same dress. Even the same socks and shoes. Identical, right down to the lacy frill at the top of each sock.

My head throbs. This is too much. I sweep the pictures off the sofa on to the carpet and press my hand over my mouth. I have to eat something or I'll be sick.

The phone rings. I pick it up, manage no more than a grunt.

'Did you switch your mobile off?' a furious voice demands.

'Esther. Sorry,' I say limply. I must have forgotten to switch my phone back on when I left Corn Mill House.

'It's lucky I never listen to you, isn't it? If I'd followed your instructions, I'd have phoned the police and made a complete tit of myself. What happened to calling me back within two hours?'

'I'll ring you back,' I tell her, and slam down the phone.

'So, you want to know what I think about everything apart from the infidelity bit. Right?'

I shovel more sauceless spaghetti into my mouth and make a sound that I hope answers Esther's question. It took me fifteen minutes to tell her everything, then another ten to get her to swear on her life that she wouldn't tell anyone, no matter what.

'Funny, the infidelity is what I want to talk about most.'

'Esther—'

'What the hell were you playing at? That could have been it, Sal—your marriage over, your happy home wrecked, and for what? A few fucks with a man you hardly know? Your children's lives ruined—'

'I'm going,' I warn her.

'Okay, okay. We'll discuss it another time, but we *will* discuss it.'

'If you say so.' I know Esther's point of view is the correct one. It's also easy, conventional, and it bores me rigid. 'Didn't I always say you're more sensible than me?' I try to make light of my newly confessed sin. 'Proof if proof be needed.'

'It's not a joke, Sal. I'm actually shocked.'

Good. 'Do you have anything to say about the rest of what I've told you? Or should I leave you in peace to consolidate your moral outrage?'

There's a pause. Then she says, 'Could the woman and girl in the photos be William Markes' wife and daughter?'

Her words make me feel numb and wobbly, as if I've stepped off a roller-coaster in the dark. 'Why?'

'I don't know.' I listen as Esther chews her fingernails. 'I just wondered if . . . I'm thinking of one family—the Markeses— trying to pass themselves off as another. I don't *know*. I need two weeks on a desert island to think about it.'

'Mark Bretherick doesn't think his wife wrote the diary.'

'Yeah. You said.' She sighs. 'Sal, isn't it obvious? You and I can't work it out in a phone call. You need to go to the police.'

'The photos weren't necessarily hidden,' I say, stalling. 'Haven't you ever put a new picture in a frame and been too lazy to take out the old one? So you put the new one next to the glass and leave the old one behind it?'

'No,' Esther says flatly. 'And especially not if one of the photos is of another girl wearing my child's clothes. You're sure they're the same? Not just similar?'

'All I know is they're both wearing a dark green dress, a green and white striped blouse with a round-edged collar—'

'Hang on. The dress is short-sleeved? If there's a blouse underneath?'

'Yeah, it's like a sort of tunic.'

'It sounds like a school uniform,' says Esther. 'What colour shoes and socks? Black? Navy?'

'Black shoes, white socks,' I say breathlessly.

'Hardly a casual Saturday-at-the-owl-sanctuary sort of outfit. Not that I'm an expert,' Esther adds with distaste.

I put down my bowl of pasta, retrieve the pictures from the floor and look at them again. She's right. What's wrong with me? Of course it's a uniform; it's the green dress that put me off—it's nowhere near as shapeless and institutional as most school tunics. Its short sleeves are fluted, the neck is shaped, and it's got a belt with a pretty silver buckle. *A uniform*. It makes perfect sense. Every school in the county, like every parent in the county, takes its children on trips to Silsford Castle's owl sanctuary.

'Sally? Hello?'

'I'm here. You're right. I don't know how I missed it.'

'You should still phone the police.'

'I can't. Nick'd find out about last year. He'd leave me. I'm not risking it.' *Please don't say it. Please.*

Esther says it. 'You should have thought about that before you shagged another man. For a week.' As if only a day's worth of infidelity would have been less reprehensible. 'This isn't just about you, Sally.'

'Do you think I don't fucking know that?'

'Then call the police! Today you were followed, yesterday someone pushed you under a bus. Do you still think it was Pam Senior?'

'I don't know. I keep changing my mind. One minute it seems so crazy and the next . . . She was so keen to help after it happened. It made me suspicious. Ten minutes earlier she'd made it pretty clear she hated me.'

'Oh, come on,' Esther says scornfully. 'There's no mystery there. She's dim, isn't she? She sounds it, from everything you've told me about her. A dim person would always instantly forgive an enemy who'd nearly died.'

'Would they?'

'Yes. Sentiment would triumph over reason. "She nearly died, so I have to like her now"—that's what Pam will have thought. Bright people continue to hate those who deserve to be hated, irrespective of contingencies.' Esther's voice is full of pride, and I know she's thinking about her boss, the Imbecile. I listen to her loud exhalations as she tries to calm down. She hates not being in charge. 'Look, Nick wouldn't necessarily find out,' she says. 'It's well known that the police protect adulterous witnesses.' She talks over my snorts of derision. 'It's true! Most of them are at it themselves. Cops are real shaggers—everyone knows that. They won't even disapprove. All they're interested in is getting the facts so they can do their job. If you tell them everything you know, they'll do their best not to involve Nick.'

'You have no way of knowing that,' I say, and put the phone down before she can argue with me. I wait for her to ring me back but she doesn't. My punishment.

All they're interested in is getting the facts. What was the Alfa Romeo's registration? I knew it this morning. I memorised it.

I've forgotten. In the hours between then and now, it has slipped out of my mind. *Idiot, idiot, idiot*.

I pick up the four photographs, take them downstairs and put them in my handbag. Then I go back to the lounge and throw the two wooden frames into the wastepaper basket. The chances of Nick noticing or asking about them are zero; for once I'm glad I haven't got a husband who's observant and on the ball.

I think about the police. *Real shaggers*. How observant can they be if they didn't find the two hidden photographs? Assuming they were hidden. Surely the house was searched after Geraldine and Lucy died. Why didn't anybody find those pictures?

I know what school Lucy Bretherick went to: St Swithun's, a private Montessori primary in North Spilling. Mark . . . the man at Seddon Hall told me. I'd heard of Montessori, knew it was a kind of educational ethos, but I wasn't sure what exactly it entailed, and didn't ask because he clearly assumed that as a fellow middle-class parent I knew all about it.

I don't, but I plan to find out as much as I can—about the school, about both girls whose photographs are in my bag, and their families. Tomorrow morning, as soon as I've dropped Zoe and Jake off at nursery, I'm going to St Swithun's.

Police Exhibit Ref: VN8723
Case Ref: VN87
OIC: Sergeant Samuel Kombothekra

GERALDINE BRETHERICK'S DIARY, EXTRACT 3 OF 9
(taken from hard disk of Toshiba laptop computer at Corn
Mill House, Castle Park, Spilling, RY29 0LE)

23 April 2006, 2 a.m.

Tonight, Michelle babysat while Mark and I went out for
dinner. I didn't have to negotiate about bedtime, how
many stories, brushing teeth. I didn't have to turn on the
night light or leave the door open at exactly the right angle. All that was Michelle's responsibility, and she was
paid handsomely for it.

'Mark's taking me to the Bay Tree, the best restaurant
in town,' I told Mum on the phone earlier. 'He thinks I'm
stressed and need a treat to cheer me up.' There was a
touch of defiance in my voice, I'm sure, and after I'd delivered my news I sat back and waited to see if Mum
would agree or disagree.

She asked her usual question, 'Who's looking after
Lucy?', her voice full of concern.

'Michelle,' I said. She always does, on the rare occasions that Mark and I aren't too shattered to venture out
at night. Mum knows this but still asks every time, to
check I'm not going to say, 'Oh, Michelle's busy tonight,
but don't worry, I found a tramp on the street earlier—
he's agreed to do it for a bottle of methylated spirits and
we won't even have to give him a lift home afterwards.'

'You won't be back late, will you?' Mum asked.

'Probably, yes,' I said. 'Since we're unlikely to set off till
after eight thirty. Why? What does it matter what time we
get back?' Every time Mark and I dare to go out for the

evening alone, I think of that poem I learned at school: *on a dark night, full of inflamed desires—oh, lucky chance!—I slipped out without being noticed, all being then quiet in my house.*

Mum said, 'I just thought ... Lucy's a bit funny at night at the moment, isn't she? This whole scared-of-monsters thing. Will she be okay if she wakes up and there's only Michelle there?'

'If you mean would she prefer to have me dancing attendance on her in the small hours, yes, she probably would. If you mean will she survive the night, yes, she probably will.'

Mum made a clucking noise. 'Poor little thing!' she said.

'Mark and I could always just have a starter and a glass of tap water each and be back here by nine thirty,' I said—another test for her to fail.

'Do come back as soon as you can, won't you?' she said.

'Mark thinks I need a break,' I said loudly, thinking: This is absurd. If I took a half-hearted overdose, everyone would be quick to say it was 'a cry for help'. But when I actually cry for help in the more literal sense, my own mother can't hear me. 'Do *you* think I need a break, Mum?' For over thirty years I was the person who mattered most to her; now I'm just the gatekeeper to her precious granddaughter.

'Well ...' She started spluttering and making throat-clearing noises, anything to avoid answering. What she thinks is that I shouldn't even be aware of my own needs now that I'm a mother.

I didn't enjoy the meal, as it turned out. Not because of Mum. I never do enjoy my breaks, long or short, from Lucy. I look forward to them intensely, but as soon as they begin, I can feel them starting to end. I feel the temporariness of my freedom, and find it hard to concentrate on anything other than the sensation of it trickling away.

Proper freedom is the kind you can keep. If you have to buy it (from Michelle), and are only granted it by someone else's kind permission (school, Michelle), then it's worthless.

When I'm not with Lucy, it's almost worse than when I am. Especially at the end of a period away from her, when 'crunch time' is approaching. I dread the moment when I first see her, when she sees me, in case it's worse than ever before. Sometimes it's fine, and then the dread goes away. I sit next to Lucy on the sofa and we hold hands and watch TV, or we read a book together, and I say to myself, 'Look, this is fine. You're doing fine. What's there to be so terrified of?' But other times it isn't fine and I run round the house like a slave pursued by the master's whip, trying to find the toy or game or hairclip that will pacify her. Mark says I set too high a standard for myself, wanting her to be happy all the time. 'No one is happy all the time,' he says. 'If she cries, she cries. Sometimes you should try just saying, "Tough," and seeing what happens.'

He doesn't understand at all. I don't want to see what happens. I want to know what's going to happen in advance. This is why I can't relax in Lucy's presence, because there seems to be no law of cause and effect in operation. I do my absolute best every single moment that I'm with her, and sometimes it works and everything is fine, and other times it's a disaster—I put on her favourite DVD and she shrieks because it's the wrong episode of *Charlie and Lola*. Or I suggest that we read her favourite book and she spits at me that she doesn't like that book any more.

When I do succeed in pleasing her, I sit beside her with a tense smile plastered to my face, trying not to do anything that might bring about a change of mood. I love Lucy too much—I can't extricate my own mood from hers, and this offends my independent spirit. I can barely express how much I resent her when she puts the itchy hook of her discontent into my mind. That one tiny action is enough to shatter my good mood. I look at her face, contorted in dissatisfaction, and I think, I can't separate myself from this person. I can't forget about her. She's got me, for ever. And then I think about how much she takes from me every day in terms of energy and effort and even my essence, even the bit of me that makes me who I am—she takes all that, without appreciating it, every minute of every day, and despite all this she chooses to make things even worse for me by whining when she's got nothing to be unhappy about. That's when I'm aware of the danger.

I've never really done anything. The only objectively bad thing I've done is drive away from Lucy once, when she was three. It was a Saturday morning and we'd been to the library. I didn't particularly want to go. I'd have preferred to go for a sauna or a manicure—something for me. But Lucy was bored and needed an activity, so I silenced the voice in my mind that was shouting, 'Somebody please shoot me in the head, I can't bear any more of this tedium!' and took my daughter to the library. We spent over an hour looking at children's books, reading, choosing. Lucy had a brilliant time, and I even started to relax and enjoy it a bit (though I was constantly aware that people who didn't have children were spending their Saturday mornings in ways that were far superior). The problem arose when I said it was time to go home. 'Oh, Mummy, no!' Lucy protested. 'Can't we stay for a bit longer? Please?'

At moments like this—and there are many when you've got children, at least one a day and usually more—I feel like a political leader wrestling with a terrible dilemma. Do I appease and hope to be treated leniently? That never works. Appease a despot and he will only oppress you even more, knowing he can get away with it. Do I steel myself for a fight, knowing that whether I win or lose there will be terrible devastation on all sides?

I knew Lucy would get hungry very soon so I stood firm and said, no, we needed to go home and have lunch. I promised to bring her to the library again the following weekend. She screamed as if I'd proposed to gouge out her eyeballs, and refused to get into the car. When I tried to pick her up, she fought me, kicking and punching with all her might. I stayed calm and told her that if she didn't co-operate and get into the car, I would go home without her. She paid no attention. She shrieked, 'I'm not happy about you, Mummy, you're making me very cross!' So I got into the car and drove away, alone.

I can't describe how exciting it was. Inside my head I was cheering, 'You did it! You did it! Hooray! You finally stood up to her!' I drove slowly, so that I could see Lucy's face in the rear-view mirror. Her angry screams stopped abruptly, and I watched the expression on her face turn from blank shock to panic. She didn't move, didn't run towards the car, but she threw her arms out in front of her, opening and closing the fingers of both hands, as if by doing that she could grasp me and pull me back. I could see her mouth moving, and lip-read the word 'Mummy!', repeated several times. Never in a million years would she have expected me to drive away without her.

I probably should have stopped the car at that point, while she could still see me, but I was full of exhilaration and, just for a few seconds, I wanted to believe that it could last for ever. So I drove quickly round the block. I pulled up outside the library again about half a minute later. Lucy was sitting cross-legged on the floor, howling. A woman was trying to comfort her and find out what had happened, where her mother was. I got out of the car, bundled Lucy up, saying 'Thank you very much!' to the puzzled woman, and we drove back home. 'Lucy,' I said calmly. 'If you're naughty and don't do what Mummy says, and if you make life difficult for Mummy, that's the kind of thing that will happen. Do you understand?'

'Yes,' she sobbed.

I hate the sound of her crying, so I said, 'Lucy, stop crying right this minute, or I'll stop the car and make you get out again, and next time I won't come back for you.'

She stopped crying instantly.

'That's better,' I said. 'Now, if you're good and make life easy for Mummy, then Mummy will be happy and we'll all have a nice time. Do you understand?'

'Yes, Mummy,' she said solemnly.

I felt a mixture of triumph and guilt. I knew I'd done something bad, but I also knew that I couldn't help it. It's hard enough behaving well when the people around you also are, when whoever you're with is leading by example. Sometimes you think, I want to do a bad, selfish thing now, but I can't because everyone else is being so infuriatingly decent. But when you're trapped in an explosive situation with someone who is determined to break all records for appalling behaviour, how, dear Gart, do you maintain your composure and do the right thing?

It isn't only Lucy who sets me off. I've often had to sit on my hands, so tempted have I been to whack a friend's child round the head. Like Oonagh O'Hara, who only has to whinge or stamp her foot to set both her parents off with their, 'Sweetie! Come for a cuddle!' nonsense. Gart, how I would love to punch Oonagh in the face. If I could do it once, I think I'd be happy for ever.

6

8/7/07

DC Colin Sellers sniffed the arm of his jacket when he was sure no one was looking. Inconclusive. He sniffed again, but couldn't tell if it was his clothes or his surroundings that stank. What was it about charity shops? He resolved never again to tell Stacey she ought to buy her clothes at Oxfam instead of Next. He hadn't been inside a charity shop for years, hadn't realised they all smelled like a stale stew of the past, layers of rancid odours piled one on top of the other like the decades of a life that has disappointed its owner.

Sellers wasn't normally prone to maudlin reflections, but the shops were bringing it out in him. He'd done all the dry-cleaners first—and the chemical stench of those had been bad enough—but now he wished he'd done it the other way round, saved the best for last. Anything was better than the charity shops.

At the moment he was in the Hildred Street branch of Age Concern in Spilling, which was, thank God, the last of them. Tonight he'd make sure to tell Stace to wash his clothes at an extra high temperature. Or maybe he'd just throw them away. One thing he wouldn't do: donate them to a manky shop for some other poor sod to buy. From now on, Sellers was against second-hand clothes. People ought to give money to these do-gooder organisations, and that's it, he thought. A nice, clean cheque that doesn't smell of grease or death or failure.

It occurred to Sellers that he had never in his life given any money to charity. Because he couldn't afford to, because he had Stacey and the kids to pay for as well as making sure Suki, his girlfriend, always had a good time and didn't get bored of him. And then there were Stacey's French lessons, which irked him more than he was able to express. *S'il vous plaît*. If he heard her say that one more time, he might actually ram her fag-packet-sized French dictionary down her throat.

Eventually, an old woman wearing a purple nylon polo-neck and a string of large, fake pearls emerged from behind the beaded curtain, holding the two colour print-outs Sellers had given her much younger and considerably more attractive assistant a few minutes earlier. One was of Geraldine Bretherick, the other of a brown Ozwald Boateng suit like the one Mark Bretherick had reported missing from his house.

'You're a policeman?' The old woman did her best to look down at Sellers, even though she was several inches shorter than he was. She looked about seventy, had fluffy white hair, several prominent moles like lumps of brown putty stuck to her face, a beak of a nose, and about ten times more skin on her eyelids than a person could ever need; each one was like a small, fleshy concertina. 'You want to know if anyone's brought in a suit like this?'

'That's right.'

'No. I'd have remembered. It's got funny lapels.' She glared at Sellers, daring him to disagree. 'I don't think our customers would like it at all.'

'What about this woman? Do you remember seeing her in the last few weeks?'

'Yes.'

'Really?' Sellers perked up. So far, the response had been a resounding 'no'. He'd been to every dry-cleaner and charity shop in the Culver Valley and he might as well not have bothered. 'Did she bring something in?'

'No.' The old lady leaned her beak towards him. 'You asked if I remembered seeing her. I do. She often went into the picture-framer's opposite. I saw her all the time, getting out of her car right outside the shop—she'd park on the double yellow line, plain as the nose on your face.' Sellers tried very hard not to look at the nose on her face as she spoke, fearing he might laugh uncontrollably. 'Usually she'd be carrying some dreadful picture—nothing more than splodges and scrawls, really, obviously by a child. Many a time I said to Mandy, "That woman ought to have her head examined." I mean, Blu-Tacking them to the fridge door is one thing, but framing them . . . And why didn't she wait and bring them in all at once? Didn't she have anything better to do?'

'Mandy? Is that your assistant?' Sellers glanced in the direction of the beaded curtain, but there was no sign of the pretty young girl who'd served him. I've already got a pretty young girl, he reminded himself: Suki's my pretty young girl.

'If she had the time to take each squiggle of crayon to the framer's individually then she had time to park her car properly,' said the old woman. 'No doubt she thought she'd only be nipping in and out, but all the same, there's no excuse for parking on a double yellow line. We've all got to obey the rules, haven't we? We can't go making exceptions for ourselves whenever we feel like it.'

'Right,' said Sellers, because he could hardly say otherwise. And he agreed, by and large. Apart from where matters of the heart were concerned. The heart and other equally important organs.

'She's dead, isn't she?' Folds of skin rearranged themselves around the old woman's eyes as she looked up at Sellers. 'I saw it on the news.'

'Right.' *And you're still worried about her illegal parking habits? Get a life, you old bat.*

'What time is it?'

'Nearly seven.'

'You'd better make yourself scarce. Our evening event's about to start.'

'I've finished, anyway.' Sellers eyed the three neat semicircular rows of grey plastic chairs in the middle of the shop. A wild time would be had by all, he didn't think.

'You should have come in the afternoon.'

'I did. You were closed.'

'Mandy was here all afternoon,' the old woman contradicted him. 'We're open every weekday from nine thirty until five thirty. And, in addition, we have our evening events.'

Sellers nodded. So Mandy had snuck an afternoon off, had she? He was liking her more all the time. He wondered if she would be taking part in tonight's event, and was about to ask what, precisely, Age Concern in Spilling had to offer him this evening. He came to his senses just in time, thanked the old woman for her help and left.

The Brown Cow pub, where he was due to meet Gibbs half an hour ago, was a five-minute walk away. As he strode along the High Street, smiling at any female with long legs and large breasts who looked as if she might be up for it, Sellers admitted to himself that he'd been thinking about other women a lot recently. Which had to mean he was a greedy bastard. He had two already; wasn't that enough? And for how long would he be able to stop at thinking? How long before he gave in to the urge that was building inside him?

Sellers wasn't good at denying himself things he wanted. He yielded to temptation instantly and gladly, and was proud of it. Much better to live for the moment and live it up than to be a puritan like Simon Waterhouse, avoiding anything that might prove to be pleasurable. Trouble was, Sellers didn't want to be saddled with a third woman who would then feel as entitled to make demands as Stacey and Suki did. His third woman—not that he'd spent much time building a profile—should be obedient, virtually silent, and want nothing from him but sex. Mandy from Age Concern seemed unlikely to fit the bill. Keen as he was to find himself a new ride, Sellers drew the line at spending his evenings in charity shops, sitting on a grey plastic school-chair listening to some bearded vegan loser give a lecture on Africa.

He bumped into Gibbs in the pub doorway.

'Thought you'd stood me up.'

'Sorry. Took longer than I thought.'

'Get a round in, then.'

Sellers ordered two pints of Timothy Taylor Landlord. At least Gibbs' taste in beer hadn't changed since his wedding. Everything else had, though Gibbs himself was either unaware of the changes or chose not to mention them. Sellers got his money ready, then glanced over to the small table in the corner to which Gibbs had retreated, never one to keep a mate company at the bar. He sat with two empty pint glasses in front of him, pushing a pool of spilled beer around the table-top with his index finger, trying to change its shape. Okay, so his behaviour was the same as ever but the way he looked . . . fucking hell, it was like being in the pub with the Madame Tussauds version of Christopher Gibbs—all bright and immaculate. What did Debbie do, put him in the washing machine?

The pub had changed too. Once it had boasted a no-smoking room; now the whole place was free of smoke. And the landlord had fallen for some wide-boy's flannel about sandalwood logs and wouldn't dream of putting ordinary wood on the fire any more, so the whole place was as fragrant as Gibbs' shiny hair.

'Nothing on the suit,' said Sellers, putting the drinks down on the table. Deliberately, he trapped Gibbs' finger under his pint glass before moving it and apologising.

'I saw Norman this afternoon.'

'Norman Bates? How's his mother?' Sellers quipped.

'Norman Computer. Geraldine Bretherick's laptop.'

'Oh, aye?'

'If she ordered GHB over the Internet, she did it from somewhere else.'

'That's possible. Maybe she went to an Internet café or used a friend's computer.' Though come to think of it there were no Internet cafés in Spilling and only one in Rawndesley. There were always the libraries, though.

Gibbs looked uneasy.

'What?' Sellers asked.

'The diary file was created on Wednesday the eleventh of July this year, Norman said. Waterhouse—the arsehole—pointed out that the eleventh of July was the Brethericks' ten-year wedding anniversary.'

'Why's he an arsehole?' Sellers was confused.

'He would be the one to spot it. In front of the Snowman.'

'I wouldn't have made the connection,' said Sellers. 'Waterhouse has got a good memory for dates.'

'He never goes on any, that's why. The original shagless wonder.'

'So,' said Sellers thoughtfully. 'Geraldine put fake dates on the entries. Either that or she wrote them by hand on those dates, then typed them up over a year later.'

'Why would she do that? And where's the hard copy? It wasn't in the house.'

'She could have thrown it away, save on storage space.'

Gibbs snorted into his pint. 'You saw the stately home. Could've stored a football team of elephants.'

'All right, so she wrote the entries for the first time on Wednesday, July the eleventh, and put dates on them that were more than a year old. Why?' Sellers started to answer his own question. 'I suppose it could have been a way of saying to her husband, "I've felt like this for ages and you haven't even noticed." But then why only choose dates from a year ago? The first entry was dated 18 April 2006 and the last one 18 May 2006. Not much of a spread. Why didn't she make the fake dates span three years instead of a month?'

'Fuck should I know?' Gibbs had ripped up a beer-mat and was floating small, ragged chunks of cardboard in the Landlord lake on the table. 'Maybe someone else wrote the diary.'

'What, someone who murdered Geraldine and Lucy? Who?'

'Waterhouse'd say William Markes.'

'Come on, for—'

'Stepford's looking shifty too—reckon he's having his doubts.'

'He's still nervous because he's new. This thing of the dates being out of kilter—it doesn't mean the diary's a fake. Think about it: if you'd murdered two people and wanted to fake a diary for one of them, to put them in the frame, you wouldn't attract unnecessary attention by choosing a cluster of dates from well over a year ago, would you? You'd make it more recent. Whereas if you're an unhappily married woman, pissed off with your husband, it's going to hit you hardest on your ten-year anniversary, isn't it? Ten long years of this shit, you'd be thinking—time to open a diary file and have a good bitch, let out some of the poison . . .' Sellers stopped when he saw Gibbs' face. He blushed. 'Looking forward to your and Debbie's anniversary, are you?'

Gibbs laughed. 'There's no danger Debbie'll feel that way after ten years with me. She's like a different woman since we've been married. She can't get enough of me.'

Sellers didn't want to hear about Gibbs being in demand. 'Anything more on the laptop?' he asked.

'Norman's still on it.'

The pub door opened and two young girls came in wearing strappy tops and miniskirts. One of them had a purple jewel in her navel. Sellers felt Gibbs' elbow in his side. 'Young enough for you?'

'Sod off.'

'Go on, go and drool over them. Colin Sellers the Chat-up King, with the stylish retro sideburns. "All right, love, wipe yourself, your taxi's here. It's four in the morning, pay for yourself if you don't mind, love."' His attempt at a Doncaster accent was appalling; it sounded more Welsh than anything else. All of a sudden Gibbs fancied himself as a comedian?

'Cocksucker,' said Sellers. He thought about Mandy and the Age Concern shop's evening event, and realised he'd made the wrong choice. The way he was feeling at the moment, he'd happily sit in a grey plastic chair in a smelly shop for the rest of his life as long as Gibbs wasn't sitting beside him.

When Charlie opened her front door and saw Simon, her heart dropped and landed with a thump on the floor of her stomach. Then, with equal speed and as little warning, it began to ascend, as if someone had filled it with helium. Simon was here; he'd made the effort to come and see her. About time.

'Hi,' she said. He was holding something behind his back. Flowers? Unlikely, unless he'd hired a private tutor in the social graces since Charlie last spoke to him.

'What's happened here?' he asked, looking at the bare hall behind her.

'I'm redecorating.'

'Oh, right. Sorry, I . . .' He craned his neck, looking for paint and dust-sheets that Charlie hadn't bought yet.

'Not *now*, at this precise second. I was just about to grab a spoon and have some cold, ready-made chilli from a jar for my dinner. Fancy some?'

'Why don't you heat it up?' Simon looked puzzled. 'You've got a microwave.'

'I suppose you'd rather it was home-made as well. With organic beef.' *You're going to drive him away before he's even through the door.*

'Why didn't you give that letter to me?' Simon produced a hostility to match Charlie's. 'About Mark Bretherick not being who he says he is? Why did you take it to Proust?' They glared at one another; it was like old times. Strange how quickly they could switch back.

'You know the answer to that.'

'No, I don't. I don't know the answer to anything. I don't know why you stopped talking to me, or jacked in CID. Do you blame me for what happened last year, is that it?'

'I don't want to talk about that. I mean it.' Charlie gripped the door, ready to close it. It was too late, of course—the shame was already in the house. It was there even before Simon had said the words 'last year'; she knew he knew, and that was enough.

Simon stared at his shoes. 'All right, so you're punishing me,' he said quietly. 'And I'm supposed to guess why.'

How could Charlie tell him that her respect for him had grown since she'd removed herself from his life? From the start Simon had had the good sense to stay away from her; he'd known there was a taint about her, waiting to happen.

'So, you'd fuck up your career just to spite me,' he said viciously. 'I'm flattered.'

Charlie laughed. 'The world doesn't begin and end with CID, you know. What about your career? Don't you think it's time you took your sergeant's exams?'

'One day someone's going to realise how ridiculous it is that I'm still a DC, and they'll do something about it. I'm not applying for anything.'

'Oh, what shit is that?' Charlie couldn't keep the words back. How did Simon do it? How did he manage to hit her bang in the middle of her temper reflex every time? 'You can't be made a sergeant unless you put in for the exams and you bloody well know it.'

'I know how many people are aching for a chance to kick me in the teeth. No way am I going begging for a promotion. I'd rather be a DC for ever and embarrass everybody by being better than them. I've got as much money as I need.'

Charlie knew no one but Simon who would adopt this attitude and stick to it. Who would really mean it. She wanted to weep. 'Look, we can't talk on the doorstep. Come in, if you can bear my shell of a house. But I meant what I said: certain subjects are closed.' She turned and headed down the long narrow hall towards the kitchen. 'What are you hiding, anyway? If it's wine, hand it over.' She took the jar of chilli out of the cupboard. There was nothing to go with it apart from some egg fried rice in a foil carton in the fridge, left over from a takeaway two days ago. It would have to do.

There was a rustle of plastic, the sound of something being taken out of a bag. Charlie looked round and saw two ugly greeting cards standing on her kitchen table. Both were creased and looked as if they'd travelled here in Simon's trouser pocket. She took in the pastel-coloured flowers and swirly gold letters. 'What are they?' she asked, moving closer. 'Wedding anniversary cards.' Strange but true. She laughed. 'Darling, don't tell me I forgot our anniversary.'

'Read them,' said Simon gruffly.

Charlie opened them both at the same time, looked from one to the other. She frowned.

'Don't worry, I've not stolen them from evidence,' said Simon. 'The originals are back at the Brethericks' house. But that's what was written in them, word for word.'

'Sam made you buy two more cards and copy out the messages? Why not just photocopy them?'

Simon's cheeks reddened. 'I didn't want to bring photocopies. I wanted you to see them as cards. As I saw them, on the mantelpiece at Corn Mill House.'

Charlie tried to keep a straight face. Who else would bother? For greater accuracy, Simon had even made sure to cast in his reconstruction cards that had been designed specifically for marriages of ten years—like the Brethericks', Charlie assumed. Both had embossed number tens on their fronts. 'Where did you buy them?'

'Garage down the road.'

'The romance is killing me.'

'Don't laugh at me, all right?' The warning in his eyes went beyond what he'd said. Something inside Charlie shrivelled and slunk away. Was he reminding her that she was no longer in a position to feel superior to him? To anyone? It didn't matter if he was or wasn't; she'd just reminded herself.

She picked up the jar of chilli, twisted open its lid and emptied it into a small orange pan. *Welcome to the most miserable dinner party in the world.* She didn't even have any lager.

'I want to talk to you about it. Geraldine and Lucy Bretherick.' Simon's voice closed in behind her. 'You're the only person I want to talk to about it. It's not the same without you. Work, I mean. It's shit.'

'Sam's been keeping me up to date,' said Charlie.

'Sam? Kombothekra?'

'Yeah. There's no need to look like that.'

'You see him? When? Where?' Simon made no attempt to conceal his displeasure.

'He and his wife have me round for dinner sometimes.'

'Why?'

'Thanks a lot, Simon.'

'You know what I mean. Why?'

Charlie shrugged. 'They're new in town. Well, new*ish*. I don't think they've got many friends.'

'They've never invited me.'

'Why don't you get your mum to ring and complain? Pathetic, Simon!'

'Why d'you go?'

'Free food, free booze. And they don't expect to be invited back, ever, because I'm single and pitiable and in need of looking after. Kate Kombothekra thinks all single women over the age of thirty live in brothels without kitchens.'

Simon yanked a chair out from under the table, scraping its legs along Charlie's new tiled floor. He sat down and hunched forward, his large hands on his knees, looking as if he might pounce. 'You don't speak to me for a year, but you go round to Kombothekra's house for dinner.'

Charlie stopped stirring the chilli. She sighed. 'You're the person I was closest to. Before. I found it—I *still* find it—easier to be with people who—'

'What?' Simon's mouth was set; his next move might be to punch her. He used to hit people all the time. Men. Charlie hoped he remembered she was a woman; you could never tell with Simon.

'People I don't know very well,' she said. 'People I can relax with, and not worry that they know exactly how I feel.'

The anger drained from his face. Whatever had been eating him up, Charlie's words seemed to have lanced it. 'I have no idea how you feel,' he mumbled after a few seconds, following her with his eyes as she walked up and down the small room.

'Bollocks! The way you said, "last year", when you first got here.'

'Charlie, I don't know what you're talking about. I just wish things could be like they used to be, that's all.'

'Like they used to be? That's your ambition? I've been miserable ever since I met you, do you know that? You make me feel too much. And this has got nothing to do with *last year*.' Charlie shouted the offending words. 'You make me want to close down and . . . become a robot!' She covered her face with her hands, digging her nails into the skin of her forehead. 'I'm sorry. Please, forget I said all that.'

'Is that sauce burning?' Simon shifted in his seat, not looking at her. Probably itching to get away. Back to the Brown Cow, where he could report to Sellers and Gibbs about how mad she'd gone. The old Charlie would never have let out so much truth in one go; she'd had too much to lose.

The ready-made chilli had got what it deserved. Charlie took the pan off the flames and dropped it in the washing-up bowl. Soapy water poured in over the sides. She stood and watched the pan sink, watched the lumpy meat and tomato sauce disappear beneath the suds until it was no longer visible.

'So Kombothekra's told you what he thinks, then? About Geraldine and Lucy Bretherick?'

'Is there any doubt? The mother killed them both, didn't she?'

'Proust doesn't think so. I don't either.'

'Why? Because of the letter I picked up at the post office? That's bound to be some dick's idea of a joke.'

'Not only that. Did Kombothekra tell you about William Markes?'

'No. Oh, yeah. The name in the diary? Simon, that could be anyone. It could be . . . I don't know, someone she met one day who annoyed her.'

'And the cards?' Simon nodded at the table.

Charlie sat down opposite him, looked at them again. 'Sam didn't mention the cards.'

'*Sam* is no detective. He hasn't noticed anything wrong about them, and I haven't told him what I think. I haven't told anyone.'

Their eyes met; Charlie understood that Simon had been saving this for her.

She opened the first card again. It was odd to see the message—a message from Geraldine Bretherick to her husband—written out in Simon's tiny, meticulous handwriting. 'To my darling Mark, Thank you for ten wonderful years of marriage. I'm sure the next ten will be even better. You are the best husband in the world. Your loving wife, Geraldine.' And three kisses. The second card—Simon's writing again—said: 'To my beloved Geraldine, Happy tenth wedding anniversary. You have made me so happy for the first ten years of our married life. I am looking forward to our future together, which I know will be every bit as amazing as the years we've had so far. All my love for ever, Mark.' Four kisses on this one; Mark Bretherick had out-kissed his wife.

'Aren't people odd?' said Charlie. 'Course, it doesn't help that it's in your handwriting. Imagine you writing something like that.' She giggled.

'What would I write?'

'Hey?'

'If I'd been married for ten years. What would I write?'

'You'd probably put "To whoever" at the top and "love Simon" at the bottom. Or maybe even just "Simon".' Charlie narrowed her eyes. 'Or you wouldn't send a card at all—you'd decide it was crass.'

'What would you write?'

'Simon, what are you driving at?'

'Come on, answer.'

Charlie sighed and rolled her eyes. ' "To whoever, happy anniversary, I can't believe I haven't divorced you yet for your gambling-stroke-laziness-stroke-unsavoury sexual practices. Love you loads, Charlie." ' She shuddered. 'I feel as if I'm taking my drama O level all over again. What point are you making?'

Simon stood up and faced the window. He always got twitchy when she mentioned sex. Always had. 'Happy anniversary,' he repeated. 'Not happy tenth anniversary?'

'I might write that, I suppose.'

'Both Mark and Geraldine seem obsessed with the number ten. It's printed on the front of both cards and they each mention it twice.'

'Isn't ten years meant to be the first significant milestone?' said Charlie. 'Maybe they were proud of their score.'

'Read the words,' said Simon. 'What sort of couple would write those things to one another? So formal, so elaborate. It's like something from Victorian times. It sounds as if they hardly know each other. In your card, your imaginary card, you made a joke about gambling—'

'Don't forget the sexual practices.'

'A *joke*.' Simon refused to be sidetracked. 'When you're close to someone, you make jokes, little comments other people might not get. These read like the phoney, stilted thank-you letters I was forced to write to my aunties and uncles as a child. Trying to say the right thing, trying to drag it out a bit so that it's not too short—'

'You can't be suspicious because there are no jokes! Maybe the Brethericks were a humourless couple.'

'It sounds as if they weren't a couple at all!' Simon's shoulders sagged. His posture became looser, as if he'd released some tension by voicing his suspicion. 'These cards are for display purposes. I'm sure of it. They go on the mantelpiece and everyone who sees them is fooled. Kombothekra's fooled—'

'You're saying their marriage was a sham?' Charlie was getting hungry. If Simon hadn't been here, she would have taken the pan out of the sink, decanted the chilli into another pan, heated it up and tried to ignore the burned bits and the taste of Fairy Liquid. 'I'm going to ring a home-delivery curry place,' she said. 'Do you want anything?'

'Curry and beer. You think I'm wrong?'

She considered it. 'I would never in a million years write a card like that. You're right, it's that polite thank-you-letter tone, and I'd hate to be married to someone who expressed his feelings in that way, but . . . well, people's relationships are peculiar. What newspaper do they read?'

Simon frowned. '*Telegraph.*'

'Delivered every day?'

'Yeah.'

'There you go, then. They probably had Lucy christened even though they never go to church, and Mark probably asked Geraldine's father for her hand in marriage and congratulated himself on his love of tradition. A lot of people are frighteningly keen on stupid formalities, especially the English upper-middle classes.'

'Your folks are upper-middle class,' said Simon, who had met Charlie's parents only once.

Charlie waved her hand dismissively. 'My mum and dad are *Guardian*-reading ex-hippies who like nothing better than a good old CND march at the weekend—it's completely different.' She opened a drawer, looking for the Indian takeaway menu. 'As for the number ten . . . Did you find lots of home-made films at the house? Lucy blowing out the candles on birthday cakes, Lucy doing not very much in a bouncy chair?'

'Yeah. Stacks. We had to watch them all.'

'Some families are obsessed with recording everything, keener on filming their lives than they are on living them. The Brethericks probably wrote their wedding anniversary cards with the family keepsake box in mind.'

'Maybe.' Simon sounded far from convinced.

'By the way, I don't think much of your expert.'

'Harbard?'

Charlie nodded. 'He was on telly again tonight.'

'Kombothekra's shy,' said Simon. 'He can get away with taking a back seat with the media if Harbard's on telly every day—CID's pet professor.'

'He seems cheap and nasty to me,' said Charlie. 'You can imagine him turning up on *Celebrity Big Brother* in a few years, once his career's hit the rocks. He looks like a fat version of Proust, have you noticed?'

'He's the Anti-Proust,' said Simon. 'Kombothekra's no expert, that's for sure. He needs a few lessons on reading and summarising an academic text.' Charlie mimed sticking her nose in the air, but he didn't notice. 'He's scraping around for anything that'll support his theory. He gave us an article today, Harbard's latest, and made a big deal about one particular paragraph that said family annihilation is a predominantly middle-class crime, because the middle classes care more about appearances and respectability. He was trying to explain away all the interviews with Geraldine's friends who swear blind she'd never have killed her daughter or herself—who *know* that she was happy. Kombothekra quoted this one paragraph, and that was supposed to prove that her happiness was just a front, that she was some kind of textbook case: someone whose life seemed perfect on the outside but whose unhappiness was building up in private to the point where she'd murder her own child—'

'You can't have it both ways,' Charlie interrupted him. 'Geraldine's happiness wasn't a sham but the anniversary cards are?'

'I'm not talking about that any more,' said Simon impatiently. And unreasonably, Charlie thought. 'I'm saying Kombothekra misunderstood the article. Deliberately, because it suited him to do so. I'll send you a copy, you can read it for yourself.'

'Simon, I don't work in—'

'This thing about affluent middle-class people killing their families because they can no longer maintain the illusion of perfection? Later on—in the same fucking article!—it makes it clear that money's always a big factor in those cases: men who have made the world believe in their wealth and success, and made their families believe it, who've been living way beyond their means and suddenly they can't pretend any longer; things have slipped too far out of their control and they can't sustain the fantasy however hard they try. Rather than face the truth, admit to everyone that they're failures, and bankrupt, they kill themselves and take their wives and kids with them.'

'Nice,' Charlie muttered.

'These men love their families, but they genuinely believe they're better off dead. The article describes it as "pathological altruism". They feel ashamed, because they're unable to support their wives and kids, who they see as extensions of themselves, not as people in their own right. The murders they commit are a sort of suicide-by-proxy.'

'Wow. Professor Harbard had better look to his laurels.'

'I got all that from the article,' said Simon. 'Kombothekra should have got it too. None of it applies to Geraldine Bretherick. She's not a man—'

'Does the article say it's always men?'

'It implies it. She didn't work—she had no financial responsibility for the family whatsoever. Mark Bretherick's loaded. They had money coming out of their ears.'

'There must be other cases that don't fit that pattern,' said Charlie. 'People who kill their families for other reasons.'

'The only other reason mentioned in the article is revenge. Men whose wives are leaving them or have left them, usually for new partners. In those cases it's murder-by-proxy rather than suicide-by-proxy. The man sees the kids as an extension of the *woman*, his unfaithful wife, and he kills them because, as revenge, it's even better than killing her. She has to carry on living knowing that her children have been murdered by their own father. And, of course, he kills himself to avoid punishment, and presumably—and this is me talking, not the article—presumably to align himself symbolically with the victims, because he feels like a victim. He's saying, "Look, we're all dead, me and the kids, and it's your fault." '

'So you're saying it's murder-by-proxy but the man doesn't feel he's the murderer?'

'Exactly. The real murder victim is the happy family and the deserting wife is the one who's killed it—that's the way he'd see it.'

Charlie shuddered. 'It's gross,' she said. 'Offhand, I can't imagine a worse crime.'

'I just thought of that last part on my own,' said Simon, looking surprised. 'Does that make me a sociologist?' He picked up the two anniversary cards and stuffed them in his trouser pocket, as if suddenly embarrassed by their presence. 'Mark Bretherick didn't have another woman on the go,' he said. 'If he had, we'd have found her. He wasn't planning to leave Geraldine. So it doesn't fit with the revenge model either.'

'Okay.' Charlie wasn't sure what he wanted her to do with all this information. 'So talk to Sam.'

'Tried and failed. Tomorrow I'm phoning in sick and going to Cambridge to talk to Professor Jonathan Hey who co-wrote the article with Harbard. I made the appointment this morning. I want to know more.'

'So why not talk to Harbard? Isn't that what he's there for?'

'He's too busy having his slap-head powdered by BBC make-up artists to talk to the likes of me. And he's obsessed with one thing and one thing only: his prediction that more and more women are going to start committing familicide. That's what gets people writing to the papers complaining about him, or applauding his bravery—that's what keeps his name in the news and gets him the media appearances he loves.'

'Why will more and more women kill their children?' asked Charlie. 'Can he get away with saying that?'

'Try stopping him. His argument's simple: in most areas of life, women are doing things that, at one time, only men used to do. Therefore women will start to kill their families. Therefore Geraldine Bretherick must have killed her daughter and herself. Does he bother trying to reconcile it with his own article, with all this stuff about financial factors and revenge? Does he bollocks. His reasoning's bullshit. So, I want to know if his side-kick's full of the same shit or if, as an expert of equal standing, his take on things is slightly different. Fancy coming with me?'

'What?'

'To Cambridge.'

'I'm working tomorrow.'

'Fuck work. I'm asking you to come with me.'

Charlie laughed in disbelief. 'Look, why phone in sick? Tell Sam you want to talk to this Jonathan Hey—maybe he'd think it was a good idea. The more expert opinions the better, surely.'

'Yeah, right. When's that ever been the philosophy? Harbard's our designated professor. I'd get the manpower-and-resources lecture if I got greedy and asked for another.'

'Won't Hey say exactly what Harbard's said?'

Simon's determination was etched on his face. 'Maybe. Maybe not. Harbard lives alone. Hey's younger, married, a father . . .'

'How do you know all this?'

'The magic of Google.'

Charlie nodded. There was no point trying to talk Simon out of it. She wasn't going to tell Sam. She'd have had nothing to tell if Simon hadn't confided in her about his plans. Now he'd made her complicit. Was it some kind of test?

'I'm starving,' she said. 'I'm going to order this curry before I faint. It'll take at least half an hour to get here and there's not a crisp or peanut in the house, I'm afraid. All I've got's eggs, stuff in tins and jars, and a packet of chicken stock cubes.'

Simon said nothing. Beads of sweat had appeared beneath his hairline.

'Do you want to look at the menu?' Charlie tried again.

'I want you to marry me.'

He sat rigid, watching her, as if he'd just confessed to having a contagious fatal illness and was waiting for her to recoil in horror. 'So,' he said. 'Now you know.'

'This is the best thing that could have happened,' Mark Bretherick told Sam Kombothekra. At least Sam knew the man in front of him *was* Mark Bretherick. He'd followed Proust's instructions and checked more times than someone with an obsessive-compulsive disorder would check, and in more ways. There was no doubt. Mark Howard Bretherick, born on the twentieth of June 1964, in Sleaford, Lincolnshire. Son of Donald and Anne, older brother of Richard Peter. This afternoon Sam had spoken to a teacher at Bretherick's primary school, who remembered him clearly and said she was positive that the man whose photograph had been on the news and in the papers was the boy she had taught. 'I'd know those eyes anywhere,' she said. 'Sad eyes, I always thought. Though he was a happy enough lad. Extraordinarily bright, too. I wasn't surprised when I heard he'd done well for himself.'

Sam knew what she meant about the eyes. Gibbs had managed to unearth a photograph of Bretherick aged eleven. He'd won a school swimming competition and his picture was in the local paper. The man who sat in front of Sam now was that boy plus thirty-two years.

Bretherick's voice on the phone, when he'd summoned Sam without explanation but insisting it was urgent, had been a little like a schoolboy's: full of the sort of anarchic, high-pitched energy that puts adults instantly on their guard. Bretherick had insisted 'something good' had happened, and Sam had hurried round to Corn Mill House hoping the situation hadn't deteriorated—though admittedly that was hard to imagine when you looked at things from Bretherick's point of view—but fearing it had, somehow.

His last comment had got no reaction from Sam, so Bretherick tried again. 'I allowed doubt to creep in,' he said. 'Because you seemed to have no doubts at all. I should have trusted my wife, not some stranger. No offence.'

Sam was gratified to hear that Bretherick had trusted him at all, however fleetingly—when? For an hour this afternoon, perhaps, in his absence?—even though the phase was now over. Bretherick's skin was grey, the whites of his eyes speckled with red from lack of sleep. He and Sam were in his kitchen, sitting opposite one another across a large pine table. The green carpet on the floor bothered Sam, made him dislike the room as a whole. Who, he wondered, carpets a kitchen? Not Geraldine Bretherick—the carpet was stained and looked at least twenty years old.

He was inclined to believe Bretherick's story. For a lie it was too elaborate; a man of Bretherick's intelligence would invent something simpler. So either it had happened or Bretherick had become delusional overnight. Sam favoured the former explanation.

'Mark, I understand that you're telling me that a woman who looked like your wife stole two photographs from your house,' said Sam carefully. 'What I don't understand is why you're happy about it.'

'I'm not happy!' Bretherick was insulted.

'All right, that's the wrong word. I'm sorry. But you said this was the best thing that could have happened, both on the phone and a few seconds ago. Why?'

'You told me Geraldine must have killed herself and Lucy because there were no other suspects—'

'I didn't quite say that. What I might have—'

'There *is* another suspect. A man who pretended to be me. The woman who was here said she'd spent some time with him last year—I don't know how long, but I got the impression she was talking about a significant amount of time. Reading between the lines, I think she might have been involved with him. Even though she was wearing a wedding ring. She said he went into detail about my life, talked to her at length about Geraldine and Lucy, about my work. Why would she lie? She wouldn't. She'd have no reason to come here and make all that up.'

'If she can steal, she can lie,' said Sam gently. 'You're sure she took these two photographs?'

Bretherick nodded. 'One of Geraldine and one of Lucy. I'd started packing up. I couldn't bear the idea of throwing things away, but I couldn't cope with having them in the house. Jean said she'd take it all, everything, until I was ready to have it back.'

'Geraldine's mum?'

'Yes. I put the two photos in one of the bags. They were my favourites, of Geraldine and Lucy at the owl sanctuary at Silsford Castle. I kept them on my desk at work, since I spent more time there than at home.' Bretherick rubbed the bridge of his nose with his thumb and index finger, perhaps as a cover for wiping his eyes, Sam couldn't tell. 'I brought them home yesterday. I couldn't keep them out where I could see them. Every time I looked at them, I . . . it was like an electric shock of pain. I can't describe it. Jean's the opposite. If anything, she's put up more pictures since they died. All Lucy's framed drawings that used to be here, on the wall . . .'

'You've been into work?' asked Sam.

'Yes. Something wrong with that?'

'No. I didn't know you had, though.'

'I have to do something, don't I? Have to fill my days. I didn't *do* any work. I just went to the office, sat in my chair. Opened sympathy cards. Then I came home.'

Sam nodded. 'Has anyone else been to the house, anyone who might have removed the photographs?'

Bretherick leaned forward, his eyes locking on Sam's. 'Stop treating me like a moron,' he said, and for the first time since he'd reported finding the bodies of his wife and daughter, Sam could imagine him giving orders to his staff of seven at Spilling Magnetic Refrigeration. 'I'm not treating you like one, although soon I might have to. The woman who looked like Geraldine, who was here this afternoon—she stole the photographs. I'd only put them in the bag an hour or so before she turned up, and no one's been here since she left apart from my mother-in-law and now you. I might be bereaved but I'm not an idiot. If there was anyone else who might have stolen them, don't you think I'd mention it?'

'Mark, I'm sorry. I have to ask these questions.'

Bretherick twisted in his chair. 'A man who pretends to be me has an affair with a woman who looks exactly like my wife—a woman who comes here this afternoon, refuses to answer my questions or tell me her name, and steals photographs of Geraldine and Lucy. I want to hear you say that this changes everything. Say it.'

This man has an interview technique, thought Sam. Not many people did, not unless they'd been trained. Sam knew his own interview technique wasn't one of his strengths as a detective. He hated to put people on the spot, hated it even more when they did it to him.

'You don't know for certain that this woman was having an affair with—'

'Irrelevant.' Bretherick cut him off, began to tap his fingers on the table one by one, as if playing the piano slowly, one-handed.

Sam felt hot and flustered. This was a show of strength; Bretherick was trying to prove he was cleverer, as if that made him more likely to be right. Perhaps it did. Talking to him was like talking to Simon Waterhouse. Whose analysis, Sam was certain, would be identical to Bretherick's.

'How many suicides have you dealt with, Sergeant?'

Sam took a deep breath. 'Some. Maybe four or five.' None since he'd become a detective. One, he corrected himself: Geraldine.

'Did any of those four or five have this many question marks surrounding them, this many strange, unexplained details?'

'No,' Sam admitted. *You don't know the half of it.* He hadn't told Bretherick that the diary file on Geraldine's laptop was opened more than a year after the date of the last entry. He was still trying to work out what he thought of this man who had already been back to the office, already bagged up his wife and child's possessions.

One detail had bothered Sam from the start, though he'd assumed he was wrong to be concerned about it since Simon Waterhouse seemed not to have registered it: when Mark Bretherick had first rung the police, he'd said, 'Someone's killed my wife and daughter. They're both dead.' The words had been clearly audible even through his hysteria. Interviewed later, Bretherick had claimed that he hadn't read or even seen Geraldine's suicide note in the lounge. He'd let himself into his house after returning from a long and tiring trip abroad, gone straight upstairs to his bedroom and found Geraldine's body in the en-suite bathroom. His wife's body, in a bath full of blood. The razor blade lying on her stomach; Bretherick didn't touch it, left it in place for the scene-of-crime officers to find. Why hadn't he called the police immediately from the telephone beside his bed? Instead he said he'd gone straight to Lucy's room to check she was all right and then, when he failed to find her in there, he looked in all the other rooms upstairs and found her dead body in the family bathroom.

Maybe it makes sense, thought Sam. If you discover that the person you assume is looking after your child can't be, because she's lying in the bath with her wrists slashed, maybe the first thing you do is panic and search the house for your daughter. Sam tried for about the two hundredth time to imagine himself in Bretherick's terrible position. He doubted he'd be capable of moving at all if he'd just found Kate dead. Would he even be able to pick up a phone? Would he think about where his sons were?

There was no point speculating. Mark Bretherick couldn't have killed Geraldine and Lucy. He was in New Mexico when they died.

'She said she'd come and see me again, but I don't think she will,' Bretherick was saying. 'I was stupid to let her go. I need to know who she is.'

It was a few seconds before Sam realised he was talking about his visitor from this afternoon, not his dead wife.

'We'll do our best,' said Sam.

'It'll be easy for you to find out. You can appeal on television. She could be Geraldine's twin, she looks so much like her. She's married . . . Oh, and she's got one of those mobile phones that shuts like a . . . sort of like a clam shell. Silver, with a jewel on the front, looks like a little diamond. You need to find her and bring her back here.'

Sam let out a long, slow sigh, hoping Bretherick wouldn't notice his sinking shoulders. A television appeal? That would be Proust's call, and Sam could guess what the inspector would say, could almost hear him saying it: Mark Bretherick had appeared on the news many times in the past few days. His was the sort of tragedy that attracted attention, and possibly visits from local nutters. This woman, whoever she was, could easily have been lying. Should Sam suggest a TV appeal all the same? Lobby for one as Simon Waterhouse might? Perhaps if he'd been there longer . . .

Sam still felt like a stranger in a strange land at work. Every molecule in his body yearned to go back to West Yorkshire, to the lock-keeper's cottage by the side of the Leeds–Liverpool canal that he and Kate had loved, with the wisteria climbing its walls. Sam hadn't known what the plant was called but Kate had gone on about it so much when they'd first seen the house, he could hardly have avoided learning the name. But Kate's parents lived near Spilling and she'd finally admitted she needed help looking after the boys so there was no way they'd be going back to Bingley. In the end, Sam thought with a mixture of pride and shame, it turns out I'm more sentimental than my wife.

'If Geraldine didn't do it—if you can prove that—I'll be able to carry on,' said Bretherick. 'For her sake and Lucy's. I expect that sounds odd to you, Sergeant.' He smiled. 'I must be the first man in the history of the world to feel relieved when he realises his family has been murdered.'

7

Wednesday, 8 August 2007

St Swithun's Montessori School is a Victorian building with a
clock-tower on its roof and green-painted iron railings separat-
ing its playground from the enormous landscaped garden of the
old people's home next door. I can hear children through the
open windows as I approach the front door—singing, chanting,
laughing, calling out to one another. It sounds as if a party is
being thrown in every room.

I stop, confused. It's the summer holidays. I was expecting to
find the place empty apart from the odd secretary. There's a sign
on the door that says 'Action Week One—Monday 6 to Friday
10 August'. I wonder if it's some kind of holiday childcare
scheme, and have the automatic thought: what are parents supposed to do for the rest of the holidays?

I walk in and find myself in a small square entrance hall with
a flagstone floor. Class photographs line all four walls: rows and
rows of children wearing green. This startles me; I feel as if I've
been ambushed by tiny faces. Beneath each picture is a typed list
of names and a date. One, to my left, is dated 1989. I see Lucy
Bretherick's green dress, over and over again.

The sight of all these children makes me ache for mine. I
found it harder than ever to drop them off at nursery this morning. I didn't want to let them out of my sight. I kept asking for
one last kiss, until Jake eventually said, 'Go to work, Mummy. I

want to play with Finlay, not you.' This made me laugh; clearly he's inherited his father's diplomacy.

I didn't go to work. I rang HS Silsford, lied to the disgusting Owen Mellish and came here instead. I've never phoned in sick before, legitimately or otherwise.

'Can I help you at all?' A soft Scottish accent. I turn and find a tall, thin woman behind me. She looks my age but better preserved. Her skin is like a porcelain doll's and her short, sleek black hair hugs her scalp like a swimming cap. She's wearing a fitted jacket, the thinnest pencil skirt I've ever seen and sandals with stiletto heels. On her ring finger there's a pile-up of gold and diamond bands reaching almost to her knuckle.

I smile, open my bag and pull out the two photographs that I found hidden behind the ones of Geraldine and Lucy. When I look up, I see that the Scottish woman's face has been immobilised by shock, and it's nothing to do with my cuts and bruises. 'I know,' I say quickly. 'I look like Mrs What's-her-name on the news who died. Everyone's been telling me.'

'You . . .' She pauses to clear her throat, eyeing me warily. 'You know her . . . her daughter was one of our pupils?'

My turn to look shocked. 'Really? No, I didn't know. I'm sorry.' I have no plan other than to keep lying until I come up with a better strategy. 'I'm sorry if I sounded flippant,' I say. 'I had no idea you knew the family personally.'

'So . . . you're not here in connection with the tragedy?'

'No.' I smile again. 'I'm here because of these.' I pass her the two photographs.

She holds them at a distance, then brings them close to her face, blinking at them. 'Who are these people?' she asks.

'I was hoping you could tell me. I don't know. I just recognised the uniform as belonging to this school.' Inspiration rushes to my aid. 'I found a handbag in the street and the photos were inside it. There was a wallet too, with quite a lot of money in it, so I'm trying to find the bag's owner.'

'Weren't there credit cards? Contact details?'

'No,' I say quickly, impatient with my own fictions. 'Do you know who the girl is? Or the woman?'

'I'm sorry, before we go any further . . .' She extends her hand. 'I'm Jenny Naismith, the headmistress's secretary.'

'Oh. I'm . . . Esther. Esther Taylor.'

'Pleased to meet you, Mrs Taylor,' she says, eyeing my wedding ring. 'This is a bit of a puzzle. I know every child at St Swithun's and every parent—we're like a big family here. This girl is not one of our pupils. I've never seen the woman before either.'

The bell rings, making my whole body shake as if in response to an electric shock. Jenny Naismith remains perfectly still, unperturbed. Doors all around us start to open, and children pour out. They aren't wearing the green uniform. Some of them are in fancy dress—pirates, fairies and wizards. Several Spidermen and Supermen. For a few seconds, maybe half a minute, they're a flood of colour, sweeping past us and out into the playground. As soon as I am able to make myself heard, I say, 'Are you sure?'

'Quite sure.'

'But . . . why would a child who wasn't at St Swithun's be wearing the uniform?'

'She wouldn't.' Jenny Naismith shakes her head. 'This is very odd. Wait here.' She points to a pair of brown leather armchairs against one wall. 'I'd better show these to Mrs Fitzgerald.'

'Who?' I call after her.

'The head.'

I start to follow her, but children are still spilling out of classrooms; by the time I've dodged the first lot I've lost sight of her.

I sit in a leather chair for a few seconds, then stand, sit then stand. Every time a door opens, I half expect a team of policemen to appear. But nothing happens. I stare at my watch and convince myself that the hands aren't moving at all.

Eventually another bell rings, startling me as much as the first did, and the sea of children pours back into school. My legs get kicked so many times that eventually I pull them up on to the seat of my chair. The pupils of St Swithun's seem to have selective vision; they see each other but they don't see me. I could be invisible.

I look at my watch again, swear under my breath. Why did I let Jenny Naismith take the photographs away? I should have insisted on going with her.

I pick up my bag and walk along a series of corridors decorated with children's artwork, large watercolour paintings of birds and animals. A passage from Geraldine's diary comes into my mind. I don't remember her exact words but it was something about spending her days enthusing about pictures that deserved to be shredded. How could she say that about her own daughter's drawings? I've kept every work of art Zoe and Jake have ever produced. Zoe, being organised and imaginative, has a real eye for colour and composition, and Jake's more casual paint-splats are no less attractive, as far as I can see, than the output of many a Turner Prize–winner.

I walk and walk, getting more lost as I move deeper into the building. St Swithun's is a maze. How long must it take a child to learn his or her way round? I end up in a big hall with white tape stuck to the floor and wooden climbing frames covering one long wall. Blue mats are arranged in lines that are slightly askew, like stepping stones. This must be the gym. It's also a dead end. I turn to leave, to go back the way I came, and bump into a young woman wearing red tracksuit bottoms, white pumps and a black Lycra vest-top. 'Oops, sorry,' she says nervously, twisting her high ponytail around her hand. Her forehead is large and flat, which gives her a severe look, but overall her face is pretty. Her breath smells of peppermint. When she notices my face, she backs away.

I haven't got the energy for a repeat performance, so I say, 'I'm looking for Jenny Naismith.'

A pause. Then, 'Have you tried her office?'

'I don't know where it is. She said she was going to find the head, Mrs Fitzgerald. That was about ten minutes ago. She's got two photographs of mine and I need to get them back.'

'Photographs?' She says it so quietly, I almost have to lip-read. 'Are you a relative?'

'Of the Brethericks? No. I know—there's a strong resemblance. It's a coincidence.'

'You obviously know . . . what happened. Are you a journalist? Police?' In spite of her soft voice, she's persistent.

'Neither,' I tell her.

'Oh.' Disappointment all over her face: there's no mistaking it.

'Who are you? If you don't mind . . .'

'Sian Toms. I'm a teaching assistant. You said two photographs?'

I nod.

'Of . . . of Lucy and her mum?'

'No. Another woman and girl. I don't know who they were. The girl was wearing a St Swithun's uniform, but Jenny Naismith said she definitely wasn't a pupil here.'

I see a flash of—could it be triumph?—in Sian Toms' eyes. 'Jenny won't tell you anything. She'll have thought you're another journalist. They've been all over—you can imagine. Wanting us to talk about Lucy and her family.'

'And did you?'

'No one asked me.'

'What would you have told them?' I hold my breath. I wonder if anyone has ever been as keen to hear what Sian Toms will say next as I am now, and I wonder if she's thinking the same thing—making the moment last.

'The only thing that matters.' Her voice vibrates with suppressed anger. 'Geraldine didn't kill Lucy—there's no way on earth she did it.' She pulls at her ponytail. A few strands of hair come loose. 'Never mind how sorry we all are, how devastating it's been for the school community, what about getting the facts right? I'm sorry. What am I doing?' She seems astonished to find herself in tears, sinking to the floor in front of a woman she has never met before.

Ten minutes later, Sian and I are both sitting on one of the gym's dusty blue mats.

'You get some children—not many—who are a dream to teach,' she says. 'Lucy was like that, always keen, whatever she was doing. She'd volunteer for everything, help organise the other children: boss them around, basically, parroting words and instructions she'd heard us say. Used to make us laugh—she was six going on forty-six. We all used to say she'd probably end up as Prime Minister. After she died, we had a special assembly to pay tribute to her. Everyone was in tears. Lucy's classmates read poems and stories about her. It was horrible. I mean . . . I don't mean I didn't want to remember Lucy, but . . . it was like, all we were allowed to do was say nice things about her and how much she'd meant to us. Geraldine's name wasn't mentioned. No one said anything about what had *happened*.'

Sian pulled a tissue out of her sleeve and twisted it into the corners of her eyes. 'Lucy could just as easily have died of . . . I don't know, some illness, from the way people here talk about it. Teachers, I mean. It really freaks me out. They're trying to be tactful, but you can tell they all believe what they've heard on the news. They've forgotten that they knew Geraldine, person- ally, for years. Haven't they got minds of their own?'

'A lot of people haven't,' I tell her, thinking of Esther, of her automatic disapproval before she'd given me a chance to ex- plain. 'How . . . how can you be so sure Geraldine didn't kill Lucy? Did you know her well?'

'Very. I take the minutes at the Parents and Friends meetings. Geraldine joined the committee when Lucy started at the school's nursery nearly four years ago. We always go for a drink afterwards, and sometimes a meal. We knew each other really well. She was a lovely person.' Sian presses the tissue into her eyes again. 'That's what's doing my head in. I'm not allowed to say I'm upset about Geraldine being dead—they'd all think I was betraying Lucy's memory. I'm sorry.' She covers her mouth with her hand. 'Why am I telling you all this? I don't even know you. You look so much like her . . .'

'Maybe you should speak to the police,' I say. 'If you're so sure.'

Sian snorts contemptuously. 'They haven't noticed I exist. I'm only the teaching *assistant*. They talked to Sue Flowers and Maggie Gough, Lucy's teachers. Never mind that I'm in the classroom too five mornings a week. I work as hard as anyone. Harder.'

'You're the teaching assistant for Lucy's class?'

She nods. 'What could I have told them anyway? They'd never have understood. They didn't see the way Geraldine's eyes lit up whenever Lucy was there. I did. You get some parents who—' She stops.

'What? Go on.'

'It's usually the mums, especially the ones who use the after-school club,' she says. 'You see them waiting at the gates at half past five—they're standing there, chatting away, and when we let the children out, just for a second you can see the strain on their faces; it's like they're gearing up for . . . some kind of ob-stacle course. Don't get me wrong, they're pleased to see their kids, but they're also dreading the hassle of wrestling them into the car.'

I nod eagerly. *Sounds familiar.*

'Then of course the children get tetchy. They don't want their mums to be tired, they want them to be excited and energetic. Well, Geraldine always was. She was raring to go—it was as if being with Lucy gave her this special energy. And she'd always arrive early for pick-up; usually by twenty past three she was hopping up and down outside the classroom. She'd peer through the window, waving and winking like a teenager with a crush or something. We used to worry about how she'd cope when Lucy left home. Some mums go to pieces.'

'You could tell the police all that,' I say. 'Why do you think they wouldn't listen to you? It sounds as if you know what you're talking about.'

Sian shrugs. 'They must have a reason for thinking what they think. I'm hardly going to change their minds, am I?' She looks at her watch. 'I've got to go in a minute.'

'The photographs Jenny Naismith's got, the ones I brought in, they came from Lucy Bretherick's house,' I blurt out, not wanting her to leave yet.

'What? What do you mean?'

I tell Sian an edited version of the story: the man at the hotel who pretended to be Mark Bretherick, my trip to Corn Mill House, finding the frames with the two photographs hidden beneath ones of Geraldine and Lucy. I'm hoping she'll be flattered that I'm telling her so much, that it'll make her feel important, make her want to stay and carry on talking to me. I don't mention that I stole the pictures. 'Did Lucy's class go on a school trip to the owl sanctuary at Silsford Castle?' I ask. It didn't occur to me to ask Jenny Naismith.

It's a while before I get an answer. Sian is still trying to take in what I've told her. 'Yes. Last year. Every year we take our reception class.' She looks at me. 'I'm not being funny, but . . . even if Jenny knew who the other girl was, she wouldn't have told you.'

Because she thinks I'm a gutter press hack. Great. For a school secretary, Jenny Naismith is a more than averagely talented actress. If she thought I was planning a big, emotive story in one of the tabloids, perhaps to publish pictures of other St Swithun's pupils, what would she have done? I press my eyes shut. She'd have taken the two photographs, locked them away somewhere, then made herself scarce.

I have no proof that those pictures exist, that I ever had them.

'So, if this girl *is* a pupil at St Swithun's, she's probably in Lucy's class,' I say.

'Not necessarily,' says Sian. 'The photo of the other girl might have been taken the previous year. Any year, really. How old did she look?'

'I don't know. I assumed she was Lucy's age because of where I found the photo, because the other woman looked roughly the same age as Geraldine.' I hear myself admitting to having made assumptions on the basis of no facts, connections that probably don't exist, and feel embarrassed. 'Is there a girl at St Swithun's whose surname is Markes?' I ask. 'Whose father is called William Markes?'

'No. I don't think so, no.'

Why would there be? My brain is rushing ahead of itself; I'm speaking without thinking.

'Did the Brethericks seem like a happy family?'

Sian nods. 'That's why I can't get my head round this thing with the photos. Mark would never . . . He and Geraldine were really sweet together. They always held hands, even at parent consultations.' I wince. Sweet? The adjective seems inappropriate as a way of describing two adults. 'Most of the parents sit with their arms folded, looking deadly serious, as if we've done something wrong. Some even take notes while they interrogate us. Sorry, shouldn't have said that, but they do harp on: is their child more than averagely creative, are we doing everything we can to stimulate them, what special talents have they got that the other children don't have? The usual competitive rubbish.'

'But not Mark and Geraldine Bretherick?'

Sian shakes her head. 'They asked if Lucy was happy at school—that was it. If she had friends, and enjoyed herself.'

'And did she? Have friends?'

'Yeah. This year the class—Lucy's class—is friendly as a whole, which is nice. Everyone plays with everyone. Last year it was a bit more cliquey. Lucy was one of the three oldest girls in the class, and they tended to hang round together. Lucy, Oonagh—'

'Wait.' I recognise the name instantly; it was in the diary Mark Bretherick made me read. Oonagh, daughter of Cordy. Could she be the girl in the picture? I open my bag, pull out my notebook—home to my many lists—and a pen. I write down the names as Sian says them, the two girls in Lucy's gang last year: Oonagh O'Hara and Amy Oliver. There were no references to Amy in Geraldine's diary.

'Is either of them skinny?' I ask, remembering the swollen-looking knees, the bony legs.

Sian looks taken aback. 'They're both thin. But . . .'

'What?'

For the first time, she seems to be holding something back. 'The woman—what did she look like?'

I describe her: short brown hair, square face, blunt features. Leather jacket. 'Why?' I say. 'Tell me.'

'I've really got to go in a minute.' Sian's eyes move to the door. 'I think the pictures you found might be of Amy and her mum. Amy's painfully thin. We used to worry about her.'

'Used to?'

'She left St Swithun's last year. Her family moved away.'

Moved away. For some reason, the words make my skin prickle.

'It'd explain why Jenny Naismith didn't recognise her,' says Sian. 'Jenny only started here in January.'

My heart is pounding. 'Tell me about Amy's family,' I say, trying not to make it sound like an order. 'The O'Haras too.' Amy Oliver could well be the girl in the photograph, but Oonagh was the one mentioned in Geraldine's diary, and there's part of me that can't allow anything to be neglected or overlooked. It's the same part that won't let me walk past a cupboard or drawer that Nick has left open and climb into bed, no matter how exhausted I am. 'You're too thorough,' he regularly tells me. 'It's easy to fall asleep even if the bedroom's a mess—look.' Three seconds later he's snoring.

Sian looks at her watch and sighs. 'You didn't get any of this from me, right? The O'Haras split up last year. Oonagh's mum went off with another man.' She rolls her eyes to indicate that she has no time for that sort of thing. Instantly, I feel defensive on behalf of Cordy O'Hara, a woman I've never met. 'Amy's parents . . .' Sian shrugs. 'We didn't see much of them, to be honest. They both worked. It was always Amy's nanny who dropped her off and picked her up. But I believe they're separated too. I'm not sure, though. You know what schools are like for rumours. It wouldn't surprise me if they'd split up.'

'Why?'

Sian rubs the strap of her watch, distracted by her need to be somewhere else. 'I'll walk with you to wherever you're going,' I say. 'Please. You have no idea how much you're helping me.'

A flush of pleasure spreads across her face, and I find myself hoping that Zoe is never so grateful for a snippet of praise from a stranger. If I could secure one thing for my children it would be confidence. *The confidence to lie, cheat on their partners, skive off work and stick their noses in where they aren't wanted?* Yes, I say silently. If necessary, yes.

Sian and I leave the gym, head out into the maze of corridors. 'Amy's dad's lovely but her mum's a bit funny,' she tells me, eager to talk now that we're moving. 'She used to make Amy write all sorts of strange things in her news-book that couldn't possibly have come from Amy. The children are supposed to do it themselves from reception age onwards—' She breaks off, seeing the question in my eyes. 'Oh, it's like a little notebook. All the children have one—the school provides them. Every weekend they're supposed to fill them in. They bring them in on Monday morning and read them out to the class: what I did at the weekend, that type of thing.'

'What kind of strange things?' I ask.

Sian scrunches up her face. 'Hard to describe, really. You'd have to see it for yourself.'

'Can I? Is it here, at school, or did Amy take it with her when she left?'

'I'm not sure . . .'

'If it's here, you've got to find it and send it to me.' I stop, tear a page out of my notebook, write down Esther's name and my address. Even though Sian is in a hurry, she waits beside me without complaining. I hand her the piece of paper.

Unbelievably, she thanks me. 'If I do find Amy's news-book, it didn't come from me, okay?'

'Of course.'

Sian pulls her ponytail loose and shakes out her hair. 'For what it's worth, I didn't much like Amy's mum. Worked for a bank, she did. In London,' she adds, as if this detail makes it worse. I wonder if Sian was born and raised in Spilling. A lot of Spilling people seem to bear a grudge against London for being the capital when clearly their home town is more deserving of the honour. 'Like Amy, she could get angry very easily, for no good reason.'

'What made Amy angry?' I ask.

Sian sways beside me, keen to get moving again. Suddenly, she stops. Opens her mouth, then closes it. 'Lucy,' she says. 'Funny, that's only just occurred to me. They were good friends, don't get me wrong, but they could rub each other up the wrong way. Amy was a bit of a dreamer—imaginative and over-sensitive—and Lucy could be a bit . . . well, bossy, I suppose. Sometimes they clashed.'

'Over what?' A pulse has started to throb behind my left eyebrow.

'Oh, you know, Amy'd say, "I'm a princess with magic pow-ers," and Lucy'd say, "No, you're not, you're just Amy." Then Amy'd have the screaming abdabs and Lucy would pester us to tell Amy off for pretending to be a princess when she wasn't. Look, I've seriously got to make a move,' Sian says.

I nod reluctantly. If I keep her here for a million years, I still won't get through all the questions I want to ask. 'One more thing, quickly: when did Amy leave St Swithun's?'

'Um . . . end of May last year, I think. She didn't come back after the half-term break.'

End of May last year. I was at Seddon Hall with a man who called himself Mark Bretherick from the second of June to the ninth. Can it be a coincidence?

Sian opens her grey bag and pulls out a large, old-fashioned brick of a mobile phone. She presses a few buttons. 'Write this down,' she says. '07968 563881. Amy's old nanny runs our after-school club—that's her number. She knows more than I do about the family, much more.'

While I'm writing, Sian takes the opportunity to escape. She stretches out an arm behind her to wave at me as she hurries away.

An hour later I'm no longer lost. I feel as if I know St Swithun's as well as any teacher or pupil—I could draw a detailed map of the place and not miss out a single crevice or passageway. What I can't seem to do is find Jenny Naismith. Everyone I've asked has 'just seen her a minute ago'. I also can't find the headmistress, Mrs Fitzgerald. I'm so angry with myself for letting go of those photographs that I can hardly breathe.

My throat is dry and my feet are starting to ache. I decide it can't hurt to go back to the car, where I'm sure there's an old bottle of water lying around in one of the footwells or wedged under a seat. At least three people have assured me that Jenny Naismith won't leave until at least four o'clock, so I can afford to have a break.

Outside, I switch on my phone and listen to four messages, two from Esther and two from Natasha Prentice-Nash. I delete them all, then key in the number Sian gave me. A chirpy female voice with a Birmingham accent says, 'Hi, I can't take your call at the moment, but leave a message and I'll get back to you.' I swear under my breath and toss the phone back in my bag. I can't bear to wait and do nothing. I need everything to happen now.

Sian's words buzz around my worn-out brain. I try and fail to make sense of everything I now know: bossy, literal-minded Lucy Bretherick with her perfect family, her adoring parents who wanted nothing but her happiness, who held hands all the way through parents' evenings; and Lucy's two friends, both from families that sound not quite so perfect . . . Yet Lucy is the one who ends up dead. Murdered by her mother. I think about envy, how it is fed by inequality.

Amy's old nanny runs our after-school club. That was what Sian said. Old as in she's no longer Amy's nanny? Why not? If the Olivers moved away, why didn't they take her with them? I've got friends and colleagues who would cut their own limbs off sooner than lose a trusted nanny.

I wish I'd thought to ask Amy's mother's name and the name of the bank she works for. Amy's mum, Oonagh's mum—did Sian mention any of them by name? It drove me mad after Zoe was born, the way I quickly became 'Zoe's mummy', as if I had no identity of my own. To annoy the midwife and the health visitor I used to make a point of calling Zoe 'Sally's daughter'. They had no idea why I was doing it and looked at me as if I was insane.

Sian said 'worked', not 'works'—Amy Oliver's mother *worked* for a bank in London. That's what you say when you haven't seen someone for a while, when you're describing what they did or how they were when you were last in touch with them. There's nothing unusual about it. So why do I fear that the Oliver family has vanished off the face of the earth?

I'm halfway across the car park when I catch sight of my Ford Galaxy. There's a jagged silver line across the paintwork, stretching the length of the car. The two tyres I can see are flat, and there's something orange lying behind one of the wheels. I swing around, breathing hard, expecting to see a red Alfa Romeo, but the only other cars in the visitors' car park are three BMWs, two Land Rovers, a green VW Golf and a silver Audi.

I move closer. The orange lump is a ginger cat. Dead. Its eyes are open, in a head that's no longer attached to its body. There's a red mess where its neck should be. A rectangle of brown parcel tape has been stuck over its mouth. I bend double, retching, but nothing comes up; there's nothing in my body apart from sharp fear. Dark spots form on the insides of my eyes.

This is when it hits me: someone wants to harm me. *Oh, God, oh, God.* Boiling-hot panic courses through me. Someone is trying to kill me and they can't, they absolutely can't because I've got two young children. After a few seconds I come down from the wave of high-pitched terror and feel only numb disbelief.

I need water. I fumble for my car keys, realise I forgot to lock the damn thing and drop them back in my bag. Keeping my head turned so that I don't have to see the cat, I struggle to open the driver door. My arms and hands have no strength; it takes me three tries. Once I've done it, I look under the driver's seat and the front passenger seat for my bottle of water. It's not there. I'm about to slam the door when I notice it sitting upright on the passenger seat. I blink, half expecting it to disappear. Thankfully it doesn't. Standing with my head tilted back, I pour what's left of the water into my mouth, glugging it down, spilling some on my neck and shirt. Then I lock up the car and, without looking back at the cat, start to run towards the centre of town.

Brown parcel tape over its mouth. A warning to me to say nothing. What else could it mean?

I run until I get to Mario's, Spilling's only remaining cheap and cheerful café. Its owner, who has two-tone black and white hair like a skunk, sings opera arias at the top of her voice all day long and thinks she's being 'a character'. Usually this makes me want to demand a discount, but today I'm grateful for her tuneless outpourings. I force a smile in her direction as I walk in, order a can of Coke so that she'll leave me alone, and find a table that's not visible from the street.

First things first: phone nursery to check Zoe and Jake are all right. I am barely able to sit still as I listen to the ringing. Eventually one of the girls answers and tells me my children are fine—why wouldn't they be? I almost ask her to check the street outside for dead cats, but I manage to restrain myself.

I'm not scared of you, you bastard.

I open my Coke and take several big gulps that fill my stomach with uncomfortable air. Then I pull two pages out of my notebook and start to write another letter to the police. I write quickly, automatically, without allowing myself to stop and think. I've got to get it all down on paper before the dizziness at the edges of my mind gets any worse. I grip the edge of the table, a pins and needles sensation prickling the skin all over my body. I really ought to eat something. Instead, I write and write, everything I think the police need to know, until I can no longer ignore the twitching in my throat. I'm going to be sick. I grab my letter and my bag and run to the ladies' toilet, where all the Coke I've drunk comes back up. Once my stomach is empty, I close the toilet lid, sit down and lean my head against the partition wall. It occurs to me that I could collect Zoe and Jake early today. I'm not working; I could go and collect them now.

My letter isn't finished. I wanted to write more, but I can't remember what. Strange, dark shapes move in front of my eyes, blurring my vision. I open my bag and pull out a white envelope that has been in there for at least a year. It's addressed to Crucial Trading, the carpet company. I was supposed to fill in a customer satisfaction questionnaire and return it to them. Nick and I spent seven thousand pounds on new wool carpets and leather and sisal rugs for our lovely old house, before we went mad and decided we needed to move next door to Monk Barn Primary School. This makes me cry. Then I realise I can't collect Zoe and Jake because my car tyres have been slashed, and cry harder.

I pull the uncompleted questionnaire out of the envelope, put my letter in, cross out Crucial Trading's name and address, and write 'POLICE' in capital letters. I can't manage any more than that one word. Stumbling back to my table, sweating, I admit to myself that I am seriously unwell. It must be the shock. I should pick up the kids and get home before I start to feel worse. 'I need a taxi,' I say to skunk-opera woman.

She eyes me with suspicion. 'Rank is outside health shop,' she says. 'You no eat?'

'Sally?' A deep, male voice comes from behind me. I turn and see Fergus Land, my next-door neighbour. He beams at me, jolly as ever, and I feel even weaker. 'I can give you a lift,' he says. 'Are you going home? Not working today?'

'No. Thanks,' I force myself to say. 'Thanks, but . . . I'd rather get a taxi.'

'Are you all right? Gosh, you're a bit off-colour. Been over-indulging? Celebration last night, was it?'

He looks so kind, so concerned. If he offered to drive me to nursery and then home in silence, I'd gladly accept, but I can't face the prospect of making conversation.

'Did you tell Nick I've got his driver's licence? He hasn't—'

'Fergus.' I grab his hand and press the envelope into it. 'Will you do me a favour? It's important. Post this for me. Don't say anything to Nick, or anyone, and don't read it. Just post it. Please?'

'The police?' He says it in a loud whisper, as if they're a con-troversial secret society, unmentionable in polite company.

'I can't explain now. Please,' I say, on my way out of the door.

'Sally, I'm not sure. I . . .'

I run out on to the street, thinking that if I can only get to Nick's work, everything will be all right. I need to speak to him. I need to tell him someone is leaving headless animals next to my car. I walk as quickly as I can to the taxi rank outside the health food shop, looking behind me every few seconds to check

I'm not being followed, and pretending I can't hear Fergus, who is standing outside Mario's shouting, 'Sally! Sally, come back!'

I stagger along the pavement. My legs feel as if they're made of wool. No red Alfa Romeo that I can see. Other red cars, though—their brightness hurts my eyes. And one green VW Golf that's driving behind me, just an inch or two behind. In the pedestrianised, access-only part of the street. I stop walking, turn back towards Mario's. Fergus has gone.

The green VW stops and the driver door opens. 'Sally.' I hear relief. 'Are you okay?'

It's as if I'm looking at him through running water, but I'm still sure: it's the man from Seddon Hall.

'Mark,' I say faintly. The street spins.

'Sally, you look terrible. Get in.'

He hasn't changed at all. His face is round and unlined, a mischievous schoolboy's face. Like Tintin. Worried, though.

'Sally, you're . . . I've got to talk to you. You're in danger.'

'You're not Mark Bretherick.' I blink to straighten out my vision, but it doesn't work. Everything's wobbly.

'Look, we can't talk now, like this. What's the matter? Are you ill?'

He gets out of the car. The scene in front of me is going grey around the edges; all the shops are shaking, distorted. I'm vaguely aware—as if it's a dream I'm watching through a gauze veil, someone else's dream—of looking up at Mark Bretherick, of his arms supporting me. Not the real Mark Bretherick. My Mark Bretherick. I've got to get away from him. I can't move. It must be him—the cat, the bus, everything. It must be.

'Sally?' he says, stroking the side of my face. 'Sally, can you hear me? Who was the man shouting your name outside the café? Who was he?'

I try to answer, but nobody's there any more. Nobody's anywhere apart from me, and I'm only in my head, which is getting smaller and smaller. I let the nothingness pull me down.

Police Exhibit Ref: VN8723
Case Ref: VN87
OIC: Sergeant Samuel Kombothekra

GERALDINE BRETHERICK'S DIARY, EXTRACT 4 OF 9
(taken from hard disk of Toshiba laptop computer at Corn
Mill House, Castle Park, Spilling, RY29 0LE)

29 April 2006, 11 p.m.

On the news tonight there was an item about two little
boys in Rwanda. Their parents had been murdered by an
enemy tribe a few years ago. The boys were only seven or
eight years old but had worked for years in a mine, doing
heavy manual work in order to survive. Unlike us pam-
pered Westerners, they had no days off. They were on the
news because finally (perhaps thanks to some charitable
initiative—I missed some of the report because Mum
phoned) they are able to stop working and go to a new
school that has opened nearby. The BBC reporter asked
them how they felt about this new phase of their lives and
they both said they were delighted; both are eager to learn
and grateful for an opportunity they thought they'd never
have.

While Mark mumbled next to me—all the predictable
responses: how sad, how shocking, how moving—I
thought to myself, Yes, but look how civilised and mature
they are. We should pity them, of course, but we should
also admire what they have become: two wise, polite, sensitive, substantial young men. You only had to look at
them to see what a pleasure they would be to teach, that
they would give nobody any trouble. It was hard not to
marvel at the vast gulf between these two lovely, respectful
boys and the two children with whom I'd spent the afternoon: my own daughter and Oonagh O'Hara. If ever two

people would benefit from a few weeks' forced labour in a Rwandan mine... well, I know it's a terrible thing to think, but I *do* think it so I'm not going to pretend I don't.

So, this afternoon, a Saturday. Cordy and I are at Cordy's house, trying to persuade our children to eat. Sausages and chips, their favourite. Except Oonagh won't eat hers because there is some ketchup on a chip, and Lucy won't eat hers because the sausages are mixed in with the chips instead of on separate sides of the plate. By the time the complex negotiations have been concluded and all the necessary amendments have been made, the food is cold. Oonagh whines, 'We can't eat our food now, Mummy. Stupid! It's cold.'

Cordy was evidently hurt, but she said nothing. Her idea of discipline is Sweetie-come-for-a-cuddle. If Oonagh called the Queen of England a scabby tart, Cordy would praise her democratic slant of mind and her confident colloquialism.

She threw away the sausages and chips and made more. I counted what, of the second batch, was eaten: four small cylinders of sausage, eight chips. Between two of them. If those two dignified Rwandan boys had been presented with the exact same spread, they would have cleared their plates and then offered to load the dishwasher—no question about it.

Later, while Cordy was upstairs trying to introduce the concept of sharing into a squabble over dressing-up clothes and Oonagh's reluctance to let Lucy wear any of her pink frilly dresses, I decided a punishment was necessary. No child should get away with calling her mother stupid. I crept into the lounge and took Oonagh's *Annie* DVD out of its case. Love of *Annie* has spread like a forest fire through the girls in Lucy's class. It makes me sick the way they've all latched on to it, as if there's cause for any of them to identify with children who have a genuinely hard time rotting in an orphanage. The craze started with Lucy, I'm ashamed to say. It's Mum's fault. She's the one who bought Lucy the DVD. I thought it would be appropriate for me to confiscate Oonagh's copy, then quickly decided that removing it wasn't enough: I wanted to destroy it.

(In the end I brought it back home, locked myself in the bathroom and attacked it with the small knife I use to chop garlic. I suffered a mild pang of guilt when it occurred to me that I was destroying Miss Hannigan—the only character in the film that I like and admire—and I sang her song under my breath as a tribute, the one about how much she hates little girls. The lyrics are the work of a genius, especially the rhyme of "little" with "acquittal". I'm sure I'm not typical or representative, but I would certainly acquit Miss Hannigan if she wrang those orphans' necks. Every time I sit through the film with Lucy, I pray that this time the orphanage will catch fire and all those whiny-voiced brats will be burned to a crisp.

I nearly stole Cordy's *Seinfeld* DVD collection and destroyed that too when she told me she was pregnant. 'It was a total accident, but we're really pleased,' she said. She's only had this new boyfriend for a few weeks. She and Dermot are still living in the same house, though in separate beds. Last I heard they were trying to work things out.

I smiled furiously. 'We?' I said. 'You mean you and Dermot, or you and your new man? Or all three of you?'

Her face crumpled. 'It was an accident,' she said in a forlorn tone.

Accident! How was it an accident, exactly? I felt like asking. Did a member of a local archery society fire an arrow that travelled from a distance to pierce New Boyfriend's condom? Did a bird of prey swoop down and use its sharp beak to extract Cordy's diaphragm when she wasn't looking? Of course not. If you choose to use no contraception and you get pregnant, that's not an accident: it's trying very hard to get pregnant in a way that you hope will 'out-casual' the enormity of pregnancy and the possibility of failure.

Let me tell you, I nearly said, what not wanting to have another child means: it means using extra-safe Durex every single time, no exceptions, and still, in spite of the condoms, sneaking to the chemist after each fuck to buy the morning-after pill—at twenty-five pounds a time, I might add—as an extra insurance policy. I've never told anyone and I probably never will (unless one day I feel like worrying Mum a bit more than usual) but I think I'm hooked on Levonelle the way some people are hooked on painkillers. My hormones must be well and truly frazzled, but I don't care; call it my sacrifice for the greater good that is childlessness.

It isn't only about avoiding pregnancy, since Gart knows I subject each condom to a rigorous examination before I allow it anywhere near me. I know I don't need the Levonelle. I also know I could go on the pill for free and save a fortune, but that wouldn't be as satisfying, wouldn't scratch the right psychological itch. The paying of the twenty-five pounds is important to me, as is the ritual of lying to pharmacist after pharmacist about when I last took Levonelle, nodding solemnly through their earnest speeches about nausea and other possible side-effects. Every time I hand over the money, I feel as if I'm paying my subscription to the only club in the world that I'm interested in belonging to.

I've often thought I ought to volunteer (not that I've got the time) to counsel infertile women. Their misery, from what I've seen, certainly seems genuine, and it occurs to no one to give them anything but sympathy by way of emotional support. Give me an hour or two and I could persuade them of how lucky they are. Has anyone ever told them, for example, that for a mother to be with her child or children in the company of child-free women is the worst kind of torture? It's like being at the best party in the world, but being forced to stand on a chair in the middle of the room with a noose round your neck and your hands tied behind your back. Around you everyone is sipping champagne and having a raucous (wild?) old time. You can see their fun, smell it, taste it, and you can even try to have a bit of fun yourself as long as you make sure not to lose your balance. As long as no one knocks your chair.

8

8/8/07

Simon was halfway up a narrow winding staircase, wondering
how it could have been designed for use by human beings, when
he found himself face to face with Professor Keith Harbard.

'Simon Waterhouse!' Harbard beamed. 'Don't tell me you're
Jon's dinner date. He kept that quiet.' In the dim, stone-walled
stairwell, the professor's breath filled the air with the thick, tight
smell of red wine.

There wasn't a lot Simon could say. The munchkin staircase
led nowhere apart from to Professor Jonathan Hey's rooms.

Harbard's mouth made a chomping motion as he considered
the implications. 'You're consulting Jonathan?'

'There's a couple of things I want to ask him.' 'I', not 'we';
Simon avoided a direct lie. He couldn't ask Harbard not to mention his presence here to Kombothekra or Proust. *Shit*. At least
he hadn't phoned in sick. Charlie's response to his marriage
proposal had cut through his illusions about what he could get
away with. If she'd said yes, he would be feeling as invincible
today as he had yesterday. As it was, he'd woken up this morning in a chastened frame of mind, determined to take no
chances. He'd phoned Professor Hey and asked if he could come
to Cambridge later than planned, after the end of his shift. Hey
had said, 'Call me Jonathan,' then added, after a small cough,
'Sorry. You don't have to. You might rather call me Professor
Hey. I mean, you can call me Jonathan if you want to.' This was

too confusing for Simon, who had resolved on the spot to avoid saying the man's name at all.

Hey had invited Simon to stay for dinner at Whewell College after their meeting. For some reason, Simon had felt unable to decline. He was dreading it; his mother had done him no favours, he knew, by insisting for years that mealtimes should be private, family only. That Hey knew nothing of Simon's hang-up would make it easier, he hoped.

'Funny little college, this.' Harbard put out his hands to touch the stone walls on either side of him. He looked as if he was getting into position to kick Simon down the steps. 'It's like the land that time forgot compared to UCL. Still, Jon seems to like it. It wouldn't suit me. I'm a London boy through and through. And the sort of work Jon and I do . . . well, I wouldn't want to be tucked away in an enclave of privilege. That's the trouble with Cambridge—'

'I'd better get on,' Simon interrupted him. 'I don't want to be late.'

Harbard made a show of looking at his watch. 'Sure thing,' he said. 'Well, I guess I'll see you around.' Simon didn't like the professor's transatlantic accent any more than he liked his way of ordering a drink: 'Can I get a glass of Australian red? And, actually, can I also get a glass of sparkling mineral water? With ice?' If Simon had been the barmaid at the Brown Cow, he'd have taken Harbard at his word and pointed him in the direction of the freezer.

When he could no longer hear the professor's heavy footsteps, Simon stopped and pulled out his mobile. He'd been meaning to phone Mark Bretherick, before Charlie's unexpected fury had made him regret everything, even the things he hadn't done. Sod it; he'd do it. He was going to get it in the neck anyway, now that Harbard had seen him, so he might as well do what he believed to be the right thing.

Bretherick answered after the second ring, said, 'Hello?' as if he'd been holding his breath for hours.

'It's DC Waterhouse.'

'Have you found her?'

Simon felt something uncomfortable lodge in his chest, something that was the wrong shape for the space it was trying to occupy. To say no would be misleading; Bretherick would assume the police were actively looking for the woman he insisted had stolen photographs of Geraldine and Lucy from Corn Mill House. Simon wasn't convinced she existed, and was beginning to wonder about the missing brown suit. 'Your wife's diary,' he said. 'You asked about showing it to your mother-in-law. What did you decide?'

'I keep changing my mind.'

'Let her read it,' said Simon. 'As soon as possible.'

Bretherick cleared his throat. 'It'll kill her.'

'It hasn't killed you.'

A flat laugh. 'Are you sure?'

'Show Geraldine's mother the diary.' Simon was shocked to hear himself. An elderly woman would be devastated, and possibly nothing would come of it.

He and Bretherick exchanged curt goodbyes, and he climbed the remaining stairs to Jonathan Hey's rooms. The white outer door, with Hey's name painted on it in black, was open, as was the wooden inner door. Music drifted out to the stone staircase. Country and western: a woman's voice with a Southern twang. The song was about someone waiting for her man who was a riverboat gambler, who promised to return and then didn't. Simon gritted his teeth. Did all sociology professors feel the need to pretend to be American? Hey's accent, on the telephone, had been well-to-do home-counties English; how could someone from Hampshire or Surrey listen to songs about the Bayou and the Mighty Mississippi without feeling like a twat?

Simon knocked on the door. 'Come in,' Hey called out. Mercifully, he switched off the forlorn American woman. Simon walked into a large, high-ceilinged room with white walls and a threadbare beige carpet, much of which was covered by a red and black patterned rug. The pattern reminded Simon of faces, specifically, the faces of the constantly moving target creatures in 'Space Invaders', the first and only computer game he'd ever played. On one side of the room there was a wine-coloured three-piece suite, and on the other a white table with a wooden top surrounded by six white chairs with flat wooden seats.

There was no sign of Hey, though his voice was representing him in his absence. 'Be with you in a sec!' he shouted. 'Have a seat!' Simon couldn't tell if Hey was in the kitchen or upstairs. Through one half-open door he could see an old-fashioned cooker with a stained top; it reminded him of the one in the student house he'd shared with four people he'd despised, all those years ago. Another door at the other end of the same wall opened on to the stairs.

Simon didn't sit. While he waited, he looked at Jonathan Hey's many glass-fronted bookcases. He read a few of the titles: *Folk Devils and Moral Panics. A Theory of Human Need. On Women. How to Observe Morals and Manners*. He saw names he'd never heard of, and felt disgusted by his own ignorance. Sexist that he was, he'd assumed sociologists were mainly male, but apparently not: some were called Harriet, Hannah, Rosa.

One whole shelf was dedicated to Hey's own publications. Simon skimmed the titles, which were variations on a theme; again and again, the words 'crime' and 'deviancy' cropped up. He looked to see if Hey had written any books specifically on the subject of what Harbard called family annihilation. He couldn't see any; perhaps the article he'd co-written with Harbard was the extent of his work on the topic.

There was a framed poster on one wall advertising the film *Apocalypse Now*. Next to it was another poster, a cartoon of a black woman wearing a headscarf and holding a baby, with the caption: 'The hand that rocks the cradle should also rock the boat'. The slogan irritated Simon, for reasons he couldn't be bothered to think about. There was nothing else on the walls apart from Hey's framed degree and PhD certificates and a truly repulsive painting that looked like an original, of an ugly adult's face wearing grotesque clown make-up beneath a white, lacy baby's bonnet.

'The picture.' Hey appeared in the room. He had a pleasant, plump face, and was about twenty years younger than Harbard. Simon noticed his clothes: a shirt and formal jacket with faded jeans and blue and grey trainers—an odd combination. 'It was supposed to be an investment, but the artist sank without trace. Who was it who wrote that poem about money talking? "I heard it once—it said goodbye." Do you know it?'

'No,' said Simon.

'Sorry, I'm wittering.' Hey extended his hand. 'Nice to meet you. Thanks for coming all this way.'

Simon told him it was no problem.

'I've been considering contacting you. I probably wouldn't have plucked up the courage, though, which would have been lazy and wrong of me.'

Simon prepared himself to receive unwanted information about Whewell College's intruder alarm system or choral scholars' cars being vandalised. A lot of civilians seemed to think that all police officers ought to make themselves available to deal with all crimes, irrespective of geography. Simon tried not to look bored in advance.

'I'm worried about this book Keith's writing,' said Hey, lowering himself into an armchair. Simon instantly changed his mind about the man. 'Keith Harbard. I know he's been working with you. He was here just before you, actually. I tried, yet again, to talk him out of it . . .'

'He's writing a book?' This was the first Simon had heard of it. 'About family annihilation killings?'

'He's planning to use the Brethericks as his main case study.'

'Mark Bretherick will do everything in his power to stop that from happening,' said Simon, hoping it was true.

Hey nodded. 'That's the trouble, for people like Keith and me. We're researching familicide, and we publish our research.

But the women whose husbands have killed their children before committing suicide don't want some academics coming along and writing about it. They see us as careerists, profiting from their misery.'

'I don't blame them,' said Simon.

Hey sat forward. 'I don't either,' he said, 'but that doesn't mean I'm going to stop working on the topic. Familicide's a terrible crime, one of the worst human beings have managed to come up with. It's important that people think about it.'

'Especially if those people get promoted as a result?'

'I was a professor long before I first took an interest in family killings. There's no more promotion for me. I work on familicide because I want to understand it, because I would like it never to happen again. All my writing on the subject is in pursuit of that sole aim.'

Simon couldn't help but be impressed by Hey's seriousness. 'All right. So you're not in it for careerist reasons. Same true of Harbard?'

Hey's face changed. He looked as if a part of his body had started to hurt. 'Keith's been a mentor to me my whole career. He was the external examiner for my PhD, my referee for this job. He took me under his wing from the start. I know he can be a bit full of himself—'

'You're defending him,' Simon pointed out. 'I didn't attack him.'

Hey sighed. 'No, but I'm about to. Much as I hate doing it.' He hesitated. Simon tried not to look too attentive, a tactic that either worked well or not at all. 'I'm worried he's out of control.'

'Out of control?' It wasn't what Simon had been expecting. He saw Harbard as a man who managed his own career with a cool, clear head, more effectively than any PR could.

'Can I get you a drink, before I launch in?' said Hey. 'Sorry, should have offered ages ago.'

Simon shook his head.

'I'd really hate for Keith to find out I'd . . . voiced any reservations. Can you make sure it doesn't get back to him?'

'I can try.'

'He's a lovely guy. I wouldn't say he's a close friend, but—'

'Why not?' Simon interrupted.

'Sorry?'

'You say you've known him your whole career, he's been your mentor—I assumed you were good friends.'

'It's always been more of a professional relationship. We don't socialise. Although . . . well, sometimes Keith talks to me about his personal life.' Hey looked slightly embarrassed. 'Quite often, I suppose.'

'But he never asks you about yours?'

Hey's guilty smile told Simon he'd guessed correctly. 'He knows the title of every book and article I've ever written, but he occasionally forgets *my* name—calls me Joshua. I doubt he has a clue that I'm married and soon to be a father of two.'

'Twins?' Simon felt obliged to ask, aware once again of the deadened space inside him where his feelings ought to be. Would he ever have a child? It was looking increasingly unlikely.

'No, no.' Hey laughed. 'Thank goodness. No, one already hatched, the second a work in progress.'

'Congratulations.'

'Don't.' Hey raised his hand to stop Simon. 'Sorry. I'm a bit superstitious. Accepting congratulations before I know everything's going to be okay, you know? There's still a long way to go. Do you believe in the idea of tempting fate?'

Simon did. He believed someone had tempted fate—on his behalf and beyond all endurance—before he was born. That would explain his life so far.

'I feel as if I'm to blame,' said Hey. 'I was the one who got Keith interested in familicide in the first place. Did he tell you that?'

'No.' Simon resisted the ignoble urge to tell Hey that Harbard had not once mentioned his name.

'I used to work more on the relationship between the criminal and society, on the social rehabilitation of criminals, attitudes to reoffending, that sort of thing. There was this one guy, Billy Cass, who I used to visit in prison a lot. You get quite close to these people, through the work. Well, you must find the same thing in your job.'

Simon said nothing. He'd never been close to a scrote in his life apart from physically, geographically. That was bad enough.

'Prisons, I should say. Billy was in and out, in and out. He's out at the moment but he'll be in again soon. That's life as far as he's concerned. He doesn't even mind it.'

Simon nodded. He was familiar with the type. Billy, he thought. William. But the surname was Cass, not Markes.

'One of the prisons he was in, there was a man they all victimised—beat him, tortured him. The guards as well. The man was in for killing his three daughters. His wife had left him, left all of them, and he wanted revenge. He killed his own children, then tried to kill himself and failed. Imagine that.' Hey paused, watching Simon to check he hadn't underestimated the seriousness of the father's actions. 'You can't imagine it,' he said. 'This man wasn't like Billy, he didn't like being in prison, didn't like being anywhere. He'd wanted to die, really wanted to, but he'd botched it. Over and over he tried to kill himself in prison—knives, ligatures, the works. He even tried bashing his head repeatedly against the wall of his cell. The guards would happily have let him get on with it, except there was a new initiative. They'd been told their suicide figures were too high. It became a way of torturing him: saving his life.' Hey frowned, stared down at his feet. 'I'd never heard anything so horrific. That was when I knew I had to do something about it.'

Simon frowned. 'You don't honestly think you and Harbard writing your books and articles is going to stop things like this from happening? Or make it easier for those who are left behind?'

'I can't bring people back from the dead, obviously,' said Hey. 'But I *can* try to understand, and understanding always helps, doesn't it?'

Simon was doubtful. Would he feel better if he understood why Charlie, in response to his suggestion that they get married, had burst into tears, screamed obscenities at him and thrown him out of her house? Eternal confusion might be preferable; some things were too hard to face up to.

'Anyway, whether you approve or not,' said Hey, with a small, apologetic shrug. 'Keith and I decided to devote ourselves, research-wise, to familicide. That was four years ago. At this moment in time, we're two of a handful of experts on the subject in the UK. From what I know about Geraldine and Lucy Bretherick's deaths, they don't fit in with any family annihilation model that we've come across in our research. Not at all.'

'What?' Simon's hand was in his jacket pocket, fumbling for his notebook and pen. 'You're saying you don't think Geraldine Bretherick was responsible for the two deaths?'

'No,' said Hey unequivocally.

'Harbard disagrees,' Simon pointed out.

'I know.' For a second, Hey looked stricken. 'I can't talk sense into him, however hard I try. He's going to write a misleading, entirely wrong-headed book, and it's all my fault.'

'How?'

Hey rubbed his face with his hands, as if he was washing. 'Familicide's not like murder, that's the first thing you need to understand. People commit murder for a variety of reasons—it's a crime with an extensive motive pool. Whereas you'd be surprised to discover how few prototypes there are for family-annihilation killings. Few enough for me to run through them all before dinner.' Hey glanced at his watch. 'First off, there are the men who kill their *entire* families—wives, children, themselves—because they're facing financial ruin. They can't cope with the shame, the sense of failure, the disappointment and disgrace they imagine their families will feel. So they choose death as the better option. These are men who have always been perceived as—and indeed, have *been*—loving, caring fathers and husbands. They can't go on—the inevitable alterations to their self-image would be too painful—and they can't envisage a life for the family with them gone. They view the murders as their final act of care and protection, if you like.'

'They're usually middle-class?'

'Right. Middle, upper-middle. Good guess.'

'It wasn't. I read it in your article, yours and Harbard's.'

'Oh, right.' Hey looked surprised but pleased. 'Okay, second model: the men like Billy's prison colleague, who kill their children to take revenge on former partners who've left them, wives who are planning to leave them or have been unfaithful. These instances of familicide usually come from the opposite end of the social spectrum—men with low incomes, manual jobs if they've got jobs at all.'

'You make it sound as if there are plenty of cases to choose from. It must be an incredibly rare crime.'

'One familicide in the UK every six weeks. Not as rare as you might think.' Hey paced the floor, from one end of his Space Invader rug to the other. 'The second prototype—the vindictive, vengeful family annihilator—sometimes he kills the woman too. The kids and the wife or partner. It varies. Depends on whether he thinks killing her would be a better revenge than leaving her alive once her children are dead. If there's another man involved, he might not want his rival to get his hands on the woman that he regards as his property, just as he doesn't want his children to end up calling another man "Dad". Sometimes he wants to end his wife or girlfriend's bloodline: he doesn't want anything of her to live on, which is why he has to kill the children too, his own children.'

'You keep saying "he". Are family . . . annihilators always men?' Simon asked.

'Almost always.' Hey perched on the arm of his sofa. 'When women do it—traditionally—it's for different reasons. Women don't kill their children to avoid facing bankruptcy; as far as we know, that's never happened, not once. And the revenge-motivated familicide is male, not female. Simple reason: even in our supposedly equal modern society, children are still seen as belonging more to the woman than the man. He kills them as a way of destroying something that's hers. Very few women would see their children as belonging more to their husbands than to themselves, so they wouldn't be destroying his treasured possessions—only their own. See what I mean?'

'So when women do it, what's their motive?' asked Simon. 'Depression?'

Hey nodded. 'Keith's told me about the diary Geraldine Bretherick left, and, granted, it sounds as if she was seriously dissatisfied. I'm not sure if she was depressed. But she wasn't delusional, and most mothers who kill their children are. They tend to have a *history* of depression dating back to childhood, linked, often, to disastrous family backgrounds and a total lack of support networks.'

'What kind of delusions?' asked Simon. He was wondering about William Markes, a man no one had been able to find.

'All kinds. Some believe that they and their children are suffering from terminal illnesses,' said Hey. 'Murder and suicide are their escape routes, to avoid prolonged suffering. They're not ill at all, of course, but they're absolutely convinced they are. Or else the women are suicidal, and feel so protective of their children, so attached to them, that they can't kill themselves and leave the children alive: that feels too much like abandonment.'

Simon wrote all this down.

'I haven't seen Geraldine Bretherick's diary, but Keith's described it to me and shown me passages from it. It's full of complaints about her daughter, right?'

'Pretty much,' said Simon.

'The women who kill their children and then commit suicide, they don't express negative feelings about their children beforehand. Love is their motivation, albeit a twisted love. Not resentment. At least, that's true of every case I've ever heard of.'

'So . . .' Simon tapped his pen against his leg, thinking. 'Harbard should know all this. Yet he's convinced Geraldine Bretherick—'

'He's convinced because he wants to be.' Hey's pained expression had returned. 'It's my fault.'

'How so?'

'There was a case a while ago, in Kenilworth, Warwickshire—a man whose business empire was falling apart. He owed millions. Meanwhile his wife and four teenage kids had no idea there was a problem, and were busy splashing out on credit cards, booking holidays, buying cars, taking their wealth and privilege for granted. The wife didn't work, she didn't think she had to. She thought she had a rich husband.'

'He killed them all?' Simon guessed.

'Stabbed them in their beds while they were sleeping, then hanged himself. His sense of identity collapsed when he was forced to confront his inability to provide for his family. Keith and I were talking about it one night, I'd had a bit to drink . . . I said it was more and more common for the woman to be the main breadwinner. Not only the breadwinner, but the one who administrates the family finances. I wondered aloud—and, believe me, I wish I hadn't—if one day we would start to hear about cases of women who killed their husbands and children for the same reason.'

'Do you think that's likely?' asked Simon.

'No!' Hey looked cornered, bewildered. 'I don't. If it was going to happen, it would be happening already. That's my hunch. I was just . . . idly speculating. But Keith's eyes lit up. He said he was sure I was right—it *would* start to happen. He seemed . . . I almost had the impression he *wanted* it to happen. No, that's a terrible thing to say, of course he didn't. But I could tell he'd latched on to the idea. Women have always borne the burden of domestic responsibility pretty much single-handedly, he said.

Which is true, even in our so-called enlightened society. Women take responsibility for the home and the kids, and often view their husband as an extra child, someone else to be looked after. Men used to be the ones who brought in the money, but even that's changing. Women are keen to work outside the home now, which means men get to have it even easier. More and more of us marry women who earn more than we do—' Hey stopped suddenly. 'Are you married?' he asked.

'No.' The word rang in Simon's ears.

'Girlfriend?'

'Yes.' Another 'no' would have been too difficult.

'Does she earn more or less than you?'

'More,' said Simon. 'She's a sergeant.'

'My wife used to earn more than I did. Embarrassingly more—my salary was pocket money.' Hey smiled. 'I didn't care, from a macho point of view. Do you?'

'No.' Simon did. Only a little, but he did.

'It often changes once you've had children. Now I'm the sole breadwinner.' Hey sounded as if he felt guilty. 'Anyway, naturally women are more nurturing and more protective than men. They shoulder burdens rather than delegate them to their husbands or partners. Often they assume a man wouldn't be able to cope in the way that they can. Plus, they want to make everyone happy, even if it's at their own expense—you know, the martyr mentality. The "have-the-men-had-enough?" mentality.'

Simon had no idea what Hey was talking about.

'Whereas men—again, huge generalisation—men tend only to care about making themselves happy. We're undeniably more selfish.'

'Apart from the men who are so distressed about not being able to provide for their families that they kill them,' Simon reminded him.

'Ah, but it's their own egos they really care about. Not their wives and children. Obviously, because they murder them. And that's why, ultimately, I don't think women *will* start to commit familicide in the same numbers as men. Women care more about their families than about preserving their own vanity.'

'You have a low opinion of men,' said Simon, both admiring and resenting Hey's honesty.

'Some of us are all right. You see, this is my point.' Hey smiled sheepishly. 'I think aloud, and it causes trouble. All I said to Keith was that I wondered if, eventually, we'd start to come across cases of *women* whose business empires collapsed and who, rather than admit that they'd failed to look after their families properly . . .' He chewed the inside of his lip. 'Two weeks later, Keith had dashed off an article predicting more familicides committed by women for financial reasons.'

'And then Geraldine and Lucy Bretherick were found dead.' Simon stood up, couldn't keep his body still when his mind was all over the place. 'You're saying Harbard's using our case. He wants Geraldine Bretherick to have proved him right.'

Hey nodded. Patches of red had appeared on his cheeks. 'I don't think she has,' he said. 'Geraldine Bretherick was a full-time mother and home-maker. She had no financial responsibilities, and she had the security of knowing that her husband was rich and likely to become richer. So that's prototype one down the pan. And the vengeful, vindictive model: Keith says there's no evidence Mark Bretherick was planning to leave her, or had another woman?'

'None,' said Simon.

Hey held up his hands. 'I just don't see it. I keep telling Keith that none of the predictions he made in his article are borne out by this case, not a single one, but he keeps insisting he was right: he predicted more women would kill their children and now Geraldine Bretherick has. That's what he says; he seems determined to ignore the specifics. It's as if all the detail we've gone into, all those years of both our lives, have just been wiped out!'

Simon looked up from his notes.

'Sorry,' Hey muttered. 'Look, it's not my career I'm thinking about. I feel responsible. I'm one of the few people in the country who know as much about this topic as Keith does. Now that I've told you my opinion . . . well, at least the police know there's another point of view.'

'You've been very helpful,' said Simon.

Hey looked at his watch. 'We'd better start heading down to dinner.'

Simon had no appetite. 'I might give it a miss, if you don't mind,' he said. 'I've had a tiring day and tomorrow's going to be another one. I ought to start driving back.'

'Oh.' Hey sounded disappointed. 'Well, if you're sure. We don't have to talk about this sort of thing. I mean, I don't want you to think my conversation's limited to—'

'It's not that,' said Simon. 'Really, I should get back to Spilling.'

Hey showed him to the door. 'If Geraldine didn't do it . . .' he said. 'Sorry, I'm thinking aloud again.'

Simon paused at the top of the stone staircase. 'We're short on suspects. That's why, from our end, everyone's lapping up Harbard and his theories.'

'The husband?' asked Hey.

'Alibi,' Simon told him. 'And no motive. They were happy. Bretherick had no one waiting in the wings.'

'I have to say this.' Hey frowned. 'It would worry me if I let you leave without having said it. When men do murder their wives . . . well, in the majority of cases the wives don't work or have any status outside the home. It's much rarer for a husband or partner to kill a woman he regards as his equal. Valued by people other than himself.'

Simon mulled this over as he walked back to his car. It was enough to make pregnant professional women give birth at board meetings, he thought. Geraldine Bretherick had been valued by her friends, but had they loved her? Needed her? Cordy

O'Hara's life would go on without her. There was her mother, of course, but Simon had a feeling Hey would say that didn't count in this context.

Apart from Mark, perhaps even more than Mark, Lucy Bretherick must surely have been the person who most valued and needed Geraldine. Lucy, who was also dead.

When Charlie opened the door to her sister, the first thing she noticed was what looked like a large book in Olivia's hands, roughly the size and shape of the Spilling and Rawndesley telephone directory. Olivia held it up; it was a Laura Ashley catalogue, Spring/Summer 2007. 'Before you complain, their prices are very reasonable. You'd be surprised. I know what a skinflint you are, and you know I don't settle for second-best. Laura Ashley is perfect—affordable designer.'

Charlie waited for Liv to notice her red nose and puffy eyes, but Liv pushed past her into the hall. She stopped when she drew level with the radiator, eyeing the stained plaster all around her. 'I know the look I'd go for,' she said. 'I've given it a lot of thought, and picked out a few goodies, nice fabrics and stuff. Obviously it's your choice . . .'

'Liv. I don't give a shit about fabrics.'

'. . . but I'm *almost* going to insist on Allegra Gold wallpaper for the hall, with a basketweave nutmeg carpet. And for the lounge, a Burlington distressed leather three-piece suite. Laura Ashley's not all country-spinster chintz and flowers, you know. They've got some strong, solid stuff too. They do everything— literally everything—and the beauty of getting it all from one place is that they come and—'

Charlie pushed her sister aside and ran up the stairs. She slammed her bedroom door and leaned against it. *Spinster.* That was her, would always be her. She heard Liv huffing and puffing her way up the stairs; more exercise than she'd done in years, probably. Charlie walked over to the bare, curtainless window. She took hold of one end of the curtain rail and ripped it off the wall. There. Now Liv wouldn't be able to hang any Laura Ashley curtains from it.

'Char?' A small knock at the door. Olivia pretending not to want to intrude. 'Look, if you don't want me to interfere, why not take charge of the decorating yourself? You can't live with bare floorboards for ever.'

'It's fashionable,' Charlie told her. 'Carpet's out. Wooden floors are in.'

Olivia flung open the bedroom door. Her face matched her pink scoop-necked sweater. 'Properly sanded and polished ones, yes. Not ones that look like this. You haven't even got a bed!'

'I've got a mattress. King size.'

'You're living like . . . like someone who's plotting a terrorist atrocity in a squat! Do you remember the shoe bomber, that ugly git with long hair and a turnip nose who tried to blow up a plane? I bet his bedroom was nicer than yours!'

'Liv, I'm upset. That's why I asked you to come round. Not so that we could talk about floorboards. Or terrorists.'

'I *know* you're upset. You've been upset for over a year. I'm used to it.' Liv sighed. 'Look, I know why you gutted the house, and I understand that you can't be bothered to sort it out. I'm happy to project-manage it all for you. I honestly think you'd feel better if you—'

'No, I wouldn't!' Charlie yelled. 'I wouldn't feel better if I had an Allegra Burlington to sit on, whatever the fuck that is! And this has got nothing to do with what happened last year—nothing! You think that's why I'm in a state?'

Olivia's eyes darted left and right, as if she'd been asked a trick question. 'Isn't it?'

'No! It's Simon. I love him, and he asked me to marry him, and I swore at him and threw him out.'

'Oh, right.' Olivia sounded deflated.

'Yeah, that's right. Boring, isn't it? Simon Waterhouse again.'

'But I thought . . . from what you said on the phone, you dealt with it. He proposed, you said no—'

'Of course I said no! This is Simon we're talking about! If I'd said yes, his feelings by now would be slightly more lukewarm than when he proposed. By the time we announced our engagement, he'd have gone off me a bit more. By our wedding day he'd be indifferent, and by the time we arrived at the honeymoon suite—hah!—I'd be all his nightmares and worst fears rolled into one.'

Olivia's eyes narrowed. 'I seem to be missing some vital components of this situation,' she said. 'Simon's never even taken you out for dinner. You've never so much as kissed!'

Charlie mumbled something non-committal. She had kissed Simon—at Sellers' fortieth birthday party, shortly before Simon had decided he wasn't interested after all and rejected her in the most humiliating and public way possible—but she'd never told Olivia. She couldn't, even now. She could hardly bear to think about that party.

'He's got a tragedy fetish,' she said. 'He feels sorry for me because of last year.'

'And because you've got a bedroom like the shoe bomber,' Olivia reminded her.

'It's not inconceivable that he loves me, is it? For all the wrong reasons.' Charlie's voice cracked. 'And if he does, and I say yes, then he'll stop. Not straight away, but he will.' She groaned.

'Char, you're . . . Please tell me you're not considering saying yes.'

'Of course not! What do you think I am, a headcase?'

'Good.' Olivia was satisfied. 'Then there's no problem.'

'Oh, forget it. You might as well go.'

'But I've brought some fabric swatches . . .'

'I've got an idea: why don't you stick your swatches up your arse and fuck off back to London?' Charlie stared at her sister, determined not to blink in case she lost the fight while her eyes were closed.

Olivia stared back. 'I'm not going anywhere until you've at least looked at the Villandry Duck Egg,' she said, her voice cool and dignified. 'It's woven velvet. Look at it, touch it. I'll leave it by the front door on my way out.'

What was Charlie supposed to say to that?

The phone rang, sparing her the effort of making a decision. 'Hello?' she said in a falsely cheerful voice.

'Charlie? It's Stacey Sellers, Colin Sellers' wife.'

'Oh.' *Fuck, fuck, fuck.* This could only mean one thing: Stacey had found out about Suki, Sellers' illicit shag, and wanted Charlie to confirm what she already knew. Charlie had dreaded this moment for years. 'I can't talk now, Stacey. I'm in the middle of something.'

'I was wondering if I could come round some time. Soon. I need to show you something.'

'Now's a really bad time, and I'm not sure when'll be better,' said Charlie. Rude, perhaps, but lying? No. 'Sorry.' She put the phone down and forgot about Stacey Sellers instantly. 'That was Laura Ashley,' she told Olivia. 'She wanted to pop round with some more swatches. She says you picked all the wrong ones.'

'Just wait till you've touched the Villandry Duck Egg. It's from heaven.'

'I was joking,' Charlie explained. 'Sorry if I jumped down your throat.'

'It's okay,' said Olivia, suspicious of her sister's attempt to appear reasonable when all the evidence suggested otherwise. 'Look, I understand, honestly I do. You'd like to be able to say yes to Simon, wouldn't you?'

'In an ideal world.' Charlie sighed. 'If just about every circumstance were different.'

The doorbell rang. Charlie closed her eyes. 'Stacey,' she said.

'Who?'

'How can she have got here so quickly?' She ran downstairs and threw open the door, preparing to repel all requests for information or advice. But it wasn't Stacey; it was Robbie Meakin. 'Oh,' she said. 'Aren't you supposed to be on paternity leave?'

'Had to cut it short,' said Meakin. 'It was doing my head in. Not being able to get away from the baby, not sleeping properly . . .'

'That'll teach you.' Charlie smiled. It was reassuring to know that other people's lives were as difficult as hers. 'You can't come and live here, I'm afraid.'

Meakin laughed. 'I'm really sorry to bother you this late,' he said. 'I thought you'd want to see this straight away. Someone hand-delivered it to the nick early this evening.' He passed Charlie a folded sheet of paper. It was small, covered in writing, and looked as if it had been torn out of a notebook.

'How is the baby, anyway?' she asked as she opened it up.

'Fine. Hungry all the time, crying all the time. Wife's nipples are like two giant scabs, caked in dried blood. Is that normal?'

'I wouldn't know. Sorry.'

'It's normal,' Olivia shouted from the top of the stairs. 'Tell her to give it time, it'll get better.'

'My sister,' Charlie mouthed at Meakin. 'She knows nothing.'

He grinned. 'Right, well, I'll be off. I thought I should get that to you as soon as possible. I heard you picked up the last one.'

'Last one?'

'Letter. About Geraldine and Lucy Bretherick. Didn't you?'

Charlie nodded. 'I'm not CID any more, Robbie.'

'I know, but . . . You know you're the only one who sent a card and present for the baby? Waterhouse didn't. Sellers and Gibbs didn't.'

'They're men, Robbie. Do you send cards?'

He flushed. 'I will from now on, Sarge.'

Charlie sighed and began to read. More interesting than she'd expected. A little hysterical, but interesting.

Suddenly she was impatient for Meakin to leave. She wanted to read the rest of the letter. She examined it with Simon's eyes, unable to respond independently of what she knew his response would be.

'I bought and sent that present,' said Olivia crossly, once Meakin had gone. 'And did I get a word of thanks?'

'Liv, bring me the phone.' Charlie held her hand out, still staring at the letter. She ignored the hearty sighs that arrived with the telephone, and rang the CID room. Proust answered after the first ring. 'Sir, it's me, Charlie. I've got another letter here about the Brethericks. It's anonymous again, but much more detailed than the first one. You need to see it.'

'What are you waiting for, Sergeant? Bring it in. And, Sergeant?'

'Sir?'

'Cancel whatever plans you've made for tonight.'

'I was planning to get a good night's sleep. My shift only finished at seven.'

'Cancel it. I need you here, helping me. Am I sleeping?'

'No, sir.'

'Exactly,' said Proust. He sounded pleased to have won the argument so decisively.

To whoever is investigating the deaths of Geraldine and Lucy Bretherick:

I wrote before, saying Mark Bretherick might not be who he says he is. I have just found a dead ginger cat by the wheel of my car with parcel tape over its mouth. Whoever left it also slashed the tyres. I believe I'm in danger—being warned off. Two days ago someone pushed me in front of a bus in the centre of Rawndesley, and yesterday a car followed me—a red Alfa Romeo, with a registration that began with a Y.

Last year, in a hotel, I met a man who told me he was Mark Bretherick. His real name might be William Markes. He might be the driver of the car that followed me.

I found pictures of a girl in a St Swithun's uniform and a woman hidden behind photos of Geraldine and Lucy in two wooden frames at Corn Mill House. They were in a bin-bag.

Mark Bretherick was going to throw them away. All four pictures were taken at the owl sanctuary at Silsford Castle. Jenny Naismith, the head's secretary at St Swithun's, has these two photographs. There was a girl in Lucy Bretherick's class last year called Amy Oliver—the pictures might be of her and her mother.

Speak to the woman who used to be Amy's nanny: her number is 07968 563881. You need to make sure Amy and her mother are still alive. And her father. Talk to anyone you can about the relationship between the Bretherick and Oliver families. Cordy O'Hara, the mother of Oonagh, who was best friends with Amy and Lucy, might know something. Talk to Sian Toms, a teaching assistant at St Swithun's. Look for more bodies in and around Corn Mill House—in the garden. When I went to Corn Mill House, Mark Bretherick was in the garden with a trowel in his hand. Why would he be gardening when his wife and daughter had just died? Search his business premises—anywhere he has access to. Ask him why he hid photographs of Mrs Oliver and Amy behind ones of his wife and daughter.

Jean Ormondroyd, Geraldine Bretherick's mother, was a small woman with a long neck and tiny shoulders. Her iron-grey hair was bobbed, and hung like curtains around her face, curling up at the edges. From her seat by the wall, Charlie could see only hair and from time to time the tip of a nose. Jean was looking at Proust and Sam Kombothekra, speaking only to them. No one had told her who Charlie was and she hadn't asked.

'I'd like you to tell the inspector what you told me, Jean,' said Sam. 'Don't worry about repeating yourself. That's what I want you to do.'

'Where's Mark?'

'He's with DC Sellers and DC Gibbs. He won't leave without you.'

Charlie hadn't needed to ask Sam how seriously the new information was being taken; Proust never sat in on interviews except in emergencies. If someone who wasn't Geraldine Bretherick had committed two murders at Corn Mill House on the first or second of August, they'd had six or seven days to cover their tracks, six or seven days of the police believing that the only murderer had made things easy for them by killing herself. Emergencies didn't come much more dire than that.

Jean addressed Proust. 'Mark showed me Geri's diary. I've been asking to see it since I first heard about it, and he finally showed it to me, thank goodness. That diary wasn't written by my daughter.'

'Tell Inspector Proust why you're so sure,' said Sam. Was he wondering why Charlie was there, why Proust had been so adamant about needing her? It can't be easy for Sam, she thought. He's trying to do my job, and I turn up to watch him do it.

'Lucy's night light,' said Jean. 'What the diary says—it's wrong. Lucy had a night light, yes, but it was a plug-in one, Winnie the Pooh. It went in the plug socket in her bedroom, next to her bed. It's about the size of a normal plug, but round instead of square.'

'The diary doesn't specify the sort of night light, does it?' Proust asked Sam.

'Let me finish,' said Geraldine's mother. Both men turned to face her. 'It says in the diary that Lucy wanted her door open because she was scared of monsters, the same reason she wanted it to be a bit light. It says that from that night, the first time she talked about being scared of monsters . . .' Jean stopped, took a few breaths. 'Every night after that, it says, Lucy slept with her door open and her night light on, but why would she have needed the door open? The night light was in her room.'

'We assumed the night light was outside Lucy's room, and the door was left ajar to let the light in,' said Sam.

'But didn't you see Lucy's Winnie the Pooh light? Didn't you find it?' Jean's voice was full of contempt.

'We did. Jean, there was no way we could have known Lucy had the light in her room and not, say, on the landing.'

'But didn't you plug it in? Didn't you see how dim it was? Just a faint gold glow. Night lights like that are designed to go in children's rooms. That's the whole point of them. You should have known.'

'I'm sorry,' said Sam. 'I didn't.'

'Someone should have known! How many detectives saw that light? Don't you have children? Don't they have night lights?'

How many detectives does it take to change a light bulb? Charlie mused.

Proust was looking at Sam, waiting for him to answer.

'My sons sleep with their bedroom doors open, and we leave the bathroom light on.'

'Mark didn't know either,' said Jean. It sounded like a concession. 'He'd heard Geri mention a night light, but he won't have known what sort, or where it was. Geri was always the one who put Lucy to bed and got up for her in the night.'

'Was Mark a good father, would you say?' asked Proust.

'Of course he was! He has to work all the time, that's what I meant. Like a lot of fathers. But it was Lucy's future he was working for. He adores that child.' Jean's head dipped. 'I still can't believe she's gone. My sweet Lucy.'

'I'm so sorry, Jean. And I'm sorry to have to put you through a second interview.'

'Don't be,' she said. 'You need to talk to someone who knows even more about Geri and Lucy than Mark does. And that's me. I can't believe you didn't show me the diary straight away. That's the first thing I'd have done, in your position. I could have helped you a lot sooner.'

'The decision wasn't—'

'I wasn't a part-time grandmother.' Jean Ormondroyd cut Sam off angrily. 'I spoke to Geri and Lucy on the phone every day. I knew every single detail of Lucy's life: what she ate for every meal, what she wore, who she played with. Geri told me everything. The night light was in Lucy's room, and the door had to be *closed*—Lucy insisted. That way the monsters couldn't get into her room from the dark bits of the house.' Jean looked at Charlie, dissatisfied with the reaction she was getting from Proust and Sam: solemn silence. Charlie smiled sympathetically.

'When Geri and Lucy came to stay the night at my house, which they often did if Mark was away on business, the Winnie the Pooh night light came too. And Lucy's door had to be shut; if we took too long to shut it, five seconds instead of two, she'd get panicky. We'd finish her bedtime story, kiss her goodnight and have to run to the door to close it before any monsters crept in.'

Proust leaned forward, rubbing the knuckle joints of his left hand with the fingers of his right. 'Are you telling me that Mark never put his daughter to bed? Not once? At weekends, on holiday? He didn't know she had a light in her room and that the door had to be closed?'

'He might have had a vague idea, but Geri was always the one who put Lucy to bed. If Mark was around, he'd do the bedtime story session downstairs. He'd always read her as many stories as she wanted. But bathtime and bedtime was Geri's responsibility. They had their routines, like most families.'

'Nevertheless,' said Proust. He pulled a small grey mobile phone out of his shirt pocket, glanced at it, then dropped it back in. 'I find it odd that he and Geraldine didn't discuss Lucy's fear of monsters and her need to have her door either open or shut.'

'They did,' said Jean. 'Mark told me on the way here: he knew there was a problem about monsters, and he knew Lucy had been fussy about the light and the door, but he didn't remember the specific details. He's a very busy man, and . . .

well, men don't remember those domestic details in the way women do.'

Charlie was beginning to admire Jean Ormondroyd, who was clearly determined not to cry. She wanted them to focus on the information she was here to give them, not on her feelings.

'It's not just the night light that's wrong,' she said. 'There are other things. Lucy had a DVD of *Annie* the musical, yes, but I didn't buy it for her. Geri did. And the conversations the diary describes between Geri and me—they never happened. I didn't buy her a mug with any book title on it—it didn't happen!'

Mug with a book title? Charlie would have to look at the diary; she hadn't a clue what Jean was talking about. I don't work here, she reminded herself. I don't have to understand.

'Jean, who do you think wrote the diary, if not Geri?' Sam asked.

'The man who killed her, obviously. I can't believe you need me to tell you. Haven't you worked it out yet? He made her write it, before he murdered her. And the suicide note. He made her write a diary that would make the police believe she was capable of doing such a terrible thing—which of course she wasn't! That's why Geri wrote things that weren't right, things he wouldn't know weren't right, as a way of signalling she wasn't doing it by choice, so that Mark and I would know.'

Charlie thought this sounded far-fetched. If Geraldine had wanted to signal to her husband and mother that she wasn't writing the diary of her own volition, would she really do it by changing the location of a night light? Or writing that Jean had bought Lucy the *Annie* DVD when she hadn't? Mark hadn't even known what sort of night light Lucy had. Had he known where the *Annie* DVD had come from? Doubtful. Geraldine could have planted an incorrect detail about his work if she'd wanted to be sure of alerting him to something being amiss.

'Jean, I need to ask you something else,' said Sam. 'Have you heard the name Amy Oliver before?'

'Yes. She was Lucy's friend at school, one of her two best friends. Of course I've heard of Amy.'

'How recently was Lucy in touch with her?'

'Not since Amy left St Swithun's, which was some time last year. Spring or summer. Amy moved away.'

'Do you know where she went?'

Jean shook her head. 'I was relieved, to be perfectly honest. So was Geri. She thought Amy was ... well, a bit unstable. Volatile. She often upset Lucy. They fought a lot, and Amy always ended up screaming and crying.'

'What did they fight about?' Sam asked.

Jean sighed. 'Lucy's ... Lucy was a real stickler for detail. She knew the difference between what was true and what wasn't.'

'Are you saying Amy used to tell lies?' asked Proust.

'All the time, according to Geri. And Lucy, who, bless her heart, couldn't stand to let things pass if they simply weren't right, she'd try to correct Amy. That's when the screaming would start. Amy lived in a fantasy world, by the sound of it, and she was over-sensitive. Not at all robust.' Jean made a dismissive noise. 'You know what little girls are like—it's the law of the jungle, isn't it? No good being a timid little mouse.'

'How did Oonagh O'Hara fit in?' Sam asked. Proust snorted quietly. Charlie knew there were many things in which the inspector had no interest whatsoever. Evidently the complex relationships that existed between primary school girls was one of them.

'That was another thing about Amy.' Jean pursed her lips. 'She wanted Oonagh to be her best friend, not Lucy's. She'd deliberately try to exclude Lucy, tell Oonagh secrets and make her promise not to tell.'

'What sort of secrets?' said Sam.

'Silly things, not even secrets. She wanted to make Lucy feel left out, that's all. She'd whisper to Oonagh, "My favourite colour's pink—don't tell Lucy." She used to say she was a princess, apparently. She was a princess and her mother was a queen. Geri said . . .' Jean's words tailed off.

'Go on,' Sam encouraged her.

'Geri said it was as if Amy wanted to . . . to punish Lucy for seeing through her, for insisting on pointing out the truth whenever she made up her silly stories.'

'Was Geraldine happy in her marriage?' asked Proust impatiently, as if to demonstrate the difference between a proper question and a pointless one. 'Did Mark treat her well? Did they love each other?'

'Why don't you ask Mark?' said Jean. 'It's unforgivable, if you're trying to make out he's guilty in some way. He's a wonderful person, and he worshipped Geri. He never raised his voice with her, not once in all the years they were together, and you're trying to find fault with him because you need to blame somebody and you can't think of anyone else.'

'Let's move on to the gloves,' said Sam. 'Jean, tell Inspector Proust—'

'You tell him. You've obviously told him already. Why do I have to say it again?'

'I'll hear it from you,' Proust barked, and the small woman shrank back in her chair. As someone who believed in the law of the jungle, thought Charlie, Jean Ormondroyd could hardly object.

'Geri had a pair of yellow rubber gloves in the drawer beneath the sink, for washing up the things that wouldn't go in the dishwasher. I used to say to her, why buy things that won't go in the dishwasher when it's just as easy to . . .' She stopped. 'The gloves aren't there any more. I was wanting to wash a few glasses, help Mark out, and the gloves had gone. Mark didn't even know they were there, so he hasn't touched them. They were always there.'

'Might Geri have thrown them away?' Sam asked.

'No. They were new ones. She'd keep a pair for ages before she'd replace them. The man who killed her wore them so as not to leave fingerprints.' She shuffled her chair forward across the floor. 'I'm not being fanciful, before you say I am. What other explanation could there be for any of this apart from what I'm saying? Well?'

Sam looked at Proust. Neither of them replied. Jean Ormondroyd's eyes came to rest on Charlie, her expression fierce and demanding. Had it occurred to her, Charlie wondered, that getting an answer—even the right one—might be worse than not knowing?

9

Thursday, 9 August 2007

I don't remember sleeping, falling asleep, but I must have, because I know I'm awake now. Awake in a room I don't recognise, long and thin with a low ceiling. I haven't seen it before, and this is the first time I've had this thought: that I don't recognise my surroundings. So I must have been asleep. My clothes are twisted, as if someone has twirled my body like a skipping rope. My skin feels sticky, especially my back and the backs of my legs. I stretch out my hands, pat the surface beneath me—material, thick and fleecy.

I try to sit up, to look around, but my head aches too much. Moving it sends streaks of fiery pain shooting down my neck and back. I lower it gently, inch by inch, until it touches the bed again, closing my eyes against the glare from the overhead light, which is already, after only a few blinks, making my brain throb just above the bridge of my nose.

My throat is so dry it's sore. Where am I? What the hell happened to me? I've had hangovers in my time, but never one as bad as this. And I haven't been drinking. Fear spreads quickly around the points of pain all over my body, submerging them the way an incoming tide fills the space around small islands. I can smell new paint and a heavy fruity smell that is familiar. I've smelled it recently, I'm sure.

The children. What time is it? I have to collect Zoe and Jake. This is more important even than knowing where I am. I picture their eager, bobbing heads at the nursery window, the leap of joy in their eyes when they see me, and yank my body into an upright position, not caring any more how much it hurts.

I look at my watch. The digital display reads 0010. *Ten past midnight—oh, my God.* My stomach and heart lurch in tandem, as if someone's tied a thick rope around them and pulled hard. That's when I remember: Mark. I fainted on the street, and he helped me. Not Mark, I correct myself. Mark Bretherick is somebody different.

'Mark,' I shout, because my voice is working more efficiently than my body. I know I can't move quickly enough.

I haul my heavy, tingly legs over the side of the bed and see that it's not a bed, it's some kind of high bench with white towels draped over it all the way along. 'Mark,' I yell again. What else am I supposed to call him? The door is open. Why can't he hear me? *Ten past midnight.* Nick will have got a phone call from nursery after I failed to turn up. By now he'll be frantic.

I need my phone. My bag is on the other side of the room, by the small convex window. I shuffle off the bench and try to stand up. *Why was I lying on white towels?* I wobble, try to perch on the bench again and fall. 'Ow!' I groan, face down on the stripy carpet. *Yellow, green, orange.* Dizzy, I manage to roll on to my back. I stare at the light, a transparent bulb inside a bell-shaped pink glass lampshade.

It comes to me suddenly: I'm in his house. Not-Mark's house. He brought me home.

I haul myself forward and up on to my knees. 'Mark! Mark, are you there?' I call out, but my voice has lost its power. My handbag might as well be a hundred miles away. A wave of nausea sweeps over me. I think about the ginger cat's head, the blood around its ragged neck, and have to put my hand over my mouth to stop myself from vomiting.

On all fours, I count to twenty and gulp in air until the sick feeling passes. There are balls of fluff on the carpet. Like on ours at home, after we replaced the red that was everywhere with a more soothing grey-green. This carpet is new. Yellow, green, rust, taupe. And orange, like the cat's head. Stripes. Chosen by a woman, surely.

'Sally?' He is here: the man I spent a week with last year. The man from my adventure. He smiles hesitantly before coming into the room, as if reluctant to trespass on my territory. His red-brown hair is wet, three small curls plastered to his forehead. I recognise the red sweater he's wearing; he wore it at Seddon Hall. *I don't buy that whole redheads-can't-wear-red philosophy*: that's what he said. He's holding a glass of water. 'Here, have a sip of this. You'll feel better.'

'My kids . . .' I start to say.

'It's okay.' He helps me to my feet, supports me when he sees that I'm about to fall. 'Nick picked them up from nursery. They're fine.'

I gulp the water. It's gone too quickly. I'm still thirsty. 'You . . .' *He spoke to Nick.* I close my eyes, see bursts of light that are quickly swallowed by blackness. 'Who are you?' I feel as if everything that's precious to me is slipping away. I can't let it go.

'You need to lie down,' he says. 'We'll talk later.' He picks me up, carries me towards the bench.

'I need to phone Nick,' I say. 'My head's pounding. I need something to eat.'

'I'll bring you some food. And a pillow too—that'll make you more comfortable.' He makes a strange noise, as if he's choking. 'Sally, how did you get in such a state? What happened to your face? What's . . . do you know what's wrong with you?'

'Who are you?' I ask again, terrified because I can't answer his question. I have no idea why I feel so bad, so weak. 'Bring me my phone. Now,' I say as firmly as I can.

'You need to rest . . .'

'I need to speak to my family!' Adrenalin sets my brain spinning. 'Who are you? Tell me! Did you leave a dead cat by my car?'

'Did I *what*? You're not making sense. Lie down. Take deep breaths.'

It's easy to let myself fall back. For once, the deep breaths seem to work. I feel more solid, more aware. Aware that I'm starving. I've got to get something inside my stomach soon or my brain will shut down completely.

'Lucy and Geraldine Bretherick,' I whisper. 'Dead.'

'I know,' he says.

'You're not Mark.'

'No.'

I open my eyes, but he is looking away. Embarrassed.

'You lied.'

He sighs. 'Sally, you're not strong enough to have this conversation now. Let me get you some food. Just lie here and rest, okay?'

'I need to talk to Nick.'

'After you've eaten.'

'No, I . . .' I try to sit up and nearly fall off the bench. He is walking towards the door, and has to run to catch me. My eyes are heavy and sore; I need to close them. I think a question in my mind: *Are you sure Nick said the children were all right?* I've used up my capacity for movement and speech. I'm being pulled away from myself. I struggle to stay in the room with the man who told me he was Mark Bretherick, but I'm too slow. My resistance breaks up, fades and flattens into calm.

From far away, I hear his voice. Soothing, like notes in a piece of music. 'Do you remember what you said to me at Seddon Hall? You were talking about how drained and used up you felt at the end of every day, days spent struggling to attend to your family's needs at the same time as giving a hundred and fifty per cent to your work, racing round like a maniac trying to pack it all in. Do you remember? And you said—it stuck in my mind—you said the hardest thing is being so exhausted you could collapse and at the same time having to pretend you're not tired at all. Having to pretend you're fine and cheerful and full of energy so that Nick doesn't give you a hard time.'

Did I tell him that? It's something I would normally only confide in my women friends, the ones with children. But it's true. I want to explain, but my voice won't start. Nick would worry if he knew how difficult I find my life, only because he cares about me. 'Why don't you go part-time?' he would say. 'Three days a week, or, even better, two.' He said that once after Zoe was born, before I'd learned I had to pretend to be zinging with energy right up until bedtime and, more often than not, after bedtime as well. 'I could cut down my hours too,' he added hopefully. 'We could both spend more time at home, relaxing as a family.' I said no, refused even to discuss it because that would have meant telling the truth: I love my work too much. I don't want to do even a tiny bit less, even if carrying on the way I am means I'll wear myself down until there's nothing left of me. I'll take the chance. And the idea of Nick cutting down his hours and his salary in order to relax more sent chills down my spine.

'Your body is telling you you're not ready to go home,' the voice continues softly. 'Listen to it. Remember what you said, about the hardest part of going home after a work trip?'

But I haven't been on a work trip. My mouth still won't work. I can't argue.

'You're ready to drop; all you want to do is walk through the front door, go straight to bed and stay there for twenty-four hours. But Zoe and Jake have missed you, and Nick has been on duty alone in your absence, so you have to take over. You have to spring into action like an entertainer at a children's party, and Nick has to be allowed to have the rest of the day off, cycling, or meeting his mates at the pub. And because you feel guilty, because you often go away overnight and Nick never does, you put a brave face on it. You dread going home after every trip because you know you're going to have to do even more work than usual to make up for the inconvenience of your having been away—as if you owe the family that extra effort, like some sort of penance.'

Is he still in the room? He's saying words, but they are my words. They're what I say when I'm at my lowest ebb. Not what I really think, not how I truly feel. *No. It's not like that. Stop.*

'I asked you why you didn't say something to Nick. Remember? You said he wouldn't understand. He genuinely believes he does his fair share. That's because he doesn't see all the other things that need to be done, the things that you take care of so that he never even notices them; they're invisible to him.'

I try to think about this, but my mind feels as if it has been wrapped in tight material.

'You take turns to get up with the kids at the weekend, but you'd almost rather get up early on Saturday and Sunday,' says the voice. My words, his voice. *He remembers every word I said.* 'You don't enjoy your lie-ins. Nick enjoys his; when it's your turn to do the early shift, he gets up at ten to find the house immaculate, the children dressed, fed and playing happily— teeth and hair brushed—and you still in your dressing gown, hungry, just starting to think about the possibility of getting some breakfast or a coffee for yourself.'

And when it's his turn, I get up at nine and find the kids hungry and whining, still in their pyjamas, and every toy we own out of its box and scattered all over the carpet, and a pile of dirty dishes in the sink, and Nick sitting at the kitchen table with his coffee and the newspaper . . .

'I remember something else you said at Seddon Hall.' The man's voice cuts into my thoughts. Now I know he's still there. Through the fug, my brain jolts. What has he been saying? Bad things about Nick. I can't trust him. *Has he drugged me? Is that why I feel like this?* 'You said you'd never regret lying, never regret our week together. You said, "If you see that no one else is going to look after you, you have to look after yourself."'

His words drop into the narrow tunnel inside my head, which soon closes into blackness.

*

When I wake up, he's gone. I look at my watch. It's quarter to four in the morning. I have a bad stomach ache and I'm horribly frightened and confused, but I can move more easily than before. I jump down from the bench and hear a clink, the sound of metal rattling. What is this thing I've been lying on? It has one wide silver leg, in the middle, with a round base. Wheels. I remember seeing but not registering it when I was lying on the carpet before. I bend and look again, to check my memory isn't playing tricks on me. It isn't. I hear another hard, metallic noise, quieter than the first.

I pull away one of the towels, then another, and stare at the beige leather I've uncovered. I frown, trying to pin down a memory. A doctor's examination table? Then my breath catches in my throat and I push away all the other towels at once. They fall in a heap on the floor. Something protrudes from one end of the long, thin leather table: a large horizontal loop, like a rigid noose, covered in the same beige leather. I knew it would be there. Still, my gut lurches.

If I didn't know what this was, the noose shape would terrify me. Recognition does nothing to lessen my fear. Because this thing shouldn't be here. It doesn't belong here; there's something horribly wrong. It's a massage table like the ones at Seddon Hall, the ones I lay on for the three or four massages I had during the week I spent with Mark.

With someone who wasn't Mark. With someone who lied.

I turn, run for the door, knowing that this time no offers of food and rest will stop me from leaving. Nothing will stop me from getting back to my home, Nick and the children.

Except that something does, and the wild scream that erupts from my throat when I remember the second metallic click, the sound I thought came from the bench—from the table—does nothing to alter the stark fact: the door is locked.

Police Exhibit Ref: VN8723
Case Ref: VN87
OIC: Sergeant Samuel Kombothekra

GERALDINE BRETHERICK'S DIARY, EXTRACT 5 OF 9
(taken from hard disk of Toshiba laptop computer at Corn
Mill House, Castle Park, Spilling, RY29 0LE)

3 May 2006, 9 p.m.

One side-effect of being a mother is that I have lost some
of my fears and some of my imaginative capacity. In some
ways, this is quite liberating. I am so overpowered by my
own feelings that I cannot believe anyone might feel differently. The perfect example: on Saturday, Cordy and I
took Oonagh and Lucy swimming. On the way back we
stopped at Waitrose. Both of the girls had fallen asleep. I
suggested to Cordy that she and I run in and out quickly,
leaving them locked in the car in the car park. I do it all
the time with Lucy, but Cordy looked shocked. 'We can't
do that,' she said. 'What if the car explodes? That happened once—I heard it on the news. Some kids died because they'd been left in a car and its petrol tank blew up.'

'What if we take them with us and Waitrose's roof falls
in and crushes them to death?' I said.

'We can't leave them alone,' she insisted. 'Some psycho
might kidnap them.'

'They're tired,' I said. 'Let's leave them to sleep. The car
will be locked.' This, I knew, was a weaker argument than
my previous one. A psycho could smash a car window and
kidnap two girls, easily. What I wanted to say, but didn't
feel able to, was that I couldn't for the life of me imagine
why anyone who didn't have to cart two five-year-olds
around with them should wish to do so. I knew Cordy

meant paedophiles when she said 'psychos'. I tried to imagine myself into the mind of a paedophile. It proved impossible, and not only for the obvious reasons. I find it hard to empathise with any adult who would seek out the company of children. I know people do it all the time, often innocently and with no evil intentions, but I still find it implausible. And what you cannot imagine, you cannot fear.

I have also, I discovered last night when Mark suggested we go abroad during Lucy's half-term holiday, lost my fear of flying. I know with absolute certainty that no plane I am on will crash, because if I died in a plane crash then I would be exempt from all future parenting duties, and Sod's Law dictates that I won't get out of it so easily. If I died in a plane crash, I would not have to spend another ten thousand Saturday afternoons standing beside bouncy castles that smell of vomit and sweaty socks, or sitting amid the debris of a game of pass-the-parcel like a tramp on a bed of newpapers while Lucy spits lumps of wet, unswallowed sandwich into my hand. I'm not saying I want to die—I simply know that I won't.

I told Mark I refused to be forced out of my home and forced out of the country at a time that's not convenient for me, just because St Swithun's has decided to award its teachers an extra long half-term. It makes me so angry: you pay a fortune for private education and they take longer holidays than in the state sector. I call that fraud.

Michelle has made it clear that I can no longer rely on her. She's going on holiday with her fat, ugly boyfriend who never speaks—the trip is already booked. I offered her an exorbitant sum of money to cancel it, but she's in love (Gart knows how and why, given the absolute lack of provocation from her love-object) and seems now to be immune to my financial incentives. If I get desperate, I might ask one of the mums from school to have Lucy for half-term; one of them's bound to be planning to ruin those two weeks of her life by spending them doing child things, so she can have my child too. I'll buy her a new vacuum cleaner or apron or something to say thank you, and Lucy can spend a fortnight picking up tips on how to sacrifice yourself and become the family slave, since life is so much easier for all females who learn this lesson well and do not think to question it.

Mum, who ought to be a great help to me, is out of the question. I rang her last night, but never found out whether she could or couldn't have Lucy to stay for that fortnight because the conversation didn't get that far. She told me I ought to want to look after my own daughter during her school holidays.

'Ought I?' I said. 'Well, I don't. I can't face a fortnight of not being able to do a single thing I want to do. I might as well spend two weeks bound and gagged in a cellar.'

Saying things I don't mean, 'barking worse than my bite', is a necessary outlet for me, one way of exercising my power and freedom. Mum should be relieved that I'm dealing with my frustration humorously, verbally. I do it—I say these terrible things—to keep myself sane. If just once Mum would say, 'Poor you, two weeks of being on mother duty, what a nightmare,' I wouldn't feel quite so negated. Or, an even cleverer response: 'You need to start putting yourself first—why don't you send Lucy to boarding school?' I'd never do that, Gart forbid. I like to see Lucy every day, just not *all* of every day. The suggestion of boarding school would stir up my maternal fervour, which (anyone shrewd would by now have worked out) might be exactly what I need.

Sadly, Mum doesn't understand about reverse psychology. She started crying and said, 'I can't understand why you had a child. Didn't you know what it would involve? Didn't you know it would be hard work?'

I told her I'd had no idea what it would feel like to be a parent because I'd never done it before. And, I reminded her, she had lied to me. She'd said, over and over again while I was pregnant, that being a mother was hard work but that you didn't mind because you loved your child so much. 'That's rubbish,' I told her. 'You love them, yes, but you *do* mind. Why should loving someone mean you're willing to sacrifice your freedom? Why should loving someone mean you're happy to watch your life become worse than it used to be in almost every way?'

'Your life isn't worse,' said Mum. 'You've got a beautiful, lovely daughter.'

'That's *her* life,' I said. 'Lucy's life, not mine.' And then, because of an article I'd read on the train yesterday, I said, 'There's a "conspiracy of silence" about what motherhood is really like. No one tells you the truth.'

'Conspiracy of silence!' Mum wailed. 'All you ever do is tell me how awful your life's been since you had Lucy. I wish there was a conspiracy of silence! I'd be a lot happier.'

I put the phone down. She wanted silence, so silence was what I gave her. I could have won the argument decisively by pointing out that I am only as selfish as I am, as reluctant to subordinate my own needs to someone else's, because from the moment I was born she treated me as if I was made of gold. Never did I get even the slightest hint that she had needs of her own and wasn't simply there to serve me. In Mum's eyes, I was an infant goddess. My every whim was attended to instantly. I was never punished; all I had to do was say sorry and I would be forgiven, and indeed rewarded for my apology. Lucy will be a more considerate woman than I am, I have no doubt, because she has grown up knowing that she is not 'the only pebble on the beach'.

My relationship with Mum has never fully recovered from the *Big Sleep* row. The Christmas after Lucy was born, Mark was away at a conference. Mum came to stay. She bought me an extra little present: a mug with a book cover on it, *The Big Sleep* by Raymond Chandler. I unwrapped it on Christmas morning after four sleepless nights in a row, four nights spent dragging myself round the house like a corpse with Lucy over my shoulder, patting her, trying to persuade her to close her eyes so that I could close mine. '*The Big Sleep?*' I snapped at Mum, unable to believe she would be so cruel. 'Is this your idea of a sick joke?'

She acted all innocent. 'What do you mean, love?' she said.

I lost my temper, started screaming at her. '*Big Sleep? Big fucking sleep?* I haven't slept for more than an hour at a time for ten fucking weeks!' I threw the mug at the fireplace and it smashed into pieces. Mum burst into tears and swore she hadn't done it deliberately. Looking back, I don't suppose she did. She's not nasty, just thoughtless—too sensible to be sensitive.

I couldn't help noticing that, having told me I ought to want to look after Lucy during half-term, Mum didn't ring back and offer to do so herself, as many a doting grandmother would have in her position. I am increasingly convinced that she only worries so much about Lucy because, in terms of offering practical help, she is willing to do so little.

10

'This isn't about me,' said Mark Bretherick. 'You'd like to pretend it is, but it isn't. Do you know what your men are doing with the earth they're digging out of my garden?' He pointed out of the lounge window at the teams of officers in overalls. Sam Kombothekra, more silent and serious than Simon had ever seen him, stood guard beside them, hands in his pockets, shoulders hunched. Simon knew he was hoping they'd find nothing. Kombothekra hated the unpleasantness crime brought with it, the social awkwardness of having to arrest a person, of having to look a man in the face and tell him you think—or know, more often than not—that he's done something terrible. Especially hard if that man is someone you're used to treating very differently.

His own fault. A bit less of the 'Mark, we understand what you're going through' and he'd have found today a piece of piss.

'Our men will repair the damage as best they can,' Simon told Bretherick.

'That's not what I meant. It's a very clever metaphor you've got going here. You look as if you're unearthing, when burying's what you're really doing. That's the true purpose of all the earth that's flying around out there!' Bretherick had finally exchanged the blue, sweat-stained shirt he'd worn for days for a clean, mustard-coloured one, which he wore with gold cufflinks.

'Burying what?' asked Simon.

'The reality of the situation. You got it badly wrong, didn't you? When facing up to that became unavoidable, you decided to make me the villain of the piece because it was easier than admitting that *I've* been right all along: that a man called William Markes, who *you* can't find, murdered my wife and daughter!'

'We don't decide to make people villains. We look for evidence that will implicate or exonerate them.'

Contempt twisted Bretherick's features. 'So you're hoping to find proof that I've committed no crime hidden beneath a begonia, are you?'

'Mr Bretherick—'

'It's actually *Dr* Bretherick, and you still haven't answered my questions. Why are you hacking my garden to bits? Why are there people at my office, disturbing my staff, going through every scrap of paper? Clearly you're looking for evidence that I killed Geraldine and Lucy. Well, you won't find any, because I didn't!'

Simon and Kombothekra had said something similar to Proust yesterday: Bretherick had long since been proved innocent of the only crime known to have been committed. Why exactly *were* they here?

'You're right, Waterhouse,' Proust had said for the first time since records began. If Simon had been wearing a hearing aid, he'd have taken it off and given it a good shake to check it was working properly. 'Be grateful you aren't in my shoes. I had to make a choice: either I end up a laughing stock, fooled into wasting thousands of pounds by some nameless fantasist's rip-roaring tale of dead cats, red Alfa Romeos and bereaved men gardening at inappropriate times, or I go down in history as the DI who dismissed an important lead and never found the bodies hidden in the perishing greenhouse. Which you can bet your police pension would be discovered five years later by a pipsqueak bobby out sunbathing on his day off.'

'Sir, either there are more bodies to find, or there aren't,' Simon had pointed out. 'It's not as if they'll only be there if you don't look for them.'

A cold squint from the Snowman. 'Don't be a pedant, Water-house. The worst thing about pedants is that there's only one way to answer them and that's pedantically. What I was trying to say—and what, frankly, anyone whose brain was in good working order would have understood—is that I *fear* our searches will yield nothing. Equally, I fear that if I ignore the information contained in the anonymous letter—'

'We completely understand, sir,' Kombothekra had chipped in hastily. For a man who wanted no trouble, he'd made an odd career choice.

'Does the name Amy Oliver mean anything to you?' Simon asked Mark Bretherick.

'No? Who is she? Is she the woman who came here, who looked like Geraldine?'

'She's a child. She was in Lucy's class at school last year.'

Simon saw his disappointment, quickly masked by anger.

'Don't you people listen? Geraldine dealt with all the school stuff.'

A quiet voice came from behind Simon. 'You didn't know the names of any of Lucy's friends?' Kombothekra had joined them.

'I think there was one called Uma. I probably met them all at one time or another, but—'

The telephone rang.

'Am I allowed to answer?'

Simon nodded, then listened as Bretherick issued a brief, baf-fling diatribe. 'It has to be client-server based, and it has to have multi-level BOMS,' was his conclusion.

'Work?' said Simon, once the conversation was over. How could Bretherick function professionally at a time like this?

'Yeah. I suppose you've tapped my phone, haven't you? If you want to know what anything means, feel free to ask.'

Patronising turd, thought Simon. 'The two photographs that you claim were stolen,' he said, deciding it was time to retaliate. 'Inside the frames, behind the pictures of Geraldine and Lucy, were two other photographs that we believe might be of Amy Oliver and her mother.'

Bretherick exhaled slowly, a frown gathering around his eyes. 'What? What do you mean? I . . . I didn't have any photographs of . . . I didn't know Amy Oliver, or her mother. Who told you that?'

'Where did the pictures of Geraldine and Lucy at the owl sanctuary come from? Did you take them yourself?'

'No. I've no idea who took them.'

'Did you put them in their frames?'

'No. I don't know anything about them. One day they just appeared on the mantelpiece. That's it.'

Fundamentally Simon believed him, but it sounded lame. 'They just appeared?'

'Not literally! Geraldine must have put them in frames and . . . she did all that, framed her favourite photos and Lucy's paintings and put them up. I saw those two and liked them and took them to my office. That's all I know about them. But why would she have put photographs of this Amy Oliver girl and her mother inside the frames? It makes no sense.'

'Were the Olivers significant to Geraldine, do you know?'

Bretherick answered with a question. 'How come you know all this, about the photographs? Have you found the woman who stole them?' He leaned forward. 'If you know who she is, you've got to tell me.'

'Mark, what sort of thing did you and Geraldine used to talk about?' Kombothekra asked. 'You know—of an evening, after dinner.'

Simon made up his mind to draw the sergeant's attention to the wedding anniversary cards, the oh-so-courteous messages inside them.

'I don't know! Everything. What a stupid question. My work, Lucy . . . Aren't you married?'

'Yes.'

'No,' said Simon quickly. He didn't want to have to sit there worrying he would be asked the same question. Better to get it over with.

Bretherick stared at him. 'Well, then you'll never know how it feels when someone murders your wife.' Simon thought that this was stretching the concept of looking on the bright side beyond its capacity.

'I know the name of every single one of my sons' friends, and their parents,' said Kombothekra.

'Bully for you,' said Bretherick. 'Do you know how to build, from scratch, a cryogen-free nitrogen-recycling cooling unit that every laboratory in the world will need to buy? That will make your fortune?'

'No,' said Kombothekra.

'And I do.' Bretherick shrugged. 'We all have our strengths and weaknesses, Sergeant.'

Simon was starting to feel inadequate; it didn't take much. He said, 'Your mother-in-law says there are things in Geraldine's diary that are factually incorrect. Jean didn't buy Geraldine a mug with *The Big Sleep* on it, for example. Geraldine didn't fly into a rage, smash the mug, accuse her mother of being insensitive to her sleep-deprived state.'

Bretherick nodded. 'Geraldine didn't write that diary. Whoever killed her wrote it.'

'Yet you only became sure of this once you'd heard what Jean had to say. Isn't that right?' Bretherick had asked why he was a suspect; Simon hoped it was becoming clearer. 'You read that diary long before Jean did—several times, I assume?'

'Over and over. I can recite much of it from memory, my new party trick. What a popular guest I'll be.'

'Why didn't you say straight away, "This didn't happen, this isn't true, my wife can't have written this"?'

Simon watched uncomfortably as Bretherick's face lost its colour. 'Don't turn that on me! You all told me Geraldine had killed herself and Lucy. You kept telling me. No, the diary didn't sound like Geraldine—it sounded nothing like her—but you said it was her diary.'

'I'm not talking about the feelings and attitudes she expressed, things you might have assumed she'd withheld from you,' said Simon. 'I'm talking about facts: the smashing of the mug, the things that simply didn't happen.'

'I don't know anything about a mug! How was I supposed to know if it happened or not? That diary's full of . . . distortions and lies. I *told* you it was all wrong. I told you someone else must have written it. I don't recognise Geraldine's voice, or her thoughts or her description of our lives. That business about God being called Gart? I never heard Geraldine or Lucy say that, not once.'

There was a tap on the lounge window, one of the search team from outside. Kombothekra, who had been leaning against the glass, turned, obscuring Simon's view of the garden. Simon watched the sergeant's back, its stiff stillness, and listened to the absence of background noise. No voices any more, no sound of shovels cutting into earth. His heart started to thump.

'What?' Bretherick saw the look on Kombothekra's face. 'What have you found?'

'You tell me, Mark,' said Kombothekra. 'What have we found?' He nodded at Simon and raised two fingers almost imperceptibly, the barrel of an imaginary gun. Either Simon had lost his ability to read signals or else two bodies had been found beneath Mark Bretherick's rectangular lawn.

What no nod could tell him—for Kombothekra couldn't possibly know at this stage—was whether these were the bodies of Amy Oliver and her mother. And now there was a new question that had leaped to the top of Simon's list. More than anything, he wanted to find out the name of the anonymous letter-writer.

How did she know so much, and how the fuck was he going to find her?

'Amy Oliver,' said Colin Sellers, looking over Chris Gibbs' shoulder at the photograph of a gangly, sharp-eyed young girl in school uniform sitting on a wall. Until today, neither detective had been in a school office since his teenage years, and neither felt entirely comfortable. Gibbs had been loathed by his teachers, and Sellers, though amiable and popular, had been berated daily for chatting to his friends when he should have been working.

'Not a happy girl,' Gibbs muttered.

'Shit.' Sellers lowered his voice so that Barbara Fitzgerald and Jenny Naismith, the headmistress and secretary of St Swithun's Montessori Primary School, wouldn't hear him. He didn't want to offend them, and imagined that because they worked with children they would be quick to take offence.

Sellers didn't fancy either of them. Mrs Fitzgerald was old, had waist-length grey hair and wore glasses that were too large for her face. Jenny Naismith was in the right age bracket and had a pretty face and good skin, but looked too neat and meticulous. Bound to be a ball-breaker.

On the plus side, both women were efficient. They had produced the two photographs and confirmed the identities of their subjects within seconds of Sellers' and Gibbs' arrival. Now Mrs Fitzgerald was hunting in a filing cabinet for a list of all the people who went on the school trip to Silsford Castle's owl sanctuary last year. Sellers couldn't imagine why she'd kept it this long. 'We keep everything,' Jenny Naismith had said proudly.

'Shit what?' Gibbs asked.

'Nothing. For a minute I thought the name Amy Oliver rang a bell.'

'From where?'

'Don't get excited.' Sellers laughed away his embarrassment. 'It's Jamie Oliver I was thinking of. That's why it sounded familiar.'

'I hate that twat,' said Gibbs. 'Every ad break, he's there telling me what to eat: "Try putting some butter on your bread. Try having some chips with your sausage."' Gibbs attempted a cockney accent. 'As if he invented it!'

'The spelling is different.' Barbara Fitzgerald abandoned the filing cabinet. 'Amy's name is O-L-I-V-A. Oliva. Spanish.'

Gibbs checked his notebook. 'So that's why her mother's called . . .' He couldn't read his own writing. 'Cantona?' He was aware of Sellers beside him, trying not to laugh. Too late, he realised what he'd said.

'Encarna.' Barbara Fitzgerald didn't laugh, corrected him matter-of-factly, as if it were an easy mistake to make. 'It's an abbreviation of Encarnación. Which is Spanish for "Incarnation". Many Spaniards have religious names. I told you, Amy moved to Spain.'

'Mrs Fitzgerald's got the most amazing memory,' said Jenny Naismith. 'She knows every detail about every child at this school.'

Gibbs altered the spelling of Amy's surname. Evidently that was something the anonymous letter-writer didn't know; had she never seen it written down? Esther Taylor: that was the name of the woman who had turned up at St Swithun's with the two photographs. Or at least the name she had given Jenny Naismith. Taylor was a common name, but Esther was more unusual, and if she looked like Geraldine Bretherick . . . well, it shouldn't be too hard to track her down.

'This list isn't leaping out at me,' Mrs Fitzgerald said apologetically. 'I'll have a proper look later, and I'll bring it into the police station as soon as we track it down.' She folded her thick, tanned arms. 'Actually, I went on that trip myself, and I'm pretty sure I could jot down most of the names for you now. Would you like me to?'

'Yes, please,' said Sellers.

'You didn't notice who took those two photographs, by any chance?' Gibbs asked. 'Or anyone taking photos of Geraldine and Lucy Bretherick?'

Barbara Fitzgerald shook her head. 'Everyone was snapping away, as they always do on school trips.' This was the first time the name Bretherick had been mentioned. The headmistress seemed unflustered by its appearance in the conversation. Jenny Naismith was still ransacking the filing cabinet. Sellers couldn't see her face.

'What can you tell us about Encarna Oliva?' he asked.

'She worked for a bank in London.'

'Do you know which one?'

'Yes. Leyland Carver. Thanks to Encarna, they sponsor our Spring Fair every year.'

'Do you have the family's contact details in Spain?'

'I don't think we were ever given a snail-mail address,' said Mrs Fitzgerald, 'but we did get an e-mail shortly after Amy left St Swithun's, telling us all about her new home in Nerja.'

'Nerja.' Sellers wrote it down. 'I don't suppose you've still—'

'No, but I do remember the e-mail address.' Mrs Fitzgerald beamed. 'It was amysgonetospain@hotmail.com. No apostrophe. My secretary and I had a long discussion about it. Not Jenny—my previous secretary, Sheila. The missing apostrophe annoyed me. Sheila said she'd never seen an e-mail address with an apostrophe in it, and I said that if one couldn't use apostrophes in Hotmail addresses, then why not avoid the problem altogether by coming up with an address that doesn't require an apostrophe?'

'Is there a computer here that I can use?' asked Gibbs. Jenny Naismith nodded and led him to her desk. 'Worth a try,' he said to Sellers.

'What about Amy's old address?' Sellers asked the headmistress. 'The people who live there now might have a forwarding address for the Olivas.'

'They might,' Mrs Fitzgerald agreed. 'Good idea. I can root that out for you, certainly.'

Sellers was relieved that she didn't know it by heart. He'd been starting to wonder if she had special powers.

When the head turned to face him again, armed with a sheet of A4 paper, she had a more reserved expression on her face. 'Is Amy . . . all right?'

Sellers was about to say something reassuring when Gibbs said, 'That's what we're trying to find out.' He didn't look up from the keyboard.

'We have to work on the assumption that she's fine unless we find out that she isn't. Which hopefully we won't.' Sellers smiled.

'Will you let me know the very second there's any news?' asked Mrs Fitzgerald.

'Of course.'

'I liked Amy. I worried about her too. She was extremely bright, very passionate, very creative, but like many sensitive, creative children, she tended to overreact. Hysterically, some-times. I think she did it to make life more interesting, actually. As an adult, I'm sure she'll be one of those women who creates drama wherever she goes. She once said to me, "Mrs Fitzgerald, my life's like a story, isn't it, and I'm the main person in the story." I said, "Yes, I suppose so, Amy," and she said, "That means I can make up what happens." '

'Number 2, Belcher Close, Spilling,' Jenny Naismith read from the piece of paper in her boss's hand. 'Amy's old address.'

'Do you want to look at our *A–Z* or have you got sat nav?'

Sellers covered his mouth with his hand to hide a grin. Barbara Fitzgerald had pronounced it as if it were the name of an Eastern deity: his venerable holiness, Sat Nav. 'We'll find it,' he said.

Was a trip to Spain likely to fall into his lap? Why couldn't it be France? He could take Stace; she could practise her French— there was no doubt she needed the practice. Sellers had done French O level, got a B, and he reckoned Stace was the sort of person who'd never be able to learn a language. She just didn't get it. She was rubbish. If he could have taken her to France, it might have helped. Maybe Spanish was easier. Maybe he could persuade her to switch. Better still, he could take Suki to Spain . . .

Barbara Fitzgerald handed Sellers a list of names. He counted them. Twenty-seven. Great. Would Kombothekra want him to collect twenty-seven accounts of a visit to an owl sanctuary in the hope that someone would remember who took which photographs? That'd be fun. Sellers was halfway out of the school office when he remembered he'd left Gibbs behind. He turned, doubled back on himself.

Jenny Naismith was walking up and down behind her desk, too polite to ask when she might once again have the use of her computer. Gibbs had stopped typing and was staring at his Yahoo inbox, blowing spit bubbles. 'Are you ready?' Sellers asked him. *How to be charming and graceful, by Christopher Gibbs.* 'You're not waiting for Amy Oliva to reply, are you? She'll be at school.'

'So? That's all schools do these days, isn't it? Buy kids computers to play with?'

'In this country, sadly, things are going in that direction,' said Barbara Fitzgerald from the doorway. 'If you're talking about the state sector, that is. In Spain, I'm not sure. But, you know, there's no point sitting there and waiting.' She smiled fondly at Gibbs; Sellers found himself feeling quite impressed. 'Forget about it for the time being and try again later.'

Gibbs grunted, abandoned the keyboard and mouse.

As he and Sellers walked back to the car, Sellers said, 'Wise words indeed, mate. Is that what Debbie says when you can't get it up? Forget about it for the time being and try again later.'

'Not a problem I have.' Gibbs sounded bored. 'Right, what now?'

'Better check in with Kombothekra.' Sellers pulled his phone out of his pocket.

'Is he Asian?' Gibbs asked. 'Stepford?'

'Of course not, pillock. He's half Greek, half upper-crust English.'

'Greek? He looks Asian.'

'Sarge, it's me.' Sellers gave Gibbs a look that Barbara Fitzgerald would no doubt have thought too discouraging, bad for morale. 'The photos are of Amy Oliva and her mother, confirmed. That's Oliva spelled O-L-I-V-A. They were brought in by a woman who called herself Esther Taylor . . . sorry? What?'

'What?' Gibbs mouthed, when the silent nodding had gone on for too long.

'All right, Sarge. Will do.'

'What, for fuck's sake?'

Sellers rubbed the screen of his mobile phone with his thumb. He thought about the helium balloons his children were given at parties and in restaurants. They tried so hard to clutch on to the strings, but they could never maintain their grip and eventually the balloons drifted up and out of reach. There was nothing you could do but watch as they escaped at speed. That was how Sellers was starting to feel about this case.

Double or nothing. He would have preferred nothing.

'Corn Mill House, in the garden,' he said. 'They've found two more bodies. One's a child.'

'Boy or girl?' asked Simon, aware that this question was normally asked in happier circumstances. He, Kombothekra and Tim Cook, the pathologist, stood by the door to the greenhouse, away from the rest of the men. Kombothekra hadn't worked with Cook before. Simon had, many times. He, Sellers and Gibbs knew him as Cookie and sometimes drank with him in the Brown Cow, but Simon was embarrassed to make this obvious to Kombothekra; he hated the nickname anyway, regarded it as unsuitable for a grown man.

'Not sure.' Cook was at least five years younger than Simon, tall and thin with dark, spiky hair. Simon knew that he had a girlfriend who was fifty-two, that they'd met at a local badminton club. Cook could be unbelievably boring on the subject of badminton, but would say little, even when urged by Sellers and Gibbs—especially then—about his older partner.

Simon couldn't believe the age gap didn't bother Cook. He, Simon, could never have a relationship with anyone twenty years older than himself. Or twenty years younger, for that matter. *Or with anyone.* He pushed away the unwelcome thought. Half the time he prayed Charlie would change her mind, the other half he was grateful she'd had the good sense to turn him down. '"Not sure"?' he said impatiently. 'That's the sort of expert opinion I could have come up with myself.'

'It's a girl.' Sam Kombothekra sighed heavily. 'Amy Oliva. And the woman's her mother, Encarna Oliva.' He turned, glanced at the makeshift grave behind him, then turned back. 'It's got to be them. Family annihilation mark two. Keeping the media at bay's going to be a nightmare.'

'We know nothing,' Simon pointed out. Sometimes he heard a phrase that he knew would be impossible to dislodge from his mind. *Family annihilation mark two.* 'Whoever they are, this can't be a family annihilation.' He resented having to use Professor Harbard's crass definition. 'Mrs Oliva can't have buried her own body, can she? Laid a lawn over herself? Or are you saying her husband killed them? Mr Oliva? What's his first name?'

Kombothekra shrugged. 'Whatever his name is, his body's buried somewhere nearby, and our men are going to find it any second now. Mark Bretherick killed all three Olivas, and he also killed Geraldine and Lucy.'

Simon wished Proust were here to give Kombothekra the slating he deserved. 'What the fuck? I know we can't avoid charging him, but . . . Do you really think he's a killer? I thought you liked him.'

'Why?' Kombothekra snapped. 'Because I was polite to him?'

'I think he's a killer,' Cook chipped in. 'Four bodies have turned up on his property in less than a fortnight.' Neither

Simon nor Kombothekra bothered to reply. Simon was thinking about the shock and fury on Bretherick's face as he was helped into the police car that would by now have delivered him to the custody suite at the nick. Kombothekra stared at his feet, mumbled something Simon couldn't decipher. 'Anyway, have I said anything about the adult skeleton being a woman's?' The pathologist returned to his area of expertise, reminded the other two men that they needed his input.

'You haven't said anything, period.' Simon glared at him.

Kombothekra looked up. 'You're saying the adult skeleton is a man's? Then it's Amy's father.'

'No. Actually, it *is* a woman.' The revelation got no response. Tim Cook looked embarrassed, then disappointed. 'It's easy to identify an adult female pelvic structure. But a young child . . .'

'How young?' asked Simon.

'My guess would be four or five.'

Kombothekra nodded. 'Amy Oliva was five when she left St Swithun's school, supposedly to move to Spain.'

'Get me dental records,' said Cook. 'Don't give the bodies names until we're sure.'

'He's right,' said Simon.

'How long dead?' Kombothekra demanded, his usual charm and tact having deserted him.

'I can't say for sure at this stage. Somewhere between twelve and twenty-four months would be my guess,' said Cook. 'There are remnants of tendons and ligaments, but not many.'

'How did they die?'

Cook made a face. 'Sorry. If we had more soft tissue, I might be able to tell you, but all we've got's bones and teeth. Unless the murder weapon made some sort of mark on a bone . . . I'll have a good look when I get them on the table, but don't bank on finding a cause of death.'

Kombothekra pushed the pathologist out of the way and headed for the house.

'Is he always like that?' Cook asked.

'Never.' Simon wanted to speak to Jonathan Hey, but felt he couldn't walk off so soon after Kombothekra had, leave Cook stranded. When he'd visited Hey in Cambridge, the professor had as good as asked him if he was sure Mark Bretherick hadn't killed Geraldine and Lucy. What exactly had he said? Something about husbands being more likely to murder wives who don't work, who have no status outside the home.

Encarna Oliva, from what Simon had picked up second-hand via Kombothekra and Sellers, had been a banker at Leyland Carver. In professional and commercial terms, status didn't come much higher than that. She must have earned a small fortune. Her body had been found in Mark Bretherick's garden, but he wasn't her husband.

It was all wrong. They were finding out more, but Simon had no sense of a coherent shape emerging.

Cook said, 'I'd better get back to it. Why do we do it? Why aren't we postmen or milkmen?'

'I worked for the post office for two weeks once, at Christmas,' Simon told him. 'They sacked me.'

As Cook wandered reluctantly back to the bones, Simon pulled out his phone and his notebook. There was time, he told himself, before Kombothekra came back from wherever he'd disappeared to. Jonathan Hey didn't answer his office telephone, so Simon rang his mobile. Hey answered after the third ring.

'It's Simon Waterhouse.'

'Simon.' Hey sounded pleased to hear from him. 'Are you in Cambridge again?'

'No. I'm at Mark Bretherick's house in Spilling.'

'Right. Of course. Why would you be in Cambridge?'

'We've found two more bodies on the property—an adult woman and a child.'

'What? Are you sure?' Hey tutted. 'Sorry, that's an idiotic question. What I mean is, you're saying two more people have died at the Bretherick house *since* Geraldine Bretherick and her daughter?'

'No, these bodies have been here at least a year,' Simon told him. 'This is highly confidential, by the way.'

'Of course.'

'No, really. I shouldn't be telling you any of it.'

'So why are you?' asked Hey. 'Sorry, I'm not being rude, I just—'

'I want to know what you think. My sergeant, when we dug up the bodies, said "Family annihilation mark two", and I just wondered—'

'Dug up?' Hey's voice was squeaky with incredulity.

'Yeah. They were buried in the garden. Under a smooth, green lawn—not quite so smooth any more.'

'That's terrible. What a horrible thing to find. Are you okay?'

'Obviously they didn't die naturally. No clothing on the bones, so either they were murdered naked or stripped post-mortem.'

'Simon, I'm not a cop.' Hey sounded apologetic. 'This is way off my territory.'

'Is it?' This was the part that held the most interest for Simon. 'Nothing's been confirmed, but we think the remains we've found might be a classmate of Lucy Bretherick's and her mother.' He spelled it out. 'Another mother and daughter, killed in the same place—or at least bodies found in almost the same place . . .'

'Geraldine and Lucy Bretherick's bodies were found in two bathtubs, weren't they?'

'That's right.'

'So they were also nude.'

It was a good point. Simon wasn't sure what it meant, but it was another connection between the first pair of bodies and the second.

'I suppose there's no reason to think the poor souls you've found today were also killed in the bath and then . . . Simon, I can't quite believe I'm taking part in this conversation. What help can I possibly be to you now?'

'What do you mean "now"?'

'Well, now that familicide's ruled out.'

'Is it, though? That's why I rang you.'

'I never thought it likely, from what I'd read and from what Keith told me, that Geraldine Bretherick had killed herself and her daughter. Now that you've discovered the bodies of another woman and child, I'd say it's virtually certain the Bretherick deaths weren't a familicide committed by Geraldine Bretherick.'

'So, what, then? What do you think happened?'

'I've absolutely no idea. Surely . . . well, isn't it likely that the same person killed all four victims?'

'I think so. Yes.'

'You said a classmate of Lucy Bretherick's; was it a boy or a girl?'

'We think a girl, but it's to be confirmed.'

'Well, if it does turn out to be a girl, that would make it ninety per cent certain that your killer's a man.'

'Why?' asked Simon.

'Because he's going round killing women and girls. Mothers and daughters.'

'Couldn't a woman be doing that?'

Hey let out a hollow laugh. 'Like the perpetrators of familicide, serial murderers are almost always men.'

'Don't say that.'

'What?' Hey sounded worried.

'Serial. It's a word we avoid if at all possible.' Simon closed his eyes. Kombothekra was expecting to find the body of Amy Oliva's father; now Jonathan Hey was suggesting that they might at any moment uncover the remains of another mother and daughter. Simon wasn't sure his mind could accommodate that possibility.

'Also . . . I mean, would a woman be able, physically, to dig up enough earth to bury two bodies?' asked Hey.

'A strong one might,' said Simon. 'If you're right, though, and one man is responsible for all four deaths, what if that one man is Mark Bretherick? Then the murder of Geraldine and Lucy could still be viewed as a familicide.' Hearing himself say this convinced Simon it had to be wrong. He believed, increasingly, in Mark Bretherick's innocence.

'You told me he had an alibi,' said Hey. 'But, leaving that aside . . . No. What sociologists mean when they talk about familicide is a very specific crime, the crime we discussed at length when you came here, to Cambridge. Male family annihilators kill only their wives, children and, sometimes, themselves.'

'Restrained of them,' Simon murmured.

'They don't kill school friends, mothers of school friends.' Hey sighed. 'I don't mean to put a spanner in your works, but none of the details fit. I mean, sometimes you get men who snap and go on a short, localised killing spree. They open fire in a shop, or restaurant—a public place. They kill strangers, and then they go back home and kill their families and themselves, but it all happens within a time frame of twenty-four hours, seventy-two at most. If the two bodies you found today have really been there over a year . . . I'm sorry, but that doesn't fit with anything I know or have ever come across. Men who commit familicide don't kill two strangers first, then wait a year, then kill their nearest and dearest. They just don't.'

'Yeah, yeah. Okay.'

'Simon? Any opinion I give you, you've got to take with a barrelful of salt, right? I'm not a psychologist or a detective.'

'Just tell me what you think. You're an intelligent person—those are in short supply.'

'Unless Mark Bretherick's alibi turns out to be false, I don't think he killed anybody,' said Hey. 'Whoever killed the first mother and daughter must have killed the second. If I *were* a police officer, and this were my case, I'd start from that assumption.'

Simon thanked him and promised to drop in next time he was in Cambridge. Hey spoke as if Simon was bound to find himself strolling past Whewell College at least once a week.

Simon wondered if it was a version of what he thought of as London syndrome: the way people who lived in London always assumed you would go to them rather than them come to you. He had a mate from university who did it all the time. 'We haven't met up for ages,' he'd say. 'When are you next going to be in London?' As if there were no trains out.

After saying goodbye to Hey, Simon went in search of Kombothekra. Tim Cook and his two assistants were busy attending to the bones. Simon stepped around the cordoned-off area, asking himself if it was safe to assume that, if Bretherick wasn't the murderer, then he had to be of great interest to the murderer, perhaps the object of the murderer's obsession. Why else would he kill Bretherick's family and bury two people on his land?

Kombothekra was in the kitchen, sitting at a large, wooden table with his arms stretched out in front of him.

'Are you okay?' Simon asked.

'I've been better. I thought I ought to tell Proust where we're up to.'

'What did he say?'

Kombothekra's expression said it all. 'It shouldn't be as bad, but it's worse,' he said quietly.

'What?'

'Finding a child's skeleton. It oughtn't to be as hard as . . . well, say, Lucy Bretherick. I mean, that got to me, but this . . .' He shook his head. 'Seeing a skeleton, the inside of a person. It makes you focus on what should be there but isn't. Skeletons look so . . . vulnerable.'

'I know.'

'Lucy Bretherick was dead, but she was still recognisable as a child.'

Simon nodded. 'Sam . . .'

'What?'

'It could be two different killers. It could.' *Even an expert like Jonathan Hey could be wrong.* 'What if Mark Bretherick killed Amy and Encarna Oliva and that's why Geraldine and Lucy were murdered—in retaliation?'

'By Amy's father?' Kombothekra's mouth twisted. 'I wouldn't let Proust hear you say that. Speculation's out. Finding out for certain what happened before close of business today is in.'

'That bad, was he?'

'I'm not allowed even to *think* these bodies might be Amy Oliva and her mother. I'm not allowed to say it, obviously, but I'm not allowed to think it either. He says he'll be able to tell from my face when he sees me if I'm still thinking it, and if I am I'll "rue the day".' Kombothekra made quote marks in the air.

Simon grinned. 'Dental records'll tell us soon enough.'

'I hope he finds cause of death.' Kombothekra nodded towards the garden. 'Grooves in the bone made by a big knife, or . . . some great big fuck-off mark from a clearly identifiable weapon. It'd be nice to know they were dead when the killer buried them.' He looked up at Simon. 'Don't tell me it hasn't occurred to you. That they might have been buried alive?'

It hadn't and it didn't now; Kombothekra's words barely registered. Simon had had an idea. *A mark from a clearly identifiable weapon . . .* He went over it once more to check it was sound. In his mind, a tangle of incomprehension began to unravel. He saw a way in which the apparently impossible might make perfect sense—the only way.

He was out of the kitchen in seconds, pulling his phone out of his pocket.

11

Thursday, 9 August 2007

Nick is lying on the sofa, which is on the ceiling instead of the floor. He has tomato sauce all over his face. Zoe is sitting on his knee, kicking the lampshade with her foot. The news is on too loud, and the television is also upside down. The children's toys are whirling in mid-air, in constant motion. Jake comes in, walks across the ceiling and asks Nick, 'Where Mummy gone?' His palms are flat, upturned—or rather downturned—and his face is set in a curious frown, a replica of the puzzled expressions he's seen on grown-ups' faces. 'Gone a London, Daddy? Back soon?'

I jolt awake and the horror rushes to meet me. No gradual dawning of awareness—it hits me all at once. I'm still here, locked in the room. How could I have fallen asleep? I remember crying and begging to be released, falling to the floor eventually, hungry and exhausted . . .

He drugged me. He must have done. The bottle of water that was on the passenger seat of my car, not in the footwell where I expected to find it . . . the water he brought me when he first came into the room . . .

I run to the door. Still locked. I start to bang and scream. When my fists don't make a loud enough noise, I hurl my whole body at the door, over and over. If it hurts, I'm unaware of the pain. My mind only has space for one thing: the need to get out of here.

My bag—it's still there, by the window. I lunge and grab it, tip the contents out all over the floor. My phone has gone. So has my watch, I notice when I try to look at it. *He's been in here while I was asleep.* I don't know how long I slept for, but it must have been a while. I can tell from the light coming through the curtains that it's daytime now.

The curtains. I yank them open. There's a small, paved yard outside, dotted with plants in pots of different sizes and styles—too many. Enough to cause an obstruction to anyone who might want to walk from the house to the tall, thick hedge that encloses the yard on two sides, as sturdy-looking as a brick wall. There is no third side to the yard, so it must turn the corner, go round the side of the house. Among the plant-pots—at their centre—there is a small fountain, a silver elephant's head on a tray. Water pours from the trunk, shows no sign of stopping. In one corner of the yard there's a wooden gazebo that's missing one or two planks from its seat. Next to this is a black-painted wooden gate, solid, the same height as the hedge. There's a padlock on it.

Nothing to indicate where this house is. No chance of a passer-by seeing me, however long I stand by the window.

I run back to the door, grab the handle with both hands and use what little energy I have left to produce the loudest scream I can. No response. I listen. Is there only silence in the rest of the house, or can I hear something? Has he gone out or is he wait-ing on the other side of the door, listening to my anguish and ignoring it? I no longer feel hungry, only emptier than I have ever felt. The air seems to ripple slightly each time I turn my head, as if it's some kind of thick, transparent liquid.

'Sally?'

'Unlock the door, let me out!' I hate myself for being pleased to hear his voice.

'All right. But . . . Sally, I don't want you to get a shock. Are you listening?'

What is he talking about?

'I'm holding a gun. When I open the door, I'm going to be pointing it at you.'

'I need to phone Nick. Please. Give me back my phone.'

The door opens. He looks exactly the same as he always has, the same helpful, concerned face. The only change is the gun in his hand.

I've never seen a gun in real life before. I've seen them in films, on television, but it's not the same. *Stay calm. Think.* The gun is small, grey and smooth.

'I'm not going to do anything stupid,' I tell him. 'But I do need to phone Nick, as soon as possible. I don't want him to worry about me.'

'He won't. He isn't. Look.' He pulls my phone out of his pocket and hands it to me. There's a message from Nick: 'Talk about short notice. Yes, can pick up kids if have to. Come back asap. Ring when you can—kids will want to speak.'

Next I read the text that supposedly came from me, the one Nick replied to. It is shorter and less informative than any message I've ever sent. It says that I have to leave for Venice immediately because of a crisis, that I'll be back as soon as I can.

For Christ's sake, Nick! When have I ever sent such a business-like text? When has my work involved a crisis so dire that I would set off abroad without making sure to speak to you first? When have I ever not signed a message 'S', with three kisses?

I clear my throat, struggle to find my voice. 'You wrote this? As me?'

The man nods. 'In spite of everything, I didn't want Nick to worry.'

'When will you let me go home?' I ask tearfully. 'How soon is soon?'

He lowers the gun, walks towards me. I flinch, but he doesn't hurt me. He wraps his arms round me, hugs me for a few seconds, then releases me. 'I expect you've got a lot of questions,' he says.

'Did you kill Geraldine and Lucy? Is your real name William Markes?' I ask because I think he wants me to. All I care about, at this moment, is when I'll see my family again; that's the question that fills my mind, along with all its possible answers.

'Who?' His body stiffens. He raises the gun. Silence swells around us.

'William Markes,' I repeat. He doesn't recognise the name. *And it frightens him. Not knowing frightens him.*

'No,' he says eventually. 'My name is not William Markes.'

'You said "In spite of everything"—you didn't want Nick to worry in spite of everything. In spite of what?'

'His mistreatment of you.'

'*What?*'

'He treats you like a skivvy.'

'No, he doesn't!'

'"I go from room to room tidying up, and before I've finished, Nick's worked his way round most of the house messing it up again, and I have to start from scratch." Do you remember saying that to me?'

'Yes, but—'

'This is the man you want to go back to?'

'You're insane.' If he wasn't holding a gun I'd call him something worse, much worse.

He laughs. '*I'm* insane? You're the one who told me what you'd do with the money if you ever won the lottery. I got all this from you.'

'I never said anything about—'

'You'd hire a full-time servant to walk round your house seven days a week, arranging each room so that it looked as you wanted it to look. That way you'd never have to encounter Nick's mess; you'd be able to walk into a room and sit down without having to repair any damage first.'

He's right. I forgot the lottery part; the rest is familiar. My words. He is taunting me with my own words. 'I love Nick and I love my kids,' I tell him, crying. 'Please, let me go! Put down the gun.'

'It's hard for Nick when you're away, isn't it? You have to hire a woman to help look after him and the kids or else things spiral out of control pretty quickly.'

Pam Senior. Pam helped Nick, the week I was at Seddon Hall. What does she have to do with any of this?

'But if *he* goes away—not that he does very often. You'd like him to go away more often. If Nick goes away, your life gets easier. You've got the kids to look after, yes, but not the strewn newspapers and the discarded banana skins—'

'Stop.' My head throbs. I want to curl into a ball on the carpet, but I can't. I have to try and get out. 'Please, stop. You can't honestly believe—'

'What do you think of this room?' He takes my phone from my hands, puts it back in his pocket and points the gun at my chest.

'What?'

'Tidy enough? It can hardly be messy. There's nothing in it apart from the massage table, you and your bag. More furniture is on its way: a bookcase, a lamp. You don't like it, do you?' His voice shakes. 'Can't wait to get out. I did it up specially for you. The massage table wasn't cheap, but I know how much you like your massages. And the carpet, and the lampshade. I chose everything for you.'

'Including the lock for the door?' I dig my fingernails into my palms to stop myself from howling.

'I'm sorry about that,' he says. 'And I'm sorry about the prop.'

'What?'

'The gun.' He waves it at me. 'I'm hoping I won't need it for much longer.'

I'm too crippled by terror to work out if this is a threat. 'Why?' I ask. 'What's going to happen?'

'That's up to you. Do you know how many times I painted these walls? At first I thought pale apricot, but it was too sickly. I tried yellow—too dazzling. And then a couple of weeks ago I thought of the obvious—white. Perfect.'

This can't be happening. It cannot be that a madman has been creating a room in which to imprison me while I've been getting on with my life, completely unaware. My thoughts become more concrete and focused as it dawns on me that what he's saying can't be right. A couple of weeks? Two weeks ago, Geraldine and Lucy Bretherick were still alive. But . . . the carpet is new and the room smells of paint. He can't have ordered the carpet since Geraldine and Lucy died. It would have taken longer than that . . .

As if he can read my mind, he says, 'Your being here has nothing to do with the deaths that have been on the news. Maybe that influenced the timing a bit, but—'

'I know who you are,' I tell him. 'You're Amy Oliver's father. Where are Amy and her mother? Did you kill them too?' I don't know anything; I'm guessing. But I'm starting to want to know. Maybe finding out the truth is the only way to understand him, my only chance of getting out of here.

'Did I kill them?' I've made him angry. 'Look at me. Do I look like the sort of man who would kill his wife and daughter?' He sees me staring at the gun. 'Ignore this thing . . .' He shakes it in the air, scowling at it as if it's attached itself to his hand against his will. 'Look at my face. Is it the face of a killer?'

'I don't know.'

He raises the gun, straightens his arm so that it's closer to my face.

'No,' I manage to say. 'You're not a killer.'

'You *know* I'm not.'

'I know you're not.'

He seems satisfied, and lowers the gun. 'You must be absolutely famished. Let's eat, and then I'll give you the grand tour.'

'Tour?'

He smiles. 'Of the house, stupid.'

He has already laid the table. The meal is pasta covered in grey, gelatinous gloop, the same colour as the gun. There are flecks of green in the sauce and funny straight sticks that look like pine needles. My throat closes. I can barely breathe.

He tells me to sit. At the far end of the kitchen there is a round wooden table and two wooden chairs. At some point someone who lived here got carried away with small square tiles in primary colours. The room looks like something from a children's TV programme.

'Linguine with a leek and anchovy sauce,' he says, putting down a plate in front of me. A spiral of leek, like a green snake, protrudes from the grey slime. The fishy, lemony smell makes me gag. 'With parsley and rosemary. Incredibly nutritious.' He sits down beside me.

So the pine needles are rosemary. I see a recipe book open on the surface beside the sink. A leather, tasselled bookmark lies across the double-page spread.

The back door has a glass panel in it, but I can see nothing that might smash it—no heavy-handled knives out on the work-surface, no chunky chopping-boards. All the counters are spotless, empty apart from the recipe book. The gun sits on the table, beside his right elbow.

He says, 'I won't offer you a glass of wine, if that's all right. But I also won't have any myself.'

I quell the scream that's rising inside me and manage to nod. What is he talking about? His words make sense, yet at the same time they are completely incomprehensible. Through the glass in the door I see a large wooden shed and more potted plants, mainly cacti. The private space is enclosed by a high hedge and an even higher brick wall.

I am in a house that will be almost impossible to escape from.

'Is the food all right?'

I nod.

'You're not really eating it.' He chews and swallows noisily, questioning me in between mouthfuls. His noises make me feel sick. In the end, I force down everything on my plate in order to convince him of my gratitude.

When we've both finished, he says, 'There's no pudding apart from the healthy kind. If you're still hungry there's plenty of fruit. I've got apples, pears or bananas.'

'I'm full. Thanks.'

He smiles at me. 'How long has it been since someone looked after you, Sally?'

'I'm fine.'

'I remember you telling me your ideal lunch was a drive-through McDonald's. Do you remember what you said?'

'No.'

'I said, "You can't possibly think McDonald's burgers taste good." And you said, "They taste brilliant to me, mainly because they're quick and easy. I don't even have to get out of the car. My taste buds are easily influenced."'

My stupid little McDonald's appreciation speech. I've recited it so often, to so many people.

'Do you remember telling me that every time Nick cooks he demolishes the kitchen, and it takes you at least two hours to reconstruct it afterwards?'

I blink away tears. I'm not sure how much more of this I can stand.

'You don't have to worry about mess with me.' He gestures around the room. 'No work for you to do at all.'

'When can I phone my children?'

His face shuts down. 'Later.'

'I'd like to speak to them now.'

'It's not even lunchtime. They're still at nursery.'

'Can I phone Nick?'

He picks up the gun. 'I still haven't shown you round. This is the kitchen, obviously. It's where I normally eat, but there's also a dining room. It's handy to have two dining areas, especially with children.' A quick glance at his face tells me he is serious.

He thinks he's introducing me to my new home.

'You've got children?' I try to sound matter-of-fact.

His face shuts down. 'No,' he says, looking away.

Fear presses down on my heart. It takes me a while to rise to my feet. He pretends not to notice the state I'm in as he leads me round the house, one hand on my arm. From time to time, he says, 'Cheer up!' in an unconvincingly hearty voice, as if my distress embarrasses him and he doesn't know how to react.

The room he locked me in is included in the tour. It's where he takes me after he's forced me to be more admiring of the narrow beige dining room than it deserves by repeatedly saying, 'What's the matter? Don't you like it? You don't seem to like it,' tapping the gun against his leg.

He tells me the room with the stripy carpet used to be a garage. 'There's still a garage,' he adds quickly, as if he imagines the lack of one might concern me. 'A double, detached from the house. But there used to be an integral one as well. We didn't need two, so we decided to turn this one into a playroom.' He sees my shock and sighs. 'I don't want you to think I'm unwilling to confide in you,' he says. 'I know it must seem as if there's a lot you don't know about me, and I will tell you, I promise, but the important thing is you, Sally. You're the only person I'm interested in now, for the time being at least. You won't get upset if I mention the past, will you?'

'No,' I hear myself say. I wish I could go back in time, into my own past, and scream at myself to stay away from him. How could I have been so stupid? If he's insane now he must have been insane last year, when I first met him. Why didn't I spot it? What's wrong with me? Is this my punishment? I didn't even fancy him that much. Was I so desperate to have an adventure, to make the most of my one week of freedom, that I missed all the obvious warning signs? I could lose Nick, my children, my whole life, because I chose to have a fling with this man of all men.

My resolve hardens. I have to get out of here, whatever it takes.

'Show me the rest of the house,' I say.

He doesn't need any encouragement. As he marches me from room to room, still holding me by the arm, I look for something

I can grab and use to knock him out. There's a wrought-iron letter-stand on a table in the hall with a small lamp beside it. Either of these might do, if only he would take his eyes off me for a second.

The lounge is the biggest room I've seen so far, full of bulky chairs and sofas upholstered in distressed brown leather, with a beige velvet-effect carpet. The walls that aren't covered with bookshelves are white. After we leave the room, I realise I didn't take in the title of a single book, and there were dozens. There was something on the wall too—a framed, brightly coloured poster with writing on it—something about El Salvador.

I must pay more attention. If I get out of here, I'll have to describe this house to the police.

Halfway up the stairs he stops and says, 'You'll have noticed there was no television in the lounge. Television in the lounge kills conversation, but I can get you one for your room if you'd like.'

It's not my room, I want to scream at him. *Nothing here is mine.*

Upstairs there are six rooms, five with their doors standing open. He walks me into each one, then out again almost straight away. One contains gym equipment—weights, a cross-trainer, a treadmill, an exercise bike—as well as a stereo, a club-style swivel chair in burgundy leather and two speakers, the biggest I have ever seen. The second is a bedroom, with pale blue walls, a blue carpet, navy curtains with a white trim and a double bed with blue bedding. Two blue towels lie neatly folded on the bed. 'This is the guest room,' he says, 'but we call it the Blue Room.'

In the next bedroom we come to, everything is pink and floral. *A little girl's room.* I feel as if I might faint. There is a single bed against one wall. Beside it are two toy cots and a plastic toy bath. I am allowed only a fleeting glimpse of the master bedroom before he pulls me into the smallest of the upstairs rooms, a boxroom. It has an aubergine-coloured carpet that is flecked with white, yellow walls, a skylight, a desk and more shelves full of books. My eyes are drawn to a novel I read while I was at university: *The Secret Agent* by Joseph Conrad. I hated it. And there are other books by Conrad too—eight or nine, titles I've never heard of: *Almayer* something. My eyes flit to the shelf above, too impatient to read the whole title.

What's wrong with this room?

A circle of pain around my arm and I'm dragged out on to the landing. Did I see something? What was it my eye landed on that didn't look right?

The man steers me towards the sixth door on the landing, the only one that's closed. He tries the handle. 'Locked, see? The plumbing's not working and I don't want a flood.' I stare at the shiny lock. It looks new. How recently did he have it put on? 'I'll show you the bathroom you can use.' He uses the gun to usher me downstairs; I can feel it against my back.

Halfway down I lose my footing and fall, hitting my side on the steps. 'Careful!' he says. I hear panic in his voice. Does he imagine he cares about me? Is that what he tells himself, his justification?

I stand up, winded but determined not to let him see I'm in pain. He is eager to show me what he calls my 'private bathroom'. In the hall, under the stairs and opposite the entrance to the kitchen, there's a door with a sloping top that follows the line of the stairs. I didn't notice it before. He opens it. Inside, there's a lavatory, shower and basin, all within a few centimetres of each other. I'm not sure there would be room for a person to stand in front of the basin if the door were closed.

'Bijou I think is the word,' he says. 'This used to be the cupboard under the stairs. I never wanted to turn it into a bathroom; this house hasn't got much in the way of storage space, and the master bedroom's got an en-suite . . .' He frowns, as if an unwelcome memory has forced itself upon him. 'I suppose it's lucky I lost the argument.'

'Argument with who?' I ask, but he isn't paying attention. He mumbles something that sounds like 'satisfied diffusion'.

'Pardon?' I say.

'Stratified diffusion.'

'What's that?' *Mark Bretherick is a scientist. Could this man be one too? Is that how they know each other?*

'En-suite bathrooms. Foreign holidays, too. It doesn't matter.' He waves his gun to dismiss the topic, nearly hitting me in the face. Mark Bretherick told me that Geraldine and Lucy's bodies were found in the two bathrooms at Corn Mill House. The door of one bathroom in this man's house is locked. Does it mean anything?

'I don't understand.' I look into his eyes, searching for a person I can reach somehow. How can I persuade him to let me leave?

'Do you want to phone Nick now?' he says.

'Yes.' I try not to sound as if I'm pleading.

He hands me my phone. 'Don't speak for too long. And don't say anything disloyal. About me. If you even try, I'll know.'

'I won't.'

'Say you're busy and you don't know when you'll be back.' He holds the gun to the side of my head.

Nick answers after the third ring. 'It's me,' I say.

'Sal? I thought you'd forgotten we exist, me and the kids. Why didn't you ring last night? I told them you would—they were really disappointed.'

'I'm sorry. Nick—'

'When are you back? We need to talk about your work situation, sort something out. Save Venice can't expect you to drop everything and go running whenever it suits them.'

'Nick—'

'It's ridiculous, Sal! You didn't even have time to ring me? I'm not surprised your employers forget you've got two young children—you act like you've forgotten too, most of the time!'

I burst into tears. *That's so unfair.* Nick gets angry so rarely. 'I can't discuss this now,' I tell him. 'The freezer's full of stuff Zoe and Jake can have for their tea.'

'When are you back?'

Hearing this question, answering it, is as painful as I imagined it would be. 'I don't know. Soon, I hope.'

A pause.

'Are you crying?' Nick asks. 'Look, sorry for moaning. It's a nightmare having to do it all myself, that's all. And . . . well, sometimes I worry your work's going to take over your whole life. A lot of women scale down their careers when they have kids; maybe you ought to think about it.'

Silently, I count to five before answering. 'No.' *No, no, no.* 'I'm not scaling down anything. This is a one-off crisis. Owen Mellish and I had to drop everything and come and sort it out.' *Come on, Nick. Think about it. Owen has nothing to do with Venice—he works with me at HS Silsford.* I've told Nick many times that I think Owen's jealous because I got the Venice job and he didn't.

'Owen Mellish?' says Nick. *Thank God.* 'The creep with the phlegmy voice?'

'Yeah.'

'Oh, right,' says my husband, sounding mystified. I wait. All I need is for him to ask if something's wrong. Even if I can't give him any details, even if all I can do is answer his questions with a yes or no, it will be enough to alert him. He will contact the police.

I wait, breathing jaggedly, nodding as if Nick is speaking so as not to arouse suspicion. The gun is touching my skin. 'Great,' says Nick after a few seconds. Something has gone wrong: he sounds amused, not worried. 'My wife's run off to Venice with Mr Phlegmy-voice. Listen, I've got to go. Ring tonight, yeah?'

I hear a click.

'What a disappointment,' says Mark. The man who is not Mark. 'You should have married a man with a career, not just a job. Nick will never understand.'

I can't speak, or stop crying.

'You need comforting so rarely—you're so strong, so dynamic and capable—but now, when you really need him, Nick lets you down.'

'Stop. Stop . . .' I want to ring Esther, but he'd never let me. Esther would know instantly that I was in trouble.

'Do you remember at Seddon Hall you told me you didn't think you were cut out for family life?'

Disloyal. I was disloyal to Nick and the children, and I am being punished for it.

'I don't think that's right.' He puts his arm around my shoulders, squeezes. 'I told you so at the time. Trouble is, you're trying to be part of the wrong family.'

'That's not true . . .'

'You're the perfect wife and mother, Sally. That's something I've realised recently. You know why? Because you know how to strike a balance. You're devoted to Zoe and Jake—you adore them, you look after them brilliantly—but you also have a life and a purpose of your own. Which makes you an excellent role model.' He smiles. 'Especially for Zoe.'

I try to jerk my body away from him. How dare he talk about my daughter as if he knows and cares about her, as if she is our shared concern?

'Don't let Nick talk you into sacrificing yourself so that his life can be even easier. So many husbands make their wives do that—it's not healthy.' He tucks the gun into his trouser pocket and rubs his hands together. 'All right,' he says. 'Lecture over. Let's go and get you settled in your room.'

Police Exhibit Ref: VN8723
Case Ref: VN87
OIC: Sergeant Samuel Kombothekra

GERALDINE BRETHERICK'S DIARY, EXTRACT 6 OF 9
(taken from hard disk of Toshiba laptop computer at Corn
Mill House, Castle Park, Spilling, RY29 0LE)

9 May 2006, 10.30 p.m.

Today I did what I've often fantasised about doing but
never believed I would. I underestimated my own audac-
ity. My mobile phone rang at ten o'clock this morning. It
was Mrs Flowers, ringing to say that Lucy had been sick,
instructing me to come and collect her. I felt as if concrete
slabs were falling inside my chest one by one, a 'domino
effect' of horrified realisation: everything I wouldn't be
able to do if I went straight to St Swithun's as I was being
ordered to.

Children are sick all the time; usually it is insignificant.
I asked how Lucy was now.

'Subdued,' said Mrs Flowers. 'She's sitting on Miss
Toms' knee, reading a story. I'm sure she'll perk up no end
when she sees Mummy.'

I heard myself say, 'I wish I could come and get her, but
I'm in Prague.' I don't know why I picked Prague. Perhaps
because its name is short and terse, easy to bark when
you're in a foul mood. 'Even if I got on the first flight
back . . .' I stopped, as if I was trying to work it out. 'No,
you'd better ring Mark,' I said.

'I already have,' said Mrs Flowers. 'He's recorded a
message on his voicemail saying he won't be back until after lunch.'

'Oh dear!' I tried to sound anguished. 'Can you cope
until then?'

Mrs Flowers sighed. '*We* can cope. It's Lucy I'm thinking of. Never mind. We'll give her lots of cuddles and try to keep her happy until we can get hold of Daddy.'

You'll try, and you'll succeed, I thought, because you're brilliant with small children. I too was thinking of Lucy, however selfish Mum might say I am. Last time I picked Lucy up early from school because she was ill, I ended up threatening her, tears of fury pouring down my face. 'I was poorly at school today, Daddy,' she told Mark later. 'And it made Mummy poorly too—she cried all the way home. Didn't you, Mummy?' Mercifully, she didn't tell Mark the rest: that I shook my finger in her face and said, 'If you're ill, you'll go straight to bed when we get home and have a long sleep; you'll sleep for the rest of the day and let Mummy get on with all the things she has to do. If you don't want to sleep, that means you're well enough to stay in school and I'll take you straight back there.' A terrible thing to say, I know, but it was a Monday. I look forward to Mondays like nobody would believe; after each weekend, my need to get away from Lucy and have some time and thinking space for myself is overwhelming. I love my daughter but I'm terrible at being a mother. The sacrifices that are required of me are against my nature, and it is time that the world—including Mrs Flowers—started to take my innate deficiencies into account. If I said I was a dreadful tennis player, no one would urge me to keep trying until I'm as good as Martina Navratilova.

We ought all of us to 'play to our strengths'. Which is why I felt betrayed when Cordy told me she is planning to give up her job when her new baby is born. So much for my theory about her leaving Dermot in order to be able to leave Oonagh and motherhood behind as well. 'I can afford not to work for a few years,' she said, in response to my asking why. 'I've got quite a bit saved up. And I haven't really enjoyed being a working mum. I want to be there for my kids myself, not have to rely on my ageing parents or a semi-literate childminder. I want to do the whole mummy thing. Properly.'

I felt bilious, and was unable to speak while I waited for the feeling to subside. So that's that, I thought: the end of the career of one of the brightest women I have ever met. Cordy could make it to the top of any profession she chose. If she doesn't like being a financial adviser she could do something else—train to be a lawyer or a doctor, write a book, anything. I have always had so much more respect for her than for the mothers who immerse themselves in what Cordy calls 'the whole mummy thing', the ones who are only so good at mothering because they have to be, because they are afraid of setting foot outside their own front doors and they need the perfect excuse. Can't hack it in the real world? Have a baby, then, and let everyone praise you for your commitment and devotion to your child above all else. Pride yourself on stuffing your child's school bag full of papayas and kiwis for snack time, instead of the small dented apples that working mothers rely on. Stand at the school gates twittering, 'All I've ever wanted is to be a mum.'

People without children can't get away with making an equivalent statement, can they? 'Excuse me, madam, but why do you sit at home all day doing sod all?' 'Oh, well, it's because I want to devote myself full-time to being a niece. I've got an aunt, you see. That's why I've decided not to achieve anything ever. I really want to pour all my time and energy into my niecehood.' People would be quite blunt and say, 'Don't you think you ought to do something else as well as being a niece?' I know the obvious answer: babies and children take up more time than aunts. Nevertheless, there is a fundamental truth in what I'm saying.

I asked Cordy if she was familiar with the ghost story about the monkey's paw. She wasn't. It didn't help that I couldn't remember all the details. I told her a trimmed-down version. 'An old couple find a monkey's paw, which enables them to make a wish. Any wish they make will come true,' I said. 'They lost their only son in tragic circumstances—he fell into a piece of machinery at the factory where he worked and got mangled so badly that he died . . .'

'They wish for him not to be dead?' Cordy guessed.

I smiled. You have to word it in exactly the right way or else the story doesn't work. 'The couple closed their eyes, held the monkey's paw in their hands and said, "Please, please, bring back our only son—that is our wish." That night, there's a knock at the door. They rush to open it, and it's him. Except it's not him as he used to be: it's a walking, breathing, bloody mangled mess, a grotesquely twisted lump of meat brought back to life, unrecognisable as human—'

'Yuck!' Cordy elbowed me in the ribs. 'Shut up.'

'I always think of that story when I think about working mothers.'

'Why, for God's sake?' Cordy asked.

I told her: because, for Gart's sake, when a woman returns to work after having a child or children, she is not the same. She is a semi-destroyed version of her former self. Mangled, virtually falling apart, she goes back to her workplace and she knocks on the door, and her colleagues are horrified to see how she's changed.'

'Christ on a bicycle,' Cordy muttered. 'Maybe I ought to give up work straight away.'

'No!' I snapped at her. She had entirely missed the point. 'The monkey's-paw mother doesn't care what she looks like. She doesn't give a damn! She knows where she belongs and she's determined to go back there, no matter how inconvenient it is for everybody else.'

Cordy looked at me as if I was weird.

'Don't sacrifice your career,' I begged her. 'Think of all the other monkey's-paw mothers struggling on, turned inside out but still fighting. If you give up, you'll be letting them down.'

She told me she'd think about it, but I had the sense she was only saying that to placate me. Later, I realised my little sermon had been pointless. You can't tell anyone anything; no one listens. Look at Mark and me. He thinks I've sold myself short, thrown away all my talents. And I think he's wrong. He would like me to paint or sculpt. He says I'd be more fulfilled, but that is utter rubbish. He wants these things for me not for my own sake but because it would make him feel better if I earned 'pocket-money'.

12

8/9/07

'Overpriced and ugly,' said Sellers, looking up at number 2 Belcher Close. 'I hate these new dolls' house estates.' He knew this would be his girlfriend Suki's view. She'd prefer a converted church or stable block—something centuries old and unusual.

'I don't mind 'em,' said Gibbs. 'They're better than your place. Debbie was after me to buy her one a while back. I told her to dream on. The four-bedroomers go for about half a million.'

Sellers' mobile phone started to ring. Gibbs began to mutter beside him, 'All right, love, wipe yourself, your taxi's here . . .' His crude impression of Sellers had become a regular perform-ance piece.

'Will you give it a rest? Sorry, Waterhouse.' Sellers turned away. 'Yeah, no problem. If they know.'

'Know what?'

'He wants us to find out Amy Oliva's dad's first name.'

'Why doesn't he ring St Swithun's?'

'School's closed, dickhead.'

Sellers rang the doorbell. A man's voice yelled, 'Coming!' They waited.

He was red-faced when he opened the door, pulling off his tie. Hair dishevelled, sticking up in odd places. Late twenties, early thirties, Sellers guessed. His suit jacket lay in a crumpled heap on the stairs behind him and his briefcase was open in the middle of the hall, its contents scattered around it.

Well-meaning but fucking useless, Gibbs was thinking.

'Sorry. Just got in from work and I've managed to lose my wallet. I was upstairs looking for it. It's been one of those days, I'm afraid. I'm sure I brought it home, but . . .' He looked down at his feet, then turned to look behind them. 'Anyway . . .'

'DCs Sellers and Gibbs, Culver Valley CID,' said Sellers, showing the man his ID.

'CID? What . . . Are my children all right?'

'We're not here with bad news,' Sellers told him. 'We're trying to trace the Oliva family. Was that the name of the people you bought this house from?'

'Huh!' said the man. 'Wait here. Just wait.' He dashed down the hall and disappeared into a room at the far end. When he came back he was carrying a pile of envelopes, about ten inches high, in both hands. 'When you find them, you can give them these. They had their post redirected for the first year after they moved, but obviously they didn't renew it because . . .' He tried to pass the letters to Gibbs, who stepped back to avoid taking them.

'Do you have a forwarding address?'

The man looked peeved. 'They left one, and a number; turns out they were fake.'

'Fake?' Sellers felt a prickle of excitement. There was about to be a development. He could often feel it, just before it happened. Suki said he was intuitive.

'I rang the number and the people there had never heard of the Olivas. I asked a few more questions and found out that the phone number didn't belong to the address they gave me. So either they got the number wrong, or they lied, didn't want us to know where they were going.' The man shrugged. 'Lord knows why. The sale went through amicably enough. We didn't bicker over curtains and light fittings, like the stories you sometimes hear.'

Sellers took the letters from him. Most were junk mail, addressed to Encarna Oliva, Encarnación Oliva and Mrs or Ms E. Oliva. There were a couple of envelopes addressed to Amy. Nothing for her father, Sellers noticed.

'Mr Oliva: what was his first name?'

'Oh . . . um . . . hang on.' The man at the door chewed his thumbnail.

'Was it a Spanish name?' said Gibbs.

'Yes! How did you . . . oh, right, because they were Spanish and went to Spain.' The man laughed, embarrassed. 'That's why you work for CID and I don't. And why I've lost my wallet. Oh—Angel, that was it. Spanish for angel, but it's pronounced Ann-hell. Different countries, different customs, I suppose. I wouldn't like to be an English bloke called Angel.'

'Do you know what he did for a living?' asked Sellers.

'Heart surgeon at Culver Valley General.'

'And what's your name?'

'Harry Martineau. That's e-a-u at the end.'

'When did you buy the house from the Olivas?'

'Um . . . oh, God, you'd have to ask my wife. Um . . . last year, May some time, I think. Yes, May. I remember because it wasn't long after the FA Cup final. We watched it in our old house, but we'd already started packing. Sorry, I'm very shallow!' He laughed.

Gibbs disliked Martineau. There was nothing shallow about remembering where you were for the FA Cup final. Gibbs had missed it this year for the first time in his adult life. Debbie had had a miscarriage; they'd spent the whole day and a night in hospital. Gibbs hadn't told anyone at work, and he'd told Debbie not to say anything in front of Sellers or the others. He didn't mind her workmates knowing, but he didn't want it talked about at the nick.

'Have you still got that address and phone number?' Sellers asked Martineau.

'Somewhere, but . . . look, could you pop back tomorrow, about the same time? My wife'll know where it is. Or, tell you what, why don't you come in and wait? She won't be long. Or you could nip back first thing in the morning. We don't leave the house until—'

'If you find it, ring me.' Sellers gave Martineau his card, keen to staunch the flow of unappealing offers.

'Will do.'

'Tosser,' Gibbs muttered as he and Sellers walked back to the car.

Sellers was already talking to Waterhouse. Gibbs listened to one end of the conversation, heard Sellers' tone change from satisfied to frustrated to baffled.

'How can that be?' Sellers wondered aloud, tapping his phone against his chin as they got into the car. Where was his intuition now? Maybe he had none; Stace never mentioned it. Maybe Suki was patronising him. 'Waterhouse says he's heard the name before,' he told Gibbs. 'Recently. He sounded worked up—you know the way he gets.' Sellers pulled the list of names Barbara Fitzgerald had given him out of his pocket: the owl sanctuary trip list. No, it wasn't there. Suddenly, all the names on the list struck Sellers as familiar somehow. Was he going mad? Was it because he'd read the list already, when the head-mistress had first given it to him?

'Waterhouse has heard the name Ann-hell Oliva?' said Gibbs. 'Then why the fuck—'

'No.' Sellers cut him short. 'Harry Martineau. Spelled e-a-u at the end. That's what he said—exactly what Martineau said. Word for word.'

Charlie Zailer sat cross-legged on her lounge floor with two swatches of fabric in front of her: Villandry Champagne and Caitlyn Biscuit. One was a ribbed light gold, the other a sumptuous crushed velvet, also gold. Charlie had been looking at them for nearly an hour and was no closer to making up her mind. How did one decide these things? It was dark outside, but she couldn't be bothered to get up and close the curtains.

Choosing between the fabrics her sister had brought round wasn't the only challenge; she would also need to pick a chair and sofa to be upholstered in the chosen material. A Winchester chair? A Burgess sofa? Charlie had spent most of the evening flicking through the pages of the Laura Ashley catalogue that Olivia had given her, flustered by her inability to decide. Despite her initial resistance, she was fascinated by the catalogue. She couldn't stop looking at its pinks and mauves, the tassels, glass beads and sequins—things she would once have hated. The luxurious, shimmering rooms pictured in the 'Inspirations' pages looked like . . . well, they looked like rooms that belonged to the sort of women men wanted to marry.

Charlie groaned in disgust, horrified by the thought. What kind of drooling, simpering slush-brain was she turning into? Still, the idea persisted: *if my bedroom looked like this one, I could marry Simon and be certain it would work. Women with butterscotch satin bedspreads don't get dumped.*

How embarrassing to be more pathetic at the age of thirty-nine than she'd been at sixteen.

Caitlyn Biscuit. Villandry Champagne. Either would do. Charlie's bones ached from sitting in the same position for too long.

The doorbell rang. She sprang to her feet as if she'd been caught out. Had whoever was at the door looked in through the window and seen her hunched over the two squares of gold cloth? Hopefully not. She looked at her watch: ten to eleven. Simon. It had to be. I'll let him choose, she thought. Thrust the two swatches under his nose and give him five seconds to pick his favourite. See what he makes of that.

It wasn't Simon. It was Stacey, Colin Sellers' wife. Charlie's smile shrivelled. Stacey was wearing pyjamas—white, with pink pigs on them—under a black belted raincoat. One of her feet was bare, the other stuffed into a navy mule slipper. The other slipper was behind her, lying on its side in the small front yard. Stacey was shaking, sobbing hard.

Charlie led her into the hall, then stood back, watching and wondering what to do. Stacey made a gurgling noise and wrapped her arms around herself. This will be easy, Charlie thought. You know nothing about Suki Kitson. You are not aware of any infidelity on Sellers' part, but at the same time you're not saying he'd never do such a thing; you simply don't know. You have no information, and you have no opinion. All you have is vodka and Marlboro Lights, and all you can spare is half an hour.

She took Stacey through to the kitchen, poured two large drinks and lit a cigarette. She only had three left so she didn't offer one to Stacey. 'What's happened?' she asked. It was hard to sound sympathetic when all she felt was anger. Stacey probably had no idea of the effect the mere mention of her name had had on Charlie ever since Sellers' fortieth birthday party. Did the sodden, bawling creature slumped over the kitchen table even remember?

Charlie did, and that was all that mattered. Stacey and two of her friends had peered into a bedroom with an open door, a room in which Charlie, stark naked, had been abandoned by Simon five seconds earlier. They'd been on the verge of getting into bed together for the first time when he'd fled without explanation, and they'd never properly discussed it since. Charlie had been too shocked and upset to run and close the door, or to grab a sheet to cover herself with. Simon's departure had knocked her to the ground, too, so she was sprawled on the carpet when Stacey and her tipsy mates had decided to have a good gawp at her. The two friends had been embarrassed and retreated instantly, but Stacey, who knew Charlie, knew she was Sellers' skipper, had giggled and said, 'Oops!' before disappearing. For that, Charlie would never forgive her.

Charlie had stayed at the party until Sellers threw everyone out, determined to prove she was able to enjoy herself in

Simon's absence. Later, in the early hours of the morning, she'd overheard Stacey gossiping about what she'd seen. Stacey hadn't spotted Charlie sitting on the sofa she was leaning against, and was busy telling her friends that Charlie had been pursuing Simon for ages, asking them to imagine how awful it must be to bag the man of your dreams finally, only to have him scarper the minute you take your clothes off. Charlie couldn't have put it better herself.

She realised Stacey was asking her something. Wanting to know if she spoke French. French? What did this have to do with Sellers screwing Suki Kitson?

'I did an A level in it, but I wouldn't say I'm fluent.'

'I thought you used to be a language teacher at Cambridge uni.'

'Anglo-Saxon, Norse and Celtic. And it was more literature and history than language. Why?'

Stacey pulled a piece of paper out of the pocket of her raincoat and pushed it across the table. Charlie stayed where she was, too far away to read it. She could see that there were two chunks of text. 'What is it?'

'It's my French homework, to do over the summer holidays.'

You've come here at night, in your pyjamas, to talk about homework? Get a life, you silly cow.

'You know I'm learning French?'

Like it had been announced on the ten o'clock news. 'I do now.'

'Our teacher gave it to us.' Stacey paused to tip some vodka into her mouth. It dripped down her chin. 'It's a verse from a song, the same verse in French and in English. We have to work out if the song was written by a Frenchman or by an Englishman. It's impossible!' Stacey wept. 'I mean, I'm as clever as the next person, and I've been doing really well with learning my vocab and my verbs, but . . . I just don't see how you can tell. It could have been written by a . . . Outer Mongolian for all I know. And Colin—I hate him! He won't help me! I've asked some of my friends, but no one's got a clue. I thought of you and . . . well, I thought you *must* be able to help me.'

Charlie felt a stirring of interest. She picked up the piece of paper, read the English text first:

> My Friend François
> My friend François is rather a giggle.
> My friend François burst into song.
> We asked him politely to put a sock in it.
> 'Keep your shirt on,' he said,
> And then there was a right hook
> And that really upset the apple cart.
> That's my friend François for you!

The French version was headed 'Mon Ami François' and, apart from being in a different language, was exactly the same. Charlie wanted to laugh. *Good on you, Mr French Teacher.* Anyone could learn lists of vocab, but not everyone had a flair for the logic of languages. 'I'm sure you won't be the only one who's stumped,' she told Stacey. 'Tell your tutor it was too hard.'

'Colin knows the answer and he won't tell me! He says if I can't work it out I'm as thick as pig-shit and I'm wasting my time trying to improve myself. He can be so hateful sometimes!'

'I used to think of him as the cuddly one, when we worked together,' said Charlie. 'But then, he was often standing next to Chris Gibbs.'

'Did he ever used to . . . mention me? Say he loved me, or how he felt about me? I thought he might have . . . because you're a woman . . .'

'No,' said Charlie flatly, sensing they were moving closer to the real reason for Stacey's visit.

'Can I stay here tonight?' Stacey asked.

'Sorry. There are no beds. Just a mattress on the floor, and that's mine.'

'I'll sleep on the floor, I don't care.'

'No, you won't.' *Absolutely not.*

The doorbell rang. Stacey howled at Charlie not to tell Sellers she was there. 'Your car's parked outside, you stupid arse,' Charlie muttered as she went to open the door. The possibility that her second late-night visitor might be anyone other than Colin Sellers did not occur to her, so she was startled into silence when she found, instead, Simon Waterhouse on her doorstep wearing his slightly puzzled grin, as if he was surprised to find himself there.

Charlie grabbed him with both hands and pulled him into the kitchen. 'You'll have to go now,' she told Stacey. 'Simon and I need to talk. Don't we, Simon?'

He had rammed his hands deep into his trouser pockets and was looking embarrassed.

'But you haven't told me the answer!' said Stacey. Her mouth hung open. The lower part of her face was covered in a shiny layer of mucus.

'It defeats the object if I tell you,' said Charlie. 'What your teacher wants to know is whether you can figure it out, and you can't.'

She watched as Stacey stumbled down the hall and out into the rain, hobbling past her second slipper without stopping to pick it up. Never before had closing the front door given Charlie so much satisfaction.

'What was that all about?' asked Simon.

As she explained, he picked up the sheet of paper that Stacey, in her distress, had left behind. He walked up and down as he read it. 'An Englishman wrote it. Right?'

'Obviously.'

'The name François's meant to make you think it's by a Frenchman, so it can't be or it'd be too easy.'

'What? You're kidding, right?'

Simon wasn't.

'Come on, it's obvious.'

'Not to me,' he said.

'Then you're as thick as Stacey Sellers,' said Charlie. 'What do you want, anyway?' She tried to sound off-hand.

'You heard what we found at Corn Mill House?'

'You want to talk about work? Your work? Go and wake up Sam Kombothekra. I'm off to bed.'

'I also wondered . . . if you'd thought any more about the other business.'

'The other business? The *other business*?' She flew at him, slamming the palms of her hands into his chest, sending him staggering across the room. 'You can't even say it, can you? Because you don't mean it! You don't love me—at least, you've never said you do. Well?' She was aware that she needed to create some silence if she wanted him to respond.

'You make it impossible for me to say any of the things I want to say,' he managed eventually.

'Tough,' Charlie snapped. 'You used to treat me like a leper and now you want to marry me, when we've never even slept together, never been out on a date? What changed?'

'You did.'

Charlie waited.

'You need me now. You didn't before. Even then, I cared more about you than I did anyone else, though I might not have shown it.'

Charlie dropped her cigarette end into what was left of Stacey's vodka. 'Maybe I should push the boat out and slit my wrists,' she said. 'Make myself utterly irresistible to you.'

Simon shook his head. 'There's no point, is there? I might as well go.'

'No. Stay. Tell me about the case.' Charlie needed time to think about what he'd said.

'What if I don't feel like it?'

'I'm not asking for a declaration of love.' Charlie smirked. 'The mood doesn't have to be right.'

He sighed. 'We think the writer of the anonymous letters is called Esther Taylor, although we've yet to find an Esther Taylor who looks anything like Geraldine Bretherick. There are a couple we've not managed to track down yet, so hopefully she's one of them. Anyway, the photographs that were hidden in the frames she took from Corn Mill House are of Amy Oliva and her mother, Encarna. That's been confirmed by the school.'

'Encarna?'

'Encarnación. They're Spanish. She was a banker at Leyland Carver in London, and Amy's father, Angel Oliva, was a heart surgeon at Culver Valley General. They're supposed to have moved to Spain, except the contact details they left with Harry Martineau, the guy who bought their house, don't check out. I could have been in Spain by now, but the Snowman wants to dig up every inch of Mark Bretherick's garden before he'll fork out for a plane fare, tight-arse that he is. He reckons we're going to find Angel Oliva's body. So does Kombothekra.'

'And you disagree?'

Simon looked away. 'The name Harry Martineau ring any bells?' he asked.

'With me? No.'

He closed his eyes, folded his hands behind his head and rubbed the top of his neck hard with his thumbs. 'I've seen it before—I know I have. Or heard it.'

'You've got a theory, haven't you?' said Charlie.

'I'm waiting for Norman to come back to me about something.'

'HTCU Norman?'

Simon nodded.

'So it's something about the computer, Geraldine's laptop?'

'I'll tell you when it's been confirmed.'

No question that it would be confirmed; Simon was sure he was right. As usual. Charlie couldn't resist. 'If I was your wife, would you tell me things before they'd been confirmed?'

'Would you tell me the answer to Stacey Sellers' French puzzle?'

She laughed. Reluctantly, Simon grinned.

'Tell you what,' she said. 'Work it out all by yourself and I'll marry you.'

He looked curious. 'Seriously? You'd do it, just based on that?'

Just based on that. He was unbelievable. Charlie didn't have the energy to be solemn, or worry about it any more. She didn't have the energy to accept or reject Simon's offer of marriage in the proper spirit of either, with the earnestness and anguished soul-searching that was required, the meticulous calculation of probabilities, the thousands of tiny equations featuring the words 'hope' and 'fear'. If she took the matter of his proposal and her response to heart, the only outcome could be terrible pain: of that Charlie was certain. So, might as well let it depend on something absurd. Send it up mercilessly. That way, the end result wouldn't matter.

'Seriously,' she said. '*Vraiment.* That means "really" in French.'

Mark Bretherick's solicitor, Paula Goddard, was waiting for Sam Kombothekra outside the custody suite. 'There you are,' she said. 'I wanted a quick word before we go in.'

Sam walked and she followed, struggling to keep up. Her legs were short and her shoes looked like instruments of torture. 'Shouldn't you be having a last-minute consultation with your client?' Sam said.

Goddard stopped walking. 'I'm not spraining my ankle to keep up with you.'

Sam considered not stopping; it was past eleven o'clock. He'd missed his boys' bedtime two nights running. They were too young to understand, old enough to know how to turn their disappointment into a weapon. His four-year-old was bound to be explicit about Sam's new position in the family hierarchy the next time he saw him. 'I don't like you any more, Daddy. I only like Mummy.' Or words to that effect.

Sam slowed down. 'Sorry,' he said. It wasn't Paula Goddard's fault that the way she'd said, 'There you are,' as if he'd been hiding from her deliberately, had reminded Sam of his wife Kate, whose there-you-ares tended to mean, 'Stop skulking in the lounge with the newspaper when there's Lego to be put away.'

Goddard folded her arms. 'Let me say from the outset: I haven't got time for the pointless battles that cops and lawyers go in for. I'm not your enemy and you're not mine, right? I know two dead bodies were found in my client's garden . . .'

'You forgot the two in his house.'

'. . . and I know how bad that looks. And you know he was in New Mexico when his wife and daughter died; that's been established to everyone's satisfaction, right?'

Sam leaned against the wall. Nothing about this case was satisfactory, nothing at all.

'I haven't been Bretherick's lawyer for long,' said Goddard. 'Less than twelve hours. His family asked around and someone recommended me.'

'Should I have heard of you, then?'

'Depends how well-informed you are. The point is . . . I've represented men who are guilty of murder and men who are innocent. I work just as hard for both. And I've never seen a more innocent man than Mark Bretherick.'

'He might be a good liar,' said Sam. 'However good your judgement is, however experienced you are, you might be wrong about him.'

'I'm not.' Goddard started walking. Sam had no choice but to follow. 'He only says he hasn't killed anyone when I ask him outright. He thinks it's that obvious, he forgets he needs to say it. Plus, he's not asking me to get him out. He doesn't want to go anywhere.'

'I can understand that. I also wouldn't want to go back to a house where four people at least had been killed.' Anticipating her next point, Sam added, 'Even if I was the one who'd killed them. Especially then.'

'That's not why,' said Goddard briskly. Either she was exceptionally talented at presenting her beliefs as solid facts or else she knew something Sam didn't. 'He thinks you lot aren't inves-tigating these murders in the right way; he's convinced Gerald-ine and Lucy were killed by a third party, incidentally. Not by Geraldine. He wants to stick around and make you listen to him. If he could, he'd glue himself to you twenty-four hours a day, Sergeant.'

'Maybe he's got a guilty conscience and that's why he's happy to be in custody,' said Sam. 'Being caught and locked up can be a relief—not having to run any more. Plus, he gets his meals cooked.'

Goddard squinted at him. 'How long have you been in the job?'

'Twenty-two years.'

'How many people have you known who want to stay locked up?'

Sam nodded, conceding the point.

'Most people prefer to have their freedom, even if that means making their own tea, for God's sake,' Goddard muttered crossly. 'Anyway, I'll let him speak for himself, but . . . I just wanted to warn you, you're wasting your time if he's your chief suspect. Mark Bretherick's killed no one.'

Sam didn't necessarily disagree with her. He was more con-cerned with what Mark knew, the information he could provide, than with what he might have done. After speaking to Cordy and Oonagh O'Hara, Sam had new questions he wanted to put to Bretherick. He had no intention of sharing these with Paula Goddard. Her little speech about lawyers and police not being enemies had been classic manipulation.

Goddard was also the second woman today who seemed to expect Sam to roll over and agree unreservedly with her every opinion. Cordy O'Hara had been adamant that neither Gerald-ine nor Mark Bretherick had killed anybody. 'You asked about Amy Oliva,' she'd said. 'Amy's mum, Encarna, now there's someone I can imagine running amok with a machete. I quite enjoyed her company—she was certainly never boring—but not many people did. She could be ferocious.'

Sam had stored this information in his mind. He'd liked Cordy's flat with its exposed brick walls, colourful woven rugs and tall, jungle-like plants. He'd liked the way she'd worn her baby in a sling against her chest while they were talking, and the baby's name: Ianthe. There was a bronze sculpture of a large, crushed tin can in the middle of Cordy's living room, with a flat bronze circle for a base. The green silk curtains had threads of pink running across them, and fell all the way to the floor, pooling on the dark floorboards. Nothing matched anything else in the way that his wife Kate decreed things ought to within a home, but somehow the ensemble worked.

Six-year-old Oonagh O'Hara, with a grave expression on her face, had told Sam a secret, after much encouragement from her mother, a secret Lucy Bretherick had told her. Sam wondered if there was any truth in it. He hoped he was about to find out.

Mark Bretherick stood up when Sam entered the interview room with Paula Goddard. 'What's happened?' he said.

'You mean other than the discovery of two dead bodies in your garden?'

'I mean what's happened since? Do you know whose the bodies are?'

'Not yet,' said Sam.

'The detective who interviewed me before, Gibbs, he kept asking about Amy Oliva from Lucy's class, and her mother. Do you think that's who they are?'

'We don't know.'

'I think that's who they are,' said Bretherick, turning to his solicitor. 'DC Waterhouse told me about the photos hidden in the frames, behind the ones of Geraldine and Lucy.'

Bretherick seemed almost as well-informed as the investigating team. 'The head of St Swithun's has seen the pictures and confirmed that they're of Encarna and Amy Oliva,' Sam told him. 'Now, I've got some questions I'd like to ask *you*, Mark.'

'Listen: if those bodies turn out to be Amy and her mother, you've got to look again for William Markes. You couldn't find him before because Geraldine didn't know him. Maybe he's an associate of this other woman—Encarna.'

Sam smiled politely, fighting down his irritation. Colin Sellers had made the same suggestion about half an hour earlier.

'You've got to take that school apart. Markes is connected to St Swithun's somehow, and it looks as if he's targeting mothers and daughters from Lucy's class. Have you done anything about warning the other families? I'd want to be warned if I were them.'

Sam turned to Paula Goddard. 'Do you want to ditch him and take me on as your client instead? Since I'm the one who seems to be under interrogation.'

'All right.' Bretherick held up his hands. 'Ask away.'

'I want to talk to you about last year, the May half-term holiday.'

'What about it?'

'The school was closed between Friday the nineteenth of May and Monday the fifth of June.'

'So?'

'You and your family went to Florida,' said Sam.

'I'm not sure of the dates, but . . . yeah, we went to Tallahassee last year, spring. We rented an apartment for two weeks. And Lucy came, so it must have been school holidays. I mean . . .' He blushed. 'I don't mean Lucy came as in we might have gone without her. Geraldine would never have done that.'

'Did you often take your family on holiday?'

'No. Hardly ever.'

Goddard rolled her eyes and leaned back in her chair.

'I went away all the time for work, never made time for holidays. I don't like being on holiday, I get fed up. I don't think you can arrange to relax. And Geraldine didn't work, so it wasn't as if she needed a break from anything, and she loved our house so much, she said, she didn't mind staying at home—'

'Yet you went on holiday to Florida for two weeks.' Sam cut short the justifications.

'Yes.' Bretherick frowned, as if worried by the discrepancy. 'It wasn't a holiday for me. I was working at the National High Magnetic Field Laboratory; hold on a minute.' He bowed his head. 'That's right. My trip had been arranged for a while when Geraldine told me she and Lucy wanted to come too.'

'She didn't normally tag along on your work trips?'

'No. That was the first and only time.' Bretherick flinched. The word 'only' hung in the air.

'Can we get to the point, Sergeant?' said Goddard.

'So why this one in particular?' Sam asked.

'I don't know. Florida's, you know ... Disney World. She took Lucy to Disney World.'

'One of Lucy's classmates claims Lucy told her she was going to Florida because Geraldine didn't want her to play with Amy Oliva during the holidays.'

Mark Bretherick and Paula Goddard said 'What?' in unison. Both looked perplexed.

'There were three of them who tended to get together during the school holidays,' Sam told Goddard. 'Lucy, Amy Oliva and Oonagh O'Hara. Oonagh went away to her grandparents' last year for the May half-term fortnight.' He turned to Bretherick. 'If Geraldine and Lucy hadn't accompanied you to Florida, Lucy and Amy would have played together most days, presumably?'

'I have no idea,' said Bretherick. 'All I know is Geraldine asked if she and Lucy could come with me, and I was delighted. It was much nicer not to go alone.'

'I've been told that Lucy said to a friend of hers, "My mummy hates it when I play with Amy. She and my granny think Amy's a bad lot." She's also supposed to have said, "Amy's not horrible all the time, but I'm glad my mummy doesn't like her because now we can go to Disney World."'

'It's possible.' Bretherick shrugged. 'Lucy's understanding of the way people's minds worked was ... advanced for a child of her age.'

'Geraldine didn't work,' said Sam to Bretherick and Goddard equally. 'We've established that she rarely went on holiday. Would someone have risked burying two bodies in her garden while she nipped to the shops or round to a friend's house? They'd have had to dig for hours, and lay new lawn afterwards.'

Bretherick's eyes sparked with excitement. 'The bodies in the garden: how long had they been there? Do you know?'

'The pathologist couldn't be precise, but—'

'They were buried while we were in Florida, weren't they? Whoever killed them knew we'd be away, knew he'd have time to . . . And that part of the garden, where they were found, isn't overlooked.'

There was something that hadn't occurred to Mark Bretherick and maybe never would: among the people who had known about the trip to Florida was Geraldine herself. Had she arranged to go abroad with her husband and daughter in order to leave the coast clear for a double murder and burial? Or perhaps only a burial—the murders might already have been committed. In which case, Geraldine had either had an accomplice or was herself an accomplice.

'William Markes.' Bretherick slapped the table with the flat of his hand. 'Find out if he's the father of a child at St Swithun's.'

'We've already checked,' Sam told him. 'There are no children with the surname Markes.'

'Is there something wrong with you mentally? What about any single mothers, or divorced ones who might have changed their names back, and their children's? What about cohabiting parents, where the kids have got the mother's name? Or mothers who have got new boyfriends or partners, father-substitutes? Start with Lucy's class and don't stop until you've checked the background of every child in the school. And then check the teachers, and their husbands and partners.'

Cordy O'Hara had a new boyfriend, baby Ianthe's father. What was his name? Sam saw Paula Goddard watching him, amused. Should he end the interview now, he wondered, or wait for Mark Bretherick to dismiss him?

He didn't have to wait long. 'Come back and tell me when you've found Markes,' said Bretherick. 'And you . . .' He swung round in his seat to face Goddard. 'Make sure they check properly. I've said right from the start: William Markes killed Geraldine and Lucy.'

13

Friday, 10 August 2007

I hear a clinking sound, like two glasses banging together. *Cheers.* A noise I've heard before. I'm not dreaming. Opening my eyes rearranges the chunks of raw pain in my head. I have to close them again.

He held the gun to my forehead and made me swallow a pill. When was that? Last night? Two hours ago or twelve? He said it was a vitamin pill and would do me good. I thought at the time that it tasted familiar and safe. I didn't mind taking it, not as much as I mind everything else. It must have knocked me out.

My feet are tied. I can't move them. I open my eyes more slowly this time and find myself face down on the leather massage table. I prop myself up on my elbows, turn to look at the rest of my body and realise what's restricting the movement in my feet: it's the hard loop at the end of the table. I'm lying the wrong way round, with my head at the bottom. He must have put me like this, with my feet threaded through the stiff noose. Why? Is there a reason for anything he's doing to me?

Zoe and Jake. I have to speak to them. I have to persuade him to give me my phone again. I see them clearly in my mind, tiny and far away, two little flares of colour and hope in the darkness: my precious son and daughter. *Oh, God, please, please, get me out of here.*

The clinking noise . . . Thinking about the children brings my memories of home into focus: it was the sound of a milkman putting down bottles, I'm sure of it. Zoe and Jake are milk addicts, and we have three pints a day delivered. Our milkman comes later than most, between seven and seven thirty. When Nick and I hear the glassy jangle of bottles banging together—the same sound I've just heard outside the window of this room—we grin at one another and say, 'Whose turn?' On my days, all three bottles are brought in together and put straight in the fridge. On Nick's, he goes down for one bottle at a time, as and when he needs them, because carrying one bottle upstairs is easier than carrying three. In winter, for added annoyingness, he says daily, 'It's as cold outside as it is in the fridge, so the bottles might as well sit out there. It's not as if anyone's going to nick them.' Once he added, 'This is Spilling, not . . . Hackney.'

'Why Hackney of all places?' I snapped.

'Didn't you know? It's the milk-bottle-theft capital of the UK.'

I swivel my body into a sitting position, trying to quell the storm of panic that's raging inside me. I love Nick. I love our flat, with its too many stairs. I love everything about my life, even every bad experience I've ever had—apart from this, what's happening to me now.

Across my shoulders and the top of my back, there are three distinct centres of pain. Did I fall on to some railings, something with sharp points? It seems unlikely. Ludicrous. I can't move or think quickly, and I know I must do both if I'm to have a hope of escaping. My chest is itchy beneath my shirt, and my clothes are as twisted and uncomfortable as they were the last time I woke up in this room.

I pick up the towel that's draped across the massage table, bring it to my face and inhale. That fruity smell again, but stronger. And—oh, God—now I recognise it: orange blossom. My masseur at Seddon Hall used it on me. I told Mark . . . I told the man who has locked me up that I loved it.

And he remembered, and he bought some, just like he bought the massage table . . .

I jump to my feet, pull off my shirt, losing a button in the process, and smell the inside of it: orange blossom. *No, no, no.* I reach over my shoulder and touch my back. It's oily; my fingertips skid. He has given me a massage. That's why there are sore patches across my shoulders. While I've been unconscious, he has been kneading and pressing my skin with his fingers. And . . . the itching on my chest. I look down. My bra is on the wrong way round: the semicircular lines of sewn-on pink roses have been rubbing against my skin.

I stifle a scream. I don't want to wake him up. The darkness is still lifting outside, the milkman's just been; it must be between 4 and 5 a.m. Which means he might well be asleep. If he doesn't wake until, say, seven, that gives me two hours.

To do what?

Crying hard, I take off my bra and check the skin beneath for oil. I find none. Next I take off my trousers and run my hands up and down my legs, front and back, over the scabs and bruises on my knees. No sign of any oil, but . . . My knickers are also on the wrong way round. I press my clenched fist into my mouth so that no sound escapes. Tears drip over my fingers and down my arm. *What has he done to me?*

Eventually, I force myself to move. I put my clothes back on and start to walk up and down the room, try to clear my head. Nick is always accusing me of working myself into a state if I can't solve the whole problem in one stroke. What would he do?

He would bring in the milk bottles one at a time.

I run to the window and pull back the yellow silk curtains. Nothing has changed.

I see no milk bottles, only the plant-pots, the thick hedges, the gate with the padlock on it, the elephant fountain. How would a milkman have got into the yard? Unless . . . maybe there's access from the street to another part of the garden, round the corner, and the milkman walked round the house. On the concrete of the yard there are wet patches near the wall, a cloudy liquid that might be milk. The rest of the yard is dry.

Opaque patches, then smaller drops leading to a point I can't see because it's right under the window.

Breathing hard, I grab one end of the massage table, drag it over to the far wall and climb up on to it. Holding the curtain pole with one hand to steady myself, I plant one knee on the massage table and the other on the narrow window sill, and press my face hard against the glass. 'Yes,' I hiss, seeing two semicircles of shiny red and silver. Semi-skimmed milk bottle tops. There must be some sort of hole or recess cut into the wall.

I climb down and start pacing again. Tomorrow. The milkman will come again tomorrow. If I could hear the bottles clinking, that must mean he would hear me if I screamed for help. All I have to do is make sure I'm not unconscious. I mustn't swallow another pill . . .

I frown. If the man is using pills to knock me out, how did he do it the first time when I passed out on the street? I hadn't taken any pill . . .

The room closes in on me as another detail clicks into place: the pill he gave me *was* a vitamin—that's why it tasted like one, like something I'd tasted before. The drug was in the water he gave me to wash it down. 'Rohypnol.' I say the word aloud, a word I've heard on the news but never imagined would be part of my life.

I walk over to the door and stick my little finger into the lock. Only the tip goes in. I grab my bag, pull my Switch and credit cards out of my wallet. Neither is anywhere near thin enough to slot into the gap between the door and the wall. *Idiot*. It's the wrong sort of lock anyway. *Pathetic, Sally, trying things you know won't work because you're terrified of admitting there's nothing you can do. Why don't you try the handle while you're at it?* I slam my closed fist down on the metal. There's a click, and the door opens with a protracted creak. I cover my mouth with my hands. He hasn't locked it. I blink to check I'm not hallucinating, unable to believe something good has happened.

As quietly as I can, I leave the room and walk down the hall. The door to the porch is slightly ajar, though the front door is closed. If he forgot to lock me in, could he also have forgotten to lock the front door?

Is it a test? Is he waiting outside in the yard with the gun?

I look up and see that something is balanced on top of the door, a small grey object. Metal. *The gun.* No, it's my mobile phone. Anger makes me shake. The sick bastard has booby-trapped the door to the porch. He deliberately left my cell door unlocked—he knew I'd try to get out. I bet he laughed at the idea of my phone falling on my head as I ran to the front door. Which is locked; it won't budge.

I reach up for my phone. He's removed the SIM card. *Of course. Stupid.* Ashamed of having believed I might free myself, I put my mobile back where I found it. If I can't escape, I don't want him to know I tried and failed.

I walk from room to room in search of another telephone, a land line. There isn't one, at least not downstairs. I look in the lounge, dining room and hall for bills or envelopes that might have his name and address on. I find nothing. In the lounge there are some novels, and lots of books about plants and gardening. There's a whole shelf devoted to cacti, the only one in the room that's full. I pull out a few books at random, in case there's a name written on the inside cover of one of them, but I find only blank pages.

The framed poster I saw yesterday but only half-remembered shows a map against a bright yellow background, with a country highlighted by a green line. Two cartoon-like arms are reaching out, as if trying to take the country away from its neighbours. 'Hands off El Salvador' is printed in big red letters at the bottom. I assume the green-edged country is El Salvador; I was always hopeless at geography.

The shelves in the lounge make me think about the tiny study upstairs and what I saw in it. *Something wrong.* A row of Joseph Conrad novels, a row of serious-looking hardbacks with complicated titles, too complicated for me to take in in my panicked state, and then ... empty shelves, lots of them. And the desk was completely bare. No computer on it, no pens, no coaster or roll of sellotape, nothing. Who has a desk without a computer on it?

The dining room ... I race back down the hall. One whole wall is covered in shelves, good quality ones, probably oak. All empty. Feeling cold all over, I run to the kitchen, pull open the six narrow drawers beneath the work-surface. I find some cutlery in one, but apart from that, nothing. If someone opened my kitchen drawers at home they'd find crayons, unpaid parking tickets, string, aspirins—just about everything.

I force my mind back to the grand tour, as he called it. In the bedrooms upstairs: no lamps, no rugs, nothing on the window sill. No photographs, clocks, pictures on the walls, combs or hairbrushes, glasses for water.

Nobody lives here.

The man hasn't brought me to his home. Maybe he lived here once, with his family, but not any more. He's brought me to an immaculate deserted house and laid out a few objects here and there to make it look as if this is where he lives: that wrought-iron letter-stand in the hall ... did he imagine it would be enough to fool me?

If he doesn't live here, where does he live? Where are the rest of his possessions? Perhaps he's not here now, asleep upstairs. Did he drug me and then go back to his wife and children? Maybe this is a second home, one his family don't know about. *One he bought to keep me locked up in for ever.*

The recipe book that he used to make that disgusting meal with the grey sauce is still open on the kitchen counter, still with the bookmark laid across it. I look around for other cookery books but see none. The open pages are glossy, unstained by spillages. *He bought the book in order to cook for me. That was the first time he used it.*

The kitchen window sill is pristine, uninterrupted white. I get down on my hands and knees and start to open the cupboards that run along the bottom of one wall. There's nothing in them apart from three saucepans, two Tupperware containers and a colander. Inside the colander there's a clear plastic syringe with measurements printed on it along one side.

My heart goes wild. I tear the lids off the saucepans, looking for a bottle of whatever he's been using to knock me out. *Rohypnol.* Does it even come in a bottle? Surely he'd keep it close to the syringe. The measurements chill me more than anything: the idea that he leaves nothing to chance. He knows what he's doing, knows exactly how long he wants me to be unconscious for, how much of the drug he needs to achieve it.

I hate him more than I thought it was possible to hate. I scramble to my feet, sweep the recipe book and bookmark off the counter on to the floor, panting with rage. The book slams shut as it lands. I read the title on the cover: *100 Recipes for a Healthy Pregnancy.*

'Which one do you fancy this evening?' says a voice from the hall.

At gunpoint, he marches me back to the room with the stripy carpet. He is wearing dark green paisley pyjamas. 'Lie down,' he says, pushing me towards the massage table. 'On your back.' His voice is stern. He doesn't look at me as he speaks.

'What have you done to me?' I whisper, afraid to raise my voice in case it makes him angry.

He wheels the table over to the wall. 'How am I supposed to have a clear head for work if you wake me up at quarter past five in the morning?' he says.

I hear myself apologise to him. I need to know, need to be told. However bad it is.

'It's okay,' he says. 'Shush. Stop crying, there's no need to cry. Now, shuffle along and down—this way, that's right—and put your legs up against the wall, so that your body makes a right angle. That's good. Now, stay in that position. Get as comfortable as you can. I want you to stay like that for an hour or so.'

Tears pour down my cheeks, collect in my ears. I can't speak.

He walks over to the window, tapping the gun against his open palm. 'I suppose, since you've obviously worked it out, there's no point in my being secretive any more. You saw the title of the recipe book.'

'I'm not pregnant!'

'You might be. You might be already, if we're lucky.'

The vitamin pill: it was folic acid. That's why the taste was so familiar. I took it throughout both my pregnancies.

'Have you raped me? How many times?'

He makes a disgusted noise. 'Thanks,' he murmurs. 'Thanks such a lot for that vote of confidence.'

'I'm sorry . . .'

'I'm not an animal. I used a syringe.' He lets out a small laugh. 'I didn't have a turkey baster, not being much of a cook. You're the only person I've ever cooked for, in fact.'

'You drugged me and undressed me and injected me with . . . with . . .'

He picks up my hand and squeezes it. 'Sally, I want us to be a proper family. I've got a right . . .' His voice wavers. '*Everybody* has a right to have a proper happy family. I've never had that, Sally. I don't think you have either.'

'That's not true, it's not true!'

'I know you need time to adjust. I wouldn't dream of suggesting we sleep together, not yet. Never, if you really don't want to. I'm not a brute.'

I dig my fingers into my legs. If I could, I'd rip out all my insides until there was nothing left of me.

'I know I should have told you about the baby but . . . well, I was eager to get the ball rolling. I'm sorry.'

'How many times have you . . . injected me?' I manage to say.

'Just twice. And I've got a good feeling about this last time.' He crosses his fingers, holds them in front of my face.

I cry while he strokes and pats my hand and makes soothing noises. I have no idea how much time is passing, how much of my life I am losing in this room: half an hour, maybe longer, since he last spoke. When I run out of tears, I say, 'Why did you give me a massage?'

'To make you feel good. You love massages.'

'I was unconscious!'

'I thought it might relax you, *sub*consciously. Sometimes the body knows things the mind doesn't. The more relaxed you are, the more likely you are to conceive.'

I feel a surge in my stomach, nearly choke on the bile that rises to fill my throat.

'Do you think I want this to be horrible for you, Sally? I don't. I truly don't.'

'I know.' *I'm going to get that gun off you and I'm going to kill you, you sick fuck.*

'You have to try to want what I want. Do you remember, at Seddon Hall, you told me you were sick of always being the one who had to arrange everything: Valentine's Day dinners, even treats for your own birthday?'

'You make it sound as if I hated my life!' I blurt out, sobbing. I can't bear to listen to him. 'I love my life—I was just complaining!'

'With good cause,' he says, tapping the gun against the side of the massage table. 'What about the Christmas when you chose and bought your own present from Nick because you didn't trust him to get the right thing: Boudoir eau de parfum by Vivienne Westwood. You even wrapped it yourself and wrote "To Sally, love Nick" on it. Do you remember telling me that? Because you were sick of wondering if Nick would remember to wrap it in time for Christmas Day.'

Why did I tell him so much?

'Can I . . . please could I have my phone, just for a few minutes? I need to speak to Zoe and Jake.'

I have said the wrong thing. He drops my hand. His eyes harden, his face as close to a portrait of pure evil as anything I've ever seen. 'Zoe and Jake,' he repeats in a wooden voice. 'The trouble with you, Sally, is that you never know when the party's over.'

Police Exhibit Ref: VN8723
Case Ref: VN87
OIC: Sergeant Samuel Kombothekra

GERALDINE BRETHERICK'S DIARY, EXTRACT 7 OF 9
(taken from hard disk of Toshiba laptop computer at Corn
Mill House, Castle Park, Spilling, RY29 0LE)

17 May 2006, 5.10 a.m.

A brilliant thing happened tonight—I thought for a while
that it might be the key to everything. Well, last night, I
suppose you'd have to say, but I haven't had any sleep. I'm
going to end up like that man I saw on that 'shock-doc'
documentary, who was so sleep-deprived for so long that
he ended up with a permanent headache. When he went
to the doctor, he was told that by not sleeping enough
he'd done irreparable damage to the nerve endings in his
brain. The doctor gave him a drug to stop the headache,
but that made him shake as if he had Parkinson's disease.
The documentary said only that he was a contract lawyer
in the city, not whether he had small children, but I'm certain he did. I think he had three children under five and a
wife who also worked full-time.

I took Lucy to the theatre last night. Not to a matinee,
not like the awful time we went to see *Mungo's Magic
Show* and we were surrounded by brats, and Lucy
screamed because I wouldn't let her eat two Cornettos.
No, this time I took her in the evening, like an adult. I
wondered if she might be more bearable if I treated her
more like a grown-up. So I booked two tickets to *Oklahoma!* the musical at Spilling Little Theatre. Mark was
away at yet another conference. I told Lucy that she and I
would be going out together for a special treat evening,
but only if she was very good. She was so excited, happier

than I've ever seen her, and she really did try hard. I told her we would go out for dinner first, and she was even more excited about that. She'd never been to a restaurant in the evening before, and she knew it was something grown-ups did, so of course she wanted to do it.

We went to Orlando's on Bowditch Street, and Lucy had spaghetti bolognese. For once she ate everything on her plate. Then we held hands and walked to the theatre, and she sat through the whole performance transfixed, as still as a statue, eyes as wide as plates. Afterwards she said, 'That was great. Thank you for taking me to the theatre, Mummy.' She said she loved me and I said I loved her and we held hands again all the way back to the car. I thought it was a turning point. I decided to do grown-up things with her whenever I could, try to treat her more like a twelve-year-old than a five-year-old.

I must have been stupid or desperate or both to think that would work. An hour ago, when I was tossing and turning in bed and wondering what Lucy and I might do together next—a manicure, the National Portrait Gallery, the cinema—I felt someone tugging on my hair. I thought it was an intruder and screamed, but it was Lucy. Normally when she wakes at night, she doesn't get out of bed; she yells for me and expects me to come running. But there she was, and she wasn't upset. She was smiling. 'Mummy, can we go to the theatre again?' she said.

'Yes, darling,' I promised. 'Very soon. But you've got to go back to sleep, Lucy, it's not morning yet.'

Could I have handled it better? No doubt my mother would say so. If Lucy had asked her, she would probably have leaped out of bed, even at four in the morning, and searched on the Internet for suitable shows, bleary-eyed but insisting she was full of energy. I've asked her, often, how she managed not to feel permanently exhausted when I was little. She puts on a smug little smile, waves her hand dismissively and says, 'Being tired has never killed anyone. You don't know how lucky you are!' Then she tells me an anecdote about someone she met in town whose daughter has triplets, no husband and seventeen low-paid manual jobs that she must do simultaneously in order to feed her family. And I envy this down-trodden la-bourer that my mother has almost definitely invented for the sole purpose of shaming me, because it sounds as if her life has probably always been appalling. Whereas I had a brilliant life before I became a parent: that is why I find it so hard to cope.

'I want to go to the theatre again now,' Lucy insisted. 'I want to go out for dinner again, with just you.' I repeated that it was night-time, that no theatres or restaurants were open. She began to scream and howl, hitting me with her fists. 'I want to go NOW, I want to go NOW,' she wailed. In the end the only way I could shut her up was by threat-ening her. I said that if she didn't quiet down and go back to sleep that instant, I would never take her anywhere again. She stopped punching and yelling, but I couldn't get her to stop crying, no matter how patiently I explained the situation. In the end I had to sit by her bed and stroke her hair while she cried herself to sleep, and I cried too be-cause my stupid special treat had ended up causing her more pain than if I hadn't bothered.

Still, at least now I know. Whether I'm kind or utterly selfish makes absolutely no difference. Even if I try my hardest, I cannot avoid the misery, inconvenience, frustra-tion and futility that make up nine-tenths of the experi-ence of having a young child. *It is simply not worth it.* Even from an investment point of view, for the sake of having grown-up children who visit you when you're se-nile and lonely, it's not worth spending the best years of your life entangled in put-your-coat-on-I-don't-want-to-put-my-coat-on-but-it's-cold-I-don't-like-that-coat-I-want-another-coat-you-haven't-got-another-coat-well-I-want-one-but-we-have-to-go-out-now-get-into-the-car-I-don't-want-to-sit-in-the-back-seat-I-want-to-sit-in-the-driver's-seat-well-you-can't-sit-in-the-driver's-seat . . . That, or a version of it, is the conversation I've been having ever since Lucy learned to talk. Why can't she simply say, 'Yes, Mummy,' and do as I ask? She hates it when I'm angry, and I've told her over and over again that this is the way to make Mummy happy.

I have never hit her. Not because I disapprove of hitting children—I have pinched and flicked Oonagh O'Hara several times without Cordy noticing—but because sometimes I want to hit Lucy so much and I know I would have to stop almost as soon as I started, so what would be the point? It would be like opening a box of delicious chocolates and only being able to eat one.

In an ideal world, parents would be able to give their children a good, satisfying kicking—a really thorough, cathartic battering—then snap their fingers and have the effects of their violence disappear. Also, it would be good if children, while being beaten, didn't feel pain; then there would be no need for guilt.

Instead they are delicate and vulnerable, which of course is their most effective weapon. They make us want to protect them even as they destroy us.

14

8/10/07

Sellers knocked on the back of the computer Gibbs was using. 'Come on, we're late.'

'Don't wait for me, or you'll be even later.'

'You don't want to miss this one.'

'Why? Something happened?'

'I've just spoken to Tim Cook,' said Sellers.

'Is he still shagging that granny?'

'I doubt it. They've been living together for nearly ten years.' Silence. 'You're supposed to laugh at that. I suppose you haven't been married long enough.' No response. Sellers tried a new approach. 'The dental records were a match. The two skeletons are Encarna and Amy Oliva. Were,' he corrected himself.

Gibbs looked up. If Sellers was right, he might as well stop what he was doing. But since he'd got this far . . . 'You go,' he said. 'I'll catch you up.'

'There's more. Amy Oliva's nanny finally— Why do I bother?' Sellers broke off, impatient. 'If you're interested, stop surfing porn sites and come to the briefing. You know they can find out what sites you've logged on to?'

'I'm in Yahoo Mail at the moment.' Gibbs grinned. 'Porn sites? How do you know about those, then?'

Sellers gave up.

Once he'd gone, Gibbs typed in his ID and password. Amy Oliva was dead. Her body had been found in Mark Bretherick's garden. It was optimistic to assume she might have replied to the e-mail Gibbs sent her yesterday.

She hadn't. The only new message was from Gibbs' sister. He opened it, saw that it had to do with arrangements for Christmas and closed it again without replying. It was August. Christmas wasn't until December. You had to draw the line somewhere.

Porn sites. He sniffed contemptuously. Sellers had to be one of those sex addicts he'd read about, like . . . was it Kirk Douglas or Michael Douglas? The HTCU lot probably had a file on Sellers twenty inches thick. Gibbs thought about Norman Grace, who wore pink shirts and thin stripy scarves wound round his neck. And slip-on shoes. Kombothekra had entrusted the hard disk of Geraldine Bretherick's laptop to a man who dressed like a woman. Once, Gibbs had seen Norman in the canteen reading a fashion magazine. If he was gay it wouldn't be so bad, but the dickhead was straight, had loads of girlfriends— fit ones, too. So what was he playing at?

Gibbs was about to get up when he had an idea. Another job for Norman. Come to think of it, he probably didn't need Norman. He could have a stab at it himself. He went to the Hotmail site. When the sign-in box appeared, he typed in Amy Oliva's e-mail address, amysgonetospain@hotmail.com. Then he clicked on 'Forgot your password?'. If it was anything like Yahoo Mail . . .

It was. Gibbs smiled when he saw the security question: 'Who wrote *Heart of Darkness*?' He typed in 'Blondie' and swore under his breath when it didn't get him in. He tried Debbie Harry, Deborah Harry and Debra Harry before remembering that the Blondie song was called 'Heart of Glass'. Bollocks. He went to Google, typed in 'Heart of Darkness' and discovered that it was a book by a bloke called Joseph Conrad. He clicked back to the Hotmail screen and gave this name he'd never heard of a try.

Result. He had to create a new password for the account in order to read the messages, since he'd claimed to have forgotten the old one. He decided on 'Debbie'. In honour of his wife, not Debbie Harry.

Amy Oliva had three new messages. Gibbs clicked on 'Inbox' and waited. His eyes widened when the next screen appeared. The unread communications were highlighted in yellow to distinguish them from the ones that had been opened. The first of Amy's new messages was from Oonagh O'Hara. The second and third were from Great Western Hotels and the Halifax bank—junk mail.

Gibbs' message, the one he'd sent from St Swithun's yesterday, was the fourth one down. It wasn't highlighted in yellow. He shivered, rubbing the back of his neck. He'd e-mailed a dead girl, believing her to be alive, and she'd opened the e-mail. Or someone had, probably the person who had killed her.

Gibbs looked at the names beneath his own. Oonagh O'Hara was a frequent correspondent, as was somebody called Silvia Ruiz Oliva—a relative, presumably. The rest was spam.

Silvia turned out to be Amy's grandmother: her messages were all signed 'Gran'. He read them all, finding them increasingly interesting as he took in the cumulative meaning. There had obviously been a family row. Silvia kept asking when she might see Amy. In one she had written: 'Please tell Mummy that if she's cross with me, I'm sorry.' Gibbs scrolled down to see if there were any messages from Amy attached to the bottom of Silvia's. There weren't. He went to the 'Sent Messages' page. Nothing. Not a single message had been copied to the folder.

He opened one of Oonagh's messages. Nothing out of the ordinary, if you didn't count the fact that its recipient was no longer living when it was written and sent. He read to the end, then breathed in sharply when he saw that Amy's original letter hadn't been deleted. Gibbs scrolled down further and found, beneath Amy's section, another message from Oonagh, probably one that was also in the inbox. Beneath that, another message from whoever was pretending to be Amy. A lengthy back-and-forth correspondence, all trailing from this one message.

Oonagh's e-mails, Gibbs noticed, contained the odd spelling mistake. Amy's written English was faultless.

Stepford had interviewed Oonagh O'Hara yesterday and she'd told him she hadn't heard from Amy since last May. Clearly she was lying. Or rather she *believed* she was lying. In fact, she'd told the truth: she had been exchanging letters with Amy's killer, not with Amy.

Gibbs raced through the messages. At the end of each of her letters, before signing off, Oonagh had written, 'Hows your mum?' or 'Is your mum okay?' In one she'd gone further and said, 'How are things with you and you're mum?' Twice, after enquiring about Encarna Oliva, Oonagh had written 'Hows Patrick?' and once, 'Hows Partick?'

Had Encarna Oliva left her husband for another man? Had Patrick worked at the bank with her? Or maybe he'd been a friend or colleague of her husband's, someone Angel Oliva had worked with at Culver Valley General Hospital. There were some women, Gibbs knew, who'd think nothing of shagging their husbands' mates. Gibbs thought it was inevitable that one day Sellers would try to bed Debbie; he was training himself to dislike Sellers in advance, so that when it happened he'd be prepared.

Amy's replies to Oonagh's e-mails were chatty but bland, full of news about watching bullfights and flamenco dancers. Clichés of Spain. Lies. Despite her e-mail address, Amy Oliva never got to Spain. She never got further than the garden at Corn Mill House. Interestingly, she—her killer, Gibbs corrected himself—had not once answered Oonagh's enquiries about Encarna and Patrick.

Why had Oonagh O'Hara lied about when she'd last been in touch with Amy? There was nothing secret or personal about any of these e-mails. 'Something weird's going on,' Gibbs said aloud.

He was on his way out of the CID room when the phone rang. It was Barbara Fitzgerald, the head of St Swithun's. 'Hello,

Christopher,' she said warmly, once Gibbs had identified himself. 'I'm just phoning to let you know I've e-mailed you a full list of everyone who went on the owl sanctuary trip last year. I did forget a few names, as it turns out.'

Gibbs thanked her.

'Is there . . . any news?'

'No.' He didn't want to be the one to tell her that another of her pupils had been murdered. Nor did he want to talk, knowing what he was withholding; guilt made him more brusque than usual and eventually Barbara Fitzgerald gave up.

Feeling unsettled, ashamed of his cowardice, Gibbs navigated his way back to Yahoo Mail. He entered his ID and password, and was waiting for his inbox to appear when he realised his mistake. Barbara Fitzgerald didn't know his Yahoo address; she would have sent the list of names to his work e-mail, the address from which he'd e-mailed her earlier. *Dickbrain.* He was about to log out of his Yahoo account when he saw that he had a new message. From Amy Oliva. No amount of blinking made it disappear.

Gibbs double-clicked on the envelope icon. The message had been sent from a Hotmail address, but a different one: amysbackfromspain@hotmail.com. It was only three words long, three ordinary words that worried Gibbs more than an overt threat would have. He got up and left the room, not bothering to sign out of his account.

Meeting room one for a team briefing? What was wrong with the CID room? Charlie had always found it perfectly adequate. She broke into a run as she turned the corner. By the time she got there she was out of breath. She knocked and opened the door. Sam Kombothekra, Simon, Sellers and Professor Keith Harbard sat in silence on comfortable blue leather chairs that looked as if they belonged in the executive row of a multi-screen cinema. Harbard was eating a muffin, dropping crumbs on the carpet around his feet.

Inspector Proust stood in the corner of the room by the water cooler with a mobile phone pressed to his ear, talking too loudly about a DVD player that was 'too complicated'. Had he phoned a shop on the other side of the world to complain?

'What's going on?' Charlie asked.

'We're waiting for Gibbs,' said Sam.

The Snowman interrupted his phone call to say, 'Round him up, will you, Sergeant?'

Charlie realised he was addressing her. *Bloody cheek*. 'I can't stay, sir. I need one of you to come with me. I think I've got something that's going to help you.' She didn't dare ask for Simon. Not in front of everyone.

'Off you go, Waterhouse,' said Proust. Charlie could have kissed him. 'Don't let it take too long, Sergeant.'

'I feel like the kid whose mother turns up two hours early to collect him from the party,' said Simon, following Charlie down the corridor.

She smiled at him over her shoulder. 'Did your mother do that?'

No reply.

'She did, didn't she?'

'What's this about, anyway?'

'By the time I've explained . . .'

They marched the rest of the way in silence. Charlie stopped outside interview room three and Simon walked into her. She grinned determinedly as he leaped back, alarmed by the unexpected physical contact.

She opened the door. A broad-shouldered woman with short spiky dyed hair and a pained expression on her face sat behind the table. She was wearing black tracksuit bottoms with pink stripes down the legs, pink lace-up pumps and a tight pale pink polo-necked jumper that clung to the rolls of flesh around her middle. 'This is Pam Senior,' Charlie told Simon. 'Miss Senior, this is Detective Constable Simon Waterhouse. I'd like you to tell him what you've just told me.'

'All of it?'

'Yes, please.'

'But . . . I can't sit here all day, I'm self-employed. I'm a child-minder. I thought you'd have told him already.'

When Charlie didn't respond, Pam Senior sighed and started to talk. A woman she didn't know had turned up on her door-step last night, she said. Late: eleven o'clock. She'd introduced herself as Esther Taylor and said she was the best friend of a woman whose children Pam sometimes looked after—Sally Thorning. She'd demanded to know what Pam had done to Sally, and tried to force her way into Pam's house.

'She called me a liar, accused me of all sorts—pushing Sally under a bus, but I didn't, I swear! Sally must have told her I did, though, and now she reckons Sally's disappeared and I must know something about it. She was threatening to go to the po-lice.' Pam's nostrils flared. She sniffed several times. 'So I thought I'd better come here first and tell you I've done nothing, absolutely nothing. What she's saying's slander, and that's illegal, isn't it?'

'Under a bus?' said Simon. 'Are you sure that was what she said? Where do you think she got that from?'

'Sally did have an accident with a bus, in Rawndesley a few days ago. I was there, I saw it. Well, I didn't see it happen, but I saw a group of people all gathered round, so I went and looked, and it was Sally. I tried to help her, offered to take her to hospital to get checked out, but she wasn't having any of it. She accused me of pushing her and shouted at me in front of everyone.' Pam's face reddened as she remembered the inci-dent. 'We'd had a bit of a row before, because of a mix-up over childcare arrangements, and I'll admit I was furious with her, but . . . what sort of person does she think I am, that I'd do that?'

'So you didn't push her?' said Charlie.

'Of course not!'

'And you didn't see if anyone else pushed her?'

'No. I told you. I've been upset about it all week. I was just starting to feel better—Sally left a message saying she was sorry, and I thought it was all over—and then this Esther Taylor woman turns up. She tried to barge into my house. Look.' Pam held out her hand so that Simon could see it shaking. 'I'm a wreck.'

'Tell him the rest,' said Charlie.

'I managed to keep her out, slammed the door on her.' Pam touched her throat. 'She started yelling outside about Mark Bretherick, asking if he was the one who ... who wanted Sally dead. I can hardly bear to say it, it's so awful. I read the local paper every night, so I recognised the name. That was what freaked me out the most.' She pulled a handkerchief out of the pocket of her tracksuit trousers; it had the initials PS embroidered on it. It had been ironed, Charlie noticed, and folded into a neat square.

'Do you know Mark Bretherick?' asked Simon.

'No!'

'Did you know Geraldine or Lucy Bretherick?'

'No, but I know how they died, and I don't want anything to do with it!'

An odd way to phrase it, thought Charlie. 'But, according to you, you haven't got anything to do with it,' she said. 'You don't know the Bretherick family. You've never known them.'

'Well, obviously this Esther Taylor knows something about them, or Sally does, and I don't want anything to do with any of them. I don't want to be attacked in the middle of the night when I've done absolutely nothing wrong!'

'All right,' said Charlie. 'Try to calm down.'

'What did Esther Taylor look like?' Simon asked.

'About my height. Short, blonde hair. Glasses. A bit like the blonde one out of *When Harry Met Sally*, but uglier and with glasses.'

'She didn't look anything like Geraldine Bretherick? Do you know what Geraldine Bretherick looked like? Have you seen her photograph in the paper?'

Pam nodded. 'No, this woman looked nothing like her.'

Charlie watched Simon watching Pam. What was he waiting for? She'd answered his question.

'Actually . . .' Pam's hanky was taut in her lap, her left and right hands waging a subtle tug of war. 'Oh, my God. *Sally* looks like Mrs Bretherick. I didn't think of it until you just said . . . Why did you ask me that? What's going on?'

'I need Sally's address and telephone number and as much detail about her as you can give me,' said Simon. As Pam spoke, he frowned and nodded, committing her words to memory. Charlie made notes. Simon looked surprised only when Pam mentioned that Sally Thorning's husband, Nick, was a radiographer at Culver Valley General Hospital. Once he'd got all the information he could out of her, he left the room.

Charlie followed him, closing the door on Pam's questions and demands. She was expecting to have to chase after Simon, but she found him standing motionless outside the interview room. 'What?' she said.

'I think I saw *When Harry Met Sally*. She said, "the blonde one out of *When Harry Met Sally*". Which is Sally, obviously, because Harry's the man.'

'I've seen it too. After a hopeless start, they get married and live happily ever after,' said Charlie pointedly.

'You're called Charlie. Charlie can also be a man's name.'

'Simon, what the fuck . . . ?'

'I know where I've seen the name Harry Martineau.'

'The man who lives in the Olivas' old house?'

'No. He doesn't exist. That's why no one's heard of Angel Oliva at Culver Valley General, the hospital where Nick Thorning works.'

'I'm completely, utterly lost,' said Charlie.

'Jones is the name. Jones: the most ordinary name in the world.'

'Simon, you're beginning to frighten me. Who's Jones? The killer? The man Sally Thorning met in the hotel?'

'No. Come on, we've got to get back to the briefing.'

'I've got my own work to do! I can't just leave Pam . . .'

Simon strode down the corridor. Charlie found herself running after him. As always, she wanted something from him that he was not making readily available. It wasn't her case, it was nothing to do with her, but she needed to know what he meant.

They hadn't got far when they saw Norman Grace from HTCU hurrying towards them. 'I was on my way to find you,' he said to Simon.

'What have you got?'

'You were wrong . . .'

'That's not possible.'

'. . . but you were also right.'

'Norman, I'm in a hurry.'

'The name's Jones,' said Norman, and Charlie's skin turned cold.

'I know.' Simon broke into a run.

Not so much as a thank you. Charlie shrugged apologetically. 'Sorry,' she said to Norman. 'He's got a bee in his bonnet.'

'Can you tell him I'm hanging on to the Bretherick hard disk for the time being? There's more, but it'll take me a while to get it into a presentable state.'

Charlie nodded, and was moving away when Norman touched her arm. 'How are you, Charlie?'

'Fine, as long as no one asks me how I am,' she said, smiling.

'You don't really want that. You don't want people not to care.'

Charlie ran down the corridor, hoping she hadn't missed anything, wondering if Norman was right. Would she prefer everyone to forget about last year? To treat her exactly as they had before?

She found Simon round a corner, on his mobile phone. He was telling somebody that he needed them to come to Spilling, saying that as soon as possible would be great. He gave the address of the nick. Charlie had never heard him sound so eager or grateful. Jealousy wasn't an issue; it was obvious he was speaking to a man. Simon never sounded so unguarded when he spoke to women.

'Who was that?' she said once they were on the move again.

'Jonathan Hey.'

'The Cambridge don? But . . . Simon, you can't just invite your own expert to the party without checking with Sam first. What about Keith Harbard?'

'Harbard knows nothing.'

When he was in this sort of mood, Charlie knew there was no point contradicting him. If he thought Hey was that much better than Harbard, he was probably right. It wouldn't stop Proust from taking one look at the second sociology professor to land at his feet and despatching him back to Cambridge without refreshments or an explanation.

Poor Jonathan Hey. What a fool, saying yes to Simon Waterhouse.

'"Change it back"?' Proust surveyed Gibbs from across the room. 'Is that supposed to mean something to us? Change what back? Change it back to what?'

'The password,' said Gibbs. 'It must be. To get into Amy's Hotmail I had to change it. Whoever set up the account must have tried to get in using the old password and failed.'

'And worked out that you changed it? How would he have known?' said Kombothekra.

'Intelligent guess. I sent a message to Amy's Hotmail address, so he knew I knew about it. He wants us to see how clever he is. Look at the new e-mail address he created, not more than a few minutes after I broke into his old one: amysbackfromspain@hotmail.com. He's trying to be witty.'

'Or she,' said Keith Harbard. 'Gibbs is right about the wit; to me that suggests a woman.'

'Have you never read Oscar Wilde, Professor?' Proust enquired.

'He's not that clever,' said Sellers. It sounded as if he might have been talking about Harbard; Gibbs suppressed a smile. ' "Change it back." How can we? We don't know what the old password was.'

'He knows that,' said Gibbs impatiently. 'It's a threat, isn't it? He knows he's giving us an impossible order.'

Harbard nodded. 'It's part of the game. Either it's a guarantee of punishment with a bit of psychological torture thrown in—she appears to be giving you a chance but it's not a real one because you can't possibly know her original password—or she's inviting you to think about what the password might have been. Maybe it was her name.'

'That's a point,' said Kombothekra. 'Thanks, Keith. I'll get on to Hotmail.'

'In the meantime, reply to the message,' said Harbard. 'She'll be flattered. Tell her you can't think of a way forward, that you need her help with the task she's assigned you.'

'Psychological expertise as well as sociological,' muttered Proust. 'Buy one, get one free. Unlike you, Professor, I don't care about our perpetrator's inner demons or what makes him tick. Give me his name, tell me where I can find him and I'll be happy. Let's concentrate on information, not speculation. We've identified the two skeletons—that's a good start.'

'Harry Martineau and Angel Oliva have become top priority,' Kombothekra told him. 'Nobody at Culver Valley General Hospital can remember a heart surgeon called Angel Oliva, and their records suggest he never worked there. So either Martineau was lying or Oliva lied to Martineau.'

'We're still checking,' said Sellers, 'but it looks as if no child or teacher at St Swithun's knows a William Markes. Cordy O'Hara's new ride's called Miles Parry.'

'The nanny.' Kombothekra nodded at Sellers.

'Yeah, I've spoken to Amy Oliva's former nanny. The number in the anonymous letter was the right one. She didn't get back to us sooner because she's in Corsica on her honeymoon, back tomorrow evening. But even before she told me that I recognised her voice on the phone.' Sellers tried not to sound proud of his own achievement.

'Have you knobbed her?' asked Gibbs. Behind his hand, so only Sellers could hear, he began to whisper, 'All right, love, wipe yourself, your taxi's here . . .'

'Corsica?' said Proust. 'Why does that sound familiar?'

'Her name's Michelle Jones,' Sellers told him. 'I knew her voice from interviewing her after Geraldine and Lucy Bretherick's bodies were found. She was in Corsica then too—I interviewed her on the phone. She was Michelle Greenwood before she got married.'

'The Brethericks' babysitter,' said Proust. 'The one who selfishly arranged a holiday with her boyfriend for the May half-term last year.'

'That's right,' said Kombothekra. 'She was also Amy Oliva's part-time nanny, so that's another connection between the two families.'

'Unfortunately, when I spoke to Michelle I didn't know we were going to draw a blank at Culver Valley General, so I didn't ask about Mr Oliva,' said Sellers. 'I've left another message for her.'

'What about this bank where Mrs Oliva worked?' Proust asked.

'I'm going today,' said Kombothekra. 'I'm hoping someone there can tell me about Patrick.'

'Ask about William Markes too,' said the Snowman. 'And Angel Oliva. Why not? Let's brandish all our names wherever we go and see what we get.' Proust would be going nowhere apart from back to his office. Saying 'we' instead of 'you' was his concession to the idea of the team.

'I spoke to the Brethericks' postman this morning,' said Kombothekra. 'He says he saw someone in the garden of Corn Mill House last spring, and he remembers it was while the Brethericks were in Florida because Geraldine had told him they were going away. He went to try and get a closer look, but by the time he got to the part of the garden where he'd seen the person, he or she had gone. Postie had the rest of his round to do, so he didn't look much beyond that spot. When the Brethericks got back, he told Geraldine he'd seen someone. She looked a bit puzzled, but said that whoever it was hadn't done any harm—there'd been no break-in. But here's the really interesting part. I asked him if he'd noticed anything else, anything at all that was unusual while the Brethericks were in Florida. At first he said no, but when I urged him to think hard, he did remember something: a red Alfa Romeo parked at the bottom of the lane outside Corn Mill House's gate. He said the car was there on at least three occasions while the Brethericks were away.'

'Bright, is he, this postman?' said Gibbs. 'Didn't he make the connection between the car and the man he'd seen?'

'He didn't,' said Kombothekra. 'On the day he saw the killer, the car wasn't there.'

'Maybe our man decided to walk that day.'

'Person,' Harbard reminded them all. 'Remember, the evidence points to a woman.'

Gibbs scowled at him. He'd made his point, why did he have to keep making it? What evidence was he talking about? Gibbs knew a man's crime when he saw one.

'So Encarna and Amy Oliva were murdered and buried while the Brethericks were in Florida,' Proust concluded.

'They were buried then,' said Kombothekra. 'We don't know when they were killed, but it was after Friday the nineteenth of May last year. That was Amy's last day at school and Encarna's last day at work. Neither of them said a word about leaving to schoolmates or colleagues. The sudden move to Spain, with no notice, was a surprise to everyone.' Kombothekra raised his eyebrows.

'The headmistress of St Swithun's, Mrs Fitzgerald, was informed by e-mail after the fact,' said Sellers. 'Apparently Encarna

Oliva was apologetic about the lack of notice and enclosed a cheque for a term's fees in lieu.'

Proust was making disgruntled noises. 'When did the Brethericks fly to Florida?' he asked crossly.

'Sunday the twenty-first of May last year,' Kombothekra told him.

'All right, then, Sergeant. Encarna and Amy Oliva were murdered at some point between the evening of Friday the nineteenth of May and . . . Sunday the fourth of June, when the Brethericks returned from Florida. If you must split hairs.'

Kombothekra looked as if he might be thinking about standing up for himself. 'Mark Bretherick was telling the truth,' he said. 'He spent the fortnight working at the National High Magnetic Field Laboratory in Tallahassee. I think we have to release him, keen though he is to hang around and tell me how wrong I am about everything.'

'That law firm Geraldine phoned, asking for a divorce and custody lawyer,' said Sellers. 'What if it wasn't Geraldine who phoned? It could have been another woman who didn't want to give her real name.'

The door banged open and Simon Waterhouse appeared with Charlie Zailer behind him. 'Has the full list come through yet from St Swithun's, the owl sanctuary trip?' he asked.

Gibbs closed his eyes. *Shit*. Barbara Fitzgerald's e-mail. Amy Oliva's message had been such a shock, he'd forgotten about the list. 'I've got it on my e-mail,' he said. 'Didn't get a chance to print it.'

'Is there a Jones on it?'

'Michelle Greenwood is now a Jones,' Sellers told Waterhouse. 'Lucy Bretherick's babysitter—she's just got married. She also worked part-time as a nanny for the Olivas.'

Waterhouse laughed and smacked the wall with the flat of his hand. 'Of course,' he said.

'I'm going to count to five, Waterhouse . . .' the Snowman began.

'No time, sir. We need to find Sally Thorning.'

'Who?'

'And Esther Taylor.' He turned to Charlie. 'Can you do that?'

'Unlikely, since I've no idea where she is.'

'I have,' said Waterhouse. 'Pam Senior said she threatened to go to the police, didn't she? She's here. Maybe she's got no further than reception, but she's here. At the nick.'

15

Friday, 10 August 2007

When I hear the key in the lock, I pull the massage table towards me so that it stands between me and the door. He comes into the room, unsmiling, his face blank. In his left hand he holds the gun and in his right the syringe, which is full. 'No,' I say. 'No. Please. It's too soon after last time . . .'

'Why aren't you lying with your legs up against the wall like I told you to?'

'It would be pointless,' I tell him. 'I didn't want to say anything before because I was scared of making you angry, but . . . I can't have any more children.'

'What?' His face twitches.

'After Jake was born I had some problems.' I know words, details, that would make this lie more plausible. I know the names of all kinds of gynaecological syndromes from the dozens of books I read when I was pregnant with Zoe. Why can't I remember any of them? 'I'm infertile. However long I lie with my legs up against the wall, I won't get pregnant. I'm sorry. I should have told you straight away.'

He laughs. 'Infertile. Not suffering from a rare genetic disorder, then, which any child you had would be likely to inherit? Of course, you couldn't say that because of Zoe and Jake.'

'I'm not lying, I swear on my life.'

'Swear on your children's lives.'

No. Not that.

'No. I would never do that. I'm telling the truth, Mark.'

'That isn't my name.'

'What is?'

He stares down at his arms, his head hanging low. 'William Markes. You guessed right first time.'

He puts the syringe down on the massage bed and points the gun at my face, holding it with both hands. 'We're going to play Conscience Roulette,' he says. 'In a minute, I'm going to ask you if you're infertile. If you are, and you tell the truth, I'll let you go. You can go back home. I want and need a family, Sally. A happy family. If you can't give me one, you're not the woman for me. But if you aren't infertile, you'll stay here with me. And if you lie and say you are when you aren't, I'll kill you. Do you understand? I'll know if you're lying. I already know.' The gun makes a clicking noise.

'I'm not infertile,' I blurt out before he asks. 'I'm sorry. I won't lie again.'

'Why are you crying? I'm the one who should be crying.' He exhales slowly. 'Lie down on the massage bed.'

Gathering together all my energy, I say, 'Please can I . . . do it myself?' I point to the syringe.

'You'd mess it up deliberately.'

'I wouldn't. I promise.'

'If you do, I'll use this.' He waves the gun. 'Not to kill you. I'd shoot you in the knee or the foot.'

'I swear I'll do it properly,' I babble, desperate.

'Good, because I'm going to be watching carefully. I'm not stupid. I'll know if you're trying to sabotage our family.'

'No!' Every nerve ending in my body is screaming a panic signal. I wish he had kept me unconscious for longer, for ever. He said he would kill me if I lied, so why didn't I? *Fear. Terror, not a desire to live, not like this.* 'Not with you watching. Please!'

'No?' He walks over to the window, turns his back on me. 'You're trying to take advantage of me. Everyone always does, because I'm soft. I never put my foot down. Do you think I don't know that you've got all the power and I've got none? Do you think I might have missed that fact, so you have to rub my nose in it?'

'I . . . I don't know what you mean,' I sob.

'I need you more than you need me. Think how you'd feel in my position. You don't need me at all, and you don't want me. So I need a gun and a syringe, locks on all the doors. And now you're asking me to leave the room, to entrust the most important thing in my world to you, when you've lied from the minute you got here. How is that fair? How is that right?'

'If you let me do this, on my own, I'll try *harder* to make it work. I promise. If you want me to help you, you have to start thinking about what I want and not just what you want.'

'Why do you care so much?' he snaps. 'Why does this tiny detail matter so much? I've seen your body before, I've touched it, every inch of it.'

Something inside me is about to break. I can't argue any more. There's no point: in his mind, he has already won every possible argument we might have.

'Let's get it over with, for both our sakes,' he says, picking up the syringe.

I walk towards the massage table.

'Wait,' he says. 'Not the table this time. I've been looking on the Internet. There are better positions for conception than flat on your back. Look.' On the carpet in front of me, he gets down on his hands and knees, holding the syringe between his teeth while his palms are flat on the floor. 'Do that,' he says, standing up. 'Right. Good.'

I stare at the stripy carpet, list the colours in my head: grey, green, rust, gold, orange. Grey, green, rust, gold, orange. Nothing happens. I don't feel his hands lifting the bottom of the dressing gown he made me put on after my clothes became too much of an inconvenience to him. Why is he taking so long?

For a beautiful moment I imagine he has died, that if I turned I would see him upright, grey and cold, eyes staring emptily.

'That doesn't look right,' he says, sounding irritated. 'I know, let's improvise a bit. Go as if to fold your arms, resting your forearms flat on the carpet. No, not . . . yes, that's it. Excellent. And then—final stage—shuffle forward on your forearms so that your body sort of stretches, so that your bottom's higher in the air than the rest of you. That's it. Stop. Perfect.'

Grey, green, rust, gold, orange. Grey, green, rust, gold, orange.

Darkness falls down on me. I twist my head to look up, see a layer of fabric. Not the ceiling. I feel air on my legs and back. He has pulled up the dressing gown, thrown it over my head. I begin to weep. 'Wait! Look up male fertility on the Internet,' I plead with him, but the words come out thick and indistinct. Only I know what I'm trying to say. 'Four times a day is less likely to succeed than every two days. I'm not lying!'

He doesn't answer.

I feel something brush against me. Not the syringe: something softer. Material. 'Please stop,' I beg. 'There's no point, not so soon after last time. It won't work! Are you listening to me? I swear, I'm not lying!'

Thick, heavy breaths come from behind me. I close my eyes, steeling myself for the syringe, pressing my face into my arms. Seconds pass—I don't know how many. I have forgotten how to count the speed at which my life is rolling away from me. Nothing happens.

Eventually, when I can't bear it any more, I raise my head and turn. He's holding the gun in the air. The bottom of his shirt has blood on it. 'What . . . ?' I start to say.

He flies across the room at me. 'You bitch!' he screams. 'Evil bitch!' I don't have time to move. I see the gun above my head, his hand coming down fast. Then a terrible crack, a burst of pain that wipes everything away.

*

When I come round, my arms and legs are twitching. That's the first thing I'm aware of. I raise my hands to pat my face and head. Something around my eyes is the wrong shape. I find a lump above my right eyebrow, hard and huge, as if someone's sliced open my skull and pushed a cricket ball under the skin at the top of my face.

My fingers are wet. I open my eyes: blood. That's right: he hit me with the gun. I look around. Tears of gratitude prick my eyes when I see he's not there. I don't mind being in this room as long as he's somewhere else.

Blood on his shirt. But that was before he hit me. Did he injure himself? How? Slowly, I rise to my feet. On the stripy carpet where I was lying, there is more blood. *Nowhere near where my head was*. I can't bear to check in the most obvious way, not after what he's done to me. I hobble over to my bag, pull out my diary and find the last page that I've marked with an asterisk. Then I count the days since then: twenty-nine. *Oh, my God.*

Knowing why he hit me frightens me as much as the click of the gun did. He can't wait. That's how mad he is. At some point in his life, he has lived with a woman and had a child; he must know exactly what the blood means.

He can't even bear to wait five or six days.

Has he given up on me and gone to find another woman?

I try the door handle. Locked. I swear at myself, knowing how ridiculous it is to be crying with disappointment. For a moment I allowed myself to hope that he had left the house in a blind fury, forgetting to take his usual precautions.

I know he has gone out. I'm sure of it. He can't stand to be around me, not now that I've let him down. I have to do something. I can't wait for the milkman tomorrow morning. I must do something now.

Why do people say, 'Where there's a will, there's a way'? Most of them will never end up in a situation like mine, forced to remember the number of times they've trotted out that idiotic platitude.

I have never said it because I've never believed it, but now I have to. I have to make it true.

Breaking down the door would be impossible. It's a thick one with metal inside, a fire door. It swings shut heavily unless someone—the man, William Markes—holds it open. That leaves the window. Double-glazed. I've looked at it hundreds of times and decided there's no way I could smash it.

I have to try. I run from the opposite side of the room, throw my body at the glass six, seven times. It doesn't move. I do it until my shoulders and arms feel as if they're about to break. I slam my fists against the window and scream, hating it for its strength.

There is clouding on one pane. It's been there since I got here, blocking a small patch of what is already a limited view. It never clears; funny, I haven't noticed before. *Moisture, trapped between the two panes of glass.* Which means that, somewhere, the seal is broken.

Climbing up on to the massage table, I unscrew the white plastic light fitting above the bulb and release the cranberry glass shade. Then I swing my arm back and hurl it at the window as hard as I can. It smashes. I leap down from the table, run to the pile of glass and choose a shard with a thin, sharp edge. I think about using it to kill myself and immediately reject the idea; if I'd wanted to die I could have lied and let William Markes shoot me—it would have been easier.

Using the pink glass triangle's sharpest point, I start to slice gently at the grey rubber seal at the top of the window. The soles of my feet sting. I stop to examine them and see that they are bleeding: small chunks of lampshade have embedded themselves in the skin. I ignore the pain and carry on cutting at the thin rubber strip. I don't care how long it takes. I will never stop. I will spend the rest of my life gouging out the corner of this window.

After what feels like hours, a curl of rubber springs towards me—I have prised it free with my makeshift spade. *Yes*. I drop the slice of lampshade on the carpet, grab the rubber and yank it as hard as I can. The strip peels away, and the glass in the window shifts slightly. I've pulled out the seal.

My body feels too battered to break anything. I push the massage table on to its side and start to unscrew the central metal leg, twisting it clockwise. It is stiff, and takes a while. I sing under my breath, 'Annie Apple, she says "Aah", she says "Aah", she says "Aah".' Zoe's Letterland song—she learned it at nursery. By the time I get to Z I'll have done it, I tell myself. I'll be free. 'Annie Apple, she says "Aah", she belongs to Mr A. Bouncy Ben says "Buh" in words, Bouncy Ben says "Buh" in words, Bouncy Ben says "Buh" in words, and then he bounces home. Clever cat . . .'

I've done it. I'm holding the sturdy metal leg. It's hollow, but still heavy enough. It should do the trick.

Running from the opposite wall, I aim the end of it at the middle of the window. The glass smashes. It cracks, then crumples and falls like hard, opaque confetti.

I sling my bag over my shoulder and move towards the open air.

Police Exhibit Ref: VN8723
Case Ref: VN87
OIC: Sergeant Samuel Kombothekra

GERALDINE BRETHERICK'S DIARY, EXTRACT 8 OF 9
(taken from hard disk of Toshiba laptop computer at Corn
Mill House, Castle Park, Spilling, RY29 0LE)

17 May 2006, 11.40 p.m.

Mum phoned this evening. I was so tired, I was barely
able to form words with my lips and tongue. 'What are
you doing?' she said. She always asks this question as if
she hopes my answer will be 'Sculpting a dolls' house for
Lucy from a piece of firewood. I'd better go now—got to
get back to my sewing machine and finish the cute ging-
ham curtains for those dollies' little windows!'

'Tidying away the toys that Lucy's scattered all over
the house,' I told her.

'I wish you wouldn't,' she said. 'You're always saying how
tired you are. You should sit down and put your feet up.'

This surprised me. Mum usually tells me I have no reason to be tired and has never before shown an interest in
the position of my feet.

'Is Lucy in bed?'

'Not yet,' I told her.

'Wait till she goes to bed, then. There's no point putting
things away that she's only going to take out in five minutes' time.'

Wrong again, Mother. There is a clear point. Tidying
up is not only about the result. The process is equally important; sometimes I think it's the only thing that keeps
me sane at home. When Lucy and I are both in the house,
I do almost nothing but walk from room to room tidying
away the mess she's made. I stand behind her, and as soon

as she's put something down I put it back in its proper place. Every time she pulls a toy or book or DVD off the shelf, five other items tumble down with it and land on the carpet. Each time she dresses up, all the play-clothes have to come out of the wardrobe to be strewn all over the bedroom. Then there are the toys I loathe most, those with more than one component: tea sets, picnic sets, hair-dresser sets, Lego, Fuzzy Felt, jigsaws. All these things end up all over my floors.

In the past Mum has said that I should make Lucy tidy up herself, but if I did she would have a tantrum, which I would then need to summon up the energy to deal with. Still, that's not the only reason why I clear up after her. Hovering behind her and putting back the things she's taken out appeals to me in a sick kind of way. I like the symbolism of it. I want to prove to all observers how hard it is for me—second by second, minute by minute—to make my life acceptable to me, to get it into an order I can live with. I want my predicament to be clearly visible to all: Lucy is constantly ruining everything and I am con-stantly struggling to repair the wreckage of my life. And I will never, ever give up. I'll be on my feet, on my hands and knees, fighting the things I hate for as long as there's breath left in my body.

How would it be if I sat on the sofa chatting or watch-ing television while Lucy spread her plastic, felt and glitter across the room? People would think I had accepted the 'status quo'. You cannot undo the act of having a child once you've had one—I know this—but my endless, fren-zied tidying is the closest I can get to the act of undoing (harmlessly, I mean).

I didn't tell Mum any of this because I knew she would start 'shoulding' me—telling me what I should and shouldn't think and feel. You can't go round 'should-ing' other people. I could tell Mum she should be more understanding, but where would that get us? Evidently she lacks the capability.

'Please don't wear yourself out,' she said. I was actually quite touched by her concern until she said, 'I'm not trying to interfere in your life. All I care about is Lucy, that's all. If you're exhausted, you won't be able to look after her properly.'

All I care about is Lucy, that's all? Couldn't she have packed a few more declarations of exclusivity into that sentence?

I was her daughter for more than thirty years before Lucy existed.

I told her not to phone again.

16

8/10/07

Sam Kombothekra realised he was going to have to watch his feet every time he moved in this strange, multi-level flat, or he would break his neck. There was a steep flight of stairs round every corner, and for added inconvenience the hall, landings and each individual step, it seemed, were littered with small, brightly coloured wooden balls. Sam had nearly been felled by a green one a few seconds ago.

He stared at the envelope in his hand, wondered when to say something and to whom. To Esther alone, to Nick alone, or to the two of them together? Maybe it was nothing.

He might not have looked at the Thornings' mail at all if it hadn't been scattered across the floor. He'd picked up the post and patted it into a tidy pile before going upstairs as a favour to Nick Thorning, who, if the state of his home was anything to judge by, was not coping well in his wife's absence. The two children, Zoe and Jake, had been safely deposited with Nick's mother. That had been Esther Taylor's idea, one she'd voiced just as Sam had been on the point of suggesting the same thing.

Simon Waterhouse had been right about Esther. Well, almost. Charlie Zailer had picked her up from reception at Rawndesley nick, where she'd been fuming because no one seemed to believe people were trying to kill her best friend. Sam had now heard her long story, which revolved around an allegedly sexually frustrated childminder who thought cosmetic breast surgery was more important than saving the eco-system of Venice's lagoon.

Esther, despite being addicted to exaggeration, nosey and bossy, had proved helpful in many ways. Nick Thorning hadn't been aware that his wife had given him a veiled message that she was in trouble. He hadn't remembered where Owen Mellish worked, only that Sally thought he was a pain in the backside. It was Esther who, when she'd phoned and Nick had told her Sally had gone to Venice with Mellish, had known something was wrong. Mellish had no involvement in the Venice work. He worked with Sally at HS Silsford, a hydraulics consultancy firm. Sam had arranged to meet Mellish at Mellish's girlfriend's flat so that he could search it. He hadn't found Sally Thorning, or any evidence to suggest Mellish had abducted her or killed anybody. All he'd turned up was several large Ziploc bags full of cocaine, which Mellish would do time for if Sam had his way.

He climbed the stairs to the lounge. Nick Thorning was sitting on the sofa with Esther Taylor beside him, holding his hand. *Whether he wants it to be held or not*, thought Sam. Simon and Charlie sat in armchairs across the room.

'What's going on?' Thorning's eyes lit up when he saw Sam. 'Is there any news?'

'I phoned the credit card company and then the hotel.' Sam tried to find a patch of carpet to stand on that wasn't occupied by a newspaper, a crayon, a bib or a nappy. 'Esther's right: it was Seddon Hall in York. Sally stayed there between the second and the ninth of June last year.' Sam nodded at Simon, who had raised an enquiring eyebrow. Yes: the second name he'd given the receptionist had also checked out, same dates. Simon looked relieved, then a little bit stunned. It was the way he always looked when he was proved right. Sam tried not to think about how often Simon turned out to be right. He might be tempted to resign if he allowed himself to dwell on it.

'Don't take it personally, Nick.' Esther stroked his hand with a rhythmic ferocity that looked likely to remove layers of skin.

'She needed a break, that's all. When the work thing fell through, she . . . I mean, she did it more for you and the kids than for herself.' Esther looked round the room, trying to garner support for her claim. 'She'd reached her limit. She needed a break in order to carry on. Don't any of your wives work?' She stared defiantly at Sam and Simon.

Kate, Sam's wife, didn't. And she was still more tired than Sam at the end of every day; he wasn't entirely sure why.

'DC Waterhouse's wife works full-time,' said Charlie. 'But then, they haven't got kids.'

Sam couldn't bring himself to give her the look he knew he ought to give her. He knew she was angry that she'd been sent to collect Esther Taylor from Rawndesley—like a skivvy, she probably thought—and angrier still that there hadn't been time to bring her up to speed.

'Is Sally's life so terrible?' Nick asked quietly. 'I thought she was happy with me and the kids.'

'She is,' Esther insisted.

'If she needed a break, why didn't she say so?'

Simon cleared his throat. 'Miss Taylor, what exactly did Sally say about meeting this man at Seddon Hall?'

'I told you. One night in the bar, they got talking. He pretended to be Mark Bretherick, who also lives in Spilling, so they had that in common—or Sally thought they had, rather—so they chatted for a while about . . . you know, local landmarks.'

'Local landmarks?' This sounded odd to Sam. 'Like what?'

'Um . . . well, I don't know exactly. I live in Rawndesley, and I'm from Manchester originally, but—'

'The memorial cross?' Simon suggested. 'The old stocks?'

'I don't mean landmarks exactly. They just talked about . . . local stuff.'

'Just the once, did they talk?'

'No.' Esther seemed more confident now. 'He was there all week. Sally kept bumping into him: in the bar, the spa . . . I think they chatted a few times.'

Sam was growing increasingly certain that Sally Thorning had done more than bump into the man they now believed had murdered four people. If some sort of sexual liaison had taken place, chances were Esther knew about it and Nick Thorning didn't. And Esther was determined to protect her friend's secret. It doesn't matter, thought Sam. What mattered was finding Sally, making an arrest before anyone else got hurt. Sellers and Gibbs might already have done both; Sam hoped to God they had.

'Sally didn't tell me either,' Esther was assuring Nick. 'Not for ages. Only when all this stuff about the Brethericks was on the news.'

'Yeah, and *then* she told you! She should have told me. I'm her husband.' Nick Thorning looked around the room as if hoping for confirmation from somebody.

'She didn't want to worry you.'

'She'll be okay, won't she?'

'Have you seen this?' Sam held the envelope in front of Nick's face.

'Yeah, this morning. What about it?'

So it meant nothing to him. Was that a good sign? 'It's addressed to Esther,' said Sam.

'I know.'

'Esther doesn't live here.'

'What?' Esther craned her neck to see the writing on the envelope. 'It's addressed to me?'

'I know Esther doesn't live here,' said Nick angrily. 'I'm not stupid. I assumed Sally would know what it was and sort it out when she got back. I just want her to come back. She will, won't she?'

'We're doing everything we can to find her and bring her safely home,' Sam told him. 'Esther, would you mind opening this?'

She tore open the envelope and pulled out a small green book, A6 size, and a postcard. 'I've no idea . . .' She looked up at Sam, frustration all over her face. 'It's addressed to me, but I haven't got a clue what it is or what it means.'

Sam was afraid he'd be equally at a loss, and was pleased to find he understood straight away. He recognised the name Sian Toms—she was a teaching assistant at St Swithun's. Sally Thorning had called herself Esther Taylor when she'd visited the school, but she must have given Sian Toms her real address.

'Dear Esther,' the postcard said. 'Here is Amy Oliva's news book, the one I mentioned when we spoke. Please don't tell anyone I sent it to you—it would go down very badly at work. Also, please can you send it back to me when you've read it so that I can put it back? Thanks. Send it to my home address: Flat 33, Syree Court, 27 Lady Road, Spilling. Best wishes, Sian Toms.'

Sam opened the news book. The first entry was dated 15 September 2005, close to the beginning of the school year that was to be Amy's last at St Swithun's. The handwriting was Amy's, or rather, it was clearly a child's: large and unwieldy. When Sam began to read the words, a shiver rippled through him.

*This weekend, Mum, Dad and I went to Alton Towers.
After hours of queuing, we went on the Log Flume, which
was mediocre. There was a ride called the Black Hole that
I was keen to go on, but Mum said I was too young and it
was only for grown-ups. I asked her if she and Dad wanted
to go on it and she said, 'We don't need to. Dad and I are
already in a black hole. It's called parenthood.'*

Sam turned to the next entry. The handwriting was the same but it was much longer.

*This weekend was excellent. I ate nothing but chocolate—
buttons, Minstrels, Milky Ways. For breakfast, lunch and
supper. I was sick on Sunday afternoon, but on balance I
think it was worth it. On Friday evening I was feeling more*

contrary than usual (those who know me well will scarcely be able to imagine such a thing) so I asked Mum if I could throw the horrid, healthy part of my tea—the part she had carefully home-cooked then saved and frozen in a small, purple plastic bowl—in the bin and instead go straight to the reward I normally only get if I eat lots of vile green things. To my surprise and delight, she said, 'You know what, Amy? You can do exactly what you like this weekend, all weekend, as long as I can too. Do we have a deal?' Of course I said yes, so she pulled all the chocolate out of the treat cupboard and threw it into my lap, and then she went and found a book she wanted to read. I asked her to put on my 'Annie' DVD for me, but she reminded me that we were both doing exactly what we wanted, and getting out of her chair to fiddle with the DVD player was not something she wanted to do. She also didn't want to do any drawing, baking, jigsaws, hair-styling, or have her house littered with squealing, pink-clad Barbie-obsessed munchkins like Oonagh and Lucy. Fair enough! Actually, her quite reasonable refusal led to a valuable insight on my part. Sometimes, I ask Mum to do things—for example to get me drinks I then don't drink, and toys and games I have no real desire to play with—not because I actually want whatever it is I'm asking for, but simply for the sake of making her do something, because I believe her role in life is to attend to my wishes. If she isn't waiting on me like a maid, something seems amiss. All Western children are the same, Mum says, because society over-protects and over-indulges them. That's why she makes a point of buying the produce, whatever it might be, of any company she hears has been using child labour. I have to admit, she's got a point. If I swept chimneys or sewed clothes in a factory from dawn until dusk, I would certainly understand that after a hard day's work, the last thing a person wants is to be given more work at home.

Under this tirade someone had written in red pen: 'No more in this vein please, Mummy. Amy gets upset when yet again she can't read her weekend news out in class or enter it in the Busy Book. Please could you allow Amy to write her news book entries herself like all the other children instead of dictating your own words for her to write down? Thank you.'

'Are you going to tell us what it is?' asked Nick Thorning.

'It's just some child's school book,' said Esther.

Sam wanted to hit her. He looked at the next and final entry in the book. Unlike the other two, it contained some spelling mistakes.

This weekend I played with my friends and went to see Mungos Magic Show at the theata. It was great.

Under Amy's handwriting there was a big, red tick. A teacher had written, 'Sounds lovely, Amy!'

Whoever that teacher was, Sam wanted to hit her too.

You learn something new every day, thought Gibbs as he waited in Cordy O'Hara's lounge for her to fetch Oonagh. Fine Art Banking. He'd spent half an hour on the phone to Leyland Carver before coming here, and found out that Encarna Oliva had been one of two people at the bank who had specialised in advising clients on which paintings, sculptures, installations and 'conceptual pieces' they ought to invest in. Gibbs hoped he'd done a good enough job of concealing his disgust. Couldn't rich wankers choose their own pictures? What was the point in being alive if you hired someone to make every little decision for you?

Gibbs liked the idea that being rich made a person stupid. He also liked feeling aggrieved. He didn't understand why—it was simply something he quite enjoyed. When he'd heard the salary Encarna Oliva had been paid to do her entirely unnecessary job, and that was before bonuses . . . Gibbs hoped Lionel Burroway of Leyland Carver wouldn't ring and complain to anyone at the nick about Gibbs' response when he'd been told the figure. 'Ms Oliva worked extremely hard, and often long hours,' Burroway had said defensively. 'Most of the private views she had to attend were in the evening, and she often had to go abroad. Her work for us brought in ten, twenty times what we paid her in new business. She was excellent at her job.'

'Right,' Gibbs had grunted. That was a new one, the idea that a person's work might actually bring in money. I'm in the wrong profession, he thought. All his work brought in was deviant scrotes that no one was pleased to see.

He had asked Burroway if Encarna Oliva had had a colleague called Patrick, perhaps a close friend. Burroway said he couldn't recall there ever having been a Patrick at Leyland Carver. When Gibbs had mentioned that Encarna might have eloped with him to Spain, Burroway's voice had cooled considerably. 'The manner in which she left us was very odd,' he said. 'I would have preferred to be informed in person rather than by e-mail with no notice, but . . . well, I suppose if she's . . .'

If she was murdered, you can't hold a grudge against her for rudeness, Gibbs had thought, grinning. Even knowing Encarna was dead, Burroway had resented having to let her off the hook.

The music Cordy O'Hara had left playing was doing Gibbs' head in. He got up, walked over to the small silver ghetto-blaster on the floor and turned down the volume ever so slightly. He examined the CD case that was balanced on top of the machine: *The Trials of Van Occupanther* by Midlake. Gibbs had never heard of it.

Large floor cushions, upholstered in bright, flowery materials that ought to have clashed but in fact looked all right, were strewn everywhere. They looked more expensive than Gibbs' three-piece suite. Amid the cushions were pottery cups that also looked pricey and were probably hand-made, some with cigarette butts in them and ash streaks down the sides. A few screwed-up Rizlas and some empty takeaway cartons lay under the green glass table that stood in one corner. It was as if a group of homeless people had broken in and had a party in the home of an interior designer.

Cordy O'Hara had her hands on Oonagh's shoulders as they came into the room, and a baby in a sling round her neck. *Like a broken arm.* 'Sorry,' she said. 'Ianthe needed changing. And sorry about the mess. Since having baby number two, I've been forced to embrace squalor, I'm afraid—too knackered to clean the flat. Oonagh, this is Chris. He's a policeman. Do you remember the other policeman, Sam? Chris works with Sam.'

Gibbs didn't like the first-names thing—he hadn't said Cordy O'Hara could call him Chris—but he said nothing. He did what Sellers would have done if he were here, and started by assuring Oonagh that there was nothing to worry about. She was only six, so he avoided referring to her having lied when Kombothekra interviewed her, and simply said, 'Oonagh, you and Amy have been exchanging e-mails ever since she went to Spain, haven't you?' He shot Cordy O'Hara a warning look. She knew Amy was dead; Oonagh didn't, and he didn't want her to find out now. The girl tried to shrink into her mother's skirt. Her round, wide-open eyes stared at the carpet. She was the image of her mother: thin, freckled face, carrot-coloured hair.

'Her dad helped her type the messages,' said Cordy. 'When Oonagh said she hadn't been in touch with Amy since Amy left school, I had no idea she was fibbing. Not until I spoke to Dermot.'

'It doesn't matter,' said Gibbs. He hated situations that required him to be sensitive. 'Oonagh, nobody's angry with you. But I do need to ask you some questions. Do you remember, in one of your messages, asking if everything was all right between Amy and her mum?'

Oonagh nodded.

'Did you have any reason to think things might not be okay between them?'

'No.' Her voice was almost inaudible.

'Did you think it was strange that Amy never answered your questions about her mother?'

'No.'

'Oonagh, sweetie, you must tell Chris the truth.'

Gibbs was instantly suspicious. Cordy O'Hara shrugged an apology at him. 'I've been trying to get it out of her. Amy used to ask her to keep lots of secrets. Didn't she, sweetie?' Oonagh wriggled, hopping from one foot to the other.

'Oonagh, you'll be helping Amy if you tell us,' said Gibbs. 'Whatever it is.'

'Please may can I go to the toilet?' the girl asked her mother.

Cordy nodded and Oonagh fled. 'Come straight back, please, sweetie,' Cordy called after her. 'They taught her at school to say, "Please may . . .", but I can't seem to drum it into her that you don't need to say "can" as well.'

'If she won't talk to me, see what you can do once I've gone,' said Gibbs.

'I've tried endlessly.' Cordy tucked her hair behind her multiply pierced ears. 'She thinks something dreadful happens to people who tell secrets; it's infuriating. If I force the issue, she'll make something up. Once, ages ago, I found her crying in bed in the middle of the night. She was distraught. Lucy Bretherick—she could be a bit of a madam, Lucy—she'd browbeaten Oonagh into telling her one of Amy's secrets. Poor Oonagh was terrified Amy would find out, that she'd send a monster to attack her in the night.'

'What was the secret?' Gibbs asked.

'I never got it out of her. Having told Lucy and felt awful about it, she was hardly going to compound her crime by telling me, poor little love.'

On the spot, Gibbs decided that if he and Debbie ever succeeded in having a child, rule number one would be no secrets from Mum and Dad. Ever.

'I feel terrible,' said Cordy. 'I was relieved when Amy moved away. Once she was gone, Lucy and Oonagh became . . . well, normal little girls. But while it was the three of them . . .' She shuddered. 'I was a horrible coward. I'm totally ashamed of myself now. I should never have exposed Oonagh to scenes like that. No wonder she was traumatised, when Lucy hounded her until she couldn't take it any more and told Amy's secret.'

'Scenes?' Gibbs asked.

'One scene, really. Though it was repeated over and over again. Lucy would take any opportunity to say to Amy, "My mummy loves me best in the whole wide world, and Oonagh's mummy loves *her* best in the whole wide world, but your mummy doesn't love you, Amy." Oh, it was heartbreaking!' Cordy pressed her hand against her chest. 'Completely untrue, too. Encarna loved Amy passionately. She just hated being a mother, which isn't the same thing at all. She was honest about how difficult she found it—that's one of the things I liked about her. She said the things no one else would say.'

'How did Amy react, when Lucy said her mum didn't love her?'

'She'd start shaking—literally shaking—with misery, and wail, "Yes, she does!" and then Lucy would try to prove her wrong. Like a barrister, taking apart a witness's case in court. "No, she doesn't," she'd say smugly, and then recite her long list of evidence: "Your mummy's always cross with you, she doesn't smile at you, she says she hates Saturdays and Sundays because you're at home . . ." On and on it went.'

'In front of you?'

'No. In the privacy of Oonagh's bedroom, but I overheard it plenty of times. I know Geraldine did too, because once I tried to raise it with her and she immediately looked guilty and clammed up; it was literally as if I hadn't spoken. The one thing Geraldine couldn't allow herself to admit was that she'd messed up. Oh . . .' Cordy waved her hand at Gibbs, as if to delete her last comment. '*I* didn't think it was her fault, obviously—children have their personalities from the moment they're born—but Geraldine and Mark had very set roles in their marriage, in the family. Mark's job was being brilliant and successful, bringing in the money, and Geraldine's was Lucy; if she admitted Lucy was capable of being mean—of actually enjoying being mean—then she'd have to admit to herself that she'd failed in her part of the bargain: raising the perfect child. And everything about Geraldine's family had to be perfect: she was so relentlessly upbeat about everything, totally unwilling to admit her daughter had faults.

'I don't know if anyone's told you this yet, and I wasn't planning to, but . . .' Cordy took a deep breath. 'Lucy Bretherick wasn't a nice girl. She wasn't kind. Clever, hardworking, high-achieving, yes. Nice? Definitely not. You know I said I was relieved when Amy moved away?'

Gibbs nodded. 'It sounds awful, and I'm sorry of course that she's dead, but . . . knowing Oonagh won't be spending time with Lucy any more is a weight off my mind.'

'After Amy left, Lucy didn't start to victimise Oonagh?'

Cordy shook her head. 'Everything was fine, like I said. But they were only six, and every bully needs a sidekick. I reckon that's the position Lucy had in mind for Oonagh—she was grooming her, subtly.'

This sounded absurd to Gibbs, but he didn't query it. 'Oonagh asked after Patrick in a couple of her messages,' he said.

Cordy nodded. 'All the girls loved Patrick. He used to play with them. They thought he was the pinnacle of cute.'

This last word made Gibbs uneasy. So Oonagh O'Hara had met Patrick. Where? At Amy Oliva's house? Had Encarna flaunted her lover under her husband's nose? 'Do you know Patrick's surname?' Gibbs asked.

Oonagh had returned. She was standing in the doorway, staring at him with something approaching scorn. She said, 'He hasn't got one, silly.'

'Sweetie! Don't dare to call people silly! Chris is a policeman!'

'I get called worse than that,' said Gibbs. 'Patrick's surname?'

Cordy frowned. 'I suppose he might have needed one to be officially registered or whatever, or for medical appointments. Good question: it could have been either, I suppose. My guess would be Oliva, though, like Amy.'

Now Gibbs was certain something strange was going on. 'Officially registered?' he said.

Realisation dawned, and Cordy O'Hara looked embarrassed. Guilty, almost. 'Oh, right, you don't know. Patrick is Amy's cat,' she said. 'A big fat ginger tom. All the girls adored him.'

17

Friday, 10 August 2007

Once I've knocked out all the glass with the leg of the massage table, I hoist myself up on to the window sill and scramble out into the yard. I run back and forth blindly, whimpering like a wounded animal, hitting the hedge and then the wall. My body feels ice cold in spite of the sun. I stop, wrap the flimsy stained dressing gown around me and tie the belt tight.

I am trapped. Again. This yard is an outdoor cell that goes round the house on two sides. There's a second wooden gate, one I couldn't see from the window, also with a padlock on it.

Three wheelie-bins stand against the wall—green, black and blue. I grab the green one and drag it over to the hedge. If I could get up on to it . . . I try, but it's too thin, the sides too smooth. There's nothing to help me get a foot-hold. Once, twice, I yank myself up, but lose my balance. *Think. Think.* Beating in my head like a pulse is the idea that the man will be back at any moment, back to kill me. I scream, 'Help! Somebody help me!' as loudly as I can, but I hear nothing. No response. The air all around me is still; not even a rumble of traffic in the distance.

I put my full weight behind one of the large, terracotta plant-pots and shunt it towards the bin. It scrapes along the concrete slabs, making a horrible noise. Panting with the effort, I finally manage to up-end the pot. Its base is wide and flat. I stand on it and climb up on to the bin lid, landing on my knees. For a few seconds I am rocking in mid-air, arms flailing, certain I'm going to lose my balance. I lunge towards the hedge, grab hold of it and manage to stand, leaning my upper body against the thick slab of twigs and leaves.

Looking over the top, I see an empty road, three street lights—the twee, mock-antique lantern kind—and the loop-end of a small cul-de-sac, around which stand several identical houses with identical back gardens. I turn and look at the house I've escaped from. Its flat beige stone-cladding façade tells me nothing. I have no idea where I am.

I'm not high enough to climb from the bin on to the top of the hedge. If the bin were two or three inches higher, or the hedge more uneven so that I could use part of it as a ledge . . . I try to stick my bare foot in, but it's too solid. I stare at its flat top, unable to believe I'm this close and still can't get up there.

What can I do? What can I do?

The milk bottles. I could take some paper and a pen from my bag, write a note and push it into an empty bottle. Could I throw a bottle far enough so that it lands in one of those back gardens? How long would I have to wait for help, even if I could?

I jump down from the bin and run round the house, back to the smashed window. Directly beneath it, a small, square alcove has been built into the wall. There are two full bottles and one with no milk in it, only a rolled up sheet of white lined paper sticking out of the neck.

The man who kidnapped and violated me has left a note for his milkman. He still belongs to the ordinary world, the one I can't reach.

I pull the note out and read it. It says, 'Hope you got my message saying not to come. If not, no more milk until further notice please. Away for at least a month. Thanks!'

Away for at least a month . . . I would have died, if I hadn't got out. He planned to leave me to die in the room. But . . . if both gates to the yard are padlocked from the inside, how can the milkman . . . ? *Oh, my God. You idiot, Sally.* I haven't even tried them. I saw two padlocks and assumed . . .

The one on the back gate that I could see from the window is locked, but the second one isn't, the one round the side of the house. The padlock has been pushed closed, which is what I saw, what misled me. But it hangs only from the gate itself; it hasn't been looped through the part that's attached to the wall. I pull it, and the gate swings open towards me. I see another quiet, empty road.

Run. Run to the police.

My heart pounding, I push the gate shut as violently as I pulled it open. *He's not coming back. Not for at least a month.* If I can get into the rest of the house somehow, I can clean myself up; I won't have to run through the streets with nothing on apart from a dressing gown that's covered in my own blood. If the police see me like this, they will know William Markes made me take my clothes off. They will ask questions. Nick will find out . . . I can't face it. I have to go back inside the house.

A heavy plant-pot would break a double-glazed window. I try and fail to lift the one that looks heaviest. Three smaller pots stand against the wall, lined up side by side on a long, rectangular concrete plinth. I move the plants and strain to pick up the base. I can lift it, just about. Holding it under my right arm like a battering ram, supporting it with both my hands, I run as fast as I can towards the kitchen window, panting. The glass cracks the second time I hit it. The third time it breaks.

I climb into the house, cutting my hands and legs, but I don't care. The recipe book has been put back on the counter. Beside it is the gun. *He hasn't taken his gun. He's given up. Given up and left me to die.* I back away, bile rising in my throat when I see the syringe lying neatly by the sink.

I can't stay in the room once I've seen it. Gagging, I run upstairs. Clothes. I need clothes. The wardrobes in the blue and pink rooms are empty. There are a few clothes on wooden hangers in the one in the master bedroom, men's clothes. His. A suit, a padded coat with paint stains on the arms and lots of keys in one of the pockets, two shirts, a pair of khaki corduroy trousers.

The idea of putting on his clothes is unbearable. I cry, wanting my own clothes. Where has he put them? Two ideas come to me at once: the locked bathroom door. A pocket full of keys . . .

I shake them all out on to the landing carpet. Some are obviously too big, too small or the wrong shape. I push these to one side. There are five left. The fourth one I try opens the locked door. The bathroom is large, almost as big as the master bedroom, with a sunken bath in one corner. In the middle of the floor, like a pyre—some kind of sacrificial mound or a bonfire waiting to burn—is a heap of somebody's possessions. Clothes, shoes, bags, school exercise books, Barbie dolls, a watch, a pair of yellow washing-up gloves, a bottle of Eau du Soir by Sisley, gold and pearl cuff links: hundreds of things. Things that once belonged to a woman and a girl. All their possessions, heaped up in this one room. And, on top, my clothes and shoes. *Thank God.*

I push my way through the pile, hear things from the top falling into the bath and basin. The loudest crash comes from a black anglepoise lamp with a chrome base. It scares me until I realise what it is. It looks like a little creature—black head, silver spine. Its bulb has fallen out and smashed in the basin.

My heart thuds harder when I find two passports. I open the first one, flick to the back page. It's her: the girl from the photograph. Amy Oliva. The other passport belongs to her mother, and her face is as familiar to me as her daughter's for the same reason. Encarnación. A Spanish name? Yes. I flicked through a book a few seconds ago that was written in a foreign language.

Amy Oliva's father. But he told me his name was William Markes.

In a plastic bag that has been loosely tied at the top, I find something slimy and green. It's a uniform: St Swithun's. Amy's school uniform. Why is it wet? Why does it smell so bad? *Did he drown her?*

I can't stay here surrounded by dead people's things. I know Amy and Encarnación are dead as surely as if I'd found their bodies. I grab my clothes, run downstairs, turn on the shower in the tiny shower room and pull off the dressing gown. There's a large dark red patch below the waist. It looks as if it's been used to wrap a severed head.

I wash as quickly as I can, watching the water around my feet turn from red to pink to clear. Then I take the blue towel that's neatly folded on top of the radiator, dry myself and get dressed.

Now I can leave, go home, call the police. I can bring them here, and they'll find . . . No. There are things I can't let them find. I have to be able to carry on living once I escape—the life I want, the life I used to have—or else there's no point.

Nobody can know what he did to me.

I go back to the upstairs bathroom. Retching, I shake Amy Oliva's foul-smelling uniform out of its plastic bag. Then I walk slowly round the house, collecting all the things I can't risk leaving: the dressing gown, the syringe, the book written in Spanish.

I begin to shake violently as I walk across the yard and out on to the street.

Police Exhibit Ref: VN8723
Case Ref: VN87
OIC: Sergeant Samuel Kombothekra

GERALDINE BRETHERICK'S DIARY, EXTRACT 9 OF 9
(taken from hard disk of Toshiba laptop computer at Corn
Mill House, Castle Park, Spilling, RY29 0LE)

18 May 2006, 11.50 p.m.

Tonight, while I was reading in the bath, trying to relax, I
heard breathing behind me. Lucy. Since she's slept with her
door open, she's felt freer to climb out of bed at night and
come and find me. I ask her every day if she's still scared of
monsters. She claims she is. 'Well, then, you're obviously
not a big girl yet,' I say. 'Big girls know monsters are made
up. Big, clever girls sleep with their doors shut.'

When I turned and saw her in the doorway of the
bathroom, I said, 'Lucy, it's half past ten. Go back to bed
and go to sleep. Now.'

'You shouldn't do that, Mummy,' she said.

I asked what I ought not to do.

'Put the night light on the edge of the bath like that. It
might fall into the water and then you'd be electrocuted
and killed until you died.' She is too young to understand
what this means, but she knows it's something bad. She
probably imagines it's the same as being hurt, like the time
she fell in the garden and scraped the skin off both her
knees.

'I'll be fine,' I told her. 'I'm careful. It's the only way I
can get enough light to read in the bath without having
the fan whirring away, and I need to read in the bath because it relaxes me.'

Why did I bother to explain? Reason doesn't work
with a five-year-old, or at least not my five-year-old. Logic

doesn't work, persuasion doesn't work, just-because-I-said-so doesn't work, begging doesn't work, lenience doesn't work, sanctions and the confiscation of toys don't work, diversion and entertainment don't work, ignoring doesn't work, and even bribery doesn't always work, or rather it only works for as long as the chocolate incentive is still being mashed in the mouth. Nothing works: the golden rule of child-rearing. Whatever you do, whatever techniques you choose, your child will reduce your soul to rubble.

In response to my attempt to answer her as I would an adult, Lucy burst into tears. 'Well, I'll be fine too!' she shouted at me. 'I never read in the bath, so I won't get electrocuted! And I won't go to heaven because you can't go to heaven until you're a hundred—Mrs Flowers told me!' She ran back to bed, satisfied she'd ruined my relaxing bath beyond all repair.

Gart knows what rubbish they've been pumping into her at that school. Lucy asked me once what heaven was. I told her it was a good thriller and a six-star hotel on a white sandy beach in the Maldives.

'Is that where Jesus went when he died?' she asked me. 'Before he came back to life?'

'I doubt it,' I said. 'From what little I know about him, I think Jesus might prefer to go camping in the Lake District.' Let no one accuse me of neglecting my daughter's spiritual education.

'So who does go to the heaven hotel?' Lucy asked.

I said, 'Has anyone at school mentioned the devil yet?'

18

8/10/07

Once he was certain 2 Belcher Close was empty, Sellers bent over, leaning his hands on his knees, and waited to get his breath back. It was clear what had happened: he'd locked her in and she'd smashed a window to get out.

Inside, keys were scattered on the landing and down the stairs. A loaded gun had been left on the kitchen work-surface. There was blood everywhere, and pieces of pink glass. Sellers was doing his best to touch nothing while he waited for scene-of-crime to arrive.

So much for his intuition. Yesterday, non-existent Harry Martineau had been oh-so-helpful, handing over the Olivas' mail, promising he'd try to find the phone number and address they'd given him. With his crumpled suit jacket and open brief-case behind him. *I've managed to lose my wallet.* Flustered, di-shevelled, harmless. And Sellers and Gibbs had fallen for it.

Sellers froze. The jacket. The suit jacket. There was a suit hanging up in a wardrobe upstairs. Sellers had been relieved to find it; he'd feared he might find a body in there.

He ran back upstairs to the master bedroom, opened the wardrobe again and stared at the suit. How the hell could he have missed it? The jacket had been lying in the hall yesterday, right in front of him. Sellers had spent hours walking round town with a photograph of the damn thing in his pocket. How many times had he taken out that photo and shown it to people?

He leaned into the wardrobe, looking for a label to confirm what he already knew. 'Ozwald Boateng', it said.

It was the suit Mark Bretherick had reported missing.

Michelle Jones sat opposite Sam Kombothekra in interview room one, crying into a handkerchief he'd given her and shaking her head every now and then, as if remembering yet another wrong that had been done to her. The healthy glow of her tanned skin was undermined by the red lines that cross-hatched the whites of her eyes. Her lips were chapped and peeling. She picked at them, crossing and uncrossing her legs continually.

Sam didn't think much of Michelle's recently acquired husband, who, instead of accompanying her to the police station, had put her in a taxi and gone home to bed. Charming. Sam's own wife Kate would have divorced him if he'd ever behaved so inconsiderately. He often heard Kate's voice in his mind and he heard it now, saying, 'Well, that's what you get for marrying someone you hardly know.' Sam and Kate had lived together for eleven years before they got married, whereas Michelle had only met her husband in April 2006, fifteen months before she married him. April Fool's Day, she'd told Sam, looking surprised that he was interested. He hoped she hadn't been fooled into making a disastrous choice, but then maybe he was overreacting. He hadn't met Jones, so he oughtn't, he supposed, to leap to negative conclusions.

Michelle had been fond of Amy but she had 'loved' Encarna; that was the word she kept using. 'I'm sorry,' she said for about the fifteenth time. 'It's crazy. I mean, it's not as if she was my boyfriend or anything, I wasn't *in love* with her.' She looked up. 'Honestly, it was nothing like that. I just . . . thought we were best friends. Very good friends,' she corrected herself.

A wealthy fine art banker, very good friends with a nanny? Sam wasn't a snob, he hoped, but it struck him as unlikely. 'You were saying Encarna got angry with you when you said you were going on holiday?' he prompted.

Michelle nodded. 'There was a half-term coming up . . .'

'Late last May?'

'Sounds about right, yeah. Encarna was in a panic because half-term was two weeks long and she needed to work and . . . well, I wasn't available. I'd always been available before, when I was single. I didn't have much of a social life, and Encarna's family were like my family; that was what she always said, that she wanted me to feel part of the family, and I *did*.' The hanky was so wet, Sam could see the pink of her fingers through the material. 'I always said yes to everything and she paid so well— miles more than any of my friends who were nannies were getting. But it was different once I had a boyfriend. It was just bad luck that he'd suggested going away for those two weeks. I was so excited, I said yes before I'd checked with Encarna, and then once it was booked . . .' She shrugged. 'I mean, would *you* have expected me to cancel?'

'It sounds like a misunderstanding,' Sam said diplomatically.

'I couldn't cancel! I had a feeling he was planning to propose and he did! It was so romantic: we'd only just met, but he said he knew. I did everything I could to help sort things out for Encarna. I phoned her mum in Spain and asked if she could come over, and she could. She was happy to, she said, but when I told Encarna she exploded. I should have realised—she didn't get on that well with her mum, and she didn't want her around for a whole fortnight.' Michelle pressed her eyes shut, squeezing out more tears. 'I thought she was going to kill me.'

'Did she attack you physically?'

'No. She just made me ring her mum back and tell her I'd made a mistake. It was awful. And I made it worse. I said I didn't understand why it would be so bad, the half-term holiday. Amy's dad had offered to have a week off work. He was always so good about doing his share—it wasn't as if he left it all to Encarna . . .'

'What was he like? Describe him.'

'Oh, a real sweetie.'

Sam found it hard not to look disgusted.

'He was lovely to Amy. Encarna used to say he had more maternal feelings than she did, and I think she was right.'

'You were saying about the half-term holiday? He offered to have a week off work?'

'Yeah, he suggested they share it,' said Michelle. 'Each stay at home for a week with Amy. I mean, that wouldn't have killed Encarna, would it? I knew she wasn't keen on doing the whole hands-on mum thing, but I didn't realise she hated looking after Amy that much. She . . .' Michelle seemed to think better of whatever she had been about to say.

'What? If you've remembered something, whatever it is, you have to tell me.'

'She didn't mean it. She said if she ended up having to take a week off work to look after Amy, she'd kill her, but she was just . . . exaggerating. Letting off steam.'

Sam leaned forward. 'What exactly did Encarna say about killing Amy?'

'Look, she only said it to make me feel bad. She wanted to ruin my holiday.' Michelle buried her face in her hands. 'She *knew* I'd never been abroad before. She *knew* the only holidays I'd been on were to my mum and dad's stupid caravan.'

'So you'd never been abroad with Encarna, to look after Amy?'

'No. I would have, like a shot, but they always went to the same place in Switzerland. Inder . . . Inter . . .'

'Interlaken?'

'That was it, yeah. It was called the Grand Hotel something-or-other, and it had a children's club that was open all day, seven days a week. It had babysitting too.' Michelle pulled her lips tightly together. 'I didn't get it myself, but there was a lot about Encarna that I didn't understand. I suppose that was what I loved about her: she was unusual. I mean, most people go on holiday to spend more time with their kids, don't they? That's the whole point. Not to leave them with Swiss nannies.'

Sam found that he didn't want to think too hard about the possibility of leaving his two sons with Swiss nannies. He and Kate could lie on sun-loungers by the pool, reading books and drinking cocktails like in the old days. The Grand Hotel Something-or-other in Interlaken. There was no point Googling it. Kate would veto the plan immediately, and he'd get bollocked for having dared to make so callous a suggestion.

'I was actually flattered that Encarna was jealous,' said Michelle bitterly. 'When I told her I had a new boyfriend, that I wasn't available to help her twenty-four hours a day any more.'

'I thought you were part-time?' said Sam.

'Officially, yeah, but more often than not I ended up staying over; it was easier. And while I was single, I didn't mind. I had pots of money. Encarna set up a little gym for me in the house. I'm a gym addict.' Michelle raised a toned arm for Sam to inspect. 'She even bought me a car. Not just a runaround, like some of my mates who are nannies have got—she let me choose.'

'A red Alfa Romeo,' said Sam.

'That's right.' She didn't ask how he knew. 'I loved it. I called it Speedy. But then she . . .'

Sam waited while she composed herself. He hated the custom of giving names to cars. His and Kate's VW Passat had a name. Sam found it so embarrassing that he'd spent years pretending he'd forgotten what it was.

'She made me give it back! When I said I wouldn't cancel the holiday. She said I'd betrayed her and I didn't deserve it any more, and she held out her hand for the keys. And I gave them to her! It was *my* car, I should have told her to piss off—sorry for swearing—but I was so shocked! She'd always been so nice to me, and suddenly she was being more vicious than anyone's ever been to me, and . . . If she'd just been a *bit* unreasonable, I'd probably have stood up to her. I'm not a doormat. But it was like she was being *so* horrible, it freaked me out. I couldn't think straight. I kept thinking, This can't be happening. And . . . she seemed so sure, I thought maybe she was right, maybe I deserved it.'

'Michelle, did Encarna love Amy?' Sam asked.

'Course she did. She just couldn't cope with being a mum. It wasn't her scene. She was dead honest about it—I really admired her for that. She'd joke about how rubbish she was. She used to say, "Saint Michelle, *please* take this child away or I'll end up hanging myself from the rafters."'

'Did she ever joke about killing Amy?' Sam asked.

A pause. 'No.'

'Michelle?'

'I've already told you. When she said she'd end up killing Amy if she had to look after her during half-term. Amy had this little black and silver night light. Like a desk lamp, really, but it used to sit just inside the bathroom, on the floor—there was a plug socket on the landing by the bathroom door—and it stayed on all night. Amy's door and the bathroom door both had to be open just the right amount, so that Amy's room wasn't too light or too dark.' Michelle started to smile, then stopped. 'Amy was quite particular. She could fly off the handle sometimes, but she was dead loving.'

'Carry on,' said Sam.

'What? Oh. Encarna used the night light when she wanted to read in the bath. She reckoned the main bathroom light was too bright, and you couldn't have it on without having the noise of the extractor fan as well, so she used to put Amy's night light on the side of the bath.'

What kind of reckless idiot would take a risk like that? Sam wondered. Then he guessed where Michelle's story was going and felt sick. 'Did she say she'd drop the night light in the water while Amy was having a bath?' he asked, wanting to get the confirmation of his worst fears out of the way.

Michelle nodded. 'Yeah. "If you abandon us, I'm going to be pushing that night light into Amy's bathwater within a few days," she said. "Everyone's always saying I'll electrocute myself, but I'm not that self-sacrificing!" It was horrendous—Amy was standing right behind her. She heard every word. Encarna didn't see her at first, and of course she felt *awful* when she did. She gave her a big hug and . . . Honestly, she totally didn't mean it. She was just a drama queen. Like mother, like daughter. That's why, after she'd yelled at me and thrown me out and nicked my car, I didn't get too upset at first. I thought she'd ring after a few days and beg me to forgive her, say she couldn't live without me. She always used to say that. But . . . I never heard from her again. I tried ringing her, over and over, but she ignored all my messages.' She looked up at Sam. 'How could she go from not being able to live without me to never wanting to speak to me again? It makes no sense.'

Sam thought it would be insensitive to point out that Encarna's death and interment might have had something to do with it. At this precise moment, he believed that Encarna Oliva had deserved to die. Kate would say so and not even feel guilty about it; she was much less forgiving than Sam was.

'Michelle, do you remember when you first told Encarna you had a boyfriend? If the two of you were friends you must have shared it with her.'

'Yeah. I told her pretty much straight away.'

'So early April last year?'

'Yeah.'

'And was she pleased for you?'

'She gave me a hug and . . .' Michelle blinked hard. 'Why is it that the good memories hurt the most? She started to cry and like . . . clung on to me. She said, "He's going to take you away from us."'

'What did you say?'

'I told her there was no chance. I said I definitely wanted to carry on working until I had a baby of my own, and that was a long way off.'

'What did she say to that?'

'She cheered up. She said, "Michelle, haven't I told you hundreds and thousands of times? You don't need to have a child, you've got Amy."'

Sam sensed more was coming. 'And then?' he said.

'And then she gave me a present: a cheque for two thousand pounds.'

'What?' Simon didn't bother with pleasantries as he threw open the door to Norman Grace's office.

Norman's face was flushed with excitement; like Simon, he was ready to launch straight in. 'I have no idea what it means, before you ask. It's your job to work that out.' He was holding a piece of paper, blank on the side that faced Simon.

'Show me.'

Norman passed him the paper, then began to read aloud over his shoulder: '"It is necessary for me that she is absent in the evenings. What I mean by that is not a large section of time, for example six until twelve—do not assume I have such wild wishes."'

'Stop,' Simon told him. 'I've got to know what this is before I read it.'

'You don't recognise it?'

Simon scanned the rest of the words. 'I recognise the sentiments, yeah. From Geraldine Bretherick's diary. But, it's so awkwardly written. Like someone on Prozac wrote it, or . . . someone from a hundred years ago. It sounds archaic.'

Norman nodded, satisfied that Simon had reached the same conclusion he had. 'After what you asked me to look for—after I found the Jones thing and realised you were right—I decided to have a shufty at the rest of the hard disk. I found a deleted file, also called "diary".' He smiled proudly. 'Lower case. The diary file we've been looking at's called DIARY, all upper case.'

Simon hardly dared to breathe.

'It's the same diary,' said Norman. 'Same dates, same number of entries, same substance and meaning. But the "diary" file, the deleted one, is quite startlingly badly written. By someone who's just come round after being knocked over the head, I thought.'

Simon read the words again. 'It is necessary for me that she is absent in the evenings. What I mean by that is not a large amount of time, for example six until twelve—do not assume I have such wild wishes. What would make me happy is two and a half hours. Between eight thirty and eleven. My body will not stay awake beyond that hour because the seconds that I have been awake in each day make me so tired. I busy myself like a good worker on amphetamines, smiling when I do not wish to smile, uttering words that are not the words I want to say. I do not eat. I am full of loud praise for pieces of art that I believe ought to be disposed of. That is a description of a usual day of my life. Because of this, no one can violate the time between eight thirty and eleven for me. If that happened, my good sense would be lost to me.'

' "My good sense would be lost to me"?' Simon muttered.

'I know. Look, here's the second version, from the DIARY file. Which was created six days after the last changes were made to the "diary" file. After that, the "diary" file was opened many times—whenever the newer DIARY file was opened, in fact—but never changed again. She didn't need to change it, did she? Because version two was a separate document.'

Simon took the piece of paper from Norman's hand. This time, he allowed Norman to read the whole passage aloud.

' "I need her not to be around in the evenings. Evenings! Anyone would think I meant from six until midnight or something extravagant like that. But no, I settle for a mere two and a half hours between eight thirty and eleven. I am physically un-able to stay up any later than that, because every minute of my day is so exhausting. I run around like a slave on speed, a fake smile plastered to my face, saying things I don't mean, never getting to eat, enthusing wildly over works of art that deserve to be chopped up and chucked in the bin. That's my typical day—

lucky me. That's why the hours between half past eight and eleven must be inviolable, otherwise I will lose my sanity."

'She's rewritten it, hasn't she?' said Norman. 'A "mere two and a half hours", "a slave on speed"—nice alliteration. And the "lucky me" at the end. She's made it more readable. Wittier, also, and more bitter. It's as if she read through her first attempt, found it to be devoid of tone and decided to . . . well, perk it up a bit. You can look at the whole thing if you want: the original and the rewrite. I can print both.'

'Print the original out in full and get it to me as soon as possible.' Simon was on his way to the door. 'We've got plenty of print-outs of the first diary file.'

'You mean the second,' Norman called after him. But Simon was gone.

Norman's face drooped. *Hoist by my own petard*, he thought. He'd said it was Simon's job to work out what it all meant, but he'd been looking forward to a bit of a discussion; he'd thought they might try to puzzle it out together. But, come to think of it, when he'd left the room, Simon Waterhouse hadn't looked puzzled. Which was puzzling.

'Why would a suicidal woman want to perk up the last desperate outpouring of her misery?' Norman asked his captive audience of computer equipment. Like Simon Waterhouse, they offered no satisfactory response.

Simon bumped into Sam Kombothekra outside the CID room. 'We've got a problem,' said Sam. 'Keith Harbard's still in reception. His cab hasn't turned up yet. When's Jonathan Hey getting here?'

'He didn't say a time. He just said as soon as he could.'

'Shit.' Sam groaned, ran his hands through his hair. 'This is all we need.'

'What does it matter?' Simon followed Sam as he sprinted down the corridor towards reception.

'They're friends. Harbard'll ask Hey what he's doing here, Hey'll tell him we've called him in as an expert to help us at the eleventh hour, Harbard'll say *he*'s supposed to be our expert.'

'So? We get rid of Harbard as politely as possible.'

'There's no way Harbard's going to leave without a fuss, allow himself to be usurped by a better expert—a man half his age. He'll be straight on the phone to Superintendent Barrow, who doesn't even know we've called Hey in!'

'That's Proust's problem, not ours. Proust agreed to Hey coming in; he can explain it to Barrow.'

'We should have gone to Cambridge. Why didn't we go to Cambridge?' Sam, using another of his wife Kate's techniques, answered his own question. 'Because you'd already invited Hey here, without checking with me or Proust or—'

'Sam?'

'What?'

'Can you hear something?'

The raised voices grew louder as they ran. One raised voice: Harbard's. Simon and Sam crashed through the double doors to reception.

'Professions . . . Professors,' said Sam, red-faced. Simon understood his nervousness. Personally, he felt oddly detached from the proceedings. He smiled at Jonathan Hey, who looked relieved to see him. Hey was eyeing Harbard anxiously. 'Is there a mistake?' he asked Simon. 'Keith said you didn't need me after all.'

'Keith's wrong.'

Harbard turned on Sam. 'What's going on? Aren't I good enough any more? You send me on my way and call in my close friend and colleague without even telling me?'

'Keith, I had no idea you hadn't been told,' said Hey, looking as uncomfortable as a schoolboy about to be caned by the headmaster. 'Look, I really feel awkward about this.' He looked at Simon, clearly hoping to be let off the hook. 'As Keith says, we're friends, and—'

Sam had recovered. 'This way, Professor Hey,' he said, leading Jonathan Hey out of reception, steering him by the shoulders so that he couldn't decide to leave with Harbard as a gesture of solidarity. The doors banged shut behind them.

'Six-six-three-eight-seven-zero,' Simon told Harbard. 'That's the taxi number. If it doesn't turn up in the next five minutes, give them a ring. Tell them to put it on our account.'

He turned his back on the irate professor and hurried after Sam and Jonathan Hey. He caught up with them halfway to meeting room one. 'What did you say to him?' Sam asked.

'Oh, just smoothed his ruffled feathers and poured oil on troubled waters.'

'Yeah, I bet.'

'I hope you did, Simon.' Hey sounded alarmed. 'Poor Keith. I'd like to phone him as soon as possible, if that's okay. I'm not happy about . . . the way this has happened. Couldn't you have warned me, or . . . ?'

'Jonathan.' Simon put a steadying hand on his arm. 'I know Keith's your mate and you don't want to offend him, but this is more important. Four people are dead.'

Hey nodded. 'Sorry,' he said. 'You know I'm happy to help if I can.'

'You've been a big help to me already,' Simon told him. 'That's why our DI's looking forward to meeting you. Sergeant Kombothekra'll tell you that Proust rarely looks forward to meeting anyone. Right, Sam?'

'Well . . . um . . .' Sam coughed to avoid having to reply. Bad form to take the piss out of your inspector in front of an outsider. Jonathan Hey looked back at Simon for reassurance. So did Sam. Simon considered how rare it was that people looked to him for comfort. Usually he unsettled those around him with an inner turbulence he found impossible to hide. Now, for once, there was no churning in his head. He hadn't had a chance to tell Sam, hadn't stuck around long enough to tell Norman Grace, but the last piece of the puzzle had fallen into place in

Norman's office a few minutes ago. Now he knew everything. Charlie would have to marry him. *If I really want her to . . .*

They arrived at meeting room one where Proust was waiting for them. The inspector sounded unnaturally courteous as he shook Jonathan Hey's hand and said how pleased he was to meet him. He looked incongruous, standing beside a tray laden with tea, coffee, sugar, milk, cups and saucers and an impressive range of biscuits—probably an entire selection box. The tray was lined with one of those lacy-doily things that Simon had never known the proper name for. Had Proust asked for that? Had Sam? Simon had told them both that Hey was well-spoken, used to the luxuries provided by Whewell College, Cambridge.

'Tea, Professor?' said Proust. 'Coffee?'

'I don't normally . . . oh, what the hell. I'll have a coffee. Thanks. White, one sugar.' Hey blushed. 'Sorry to sound like a wuss. If I drink too much caffeine I have stomach problems, but one cup won't hurt. Endless peppermint tea depresses you after a while.'

'I'm a green tea man myself,' said Proust. 'But since there's none here, I might risk a cup of builders' finest. Sergeant? Waterhouse?'

Both nodded. Was Proust actually going to pour drinks for all four of them? Incredibly, it seemed he was. Simon watched as he put the milk in the cups first, then tea in three of them, sugar in one, coffee and sugar in the fourth. *He knows Sam doesn't take sugar and I do—he must have noticed, stored the information away.* Simon felt a pang of affection for the Snowman.

Having made the drinks, Proust left them sitting in a row on the tray and stood back to admire them, pleased with his little line-up. Hey was talking to Sam about his drive to Spilling, how long it had taken from Cambridge. Had Sam asked him? Simon hadn't heard if he had.

'It's the A14 that can be a real killer,' Hey was saying. 'Bumper to bumper, crawling forward. There's always an accident.'

'But you managed to avoid the A14 tonight,' Simon chipped in.

Hey looked confused. 'No, I . . .' When he saw Proust walking towards him, he put out his hands and smiled, ready to take his cup of coffee. Then he saw what the inspector was holding and took a step back.

It was a pair of handcuffs.

'Jonathan Hey, I'm arresting you for the murders of Geraldine and Lucy Bretherick,' said Proust, 'and for the murders of Encarnación and Amy Oliva—your wife and daughter.'

19

Friday, 10 August 2007

I walk and walk, head down, looking at none of the people I pass, speaking to nobody. An endless network of suburban streets. It's only when I get to the main road and see the Picture House and the Centre for Alternative Medicine in the distance that I realise I'm in Spilling.

In front of the Picture House, there's a lamppost with a dust-bin attached to it. It's almost full, a lager can and the remains of a kebab at the top of the pile. I place the plastic bag on top of these and press the whole lot down. The syringe, the blood-soaked lilac dressing gown—I will never see them again.

I'm walking away when I remember the third item in the bag: the book with the black cover. *Spanish*. I stop. I ought to leave it where it is, I know I ought to, but I can't. Looking round to check no one's watching me, I go back to the bin. Someone is watching me: an old man sitting on a bench across the street. Staring. He isn't going to move, or look away. I hesitate for a few seconds, then decide it doesn't matter. Each small decision is a struggle. I pull the carrier bag out and rescue the book. Open it. There's a letter inside that's been written on a small lined sheet of paper, but it's nothing interesting, only a note somebody has written to Encarnación Oliva, giving lots of details about when they plan to go away and when they're getting back, dates and times, followed by something about Amy's school that is too complicated for my brain at the moment. It's addressed to

'Dear Encarna', but I don't know who it's from because it hasn't been signed. *Odd.*

I tuck the letter inside the book, put the plastic bag back in the dustbin and start to walk home. It will take me half an hour. Longer, unless I walk faster. It's hard—the soles of my feet are stinging so badly from standing on broken glass. I've got money in my purse, I could get a taxi. Why aren't I desperate to get home as soon as I can? What's wrong with me?

I stop walking. For a moment, I'm convinced I can't do it. Nick. Home. I will have to say something. I cannot envisage speaking to anybody ever again. All I want is to disappear.

Zoe and Jake. I start moving again. I want my children. I walk faster and soon I don't notice any more that my feet hurt. It will be okay. Everything will be like it used to be.

My street looks the same. Everything is the same, except me. Esther's car is parked outside my house. All I have to do is take my keys out of my bag and let myself in.

My head starts to tilt and twist when I see Jake's pink football in the hall. My breath catches in my throat. The ball is in the wrong place. I need everything to be where it belongs. Jake's football should be in the cupboard in his bedroom. I pick it up, dropping the Spanish book at the same time. Now there are definitely too many things on the floor: a pink plastic doll's dummy, a rolled-up copy of *Private Eye.* I can't pick them up. Neither can I walk past them.

'Sally? Sally, is that you?' A woman's voice. I look up, expecting to see Esther, but this woman is tall and thin with short brown hair. I've never seen her before. 'It's okay, Sally,' she says. 'You're okay. I'm Sergeant Zailer. I'm a police officer.'

The word 'police' startles me. I take a step back. *Everybody knows. Everybody knows what happened to me.*

I open my mouth to tell the policewoman to leave. 'I'm going to fall,' I say. The wrong words. My legs buckle. The last thing I'm aware of seeing is the black cartoon animal face on Jake's pink ball, right next to my eyes, enormous and terrifying.

20

Saturday, 11 August 2007

I open my eyes. This time I think I might be willing to keep them open for a while, see what happens. Everything appears to be in order. I'm still in my own bed. My favourite picture is still on the chimney breast in front of me. It's a Thai folk painting, a present from a company I did a scoping study for in Bangkok. It's painted on tree bark, and shows a chubby baby sitting cross-legged against an iridescent yellow background, holding a fish in its lap. Nick's not keen on it—he says it's too sickly—but I love it. The baby's skin is plump and pink. The picture reminds me of my children as newborns.

'Jake,' I say. 'Zoe?' I haven't seen them yet, haven't heard them shouting and singing and demanding things. Then I remember the police were here. Did they send my children away?

I am about to call out again when I hear voices, a man's and a woman's. Not Nick. Not Esther. I blink several times as their conversation gets nearer, to check this is real. Their words make no sense to me.

'He's not with his family, not at home or at work, not at his mother-in-law's . . .'

'Simon, you're not his babysitter. He's a free, innocent man.'

Simon? Who is Simon?

'Yeah, yeah.'

'You don't . . . there's nothing you're not telling me, is there? He *is* innocent?'

I think the woman is the cop from . . . when was it that I arrived home? How long ago?

'There's a lot I've not told you,' says the man called Simon. 'There's been no time.'

'What's wrong with now?'

She sounds tired. As if she can't be bothered any more.

'The French/English song. Stacey's homework—'

'Simon, for fuck's sake! I want to know why four people have died, not—'

'An Englishman wrote it. All the phrases in it—"rather a giggle", "burst into song", "put a sock in it", "keep your shirt on"—they're all English sayings. The French versions of them, translated literally, wouldn't mean the same thing. They wouldn't mean anything, they'd be gibberish. So the French version can't be the original. I doubt "put a sock in it" in French means give it a rest, like it does here.'

'I doubt "give it a rest" means give it a rest.'

I have no idea what they are talking about. My home has been invaded by people who make no sense.

'Exactly,' Simon agrees. ' "Give it a rest" would mean—'

'Let it have a nice long sleep?' The woman laughs. I hear clapping. 'Full marks, Detective.'

So Simon is also a police officer.

'Remember the promise you made?'

More sniggering from the woman. 'Are you quoting Cock Robin?'

'What?'

' "The Promise You Made" by Cock Robin. It was in the charts in the eighties.' She begins to sing. A policewoman is singing outside my bedroom door.

I burst into tears. I remember the song. I loved it. 'I want my children!' I yell.

The door to Nick's and my bedroom is flung open and the woman walks in. Sergeant . . . I've forgotten what she said her name was.

'Sally, you're awake. How are you feeling?'

The man who follows her into the room—Simon—is tall and muscly, with a prominent jaw that reminds me of the cartoon character Desperate Dan and a nose that looks as if it's been smashed to pieces more than once. He looks wary, as if he thinks I might leap out of bed and lunge at him.

'Where are my kids? Where's Nick?' I ask. My voice sounds rusty.

'Zoe and Jake are fine, Sally,' says the woman. 'They're at Nick's mum's, and Nick's at the shops. He'll be back in a minute. Do you feel able to talk to us? Would you like a glass of water first?'

It comes from nowhere: a wave of panic that forces me upright. 'Who is an innocent man?' I gasp.

'What? Calm down, Sally.'

'You were talking about him before. Who isn't with his family, or at work or home? Tell me!'

The police officers exchange a look. Then the woman says, 'Mark Bretherick.'

'He's killed him! Or he will! He's got him, I know he has . . .'

Simon has gone before I can explain. I hear him thudding down the stairs, swearing.

Sergeant Whatever looks at me, then at the door, then back at me. She wants to go with him. 'Why would Jonathan Hey want to kill Mark Bretherick?' she asks.

'Jonathan Hey? Who's he?'

She stands up and shouts the name Sam.

21

8/11/07

Charlie gripped the bottom of her seat as Simon overtook a Ford Focus and a Land Rover by swerving to their left and speeding ahead of them in the narrow gap between their sides and the kerb, to a chorus of angry beeps. Charlie could imagine what the drivers of the other cars were saying to their passengers: 'Probably being chased by cops.'

'I don't get it,' she said. 'Hey's in custody—ask him.'

'And if he won't tell me, or denies it? I'd have wasted time I can't spare, not if I want to have a chance of finding Mark Bretherick alive. Hey locked Sally Thorning in a room and left her to die. What if he's done the same to Bretherick?'

'Why are you and Sally Thorning so sure Hey would want to harm Bretherick?'

'I believe her. She's spent time with him. She knows his mind better than I do.'

'But . . . he killed them all, right? Geraldine and Lucy, and Encarna and Amy?'

'Yeah. All of them,' said Simon.

'Why? Slow down!' He had scraped the side of a van, was driving at twice the speed limit.

'I don't know.'

'*What?*'

'You heard.'

'If you don't know why, Simon, then you don't know he did it. Not for sure.'

'He had Bretherick's suit in his wardrobe and a bloodstained shirt and pair of trousers in his bathroom—the clothes he was wearing when he cut Geraldine's wrists. Oh, and he's confessed.'

He was toying with her. Charlie refused to rise to it. She flinched as a red Mercedes had to swerve to avoid them.

'To all four murders. He just won't tell us why.'

'How did you know it was Hey? Before Sellers saw the suit, before you had evidence?'

'Something Sam said started me thinking. At Corn Mill House, when we found Encarna and Amy Oliva. He said something that stuck in my mind: "Family annihilation mark two." It's a funny expression, isn't it? Not one I'd ever use myself. I'd have said number two, not mark two. For some reason it kept going round and round in my head.'

His speed was down to fifty-five. Talking was good for him.

'I had that the first time I heard that mares-eat-oats-and-does-eat-oats rhyme,' Charlie told him.

'And little lambs eat ivy.'

'Couldn't get it out of my head for months, years, after I first heard it. Drove me mad!'

'Another thing I couldn't get out of my head—Geraldine's diary,' said Simon. 'From the start I was sure there was something wrong about it. I knew Geraldine hadn't written it.'

'Hey wrote it?' Charlie guessed.

'No, that's what was wrong. I only realised much later, but deep down, subconsciously, I didn't think Geraldine's killer had written the diary either. It didn't sound . . . made up. When I thought about it, I didn't see how it could have been a fake. It was so detailed, so convincing. The voice was . . . A whole person, a whole life and world radiated from those printed-out pages whenever I looked at them. It sounds daft, but I felt a . . . a presence behind the writing, so much that was unsaid, so much more than the words in front of me.

Could the killer really have created that illusion? Plus, we found out that the diary file was opened long before Geraldine and Lucy died.'

His speed was down to fifty.

'So, whose diary was it?' Charlie asked.

'Encarna Oliva's.' Simon frowned as he saw the tailback in front of them. The centre of Spilling on a Saturday afternoon: always the same.

'Which Hey kept after he'd killed her.' Charlie worked it out as she spoke. 'And after he'd killed Geraldine, he typed up Encarna's diary on to Geraldine's laptop . . . but you said the file was opened before Geraldine died?'

'It was.'

'I don't get it.' Charlie fumbled in her bag for her cigarettes and lighter. 'Did Geraldine write the suicide note?'

'Yep.' Simon tapped the steering wheel impatiently. 'Freely and willingly. It wasn't a suicide note, that's all.'

'Then what was it? And what's any of this got to do with Sam saying "family annihilation mark two"? Simon!' Charlie clicked her fingers in front of his face.

'Remember William Markes? "A man called William Markes is very probably going to ruin my life"?'

She nodded.

'We couldn't find any William Markes in Geraldine Bretherick's life—'

'Because the diary wasn't Geraldine's,' said Charlie eagerly. 'William Markes was someone Encarna Oliva knew.' Was she catching up at last?

'No. There is no William Markes.'

'*What?*'

'Find and replace. "Family annihilation *mark* two"—"mark" is a word as well as a name: full marks, mark that essay, a marked man. When we found Encarna and Amy's bodies, Sam said he hoped Cook would find clear *marks* on the bones, to show how they'd died.'

'Will it help if I beg?' Charlie lit a cigarette. The traffic had begun to edge forward.

'You've got Encarna Oliva's diary on Geraldine Bretherick's computer. You want people to believe it's Geraldine's. It's full of gripes and complaints, exactly the sort of thing, you imagine, that would make Geraldine's suicide more plausible. But the complaints aren't about Mark and Lucy Bretherick, are they?'

'No. Encarna would have complained . . . about Jonathan and Amy. Oh, my God!' This time Charlie knew she understood.

'The names had to change, if we were going to believe it was Geraldine's diary. Quickest way? Find and replace all. Any idiot can do it in a keystroke.'

'So all the Jonathans became Marks. Amy became Lucy.'

Simon nodded, playing bumper cars with the Audi in front of him. 'Come on!' he muttered through gritted teeth.

'But . . . So William Markes . . . ?'

'Encarna Oliva called her husband Jon. And the "find and replace" manoeuvre did a bit more than Hey wanted it to. It changed Jon to Mark wherever necessary, yes, but Hey forgot that the letters j-o-n, like m-a-r-k, might crop up in other contexts too.'

Charlie chewed the skin around her thumbnail. 'Which would make William Markes . . . William Jones?'

'Right,' said Simon. 'The husband of Michelle Jones, who used to be Michelle Greenwood—Amy Oliva's nanny. When Michelle told Encarna she had a boyfriend, Encarna was terrified he'd want to marry her; she was right, as it turns out. She was scared Michelle would have a family of her own, a *life* of her own. That's what she meant when she said that a man called William *Jones*—a man she hadn't yet met, but had heard about from Michelle—was probably going to ruin her life.'

'Simon, you are a marvel of the modern world.' Charlie inhaled deeply. This would be the best cigarette she had ever smoked, she could tell immediately. 'But hang on . . . So you'd worked out that someone had done find and replace, but how did you get from that to knowing it was Jonathan Hey? How did you know Mark had replaced Jon, rather than, say, Paul or Fred?'

'I got it wrong at first,' Simon muttered, embarrassed. 'When Sellers told me Amy Oliva's father's name was Angel. I assumed William Markes was William Angeles; thank God I didn't go straight to the Snowman with it. Maybe on some level I knew it didn't sound right. Because it wasn't. Hey sent us on a wild-goose chase, pretending to be the man who'd bought the Olivas' house, calling himself Harry Martineau. He invented a completely made-up father for Amy: Angel Oliva, a heart surgeon at Culver Valley General.'

'Where Sally Thorning's husband works,' said Charlie.

'Yeah, Hey knew that. No doubt it was his inspiration. This is no good.' Simon jerked the car to the left and started to drive too fast along the pavement.

'Simon, no! You'll—'

'Hey was obsessed with Geraldine Bretherick. He pretended to be her husband when he met Sally Thorning at Seddon Hall. One reason for pretending to be a man is envy: if you covet his wife and daughter—'

'*Covet?* Have you been at the Bible again?'

'But he ended up killing Geraldine, maybe because she didn't want him. So who's the next best thing? Sally Thorning, carbon copy of his murdered love object, a woman he's already met a year previously. He kidnaps her—this time he's not going to risk rejection. He transfers his fixation from Geraldine to Sally. And when he next needs a persona to hide behind, when Sellers and Gibbs are knocking on his door, Hey makes himself a colleague of Nick Thorning, Sally's husband.'

'But . . . if Harry Martineau was Hey's invented alias, why did you think you recognised the name?' asked Charlie, confused.

'I thought I'd come across it before, but I hadn't. Not as a man's name, anyway,' said Simon. 'It hit me when Pam Senior started talking about *When Harry Met Sally*. The fictional Harry Martineau was a tribute to one of Hey's idols: Harriet Martineau, the sociologist. I saw her name on dozens of books in his office in Cambridge—books about her, books by her. That's why the name seemed familiar.'

The traffic had started to flow freely again. Simon drove back on to the road and speeded up to sixty. Ten seconds later he had to slam on the brakes as they approached the falling arms of the level crossing. 'Fucking hell! Come *on*!'

Charlie could see the tension in his shoulders. She thought about massaging the back of his neck with her fingertips. Impossible. She said, 'Assuming you're right about Hey killing Geraldine because she didn't want him, why kill Lucy too?'

'I don't know. I could guess.'

Charlie waited.

'He didn't only want Geraldine. He wanted Geraldine and Lucy, the whole happy family package, exactly what Mark Bretherick had. Like a lot of people, Hey saw the Brethericks as the perfect happy family—the dream, the ideal. If he'd killed his own wife and daughter in order to replace them with that ideal and then Geraldine rejected him . . .' Simon shrugged. 'Just a theory,' he said.

'The note,' said Charlie. 'You said it wasn't a suicide note.'

Simon's shoulders lost a little of their stiffness. He was back on safe ground: answers he knew for certain. 'Sally Thorning was carrying a black-covered book when she let herself into the flat last night. Did you notice?'

'No. I was too busy scraping her up off the floor.'

'I found the first page of a letter tucked inside the cover, a letter in Geraldine Bretherick's handwriting. First thing this morning I put it together with the so-called suicide note . . .'

'Second page of the same letter?' Charlie guessed.

Simon nodded. 'Geraldine used two sheets instead of turning the first one over and writing on the back of it. I made copies of the full letter; there's one on the back seat. Lean over, you might be able to grab it.'

Charlie was already unbuckling her seat belt. With her cigarette in her mouth, and using her index finger and thumb as pincers, she gripped the sheet of paper and swung back round. You could see the join where the two sheets of paper had been placed side by side, a grainy grey line on the photocopy.

She started to read.

Dear Encarna,

I very nearly didn't write this letter. I was scared of being honest, as people so often are, but a rumour got back to me that you didn't believe we were really going away, and I simply couldn't let that go unanswered. We have rented a place in Tallahassee, Florida, for the whole of half-term. We fly from Heathrow on Sunday, 21 May at 11 a.m. Our flight number, if you want to ring up and check, is BA135. We fly back on Sunday, 4 June, setting off at 7.30 a.m., and the flight number for our return flight is BA136. I have the tickets at home, and would be happy to let you see them if it would help.

If I were not going away, if I were planning to spend the whole holiday here in Spilling, I hope I would have had the courage to say no to having Amy for two weeks anyway, no matter what gifts or payment you offered me. Your offers were hugely generous, and I'm flattered that you thought of me, and I hope you'll believe me when I say I mean you no ill-will. I don't blame you for anything—I don't agree at all with the whole blame-the-parents line. I've always liked and respected you, and thought you hilariously outspoken and brave and assertive in a way I could never be, which is why I want to be absolutely honest with you. You know that I, along with many of the other parents from Form 1, have certain issues about Amy's behaviour, particularly around

the matter of truthfulness. I know the teachers as well as
some of the parents have spoken to you about it. I hope that
you know by now these problems are genuine and serious
and not just all of us being over-protective mother hens. Put
yourself in my position: how could I ignore my concerns and
say yes? Mark and I have brought Lucy up to be totally open
and honest, and so it's upsetting and confusing for her to be
around Amy.

The rest, the second page, Charlie had read once before, but she read it aloud now for the first time, knowing its author had not planned to take her own life. ' "I'm so sorry. The last thing I want to do is cause any hurt or upset to anyone. I think it's better if I don't go into a long, detailed explanation—I don't want to lie, and I don't want to make things any worse. Please forgive me. I know it must seem as if I'm being dreadfully selfish, but I have to think about what's best for Lucy. I'm really, truly sorry. Geraldine." '

'Hey must have felt like the cat who got the cream when he realised he could use the second page of that letter as Geraldine's suicide note,' said Simon.

Charlie read it again. 'Encarna obviously accused her of lying about the Florida trip. What a cheek.'

Simon turned into the lane that led down to Corn Mill House. 'Nearly here,' he said. 'Probably too late.'

Charlie blinked. She hadn't noticed that they weren't still stuck at the level crossing. Her seat belt clicked and stiffened each time she banged against it. Simon was driving as if in training for an Olympic hurdling event. 'Watch out,' she yelled. 'You can drive around potholes, you know. Use the steering wheel!'

A heavy sigh, but he did as she suggested.

'The diary file,' said Charlie, throwing her cigarette end out of the car window. 'If it was on Geraldine's laptop before she died . . .'

'Weeks before,' said Simon. 'And it wasn't all done in one go—the file was opened more than once. Norman gave me the dates. Every time it was opened apart from the last time, Geraldine was still alive.'

'But not the last time?'

'No. That was the third of August—she was dead by then. Hey opened it after he'd killed her. Oh, no, I don't believe it!' Simon smacked the steering wheel with both hands. A DHL delivery van was approaching them head-on and there was no room for it to pass. 'I hate this fucking lane. No! No, *you* reverse, you fucking wanker!'

'Look at his face,' said Charlie. 'He's not going to budge. We'll have to go back. What are you ... ? Simon, by the time you've got out and told him you're CID ... We'll get there quicker if we go back and let him out!'

Simon slammed his door shut and started to jerk back over the potholes. Charlie pictured herself getting married in a neckbrace. To stop Simon swearing continually under his breath, she asked another question. 'How did Hey get access to the Brethericks' computer while Geraldine was still alive, then?' *Are men like babies? Is trying to distract them a better tactic than asking them to behave reasonably?* 'And does that mean Hey had been planning Geraldine and Lucy's murders for months, or weeks? If he opened the diary file long before—'

'He didn't,' said Simon.

'He *didn't*? Then who did? Encarna herself?'

'She'd been dead over a year.' Simon almost smiled. 'The book Sally Thorning was holding when she walked in last night—you haven't asked me what it was.'

'Oh, God, *I'm* going to start drafting a suicide note in a minute.'

'It was Encarna Oliva's diary. Written in Spanish. Remember where Geraldine Bretherick worked?'

'She was an IT helpdesk bod, wasn't she?'

'Yeah, but where?'

'Um ... I don't know!'

'The Garcia Lorca Institute—a language school. A *Spanish* language school.' Charlie's eyes widened; she said nothing. 'The diary we found on Geraldine's laptop was a second draft. Norman found the deleted first draft: the writing was stiff and wooden. It made sense, but it was clumsy—'

Charlie gasped. 'Did Geraldine speak Spanish?'

'I phoned the Garcia Lorca Institute the second I left Norman's office. Yes, she did. They've got a policy: all their employees must be fluent in Spanish, even the techies.'

'Oh, my God! Geraldine *translated* Encarna's diary. She translated it for Hey. That's why it was on her computer.'

Simon nodded. 'But I've got to make him talk if I want to find out why.'

The DHL van had passed them. They were going forwards again. 'I could and should have made the connection sooner,' said Simon. 'Between Geraldine's old workplace and Encarna Oliva being Spanish. The diary: it's full of words and phrases inside quotation marks, things Encarna thought were best expressed in English. "Hunky-dory", "crunch time", "status quo" . . .'

'That's Latin,' Charlie pointed out.

'In the original handwritten diary, hunky-dory and most of the other phrases in speech-marks are written in English. Geraldine, when she translated the diary, must have decided to keep the quotes around those words.'

'That's how you worked it out.' Charlie shook her head in disbelief. 'Stacey's French assignment, "My Friend François".'

'I'd have got it anyway,' he said.

'You don't know that,' said Charlie crossly. His solving the puzzle had been accidental, a by-product of doing his job. He hadn't sweated over it . . . 'You cheated,' she said quietly.

They pulled up outside Corn Mill House. In the heat's haze, the house and garden seemed still and remote, like an apparition more than a real physical presence. Bretherick isn't here, thought Charlie, feeling the emptiness all around her.

Simon rang the doorbell, then smashed a side window when he got no answer. There were a few frantic minutes of running, up and down the stairs, opening every door, looking underneath and behind every piece of furniture. And of course the bathrooms: Charlie noticed that Simon left it to her to check both of them.

They did not find Mark Bretherick. They found nothing but silence and rooms full of air that felt unnaturally cool, given the temperature outside.

'What do you reckon that line means?' Sellers asked Gibbs, looking at the long, thin strip of red tape that bisected the floor area. They'd got a key to the premises of Spilling Magnetic Refrigeration from Hans, Mark Bretherick's second-in-command, an earnest, stick-thin German whose baggy corduroy trousers and enormous white trainers looked as if they weighed more than he did.

'Some kind of health and safety shit,' said Gibbs, stepping over the red line.

'Careful,' said Sellers. 'Something might explode.'

'We can't just look in the office and leave it at that. He might be in here somewhere.'

Sellers sighed and followed him. He'd been rubbish at science at school, had been slightly afraid of it and hated all the trappings—Bunsen burners, goggles, pipettes. He had no desire to leave the beige-carpeted, potted-plant-studded haven of the office and venture into the workshop, with its metallic smell, harsh spotlights and dusty concrete floor.

'He isn't here, though, is he?' Sellers complained, looking around at what was. Six large silver cylinders were lined up against one wall: were these the fridges Mark Bretherick made? They looked very different from Sellers' idea of a fridge; perhaps they were units for storing . . . oh, who the fuck knew what they were?

Wooden shelves covered another wall, on which were piled coils of wire, cables, drills, something that looked like a large steel snake, something else that looked like a television remote control, a machine that resembled a cash register. It had to have some more confusing scientific purpose, one Sellers wouldn't be able to fathom if he examined it for a million years. His eyes were drawn to a small machine with a part attached to it that might rotate, or looked as if it might. Part of a magnetic refrigeration unit? Does rotation cause coldness?

On a cork notice board, several sheets of paper were held in place by drawing pins with round, red heads. Sellers tried to read one that was headed 'SMR Experimental Insert', but was quickly deterred by words he'd never heard of: flange, brazing, goniometer, dewar, baffles. Baffled—now there was a word Sellers understood. He thought about doing an OU degree.

'Bretherick's not here,' he said. 'Let's ring Stepford and head back.'

'Wait,' said Gibbs. He nodded at the silver cylinders. 'We need to check those, and the wooden crates next to them; anything big enough to fit a body in.'

'Oh, come on! Hey hasn't killed Bretherick. Why would he?'

Gibbs shrugged. 'He enjoys killing people? He's clocked up four so far. Would have been five if Sally Thorning hadn't fought back.'

'Bretherick's not here,' said Sellers. 'I can feel it.'

'So where is he? Why hasn't he been in touch? He'd want to keep tabs on our progress. There's no way he'd go off somewhere and switch off his mobile. I don't buy it.'

'I do,' said Sellers. 'First we accuse his wife of murder, then him. Then we say, "Oh, sorry, mate, we fucked up. You're in the clear, so's your missus. Pity she's dead." I'm not surprised he wants nothing to do with us.'

Gibbs dragged a chair from the office through to the workshop. Sellers watched as he moved it and himself patiently along the line of large silver vats, looking inside each one. 'Well? What's in them?'

'Long, transparent tubes, looks like. With little—'

'Not Mark Bretherick, then? He's all we're looking for.'

One by one, Gibbs threw open the doors of the seven large wooden packing crates. 'Empty,' he said. 'Come on, let's go.'

'I'll just ring Stepford and . . .' Sellers fiddled with his mobile phone. 'Can't get a signal.'

'Use a phone in there.'

Sellers headed back to the office area and Gibbs followed, carrying the chair in front of him. He'd almost reached the red line, about to cross to safety, when he heard Sellers shout, 'Watch out, there's—' It was too late. Gibbs was on the floor clutching his shin, trying to swallow the loud, undignified noises he wanted to make. Next to his face was a cylinder of solid metal with a rounded edge, about twenty inches across and four inches high. It was sticking out of a hole in the floor. He'd tripped and banged his shin on the cold, hard metal.

'Are you okay? Let's have a look.'

Gibbs wasn't going to roll up his trouser leg and let Sellers inspect his wound like an old woman. 'I'm okay,' he said, though the pain felt as if it was ripping through his whole body.

Sellers grinned. 'Shouldn't have crossed the red line.' He swore under his breath. 'This phone's not working either.'

'You'll get a signal outside.'

'Chris? None of the phones in this office are working. All the wires have been cut.' Sellers waved a length of white cable in the air.

'He was here.' Gibbs tried to stand.

'Those wooden crates . . .'

'They were empty.'

'Do you reckon they're for the silver barrel-things to go in? You know, to be delivered?'

'Maybe. Why?'

'There's seven of them, but only six barrels.'

Sellers and Gibbs stared at one another.

'What did I trip over? What fucked up my leg?'

'Looked like the lid of my cocktail shaker at home, but bigger.'

'A lid?'

Gibbs hobbled after Sellers as he ran towards it. Sellers pointed to the far wall. 'Look at those monsters. The only opening's at the top. They'd need a way of lowering them, wouldn't they, to insert whatever needs to go inside—the plastic tube, or whatever? The hole this thing's in must have some kind of platform underneath it, so they can raise and lower the vats. Give us a hand, I can't get this to budge.' He was trying to loosen the round metal cap that had felled Gibbs.

Together the two detectives tried to twist it. Nothing. 'Try the other way,' said Gibbs. 'Look, it's . . .'

They pushed in the opposite direction and the lid came loose. It was heavy; it took both of them to lift it. Both hoped they would find the seventh silver cylinder empty.

They saw dark hair, and blood, and heard breathing. *Breathing*. Bretherick was alive.

'Mark? Mark, it's DC Colin Sellers. You're going to be okay. You're going to be fine. We'll have you out of here in no time. Mark, can you speak? Can you look up?'

The hair moved. Sellers saw a patch of forehead, streaked with blood. Gibbs had gone outside to phone for help.

'That's good. Talk to me, Mark. Stay awake and talk to me. Say anything.'

Bretherick's voice was a scratchy whisper. 'Leave me,' he said, and then something that sounded like 'peace'. Sellers heard a choking sound, and saw the head beneath him drop down.

22

8/12/07

'You helped us.' Simon faced Jonathan Hey across the table. 'Everything you told me—that Geraldine didn't kill herself and Lucy, that the same person who killed Geraldine and Lucy killed Encarna and Amy—why did you tell me all that?'

'I hate it when things are wrong,' said Hey. 'I can't stand for anything . . . not to be right. I wanted to be helpful.' He wouldn't meet Simon's eyes, or Charlie's. Yesterday he had been hysterical. Today his face was blank.

'You mean you wanted us to find out the truth?'

'No. Not that.' A pause. 'I was the person who knew everything you wanted and needed to know. You needed me. So I told you a small part of what I knew. And then I panicked, that I'd told you too much and you'd realise. So I tried to mislead you . . . and made things worse, all wrong again.' Hey shook his head. 'I liked you, Simon. If it counts for anything, I still do.'

'You don't know me.' *Nobody does—nobody ever has—so what makes you so special?* 'When we found Encarna and Amy, you must have known it was only a matter of time. But you still lied, as if you believed you might get away with it—Harry Martineau, Angel Oliva. And when I told you we needed you here at the nick—'

'You laid a trap for me,' said Hey. 'You could have arrested me without the pantomime if you'd wanted. It didn't occur to me that you'd be so indirect about it.' His mouth wobbled. 'You think I've let you down. I'm sorry. I truly wanted to help, Simon. I never wanted to be your bad guy.'

Charlie cleared her throat. It broke the tension in the air.

Simon felt freer to speak. 'You can still help,' he told Hey. 'Why did you kill them—Encarna and Amy, Geraldine and Lucy?'

Silence. As if the question had not been asked.

'All right, how about starting with some smaller points,' Simon suggested. 'Did you follow Sally Thorning to Seddon Hall last year?'

Hey nodded. 'After what happened . . . to my wife and daughter, I was in a state. I couldn't do anything, couldn't work, couldn't think. I ended up at the train station.'

'After killing Encarna and Amy and burying their bodies in the garden at Corn Mill House, you were in a state,' said Simon. 'So you went to the train station. Were you planning to leave the country? Leave your job in Cambridge and start from scratch?'

'I only got my chair at Cambridge in January of this year. Before that I taught at Rawndesley.'

'At the university?'

'I suppose so. Now that I've experienced Cambridge, I think it's stretching it a bit to call Rawndesley a *university*, but . . . yes, that's where I taught.' He paused, seeming to think through what he was about to say. 'I don't know why I went to the station. I had no plan. I saw Sally there . . .' He flinched. 'I've messed things up with Sally.'

'You noticed Sally immediately, because she looked like Geraldine,' said Simon. 'And you liked Geraldine.'

'We liked each other. Nothing happened between us. Nothing ever would have, even after . . . even when I was on my own and lonely and maybe a bit . . . careless about breaking up other people's families.'

An understatement if ever Simon had heard one.

Hey seemed unaware of what he'd said. He also seemed content to talk, as long as nobody brought up the four murders he'd committed. 'Geraldine would never have left Mark or had an affair. I once said to her, "Mark would never need to know." She said, "*I'd* know." She'd have hated herself.'

Charlie leaned forward in her chair. 'But you knew she had feelings for you. If circumstances had been different . . .'

'Yes,' said Hey without hesitation. 'If circumstances had been different, Geraldine would have married me.'

Simon was unconvinced. Hey might have mistaken a diplomatic knock-back for a fated but forbidden love.

'So Sally Thorning was just a fling at first,' said Charlie. 'She looked like Geraldine, but she wasn't the real thing. You still hoped Geraldine would see sense and leave Mark for you.'

'Don't belittle Sally.' Hey sounded injured. 'She saved my sanity. I thought . . . seeing her at the station like that, it was as if someone or something was trying to tell me everything would be okay. Sally was wearing a T-shirt from Silsford Castle's owl sanctuary. I'd been there with Geraldine, on the school trip . . .' A sharp look came into his eyes. 'Sally was the one. Not Geraldine. I realised too late. Geraldine was too perfect, too good. I had to hide so many things from her. All the time I wasted pursuing her when it should have been Sally. Sally's like me. I could be my real self with her.'

Simon was itching to bring up the four murders again. He restrained himself. This way was better; at least Hey was talking.

'You followed Sally to Seddon Hall,' said Charlie. 'Booked a room, introduced yourself—'

'And spent the week with her. Yes. You know all this.'

'Spent the week having sex with her?'

'Among other things, yes.'

Simon and Charlie exchanged a look. Sally Thorning had told them repeatedly that she and Hey had talked in the hotel bar a few times, nothing more. If anyone asked Simon, he'd tell them he believed her. She was sane, Hey wasn't. It was her word against his.

'Sally was easy to get into bed,' said Hey. 'Geraldine . . . I had no chance with her. That's what distracted me, made me believe

Geraldine was the one I ought to fight for, when all the time Sally was there, available. But I'd had her already, you see. And, like an ignorant Neanderthal, I undervalued her because of it. Until Geraldine was gone.'

'Jonathan, I want to ask you about the photographs,' said Simon. 'At Corn Mill House there were framed photographs of Lucy and Geraldine taken at the owl sanctuary. Inside the frames were photos of Encarna and Amy taken in the same spot. Can you tell us anything about that?'

Hey looked curious. Mildly. 'You found them at Corn Mill House? They weren't there when . . .'

When you drugged Geraldine and Lucy and killed them. 'No, they were at Mark Bretherick's office when Geraldine and Lucy were murdered.'

Hey closed his eyes. 'I looked all over the house for those pictures.'

'Tell us,' said Charlie.

'It was one of those stupid embarrassing things. They happen to me often. I persuaded Encarna we ought to go on the owl sanctuary trip. Parents were invited too. We were always so busy. I thought it would be nice to take a day off work, to be with Amy for once.' He shook his head. 'Encarna kept threatening to demand a day's school fees back, because she and I were looking after Amy on a day when we'd paid the school to do it. The trip was a disaster.'

'The pictures?' Charlie reminded him.

'Geraldine had forgotten her camera. I'd brought mine. I offered to take photos of her and Lucy.'

Simon and Charlie waited.

'The owl sanctuary trip was just before . . . just before Encarna and Amy died. By the time I got round to thinking about developing the pictures, I knew I needed both sets. I needed photographs of my wife and daughter—' He broke off. 'Sorry,' he said. 'Give me a second.'

'I think I understand,' said Simon quietly. 'You also wanted the pictures you'd taken of Geraldine and Lucy. You hoped that, given time, they would become your new family.'

Hey nodded. 'I was selfish. I could have made copies for Geraldine, but I didn't. I didn't want Mark to have them. At first I put Encarna and Amy in the frames, on a shelf in the lounge. After a while, I couldn't bear to see them staring at me.' He shuddered. 'I couldn't bear to throw them away either, or to put them in the bathroom with everything else. That would have felt like . . . stamping out their last glimmer of life. Does that make sense?'

Simon nodded. No, it didn't make sense—not in the way he wanted it to. His feeling of unease was growing. Something was wrong with the story that was taking shape, but what? What was it?

'So you put the photographs of Geraldine and Lucy in the frames instead,' he said.

'Not instead,' Hey snapped. 'As well. I never once took Amy's photograph out of that frame. Or Encarna's. I loved Geraldine, yes, but not the way I loved my family.' He began to cry, making no attempt to wipe away his tears. 'Whatever I've done, however wrong it was, I loved them. Like I loved Sally—she was my true family. Or she could have been. Can't you understand? I just wanted to make things *right*.' He looked at Simon. 'Have you always been the person you are now? I haven't. I was a different person once.'

'How did the four photos you took at the owl sanctuary end up in Mark Bretherick's office?' asked Charlie.

'An unforeseen disaster,' said Hey. 'Geraldine popped round one day unexpectedly. She never did that. I was rarely in, anyway. After I lost Encarna and Amy I spent most of my time at the university. She came round because she'd not heard from me for a while, she was worried about me. I'd told her Encarna had left me, taken Amy to Spain. When I got back from Seddon

Hall, I went to see her. Sorry, I'm telling this in the wrong order.' Hey stopped to take a deep breath.

'You lied to make her feel sorry for you.'

'I felt sorry for myself,' Hey conceded. 'I was completely alone. Do you know how horrible that is? No loving family around you? No one to ask you how your day's been, no one to make you feel you really exist?' He didn't wait for an answer. 'When Geraldine turned up on my doorstep, I thought . . . I was thrilled to see her. I completely forgot about the photos. I realised almost straight away, but by then she'd walked into the lounge. The pictures of her and Lucy were up on the shelf—if she'd looked to her right she'd have seen them. What would I have said?'

'What did you do?' Charlie asked.

'I told her to close her eyes, said I had a surprise for her. I grabbed the photos off the shelf and gave them to her, told her I'd had them framed as a present for her and Mark. I made sure to say Mark too, so she wouldn't think it was . . . anything untoward.'

'And she took them home,' said Simon. 'Unknowingly taking the photos of Encarna and Amy as well. Weren't you scared she or Mark would open the frames and find them?'

'What do you think?' Hey's voice shook. He blinked away tears, tutted. 'I started to go round more often, pretending I was just dropping in for a chat. I wanted those pictures back—I needed them—but I couldn't find them anywhere at Geraldine's. Now I know why: they were in Mark's office.' He clenched his hands into fists. 'I felt as if I'd betrayed my family. I'd sworn to myself that even though I couldn't bear to look at the photographs, I would always keep them there, in their frames, on the shelf. But I hadn't even managed to do that.'

In their frames on the shelf, behind pictures of another woman and child—their replacements. Hey's derangement had its own inner logic that put him beyond Simon's reach.

'You say you loved Encarna and Amy, and Geraldine—' said Charlie.

'And Sally,' Hey insisted. 'It just took me a while to realise I'd been searching for something I'd already found.'

'What about Lucy?'

'Lucy?' Hey's eyes clouded over. He looked annoyed, as if something irrelevant and inconvenient had been placed in his path. 'Geraldine loved her. She was Geraldine's daughter.'

'We know that,' said Charlie gently. 'How did you feel about Lucy?'

Hey glared at her.

Simon wanted to lean across the table and grab him, shake the truth out of him. A look from Charlie warned him not to. 'We don't have to talk about Lucy if you don't want to,' she said. 'Would you rather tell us about Encarna's diary? Geraldine's translation?'

Hey looked at Simon. 'I only found the diary after Encarna . . . once she was gone. She knew I didn't speak Spanish. That's why she wrote it in Spanish. I had to know what was in it, in case . . . Encarna wasn't like Geraldine. She was capable of anything.'

'She was dead,' Simon reminded him.

'I had a right to know.' Hey's tone was defensive.

'So you asked Geraldine to translate the diary?'

Hey nodded.

'Did you pay her?'

'Of course not. She did it as a favour to me.'

Charlie and Simon waited.

'Geraldine knew how much I loved Amy. She was always saying what a great dad I was. I'd never have let Encarna steal Amy, take her to Spain where I'd never see her. I told Geraldine I was going for custody. I was sure Encarna's diary was one long rant about how much she hated being a mother.' He shrugged. 'You can guess the rest. I'm not proud of having lied.'

'You told Geraldine her translation of the diary would help you win custody of Amy,' said Simon, all the more disgusted because of the respect he had once had for Hey.

'It was a terrible mistake.' Hey's voice shook. 'One of many. Geraldine started making excuses not to see me. At first I thought Encarna must have written something in the diary that showed me in a bad light, some lie or distortion—she was good at that. But when I finally persuaded Geraldine to talk to me about it, it turned out not to be that at all. She was thinking of me. Putting others before herself, as she always did.' His eyes filled with tears again. 'She asked if I was sure the diary would make a difference in court. She wanted me to talk to my lawyer, check it would be decisive. I told her there was no need, but she kept going on about it.'

'Because she wanted to spare your feelings, and Amy's,' Simon deduced aloud. A detail slotted into place: Geraldine Bretherick's phone call to a firm of solicitors. She'd wanted to consult an expert before letting Hey see the destructive words his wife had written, words she believed might ruin not only her friend's future but his past too, retrospectively. How she must have regretted agreeing to do the translation.

Hey used his sleeve to wipe his eyes and nose. 'All she'd wanted was to help me get Amy back, and she ended up having to . . . show me that poison, page after page of it.'

'Is that why you killed her?' asked Charlie matter-of-factly. 'You couldn't forgive her for showing you the truth?'

'How was it Geraldine's fault?' said Hey. 'I gave her the diary, I asked her to translate it.' He looked bewildered.

'Why didn't you tell Sally Thorning your real name at Seddon Hall? Why pretend to be Mark Bretherick?'

'I didn't think about it. I just said it. After what I'd just done, I didn't want to give my real name. And . . . I thought about Mark all the time. My wife and daughter were . . . I'd . . .'

'You'd buried them in his garden,' said Charlie.

'He and Geraldine were in Florida. I knew that. Having a lovely, happy time. I wanted to ruin it. I wanted to ruin something of theirs.'

'Were you jealous of Mark?'

Through his tears, Hey made an impatient noise. 'People like me are jealous of almost everybody, Sergeant.'

'You must have regretted using Mark's name,' said Simon. 'Once Geraldine and Lucy were dead, and it was all over the news. You must have known Sally Thorning would see Mark on TV. Is that why you tried to kill her by pushing her under a bus?'

'I didn't push Sally under a bus.'

'You expect us to believe that—'

'I pushed Geraldine.' A long pause. 'I'd been in a terrible state for days. They were all dead, all the people I loved. And then I saw . . . I *thought* I saw Geraldine in Rawndesley.'

'You'd spent a week with Sally Thorning and you didn't recognise her?'

'He'd forgotten Sally,' said Simon, keeping his eyes on Hey. 'He'd used her and discarded her, hadn't seen her for over a year. Isn't that right, Jonathan?'

Hey let out a loud sob, too distressed to reply.

'Geraldine was the one who knew he'd lost Amy, who felt sorry for him, who was helping him by translating the diary. Geraldine was the one he'd just killed, and so at the forefront of his mind. And suddenly there she was in Rawndesley, alive and well. So he tried to kill her again.'

'I . . . I panicked. I . . .'

'Where did you get the GHB?' asked Charlie.

'It can't have been hard,' said Simon. 'You told me in Cambridge; you have to get close to the scrotes in order to write your books about them.'

'Who?'

'Criminals. Offenders. Like Billy—remember telling me about him? You've got contacts who can get you whatever you want, I reckon. A gun, for example.'

'Why did you kill Geraldine and Lucy, Jonathan?' asked Charlie. 'Tell us. You'll feel better.'

His eyes glazed over. 'She would have been happy with me. Geraldine. I redecorated Amy's playroom for her. I wouldn't have rushed things. I wanted her to have her own space.' Looking down at his hands, he started to mumble, 'She loved cranberry glass. Mark wouldn't let her have it in the house; he said it was too feminine.'

'And Lucy?' said Simon. 'Did you have a room for her?'

Hey's face shut down. *What was it about Lucy?*

'Tell us about the massage table.'

'After I saw Sally in Rawndesley, I . . . I realised, of course. Almost instantly, after the shock had faded. I knew Geraldine was dead. Sally . . .'

'We understand,' said Charlie. 'Sally was still alive. Geraldine's room became Sally's room. You bought the massage table for Sally.'

Hey hunched forward in his chair. 'You've got to stop,' he said. 'You're making it sound so . . . bad. It is bad. I know it is. There's nothing you know that I don't, believe me.' His eyes seemed to challenge Simon. 'I wanted a happy family. That's all. Please, don't let Sally think it was like that, the way you've just described it. Don't say I was on the rebound. She'll never forgive me if you tell her that.'

'Why did you try to kill Mark Bretherick?' asked Simon.

'Is he alive?'

'Yes.'

'Tell him I'm sorry. I can't forgive him, but I'm sorry.'

'Forgive him? For what? For having the happy family you wanted? For having Geraldine?'

'Was your family ever happy, Jonathan?' Charlie asked. 'You, Encarna and Amy?'

'Before Encarna went to work for a bank, yes,' Hey said bitterly. 'A bank! I couldn't believe it. She was so brilliant, so talented, she could have done anything. But she chose to be a cog in the capitalist machine. She used to say making money was an art, and mocked me for disapproving. This is the woman who got the highest first in her year at Oxford.' Hey shook his head. 'Not just in History of Art—in any subject.'

'What did Encarna think about your work?' asked Simon. 'She must have known you and Keith Harbard were working on family annihilation killings.'

Hey stared down at the table, eyes wide, body tensed.

'Did your work put the idea into her head? She hated being a mother, and—'

'No!'

'Did she know that you and Harbard had been discussing whether women might start to commit familicide with increasing frequency?'

'What are you saying?'

'Encarna killed Amy, didn't she, Jonathan?' It had to be. Nothing else made sense. Something had to have tipped Hey over the edge. He hadn't always had it in him, this madness, the ability to kill. 'And you blame yourself, for putting the idea in her head. She committed murder and suicide in the same instant.'

'No! She never would have—'

'You came home and found their bodies in the bath. And Amy's night light. And you couldn't stand for the world to know: the professor whose life's work is to explain and prevent this terrible crime—'

'No! No!' Hey's face was red and wet. 'Encarna would never have hurt Amy. Look, please, believe me! I . . . I can't prove it, but—'

'You're doing it again, Jonathan,' said Charlie, standing up.

'What?' Simon could have smacked her in the face. He'd been so close to breaking Hey; what was she playing at?

'You mislead us, then you tell the truth. More lies, more truth. You can't decide what you want us to believe, can you?'

'Stop, please . . .'

'At first you hoped to pass off Encarna and Amy's deaths as a family annihilation killing. Your speciality. That's why they were both naked in the bath: you wanted us to believe Encarna did it. But now, when you hear us say it, when we're in danger of really believing it, you can't allow that, can you? You have to defend Encarna, because if you don't who will?'

Charlie stopped. Hey was convulsing, and Simon was staring at her, outraged. 'Encarna didn't kill Amy, or herself,' she told him. Seeing Simon's eyes move towards Hey—guessing he was reverting, mentally, to his original theory—she said quickly, 'No. Jonathan didn't kill them either.'

23

Monday, 13 August 2007

'Fay bootball? Fay cwicket bat, Mummy?' Jake stands hopefully at the foot of the bed, holding a walking stick that the previous owners of our flat left in the airing cupboard, unaware it would become my son's favourite toy, and his pink plastic ball. Zoe is sitting in bed with me, her arms round my neck. It makes me feel safe: protected by a fierce four-year-old.

'Mummy's not well enough to play cricket, Jake,' Esther tells him. 'Anyway, that looks more like a hockey stick than a cricket bat. Why don't you ask Zoe if she'll play hockey with you?'

Jake's bottom lip juts out. He says, 'Go back your house, Stinky.'

'Don't take it personally,' I say.

'Affawuds? Affawuds, Mummy?'

'Jake, Mummy needs to rest,' Zoe tells him firmly. 'We need to look after Mummy.'

'Yes, darling, I'll play football and cricket with you afterwards, I promise.' Being with my children again makes me almost breathless with joy. Seeing their faces, after I feared I might never see them again. I've told them I love them so often since I got back, they've started rolling their eyes whenever I say it.

Jake runs out of the room. Zoe leaps up off the bed and follows him, saying, 'Walk, don't run, Jake. We have to be extra good. It's a mergency.' A few minutes later I hear a muffled crack that comes from the direction of the lounge. Zoe shrieks,

'No, Jake! That's *my* Barbie!' Nick makes them both laugh by doing his impression of a frog. I'd have got upset and confiscated the stick, and got a much worse result.

How will I ever be able to leave home again? How will I let Zoe and Jake out of my sight?

I catch Esther scrutinising my face, as she has taken to doing. 'Stop it,' I tell her.

'What happened in that man's house, Sally? What did he do to you?'

'I've told you. Nothing.'

'I don't believe you.'

'That's up to you.' I give her a tight smile.

'Are you going to tell Nick?'

'There's nothing to tell.'

Nick knows what the police know: that Jonathan Hey imprisoned me in his house, and eventually hit me with a gun and left me there to die. The police have accepted my story for the time being. Nick has accepted it full-stop; he won't ask any more questions. He thinks he understands the what and the why of it: Hey wanted to kill me because he's a murderer, simple as that. Because he's mad.

Nick has no time for anything strange, frightening or unpleasant. He refuses to make space for it in his head. This morning he brought me some flowers to cheer me up. The last time he bought flowers was to apologise, the day we moved to Spilling. I was busy in meetings all morning, and drummed it into him that he mustn't forget to pack and bring the washing that was still wet in the machine. When I arrived at Monk Barn Avenue for the first time that afternoon, I found my black bra and several of my embarrassingly holey-toed socks lying in the hall, draped over sofas and chairs, hanging from wardrobe handles. My Agent Provocateur camisole was in the shower stall. Nick hadn't bothered to put the wet clothes in a bag; he'd simply scooped them up out of the washing machine's drum and chucked them into the back of the removal van.

I can't help smiling, thinking about the absurdity of this.

'What?' says Esther suspiciously. 'What was that envelope Sergeant Kombothekra gave you before?'

I remind myself that Esther is my best friend. I used to want to tell her everything. 'A letter from Mark Bretherick. Thanking me for saving his life.'

Who saved my life? I have become obsessed with this question. Did I do it myself? Was it Esther? My thoughts keep coming back to Pam Senior. It's odd to think that when she stood in the centre of Rawndesley and screamed abuse at me, she set in motion a chain of events that took her to the police station several days later. It was from Pam that the police first heard my name. If I hadn't managed to escape from Jonathan Hey's house, it would have been Pam's visit to the police that led to my rescue.

'Mark wants us to meet. Talk,' I tell Esther.

'Stay away from him, Sally. He's just lost his wife, remember.'

'Charitable.'

'Stay away,' she warns me. 'What good could it possibly do?'

'It might do him good. He must think it will, or he wouldn't ask.'

Jonathan Hey smashed his skull with a metal bar, nearly killed him.

Nick's appearance in the room prevents her from responding. 'Sam Kombothekra phoned while you were asleep,' he says. 'I said you'd ring him back.'

'What did he want?'

'Another update, I think.'

'Bring me the phone.' I would rather get it over with, whatever it is.

'Sal? There's something I want to ask you,' says Nick. 'It's been bugging me.'

Esther gives me a pointed look as she leaves the room.

'Can you make her go home?' I ask Nick once we're alone. 'It's like being looked after by Count Dracula.'

'That black notebook, Encarna Oliva's diary: why did you bring it back with you?'

'It was written in a foreign language. I opened it and . . . couldn't understand what was in it.' The truth. No part of what I said was a lie.

'So you thought it might be something important?' Nick looks at me expectantly. I nod. I assumed Amy Oliva's father might be bilingual, since her mother was Spanish. When I found the notebook in his bathroom and saw Spanish handwriting, I thought he might have written something about me—how he felt about me, what he was doing to me or planned to do. I brought the black notebook home with me so that I could destroy it. Instead, I passed out and dropped it on the carpet in front of the police.

I've never seen myself as the passing-out sort, but since I've come home I keep waking up without having realised I'd fallen asleep. I am still so tired. Sam Kombothekra says it's the shock.

Nick is impressed. 'So, you were escaping from the house of a psychopath and you had the presence of mind to bring an important bit of evidence with you. That's . . . efficient.'

'It's called multi-tasking,' I say as my eyes close. 'I'll tell you about it some time.'

24

8/13/07

Sam braced himself, then walked into the interview room where Simon, Charlie and Jonathan Hey were sitting in silence. He emptied the contents of a labelled evidence bag on to the table: a pile of green clothes—wet, rank-smelling. 'Amy's uniform,' he said.

Hey recoiled.

'She was wearing it when she died,' said Charlie. 'You stripped her. If I'm wrong, tell me what these clothes mean. Why are they wet and mouldy?'

Nothing. No response.

'It was Amy,' said Charlie. 'Amy killed Encarna.'

Hey shook his head, glassy-eyed. He had refused a lawyer, so there was nobody present to stop Charlie from putting the same suggestion to him nearly forty times. Lawyers—like bankers, Hey claimed—profited by exploiting others.

Sam didn't know what to think. He trusted Charlie's judgement, and it counted for a lot that Simon was backing her theory, but he needed to hear Hey say it before he could be sure.

'Who but Amy would you want to protect so badly that you'd be willing to take the blame for two murders you didn't commit?' said Simon. 'With vultures like Harbard waiting to write their articles and books about the five-year-old girl who killed her mother.'

'I'd kill him,' Hey whispered.

'He wouldn't care about your pain,' said Charlie. 'He'd write whatever suited him, you know he would. He'd say it on television too, on documentaries and discussion programmes. Think of who Harbard is, what he does, and then think how close he is to this, because of you.' She leaned forward. 'If you tell us the truth, the whole story, he won't be able to capitalise on your tragedy. He won't be able to write a book saying Encarna was a family annihilator.'

Sam watched with interest. A new approach: threatening Hey with the devil he knows. He prayed it would work.

'She's right,' said Simon. 'Harbard'll do what he's so fond of doing: invent his own conclusions, in advance of any evidence. If we don't charge you with Amy and Encarna's deaths—which we're not going to—what's he going to think? You told me he wanted to write a book about Geraldine Bretherick, but he now knows she didn't kill herself and Lucy. How long do you think it'll be before he latches on to Encarna as a replacement? If you tell us the truth, no one will be interested in listening to Harbard, Jonathan, I promise you.' Simon's voice cracked. He and Charlie had been questioning Hey for days. 'You've got to speak for your family now. Don't leave it to someone who didn't know them or care about them.'

Hey's head moved. Was it a nod? A small nod?

'Tell us what you found, the day Encarna and Amy died,' said Sam calmly, though he felt anything but calm. 'When you came home. Where had you been?'

Hey fixed his eyes straight ahead and stared, held by an invisible horror, watching it unfold.

'You called out, but no one answered?' Sam suggested.

'I'd been at a colleague's leaving party. Not even a colleague I liked. I got back late. If I hadn't gone, Amy and Encarna would still be alive.' He covered his eyes with his hands. '*Everybody* would still be alive.'

'What did you find in the bathroom, Jonathan?'

'They were dead in the bath. Both of them. And there was . . . a lamp. That was also in the water. Amy's night light. And the book Encarna had been reading.'

'They'd been electrocuted,' said Simon gently.

'Yes. Amy was . . . lying on top of Encarna, still in her school uniform. It was soaked. I thought it was an accident,' Hey sobbed. 'The lamp fell in, and Amy, seeing Encarna was in trouble, must have grabbed her, tried to pull her out, and because the bath was set into the floor, so damned low . . . She *must* have tried to pull her out, she'd grabbed hold of Encarna's arm. I had to prise her fingers off.' He shuddered. 'She was only five! In that split second of panic, seeing her mother dying, she wouldn't have known that by putting her hands in the water she was risking her own life! She wouldn't have meant to kill Encarna either, not really—a five-year-old doesn't know what it means to kill someone.'

Sam tried not to picture the events Hey was describing. It was hard.

'You wanted to believe it was an accident,' said Charlie. 'But you didn't. Not deep down. You suspected that, however briefly, Amy had meant her mother harm. At the very least, you feared it. You feared she'd pushed the lamp into the water deliberately.'

'No.' Hey's eyes were wild. He ran his hands through his hair repeatedly. 'No, no.'

'No? Then why not call an ambulance, if it was a tragic accident? Why bury their bodies in the Brethericks' garden?'

'I don't know. I don't know why I did it.'

'You don't have much self-confidence, do you, Jonathan?' said Simon. 'In spite of your professional success. You thought the bodies you'd taken such care to hide might be found one day—because it would be just your luck, wouldn't it? And you had to protect Amy from people knowing what she'd done. You stripped her so that she too would look like a victim, if someone found her and Encarna.'

Hey looked as if he might faint. 'Yes,' he breathed.

Charlie took over. 'Everyone knows murderers aren't stripped naked and buried. Victims are. You removed Amy's clothes to convince yourself as much as anyone else: that it might have been an accident. That Amy and her mum were having a bath together, perhaps, and the night light fell in. Was that the story you'd planned, if the bodies were found? Jonathan?'

'Or did you plan to pretend Encarna killed both of them?' asked Simon. 'A family annihilation. Your wife took her inspiration from your work, that's what you could have told everyone, and you buried the bodies to protect *her* reputation. If you'd said that, no one would have suspected it was Amy you were really trying to protect.'

'I don't know,' said Hey. 'Maybe.'

'Did Amy ever tell you she wanted to kill her mother?' Sam asked.

'You know enough now. I've told you enough.'

Sam thought of the e-mails to Amy from Oonagh O'Hara. *How's your mum? Is your mum okay?* Oonagh had asked that question, or a version of it, at the end of every message. 'She told him,' he said to Simon and Charlie. 'She told Oonagh O'Hara too, and Oonagh told Lucy Bretherick.' That had to be the secret Lucy had forced out of Oonagh, that Oonagh had felt so bad about revealing. 'That's why you killed Lucy.' Sam wasn't sure he was right until he saw Hey's face.

'What sort of child would say such a thing?' Hey spat, his sadness overlaid by a vicious, contorted hatred. 'Everyone thought Lucy Bretherick was an angel. Would an angel say that to a father about his own child?' He didn't wait for an answer. 'Let me tell you what Lucy was really like. Encarna and I couldn't stand her. She was a bossy show-off, an irritating, insensitive, arrogant, self-satisfied . . . creature. Her parents had made sure she was in no doubt about her importance in the world, made her believe she was better than everyone else. She was repugnant! Oh, I tried, I really did. I tried so hard to like her, for Geraldine's sake. I so wanted it to work for us as a family. But it never would have, I can see that now. Your children have to be your own.'

Simon felt a coldness inside his bones. 'What happened on the day Geraldine and Lucy died?' he asked. 'You were at Corn Mill House. Because of the diary?'

Hey nodded. 'Geraldine had finished translating it. She was terrified I'd be angry with her and kept saying I shouldn't read it, but I wasn't angry. She was in tears. I ended up comforting her. Nothing in the diary surprised me—it was just more of what Encarna said all the time. She'd written some horrible things about Lucy, about wanting to hit and punch her. I managed to persuade Geraldine that she didn't really mean it, that she was just sounding off.'

'When was this?' asked Simon. 'What day?'

'Why?' Hey was impatient. 'It was the first of August.'

Less than a fortnight ago, thought Sam. Was it possible?

'Carry on,' said Simon.

Unexpectedly, Hey smiled at him. It was a humble smile, as if he was grateful to be allowed to talk. 'There were several references in the diary to Amy's night light.'

'We know. We've had it translated, all of it.'

'Geraldine didn't understand one of them. She didn't understand why Amy would have crept up on Encarna in the bath and shouted, "I won't get electrocuted but you will."' Hey made an anguished noise, then apologised. 'I deleted the last part of that sentence, of course. Once Geraldine was dead.'

'Tell us about Lucy,' said Sam.

'We didn't know she was there. She came up behind us, we were talking . . . The *angel* eavesdropped on our conversation. I lied, told Geraldine I had no idea what Amy might have meant—I said it meant nothing to me. And then Lucy piped up, "Amy says she's going to kill her mummy." She looked pleased with herself, as she always did, as if she expected praise. Geraldine was furious. She told Lucy not to be rude and nasty, but Lucy wouldn't shut up. She said Oonagh O'Hara had told her that Amy had said she was going to kill Encarna by pushing the lamp into the water next time Encarna was reading in the bath. The only reason Oonagh's still alive is because I couldn't see a way to get to her.'

Charlie nodded. 'So you had to kill Geraldine and Lucy. Because they knew. They knew Amy's secret, and you had to protect your daughter.'

'I'd have killed Lucy with my bare hands, but I . . . cared about Geraldine, as I've said. I didn't want to upset her.'

'So you made your excuses and left,' said Simon. 'You went in search of a drug, something to knock them out.'

'I couldn't have killed Geraldine if she was . . . awake. I'm not a killer, Simon.' There was a plea in Hey's eyes. 'I just couldn't have done it. You were right. I went to see my . . . what was the word you used? Scrote? It's a horrible, demeaning word, by the way. You shouldn't use it.'

'Thanks for the tip.'

'I saw Billy. He gave me what I needed and told me what to do with it. When I went back to Corn Mill House later that day, Lucy apologised to me. She said she'd been fibbing. Geraldine was so relieved, so pleased to see me.' Hey's face lit up. 'I'll never forget that. She said, "Thank God! I was so worried about you." Her eyes were red, and so were Lucy's. They never usually fought, but . . . Geraldine had obviously given her the telling-off of her life.'

'What happened next?' asked Charlie.

'Nothing.'

Nothing? The man's incredible, thought Sam.

'I made us all a drink. I put GHB in Geraldine's and Lucy's.' Hey met Simon's stare. 'I didn't want to, but . . . Lucy never fibbed. That child was obsessed with telling the truth. If even I knew that, Geraldine must have known it too; she might have started to wonder if Encarna and Amy were really in Spain.' He coughed. 'I'd rather not talk about the next part.'

'The murders,' said Simon.

'Afterwards, I ... found the diary file on Geraldine's computer. I changed the names, deleted all the entries or parts of entries that were too specific to be passed off as Geraldine's, anything with too much detail about Encarna's life or her work. I ended up with just a few abstract-ish passages.'

'Not that abstract,' Simon pointed out. 'Geraldine's mother was able to tell us that the row about the *Big Sleep* mug had never taken place.'

'I was in a state. I missed bits. I got things wrong.'

'Encarna only started writing her diary in April,' said Charlie. 'She wrote twenty-two entries between the tenth of April and the eighteenth of May. Most people start diaries in January.'

'She started when she found out Michelle had a new boyfriend,' said Hey. 'Encarna was terrified Michelle would desert us. That was when her moods got worse, much worse. It was also when the black notebook appeared.'

Nobody spoke for a few seconds. Then Sam said, 'Thank you, Jonathan. Thank you for telling us the truth.' He felt Simon's disapproving eyes like a burn on his skin. It was the one thing Sam disliked about Simon: that he never pitied or forgave anybody.

Incredibly, Hey said, 'Thank *you*, Sergeant. All of you. You've made me feel more real than I have for a long time. You've made me understand that I have to be genuine before I can be happy. I only hope I get a chance to explain everything to Sally one day. Simon?'

Unwillingly, Simon looked at him.

'Remember the most important part of what I've told you,' Hey said. 'Amy tried to save Encarna. That's why she ended up in the water. She died a ... a good death.' A shaky smile spread slowly across his face. 'The moment she died was the moment she decided to try and save her mother.'

8/16/07

'You wanted to see me, sir?' said Charlie. What could the Snow-man want? There was no vacancy in CID; Sam Kombothekra had Charlie's job. *That's the way you wanted it, remember?*

'It's always a pleasure to see you, Sergeant.' Proust traced the rim of his 'World's Greatest Grandad' mug with his index finger. 'Even to discuss the unsavoury matter of Encarna Oliva's diary. Am I right in thinking we've ended up with *three* versions of the perishing thing, not including the Spanish original?'

'That's correct, sir.'

'And those three versions are . . . ?'

'Geraldine Bretherick's first literal translation, Geraldine Bre-therick's tweaked translation, and a third translation by an ex-colleague of mine from Cambridge, Manolo Galan.'

'Whose interpretation bears little resemblance to Geraldine's second version.' Proust frowned at his mug. 'It's a translation of the same text, yet it somehow manages to be completely different.'

'Yes, sir.'

'You agree?'

'Yes, sir.'

'Describe the difference, as you see it.' Proust leaned back in his chair.

'Geraldine's tweaked translation—'

'Will you stop using the word "tweaked"? Do you mean "edited"?'

'Geraldine's edited translation is . . . I don't know, more energetic, more . . . I know it sounds sick, sir, but more entertaining.'

'Professor Galan's version is bland and toneless, and all the more bleak for that,' Proust snapped. 'Geraldine Bretherick's is . . . in places it's almost as if she wants to make us *laugh*.'

'I know what you mean, sir.'

'Why would she? What's your take on it?'

'What do Simon and Sam think?' Charlie avoided the question.

'That Mrs Bretherick was too good, kind and naïve a person to allow Encarna Oliva to come across as the monster she undoubtedly was,' said Proust. 'You disagree?'

'I'm not sure—'

'Out with it, Sergeant.'

Charlie thought about the Brethericks' wedding anniversary cards, the messages inside that were so elaborately formal, so . . . courteous. It must be hard to be polite to your husband all the time, however much you love him. She thought about Lucy Bretherick, and how difficult Geraldine might have found it, trying to be the perfect mother at the same time as realising the daughter she adored wasn't perfect, was capable of hurting other children.

Your mummy doesn't love you, Amy.

'I wondered if Geraldine sympathised with Encarna ever so slightly,' Charlie said. 'With her frustration. If you sympathise with someone and understand how they feel, maybe feel that way yourself sometimes . . . well, you're bound to portray them more sympathetically.' She sighed. She'd got this far: might as well let Proust hear the rest. Being a man, he would no doubt react dismissively. 'Perhaps Geraldine was sick to death—sorry, bad choice of words—sick of being the perfect wife and mother. At the same time as wanting to help Jonathan Hey with his non-existent custody case, she used the opportunity of translating the diary to develop a bit of an alter-ego. She'd been given licence to speak in the voice of a bad girl, a convenient vehicle for expressing thoughts that would be utterly forbidden if she'd said them as herself . . .' Charlie saw Proust's eyes hardening against her words. She stopped.

'You can't be suggesting, surely, that Geraldine Bretherick felt the way Encarna Oliva did about motherhood?'

'Not at all. But, I don't know, maybe she'd felt a tiny amount of something similar once or twice, and . . .'

'And what, Sergeant? Spit it out.'

Charlie decided to be brave. 'Haven't you ever allowed yourself to recognise feelings that you would never want to own? And there's a certain pleasure in that recognition?'

'No,' said Proust impatiently. 'Let's not get bogged down in analysis, Sergeant. We got a result. That's all that matters.'

'Yes, sir.'

Charlie was at the door when Proust muttered. 'Lizzie agrees with you. About the diary, Geraldine . . .'

'She does?'

'No wonder women are still lagging behind men in terms of achievement, if that's the way your minds work. Lizzie also said I must congratulate you. Congratulations, Sergeant.'

Charlie nearly laughed; he'd never looked grumpier or less enthusiastic. 'On what, sir?'

'You and Waterhouse. Your impending nuptials.' Proust tapped his mug. Evidently he wanted the conversation to be over, and he wasn't the only one.

Charlie felt her mouth drop open. 'Sir, I . . . it's not quite as—'

The Snowman held up his hand. 'I don't need the process, Sergeant, only the outcome. No doubt you have your reasons—your *emotional* reasons—for hatching such a plan.' He shook his head. 'Since you haven't asked for my opinion, I won't give it to you.'

What could Charlie say? She mumbled her thanks and fled, red-faced and in a silent frenzy. *Bloody Simon—that stupid, arrogant, misinformed . . . mental case.* He'd told Proust they were getting married? What the hell was he playing at?

Acknowledgements

I am immensely grateful for the help I received from the following people: Mark and Cal Pannone, Kurt Haselwimmer, Caroline Fletcher, Guy Martland, Isabel Galan, Tom Palmer, James Nash, Ray French, Wendy Wootton, Narmal and David Sandhu, Dan, Phoebe and Guy Jones, Jenny, Adèle and Norman Geras, Susan Richardson, Suzie Crookes, Aimee Jacques, Katie Hill, and Joanne Golenya.

This is my third crime novel, and it's high time I gushed in a most un-English way about the dedicated and inspiring people who have helped me from the start: the brilliant Peter Straus, Rowan Routh and Jenny Hewson at Rogers, Coleridge & White, and the fantastic team at Hodder: Tanya, Lucy, Laura, Liz, Richard, Ron, Aslan, Martin, Jamie, Lisa, Nick, Sue, Kelly, Pippa, Helen, Suzie, Alex, Alix, Auriol, Diana, Rebecca, Anneberth, Francesca, Jen, Toni, Kerry, Leni, Emma, Emma, Will, Peter, and Henry, all the reps: Ian, Julia, Phil, Jack, Bob, Andy, Bettina . . . when I say everybody I really mean everybody! Extra huge thanks to Carolyn Mays, Kate Howard, and Karen Geary—in the leisure industry, there's a prize called 'The Seven Stars and Stripes Award for World-level Perfection', and you all deserve to win its publishing equivalent!

Thank you to John Gould for kindly allowing me to use the lyrics of his song *Mon Ami François*, and to David Wood for helping me to find John to ask his permission.

Sophie Hannah's first novel is available
from Penguin in paperback.

Read on for the first chapter of . . .

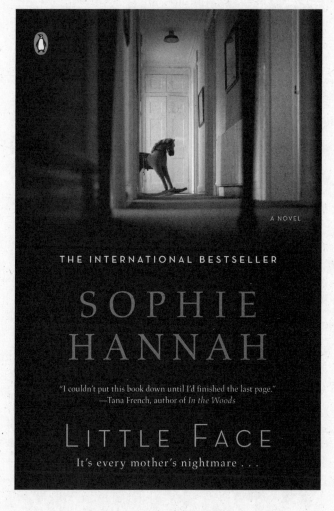

THE INTERNATIONAL BESTSELLER

SOPHIE
HANNAH

"I couldn't put this book down until I'd finished the last page."
—Tana French, author of *In the Woods*

LITTLE FACE

It's every mother's nightmare . . .

ISBN 978-0-14-311408-6

1

Friday, September 26, 2003

I am outside. Not far from the front door, not yet, but I am out and I am alone. When I woke up this morning, I didn't think today would be the day. It didn't feel right, or rather, I didn't. Vivienne's phone call persuaded me. 'Believe me, you'll never be ready,' she said. 'You have to take the plunge.' And she's right, I do. I have to do this.

I walk across the cobbled yard and down the mud and gravel path, carrying only my handbag. I feel light and strange. The trees look as if they are knitted from bright wools: reds and browns and the occasional green. The sky is the colour of wet slate. This is not the same ordinary world that I used to walk around in. Everything is more vivid, as if the physical backdrop I once took for granted is clamouring for my attention.

My car is parked at the far end of the path, in front of the gate that separates The Elms from the main road. I am not supposed to drive. 'Nonsense.' Vivienne dismissed this piece of medical advice with a loud tut. 'It's not far. If you followed all the silly rules these days, you'd be terrified to do anything!'

I do feel ready to drive, though only just. I have recovered reasonably well from the operation. This could be thanks to the hypericum that I prescribed for myself, or maybe it's mind over matter: I need to be strong, therefore I am.

I turn the key in the ignition and press my right foot down hard on the gas pedal. The car splutters awake. I turn on to the road and watch my speed rise steadily. 'Nought to sixty in half an hour,' my dad used to joke, when the Volvo was still his and Mum's. I will drive this car until it falls to pieces. It reminds me of my parents in a way that nothing else ever could. I feel as if it is an old, loyal member of my family, who remembers Mum and Dad as lovingly as I do.

I wind down the window, inhale some of the fresh air that hits me in the face, and think that it will take many more horror stories of gridlock before people stop associating cars with freedom. As I hurtle along the almost empty road past fields and farms, I feel more powerful than I am. It is a welcome illusion.

I do not allow myself to think of Florence, of the growing distance between us.

After four miles or so of open countryside, the road on which I am driving becomes the main street of Spilling, the nearest small town. There is a market in the middle and long rows of squat Elizabethan buildings with pastel-coloured fronts on either side. Some of these are shops. Others, I imagine, are the homes of old, rich snobs, bi-focalled bores who witter on endlessly about Spilling's historical heritage. This is probably unfair of me. Vivienne very definitely does not live in Spilling, even though it is her nearest town. When asked where she lives, she says simply 'The Elms', as if her house is a well-known municipality.

Waiting at lights, I rummage in my bag for the directions she gave me. Left at the mini-roundabout, then first right, and look out for the sign. I see it eventually: 'Waterfront'—thick, white, italic letters on a navy blue background. I turn into the drive, follow it round the square domed building and park in the large car park at the back.

The lobby smells of lilies. I notice that there is a tall, rectangular vase of them on almost every flat surface. The carpet—navy blue with pink roses—is expensive, the sort that will not look dirty even when it is. People with sports bags walk back and forth, some sweaty, some freshly showered.

At reception, I meet a young girl with blonde, spiky hair who is keen to help me. She wears a badge that says 'Kerilee'. I am glad that I chose the name Florence for my daughter, a real name with a history, rather than something that sounds as if it has been made up by a fifteen-yearold pop star's marketing team. I was worried that David or Vivienne would veto it, but luckily they both liked it too.

'My name is Alice Fancourt,' I say. 'I'm a new member.' I hand over the envelope that contains my details. It strikes me as funny that Kerilee has no idea of the significance of this day for me. The meaning of our encounter is completely different in our two minds.

'Oh! You're Vivienne's daughter-in-law. You've just had a baby! Couple of weeks ago, wasn't it?'

'That's right.' Membership of Waterfront is my present from Vivienne, or rather my reward for producing a grandchild. I think it costs about a thousand pounds a year. Vivienne is one of the few people who is as generous as she is rich.

'How is Florence?' asks Kerilee. 'Vivienne's absolutely besotted with her! It'll be lovely for Felix to have a little sister, won't it?'

It is odd to hear Florence referred to in this way. In my mind she is always first—my first, the first. But she is David's second child.

Felix is well known at Waterfront. He spends almost as much time here as at school, taking part in junior golf tournaments, swimming lessons and Cheeky Chimps play days while Vivienne divides her time between the gym, the pool, the beauty salon and the bar. The arrangement seems to suit them both.

'So, are you recovered?' Kerilee asks. 'Vivienne told us all about the birth. Sounds like you had quite a time of it!'

I am slightly taken aback. 'Yes, it was pretty horrendous. But Florence was fine, which is all that matters, really.' Suddenly I miss my daughter terribly. What am I doing at the reception desk of a health club when I could be getting to know my tiny, beautiful girl? 'This is the first time we've been apart,'

I blurt out. 'It's the first time I've been out of the house since getting back from hospital. It feels really strange.' I wouldn't normally confide my feelings in a total stranger, but since Kerilee already knows the details of Florence's birth, I decide that it can do no harm.

'Big day, then,' she says. 'Vivienne said you might be a bit wobbly.'

'She did?' Vivienne thinks of everything.

'Yes. She said to take you to the bar before we do anything else, and give you a large cocktail.'

I laugh. 'I have to drive home, unfortunately. Though Vivienne . . .'

'. . . thinks the more tipsy you are, the more carefully you drive,' Kerilee completes my sentence and we both giggle. 'So, let's get you on to our system, shall we?' She turns to the computer screen in front of her, fingers poised above the keyboard. 'Alice Fancourt. Address? The Elms, right?' She looks impressed. Most local people know Vivienne's home by name even if they do not know its owner. The Elms was the last home of the Blantyres, a famous Spilling family with royal connections, until the last Blantyre died and Vivienne's father bought the property in the nineteen forties.

'Yes,' I say. 'At the moment it's The Elms.' I picture my flat in Streatham Hill, where I lived until David and I got married. An objective observer would have called it dark and boxy, but I loved it. It was my cosy den, a hideaway where no-one could get to me, especially not my more threatening and obsessive patients. After my parents died, it was the one place where I felt I could be myself and express all my loneliness and grief without there being anyone around to judge me. My flat accepted me for the damaged person that I was in a way the outside world seemed unwilling to.

The Elms is too grand to be cosy. The bed David and I share resembles something you might see in a French palace with red rope around it. It is enormous. Four people would fit in it, or possibly five if they were all thin. Vivienne calls it God-size. 'Double beds are for gerbils,' she says. Florence has a spacious nursery with antique furniture, a window seat and a hand-carved rocking horse that was Vivienne's when she was a child. Felix has two rooms: his bedroom, and a long thin playroom in the attic, where his toys, books and cuddly bears live.

The views from the top floor of the house are breathtaking. On a clear day you can see as far as Culver Ridge on one side and the church tower at Silsford on the other. The garden is so big that it has been divided into several different gardens, some wild, some tamed, all ideal for pram walks on a warm day.

David cannot see any reason to move. When I suggest it, he points out how little we could afford to spend on a house. 'Do you really want to give up everything we've got at The Elms for a two-bedroom terrace with no garden?' he says. 'And you work in Spilling now. It's convenient for us to live with Mum. You don't want a longer commute, do you?'

I haven't told anyone, but gloom settles on me like a fog when I contemplate going back to work. I see the world in a different way now, and I can't pretend that I don't.

'I'll just get Ross, our membership advisor, to give you a tour of the facilities.' Kerilee's voice brings me back to the present. 'Then if you want to, you can have a swim, or use the gym . . .'

My insides clench. I imagine my stitches tearing, the still-pink wound gaping open. 'It's a bit soon for that,' I say, one hand on my stomach. 'I've only been out of hospital a week. But I'd love to look round and then maybe have that cocktail.'

Ross is a short South African man with dyed blond hair, muscly legs and an orange tan. He shows me a large gym with a polished wooden floor that contains every sort of machine imaginable. People in lycra sportswear are running, walking, cycling and even rowing, by the look of it, on these sleek black and silver contraptions. Many of them are wearing ear-plugs and staring up at the row of televisions suspended from the ceiling, watching daytime chat shows as their limbs pound the metal and rubber. I begin to realise why Vivienne looks so good for her age.

Ross shows me the twenty-five metre swimming pool and draws my attention to the underwater lighting. The water is a bright, sparkling turquoise, like an enormous aquamarine gemstone in liquid form, throwing and catching light as it moves. The pool has a stone surround and roman steps at both ends. Beside it, there is an area ringed by pink marble pillars that contains a round, bubbling jacuzzi. It is full to the brim, foam and froth seeping over the edge. On the other side of the pool there is a sauna with a sweet, piney smell, and a steam room, the glass door of which is cloudy with heat. A sudden drumming sound startles me and I look up to see rain hitting the domed glass ceiling.

I inspect the ladies' changing room while Ross waits outside. Like everything else at Waterfront, it transcends the merely functional. There is a thick plum-coloured carpet on the floor, and black slate tiles in the toilets and showers. On each surface there seems to be a pile of something tempting: fluffy white bath sheets, complementary bathrobes emblazoned with the Waterfront logo, hand creams, shampoos and conditioners, body lotions, even nail files. Three women are drying and dressing themselves. One rubs her stomach with a towel, making me feel faint. Another looks up from buttoning her shirt and smiles at me. She looks strong and healthy. The skin on her bare legs is pink with heat. Fully clothed, I feel fragile, awkward and self-conscious.

I turn my attention to the numbered wooden lockers. Some are open a fraction and have keys dangling from them; others, without keys, are shut. I circle the room until I find Vivienne's, number 131, chosen because Felix's birthday is the thirteenth of January and because it occupies an enviable position, close both to the showers and to the door marked 'Swimming Pool'. Vivienne is the only member of Waterfront who has her own dedicated locker that no-one else is allowed to use. They keep the key for her behind reception. 'It saves me carting all my possessions in and out every day like a refugee,' she says.

Ross is waiting for me in the corridor by the towel bin when I emerge from the changing room. 'All satisfactory?' he says.

'Very.' Everything is exactly as Vivienne described it.

'Any questions? Did you figure out how the lockers work? It's a pound coin in the slot to close them, which you get back, of course.'

I nod, waiting for Ross to tell me that I too will have my own locker, but he doesn't. I am slightly disappointed.

He marches me round Chalfont's, the health club's smart restaurant, and a cheerful, noisy, mock-American café bar called Chompers which I know Vivienne loathes. Then we go to the members' bar, where Ross hands me over to Tara. I decide to be bold and have a cocktail, in the hope that it will make me feel less on edge. I pick up the menu, but Tara tells me she has already prepared something for me, a fattening concoction of cream and Kahlua. Vivienne, it turns out, has ordered it in advance.

I am not allowed to pay for my drink, which is no surprise. 'You're a lucky girl,' says Tara. Presumably she means because I am Vivienne's daughter-in-law. I wonder if she knows about Laura, who was not quite so lucky.

I gulp down my cocktail quickly, trying to look calm and carefree. In actual fact, I am probably the least relaxed person in the building, so keen am I to get home, back to The Elms and Florence. I realise that, deep down, I have been itching to return from the second I left. Now that I have seen everything Waterfront has to offer, I am free to go. I have done what I set out to do.

Outside, the rain has stopped. I break the speed limit on the way home, alcohol buzzing through my veins. I feel brave and rebellious, briefly. Then I start to feel dizzy, and worry that I will drive past Cheryl, my midwife, who will gasp with disapproval to see me speeding along in a clapped-out Volvo only a fortnight after my daughter's birth. I could kill someone. I am still taking the pills they gave me when I left hospital. And I've just downed a strong cocktail . . . What am I trying to do, poison myself?

I know I should slow down but I don't. I can't. My eagerness to see Florence again is like a physical craving. I accelerate towards traffic lights that are on amber instead of braking as I normally would. I feel as if I have left behind one of my limbs or a vital organ.

I am almost panting with anticipation as I pull into the driveway. I park the car and run up the path to the house, ignoring the strained, bruised feeling in my lower abdomen. The front door is ajar. 'David?' I call out. There is no reply. I wonder if he has taken Florence out in her pram. No, he can't have done. David would always close the door.

I walk through the hall to the living room. 'David?' I shout again, louder this time. I hear a creaking of floorboards above my head and a muffled groan, the sound of David waking from a nap. I hurry upstairs to our bedroom, where I find him upright in bed, yawning. 'I'm sleeping when the baby sleeps, like Miriam Stoppard said I should,' he jokes. He has been so happy since Florence was born, almost a different person. For years I have wished that David would talk to me more about how he's feeling. Now any such talk seems unnecessary. His joy is obvious from his sudden new energy, the eagerness in his eyes and voice.

David has been doing the night feeds. He has read in a book that one of the advantages of bottle-feeding is that it gives dads the opportunity to bond with their babies. This is a novelty for him. By the time Felix was born, David and Laura had already separated. Florence is David's second chance. He hasn't said so, but I know he is determined to make everything perfect this time. He has even taken a whole month off work. He needs to prove to himself that being a bad father is not hereditary. 'How was Waterfront?' he asks.

'Fine. Tell you in a sec.' I turn my back on him, leave the room and walk on tiptoes along the wide landing towards Florence's nursery.

'Alice, careful not to wake her up,' David whispers after me.

'I'll just have a little look. I'll be quiet, I promise.'

I hear her breathing through the door. It is a sound that I adore: high-pitched, fast, snuffly—a louder noise than you might think a tiny baby could make. I push open the door and see her funny cot that I am still not used to. It has wheels and cloth sides and is apparently French. David and Vivienne spotted it in a shop window in Silsford and bought it as a surprise for me.

The curtains are closed. I look down into the cot and at first all I see is a baby-shaped lump. After a few seconds, I can see a bit more clearly. Oh God. Time slows, unbearably. My heart pounds and I feel sick. I taste the creamy cocktail in my mouth again, mixed with bile. I stare and stare, feeling as if I am falling forward. I am floating, detached from my surroundings, with nothing firm to grip on to. This is no nightmare. Or rather, reality is the nightmare.

I promised David I would be quiet. My mouth is wide open and I am screaming.